Pirates, Prostitutes and Pullers

For

the Peace Corps Generation of the 1960s who made Australia their home

and

whose distinction of intellect and character innovatively moved the boundaries of teaching and research in Asian Studies

John Butcher
Malcolm Mintz
Craig Reynolds
Carl Trocki
and
Carol Warren.

Pirates, Prostitutes and Pullers

Explorations in the Ethno- and Social History of Southeast Asia

James Warren

University of Western Australia Press

First published in 2008 by
University of Western Australia Press
Crawley, Western Australia 6009
www.uwapress.uwa.edu.au

This book is copyright. Apart from any fair dealing for the purpose of private study, research, criticism or review, as permitted under the *Copyright Act 1968*, no part may be reproduced by any process without written permission. Enquiries should be made to the publisher.

Copyright © James F. Warren 2008

The moral right of the author has been asserted.

National Library of Australia
Cataloguing-in-Publication entry:
Warren, James F. (James Francis), 1942– .
    Pirates, prostitutes and pullers: explorations in the
    ethnohistory and social history of Southeast Asia.

    Bibliography.
    Includes index.
    ISBN 9780980296549 (pbk.).

    1. Pirates—Southeast Asia—Social conditions. 2. Piracy—
    Southeast Asia—History. 3. Prostitutes—Southeast
    Asia—Social conditions. 4. Prostitution—Southeast Asia—
    History. 5. Rickshaw men—Southeast Asia—Social
    conditions. 6. Chinese—Foreign countries.
    7. Ethnohistory—Southeast Asia. 8. Southeast Asia—History.
    I. Title.

959

Cover image: The entrance to Jolo Town (Sulu) in the late 1830s.
The trading *prahu* is Taosug and appears to be crewed by Chinese.
(Source: M. Dumont D' Urville, Voyage au Pole sud et dans L' Oceanie,
Vol. II, 1837–40, Plate 139)

Consultant editor: Edward Caruso
Designed by Rosalie Okely
Cover design: Anna Maley-Fadgyas
Typeset in 10 pt Minion by Lasertype
Printed by McPherson's Printing Group

Contents

List of maps		vi
List of tables		vii
List of figures		viii
Foreword		ix
Acknowledgements		xiii
Introduction		1
Chapter 1	The Sulu Zone: Commerce and Evolution of a Multi-Mthnic Polity, 1768–1898	27
Chapter 2	Joseph Conrad's Fiction as Southeast Asian History: Trade and Politics in East Borneo in the Late Nineteenth Century	33
Chapter 3	Who Were the Balangingi Samal? Slave raiding and Ethnogenesis in Nineteenth-century Sulu	47
Chapter 4	The *Prahus* of the Sulu Zone	61
Chapter 5	Slavery and the Impact of External Trade: The Sulu Sultanate in the Nineteenth Century	70
Chapter 6	The Balangingi Samal: The Global Economy, Maritime Raiding and Diasporic Identities in Nineteenth-century Philippines	93
Chapter 7	Savagism and Civilisation: The Iranun, Globalisation and the Literature of Joseph Conrad	120
Chapter 8	Rickshaw Coolie: An Exploration of the Underside of a Chinese City outside China, Singapore, 1880–1940	146
Chapter 9	The Singapore Rickshaw Pullers: The Social Organisation of a Coolie Occupation, 1880–1940	154
Chapter 10	Social History and the Photograph: Glimpses of Chinese and Japanese Labour in Singapore in the Early Twentieth Century	173
Chapter 11	Living on the Razor's Edge: The Rickshawmen of Singapore between Two Wars, 1919–39	198
Chapter 12	Placing Women in Southeast Asian History: The Case of Oichi and the Study of Prostitution in Singapore Society	220
Chapter 13	Lives of the *Ah Ku* and *Karayuki-san* of Singapore: Their Lives, Sources, Method and a Historian's Representation	234
Chapter 14	*Karayuki-san* of Singapore: 1877–1941	249
Chapter 15	Prostitution and the Politics of Venereal Disease: Singapore, 1870–98	284
Chapter 16	A Tale of Two Centuries: The Globalisation of Maritime Raiding and Piracy in Southeast Asia at the End of the Eighteenth and Twentieth Centuries	309
Notes		333
Glossary		381
Bibliography		385
Index		403

List of Maps

Map 1.1	The Sulu Zone	29
Map 2.1	Joseph Conrad's Eastern World showing the various places referred to in the text	36
Map 3.1	The Sulu Zone	48
Map 4.1	The Sulu Zone	62
Map 4.2	Balangingi slave raiding in Southeast Asia	63
Map 4.3	Slave raiding in the Philippines	64
Map 5.1	The Sulu Zone	73
Map 5.2	Slave raiding in the Philippines	76
Map 6.1	A mid-nineteenth century Spanish map of Balangingi	94
Map 6.2	Balangingi slave raiding in Southeast Asia	95
Map 6.3	The Sulu Zone	96
Map 7.1	Iranun–Balangingi maritime raiding and the Malay Archipelago in the first half of the nineteenth century	124
Map 11.1	Singapore municipality	207

List of Tables

Table 2.1	Trade from Singapore to Berau, Bulungan and Makassar: 1864–1879	40
Table 2.2	Trade with east Borneo in selected years from Makassar between 1868 and 1883, compiled from the 'Shipping News' in the harbour column of the *Makassarsch Handelsblad*, 1868–1883	41
Table 9.1	Estimated number of Jinricksha coolies, 1888–1917	159
Table 9.2	Age distribution of 102 rickshawmen who appeared in the Coroner's Records between 1902 and 1939	160
Table 9.3	Prices for hiring rickshaws	166
Table 13.1	Schematic representation of the social history of the *ah ku* and *karayuki-san*	243
Table 13.2	Japanese and Chinese prostitutes: suicide	244
Table 14.1	Showing how unreliable the estimates were on the increase in both the number and percentage of Japanese women arriving in Singapore between 1877 and 1914	262
Table 14.2	The size of brothels in selected streets in the Southern Area in 1877 and 1905	269
Table 14.3	The size of Japanese brothels in selected streets in Singapore in 1905	270
Table 15.1	VD admissions into hospitals in Hong Kong and Singapore in 1884 and 1896	298
Table 15.2	Prisoners with VD admitted to the criminal prison between 1890 and 1896	301

List of Figures

Figure 4.1	A *lanong (joanga)*	66
Figure 4.2	A Balangingi *garay or panco*	66
Figure 4.3	A *salisipan*	67
Figure 4.4	Drawing and sketch plans of a *lanong (joanga)*	68
Figure 4.5	Drawing and sketch plan of a *garay*	69
Figure 6.1	Spanish plans of the heavily fortified Samal stronghold *(kota)* of Sipac	107
Figure 7.1	An Iranun sea raider	122
Figure 7.2	Copy of a bill of lading from the SS *Vidar*	139
Figure 10.1	Young rickshaw puller	177
Figure 10.2	Jinrickisha Station c. 1910	178
Figure 10.3	A typical Singapore traffic scene in New Market Road during the mid-1930s	179
Figure 10.4	Rickshaws lined up neatly outside Tank Road Railway Station, Singapore	179
Figure 10.5	A rickshaw coolie	180
Figure 10.6	Upper floor passage of a tenement house	181
Figure 10.7	Tenement house cubicle with no windows and no means of light	181
Figure 10.8	A view of South Bridge Road at the turn of the century	182
Figure 10.9	A rickshaw puller in full stride	182
Figure 10.10	Rickshaw stand near Raffles Hotel, 1921	183
Figure 10.11	Group of rickshaw coolies in front of the Clyde Terrace Market on Beach Road in the 1930s	183
Figure 10.12	Food hawkers set up near rickshaw pullers	184
Figure 10.13	The new Rickshaw Station, opened in 1903 by the Jinrikisha Department for the licensing and inspection of rickshaws	184
Figure 10.14	Picture postcard of *karayuki-san*	186
Figure 10.15	Registration portrait of a Japanese prostitute	187
Figure 10.16	The black and white arrival portrait of a *karayuki-san*	187
Figure 10.17	Kimono-clad 'hostesses' from Middle Road, c. 1900	188
Figure 10.18	Studio portrait of a young *karayuki-san*	190
Figure 10.19	The *karayuki-san*, Miyasaki Kechi, in Singapore, 1892	191
Figure 10.20	A *karayuki-san* sitting in a wicker chair under the veranda at 26 Hylam Street, c. 1914	192
Figures 10.21 and 10.22	Group photographs of *karayuki-san* in Singapore	195
Figures 10.23 and 10.24	Singapore postcards, 1903, depicting *geisha* rather than *karayuki-san*	196
Figure 12.1	Kimono-clad 'hostesses' from Middle Road pose against a studio backdrop in the 1930s	232

Foreword

James Warren's work over the past three decades has become essential reading to anyone interested in the modern history of Southeast Asia as a region. The word 'region' is important in this context, because Warren imagined Southeast Asia differently than many scholars before him—his project was not a national one, but rather a trans-national and indeed trans-regional one from the outset, reaching back to his first forays into monograph-length publishing with the appearance of *The Sulu Zone* in 1980. Though this was the heyday of nation-based histories of the region, Warren started from a different direction—he imagined spaces that were not 'national' in character, but rather that had survived at the interstices of developing colonial states, whether these were in the Philippines, British Malaya, or the evolving Dutch East Indies. *The Sulu Zone* defied national categories, and stood out as different in this era when writing histories of the nation was all the rage. I still remember picking up this book for the first time as a graduate student in the early 1990s, and putting it casually on the edge of my desk; it had a solemn weight to it, and I eyed it warily in thinking how much time it would take to digest. Hours became days, and days become weeks, and before I was done I had written twenty-five pages of tiny chicken-scratch notes (we took notes by pen in those days) on the entire corpus of its findings. I suspect that Warren's work has found its way into the lifeblood of many historians in this same way, a process of osmosis over long periods of time spent poring over his texts.

No one can doubt that Warren is an archival historian. He has paid his dues in the archives more than most scholars of his generation. His books have the scent of the archives, and he even has gone into detail in a few of them about where and how he found certain still-undiscovered sources, sometimes finding ant-chewed papers in damp heaps on the floors of Southeast Asian basements. His footnotes are small essays unto themselves, occasionally—data is almost sacred in Warren's historical world, where he has sought to pull together stories that others have not yet seen. Yet to envision Warren as a purely archival scholar would be a mistake of the first order. While the archives form the bare bones of his narratives, his stories are fleshed out very clearly from his own vision of 'what matters' in Southeast Asian history. This vision has been remarkably constant over time—a concern with subaltern voice, and the experience of those whom History leaves behind; a penchant for re-ordering geography, so that liminal places become central, and central places liminal, over what Fernand Braudel called the *longue duree*; and a moral concern to explain suffering, usually endured on the backs of the region's urban poor. All of these themes stand out in Warren's histories—they are the meat and potatoes of historical writing to him, or perhaps more properly the water and rice of what was left to those who had few options in life. Reading Warren can be a depressing enterprise, but only because he has taken the downtrodden to be his muse, and we feel their collective pain—often in extraordinary detail—when he writes.

The essays in this collection skirt the three great projects of his scholarly life thus far. The volume starts off with several musings about the Sulu Zone, the open, maritime space separating modern Malaysia, Indonesia, and the southern Philippines in a realm of small islands and open water. In this space new possibilities of the evolving global economy, or what Wallerstein called the 'world-system', came into being in the late eighteenth and early nineteenth centuries. The Taosug and their client sea-peoples, the Balangingi Samal and the Iranun, forged a production regime whereby other sea-peoples, mostly notably the Bajau, were predated upon to collect sea-produce for eventual shipment to Chinese markets. All of this was accomplished under the eye of a powerful sultanate; Europeans in other parts of Southeast Asia could only marvel at the strength of Sulu for many decades. This system empowered some people and enslaved many others, and it also became one of the main engines of inter-Asian trade at the dawn of the modern era. When Spanish gunboats and declining fortunes eventually weakened the Sulu Sultanate in the second half of the nineteenth century, a way of life over large parts of maritime Southeast Asia finally ended, after a long period of operation which had fundamentally transformed the region. Warren studies these processes from a variety of vantages and through many different sources, piecing together a story that had never previously been told. His essays and books on the Sulu Zone announced a new way of looking at Southeast Asian history, where the 'edge' was the center and where 'margins' were worth as much critical review as any other 'central' place.

The middle essays of this book take the trope of the margin to a different place—to the heart of the very 'center' itself. Spun from the author's book *Rickshaw Coolie*, these articles tell the story of the rickshaw pullers of Singapore, a desperate class of men who journeyed far from their homes in Southern China to try to make a life in the 'Southern Ocean'. Histories of Singapore up until this time were fairly uniform, and even the most accomplished of them stressed a normative narrative of British expansion and the establishment of colonial control, which certainly did happen from 1819 onwards. Warren, however, took a different tack. He asked how the poorest of the poor lived in this age of expanding possibilities, which offered them manual labour but little else in the founding of Singapore's 'miracle'. Warren's rickshaw-pullers lived lives of near-constant deprivation: the depravation of calories, as they strove to feed their meager bellies; the deprivation of families, as most were too poor to even hope to marry; even the deprivation of hope, as the option of returning home to China became more and more distant. The rickshaw-men pulled their loads all day for a tiny recompense, and endured the full heat of the sun and the full fury of monsoon rain in accordance with the seasons. Many were broken men by the time they slipped out of 'the life'—they could no longer pull their rickshaws, and a number of them turned to suicide when it became clear that they would no longer have a way to support themselves as they aged. Yet even here, Warren finds agency, and occasionally, the possibility of small happiness: a hit of opium to kill the pain of physical labour; a game of chance, in one of Singapore's numerous gambling dens; a night with a prostitute, who would have to stand in for the possibility of having a wife. These were meager chances of pleasure for these men, but it was all they had in many cases, and we are given an unparalleled glimpse into the lives of the working poor in the pages of Warren's texts.

These same prostitutes—forlornly awaiting the visits of the rickshaw-men, and others besides them—make up the essays in the last third of this book. If the rickshaw-men had few chances to attain any kind of happiness in the modernisation of colonial Southeast Asia, then these women had fewer still. Most came from poverty-stricken areas of Southern Kyushu and South China; almost all endured years of back-breaking work in the region's colonies, sometimes in the cities but also on plantations and in the mines. Warren focuses his research down onto the thousands of women who serviced Singapore's sex industry, and made it a famous port-of-call for men looking for 'any race of girl'. The essays here tell the stories of the *ah ku* and *karayuki-san* as an occupational group, but they also narrate the lived experiences of several women in particular—faces who stay with us because we know of their sorrows and trials as individuals, and not just as an exploited group. It might be argued that Warren's study of the *ah-ku* and *karayuki-san* is his most powerful work—it is probably the part of his research that has most seized public imagination, so that even theatre productions have been based upon it. Taken together with the experiences of the rickshaw-men, Warren's accounts tell the stories of an entire range of ordinary Singaporeans whose lives had been virtually un-chronicled before his work came along—everyday men and women who possessed almost nothing in their countries of origin, but who at least had a chance if they came to the South Seas to try to make a future, in a seemingly-limitless new landscape. The fact that most of these laborers—pullers and prostitutes alike—never realised their dreams is central to Warren's story, and to the labouring history of places like Singapore. What held promise from afar very often turned out to hold far less than that upon arrival, and the chapters of Warren's books are often chronicles of failure, paved with sweat, tears, and the loss of hopeful intent.

The final essay rounds out the collection by focusing on the relationship between transnational crime—piracy and human trafficking—and the second opening of China in the twenty-first century. This study brings together these essays in one volume, so that the reader gets a sense of these narratives in a single, convenient book. More perhaps than any other historian, Warren has staked out the underside of Southeast Asian history as his scholarly domain, a place rife with disappointment and hardship, but also with the seeds of hope and the promise of a better life. Bajau slaves in Sulu, rickshaw-men in Singapore, and prostitutes in the bellies of coal-steamers all felt these emotions, from the anticipation of potentially-better times to the disappointment of how their journeys ultimately turned out. These are sad stories but they are necessary stories, and over the course of time they have become part of the essential revisionism of Southeast Asian history as a coherent, true-to-life whole. Much of this fact is thanks to James Francis Warren.

Eric Tagliacozzo
Associate Professor
History Department and
Southeast Asia Program
Cornell University
Ithaca, April 2007

Acknowledgements

Many people have contributed towards the writing of these essays, which span more than a quarter of a century. I am indebted to the following colleagues for their valuable comments, criticisms and encouragement over the years in helping me to revise these essays for publication—Gregory Bankoff, Jeremy Beckett, Carolyn Brewer, John Butcher, Bruce Cruikshank, Shinzo Hayase, David Henley, Reynaldo Ileto, S. J., Maria Jaschok, Tsuyoshi Kato, Adrian Lapian, John Legge, Alfred McCoy, Lenore Manderson, Suzanne Miers, Malcolm Mintz, Norman Owen, Anne L. Reber, Anthony Reid, John Schumacher, William Henry Scott, Sow Theng Leong, Jonathan Spence, Paul Stange, Kurt Stenross, Heather Sutherland, Eric Tagliacozzo, Nicholas Tarling, Carl Trocki, Esther Velthoen, Wang Gungwu, Carol Warren, O. W. Wolters, Tim Wright, Yen Ching Hwang, and Brenda Yeoh.

Most of the essays in this collection are based on a series of books written at Murdoch University and during several periods of residence in the History Department, and the Institute of Advanced Studies, The University of Western Australia. I want to express my gratitude to my friends and colleagues in a range of disciplines at both institutions who have provided fellowship and scholarly support for these major book projects over the years. I am also grateful to the postgraduate students who have worked with me during these years for their friendship and insights on the teaching and writing of history.

I want to take this opportunity to thank Murdoch University for its generosity and support during the past three decades. I also want to express my gratitude to the Australia Research Council for several large grants that have assisted me greatly in researching and writing the various books on which these essays are primarily based.

I wish to particularly express my gratitude to Carolyn Brewer, colleague and friend, for her intelligent and efficient assistance in preparing the final draft of this essay collection for publication. I am also equally indebted to the editors of the following journals for permission to reproduce material for this book: *Archipel*; *Asian Ethnicities*; *Brunei Museum Journal*; *Bulletin of Concerned Asia Scholars*; *Itinerario*; *Journal of Asian Studies*; *Journal of the Malaysian Branch Royal Asiatic Society*; *Journal of Southeast Asian Studies*. Finally, I want to express my gratitude and appreciation to my wife, Carol, and to my daughter, Kristin, who, as scholars and teachers, have helped and encouraged me over the years.

Introduction

Passing Over: Some Reflections on the Writing and Teaching of Southeast Asian Modern History

Passing over

I would like to begin by introducing John Dunne's notion of 'passing over' as a way to comprehend a variety of autobiographical experiences and standpoints from which a life—that of mine as an historian—can be understood. The process of passing over is essentially a matter of sympathetic understanding. It entails the experience of 'passing over' from one culture to another, from one way of life to another. It also entails a shift of standpoint, a crossing over to the standpoint of another culture, another way of life, another human being. It is followed, as Dunne stresses in his deeply personal masterpiece, by an equal and opposite process—'coming back,' returning with new perceptions about one's own culture, one's own way of life, self, and possible pasts and futures.[1] There is a depth, call it an abyss or chasm, which appears in the most common human experience. An individual crosses this abyss in the course of passing over by sympathetic understanding to another culture and crosses it again in coming back to oneself, returning with new insights that lift the mind, the heart and the soul. What I will be doing in this section, therefore, is leaping over this abyss, crossing it and crossing it back again, albeit swiftly and briefly, going down into it and coming out again, to map a life on time.

New York born, to second-generation Irish and north-eastern European Jewish parents, I never intended to end up in Southeast Asia. While teaching African history at a suburban upper Westchester County High School, north of New York City in the mid-1960s, and passing over once a week, under the auspices of Columbia University's Afro-American College Assistance Programme, into the streetwise world and emotional milieu of the black revolution sweeping Harlem, I had my future mapped out: finish my master's thesis on the slave trade between West Africa and Brazil, and then join the Peace Corps in Peru. I wanted to learn Quechua and pass over the cultural frontier of the Altiplano, the high plateau, to live with vanquished Indian descendants of the great empire builders, the Incas. But when the United States government cut Corps funding to that area, my wife and I—we were then newly married—

were given a choice of destination(s): initially, only Liberia, but several months later also either Korea or Malaysia. We chose the latter.

I (we) lived for two years as a Peace Corps volunteer in Semporna, on the east coast of Borneo (1967–69). The period from January to November 1969, spent in Kampong Bangau Bangau, a Samal Bajau Laut village consisting of a flotilla of boat-dwellers and a semi-sedentary population of Bajau Laut in varying stages of adaptation to a house-dwelling way of life, was particularly memorable. It was the rapid abandonment of sea nomadism—a lifestyle that has characterised the Samal Bajau Laut as a people and from which they drew their sense of identity—which first motivated my interest in Southeast Asian history. My subsequent experience of attempting to write my master's thesis on the Samal Bajau Laut under North Borneo Chartered Company rule, a history involving a non-Western people based primarily on written (British) records, pointed out the extreme difficulty of presenting a balanced interpretation, using only traditional historiographical methods. It impressed upon me the vital importance of oral traditions and an ethnohistorical perspective in any future effort to investigate changes in identity, cultural values, social organisation, economic systems and political patterns of the maritime people of Southeast Asia; transformations and transition(s) initiated by the world capitalist economy, colonialism and modernity. There remained the need then to attempt to integrate my small-scale investigation of the problems of cultural ecological adaptation of the Samal Bajau Laut with the study of world historical events and experiences, and to show how they linked together as a world historical process. I felt the necessity too, to expand the temporal reach of analysis to better understand the response of a loosely structured port polity—centred around the Sulu Sultanate and the nearby areas of northern Celebes (Sulawesi), north-eastern Borneo (Sabah) and the central and western territories of Mindanao—to the ascendance of global capitalist expansion and the imperialism of European dominance. While lying behind it all there was still the prewar challenge and vision of the Dutch sociological historian, J. C. Van Leur, to see the past through the eyes of those subject and subordinate people who became mere objects of conventional postwar Southeast Asian history.

Hence the origin of my work began in personal experience rather than with books and formal training. In a very real sense, my interest in studying Southeast Asian society and history, both from interdisciplinary and cross-cultural perspectives, started at the edge. The reason is twofold. First, my introduction to Southeast Asia was based on witnessing the traumatic experience of adjustment of a maritime-nomadic people to a sedentary way of life—a pariah people who, socially and politically, were situated at the edge, on the margin of society and history. Second, to acquire the socio-historical methodology necessary to investigate problems of cultural-ecological transformation, such as their continuing adjustment to a sedentary way of life, I subsequently chose to study for my doctorate in Southeast Asian modern history at the Australian National University in 1971, rather than at Cornell University, at that time arguably the undisputed intellectual centre of the world for the study of Southeast Asia. The choice to opt for Australia, at that time considered in certain respects to be at the edge of Southeast Asian studies, was deliberate. It allowed me the ultimate practical experience of 'passing over' into another culture and society situated on the margin of Southeast Asia, and the chance of studying and working in a different system of education, which at the postgraduate level primarily emphasised research and participation in a variety of intra-university inter-disciplinary seminars. More importantly, the process of passing over was to provide the opportunity, albeit in a modest way, to help redefine where the centre and the edge were located for the international study of Southeast Asia over the next quarter of a century.

The Sulu Zone: Seeing the 'zone'

In contemporary ethnohistorical studies of Southeast Asia the 'zone' and/or 'border' have recently become chosen metaphors for theorising the historically complex and contradictory ways in which cultural difference and ethnic diversity have been articulated in social relations and in political and economic practice across time. At that time, my doctoral research aimed to explore global cultural interconnections and interdependencies in the Southeast Asian world of the late eighteenth and nineteenth centuries with particular reference to a polity and world that I dubbed the 'Sulu Zone'.[2] The thesis aimed to enhance critical understanding and discussion of historiographical methods and models used in problematising and investigating economic and cultural 'border zones' in a changing global–local context. My emphasis was on a 'zone' created through the intersections of geography, culture and history centred around the Sulu and Celebes seas, as well as China's and the West's complicated place within its long history of globalisation that can readily be traced back to the eighteenth century, if not earlier. Hence my approach, to framing and re-presenting the ethnohistory of the Sulu Zone on its own terms from the late eighteenth century, rather than merely as a corollary of the history of Western imperial expansion in Eastern Asia, was to tease out and, albeit, unravel the economic, cultural and ecological interconnections embedded in the world capitalist economy with particular reference to the evolution and transformation of the 'zone': namely, globalised connections that have non-Western as well as Western origins. This broad conceptual schemata also aimed to enhance understanding of these global systemic links and interactions between geo-political core areas, notably China and Europe, and strategically positioned 'zones' or places with loosely structured polities, strong trading bases and thin populations like the Sulu Sultanate, which encompassed a variety of economic sub-regions and extremely specialised territories.

My initial thinking about how the late-eighteenth-century global economy created a 'borderless world' or 'zone', both spatially and historically in the area of the Sulu and Celebes seas, owed much to the influence of John Smail's thought about autonomous histories and perspective in historical writing. Smail, in turn, had been strongly indebted to the writings of Van Leur and the hemispheric cross-regional historical orientation of Marshall Hodgson, who attempted to locate the history of Islamic civilisation and situate the history of European modernity in a parallel move within a world historical framework. Templates for the 'zone', and possible centre–periphery and trade-process models, were provided by the path-breaking works of E. R. Leach and Fernand Braudel, and Andre Gunder Frank. The inherent advantages of such a conceptual–theoretical, evolutionary–ecological approach for framing and interpretation in a shifting upland agricultural context were already apparent to me in Leach's pioneering work on the political systems of highland Burma. In the Sulu context, however, insular Southeast Asia was a region in which the sea served as a major means of communication for a wider inter-regional economy in which national boundaries were fluid and by no means fixed.[3] Following in the footsteps of Leach and Braudel, I abandoned the blinkered geographic perspective of earlier historians of the Philippines, Indonesia and Borneo, for a more dynamic definition of the Sulu Sultanate's boundaries. It was based on larger scale processes of social-cultural change and a 'borderless' history of a global maritime trade network oriented towards China, Europe and North America. A history without borders was about entangled commodities and patterns of consumption and desire, which were linked to slavery and slave raiding, the manipulation of ethnically diverse groups, the formation and maintenance of ethnicity, and the meaning and constitution of 'culture' as all part of the same system of world commerce and economic growth. To be released from the conceptual constraints of conventional historical geography, I called this wide-ranging web of economic influence and interpersonal relations that centred on the polity of the Sulu Sultanate a 'zone'.

My framing and interpretation of the 'zone' as a spatial system rested on the axiom that it was 'inherently unstable and generally dynamic',[4] and that it was thrust on the global stage at a specific moment or era in 'regional time'. Leach's remarkable work on state and community structures in highland Burma aimed at tracing the pattern of the shifting balance between two representations of political order and social phenomena over some 150 years. Similarly, for me the 'zone' was also a process in time.[5] It was a recognition that all ethnic groups and communities were being shaped and reshaped by the interplay between internal social and cultural forms, and ongoing, external courses of action and extrinsic factors. In a very real sense, the peoples of the 'zone'— the Taosug *datus*, Iranun and Balangingi slavers, and the huge numbers of displaced captives or slaves—were in fact 'products' of large-scale processes of global socioeconomic change which had made them what they were and which continued to shape their responses in reaction to the uncontrollable and rapid impact of these globalising forces. The holism of the zone as a 'spatial system' was posited, both as a model and a necessary analytic fiction, not a given. The invisible connections linking the processes of structural change and the dynamic movement of local systems and networks of this complex, albeit difficult to see, 'zone' to the wider economic and political world(s) of colonial capitalism and free trade, of which it was becoming a part, had to be traced and explained in 'regional time'. To rectify the presuppositions of earlier studies, I developed an ethnohistorical research strategy utilising a global, cultural-ecological perspective and framework where the interdependence of all states and societies could be seen at once, and their interconnectedness to one another within the framework of the world economic system was readily apparent.[6] It is crucial to an understanding of the more flexible trans-disciplinary approach required to write *The Sulu Zone* that it was based on devising a new conceptual, analytical framework guided by the assumption that history and ethnography are inextricably linked. It was a conceptual framework and a paradigm of sorts to enhance our understanding of crucial economic and social processes in insular Southeast Asia—a broad, loose but nonetheless coherent explanation and model about the nature of a Southeast Asian polity and economic region that responded to a set of interdependent connections and relationships fostered by the 'modern' world system from the end of the eighteenth century. Apart from offering a panoramic perspective and a means of explanatory power for the understanding of these global–regional interrelationships, the diagrammatic 'model' and role of the zone provided the major principle for framing and organisation of the narrative; it was the essential backdrop or stage against which to begin unravelling the main elements in the development of these separate but increasingly related interregional and local histories of various societies and cultures in East and Southeast Asia, and beyond.

The Sulu Zone—The meaning and constitution of 'culture'

By arguing for a broader interconnected global economic perspective, interesting complex questions were raised about what constitutes our conception of 'culture' and ethnicity. While thousands of captive people were allocated throughout the zone each year as slaves, in the period under consideration the borderlines of race, 'culture', and ethnicity were increasingly blurred by the more inclusive practices of incorporation and pluralism in a traditional Muslim social system. I maintained in *The Sulu Zone* that the Taosug, Iranun and Samal not only lived in an increasingly interdependent world, but that they also lived in an emergent multi-ethnic polity and society, the multicultural inhabitants of which came from many parts of Asia and elsewhere in the world. How are identities—single or multiple—forged? What symbols, rituals and perceptions create a strong sense of collective identity? The traditional assumption of a 'culture' as enduring over time despite outward changes in people's lives and value orientations is both 'empirically misleading and deeply essentialist'.[7]

As Roger Keesing noted, there is no part of Eastern Asia where both the production and reproduction of 'culture' and cultural meaning can be characterised as unproblematic, without glossing over or disguising radical changes in relation to ethnicity, power and hierarchy that have differentially affected states like Sulu and marginal settings like the zone.[8] In terms of questioning the ethnic boundedness and cultural homogeneity of an emergent way of life unfolding in the zone at the end of the eighteenth century, I gradually recognised the power of language, commodities and memory as key elements and symbols in the construction of new identities and communities. Filling a conspicuous gap in the literature, this aspect of the book's ethnohistorical research explored the accomplishment, or re-invention, of ethnicity as a consequence of developing ties to world commerce and economic growth, and to the expanding world of Darul Islam. The questions of the conditions under which these new identities were formed and the ethnicity accomplished throughout the zone, especially in the first half of the nineteenth century, have aroused considerable subsequent interest. I stressed in *The Sulu Zone* the inextricable relationship between slave raiding, displacement and forced migration on the one hand, and 'homeland' and identity on the other, as absolutely critical factors that led to the emergence of new communities and diasporas. This way of historically conceptualising the 'ethnicity' and 'culture' of maritime communities leads us to consider new ways of framing and re-presenting a sense of kinship, group solidarity, common culture and conflict, particularly political struggles, in the history of Southeast Asia. By stressing the problems of self-definition and the reconstruction of identities, and the meaning of homeland and lost places, that reveal social and psychological processes in their own right, *The Sulu Zone* challenged lineal notions of history with their origin in Western Europe and bounded static conceptions of 'culture' and ethnic groups that were imposed, imagined and maintained by Europeans both before and after colonisation.

This expedient reinvention of ethnicity resulting from the interconnected force of circumstance generated by the China trade compels us to think about related notions of society and 'culture' in more processual ways.[9] Historians and ethnographers of the region need to locate the emergence, maintenance and abrogation of populations and the 'cultures' they encompass within the framework of a series of historically changing, imperfectly bounded, multiple and branching yet integrated set of local, regional, global social and economic alignments. Here, some of the questions posed about the birth and accomplishment of ethnicity and border identities in *The Sulu Zone* help us understand that both the recent and more distant past—especially on the margins of states and beyond the frontier(s) in Southeast Asia—are far-reaching, particularly if one considers the contemporary complex theoretical cultural implications of the nature of 'ethnicity' (often associated with economic and political conflict in developing societies) as key factors for unravelling the development and history of the terms 'Indonesian', 'Malay', 'Thai', 'Burmese' and 'Vietnamese'. These labels have been successfully created as part of a national imaginary by modern states in the interest of forging national unity and to mythologise history. This case-based discussion of the concept of Asian 'cultures' and the creation of 'imagined communities' of nationalities as problematic, and recognition of the crucial factors which led, as part of one interconnected and interdependent process, to the accomplishment of ethnicity in the Sulu Zone, provides some of the basic building blocks for future comparative and theoretical analyses of the interpretation of culture.

The Sulu Zone—In search of 'evidence'

The chronic problem facing ethnohistorians of Asia, Africa and Latin America is the uneven nature of the source material available for certain people, places and times. How can one provide a well-detailed historical reconstruction and measure change if the documents as 'instruments of measurement' are scarce, non-existent, or themselves changing?[10] The effort has to be made to bring to bear as wide a range of evidence as possible, on critically specific points, to emphasise the global interconnections and interdependencies of particular societies and regions, in order to frame a holistic or 'total' explanation of their mutual encounters, interactions and conflicts in a contemporary 'borderless world', a world that has a long history, created in part by an evolving world capitalist economy. Hence, it proved necessary, in researching and writing this book, to seek out as much evidence wherever it could be found, especially because of the accidental generation and destruction of historical records concerning the ethnohistory of the Sulu Zone. Consequently, I used an extremely varied, in fact eclectic, body of documentation from twenty-six different archives, libraries and repositories around the world, to resolve the problem of explaining the significance of the China trade in the transformation of Taosug society and culture of the late eighteenth century. I went in search of all forms of evidence—archaeological, anthropological, historical and oral testament—and not a page was meant to be left unturned along the way.

In the late eighteenth and nineteenth centuries, the population of Sulu was heterogeneous and changing—socially, economically and ethnically. This was a direct result of global trade. The importance of populating of the Sulu Zone by captives from the Philippines and various parts of the Malay world and their role in the redistributional economy centred at Jolo, the capital of the sultanate, should not be underestimated. The perennial problem confronting the historian has always been to achieve a balance in the historical record. Frequently this record is written by the empowered. As such, their observations are, naturally enough, laden with their own preconceptions, social bias and self-interest. Their accounts have often been employed to provide a 'contrast' and sometimes justification for a particular policy or historical attitude. However, in colonial and national archives sometimes there are misplaced or forgotten documents and neglected objects of material culture that have miraculously survived the passage of time to tell a different story: the deeds and even authentic speech of the captives of the Iranun and Balangingi recounting their stories of the middle passages; the letter of a Balangingi female prisoner of war asking to join her incarcerated husband on death row; the harrowing report of a Spaniard captured and sentenced to a Balangingi *prahu* as a galley slave; an artist's sketch here, a misplaced oil painting there—all awaiting rediscovery and analysis by a young ethnohistorian, searching after the fact(s) in order to understand various enigmatic processes in the Sulu Zone.

To understand the economic and social role played by slaves in the economy, previous historical studies of the sultanate depended largely on published colonial records and accounts rather than on records inadvertently produced by the slaves themselves. Slavery in Sulu was observed through the eyes and preconceptions of European observers and writers who viewed Sulu as the centre of a world fundamentally hostile to their interests—a traditional Islamic world whose activities centred on piracy and slavery. A unique alternative to this Eurocentric perspective was presented to me by the discovery, and subsequent compilation, of the scattered statements of fugitive captives from the Sulu Sultanate. Carlo Ginsburg, a gifted Italian historian whose classic works have challenged us to retrieve social worlds that more conventional history does not record, describes particular types of legal-juridical documentation, as 'written records of oral speech'.[11] For example, according to Ginsburg's way of thinking, the written proceedings and statements of the fugitive captives, which proved so essential to writing *The Sulu Zone*, could be considered comparable in certain respects to the notes or notebook of an ethnographer, who had studied a cultural system where slavery and ethnogenesis were a common occurrence. Consequently, following the logic of this line of thought, the handpicked naval commanders of various colonial powers struggling to rid Southeast Asia of Iranun–Balangingi raiding and the slave trade, momentarily transformed on the deck of a gunboat, as anthropologist and inquisitor, performing a deadly type of 'fieldwork' in the waters of the zone several centuries ago.

What the direct testimony of the fugitive captives contained was 'life': a freshness and wealth of small-scale detail that could be used to explore the mentalities and material world of several generations of slaves; an exceptionally rich source, containing singularly invaluable textured accounts around which to base, on a cultural level, a historical ethnography, case studies and a collective biography. I made extensive use of this neglected source of social history in the book to reconstruct the social organisation of Sulu slave raiding, slave life in the zone and to make slave voices speak.[12] The macro-empirical trade data based on the shipping returns of the port of Manila (particularly the *estados* and the *almojarifazgo*) and the statements of the fugitive slaves complement one another, and together enabled me to resolve fundamental questions about the scope and magnitude of the Sulu Zone's global–regional trade, its flourishing slave population, and how these changed over time as a consequence of the impact of the China trade and the machinations of the world capitalist economy. The methodological search for a way to link the experience of individuals and related events in their lives, to larger, impersonal systems, as described and analysed in *The Sulu Zone*, was most tenable at the intersection(s) bridging the 'narrative space of ethnography',[13] the use of quantitative methods for the prosopographer, and the study in depth of the small scale. In this way, I adapted the methods of social anthropology and historical computing to do historical research and ethnography in the archives, in order to understand the 'otherness' of a previous era, and place the Sulu Zone, or, as the French social historian, Robert Darnton, phrased it, to do 'history in the ethnographic grain'.[14]

A key problem in focusing on the collective identity of particular social groups in the book—slaves and Iranun and Samal Balangingi raiders—was to choose a sample which represented the total regional and social population(s) of the zone. Spanish naval officers, specialists in 'contemporary Sulu affairs', interrogated the fugitive slave informants, and more than a century and a half later, I used both content and statistical analysis to create a multi-source, integrated database, as a prosopographer. The difficulties that attended an analysis of the social and ethnic complexity of the historical situation(s) of the slaves and their Taosug and Samal masters could only be depicted through a prosopography: a collective biography, resting on a scaffolding of empirically integrated fragments of life histories. The effort to recover their stories from abstruse sources for this book, the raw material for both history and anthropology, is based on the capacity of a creative imagination to evoke the everyday life of a 'little people'—namely, captives and slaves—and the conviction that carefully accumulated detail or 'thick description,' emphasising both experience and explanation, is the best way to reconstruct a sense of their time and place.

The Sulu Zone—some conclusions: Slavery, transformations and rethinking globalisation

My understanding and discussion of global economic–cultural interconnections and interdependencies about the Sulu Zone and the China trade were based on the premise that these intersections were governed by particular economic systems and set in a specific era and locality. The Taosug lived in a singular time and time meant change. They also lived in a singular place and geography meant destiny. The zone was a place where borders were becoming ever more porous, less bounded, less fixed, stimulated in large measure by global–regional flows of commodities, people and ideas; a kind of powerful magnet whose force European and Chinese traders were drawn to because that was where a lot of the exotica for Chinese cuisine and medicine and other commodities for the Canton market were being collected and processed. What then is the importance of *The Sulu Zone*'s thesis about the China tea trade's complicated place within its 'borderless' history? It has been a central argument of this book that we cannot think of societies and cultures in isolation, as self-maintaining, autonomous, enduring systems.[15]

In the pages of *The Sulu Zone* the world has changed through the intersections of the global trade economy centred on the Sulu and Celebes seas, as well as the Sultanate's critical place within it. Here, ordinary Southeast Asian farmers and fishers were traumatically uprooted and forced to live in a distant economic region. This world was comprised of winners responding to new economic opportunities of 'globalisation', and losers who were those forced to live in ways unanticipated before that moment of capture and enslavement. Trade debts in Jolo were paid off by slaves serving Taosug masters in the fisheries and forests of the zone. The point is that tens of thousands of ordinary Southeast Asians lived among maritime peoples completely removed from those with whom they had been born and grown up. They found themselves abroad in the seascape of the zone. First, because advanced technologies and new social alignments made long-distance slave raiding relatively easy and second, because revolutionary economic historical developments forcefully landed them in an unintended place—the zone. European traders joined with Taosug *datus* to spark one of the largest population movements in recent Southeast Asia history, with hundreds of thousands of individuals sent into slavery across the zone. Turnover in Iranun–Samal slave trafficking was in excess of millions of dollars a year: human cargo and Chinese tea then were as profitable as drugs and guns. Hence, all these commodities became inextricably entangled with one another in a deadly global trade. One of the most intractable problems facing the Southeast Asian world in the eighteenth and nineteenth centuries was connected with the huge number of captive people being taken to the Sulu Zone, never to return. However, displacement need not necessarily always be equated with social death.

Let us briefly contemplate here the force of circumstance and fate of the indigenous women of the Visayas and Luzon, who were unmercifully targeted by the Iranun and Balangingi slave raiders. Strand gatherers, these women were picked up from the beaches in the grey light of dawn as they fossicked along the shoreline. Their husbands were often slaughtered on the spot and the bodies left as a grim warning to others. In their time, these women of Luzon, the Visayas and other coastal stretches of Southeast Asia knew something of fear and real despair. For women around the region seized as captives, life in the middle passage could look like a valley of dry bones with no signs of hope of a new life. Yet out of such a tragic reality, the traditional Muslim social system could inspire new life, new beginnings and new hope—if captives were prepared to cross the line and renounce their previous ways of life and faith. The newly widowed women (sometimes with their children) were transported as slaves to the powerful sultanate(s) in the south of the archipelago where they were expected to work on providing lucrative goods to be traded with the English, Chinese and Americans—or where they became concubines or secretaries (if they could read and write) of the already rich and powerful. By the start of the nineteenth century, slave identities in the zone were being shaped and changed by the forces of 'globalisation' as distinctions of ethnicity and culture blurred and were broken down; thousands of 'outsiders' were being incorporated into the lower reaches of a rapidly expanding Islamic trading society. Sulu provides an outstanding example of how a collective identity was established, made real, and how it assumed a particular cultural content.[16]

There are no statistics on the overall number of slaves imported into Jolo between 1768 and 1878, except the estimates of European observers and local informants. In *The Sulu Zone*, I have argued that slave imports to the Sulu Sultanate during the first sixty-five years probably averaged between 2,000 and 3,000 annually. The steepest rise in the estimated number of slaves annually brought to Sulu, between 3,000 and 4,000, occurred in the period 1836 to 1848, and slackened considerably in the next several decades, with imports ranging between 1,200 and 2,000 slaves a year until the external trade collapsed in the 1870s. The figures appeared to show that between 200,000 and 300,000 captives were transported in Iranun and Samal Balangingi vessels to become slaves in the Sulu Sultanate in the period from the late eighteenth to the late nineteenth century. However, now, earlier estimates of the scale of the slave traffic described and analysed in *The Sulu Zone* have to be revised further upward for the first half of the nineteenth century, especially as the trade with China reached its zenith between the 1820s and 1840s. In July 2004, I discovered a hitherto unknown confidential report on the number of slaving vessels entering the port of Jolo, with detailed data provided by a Spanish merchant captain on the numbers captured and brought to be sold there. The stunning findings of the confidential log or 'census' suggests that between 4,000 and 6,000 Visayans, expert divers and seafarers, alone were being enslaved on an annual basis by the Iranun and Balangingi by 1845.[17]

Certain lessons and examples from history about global economic–cultural interconnections and interdependencies in this book also tended to explain patterns and events that have been formally glossed over; for example, sugar 'demanded' slaves and the Atlantic slave trade. Similarly, tea, inextricably bound to sugar as product and fate, would also inadvertently 'demand' slaves in the Sulu Zone and thus lead to the advent of Iranun–Balangingi long-distance, maritime slave raiding. Since the Europeans and Americans primarily wanted sea cucumber, shark's fin, pearls and bird's nests for the trade in China tea, the issue of the nature of productive relations in the Sulu Sultanate—slavery—suddenly became of primary importance. The soaring demand for certain local commodities in return for foreign imports affected the allocation and control of labour and the demand for fresh captives throughout the Sulu Zone. In this globalising context, tea was more than simply the crucial commodity in the development of trade between China and the West. In this history of the Sulu Zone, filled with so many deals and intrigues and such geographical scope, tea was also a plant that was instrumental in the stunning systematic development of commerce, power and population in the Sulu Zone which changed the regional face and history of insular Southeast Asia. Nevertheless, in a comparative diasporic context, the statistics on the explosion of displacement and production in *The Sulu Zone*, to satisfy the trajectory of a craving and taste, are small when compared to eleven million Africans who endured the middle passage to the New World during the three and half centuries of the Atlantic slave trade.

The Sulu Sultanate was an exceptional case for ethnohistorical investigation because the history of the zone demonstrated clearly the links between large economic and cultural systems and social mechanisms and institutions, on the one hand, and on the other, the making of collective worlds of more localised smaller communities. In short, as Kenneth Prewitt puts it, 'The global-local notion is not a metaphor invented by social theorists.'[18] Rather, it was the lived experience of millions of people in the zone and on several continents, inextricably bound to one another as product and fate. Part of the challenge for me had been to identify and link broad patterns and variations in interactions of the global economy and macro-historical trends with the 'autonomous-local history' of a barely recognised economic region in Southeast Asia. The long-term changes that occurred in these patterns and trends, based on economic interconnections and imperatives of the world capitalist economy and colonialism, had to be explained and understood through their interdependent effects in the environment, on ideas, on events, on human nature, and on the social and cultural transformation of the world(s) of the 'zone'.

The patterns revealed by the book threw up some unavoidable conclusions. The first is that the implications of the framing and analysis of the economy, culture and society of the Sulu Zone, perhaps could be applied in a wider framework not only to elucidate the development of states and the elaboration of ethnic diversity in insular Southeast Asia, but also to develop a comparative framework with mainland states and cultures, concerned namely with the impact of foreign trade; the rise and demise of populations; the rapid and expansive circulation of commodities, ideas and genes; and colonial interventions.[19] A second conclusion concerns an observation that can be made about the nature of researching and writing Southeast Asian modern history. Namely, it is the trans-historical, trans-cultural, trans-disciplinary, methodological approach linking detailed research of a local situation to wider global–regional economic systems and issues that underpins this book.

Finally, a third inescapable conclusion of *The Sulu Zone* entailed something more: the making of this ethnohistory not only involved an extension of the content and meaning of ethnicity and 'culture' in the pursuit of history, it also implied a revision of that content. What I suggested more than a quarter of a century ago, in *The Sulu Zone* and elsewhere, is that in a new history of insular Southeast Asia, the 'little people' (fishers, 'raiders', divers, traders, highlanders, forest-dwellers, 'squatter' agriculturalists, refugees, asylum-seekers and slaves, both men and women) should be prominent and visibly present, as part of the cultural landscape and complex geographical environment of a series of regional economic 'zones'—areas that are often on the margins of states, enmeshed in the hemispheric framework of the larger changing contemporary globalised world of cultural flows and economic interactions, replete with their relentless painful accounts of intrigue, displacement, paradox and insights into the human condition about courage and the will to survive. This methodological approach is especially relevant today, in a world where globalisation has become critically important in the first decade of our new century. So much controversy has filled history, so much research and analytical storytelling skills are required. The fundamental problems of North–South intersections and interactions encountered in the everyday lives of peasants, maritime and tribal peoples—making their livings and losing them, entangled in globalising events beyond their own local geographic borders and worlds—is the work of future concerned historians of Asia.

Singapore: Towards the making of a trilogy

I also became increasingly preoccupied in the mid-1970s with the local viewpoints and local understandings of ordinary Southeast Asians, past and present. Often, like the Samal Bajau Laut, they were at the edge of history—dispossessed and abandoned. Much of this population—coolie and peasant—was seemingly inarticulate and had left less in the way of historical records than the more prominent few. I wanted somehow to resurrect their views, concerns and desire to make their choices a reality. But how does one manage to write a People's History? Are there new sources to be tapped, or new ways of using the more traditional ones? Whereas historians of the past found their images of the Southeast Asian world in the fates of governors, generals, aristocrats and literati, I sought its images in the daily life of ordinary urban and rural-dwellers, in the experience of rickshaw coolies and prostitutes, the working sons and daughters of impoverished Chinese and Japanese peasant farmers. What I wanted to create was a personal history of their times—an inner history—closely based on lived experience, while, at the same time, paying careful attention to the larger historical influences—the institutions, processes and interactions—which determined their fates.

My study of the rickshaw coolies and prostitutes of Singapore in the late nineteenth and twentieth centuries has been an individual project nearly thirty years in the making. It emerged from a somewhat different historical and political context from *The Sulu Zone*. The books were based on my experience and vocation as a teacher of non-Western history in a post-colonial world. A passion for a forgotten past of people who have stood outside history and recovery of a whole set of social relations have been central preoccupations running through all my work. This is especially so in the case of *Rickshaw Coolie* and *Ah Ku and Karayuki-san*. The books insist on seeing things relationally using concepts and techniques from sociology and anthropology. The lessons in both of these disciplines for the study of history suggest how to create a total set of social relations—a socio-cultural system—in a historical past. This sociological–historical approach, which also entails elements of an ethnohistorical research strategy, is something I have stressed in my teaching, and tried to put into practice in my writing.

The underside of Singapore Chinese society and the city's development, as a commercial centre and entrepôt port from 1870 to 1940, have been the setting for much of my work for the past two decades. Both *Rickshaw Coolie* and *Ah Ku and Karayuki-san*, the two recent social histories in an envisaged trilogy, deal with the same part of Southeast Asia—turn-of-the-century Singapore, wedged between British Malaya and the Netherlands Indies—with its own startling tough 'history from below' and idiosyncrasies as a Chinese city outside China. These books examine the social conditions that spawned the rickshaw and prostitution industries and the way the rickshaw pullers and prostitutes lived the meaning of their lives in conjunction with the big changes taking place in the development of colonial Singapore and Asia. Mass migration, rural unrest and change, industrialisation in Japan, high finance and the Depression (the dark side of urbanisation in Singapore)—these topics all received their due in both works, albeit with somewhat different emphases, given my particular historiographical and thematic concerns in the respective volumes.

Discovery—1978

But, let me pause for a moment here, in order to travel back in time, to consider, briefly, the 'context of discovery' of the most important source for attempting to write this trilogy, as a social history from below—the Coroner's Records for Colonial Singapore, 1883–1940. It is late January 1978 in Singapore; I am stymied. I was fast running out of government repositories and libraries in a desperate search for documents that would provide insight into the singular identity and sociability of ordinary Chinese men and women. Since completing *The Sulu Zone* two years earlier, I had been thinking seriously of writing a historical survey about labour, migration and social transformation in a colonial city like Singapore. Perhaps, I asked, in a race against time, does the elderly court clerk know of the whereabouts of records which would help me place the lives of his parents' and grandparents' generation in a meaningful historical context. The old Chinese man did not think he could be of any real assistance but said that he still remembered the location of 'some old things' in the huge modern Court building. The two of us arranged to visit the Subordinate Court storeroom just two floors above the following morning. When the door was unlocked for me, after several months of fruitless searching, to a still largely empty storeroom in the new Subordinate Courts building, I gained entry to a collection of several hundred unclassified quarto size volumes stacked high against a wall, to a height of over one metre. The floor itself in several spots was also covered with piles of unsorted Certificate of Coroner's Views and miscellaneous documents into which everything had been dumped, higgledy-piggledy—a horizontal load filling an area more than twice the size of my office!

I can still remember my surprise when the mindful clerk standing in the open door pointed across the large room towards the mass of documents. Not sure where to start without a checklist or guide of some sort, I began to rummage among the stacks closest to me. I started to dig in and there was just about everything—Coroner's Inquests, Coroner's Views, suicide notes, drafts of letters, even recipes and household bills! The first two hours or so were both thrilling and somewhat confusing. Without stopping for a rest over the entire day, I was introduced to the beginning of an absolutely enormous cast of ordinary men and women whose life experiences were situated at a point in time in a 'visitable past'[20]—rickshaw pullers, construction workers, the homeless, parents, addicts, prostitutes, petty criminals and many others—and I immediately wondered how their stories all might fit together. Sensing the historiographical possibilities these documents offered for the study of ordinary Chinese men and women, and the fact that their experiences all might fit together, as I gradually learned, was one of the major turning points towards envisaging the trilogy. Initially, I randomly picked up, and with great excitement read the Coroner's view of the suicide of the *karayuki-san*, Oichi.[21] This was my first encounter with this extraordinary source. I shall never forget it. In a very real sense, Oichi's way of dying was the thread I pulled to begin to untangle the whole fabric of the changes occurring in the underside of Singapore society. As I dug deeper, solitarily standing in the storeroom where an elderly clerk had inadvertently revealed this treasure trove, and read the first inquest statements of rickshaw pullers and their kin and of prostitutes and their clients, finding expressions of their personal grief, of pain and frustration, of the misery that colonial rule and the Depression had inflicted upon them, of an extreme structural poverty reflected in the incidence of suicide, and of life's small pleasures like a special meal of chicken, rice wine and noodles shared with friends, I shelved the idea of merely surveying the 'inner history' of the city in a single volume.

Nonetheless, as I explored the documents another sort of reality bore down on me. As with the statements of the fugitive slave accounts of the Sulu Sultanate, I learned there was no substitute for seeing the literal evidence of a life and material circumstance—the carefully penned note, of a forlorn *karayuki-san*, a midday account of a ritual meal with the recipe still extant as if ready to prepare or pointing eerily in the direction of the vanished cook, or an ironic mention of an old rickshaw wheel, stored above a beam across the top of a latrine, which a rickshaw puller used to commit suicide. The search for this past reality was my real purpose for having come to Singapore—to resurrect events and images that would fill out and revise the story in the history books, to mark and memorialise this city as the rickshaw men and prostitutes knew it, and to waken the ghosts of Victoria Street and Duxton Road, and Malay and Smith Streets, in order breathe life into the past and to make dead people live again.

The material I found was breathtakingly exciting, not only for the light it threw on Singapore's prewar society and economy, but for the way it illuminated in sharp detail the dramatic changes that occurred in Singapore Chinese culture and history, yet within the memory of a visitable generation, still close enough to be grasped, especially the period from the early 1900s to the late 1930s. I set to work, travelling back and forth for several years, between a tiny corner of the Subordinate Court's library in Singapore and my own university office, reading, analysing and getting the material in order. The contents of this repository would yield up with skill and patience, the living testimony of Chinese people who did not know how to express themselves in print and who did not have direct access to people in power. Obviously, there was a great deal to learn from this trove of inquests and inquiries. 'It was when life was framed in death that the picture was really hung up,' observed Henry James.[22]

Giving voice

I wanted to write a history of the Chinese in Singapore full of 'imaginative drama and narrative sweep',[23] one that would be primarily about ordinary individuals and the incalculability of their lives. The stories emerge from the texts of the inquests and inquiries complete with deeply impressive dialogue. The Coroner's work is stunning, and thoroughly purposeful. It seemed to me writing about these cases of death from the point of view of anthropological history was a way of framing and re-presenting what had actually happened in life to rickshaw coolies and prostitutes, and for giving voice—preferably their own voice or voices of family and friends, and enemies or strangers in association with them—to passengers, clients, lovers, samaritans or assailants.

All the fundamentally great themes of power and innocence, friendship and loyalty, goodness and evil, love and betrayal in all its forms and fathomless complexities were found in the Coroner's cases about the lives of these very ordinary, sometimes dangerous, often inarticulate men and women. Until that moment of 'discovery' there was no knowledge of such vanished feelings and 'events' to speak of whatsoever. And I think that was very important because, when I was working on *Rickshaw Coolie* and *Ah Ku and Karayuki-san*, I tried to recreate such emotions and moments through the complex voices with which the Coroner and others spoke of the dead, and by travelling back in time in my imagination, not just along the busy thoroughfares lined with rickshaws, but into the *kongsi* foyers and on to the brothel verandas and beyond. Both volumes were an attempt to understand the character of a tidewater colonial city and important relationships and experiences in the lives of coolies and prostitutes, linking behavioural codes, cultural attitudes and work that left many fumbling for a livelihood and unsure of their emotional ground in the face of grief, loss of employment, or resentment over the failure of relationships.

I have not mentioned the necessity of a strong stomach in researching and writing this social history, as I was seriously interested in addressing the great themes of life, work, love and death. The business of life and death in the history of Singapore Chinese society and culture had to be faced. It was one of the weightiest things in the existence of the city—very heavy. Of course, a wide angle, deeply focused reconstruction of the mental, emotional and material life of previously unknown worlds is hardly novel territory for social history over the past several decades. But I think conflict was still the essence of the social drama of it all, no matter how I attenuated or conceptualised these themes. Winning and losing, as cases about the rickshaw and prostitution industries demonstrated, were still endings that people—coolies and prostitutes—passionately cared about, but the 'events' or 'knots' that triggered an ending were not always part of a sensible life, and last-minute winnings and losses of power, face, innocence, trust and wellbeing were often the most dramatic and ironic of all. Reversals of expectations about the nature of particular coolies' and prostitutes' lives and their choices were not foolproof. The repercussions of their decisions often put them on a well-trodden path that generally ended dangerously, as the 'events' in the Coroner's Inquests repeatedly proved to me. However, even stories that divulged a calculated manipulation implicit in such unexpected reversals, could also disclose, on closer examination, a path of great courage.[24]

To discover the links between the experience of the rickshaw pullers and prostitutes and the larger events in their lives, I have depended on different branches of social inquiry. Micro-sociology and ethnohistory have been critical in showing how empirical research can be shaped and changed. This approach to the history of rickshaw pulling and prostitution has necessarily combined the broader concerns of social and economic transformation with tracing the experiences of these men and women's lives. By expanding the temporal reach of analysis it was possible to provide an account of the typical career pattern of a rickshaw puller or an *ah ku* and how they lived the 'big changes' in Singapore at the turn of the century. An obvious result of this approach has been to clarify the process of moving the boundaries in historical methodology and thought, as the questions asked of Singapore history in these volumes changed, and new expectations of the craft were imposed.

The difficulties that attended an analysis of the emotional complexity of the historical situations of the rickshaw pullers and of the *ah ku* and *karayuki-san*, and the contradictions inherent in their lives—the exact combination of motives, pressures, values and feelings—perhaps, could only be depicted in these volumes through a prosopography or collective biography. This technique compelled me to pay close attention to the disparate experiences, values and motives of a relatively small group of coolies and prostitutes in diverse contexts and sequences of action, in order to piece together in a convincing manner the pattern and meaning of their lives for the majority of rickshaw pullers and *ah ku*.

Grounded in solid archival research, blending anthropological–historical techniques with literary imagery, both books, in the end, are about the experience of trying to maintain personal and cultural dignity in the face of overwhelming historical assault. It is the story of Chinese men and women and Japanese girls tearing up their roots to work offshore on the streets and in the brothels of colonial Singapore; social histories that relate their life experiences, their instincts for survival and what they knew, or did not know, and their courage and weakness in a world that often denied them freedom and love, which made many of them very complex characters. The excruciatingly personal records of the rickshaw pullers and prostitutes' lives speak to us, as individuals in the twenty-first century, about the traditional virtues of humility and endurance, of poverty, work and family, of sexual inequality and social repression, of pain, grief and (com)passion, and of loneliness and death.

Singapore return: *Broken Birds*

In March 1994, while sitting under the stars with Singapore's old Fort Canning Centre as a backdrop, I was treated to a two-hour multimedia extravaganza about young Japanese prostitutes broken by the harsh lives they were forced to lead abroad. A century ago, Japan had only a limited number of major exports—silk, coal and women. In my book, *Ah Ku and Karayuki-san*, young women were either abducted or lured from the villages of Japan to Singapore with promises of abundant wealth. *Broken Birds: An Epic Longing*, inspired by my book, also tells the story of the Japanese women forced by circumstances to work as prostitutes in Singapore from the 1870s until the 1920s.

Broken Birds was a visual spectacle and a different theatrical event from the usual cloistered indoor experience. It was ironic that this avant-garde production about Japanese women of the Meiji–Taisho eras should be re-enacted in Singapore's oldest cemetery, along Percival Road. The dramatic presentation and the extraordinarily beautiful singing voices set against the backdrop of such an unusual venue were mesmerising. The outdoor opera-type production in seven parts with a cast of twenty-four, was played out in dance, drama and music. The action unfolded through evocative one-line statements from my book based on actual oral accounts and Coroners' reports, because many of the women and girls died violent deaths. There is no attempt to build up proper characters. Ong Keng Sen, one of Singapore's most creative directors, hoped to have audiences understand intuitively and emotionally what these lives signified. The play was not about characters; it was a collection of voices—a collage that had been fused and reconstructed in time—theirs and ours. Ong felt that the power of these anonymous voices, instead of just having specific characters speaking, could not be underestimated. Lines like 'I don't think it's wrong to sell our daughters who we raised ourselves' are startling, and that is why Ong allowed the words to speak for themselves.

Broken Birds provided gripping viewing; it raised profound issues about the human condition, especially when read together with *Ah Ku and Karayuki-san*. Both the production and the book, inadequacies notwithstanding, set the mind to spinning around several of the central questions of our human condition. One of the most important issues, so old, yet so current, is the relationship between good and evil. Ong and I confront the viewer and reader with the complexity of the relationship between good and evil, the difficulty of defining either, and the way in which all of us embrace at least some of both. Evil, for Ong and me, exists. But it cannot be defined simply. As much as its causes lie in the human heart, they also lie in economic and political systems. Ong was deeply affected by the film, *Schindler's List*, in which he saw the sweep of humanity, and the horror of the Holocaust that swept away my mother's family in Lithuania. In the same way, events like the traffic in *karayuki-san* that happened in the name of economic and political gain would not be repeated in time if we listened to history more carefully, stated Ong soberly. 'The genocide in Cambodia; Bosnia would not carry with it the echoes of the Jewish extermination—the collective memories and tears of humanity. More voices must be heard.'[25]

For a theatre production that was both sometimes quasi-operatic but more a concert piece, for which a semi-staged production was necessary, there was one element in *Broken Birds* that no audience could miss—the music. It was haunting. *Broken Birds* elevated the importance of music in productions that are neither musicals nor operas. It elevated the importance of music from being incidental to crucial. *Broken Birds* also bridged another gap: that between history and the performing arts. Such a venture certainly makes history far more accessible. While historical facts—for example, details from a suicide note—can be overlooked easily in a book like my own, it becomes much more immediate when it is performed with music and movement. Here history has given material about Japanese women abroad for theatre, and theatre has given a wider audience for history. I have learned, because of the immediacy of theatre and its wider reach, that historians should consider collaborating with theatre practitioners as another means to communicate the results of their dialogue with the past.

There is also the question of audience, too. There are additional audiences to be addressed, and academically trained historians owe it to themselves as well as to the public at large to address these larger audiences. We need to speak not only to our colleagues, but also to special interest groups, historical societies, community and civic organisations, and to young people. If we fail to engage the broader audience while talking only to ourselves, then journalists, filmmakers and public relation specialists will deliver history to the public and influence the way people create historical memory and meaning.

The future

I have had further thoughts about *The Sulu Zone* since the ideas associated with the book first came to me in the years between 1970 and 1975. In the 1990s I was given the opportunity to 'pass over' twice into Japanese society and culture at the behest of colleagues, former students and friends in Japan. In 1996, on the occasion of my second visit for one year, the Center for Southeast Asian Studies, Kyoto University, asked me to write a small book that would explore various aspects of my thinking about the framing and writing of *The Sulu Zone*. After a hiatus of more than fifteen years, while I worked on other major projects in Singapore and the Philippines, I returned to the broad canvas of the Sulu Zone to begin exploring the ethnohistory of the Iranun and Balangingi anew, and also to inquire into the global struggles and misunderstandings that linked patterns of consumption and 'frontiers of desire' in Europe, China and Southeast Asia with particular entangled commodities, maritime spaces and cultural geographies. Apart from the remaining volume in the envisaged trilogy about suicide in Singapore Chinese society and culture, and the longstanding project about the impact of the typhoon on Philippine society and history, the aim of my recent book, *Iranun and Balangingi*, was to explore ethnic, cultural and material changes in the transformative history of oceans and seas, commodities and populations, mariners and ships, and raiders and refugees in Southeast Asia, with particular reference to the Sulu–Mindanao region, or the Sulu Zone: the oceans and seas of Asia. East by south, from Canton to Makassar, and from Singapore to the Bird's Head coast of New Guinea, crossed by Iranun and Balangingi raiding and slaving ships, Southeast Asian merchant vessels and colonial warships have been the sites of extraordinary conflicts and changes often associated with the formation of ethnic groups and boundaries, political struggles and national histories. Examining the profound changes that were taking place in the Sulu–Mindanao region and elsewhere, this book, the companion volume to *The Sulu Zone*, charts an ethnohistorical framework for understanding the emerging interconnected patterns of global commerce, long-distance maritime raiding, and the formation and maintenance of ethnic identity. I begin by tracing the evolution of Iranun maritime raiding from its late-eighteenth-century origins to support the English supplies of tea from China, into the nineteenth century's systematic, regional-based slaving and marauding activity. I then draw out the implications of that evolution for colonial systems of domination, development and discourse in the context of trans-oceanic trade, cross-cultural exchange and empire building.

The Iranun dramatic expansion west across Southeast Asia and south to the fabled Spice Islands in the 1780s is still poorly understood. What made the Iranun leave their homeland in south-western Mindanao? How did they so successfully navigate the length and breadth of Southeast Asia, and beyond? When and why were the Iranun settlements in the Philippines, Indonesia and Malaysia established and why did the majority of them eventually disappear? Answers to these questions were found in many places: fragile, long-forgotten objects in museum collections in Singapore, Spain, London and the United States. Archaeological sites and place names in the Philippines, Borneo and east Sumatra were also used to track the Iranun's western and southern expansion at the end of the eighteenth century. Manuscripts in the Philippine National Archive, Arsip Nasional, Algemeene Rijksarchief, the Archive of the Indies, the Museo Naval and the British Library, preserving the deeds and even the words of the Iranun and Balangingi tell their own part of the story. There are also rare illustrations from the pre-camera era—images on paper and canvas reminding us about new dimensions of worlds seemingly lost. The use by the Spanish of *kapal api* ('fire ships' or steam gunboats) against the palisaded fort at Balangingi in 1848 was the start of a new era of conflict—an era that was to bring about the end of the Iranun Age and the long-distance maritime raiding that characterised it. I discovered an oil painting of this battle in a naval archive in Spain. However, this painting does not capture the terror of the Balangingi women and children as they sheltered in makeshift bunkers below the main fort while Spanish soldiers and marines attacked; nor does it depict the traumatic deaths of some of the women and children—killed by Balangingi warriors—to prevent their being seized and becoming spoils of war for the Spaniards. But my words attempt to evoke the near total horror of the situation when their world and entire way of life was shattered forever in that defining moment of the trauma of conquest.

The broader issues of economic integration and identity formation that underpin this book also provided an apt backdrop to the current Muslim contestations and state and ethnic politics in the Philippines. Few other ethnic groups in Southeast Asia have developed such a notorious legacy of 'piracy' as the Iranun and Balangingi. This book throws light on the principal fact that these maritime Muslim groups in the Sulu Archipelago and south-western Mindanao have always been very autonomous and led a free-roaming existence in Southeast Asian waters. These vikings of Asia laid claim to being the true lords of the eastern seas in the age of sail. But it all came to an abrupt end in the mid-nineteenth century with the advent of steam gunboats. The Dutch, the British and the Spanish, in a rare instance of cooperation, banded together and put steamboats, armed with massive firepower, in the major channels and straits across the region. Soon, the hunters became the hunted. They tried to defend the frontiers of their world(s) against the West, but in vain. The concerted powerful Western response started in 1848; after only twenty years, the *musim lanun* or season of the Iranun was over. It was the end of a way of life of a people who dominated the seas for hundreds of years. *Iranun and Balangingi* clearly demonstrated the economic motivation, geographical realities, cultural nexus and religious impetus to 'piracy' in the area. Without that insight, it would be difficult to fully understand why Muslim autonomy remains such a burning issue in the Sulu Archipelago and south-western Mindanao today. While this ethnohistory deals with the historical legacy of 'piracy', the book was also a pertinent reminder of how cultures and ethnic identities are embedded in seafaring lifestyles and political processes that have not, in certain aspects, changed dramatically over the last two centuries. Today, there are some 149,000 who still identify themselves as Iranun in the coastal areas about Polloc Harbour and Illana Bay east of Zamboanga, and a small group still called Illanun of over 4,000 people on the western coastal plains of Sabah (North Borneo); remnants of their culture are still evident in their blacksmithing, their dances and songs, and their weavings. The end of their maritime rule meant that they had to adapt as best they could to the changing times, and with the influx of Christian migrant 'newcomers' to the 'final frontier' that was Mindanao, the Iranun became a minority. The adjustment was even more traumatic for the Balangingi: the Spanish had them deported in the hundreds, and they never regained anything approaching their old status, even in the Muslim world. It was the end of an era. The Iranun and Balangingi remain marginalised from the Filipino nation state and their intractable cause has only emboldened them to fight for ethnic identity, progress and autonomous statehood.

This ethnohistory comprised the second volume in a newly envisaged series. The first book, *The Sulu Zone*, was published in 1981; the second was *Iranun and Balangingi*, while the final volume will deal with slavery and collective biography in the Sulu world. The continuing impetus for this project stems from some ideas developed in the essay written in Japan in 1996 and subsequently published as a small book in the Netherlands, entitled *The Sulu Zone, the World Capitalist Economy and the Historical Imagination*.

At the beginning of the first decade of the new millennium, I temporarily 'passed over' from the School of Asian Studies, Murdoch University—my intellectual 'home' for the past quarter of a century—to the newly established Asia Research Institute, National University of Singapore. The Asia Research Institute is committed to negotiating the disciplinary fault lines between the Social Sciences and Humanities, pioneering thematic, collaborative, transdisciplinary research about Southeast Asia. Manning Clark tells us that the historian has to possess a vision that can allow the individual to research, write and teach about the things that really matter.[26] I have attempted in the course of my life to research and write history with a belief in the possibility that my vision will stir up a response in my students and audience. I also hope that I have used my time 'in the field' well, passing over the abyss or chasm and coming back, in order to write and teach about Southeast Asian Modern History from the perspective of the edge. I have been committed to teaching and context-sensitive research—with a strong cultural–ecological orientation for over three decades. A trans-historical, trans-cultural and trans-disciplinary approach is essential to the study of Southeast Asia. It is especially critical in opening up new horizons, developing theoretically informed historical analyses, and nurturing empathy for other peoples and places, and to understand their pasts and futures. Finally, to paraphrase Joseph Campbell, brilliant scholar, teacher and interpreter of some of our most sacred traditions, on the challenge of living, in the field and in the world, a closing reflection. As you attempt to live the meaning of your life and follow the way of the historian you will most certainly encounter John Dunne's abyss or chasm.

>Leap.
>Pass over.
>It is not nearly as wide as you might think.[27]

Chapter 1

The Sulu Zone: Commerce and Evolution of a Multi-Ethnic Polity, 1768–1898[1]

> It seems to me inaccurate to dispose of such Indonesian States as Palembang, Siak, Achin, or Johore with the qualifications corrupt despotisms, pirate states, and slave states, hotbeds of political danger and decay. Inaccurate, if for no other reason, because despotism, piracy and slavery are historical terms, and history is not written with value judgements. To choose examples from the field of Dutch history, the town of Flushing based its existence in the seventeenth and eighteenth centuries in no small measure on privateering and smuggling, and Middleburg's renowned trading company of 1720 occupied itself with privateering, smuggling to and from Spanish America and slave trade…The chief point is something else; what was the power—political-maritime-economic—of the harbour principalities.
>
> J. C. Van Leur

Of the many topics in the history of the Indonesian Archipelago, attention should be drawn especially to those that concern Asian social and economic history. Despite the stress Van Leur gave to illuminating the study of Indonesian trade and society four decades ago,[2] few since then have looked beyond the European experience.[3] In the north-eastern corner of the archipelago, historians continue to pursue the 'trade and empire' approach, while the region's separate history remains in Van Leur's words, 'grey and undifferentiated'.[4] Significant among the neglected aspects of its history is a reconstruction of the character of commerce and power. To date the expansion of external trade and the growing incidence of slave raiding in the region at the end of the eighteenth century have claimed the attention of most historians only when those social forces collided with or were affected by European policy.[5] Political and administrative in preference to social and economic, the histories of few Western scholars have dealt carefully with the interrelationship of commerce, marauding and servitude in a Southeast Asian harbour realm.

In a recent study, I have drawn upon anthropological concepts, particularly the idea of a 'segmentary state', European documents and local accounts to examine the economic vitality of the independent Sulu Sultanate's role as entrepôt for European as well as Asian commerce in the China trade from the late eighteenth to the end of the nineteenth century.[6] The Sultanate provided an ideal basis for such a study on several grounds. Solid anthropological fieldwork had been done over the course of the last two decades among the Taosug of Jolo, the Balangingi Samal, the Samal Bajau Laut, and the Yakan of Basilan in the Sulu Archipelago and Northeast Borneo, and among the Maranao and Subanun of Mindanao.[7] Without the ethnographic materials that have been published as a result of this fieldwork, it would have been difficult to assess the value of European historical sources and to place them in context.

There were ample sources for the study of the commercial-marauding patterns of the Sulu Sultanate in the period 1768–1898, but they were dispersed in several European archives and in Manila and Jakarta. While much of the material in English on Sulu had been exploited (although only from the point of view of European policy and trade in the Indonesian Archipelago), primary source material in Spanish and Dutch archives had been generally neglected. There remained then a need for research into these archival collections to present a coherent picture of Sulu's commercial position from the mid-eighteenth to the late nineteenth century.

Among the more important sources I have used are the manuscripts in the archives of Spain (principally Seville) on trade from Manila to the Sulu Sultanate between 1786 and 1848. When compiled and ordered as a time series, these documents (particularly the *estados* and *almojarifazgo*) suggest the overall level of commercial activity, shifts in market preferences, and the economic interdependence of Manila and Jolo in the period.[8] This datum goes far towards rounding out the detailed evidence which Van Leur saw to be lacking for maritime powers in the Indonesian Archipelago. The statements of fugitive captives of the Sulu Sultanate are another interesting source I have drawn upon. They throw very considerable light on the internal processes— the ethnic and social transformations—in the Sulu trading zone during the nineteenth century.[9]

The Sulu Zone

The Sulu Archipelago bridged two worlds and lay at a most strategic point for the maritime trade of the nineteenth century. China, the Philippines and Mindanao were situated to the north; Borneo to the south-west; and to the south-east, the Celebes and Moluccas (see Map 1.1). The Sulu chain of islands separated the autonomous Muslim, maritime world of Eastern Indonesia in

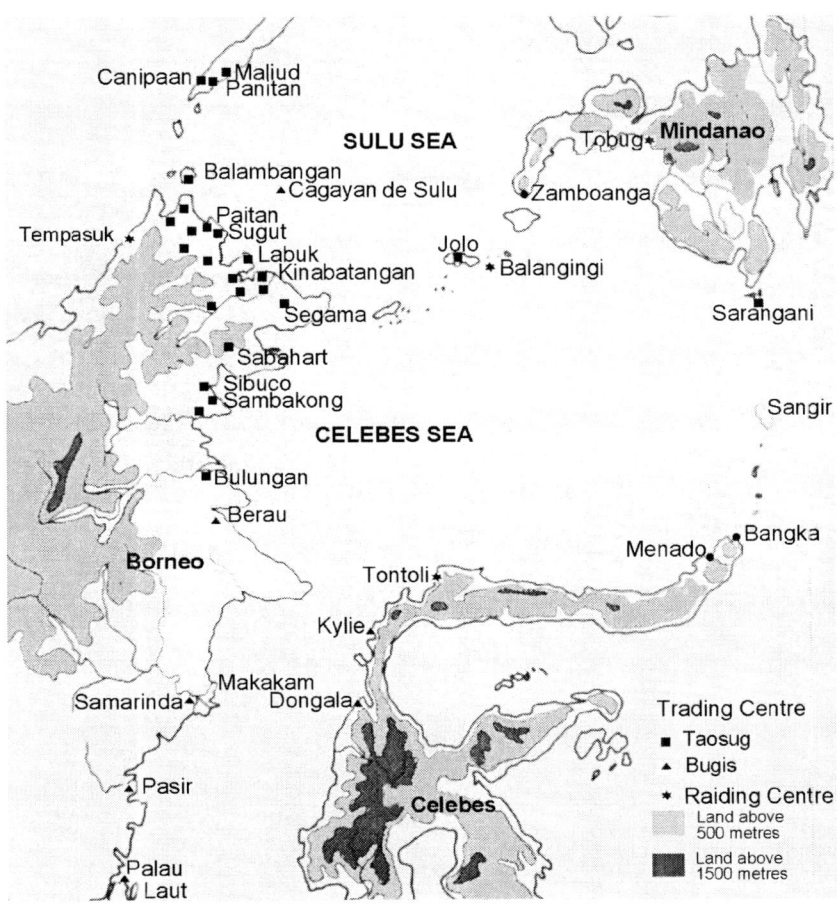

Map 1.1 The Sulu Zone

the eighteenth and nineteenth centuries from the Philippine Archipelago to the north—agrarian, Christianised and administered by Spanish colonial authorities from Manila. The crystallisation of Jolo, the capital of the Sulu Sultanate, at the end of the eighteenth century as the focal point of a broad system of trade, and centre for the marketing of slaves, outfitting of marauders and defiance of Spanish incursion, was in large measure attributable to its geographical location astride the arterial trade routes near the centre of the Eastern Malaysian seas.

Fundamental to understanding Sulu's political and commercial ascendancy after 1768 is the necessity of interpreting the Sultanate's historical experience within a wider regional framework. To explain social interaction between ethnic groups within the region, I have used the framework of a 'centre–periphery' concept. 'Hinterland' refers not only to the interior of a large land mass such as Mindanao or Borneo, but also includes island clusters within the Sulu Archipelago that depended on the port sultanate at Jolo.[10] This mode of analysis provides a means of interpreting the tensions prevalent in a region where traditional states were defined by varying relationships to the centre rather than fixed geographical frontiers.

In the late eighteenth and nineteenth centuries, there existed in the zone comprising the Sulu Archipelago, the north-west coast of Borneo, the foreland of southern Mindanao and the western coast of Celebes, a loosely integrated political system that embraced island and coastal populace, maritime, nomadic fishers, and slash-and-burn agriculturalists of the coastal rim and interior foothills. This network of interpersonal relations that was fluid across time and easily subject to disruption was integrated by the commercial-marauding patterns that came to be focused on Sulu, as the prime redistributive centre for the zone in the late eighteenth century.

Commerce and the evolution of a multi-ethnic state 1768–1898

Two perspectives have dominated the historiography of the Sulu Zone and have tended to obscure the complex but integrated patterns of trade, raiding and slavery. On the one hand, the 'decay theory' has presented Muslim marauding as a symptom of the decline of trade and the deterioration of the Malayo-Muslim State.[11] On the other, raiding is interpreted within the framework of the 'Moro Wars' as retaliation against Spanish colonialism and religious incursion.[12] Both theories have underestimated the relationship of slavery and raiding activity to the economy of the Sulu Sultanate.

My hypothesis concentrates on the social forces generated within the Sulu Sultanate by the China trade, a trade that dominated so much of the economic life of Southeast Asia—namely, the advent of organised, long-distance slave raiding and the incorporation of foreign peoples on a large scale into Sulu society. Under the stimulus of the China trade the Sulu Sultanate experienced tremendous economic growth. The period 1768–1848 witnessed a florescence of political and economic life that accompanied the large-scale infusion of captives, European trade goods and arms. During this period, when regional trade was firmly in the hands of the Taosug (the dominant ethnic group), Jolo became the common market for the zone at the expense of its erstwhile more powerful neighbours, Cotabato and Brunei.

Trade created the zone. In their efforts to obtain *tripang*, bird's nest, wax and camphor for Chinese consumption, Taosug *datus* forged trade pacts with tribal peoples of east Borneo and Bugis traders to the south (see Map 1.1). Captives and trade commodities were introduced along the rivers by Taosug and their trading partners. Taosug who intermarried with tribal people and lived at the middle reaches of the rivers on Borneo's north-east coast formed a commercial link between ethnic groups at the periphery and their Taosug kindred at the centre. Within Sulu's economy, the unprecedented demands of international trade for marine and jungle produce created the need for large-scale recruitment of labour. As the China trade grew so did the demand for labour-power to do the labour-intensive work of procurement. Driven by their patrons' desire for wealth and power, the Iranun and Samal surged out of the Sulu Archipelago in search of slaves. Within two decades their raids encompassed all of island Southeast Asia. Their well-armed *prahus* scoured the coasts of the Indonesian world and sailed northwards into the Philippines. In the course of these raids, they combined with other Iranun and Samal speaking groups living at satellite stations on the coasts of Borneo, Celebes and Sumatra. Navigating with the monsoon, their *prahus* returned to Jolo loaded with captives to be exchanged with Taosug for rice, cloth and luxury wants.

By the dawn of the nineteenth century, slavery and slave raiding were fundamental to the state. The Taosug aristocracy depended for its prosperity on the labour of slaves and sea raiders, who fished for *tripang*, secured pearls and provided crews for the fleets. The Balangingi formed the bulk of the crews of the slave raiders. The infamous reputation Sulu acquired for slave-mongering and piracy in the nineteenth century is attributable to the activities of the Balangingi, an 'emergent society' increasingly composed of *Indio* (Filipino) captives and their descendants who were brought to the Sulu Archipelago, and in many cases assimilated within a single generation to become the predators of their own people.

The raiding system enabled the sultanate to incorporate vast numbers of people from the Philippines and eastern Indonesia into the population. Traffic in slaves reached its peak in Sulu in the period from 1800 to 1848, founded on the basis of trade with China and the West.[13] The process was dynamic. Trade demands kept forcing the sultanate to incorporate more people, rewarding those *datus* who provided the most produce and forcing them to acquire more wealth-producing persons if they wanted to stay on top of their rivals. Thus, the volume of produce collected kept rising, forcing up the number of people needed to procure it, and providing *datus* with the arms necessary to exercise control over the trade net.

Conclusion

The period from 1768 to 1848 had been one of growth and cohesion for the Sulu Sultanate. It put up stubborn opposition to European imperialism and proved more than a match for Western powers. This changed after mid-century. With cooperation among European navies and more effective use of steam vessels, the Sulu world began to shrink. The trade of the region began to deteriorate. The *datu's* main source of wealth was his following. The destruction of Balangingi and Jolo by the Spanish between 1846 and 1852 placed serious constraints on the ability of Taosug to retain control over the Balangingi Samal, their principal source of slaves. The grooved cannon and gunpowder of the West that had first attracted Iranun and Samal to Jolo as clients and suppliers of captives were now operating to drive them apart. There was a progressive fragmentation of Samal groups because of Spanish incursions and disruption of the Taosug economy.

The collapse of the system only came with the concerted effort of Spain to end Sulu's autonomy. In the 1870s the Spanish navy waged a campaign to systematically destroy all *prahu* shipping in the Sulu Archipelago and force the Taosug to settle down in villages as agriculturalists. This policy and the immigration of large numbers of Straits Chinese to Sulu, in spite of—or perhaps because of—the naval campaign, had disastrous consequences for the Taosug. They were forced to curtail their commercial activities and become dependent on the merchant immigrants with contacts in Singapore. The traditional redistributive role was taken away and the zone disintegrated.[14]

Chapter 2

Joseph Conrad's Fiction as Southeast Asian History: Trade and Politics in East Borneo in the Late Nineteenth Century[1]

It was the artistic genius of Joseph Conrad that evoked the spirit of the changes in the Kuran/Berau region in the late nineteenth century. The source of the novels, *Almayer's Folly, An Outcast of the Islands* and *Lord Jim*, was Conrad's experience as a first mate in the Singapore-based, Arab-owned steamer, the *Vidar*, in which he made several trips to the east coast of Borneo. From conversations and personal observations during the short space of nineteen weeks in the *Vidar* in 1887 and 1888, Conrad was able to sketch accurately the character of the men and the shape of the historical forces at work in the development of that part of Borneo.

Until quite recently, the historical significance of Conrad's writing for understanding the nature of pre-colonial trade and legal conditions in the smaller states of the *buitengewesten* (outer islands; area beyond Java) in the late nineteenth and early twentieth centuries has been ignored. Dutch scholars, for the most part, found themselves at odds with Conrad's description of a Malay world that flatly contradicted their concept of a monolithic Netherlands East Indies—*óns Indië* (see Map 2.1). It was left to Professor G. J. Resink to place Joseph Conrad's work in its proper perspective for the study of Southeast Asian history. Since his article 'De Archipel voor Joseph Conrad' appeared in 1959, several books have been devoted partially or entirely to Conrad's Southeast Asian experience, although more from a literary–historical point of view than a historiographical one.[2]

In *Almayer's Folly* and *An Outcast of the Islands*, Conrad describes the transformation that occurred in trade along the southern periphery of the Sulu Zone[3] through the careers of William Lingard (the Tom Lingard of his novels), the *Raja Laut* whose trade activities were already legend in the Singapore of Conrad's day; Charles Olmeijer, the Eurasian trader of Tanjong Redeb who was to become the protagonist of his first novel; and finally the Singapore Arabs who came with their steamboats to monopolise the trade in gutta-percha and rattans in the 1880s.

The Raja Laut

Contrary to popular belief, the first European to trade on the Berau River was not William Lingard but George Peacock King, a Bengal-born Englishman who had monopolised the rice trade to Lombok in the 1830s.[4] In 1845 he left Lombok to establish his trading headquarters at Samarinda aboard an old hulk that had been hauled up on the shore of the Mahakam River and fortified. In less than three years King had sent his *prahus* and agents to the Berau River to trade and at one point considered building a trading post at the confluence of the Segah and Kelai rivers.[5] He soon abandoned this project and devoted his full attention to Kutai's foreign trade and the development of a local coal industry.[6] As a result of King's example, a direct Western trade route developed to that part of Borneo. Trading houses on Java, Bali and Hong Kong sent vessels and agents to Samarinda and Makassar in the 1850s—William Lingard was among them.[7]

Lingard was never the only merchant-adventurer to trade at Gunung Tabor, but by discovering a way for a large sailing ship to pass through the labyrinth of mangrove swamps and tidal flats along one of the mouths of the Berau estuary, he made Gunung Tabor his trade domain for almost two decades. The discovery of the new passage, the 'Baak van Lingard' of official charts and surveys, occurred sometime between 1859 and 1863. Lingard had extended his trading activity at that time, on account of his shipowner, an Englishman, Francis James Secretan,[8] from Ampenan, Surabaya and Makassar to Berau and Bulungan. Once Lingard had placed buoys in 'his' channel,[9] he was able to reach the upriver settlement of Gunung Tabor more easily than his rival, a Makassar-based trader named van Hardrop, and became a prominent local figure.[10]

In 1862, Lingard, quick to recognise the trading opportunities that had been opened up by his pioneering efforts, persuaded the sultan of Gunung Tabor to elevate him to the status of *Pangeran*, and confer the title of 'Raja Laut Kapitan de Berau' (literally, Admiral of Berau) on him and that of 'Anja Kansanan' (a local Malay rank title of royalty) on his consort, in order to evade the terms of a Dutch contract with the petty state, which stipulated that foreigners were forbidden to settle in the sultan's territory without Batavia's expressed permission.[11] Within two years, Lingard had left Secretan's employ, established business connections in Singapore, where he bought an interest in the sailing vessel, *Coeran*, and set himself up as an independent trader to ply between Singapore, East Borneo and Makassar.[12]

In Batavia, Netherlands East Indies officials were apprehensive when news began to reach them that another Englishman had become a Raja on Borneo;

they feared that this new 'sovereign' might follow James Brooke's example and establish himself as an independent ruler. The authorities ordered an on-the-spot investigation by the commander of the Dutch warship, *Celebes*, in 1863.[13] This report, and a separate inquiry ordered by the governor of Makassar, demonstrated that the title of Raja Laut had been genuinely conferred on Lingard, who was sufficiently proud of his rank to have worn the official garb and displayed the *barang karajaan*, the symbols of his office (a *mandau*—ceremonial sword—and pike), on several public occasions.[14] But the report correctly surmised that Lingard, unlike James Brooke, had no serious territorial ambitions and was content to restrict the use of his considerable influence to matters of private trade.

In the course of the next few years, Lingard established firm trade relations with the hinterlands of Berau and Bulungan. It was the sort of operation that required at least two men—one to sail the vessel between East Borneo and Singapore, a journey of up to four months, and another to remain at the distant outpost to collect forest products. Lingard had been provided with sheds for storing rattan and wax since 1863 by the sultans of Gunung Tabor and Bulungan.[15] He and his partner Craig appear to have taken turns collecting and organising this cargo for export, and swapping voyages between Singapore, Makassar and Berau as alternate masters of the *Coeran* from 1864 to 1866 (See Table 2.1).[16] Lingard bought out Craig in 1866 but this arrangement—two men sharing the trading interest—continued until 1870 when the Raja Laut placed his wife's cousin, Charles Olmeijer,[17] in Tanjong Redeb as his trading agent. Olmeijer, who was to spend almost three decades at this out-of-the-way trading centre, assiduously developed the trade in gutta-percha and rattans for Captain Lingard. He made extended trips into the interior to collect produce and to search for gold.[18] Olmeijer befriended the Segai-i, slash-and-burn cultivators, with whom he traded at the upper reaches of the Berau; in later years, one of his sons was to be ritually adopted as a blood brother by a group of Kenyah.[19]

In Berau, the memory of Olmeijer and his trade activities lingered among the Kenyah and could still be recounted in the early 1950s—some longhouses possessed muzzle loaders, now heirlooms, which according to oral tradition were brought upcountry by Olmeijer.[20] When Conrad first saw him in 1887, 'from the bridge of a steamer moored to a rickity little wharf forty miles up, more or less, a Bornean River,' Charles Olmeijer had been at Tanjong Redeb for seventeen years and was already something of a legend:

> I had heard of him at Singapore; I had heard of him on board...I had heard of him in a place called Pulo Laut...I had heard of him in a place called Dongala,

in the island of Celebes...and I overheard more of Al-mayer's name amongst our deck passengers (mostly wandering traders of good repute) as they sat all over the ship—each man fenced around with bundles and boxes—on mats, on pillows, on quilts, on billets of wood, conversing of Island affairs.[21]

It was at Berau that Conrad also came to know Jim Lingard, the nephew of the Raja Laut. The local nickname of this tall, young, dignified trader—Tuan Jim—was to provide Conrad with the title for his novel, *Lord Jim*.[22] He had been initiated into the family business by his uncle at the Lingard and Company post in Bulungan in 1875. Five years later, Jim was transferred to Berau where he settled and worked as a commercial trader, first for Captain Lingard and later on as a tax collector for the sultan of Sambaliong in his 'Kebun Rotan'.[23]

Table 2.2 reveals the trade scramble for jungle products that Lingard and the members of his family became caught up in at Berau; among the most important was gutta-percha, the raw rubber made necessary in the West by the demands of a machine age. Prior to 1868, it was only the vessels of the Makassar firm, Weijergang and Son, that the Raja Laut had to contend with, but within five years the busy trade of Berau had attracted the Buginese and Chinese of Makassar (see Table 2.2). By 1875, two Makassar trading houses had their agents at Gunung Tabor.[24]

Map 2.1   Joseph Conrad's Eastern World showing the various places referred to in the text

The flow of shipping entering and leaving Singapore and Makassar shows that Lingard was more than able to cope in the period from 1870 to 1875, when he had the full support of his family and associates, and owned at one point four ships,[25] and conducted trade from Bulungan and Gunung Tabor to Makassar and Singapore.[26] Although Lingard is not mentioned by name in the *Kolonial Verslag* of 1875, except as an Englishman who had traded for years between Gunung Tabor and Singapore, a brief glimpse of the scope of his trade activity at this time is provided in a sarcastic letter that he wrote to the editor of the *Makassarsch Handelsblad* which chided the Dutch for not guarding 'their' Bornean coastline against 'piracy'.

> On Monday morning 22 November (1875)...I left the *West Indian* in the small steamer *Johannes Carolina* with my wife to visit Goenoeng Tabor to see how things were going on, and to get gutta-percha etc. to take to Singapore. On Wednesday night left Brow and overtook my schooner *Fanny* outward bound to Boeloengan with cargo of rice, etc. took her in tow and towed outside the river...On Thursday morning left her and proceeded up the inner channel between the reefs to pass inside Po. Raboe.[27]

The cargo information on shipping arriving from Berau and Bulungan at Makassar supports Conrad's description in *Almayer's Folly* of the various sorts of trade goods brought from the outside world by Lingard and others to East Borneo: 'Into that river...Lingard used to take his assorted cargo of Manchester goods, brass gongs, rifles and gunpowder.'[28] It was Olmeijer acting as Lingard's 'broker' who exchanged the food items—salt, rice and sugar—Javanese tobacco and opium, textiles and hardware, as well as firearms and gunpowder for the raw rubber, rattans and wax brought to Tanjong Redeb by interior Kenyah.

Upriver longhouses came to rely on the market at Tanjong Redeb as an outlet for jungle and agricultural produce; and as a source of staples, clothing, tools and weapons. There was a considerable trade by the Kenyah in firearms that found their way into the interior along the route from the Sibuco to Kwarmote and the Kinabatangan. Kenyah traders bartered them to tribes in the interior of North Borneo for jungle produce that they removed by way of the rivers to Berau and Bulungan for export.[29] This problem—the leakage of jungle products from the north central hinterlands to the watersheds of the southern rivers 'was to vex the North Borneo Chartered Company well into the twentieth century.'[30] Although Olmeijer and Jim Lingard made long trips into the interior, most traders were discouraged from doing so and the trade of the hinterlands of these rivers, which involved thousands of people, was brought down by the Segai-i and the slaves of the sultan and local chiefs who also went into the forests in search of jungle produce.[31]

An approximate measure of this barter trade is the kind and quantity of raw products the Segai-i furnished for the private traders who came to Berau and Bulungan. Steamships like the *Tromp, Vidar* and *Paknam* with their increased cargo capacity, speed and organised schedules, making six or more journeys a year to these small riverine centres, were responsible for a further intensification of the trade; they exported tens of thousands of piculs of gutta-percha and rattans in the 1880s.[32] By that time, when gutta-percha was selling in Singapore for as much as eighty-five dollars a picul,[33] William Lingard had lost his monopoly of the export trade of Berau and Bulungan. A relentless competition for the control of the inter-island trade of Southeast Asia had begun several years earlier between steam navigation and sailing ships. On the east coast of Borneo, it proved to be a one-sided contest.

The combination of the new technological innovation, the steamboat, and the inflated prices for gutta-percha quickly brought the Arab traders of Singapore to Berau. Among the most important of these were representatives of one of the Strait's settlement's wealthiest Arabs, Syed Mohsin bin Saleh Al Joofree.[34] Members of Syed Mohsin's family established a trading post with warehouses, offices and a wharf on the Kelai branch of the Berau.[35] This station, which was responsible for much of Olmeijer's misfortune as an independent trader,[36] was operated for more than twenty years by Syed Mohsin's son, Syed Abdulla, with the assistance of Haji Mohammad Nohr and a local Buginese, Daeng Marola.[37]

The Arabs used a small steamer, the *Emily*, to run between Bulungan and the various rivers between Berau and Batu Tinagat,[38] and placed the schooner-rigged steamer of 304 tons, *Vidar*, on a trade circuit linking Singapore to Banjermasin, Dongala, Kutai, Berau and Bulungan. The round trip took three weeks and the steamer only stayed at each place long enough to load cargo, a day or two at the most.

Once the Singapore Arab steamer and similar vessels from Makassar began to sail on regular runs to East Borneo, the competition gradually became unbearable for the Raja Laut, who, unlike his close friend John Ross, remained a strong advocate of sailing ships and did not fully appreciate the new technology until it was too late. In the end he was forced to give up Singapore as a home port and clear out of Berau as the Arabs took over the trade, but not before chartering the steamers *Paknam* and *Banca* to bring his cargo to Elopura (Sandakan) and Makassar between 1882 and 1886 (see Table 2.2).[39]

Conclusion

The disappearance of the Raja Laut signified the end of an era of Asian forms of shipping and trade within the Sulu Zone. The statistics which I have compiled show that local products were exported in exchange for foodstuffs, luxury goods and arms by Asian and European traders who operated on an equal footing in independent local states or stateless societies. The colonial conquest of the outer islands by the Spanish and Dutch, and the advent of steam shipping lines on the eve of the twentieth century, introduced a new era in which the traditional patterns of political and commercial life portrayed in Joseph Conrad's fiction lost their basis of importance.

Table 2.1 Trade from Singapore to Berau, Bulungan and Makassar: 1864–1879

Ship	Master	Departed for	Arrived from	Ship	Master	Departed for	Arrived from
Coeran	Craig	Makassar – Jun. 1864		West Indian	Lingard		Berau – Aug. 1872
	Lingard		Makassar – Nov. 1864		Lingard	Berau – Sept. 1872	
	Lingard	Borneo – Dec. 1864			Merry		Borneo – Feb. 1873
	Craig		Borneo – Mar. 1865		Merry	Berau – Feb. 1873	Borneo – Aug. 1873
	Lingard		Surabaya – Jul. 1865		Lingard	Berau – Sept. 1873	Borneo – Feb. 1874
	Lingard	Borneo – Aug. 1866	Borneo – Oct. 1865	Coeran (sold Feb. 1874)	Avery		Borneo – Oct. 1873
	Craig	Borneo – Nov. 1865	Berau – May 1866	West Indian	Mackay		Borneo – Aug. 1874
	Lingard	Surabaya – Jul. 1866 and Borneo	Borneo – Nov. 1866		Mackay	Berau – Oct. 1874	
	Hanisch	Labuan – Nov. 1866			Donald		Berau – Nov. 1874
	Hanisch		Berau – Jun. 1867		Mackay		Berau – Apr. 1875
	Hanisch	Borneo – Jul. 1867			Lingard	Borneo – Aug. 1875	Bulungan – Dec. 1875
	Hanisch		Berau – Mar. 1868		Lingard	Samarang – Jan. 1876	Makassar – Jul. 1876
	Partridge	Berau – Apr. 1868			Lingard		Berau – Dec. 1876
	Lingard	Bulungan – Jul. 1869	Borneo – Jun. 1869		Lingard		Berau – May 1877
	Lingard	Borneo – Apr. 1870	Borneo – Mar. 1870		Lingard	Berau – May 1877	Borneo – Aug. 1877
	Lingard	Borneo – Sept. 1870	Berau – Aug. 1870		Lingard	Borneo – Oct. 1877	Berau – Jan. 1878
	Ewing		Borneo – Mar. 1871		Lingard	Makassar – Jan. 1878	Borneo – Jul. 1878
	Lingard	Borneo – Apr. 1871	Kutai – Jul. 1871		Lingard	E. Coast – Sept. 1878	
West Indian bought in Apr	Moss		Makassar – Dec. 1871	(up for sale)	Hugill		Kutai – Dec. 1878
Coeran	Lingard			Rajah Laut	Lingard	Makassar – Jan. 1879	Makassar – May 1879
	Palmer		Makassar – Jun. 1872		Lingard		Borneo – Nov. 1879
	Merry	Berau – Aug. 1872					

Table 2.2 Trade with east Borneo in selected years from Makassar between 1868 and 1883, compiled from the 'Shipping News' in the harbour column of the *Makassarsch Handelsblad*, 1868–1883

Ship	Master	Departed for	Arrived from	Export cargo	Value (Florins)	Import cargo	Value (Florins)
1868							
N.I. Schooner, *Celine*	Saja		Bulungan 6 May 1868			70 piculs gutta-percha, 18 piculs wax, textiles, silver coinage	4,000
Celine	Saja	Bulungan 28 June 1868	Bulungan 16 November 1868	352 piculs rice, sugar, spices, opium, textiles 320 florin silver coins	3,500		
Eng. Schooner, *Dorothea*	Camaron		Kutai 29 May 1868			120 piculs gutta-percha, munitions, textiles	
Eng. Schooner, *Fanny*	Kennedy		Berau 21 May 1868				
Eng Schooner, *Fanny*	Kennedy	Bulungan 21 June 1868					
N.I. Schooner, *Fanny*	Lantu	Bulungan 1 June 1868	Bulungan 24 September 1868	Cotton textiles, opium, beads, 5 piculs spices, 108 piculs salt, 260 piculs rice and assorted goods	743		
Eng. Schooner, *Coeran*	Lingard		Berau 3 June 1868				
Coeran	Lingard	Sourabaya 21 June 1868					
N.I. Cutter, *Sussana Cornelia*	Mulder		Berau 4 June 1868				
N.I. Schooner, *Jonge Jan*	Manusama		Berau 22 June 1868				

Ship	Master	Departed for	Arrived from	Export cargo	Value (Florins)	Import cargo	Value (Florins)
N.I. Schooner, *De Eersterling*	Mhd. Jassing	Berau 11 July 1868		32 piculs rice, opium, cotton textiles from Europe (Agent Chong Kong Sing)			
N.I. Schooner, *Jupiter*	Amalo	Bulungan 13 July 1868					
N.I. Schooner, *Suruhan*	Sian Tong	Bulungan 13 July 1868					
N.I. Schooner, *Bintang*	Daeng Pawata	Bulungan via Kutai 17 October 1868					
N.I. Schooner, *Fathul Majid*	Si Pabolo		Bulungan 18 October 1868			215 piculs gutta-percha, 120 piculs rattan (Agent Si Pabolo)	
N.I. Schooner, *Jacoba Elizabeth*	F. Hausing		Berau 4 November 1868			39 piculs gutta-percha, 9 piculs wax, 350 piculs rattan (ordinary) 6 piculs rattan (fine) (Agent P. van Hardrop)	
Jacoba Elizabeth	F. Hausing	Berau 7 December 1868					
N.I. Schooner, *Jorge Jan*	Manusama		Berau 4 November 1868			65 piculs gutta-percha, 65 piculs wax, 300 piculs rattan, 13 piculs tripang	
Jorge Jan	Manusama	Berau 27 November 1868		650 piculs rice, 13 piculs salt, textiles, crockery, hardware, opium, arms			
N.I. Schooner, *Jeannete*	Kiramong	Bulungan 12 November 1868				166 piculs gutta-percha, 20 piculs wax	

Ship	Master	Departed for	Arrived from	Export cargo	Value (Florins)	Import cargo	Value (Florins)
Eng. Schooner, *Fanny*	Kennedy		Berau 24 November 1868				
N.I. Schooner, *Fanny*	Lantu	Berau 26 November 1868		308 piculs rice, opium, spices, sugar, cotton textiles, hardware	3,151		
1873							
N.I. Schooner, *Suruhan*	Sian Tong		Berau 7 January 1873			95 piculs gutta-percha (Agents J. G. Weijergang & Co.)	
Eng. Schooner, *Coeran*	Avery	Berau 13 February 1873		1,210 piculs rice, cotton textiles			
Eng. Schooner, *Fanny*	J.D. Voll		Berau 18 February 1873			136 piculs gutta-percha	
Fanny	J.D. Voll	Berau 31 March 1873		Textiles, munitions, parangs, beads, 468 piculs rice, 2,200 pounds brown sugar	8,000		
N.I. Schooner, *Celine*	Brugman		Bulungan 10 March 1873			80 piculs gutta-percha, 15 piculs dammar, 20 katties white bird's nest	
Steamship, *Vidar*	H.G. Reynolds		Singapore 19 May 1873				
Steamship *Vidar*	H.G. Reynolds	Surabaya 4 June 1873					
N.I. Schooner, *Jupiter*	Oosthoek		Berau 26 June 1873				

Ship	Master	Departed for	Arrived from	Export cargo	Value (Florins)	Import cargo	Value (Florins)
Eng. Steamship, *Augusta*	Schuck	Singapore 28 June 1873					
Eng. Schooner, *Coeran*	Avery		Berau 29 June 1873			305 piculs gutta-percha, 227 piculs rattan, 5 piculs tripang, 12 piculs wax 3 piculs dammar	
Coeran	Avery	Berau 23 July 1873		453 piculs rice, cotton textiles, 603 piculs tobacco, assorted hardware	1,000		
N.I. Schooner, *Celine*	Roskamp	Berau 3 August 1873		Cotton textiles, woollens, hardware, 15 piculs Javanese tobacco, 271 piculs rice, 40 piculs salt			
Eng. Bark, *Amy Warwick*	Karstues		Sandakan Bay 8 August 1873				
N.I. Schooner, *Jacoba Elizabeth*	Aru		Berau 25 August 1873			100 piculs gutta-percha, 320 piculs rattan, 13 tons coal	
Jacoba Elizabeth	Aru	Berau 26 October 1873		400 piculs rice, 150 piculs salt, 20 piculs sugar, assorted trade items			
N.I. Schooner, *Jupiter*	Oosthoek	Berau 31 August 1873	Berau 16 November 1873	960 piculs rice, cotton textiles, opium tobacco, assorted trade items	1,000	225 piculs gutta-percha, 730 piculs rattan, 85 piculs mother-of-pearl, 5 piculs wax	
N.I. Schooner, *Jorge Jan*	Aha		Bulungan 26 September 1873			60 piculs gutta-percha, 70 piculs rattan	
N.I. Schooner, *Fathul Rahman*	Si Pabolo	Bulungan 19 November 1873		500 piculs rice, 300 piculs tobacco, 5 piculs sugar		1,600 piculs rattan, 5 piculs gutta-percha	
Eng. Steamship, *Vidar*	Barrow		Singapore 16 December 1873				

Joseph Conrad's Fiction as Southeast Asian History

Ship	Master	Departed for	Arrived from	Export cargo	Value (Florins)	Import cargo	Value (Florins)
1878							
German Schooner, *Astrea*	Sandelfeldt		Berau 6 January 1878			900 piculs rattan, 26 piculs gutta-percha, 130 tons coal	
N.I. Schooner, *Jonge Jan*	Kobies		Berau 11 January 1878				
N.I. Steamship, *Tromp*	Deighton	Berau 21 January 1878	Berau Feb. 24, 1878			800 piculs gutta-percha, 50 piculs wax, 60 piculs dammar, 110 tons coal	
N.I. Steamship, *Tromp*	Deighton	Gorontalo 24 February 1878					
N.I. Schooner, *Fathul Majid*	Baginda		Bulungan 28 February 1878			900 piculs gutta-percha	
Eng. Bark, *West Indian*	Lingard	Berau 8 March 1878		Cotton textiles, opium, 340 piculs salt, assorted trade goods	7,500		
N.I. Steamship, *Tromp*	Winter		Berau 12 June 1878			976 piculs gutta-percha, 35 piculs dammar, 80 piculs wax, 1 picul bird's nest, 350 piculs rattan	
N.I. Steamship, *Tromp*	Wunter	Berau 1 July 1878	Bulungan 13 November 1878	6,000 pieces cloth, 90 bundles textiles, 75 dozen jars, 206 piculs coffee, 80 piculs tobacco, 151 piculs rice, opium	10,000	400 piculs gutta-percha, 38 piculs dammar, 50 piculs wax, 150 piculs rattan, 3 piculs bird's nest	
N.I. Schooner, *Radja Wali*	Brugman	Bulungan 13 August 1878					

45

Ship	Master	Departed for	Arrived from	Export cargo	Value (Florins)	Import cargo	Value (Florins)
N.I. Schooner, *Jorge Jan*	Kobies		Berau 11 September 1878				
N.I. Schooner, *Radja Wall*	Aha		Berau 29 October 1878			280 piculs rattan, 67 piculs gutta-percha, 7 piculs dammar	
N.I. Schooner, *Radja Wall*	Aha	Berau 29 November 1878					
N.I. Schooner, *Jupiter*	Tonrang	Berau 2 November 1878					
1883							
N.I. Steamship, *Tromp*	Roe	Bulungan via Berau 31 December 1882	Berau & Bulungan 22 January 1883				
Eng. Steamship, *Paknam*	Lingard		Sourabaya 2 February 1883				
Eng. Steamship, *Paknam*	Lingard	Gorontalo 7 February 1883	Gorontalo 26 February 1883				
N.I. Schooner, *Zeus*	Casseus		Bulungan 8 February 1883				
Eng. Steamship, *Paknam*	Lingard	Berau 1 March 1883	Bulungan 10 July 1883				
Eng. Steamship, *Poh Ann*	Craig		Singapore 17 April 1883				
N.I. Steamship, *Tromp*	Roe	Berau & Bulungan 21 April 1883					
N.I. Steamship, *Tromp*	Roe	Berau & Bulungan 10 July 1883					

Chapter 3

Who Were the Balangingi Samal? Slave raiding and Ethnogenesis in Nineteenth-century Sulu[1]

The problem of ethnic identification is an important but neglected theme in Southeast Asian history. Historians of the region are indebted to Leach, F. K. Lehman and M. Moerman for their pioneering work on the nature and history of upland societies in Southeast Asia.[2] In the *Political Systems of Highland Burma*, Leach demonstrates that culture and ethnic identity are not necessarily synonymous. He points out that the process of identification among tribal people like the Kachin is never simple; it entails migration, intermarriage, barter trade relations, warfare, inter-penetrating political systems, and values and beliefs shared with non-Kachin. Manifest in the work of all these anthropologists is a conscious effort to define the nature of social categories applied to ethnic groups in Southeast Asia across time. Their work has led to a more complete understanding of the nature of ethnic groups and the processes responsible for 'accomplishing ethnicity' among upland peoples in Southeast Asia.

These studies reveal more of the Southeast Asian past than was thought possible a generation ago, but our understanding of the development of the present extraordinary ethnic diversity of insular Southeast Asia still remains far from perfect. Historians of island Southeast Asia in particular have generally been inclined to accept 'ethnicity' as a fixed premise. Such a formulation has hindered necessary reappraisal of available evidence on the nature and history of particular 'societies'. An outstanding example of this is the case of the Balangingi Samal, a little-known but important population group in the nineteenth-century island world. Before the beginning of that century, the Balangingi Samal did not exist. Yet by the 1830s, Balangingi Samal slave raiding activities, which were an important component of the wider island economy of the Sulu Sultanate, had made them a group renowned and feared throughout Southeast Asia. How did this come about?

The zone encompassing the Sulu Sultanate is the historic home of peoples, languages and cultures as varied as its landscape (see Map 3.1). The Taosug ('peoples of the current'), the dominant ethnic group in the Sulu Archipelago (now part of the Philippines), are the sole residents of Jolo Island, the historical seat of the Sultanate.[3] Originally fishers and traders with martial skills and a flair

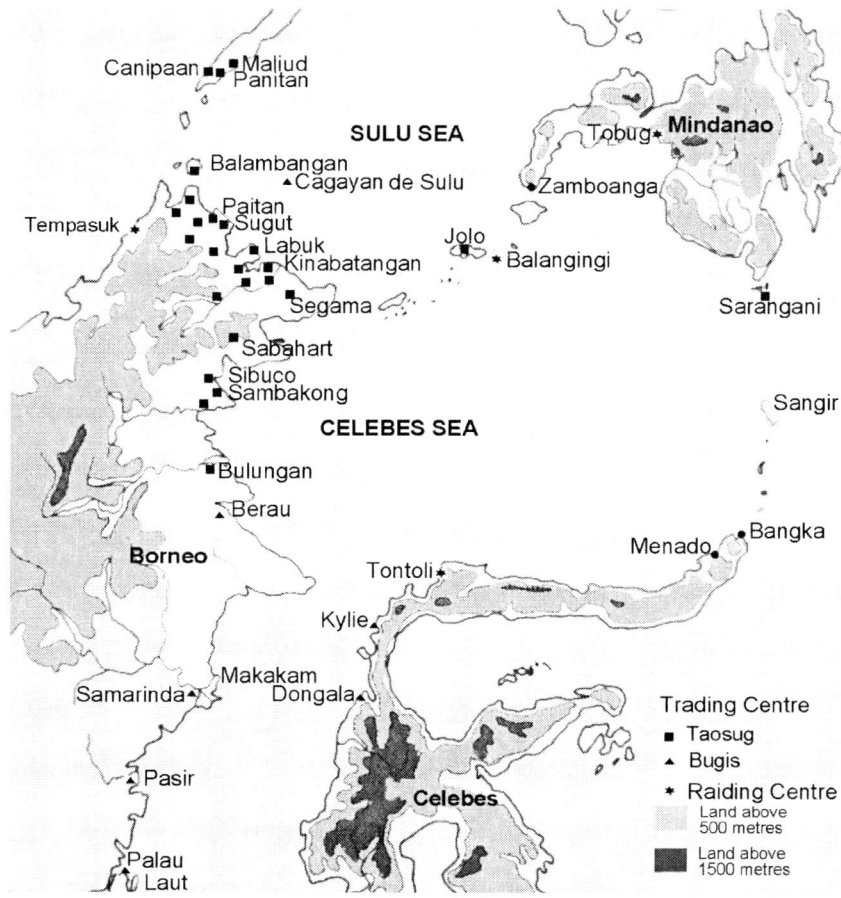

Map 3.1 The Sulu Zone

for organisation, numbers of them adopted agriculture. With the introduction of Islam, about the fifteenth century, they evolved a well-articulated political and economic system.[4] The institution of the sultanate established formal dominance of the Taosug over indigenous Samalan-speaking peoples and later migrants to Sulu.

The Samal, strand-dwellers with close ties to the sea, possessing highly developed boat-building techniques and sometimes practising simple garden agriculture, are the most widely dispersed of all ethnolinguistic groups in the Sulu chain. Manifesting the greatest degree of internal linguistic and cultural differentiation, Samal communities predominate on the coralline island clusters of the northern and southern parts of the Sulu Archipelago, as well as on north Borneo and on Celebes. The Samal distinguish among themselves by dialect, locality and cultural–ecological factors (principally between sedentary Muslim shore-dwellers and nomadic animistic boat-dwellers).[5]

Samals tend to identify themselves with a particular island, island cluster or regional orbit. In the late eighteenth and early nineteenth centuries, they comprised several groups that occupied non-contiguous territories along the southern Mindanao shore; on the south coast and in the near interior of Basilan; and on the islands of the Tapian Tana group, Cagayan de Sulu and the Balangingi cluster. Expert voyagers at sea, particular Samal groups had fixed bases of operation on a series of low coral-and-sand islands flanking the north-eastern side of Jolo. This group of islands, named Los Samales by the Spanish, was a springboard for launching seasonal raids against coastal villages from Luzon to Celebes. The most important island was Balangingi, dwelling place and organisational centre of the major slave-retailing group for the Sulu Sultanate in the first half of the nineteenth century (see Map 3.1). A related group of marauders, the Iranun, Maranao-speaking migratory strand-dwellers, established their principal settlements along the river mouths of the southern coast of Mindanao.

The history and organisation of the Balangingi Samal can be related generally to factors affecting ethnic and social transformations in the Sulu trading zone during the later eighteenth and the nineteenth centuries. Elsewhere, I have explained these changes in terms of stimuli supplied by a rapidly expanding foreign trade that encouraged the dependent peoples of the Sulu Sultanate to procure marine-forest produce.[6] Seasonal raiding programs in search of additional labour-power to service the procurement of trading produce— *tripang* (sea cucumber), bird's nests, wax, camphor, mother-of-pearl—became fundamental to the Sulu Sultanate as its economy expanded and it established itself as a powerful commercial centre.

After 1768, Sulu fitted into the patterns of European trade with China. The marine and jungle produce were new products for redressing the West's adverse trade balance with China. This commerce—involving trade with English merchants from Bengal, with Manila to the north, with Yankee adventurers from the New England seaboard, with Singapore and later Labuan—formed a complex set of interrelationships through which the Sultanate was able to consolidate its regional dominance. Under the stimulus of this international trade, the Taosug state experienced tremendous economic growth. The interdependent patterns of external trade contributed towards the Sultanate's ability to promote organised raiding, and hence its rise to power. The country traders of Bengal provided the Taosug with the sinews of marauding—shot, powder, ball and large cannon. The Manila merchants supplied basic foodstuffs in bulk because the Taosug needed a reliable source of food for the tiny archipelago's expanding population, so that they could employ their human resources in procurement and raiding rather than in agriculture. The period from 1768 to 1848 witnessed a large-scale infusion of captives, European trade goods and arms, accompanied by a florescence of political and economic life.[7]

The fishers of men

The unprecedented international trade demands for maritime and jungle products created the need for large-scale recruitment of labour in Sulu's economy. As the China trade grew, so did the demand for labour-power. Trade demands kept forcing the Sultanate to incorporate more people—rewarding those Taosug who provided the most produce, and forcing them to acquire more wealth-producing persons in order to compete with their rivals. Driven by their patrons' desire for wealth and power, the Iranun and Balangingi Samal surged out of the Sulu Archipelago in search of slaves.

From the end of the eighteenth century to the middle of the nineteenth, insular Southeast Asia felt the full force of the slave raiders of the Sulu Zone. Their harsh exploits were carried out on a large scale; well-organised fleets of large, swift *prahu* navigated along the west coast of Borneo and crossed the South China Sea to the Straits of Malacca and the Bay of Bengal. In the south, their raiding vessels thrust through the Makassar Strait and fanned out over the Indonesian world. They crossed the Banda Sea to New Guinea, made raids along the coasts of Java, and circumnavigated Borneo. In pursuit of captives, Iranun and Balangingi terrorised the Philippine Archipelago. They preyed on the poorly defended lowland coastal villages and towns of southern Luzon and the Visayan Islands. They even sailed and rowed their warships into Manila Bay, their annual cruises reaching the northern extremity of Luzon and beyond. They earned a reputation as daring, fierce marauders who jeopardised the maritime trade routes of Southeast Asia, and dominated the capture and transport of slaves to the Sulu Sultanate.

Historical studies have invariably failed to place Sulu's raiding activity in its proper context. Past and present historians of the colonial period, in considering the Sulu raids, have uncritically adopted the interpretation perpetrated by interests 'on the right side of the gunboat'.[8] They have relied heavily on sources inherently antagonistic to the nature of the society and values of the raiders: the hostile accounts of the Spanish friars, the printed reports of Dutch and English punitive expeditions, and Sir Stamford Raffles' and James Brooke's influential reports on 'Malay piracy'.

Ann Reber has shown that Raffles' writings were largely responsible for the genesis of a 'decay theory' of Malay piracy. Raffles forcefully argued that the monopolistic trade practices of the Europeans (particularly the Dutch) in the eighteenth century tore away the props that supported the economic foundations of many of the indigenous coastal and island realms; and that, severely weakened, these polities turned to piracy, the 'nemesis' of native trade and European commercial involvement in the Malay world.[9] Meant primarily for English consumption, Raffles' and Brooke's writings about the 'nefarious activities' of the Iranun and Balangingi relegated the Sulu Sultanate to the status of a mere 'pirates' nest' in the 1840s. This propaganda portraying the Sulu world as the scourge of the seas from Singapore to Papua became grist for anti-piracy campaigns mounted to destroy these seafarers whose demonstration of power aroused colonial governments from their lethargy. The decline-and-decadence interpretation gained currency with the passage of time, and is widely upheld by contemporary historians of the area.[10]

It is inadequate to explain the explosion of the Iranun and Balangingi into the mainstream of Southeast Asian history after 1768 purely in these terms. Imperative to an understanding of the nature and evolution of their marauding activities is a consideration of the relationship of Iranun and Balangingi raiding to the indigenous society and economy of the Sulu Sultanate. Much information can be gleaned from the heretofore virtually ignored statements of captives and records of trials and interrogations; these provide invaluable detail on the genesis and ethnic identity of particular Samal populations, and on the place of slaves and raiding in the Sulu world, from the perspective of the indigenous participants themselves.[11]

Ethnic identity and ethnogenesis: The Balangingi Samal

Considerable confusion has surrounded scholarly efforts to pinpoint the ethnic identity, and significance of the role and raiding activities of the Iranun and Balangingi in Southeast Asia's recent history.[12] These societies being labelled—in response to colonial governments and other authorities—Moros (Muslims), Sulu Zeeroovers (Sulu pirates) or Illanun (pirate) has bedevilled researchers who expect such populations to place themselves in one of the official categories. The ethnic nomenclature and ascription traditionally applied to the Iranun and Balangingi is particularly unreliable. Travellers, officials and academics have frequently failed to recognise the ethnolinguistic distinctions perceived by these raiding populations.

The name *I-lanaw-en*, a word of Magindanao origin meaning 'people from the lake', is a clue to the origins of the Iranun marauders. It suggests that they were originally Maranao, 'people of the lake' from the lofty tableland around Lake Lanao in central Mindanao.[13] The term was popularised by the coastal inhabitants of the Philippine Archipelago, the Malay Peninsula, Java, Sumatra and their European rulers as 'Illanun' (Iranun; Illanaon; Lanun; Illano)—and was erroneously extended to include the non-Maranao-speaking people of southern Mindanao, the Taosug of Jolo and the Samal of the Sulu Archipelago. On the other hand, to the shore-dwellers of Celebes, these seaborne raiders became known as 'Magindanao'. While they were rarely able to distinguish among the several ethnic groups that brought devastation to their coast every year, the people of the Celebes never forgot whence came the first Iranun marauders—southern Mindanao, opening like a window on Celebes; the label Magindanao was still being used in that aggrieved area to describe the Balangingi Samal in the 1850s.[14] Only Magindanao, Maranao and Iranun were called 'Illanun' by the Taosug of Jolo.[15]

The English used Illanun indiscriminately to denote simply 'Sulu pirates'. The Dutch considered the Illanun a 'vile race', identifying them as the shore-dwelling people of southern Mindanao, Sulu, and several places on the coasts of Borneo and Sumatra. The Spaniards viewed Jolo as the centre of a world fundamentally hostile to the interests of Spain and Catholicism—an Islamic world whose activities centred around piracy and slavery. In official reports to the Crown, they often referred to Iranun and Samal populations as *los Moros infieles* (the Muslim infidels). In the correspondence of the commanders of imperial gunboats who hunted them, in colonial gazettes, and in published works, the labels Moro, Zeeroover and Illanun were still being used as late as 1862 to classify various maritime peoples whose ethnic origins did not always correspond to linguistic and political affiliation.[16]

As Sulu's trade expanded at the end of the eighteenth century, Taosug *datu* (aristocrats) increasingly retained neighbouring groups of Samal as slave raiders. From Balangingi and related communities on other islands, Samal-speakers voyaged great distances; they swept the coasts from Luzon to Brunei and from Singapore to Menado, capturing slaves (see Map 6.2). But who were the Balangingi? Although Francisco Combes and Thomas Forrest described the warlike activities and trade of the Samal in earlier periods, there are no historical references to the Balangingi as a separate group before the nineteenth century.[17] In Western sources, marauders are first mentioned as Balangingi rather than Iranun in the area of Singapore and East Malaya in the 1830s.[18] From that period, the label Balangingi began to supersede Illanun in the

European literature as synonymous with 'pirate'. The Balangingi Samal seem to have acquired ethnic distinction only because they specialised in raiding activity and incorporated an incredible number of non-Samal peoples into their number.

The Balangingi Samal lived, along with Iranun and other Samal-speaking groups, in a dozen or more villages scattered along the southern Mindanao coast, on the southern shore of Basilan, and on the islands of the Samalese cluster of which Balangingi was dominant. The Samalese group comprised Balangingi Island (6 square miles) and Tunkil, a cluster of four islets (9.5 square miles) situated in the centre of the Sulu Archipelago, midway between Borneo and Mindanao. The islets were subject to change of size and shape with tidal variations and modulations in the wind and weather patterns, separating into small parcels of rock when inundated at high tide. They were fringed with mangrove swamps, and separated from neighbouring islands by reefs and winding channels through which swirled strong currents and counter-currents.[19] With no surface water, and little flora except the ubiquitous coconut palm, they were incapable of providing the subsistence base necessary to support a dense population.[20] On these islands, the Balangingi Samal constructed wells and four forts (Balangingi, Sipac, Bucotingal and Sangap) to guard their villages and *prahus*. The forts (*kota*), situated on raised ground and protected by coral reefs on three sides, were stockades of two, three and four tiers of stout tree trunks, packed with earth and coral to a height of six metres and defended with heavy cannon.[21]

The islands and shallow seas upon which the original Samalan-speaking people of the Balangingi cluster lived placed them in an ecological bind that shaped their character and relationship to the Sulu Sultanate. The sole orientation of the Samal was, of necessity, towards the sea. From it, as specialists in maritime raiding and marine procurement, they derived their strength, security and—ultimately—wealth. Lack of self-sufficiency bound the Samal to Jolo. Its proximity to Jolo as an outlet for retailing captives; its dependence on larger, volcanic islands like Jolo and Basilan as sources of rice, fruits and vegetables, and trade goods; and the natural barriers surrounding it help to explain why Balangingi became the natural home of one of the most feared piratical groups of island Southeast Asia.[22]

In the nineteenth century, the Balangingi were integrated within the Sulu Sultanate by a three-level class system comprising aristocrats, freemen and *a'ata* (slaves). The sultan appointed a *panglima* to represent him, but *datus* exercised titular rights and imposed jural authority over specific Samal islands and populations.[23] All *datu* were Taosug, but not infrequently *panglima* were

Samal. The Samal paid tribute in *tripang*, pearl shell and salt; and as clients of powerful *datu*, they offered their services for slaving expeditions, in return for trade opportunities and for protection from rival Taosug. *Datu* who exercised supervision over Samal populations were frequently associated with—if not directly related to—the sultan, and often resided in or near Jolo. In the first half of the nineteenth century, the most important Taosug patrons of Samal communities were Datu Dacula (Sipac), Datu Tahel, Datu Molok and Maharaja Leia (Balangingi).[24]

To understand the important role played by the Balangingi in the slave trade in Southeast Asia, it is necessary to trace their history as an ethnic group. The only historical work that deals with the Balangingi does not consider their ethnic origins.[25] Avoidance of this question presents a deceptive picture of a static 'society' with a homogeneous population. Samal groups in the Sulu Archipelago were emergent populations; the success of the Balangingi as slave raiders was due in large measure to their ethnic heterogeneity. Captives' statements present a picture of Samal populations undergoing constant readjustments until 1848. At the beginning of the nineteenth century, there was an infusion of ethnically diverse captive people among the Balangingi—mostly through demands for their labour on raiding *prahus*, and in the *tripang* and pearl fisheries that complicated the identity of the Samal populations.

Many of the captives or slaves who were brought to Balangingi turned Samal—borrowing language, religion and customs. Insufficient data prevent a precise reconstruction of the overall size and origin of Samal populations at that time. What information there is for the nineteenth century has survived in the statements of fugitive captives; these show that the incorporation of foreign elements took place on a large scale, especially in the second and third generations. In 1836 it was estimated that only one-tenth of the male population were 'true' Balangingi Samal; the remainder were *renegados* (renegades), more particularly Visayan and Tagalog *indios* (Filipinos), and other captives.[26]

The Taosug economy was expanding rapidly enough at this time for Samal populations to absorb larger and larger numbers of captives. An apparently conscious recruitment policy of the *datus* changed the numerical structure and ethnic composition of Samal groupings in less than two generations (1820–1848). F. Barth considers drastic a 10 per cent rate of incorporation in a generation.[27] By those standards, the flexibility of the Sulu system was incredible. Village populations in 1836 appear to have ranged from just over 300 people with ten to twelve raiding *prahu* at Tunkil to more than 1,000 people, with thirty to forty *prahu*, at Balangingi.[28] In less than a decade, Balangingi's population roughly quadrupled; in 1845 the village had an estimated 4,000 people and 120–150 large vessels.[29] The overall Samal population devoted to slave raiding reached an upper limit, in 1848, of 10,000 people with 200 raiding *prahu*.[30] The consequence of this extraordinary growth was the creation of an 'emergent' slave raiding population within the Sulu Sultanate—the Balangingi.

The social organisation of raiding

The general importance of the relationship of Balangingi raiders to the history of island Southeast Asia is widely recognised; but thus far, scholars have concentrated primarily on the Samal as 'pirates', and on their suppression by colonial navies.[31] These explanations of Samal piracy fail to recognise the central relationship of ethnogenesis to Sulu's redistributive economy, its exponential growth and its dependence on raiding. Clearly, much of the sultanate's power and much of the rapid growth of the Balangingi population in the first half of the nineteenth century stemmed from the traffic in slaves, and incorporation of them into the society.

For the Taosug, slave raiding was significantly related to power and wealth. A *datu* who could acquire large numbers of slaves could also engage more dependent people in procurement activities and trade. The surplus value of the wealth that the slaves produced enabled a Taosug aristocrat to attract other free men to him. J. Hunt recognised that the power of the *datus* derived from the number of wealth-producing persons—clients and slaves—in their retinues: 'Their principal passion appears to be a lust for power…and the object of their life is to increase their number of *ambas* (slaves).'[32] Thus, the principal aim of Taosug-sponsored Iranun/Balangingi attacks on Southeast Asian villages and *prahu* shipping was the capture of slaves who could be converted into a source of wealth.[33] Slave raiding in the Sulu Sultanate was highly organised. There were several types of expeditions: some equipped by the sultan and his kindred, some independently recruited with the encouragement of the sultan, and some conducted without the sanction of the sultan. The right to organise raiding expeditions resided at all levels of the Taosug political system; however, the sultan and certain *datu* on the coast—by virtue of their control over foreign trade and their more expansive network of alliances—were in the best position to actually carry it out.

The sultan's main source of wealth was from trade, harbour and market fees, and tribute. His income was supplemented, however, by slaves—given in repayment for commissions to raid, for assistance to raiding parties, and for harbour fees. Hunt charges the sultan with a principal role in the organisation of slave raids, stating that Samal raiders handed over to him and to other aristocrats a certain number of captives, on the basis of previous agreement.³⁴ The statements made by fugitive captives in the 1830s tend to corroborate this allegation. But the disclosures that directly implicate the sultan as an important backer are contained in the statements of Balangingi prisoners taken on board HMS *Wolf* after the capture of their *prahus* in West Malayan waters, and at Singapore's Paupers Hospital in 1836. As a captured slave, Silammkoom said, 'Orang Kaya Kullul informed us that the Sultan had desired him to plunder and capture all nations save Europeans.'³⁵

The military and economic activities of Samal populations were closely regulated by their Taosug patrons, who encouraged the Balangingi over a number of generations to become fishers of men. To meet the increased demands for slave labour in the Sulu Zone between 1800 and 1848, *datus* not only equipped Samal vessels but also provided credit to the Iranun—with advances in boats, powder and ball, cannon, rice, opium and additional crew.³⁶ Everything was to be repaid in captured slaves. In this context, slaves were considered not only chattels but currency as well; they provided a valuable medium of exchange that was readily transferable. For example, the value of a slave in the 1850s, as an article of barter in transactions between *datu* and Samal raiders, was roughly equivalent to 200–300 *gantangs* of rice. A *prahu* could be purchased for six to eight slaves; boat rental amounted to only two or three slaves. A rifle (often defective) could be rented for five pieces of linen of twenty fathoms; a portable cannon was loaned at the rate of one slave.³⁷

Most *datu* lacked the necessary means to equip expeditions on a large scale. The few *datu* who possessed such resources were inevitably involved in Sulu's external trade. Their strict supervision of external trade enabled them to maintain control over the supply and distribution of guns to client military groups. In the first half of the nineteenth century, there was a crucial struggle between the sultan (and his supporters) and other *datu* to establish exclusive control over the gun trade. By 1842, the sultan had lost dominance over external trade and particular Samal populations. As Charles Wilkes explained, 'The whole power, within the last thirty years, has been usurped by one or two *datus*, who now have monopolised the…foreign trade that comes to these islands.'³⁸ Two chiefs emerged paramount from a factional struggle spanning the three decades from 1810 to 1840: the Datu Molok, the prime minister, described in European accounts as an enterprising, intelligent man, owning four trading ships and a large quantity of arms (25 cannon and 100 muskets) and reputed to be worth 150,000 pesos; and Datu Tahel (the son of Datu Emir Bahar), a powerful figure in Sulu's foreign trade in the 1830s, and principal organiser of Balangingi raiding expeditions.³⁹

In the political organisation of slave raiding can be seen the elements responsible for Taosug military efficiency and predominance in the zone. The sultan and *datus* formed alliances with *panglimas* to authorise Samal groups to engage in raiding.[40] When permission was given to carry out a raid, the *panglima* acted as the organiser. It was he who obtained from the Taosug *datu* (who received, in return, a share of the captives) the supplies necessary to outfit the expedition. And it was he who appointed the *nakodah* (the *prahu* commanders).[41] Each *nakodah* was responsible for recruiting his own crew; he mustered them from his support groups in the village, personal kindred, dependent followers and others with whom he was allied. This pyramiding of authority and responsibility in the organisation of the raiding was commented on by British officials in 1838:

> It is also pretty certain from statements of [the] prisoners...that the six boats were under the command of Orang Kaja Koollul [who is]...reported to be related to *Panglima* Alip, the local chief of Bangeenge [Balangingi] who is again subordinate to the Sultan of Sulu.[42]

An expedition was commanded by a *panglima* or an *orang kaya* (a notable). Each *prahu* had its own *nakodah*; and a large part of the crew would be his kindred, followers and slaves. The successful execution of a slave raiding expedition was difficult and dangerous work, and depended largely on the skill of its personnel. Many renegades held important positions—*nakodah*, occasionally even squadron commander—in slaving expeditions; in return, they acquired wealth and slaves, who complemented their personal followings. Visayan *indios* in particular demonstrated their talent and courage as *nakodah*, and developed a fearful reputation in the Philippines;[43] but captives from other parts of the Malay world, who had knowledge of dialects and of their former localities, proved equally skilful boat commanders.[44]

Once the *panglima* and *nakodahs* determined the course, they rarely left the *prahus* during the voyage. They had several experienced officers to assist them: the *juru mudi* (*julmuri*), of whom there were two or more on each vessel, acted as steersmen and were responsible for the crew (*sakay*) and the maintenance of the boat; the *juru batu* (pilot) tended the anchor and kept watch for reefs, shoals, rocks, trading ships and the enemy. Accompanying a fleet was at least one *hatib* or *imam*, who read the Qur'an, led prayer recitation, and acted as legal arbiter and judge (*hakim*) when disputes arose between the commanders and their crews. In this way, strict discipline was maintained in the fleets. Most vessels appear to have carried several robust youths (12–15 years old), who could provide assistance at the oars in difficult situations as part of their apprenticeship while learning the fine points of raiding technique and navigation. Often there would be an elderly chief (*orang tua*) on board—a man no longer strong enough to be in command, but placing his rich store of experience at the disposal of the expedition.[45] Women rarely went on expeditions, except occasionally as consort of a commander.

The crewmembers consisted partly of Balangingi whose task was to fight, partly of trusted slaves who had accompanied the raiders since their youth, and slaves who had been seized on earlier expeditions. The officers and even ordinary crew brought slaves with them to cook, fetch water and assist them from time to time with their shipboard duties. The slaves were not armed, but were considered an integral part of the crew; it was their job to row, bail, clean and repair the *prahu*.[46] The size of the crew depended, of course, upon the size of the vessel. At the end of the eighteenth century, the largest Iranun raiding boats carried from fifty to eighty fighting men and about one hundred rowers. But in the nineteenth century, when slave raiders used smaller craft, the biggest Balangingi Samal *prahu* was only sixty to seventy feet long and carried a complement of no more than a hundred men including slaves. An average-size crew numbered about forty men. Smaller, less heavily armed boats carried twenty-five to thirty men.[47]

The size of the expedition depended not only upon its purpose, but also upon complex factors such as the overall length of time of the cruise, the participants' relative familiarity with the target areas, and—more importantly—the ability of the organiser to mobilise followers for the venture. Small expeditions could be managed by individual communities; sometimes whole crews came from a single village. However, composite crews were not uncommon in expeditions of less than ten *prahu*. Balangingi vessels frequently left with a skeleton crew of ten to fifteen men and travelled to neighbouring Samal villages and islands to fill out their complements.[48] It was common for masters to send unaccompanied slaves on these *prahu*, but *nakodah* were reluctant to take those who objected to their master's wish. Large-scale enterprises entailing thirty, forty and even fifty *prahus* required the cooperation of many communities on a regional basis. Organisationally, such expeditions reflected the alliance networks of powerful *datu*. For example, of the twenty-six 'Balangingi' vessels that seized Francisco Basilo and 350 other people in 1836, nine were from Balangingi, four from Tunkil, five from Basilan, two from Pilas, and six from Iranun settlements on Mindanao.[49] These groupings did not have any permanence beyond the immediate expedition. Expediency was paramount; leaders and groups of boats were constantly realigned to conduct forays and independent missions patronised by Taosug *datus* and *panglimas*.

Of course, not all Samal populations were loyal to their patrons; on occasion, Samal islands were known to have switched their allegiance. Further, there were instances of unsanctioned slave hunting by Balangingi, and defiant refusals by their *nakodahs* to pay the sultan's harbour fee—especially after 1836, when the expanding population of the Balangingi Samal, the success of their raiding, and the growing strength and political independence of their *panglimas* began to challenge the influence of the dominant ethnic group, the Taosug.

A *datu's* main source of wealth was his following. The destruction of Balangingi and Jolo by the Spanish between 1846 and 1852 placed serious constraints on the ability of the Taosug to retain control over the Balangingi Samal, their principal source of slaves. The Western grooved cannon and gunpowder, which had first attracted the Samal to Jolo as clients and suppliers of captives, were now operating to drive them apart. There was a progressive fragmentation of Samal groups because of Spanish incursions and disruption of the Taosug economy.

After mid-century, some Balangingi did remain loyal to their Taosug patrons. Others relocated on the southernmost islands of the archipelago in the Tawi-Tawi chain, openly challenging Taosug authority; a smaller number experienced the humiliation of enforced settlement in and near Zamboanga. With closer cooperation among European navies and more effective use of steam vessels, dispersed Balangingi on Tawi-Tawi (known in the European records as 'Tawi-Tawi pirates') who continued to pursue the old way of life suffered fearful casualties. No longer could their swift fleets expect to find distant coasts unprotected and towns defenceless. By the 1870s, it was clear even to these groups: the era of long-range slave raiding in insular Southeast Asia was over.

Conclusion

In this chapter, I have taken a new look at the genesis of an ethnic group of insular Southeast Asia, the Balangingi Samal, and their role as slave raiders in the economy of the Sulu Sultanate. I have concentrated on the social forces that external trade generated within the Sulu Sultanate—namely, the large-scale incorporation of foreign peoples into Samal society, and the advent of organised long-distance slave raiding in Southeast Asia. By the dawn of the nineteenth century, slavery and slave raiding were fundamental to the state. The Taosug aristocracy depended for its prosperity on the labour of slaves and sea raiders, who fished for *tripang*, procured pearls and manned the fleets. Marauding became the exclusive vocation of the Samal-speakers of Balangingi and other small islets, as they fused their activities with certain Iranun groups from the north coast of Jolo and Mindanao. The raiding system enabled the sultanate to incorporate vast numbers of people from the Philippines and Eastern Indonesia into the population. From the point of view of Philippine history and the larger history of island Southeast Asia, it is important to understand the genesis of this particular ethnic group, to know that the infamous reputation Sulu acquired for slave mongering in the nineteenth century is attributable to the activities of the Balangingi, an 'emergent society' increasingly composed of *indios* captives and their descendants who were brought to the Sulu Archipelago and in many cases assimilated within a single generation to become the predators of their own people.

Chapter 4

The *Prahus* of the Sulu Zone[1]

The Sulu Sultanate lay at a most strategic point for the maritime trade of the nineteenth century. China, the Philippines and Mindanao were situated to the north, Borneo to the south-west, and to the south-east, Sulawesi and the Moluccas. The geopolitical and commercial advantages inherent in the Sultanate's location in this 'zone' were both enviable and unique (see Map 4.1). This maritime trading zone was to provide a socio-cultural context for inter-societal relations and commerce within the sultanate and beyond after 1780. By fitting into the patterns of European trade with China in the late eighteenth century, the Sulu Sultanate established itself as a powerful commercial centre. The Sultanate's geographical position in relation to Asian routes of trade and exchange and its abundant natural resources for export to China attracted the attention of the West. The maritime and jungle products to be found within the Sulu Zone and in the area of its trading partners—*tripang* (sea cucumber), bird's nest, wax, camphor and mother-of-pearl—were new products for redressing the British East India Company's adverse trade balance on the Canton tea market with China. The trade that Sulu established with Bengal, Manila, Macao and Canton, and later Labuan and Singapore, initiated large-scale importation of weapons, luxury goods and foodstuffs. Taosug (Sulu) merchants on the coast and their descendants developed an extensive redistributive trade with the Bugis of Samarinda and Berau to the south, which enabled the Sulu Sultanate to consolidate its dominance over the outlying areas of the zone.

Slave raiding became fundamental to the Sulu Sultanate as its economy expanded and in the period between 1768 and 1848 contributed significantly towards making Sulu one of the most powerful states in Southeast Asia. As the sultanate organised its economy around the collection and distribution of marine and jungle produce, there was a greater need for large-scale recruitment of labour in Sulu's economy to do the labour-intensive work of procurement. Slaving activity carried out by the Iranun and Balangingi developed to meet the accentuated demands of external trade. Jolo, the seat of the Sulu Sultanate, became the nerve centre for the coordination of long-distance slave raiding. From the end of the eighteenth century to the middle of the nineteenth, Southeast Asia felt the full force of the slave raiders of the Sulu Zone. They earned a reputation as daring, fierce marauders who jeopardised the maritime

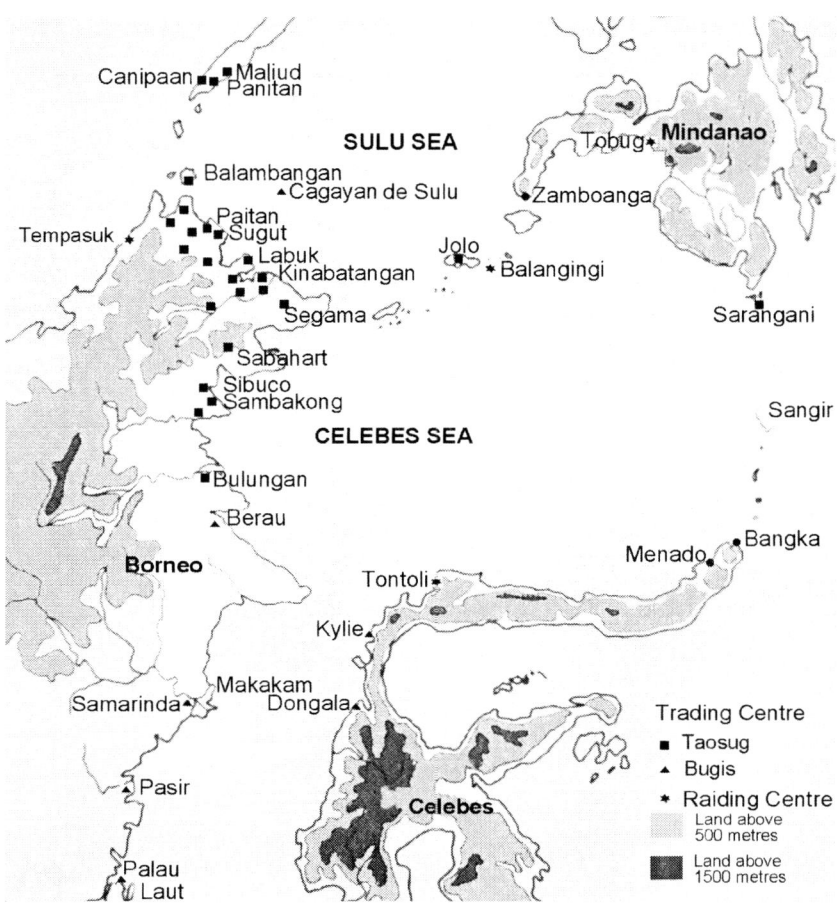

Map 4.1 The Sulu Zone

trade routes, subsistence agriculture and settlement patterns of Southeast Asia, and dominated the capture and transport of slaves to the Sulu Sultanate (see Map 4.2). The Sulu aristocracy depended for its prosperity on the labour of slaves and sea raiders, who fished for *tripang*, procured pearls and crewed the raiding vessels. Trade created the material and social conditions for the large-scale recruitment of slaves and the exploitation of dependent communities. At the same time, the labour of captive and tributary peoples provided the raw materials for expanding trade. More than anything else it was certain sets of economic and cultural practices, namely, long-distance maritime slave raiding, and the systematic harvesting, on an unprecedented scale, of key commodities for the China trade, that gave Sulu its nefarious reputation in the eyes of nineteenth-century Europeans, as a hotbed of despotism and piracy.

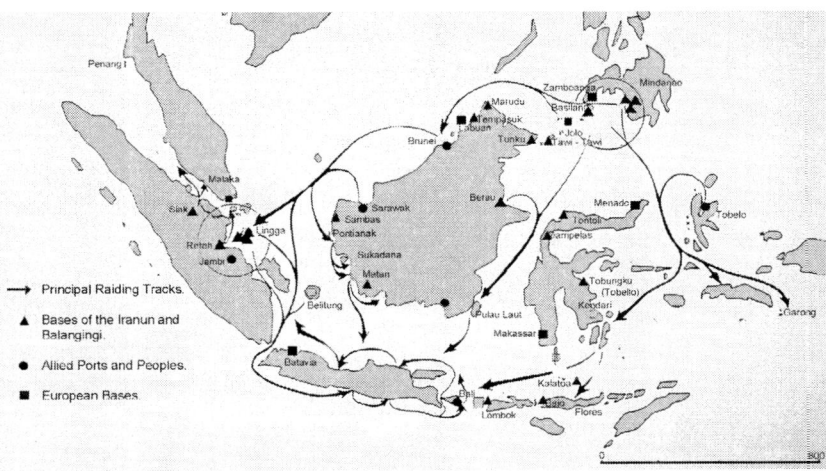

Map 4.2   Balangingi slave raiding in Southeast Asia

The *prahus*

The trading and raiding activities that forged the Sulu Zone in the late eighteenth and nineteenth centuries were predicated on specialised craft. Three basic *prahu* types were associated with Iranun/Samal maritime activities: *lanong* (*joanga*), the large, heavily armed Iranun vessel; *garay* (*panco* or *penjajap*), a raiding ship of lighter construction used by the Balangingi as their principal craft; and *salisipan* (*vinta, baroto,* or *kakap*), a canoe-like vessel with or without outriggers employed as an auxiliary craft for inshore raiding.

Boat building was an art in the Sulu Zone. The shell of Iranun and Samal vessels was built up from the keel (a hollowed-out log) without nails.[2] Fibre lashings were used to bind clinkered planks and ribs together to form the hull. Certain communities specialised in building *prahus* and shipwrights transmitted their techniques from one generation to the next. Forrest observed the construction of many *lanong* at Cotabato along the banks of the Pulangi River.

> In that part of the town…live a few Chinese; but many Magindanao mechanics, vessel builders and merchants. They build their vessels of various dimensions, and employ them in trading from one part of the coast to the other; often in cruising amongst the (Bisayan) Philippine Islands, for slaves and plunder. They cruise also as far as the coast of Java, and the islands of Celebes and Borneo…These vessels are always very long for the breadth, and very broad for their draft of water.[3]

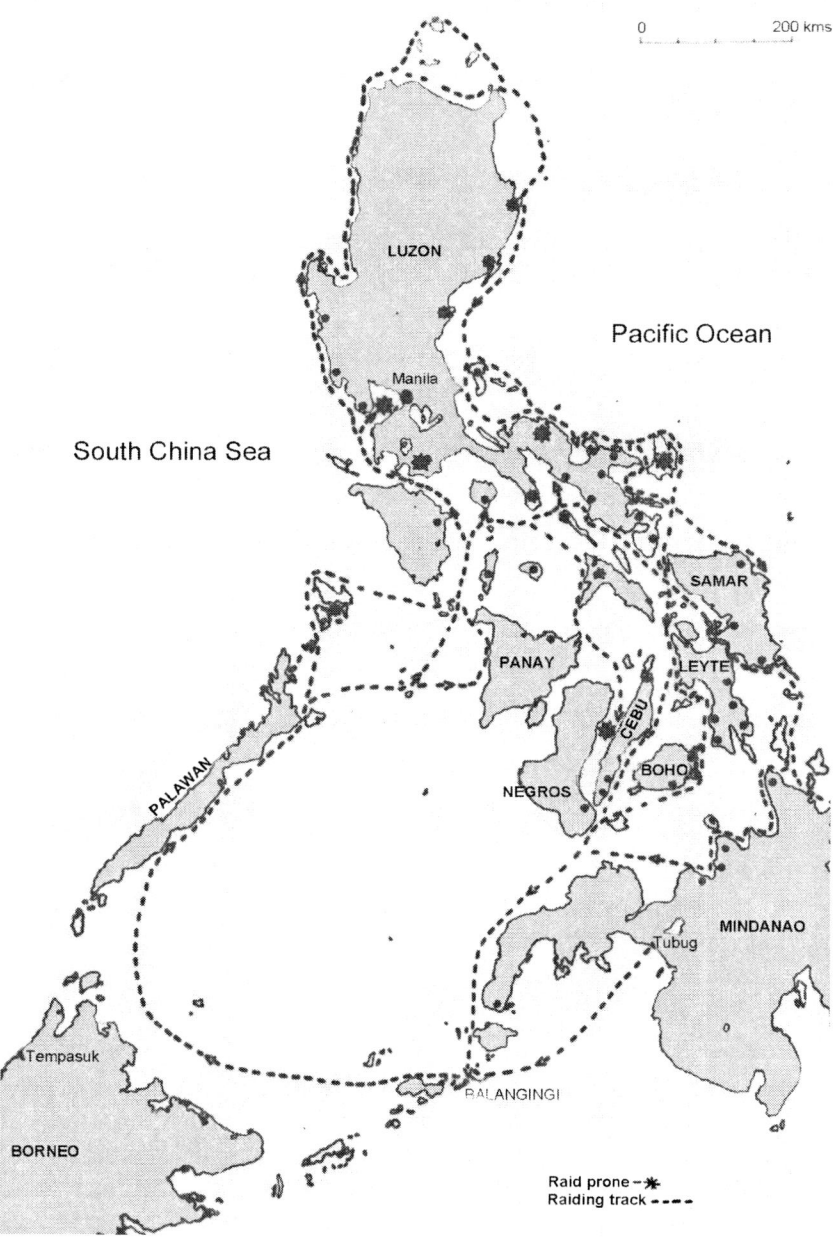

Map 4.3   Slave raiding in the Philippines

The Magindanao also constructed vessels on the coast of Sibuguey Bay in 1775, as Forrest explained, 'Here [Sibuguey Bay]…are built many stout vessels, good timber being in great plenty.'[4]

By 1790 the centre of boat-building activity in the zone had shifted away from Cotabato to the Sulu Archipelago. Basilan and nearby islands were especially rich in shipbuilding materials, and the Samal of Maluso became celebrated boat-builders.[5] Jolo island itself was fairly well supplied with timber, and Parang was the most noted place on the island for making *garay*.[6] The Samal diaspora of 1848–52 forced many boat-builders to move south and relocate on Tawi-Tawi. The transport of excellent hardwood timber from the forests to the bays for *prahu* manufacture was easy on this narrow island. Balimbing, Banaran, and Bilitan on Tawi-Tawi, and Sibutu Island were highly reputed places for making large *prahus* in the second half of the nineteenth century.[7]

The watercolour sketches of Rafael Monleon y Torres done in 1890 of the vessels of the Sulu Zone are based on models built by indigenous craftspeople that were brought back to Spain by members of scientific and naval expeditions throughout the nineteenth century. The sketches present a wealth of detail concerning the proportions, materials, construction and type of ships employed by various ethnic groups that is lacking in the literature.

The *lanong*

The *lanong* was made for long cruises and it was this ship which composed the flotillas that raided the Straits Settlements under the leadership of the Iranun of Tempasuk and Reteh. The length averaged 24–27 metres, and the hull breadth 6 metres amidships. A dug-out keel formed the lower hull, with sides built up of planks. The stern and bow were built up and overhung the keel. The *lanong* had one large mainsail forward and two tripod sheers that could be raised or lowered on a moment's notice. Much of the main interior was occupied by a fighting platform and cabin. The latter served as the *nakodah's* quarters and a powder magazine. The vessel depicted (see Figure 4.1) carried 34 oars a side; double-banked and steered with two rudders. Armament consisted of a strong bulwark at the bow, mounting a long gun (6–24 pounder) as well as several swivel guns. Shields were fixed along the side of the platform, and many *lanong* carried a boarding bridge. The crew consisted of 150–200 men, with the warrior-sailors occupying the upper platform. A triangular flag of the commander was affixed to the stern. By 1830 the *lanong* had been replaced by the swifter, lightly armed Balangingi *garay*.

Figure 4.1 A *lanong* (*joanga*) is an Iranun warship of the late eighteenth century with three banks of oars under full sail. Upward of 30 metres long, these vessels were provided with large bamboo outriggers; both sides were rowed and paddled by more than 190 men. The biggest Iranun slave raids in Southeast Asia were directed against the Philippine Archipelago.

Figure 4.2 A Balangingi *garay* or *panco* with two banks of oars under full sail. At the beginning of the nineteenth century Brunei was within easy range of the Balangingi Samal, and a squadron of *garay* hovered about southern Palawan from the middle of March to the end of November to seize Brunei inhabitants and cut off trade to north Borneo. The attacks were an important factor contributing to Brunei's regional decline. The Balangingi were alleged to have a saying that 'It is difficult to catch fish but easy to catch Borneans.'

The *garay*

The Balangingi *garay* was a beautifully built vessel of wood, bamboo, nipa and rattan. The size of the largest *garay* was 24 metres in length, and the breadth of the beam was 6 metres with a projecting stage of about 30 centimetres along the sides. The *garay*, very sharp fore and aft with a great beam, drew from three to five feet of water. The large beam enabled the vessel to carry an enormous rectangular sail on a tall, collapsible tripod of bamboo and move over reef-studded seas at better than ten knots (see Figure 4.2). The *garay* was also oar-propelled; thirty to sixty oars were used on big vessels. The upper tier of rowers sat on the projecting stage. The *garay* was either open hulled or decked with split cane from stem to stern. The deck of nibong palm was cut into lengths so that any part of it could be taken up. For armament a fixed gun was carried in a bulwark at the bow. The crew of the largest *garay* numbered upward of 100 men and the smallest 25–30 men. Because the *garay* sailed well and was light enough to be rowed swiftly, it possessed the manoeuvrability and striking power necessary for inshore raiding in the nineteenth century (see Map 4.3).

The *salisipan*

The *salisipan* was amphibian. It was a long, low, narrow, oar-propelled vessel that was easily hauled ashore (see Figure 4.3). It was open, provided with an oar

Figure 4.3 Much of the in-shore raiding on coastal settlements and beachheads was done with the *salisipan*—a long, narrow, oar-propelled craft that was easily hauled ashore.

at the stern for steering, and the crew used either oars or sculls. The *salisipan* carried one mast with a single square sail. The largest were 9 to 10 metres long, and were crewed by members of the *garay* to which the *salisipan* belonged. One could be sure that when a *salisipan* was encountered, a *garay* was not far off. In calm weather the Balangingi ran along the shore in *salisipan* or ascended small rivers, relying on their rapidity of movement. This craft proved a dangerous enemy for all the coastal peoples of Southeast Asia.

Figure 4.4 The *lanong (joanga)* was made for long cruises, and flotillas of these ships raided the Straits Settlements under the leadership of the Iranun of Tempasuk and Reteh.

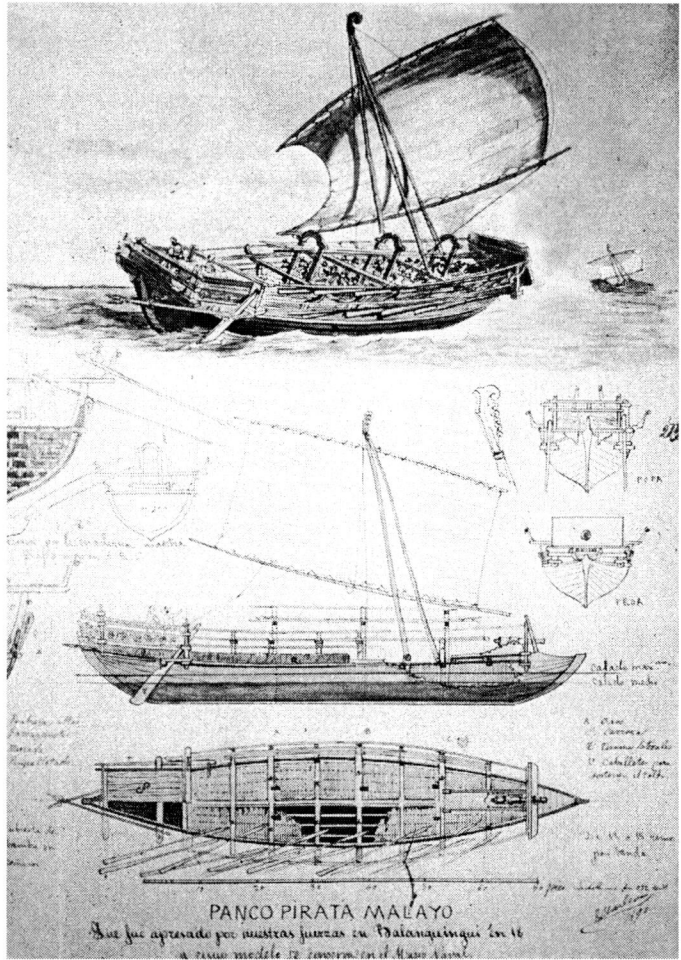

Figure 4.5 Drawing of a *garay* under full sail—a Balangingi slave raiding vessel built for speed, manoeuvrability and striking power.

Conclusion

In the Museo Naval (Naval Museum), Madrid, Monleon's extraordinary 1890 aquarelle sketches of the Iranun and Samal vessels of the Mindanao–Sulu region were both based on the small-scale models sent to Spain in the nineteenth century. These sketches and paintings present a wealth of technical, nautical and ethnographical detail. They depict ship construction, general layout, rig and sailing practice, the mechanics of these sailing vessels and the seafarers employed according to their respective ethnic groups.

Chapter 5

Slavery and the Impact of External Trade: The Sulu Sultanate in the Nineteenth Century[1]

During the late eighteenth and nineteenth centuries, a strong state emerged within the Sulu trading zone—an extensive region encompassing the southern rim of the Sulu Sea and the whole of the Celebes Sea basin.[2] The formation and prosperity of the Sulu Sultanate, as this account of its social history indicates, was based above all else on slaves. It was the role of the Sulu state, within its larger trading zone, to maintain the material and social conditions for the recruitment and exploitation of slaves.[3]

The zone encompassing the Sulu Sultanate is the historic home of peoples, languages and cultures as varied as its landscape. The Taosug (people of the current), the dominant ethnic group in the Sulu Archipelago (now part of the Philippines), are the sole residents of Jolo Island, the historical seat of the sultanate. Originally fishers and traders with martial skills, a number of them adopted agriculture.[4] With the introduction of Islam in about the fifteenth century, they evolved a highly organised political and economic system.[5] The institution of the Sultanate established formal dominance of the Taosug over indigenous Samalan-speaking peoples and later migrants to Sulu.

The Samal, strand-dwellers with close ties to the sea, possessing highly developed boat-building techniques and sometimes practising simple garden agriculture, are the most widely dispersed of all ethnolinguistic groups in the Sulu chain. Manifesting the greatest degree of internal linguistic and cultural difference, Samal communities predominate on the coralline island clusters in the northern and southern parts of the Sulu Archipelago, Northern Borneo and Celebes. The Samal distinguish among themselves by dialect, locality and cultural–ecological factors (principally between sedentary, Muslim shore-dwellers and nomadic animistic boat-dwellers).[6]

The Samal people tend to identify themselves with a particular island, island cluster or regional orbit. In the late eighteenth and early nineteenth centuries they comprised several groups that occupied non-contiguous territories along the southern Mindanao shore, on the south coast and in the near interior of Basilan, and on the islands of the Tapian Tana group, Cagayan de Sulu and the Balangingi cluster. Expert voyagers at sea, particular Samal groups had fixed bases of operation on a series of low, coral and sand islands flanking the north-eastern side of Jolo. This group of islands, named Los Samales by the Spanish, was a springboard for launching seasonal raids against coastal villages from Luzon to Celebes. The most important island was Balangingi, dwelling place and organisational centre of the major slave-retailing group for the Sulu Sultanate in the first half of the nineteenth century. A related group of marauders, the Iranun—Maranao-speaking migratory strand-dwellers—established their principal settlements along the river mouths of the southern coast of Mindanao.

The Sulu Archipelago's location, between the Asian mainland and the large islands of Mindanao, Borneo and Celebes, its varied and productive resource base, and its sizeable population as early as the eighteenth century attracted merchants from south China and Makassarese–Buginese mariners from Celebes. The annual arrival of Chinese junks and Bugis *prahus* at Jolo reflected a regular demand for local products procured principally from the Sultanate's essential domain—the sea.[7] It is important to note, however, that this traditional trade between Southeast Asian ports and the world outside was limited in scale.

By 1800, regional redistribution had become the main pattern of the economy of the Sulu Sultanate. Indirectly, it was the insatiable demand for tea that initiated European interest in Sulu's natural products and its sudden rise to regional primacy. During the eighteenth century, tea replaced ale as the national beverage in England and was especially popular among the poorer classes. China was almost the sole supplier of tea to England. These merchants were quick to recognise the potential of participation in the longstanding Sino–Sulu trade as a means of redressing the one-way flow of silver from India. Marine and jungle products, highly valued in China, were needed to stem it. Sulu's ascendancy towards the end of the eighteenth century developed out of the expanding trade between India, Southeast Asia and China.[8] Commercial and tributary activity became linked with long-distance slave raiding and the incorporation of captured peoples in a system that made Jolo a principal entrepôt for extracted produce for the China trade.

The first section of my study, revolving around the interrelated themes of external trade, slave raiding and state formation, examines the need for Sulu's maritime products in the British China trade. By fitting into the patterns of European trade with China, the sultanate established itself as a powerful commercial centre. The maritime and jungle products to be found within the Sulu Zone and in the area of its trading partners—*tripang*, bird's nest, wax, camphor, mother-of-pearl and tortoise shell—were new products for redressing the British East India Company's adverse trade balance with China.

Of importance for Sulu were textiles and other imported manufactures, opium and also guns and gunpowder, which contributed to the sultanate's physical power. Taosug merchants on the coast and their descendants developed an extensive redistributive trade in which they wrested the function of the collection and distribution of commodities from traditional competitors—the sultanates of Brunei and Cotabato. This commerce—involving trade with the Bugis of Samarinda and Berau to the south, with Manila to the north, and with Singapore and Labuan to the west—formed a complex set of interrelationships through which the segmentary state of Sulu was able to consolidate its dominance over the outlying areas of the zone along the north-east Borneo and western Mindanao coasts.

As the sultanate organised its economy around the collection and distribution of marine and jungle produce, there was an increased need for large-scale recruitment of workers in Sulu's economy to do the labour-intensive work of procurement. Slaving activity developed to meet the accentuated demands of foreign trade. Jolo became the nerve centre for the coordination of slave raiding. The second part of the study analyses the technical aspects of the seasonal raiding programs in search of additional labour to service the procurement of trading produce (see Map 5.2).[9] The final section delineates the parameters of slavery as an institution in Sulu and describes in some detail how 'slaves' who were captives served as dependants of the Sulu elite and were able to better their condition and end up, at least in the second generation, as assimilated members of the Taosug and Samal population.[10]

I have drawn upon anthropological concepts, particularly the idea of a 'segmentary state',[11] European documents in several languages with excerpts and examples from official reports, diaries, letters, journals and newspapers, and local accounts, to examine the economic vitality of the independent Sulu Sultanate's role as an entrepôt for European and Asian commerce in the China trade from the late eighteenth to the late nineteenth century, and its effect on the way slaves worked, lived and interacted with their masters.[12]

In the late eighteenth and nineteenth centuries the population of Sulu was heterogeneous but changing—socially, economically and ethnically. This was a direct result of external trade. The importance of populating of the Sulu Zone by captives from the Philippines and various parts of the Malay world—primarily from Celebes and the Moluccas—and their role in the redistributional economy centred at Jolo should not be underestimated. It has not been explored in detail. Previous historical studies of the sultanate depended largely on published colonial records and accounts to understand the economic and social role played by the slaves in the economy, rather than on records

Map 5.1 The Sulu Zone

produced by the slaves themselves. Slavery in Sulu was observed through the eyes and preconceptions of European observers and writers who viewed Sulu as the centre of a world fundamentally hostile to their interests—an Islamic world whose activities centred upon piracy and slavery.[13] Nevertheless, it is still possible to research aspects of the social history of the ethnically diverse slaves of the Sulu population.

I have drawn upon the statements of the fugitive slaves of the Sulu Sultanate that present a unique account from the perspective of the slaves themselves. From over 180 fugitive slave accounts, manuscript sources and travel literature, clear patterns of social life and economic activity can be constructed.[14] As a historical source, the published and unpublished testimonies of the fugitive slaves of the Sulu Sultanate are both invaluable and neglected. The testimonies tell us much about the experience of slavery in Sulu that could never be found in more traditional sources. The experiences of captives from the moment of seizure, and their passage in the slave *prahus* to their settlement, life and labour in Sulu, emerge from anonymity in the slave testimonies. The total effect of these individual lives and cases of fugitive slaves is to throw very considerable light on the internal processes—the ethnic and social transformations—in the Sulu trading zone during the nineteenth century.[15]

The trade data and the statements of the fugitive slaves complement one another and together enable us to resolve many fundamental questions about the size of Sulu's indigenous trade and its flourishing slave population; about how these changed over time as a consequence of external trade; and where, how and in what quantities the natural produce was harvested.

Slavery and external trade in Sulu

The impact of external trade on the pre-industrial economies of African kingdoms has received considerable attention from Catherine Coquery-Vidrovitch, Samir Amin and Yves Person.[16] In their analyses of indigenous African trade and markets, they stress that the wealth and power of the aristocracy is based on the careful regulation of external trade in the form of rights and tolls. According to Emmanuel Terray, however, such a viewpoint that stresses the monopoly or highly centralised political control of the trade can underestimate the role of slave labour in producing the surplus that is the foundation of the social and political hegemony of the aristocracy. Terray shows that the central concern of the political leaders of the Abron kingdom of Gyaman was labour.[17] In this society external trade enabled the aristocracy to 'realise' the surplus productivity extracted from the labour of its slaves. Above all, it was labour-power and not foreign trade that was the direct and immediate foundation of the political economy of Gyaman.

The importance of a mode of production based on slave labour in the Sulu Sultanate is perhaps more apparent. Power and wealth in Sulu were defined only secondarily in terms of territory. The power and status of leaders was based more on their control over personal dependants, either slaves or retainers, that could be mobilised at a given moment for what was deemed to be either commercially or politically expedient, than on the formal state structure. A report expressly prepared in 1812 for Sir Stamford Raffles, the lieutenant governor of Java, by J. Hunt, who lived in Jolo for six months, recognised the significance of the slave mode of production in Sulu's social formation:

'The power and weight of the chiefs arise solely from their wealth, or like the Barons of old amongst us, from the number of *ambas* [slaves] or retainers each entertain.'[18]

The accumulation of wealth and the transmission of power and privilege in Sulu was facilitated by the ownership of slaves. This was even more the case after the advent of European trade in the Sulu Archipelago in the late eighteenth century. The establishment of European and Asian enterprise and capital at Jolo on a hitherto unprecedented scale stimulated the production of *tripang* and other strand commodities, and made labour the chief source of wealth. Slave labour in the *tripang* and pearl fisheries helped to provide the products introduced into the external trade. The expansion of slavery in Sulu occurs then as a direct consequence of developments similar to those in the Abron kingdom of Gyaman.

An abundant supply of labour was of considerable significance in producing power and wealth among the Taosug aristocracy. A *datu* who could acquire large numbers of slaves could engage more people in procurement activities and trade, and with the surplus wealth they produced attract others to him. The efforts of ambitious Sulu *datus* to participate in this burgeoning international trade, with its extraordinary profits, forced the demand for additional labour up and swelled the flow of external trade. The need for a reliable source of labour was met by the Iranun and Balangingi—the slave raiders of the Sulu Zone. Indeed, the rapid growth of slave raiding was to keep pace with Sulu's foreign trade by providing the prime requisite for the continued growth and prosecution of the littoral and riverine procurement trade—labour-power. Thus, the Sulu state created and reproduced the material and social conditions for the recruitment and exploitation of slaves. More than anything else it was this source and application of labour that was to give Sulu its distinctive predatory character in the eyes of Europeans in the nineteenth century as a 'pirate and slave state'.

The social integration of slaves in Sulu

The testimonies of fugitive slaves and historical accounts leave no doubt that slavery was an essential element in determining the economic, military and social patterns of the Sulu state. In large measure it was the slaves who held the fabric of Taosug society together in the period under consideration. In contrast to the industrial-plantation slavery of the West, slaves in Sulu were not solely defined in terms of their status as property. Slavery in Sulu as in other areas of Southeast Asia was primarily a property relation but not exclusively

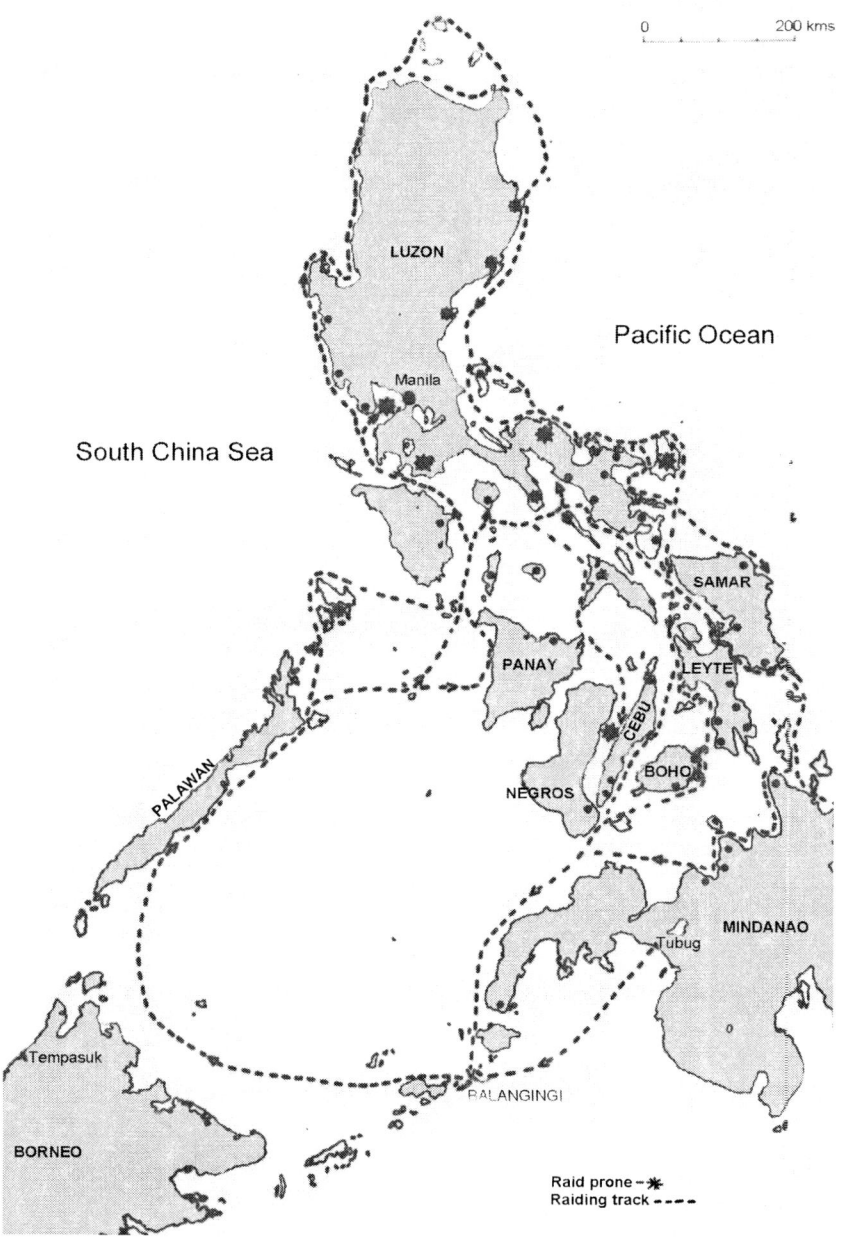

Map 5.2   Slave raiding in the Philippines

so, and a slave's social position was determined by a number of factors, often independent of their servile status.[19] In the Sulu Sultanate, *banyaga* (chattel-slaves) could have family roles as husband or wife, they could own property, and they often filled a variety of political and economic roles—as bureaucrats, farmers and raiders, as concubines and traders—by virtue of which they were entitled to certain rights and privileges accorded to other members of the community.

Slavery was a means of incorporating people into the Taosug social system. *Banyaga* were enrolled in the followings of *datus* for political support, but far more than anything else they were needed to work in the fields and fisheries to maintain an expansive redistributional economy and the flow of external trade. They were predominantly Visayan, Tagalog, Minahassan and Buginese speakers, although almost every major ethnic group of insular Southeast Asia was to be found among their ranks. Some inherited their status. Others were obtained as a form of tax or in fulfilment of debt obligations. But all *banyaga* or their ancestors had been seized by professional slave raiders and retailed in communities throughout the Sulu Zone.[20]

A distinction was drawn by Taosug between chattel-slaves (*banyaga, bisaya, ipun* and *ammas*) and bond-slaves (*kiapangdilihan*). *Banyaga* were either the victims or the offspring of victims of slave raids. *Kiapangdilihan* were persons from the ranks of commoner Taosug whose servility was the direct result of personal debt.[21] The familiar roads to recruitment into slavery were capture and birth. Capture in raiding was the principal mode of recruitment as the pressures of international trade sustained continued Balangingi slave raids throughout the first half of the nineteenth century. In addition, debt and fine obligations among the Taosug themselves provided a significant number of *kiapangdilihan*. A person might also be reduced to slavery by legal process. For example, convictions for criminal offences such as stealing and acts of sexual impropriety, particularly adultery, were punishable by heavy fines.[22] Inability to pay or offer some form of security for the fine imposed reduced people to the status of *kiapangdilihan*. *Kiapangdilihan* were an integral part of a creditor's following but with a lower status than freemen who voluntarily attached themselves to a leader. The creditor claimed rights over only the *kiapangdilihans*' economic services and, in theory, was not allowed to harm them physically. In return for subsistence, *kiapangdilihans* were obliged to work for their creditors but their services did not generally count towards repayment of debts. Many *kiapangdilihan* became dependants for life and their families could have remained obligated for several generations. Indebtedness enabled *datus* to command the labour of Taosug commoners to ensure the labour-power reserves they required in the functioning of the social formation. Debt bondage as an economic institution in Sulu was most fully developed at the end of the nineteenth century, when the Taosug could no longer rely on Balangingi raids to supply sufficient numbers of *banyaga* for their retinues, by increasing the amount of tribute ordinarily collected from clients and making the fines in the legal codes prohibitive.[23]

The legal position of a *banyaga* in the Sultanate of Sulu was determined by the Sulu code, a body of law codified from custom and precedent, as well as Islamic law.[24] In theory, as defined in the Taosug codes, a *banyaga* could be transferred, bought or sold at will; and a master held the power of life and death over a *banyaga*, who could be punished for the slightest infraction of the law. The legal expression of social distinction is exemplified in the scale of penalties and fines in the codes for the offences of murder, adultery, theft and inheritance. Punishments were much more severe for *banyaga* than for members of other social classes. For example, if a male *banyaga* had sexual intercourse with a free woman, he could either be killed outright or be severely punished and become the property of the woman's husband or family.[25] On the other hand, if a free man had sexual relations with a married female slave he need only pay a fine of 20 lengths of cotton cloth.[26] Less severe penalties for adultery between *banyaga* derived from their inferior social status. The Taosug commonly associated such degrading behaviour with slaves.

Although these laws provided institutional opinion on the debasement of people, and further reflected the low opinion of slaves held by masters, in fact, *banyaga* were often socially and economically indistinguishable from freemen and in some respects more secure. The actual situation of many individual *banyaga* as revealed in their testimonies contradicted their legal status as a group. *Banyaga* were encouraged to adopt Islam and marry; some *banyaga* were permitted to purchase their freedom and assume a new status and ethnicity; the children of a female *banyaga* and a freeman inherited the status of their father; some *banyaga* could bear arms; slaves could own property which reverted to their master at death.

The basic differences between slavery among the Taosug and slavery as it was generally understood in the West was the variability of social distance that existed between slave and master. William Pryer stated that on the east coast of Borneo the relation was that of follower and lord rather than slave and master.[27]

The power and wealth of a *datu* were commensurate with the number of slaves he owned. The more slaves a *datu* acquired, the greater was his reputation and the willingness of people to seek protection within his settlement in return for services. *Banyaga* were often well clothed, carried fine *kris*, and were entrusted with long journeys for their masters.²⁸ The personal and economic ties of slaves in the Sulu Sultanate 'provided a sense of security which bound them to their masters and gave them identity and...[incentive] to labor.'²⁹ A master was constrained to feed and clothe his slaves or give them sufficient opportunities to earn a living; otherwise his slaves might demand to be sold.³⁰ It appears to have been a common practice in the Sulu Sultanate to allow a *banyaga*, when he desired, to change masters rather than risk desertion.

Nevertheless, there are statements of fugitive slaves and other reports that present the master–slave relationship in a much more severe light. In principle, the master's ownership was absolute and his authority unbounded. *Banyaga* could suffer bodily degradation and be put to death; they could be sold, bartered or given away if it served their master's interests.³¹ Pryer noted the ambivalence in theory and practice that existed in the relationship between slave and master:

> Masters have the power of beating them [slaves] or even chopping them, but as a rule slavery here [Sandakan Bay and the coastal area] is regarded much as servantism is elsewhere...but a former Dato here cut one of his slaves to pieces for trying to escape.³²

While there is evidence of contrasting degrees of benevolence and hardship, what is important to ascertain in assessing the system is whether cruelty and maltreatment were modal characteristics of slavery in the sultanate. The fact that a *datu* defined his economic power in terms of the number of slaves he possessed, and that slaves were able to run away to another *datu* or try to escape to Zamboanga or Menado, placed important constraints on his actions. A purely antagonistic relation would little benefit a master if only because the successful exploitation of Sulu's natural produce hinged on the large-scale organisation of the cooperation of the slaves and their depandents. In 1842, an American sailor who accompanied the Wilkes expedition wrote:

> We saw several captives here who had been captured among the islands in the Sooloo Sea [Visayas] or Philippine group. One was taken out of a fishing boat in the harbour of Batavia...This man, who belonged to Batavia, spoke some English, but very imperfectly. He states they were treated well by their masters, and did not seem anxious to obtain their freedom.³³

Masters were liable to neglect or mistreat *banyaga* who were remiss in their duties, but the statements of escaped slaves and travel accounts of observers reveal that slaves, and especially those with knowledge and skills, had good relations with their masters and were not easily distinguished among his following.

Manumission was commonly practised in the Sulu sultanate and freed slaves were merged into the general population, assuming a new ethnicity and status.[34] For *banyaga*, conversion and marriage were prerequisites to manumission. The process of manumission in the Taosug social system (occurring primarily among those *banyaga* in close contact with their masters), tended to be a gradual one in which incorporation was implicit.[35] An *indios* who altered his ethnic identity by becoming a Muslim and thereby achieving manumission found a new range of opportunities open to him as a freemen and a 'Taosug'.

Banyaga could purchase their freedom in the Sulu sultanate.[36] This was frequently the case among those *banyaga* who had an aptitude for trade. Their owners often found it best to allow such slaves to acquire property so as to encourage initiative and establish their loyalty. In time these slaves might purchase their freedom with the backing of their owner, having profited from participation in his commercial affairs. Once free, reciprocal obligations continued to bind them—now as patron and client instead of owner and slave.

Manumission was an important feature of the Taosug social system. The steady leakage of manumitted slaves swelled the ranks of a *datu's* retainers and hence increased his political hegemony and prestige. The likelihood of manumission was essentially a function of occupation. *Banyaga* who provided immediate and indispensable services to their owners, who served in their households or on their trading vessels, had better chances of manumission than those who laboured in the fields or fisheries.

But for many slaves among the Taosug and Samal, escape rather than manumission remained their central ambition. Naturally, it was during the early years of captivity that the desire to escape was greatest. This was particularly the case of *indio* men who had been torn away from their homes and families, and who had experienced the hardships of the Balangingi traffic.[37] The initial social isolation created by differences in language, customs and status exacerbated the loneliness and yearning for the lost past. Some never did find the 'indispensable margin of social and psychological space'[38] necessary to overcome the trauma of transition and to settle down. They constantly reworked their past lives; the remembrance of their *pueblos* and *kampongs*, family and companions did not fade away.[39] One can feel in reading the statements of some of the fugitive slaves their desperation and incredible determination to secure freedom and reknit the fabric of their family and community life. All such *banyaga* lived in expectation of that eventual return.

The Taosug system was such that controls were difficult to apply, and 100 to 200 *banyaga* who chafed under oppression fled annually to foreign vessels at Jolo, to the interior of Jolo, to some other island in the archipelago, or to Zamboanga and Menado.[40] Very little is known about the fate of those *indios* who actually managed to return to their *pueblos*. Undoubtedly, a male *indio* sometimes reached home to find some or all of his family dead, his wife remarried, and outstanding debts and reciprocal obligations remaining to be fulfilled.[41] Many who escaped were left to make a new life, the reality of which was harsher than that which they had fled.

The economic integration of slaves

Slavery, I have emphasised, became crucial to Sulu's economic and cultural life towards the end of the eighteenth century. Most accounts of the Sulu Sultanate written before 1780 indicate that the internal demand for slaves at Jolo was on a much smaller scale than it was destined to become in the nineteenth century.[42] The impact of the West's commercial intrusion in China was a watershed in the formation of the Sulu State. Slaves who were valuable for the variety of their labours that were essential to the growth of the state came to play a more avowedly important role in Sulu at this time. For example, among the Taosug, *banyaga* were used in trading ventures, in diplomatic negotiations, as slave raiders, as concubines and wet nurses, as tutors to their owners, as craftworkers, and as peasants and fishers.[43]

There was a clear division of labour between the work of male and female *banyaga*. Heavy work was performed generally by male slaves. Physically able men assisted their owners in clearing virgin forest, in ploughing, in harvesting timber, in building and maintaining boats, and hauling water.[44] Male *banyaga* also laboured in the fisheries in search of mother-of-pearl shell and *tripang*, they manufactured salt, accompanied their owners on trading expeditions, and sailed as crew on Balangingi *prahus*. Included among the major tasks of female *banyaga* were the sowing and weeding of rice fields, the pounding and threshing of rice, and the gathering and preparation of strand products.[45] Female *banyaga* were also included in the entourage of their 'mistresses' as attendants, and some enjoyed positions of trust and some comfort as concubines of leading *datus*.

Mother-of-pearl shell became one of Sulu's most profitable exports by the beginning of the nineteenth century. Mother-of-pearl had previously been sought for the China market only on a limited scale.⁴⁶ The trade increased from 2,000 piculs in 1760 to an estimated 12,000 piculs per annum by 1835.⁴⁷ Once Asian and European traders realised the shell's value to manufacturers of jewellery, cutlery and furniture in Ceylon and Europe, they became the chief customers of this commodity,⁴⁸ which, along with *tripang*, was among the most important items of export from Jolo. It can be roughly estimated from trade statistics that some 68,000 fishers, slave and free, must have been engaged in diving for mother-of-pearl and fishing for *tripang* for hundreds of Taosug *datus* and Samal headmen during the 1830s.⁴⁹

If the labour-intensive economy of the Sulu Sultanate relied on the sea as an abundant source of produce for external trade, the wilderness of Borneo was its second mainstay. It was principally from this environment that the sultanate was supplied with specialties for the China trade.⁵⁰ Bird's nest, procured primarily from limestone caves, and wax were obtained in abundance by thousands of slaves who initiated expansion of settlement and mined the riches of the forests of east Borneo for their Sulu overlords.⁵¹

Banyaga of initiative and energy were entrusted with their master's property and sent on trading voyages. Hunt noted that the Taosug employed slaves in their *prahus* not only as crew but also as traders.⁵² Slaves regularly traded from Jolo to Balangingi and Palawan on behalf of their masters in the 1830s.⁵³ The more capable *banyaga* were employed in trading excursions to the north-east coast, as Pryer noted:

> The most intelligent of them are picked out as traders and perform long journeys sometimes of months duration, trading to different ports without ever thinking of running away. Many of these slaves amass considerable sums of money and have houses and belongings even finer than their masters.⁵⁴

Aristocratic women were given *banyaga* to assist them in their business activities, primarily local marketing.⁵⁵ By the mid-nineteenth century, some of the leading local traders in Sulu were women, as Spenser St John noted:

> In Sulu the wives of the chiefs are entrusted with the principal management of accounts and carry on much of the trade; it is said that they have acquired considerable knowledge from the Manilla captives, who are often of a superior class.⁵⁶

Ordinarily, the vending of cloth, vegetables and other trade goods in villages, at the open market, or to foreign vessels, was done by *banyaga*. Noble women, by virtue of their station, lacked the liberty to barter produce, which entailed wandering among the houses, visiting the Chinese quarter, or rowing into the bay to a trading ship. It was common for Taosug women to send one or two Spanish-speaking slaves into the roadstead in small canoes on the arrival of a European vessel. The boats carried fruits, vegetables, coils of *tali lanun* (cheap rope of excellent quality), weapons and curiosities. Slave vendors were instructed to barter a specified minimum amount of produce by evening. They commonly accepted from European sailors only such trade items as cups and saucers, scissors, buttons, empty bottles, tobacco and opium.[57] Slave hawkers were an important source of wealth to their mistresses. It was at the same time an attractive and profitable way of life for many, as Melchior Yvan explained:

> [O]ne day I was talking to a Malay, of whom I had just bought some coconuts, when he informed me that he also was a captive…upon which I enquired why he did not profit by the opportunity to escape, and revisit his country. 'Why should I do so?' he replied, 'there is something to regret everywhere; here I am well enough, my master treats me as if I were one of his kindred, I am well paid, and could save money if I wished; in my own country I know I could not do better, and perhaps should not fare as well; therefore, I prefer remaining here.'[58]

The prosperity of the Sulu Sultanate depended to a large extent on the labour of the *banyaga* who crewed the slave raiding *prahus*. They augmented the strength of client communities that specialised in slaving, and as hirelings enriched their masters through active participation in raids. Wilkes observed that *datus* 'receive a high price…for the services of their slaves.'[59] The *banyaga* cooked, fetched water and firewood, and assisted the crew from time to time with their shipboard duties.[60] The *banyaga* were not armed, but they were considered an integral part of the crew and it was their task to row, bail, clean and repair the *prahus*.[61] It was common for masters to send unaccompanied *banyaga* on these *prahus*, but fleet leaders (*nakodahs*) were reluctant to take those who objected to their master's wish.[62] Undoubtedly, *datus* were constrained to reward such slaves; otherwise they would have been far more reluctant to participate in such a hazardous undertaking.

Under the Taosug, some of these *banyaga* enjoyed considerable social mobility. The successful execution of a slave raiding expedition was difficult and dangerous work, and depended largely on the skill of its personnel. Proven ability and experience during a raid was one of the most important criteria for leadership. Some *banyaga* held important positions as *nakodahs* and occasionally as squadron commanders in slaving expeditions, and in return they acquired wealth and slaves who complemented their personal followings. Visayan *indios* in particular demonstrated their talent and courage as *nakodahs* and developed a fearful reputation in the Philippines,[63] but *banyaga* from other parts of the Malay world, who had knowledge of dialects and of their former localities, proved equally skilful boat commanders.[64]

Raiding seems to have provided other such slaves with opportunities for modest social advancement, especially if they showed a talent for fighting. Jadee, a Batak retailed to 'Sulu pirates' for trade goods on the east Sumatran coast, was 'made at first to row, and bale water out of their *prahus* [but] he gave such proofs of courage and address, that in a short time they advanced him to the rank of fighting man.'[65]

Despite the emphasis placed upon external trade in the formation of the Sulu State, agriculture remained the main activity for the majority of Taosug who still resided inland on the volcanic high islands of the Tapul group and on Pata and Siassi.[66] The sultanate needed a reliable source of food for its expanding population. The increased development of a slave mode of production conditioned the integration of the subsistence sector as a major component of the redistributive system. *Banyaga* employed in agriculture contributed towards providing the food supply that maintained the community and freed a *datu* and his retinue from subsistence pursuits, to devote their labour to trading and raiding.[67]

Small, dispersed farming communities comprised of *banyaga* dotted the interior of the larger fertile islands, especially on Jolo, Tapul and Pata. Masters allotted their *banyaga* a bamboo hut large enough to accommodate a single family, and a farm plot.[68] The huts were scattered about over large tracts of land. The slave statements suggest that in at least some cases these subordinate agricultural settlements were homogeneous in language and religion. The size of such settlements is not known and would have depended on the number of farm slaves a *datu* owned, but they must have contained up to several hundred persons. These *banyaga* were encouraged by their masters to marry other *banyaga* and establish homesteads. Farm slaves were expected to provide for their own wants from the fields and gardens that had been given to them.[69] They were obligated to remit a fixed minimum portion of this produce to their master through the agency of the village headman, who could be of slave or non-slave origin. Farming was their major economic obligation, but *datus* demanded also that villagers near the coast collect *tripang* and pearl shell for them, although for this they received barter goods in exchange. All were liable to be called upon for military services.[70]

In prominent trading centres like Jolo, Parang and Bual, where agriculture was of secondary importance, talented *banyaga* engaged in a wide range of activities and included among their numbers bureaucrats, tribute collectors, artisans, musicians, scribes and commercial agents. The opportunities for social mobility among these slaves stood in marked contrast to those of slaves engaged in farming or fishing.

Banyaga recruited by the sultan as officeholders enjoyed considerable prestige. The sultan appointed them to administer trade and subject peoples in different parts of the zone in order to centralise his authority and thwart the ambitions of rival elements among Taosug aristocrats. Because of their inferior social status, *banyaga* did not have the political aspirations of the *datu* class, and the sultan's power was strengthened by the use of such persons as administrators. The interests of these slaves by virtue of their elevation to political office lay unquestionably with the sultan and they made loyal followers.

Banyaga played leading roles as bureaucrats on the Samal islands, acted as tribute collectors throughout the zone, and staffed tariff stations on Bornean rivers.[71] Chrishaan Soerma commanded a large *prahu* that collected tribute from Parang, Tapul, Tawi-Tawi and Sandakan Bay in the 1830s.[72] A Chinese seized near Banjermasin by the Iranun named Banjer was a sultan's man and had once been put on a trading station to control inland commerce along the Kinabatangan River.[73] The sultan also made use of *banyaga* to exercise control over subject groups on the north-east coast of Borneo. In 1878, Pryer wrote, 'it is not considered particularly degrading to be a slave, most of the leading men here have been so.'[74] One of the most influential of these slave headmen was Tuan Iman Gelanee, who dominated the Samal Bajau Laut on the north-east coast after mid-century. According to William Pryer:

> Tuan Emum is a Bugis, he was captured when young by Sooloo pirates and taken over by the Sultan himself who finding him to be a man of ability sent him over here, Sandakan then apparently being pretty much in the hands of the Badjus, Emum married the queen of the Badjus, [and] became the headman amongst them.[75]

As Taosug trade became more complex and the political problems posed by the West grew, so did the amount of work that required literacy. The uses of written documents were no longer confined principally to the records of the genealogy of the sultan, the appointment of officials, and the collection of tribute and legal fees. After 1768, writing was required for diplomatic and trade correspondence with the Spanish, Dutch and English, for recording grants of land and the terms of treaties of various sorts with the West, and to keep track of the accounts of *datus'* commercial enterprises.

Paradoxically, few Taosug aristocrats could read and write, and *banyaga* with education who could serve as scribes, interpreters and language tutors were much sought after.[76] The majority of these scribes were male slaves drawn from different parts of the Malay world, but female *indio* slaves served as the sultan's secretary at different times.[77] While most other slave specialists—artisans and craftsmen—were more or less expendable, the skills of the educated *banyaga* could not easily be learned by others and were considered indispensable to the business enterprise of *datus* who employed them. *Banyaga* who could speak or write one or more foreign languages were engaged as trading agents by *datus*, enabling them to amass considerable personal wealth: 'These [educated slaves] are not denied the right of holding property which they enjoy during their lives, but at their death it reverts to their master. Some of them are quite rich.'[78] Wilkes described such a *banyaga* who appears to have been of some assistance to his expedition:

> All accounts of the Datu of Soung are kept in Dutch, by a young Malay from Ternate, who writes a good hand, and speaks English, and whom we found exceedingly useful to us. He is a slave of the Datu who employs him for this purpose only he told me he was captured in a brig by the pirates of Basilan and sold here as a slave, where he is likely to remain for life, although he says the Datu has promised to give him his freedom after ten years.[79]

The number of slave artisans—goldsmiths, silversmiths, blacksmiths and weavers—was never large, and comprised only a small fraction of the total slave population. Gifted *banyaga*, whose raw materials—brought by trade or tribute—were transformed into jewellery, tools, weapons and armour, were full-time artisans, while others who were less talented pursued their occupations on a part-time basis. Not surprisingly, the arbitrary distribution of *banyaga* left some talents wasted. Jose Ruedas, a silversmith, spent three years as a fisher and gatherer of pearl shell before being taken by his owner to be exchanged for a bundle of cotton cloth at Jolo, where he resumed his craft.[80] While some slaves found their skills superfluous in a particular island's economy, others appear to have had the opportunity to acquire training in critical occupations, especially as blacksmiths and armourers.[81]

It is clear from the accounts of Forrest, Hunt, D. D'Urville and Wilkes that slaves were called upon to perform instrumental music and sing, sometimes in

Spanish, or recite Visayan poetry for religious festivals and when Europeans visited Jolo.[82] Under such circumstances, there was ample opportunity for *banyaga* with musical talents to improve their condition. Furthermore, some *datus* played the flute, violin or guitar and all were fond of Spanish songs and dances.[83] *Indio* slaves could and did act as their music instructors and entertained them at night while they smoked opium and discussed trade and politics.

I have emphasised that slave holding was the primary form of investment for the Taosug, but have not yet mentioned the slave's significance as an object of exchange in a society and trade where general-purpose money was lacking. As a form of wealth, *banyaga* were a tangible asset in readily transferable form. In this context, *banyaga* were considered not only to be chattel but currency as well. For instance, the value of a *banyaga* in the 1850s, as an object of exchange in transactions between Taosug *datus* and Samal raiders, was equivalent roughly to ten *kayus* (pieces of coarse cotton cloth 20 fathoms in length), or two bundles of coarse *kain* (sarongs), or 200–300 *gantangs* of rice. *Prahus* could be purchased for six to eight slaves while boat rentals amounted to only two or three slaves. Portable cannons were loaned at the rate of one slave; and rifles (often defective) could be rented for five pieces of linen of 20 fathoms.[84] Slaves were exchanged over and over again. *Datus* rarely traded their own followers, especially the younger ones, who were considered more malleable and educable, but they trafficked extensively in slaves who were given to them by Iranun and Balangingi as tribute, in payment of debts and fines or as captives. It was not at all uncommon for slaves to have had two, three and even possibly four owners in his lifetime, to have lived among several ethnic groups in very different parts of the zone, to have fulfilled a variety of economic functions, and experienced varying degrees of hardship and servitude.[85] The ease with which slaves could be moved about reflects their centrality to the economic system.

Slavery then was of decisive importance in the economic and military organisation of the Sulu sultanate in the nineteenth century. *Banyaga* were encouraged to participate actively in the economic life of the state, and hence obtain a degree of social and cultural autonomy within the society. As Wilkes explained:

> At Soung, business seems active, and all, slaves as well as masters, seem to engage in it…these circumstances promote the industry of the community, and even that of the slave, for he [sic] too as before observed, has a life interest in what he earns.[86]

Many *banyaga* ultimately achieved a status and living standard that, though modest enough, was still in their view an improvement over their previous social condition under colonial overlords who did not scruple to thrust their own subjects into bondage. A minority were able to become wealthy; they maintained their own households in the principal towns, living out their lives in a style similar to that of their owners. Some of these *banyaga* who were wealthier than most Taosug commoners and even than some aristocrats owned mats, chests, fine clothes, brass utensils, weapons and gongs. A *banyaga* of standing had a *prahu* and owned a few other slaves to do his trading.[87] Of the condition of slaves in Jolo, Manuel de los Santos observed: 'those slaves who wish to marry can do so because there are many women. I have seen some of them bear arms. Others who were slaves formerly, now are wealthy and free.'[88] Jose Ruedas stated: 'There are many Christian captives in Jolo some of whom are happily married and wealthy.'[89]

The slave statements demonstrate that status discrepancy was common in nineteenth-century Sulu. Among the hierarchy of *banyaga*, those who functioned as bureaucrats, artisans, scribes and concubines often had a greater degree of power and privilege than Taosug commoners. Wilkes remarked of such slaves, 'Some of them are quite rich, and are invariably better off than the untitled freemen.'[90] There is some evidence illustrating that in rare instances, *banyaga* of remarkable talent rose to the rank of *orang kaya* and *datu* as protégés of their owners.[91]

My discussion of slavery in Sulu thus far testifies to the view that the aristocracy was bent on attracting the flow of external trade to Jolo because it was the principal means of 'realising' the surplus they extracted from the labour of their slaves.[92] Slaves were what the *datus* needed in order to obtain the new luxury products brought by the trade. By the beginning of the nineteenth century the Jolo market offered British-manufactured brassware and glassware; Chinese earthenware and ceramics; fine muslins, silk and satin garments; Spanish tobacco and wines; and opium from India.[93] There was a constant increase not only in the variety but also in the quality of these objects of trade. These luxury goods for personal adornment and pleasure, and for the household, were translated into power and prestige factors by the aristocracy to form the material basis of their social superiority.

More importantly, the political and commercial growth of the Sulu State was reflected in the enormous increase in war stores in the Jolo market at the end of the eighteenth century—lead, iron, shot, gunpowder and cannon.[94] The Taosug aimed at monopolising control over the exchange and distribution of these goods which, with slaves, enabled the reproduction of the social formation; the

European firearms and gunpowder supplied by the international trade enabled coastal-dwelling Taosug to advance their commercial interests in the intersocietal exchange network, to promote raiding on a large scale and keep the zone free of undesirable intruders and competitors. As Terray emphasises, it is only in this sense that external trade is a vital element in the overall functioning of the social formation: 'Like every distributive mechanism, it created no wealth that was born in the process of production; but it gave a concrete form appropriate to the requirements of reproduction.'[95]

It is worth emphasising again the powerful economic forces that were pushing the Taosug aristocracy in the direction of acquiring more and more slaves. In the first place, their demands for all kinds of products coming in from external trade had to be satisfied—demands that were constantly increasing. These demands were both a consequence and cause of slavery. In order to trade, it was necessary for the Taosug to have something to give in exchange. Hence the collection and redistribution of produce was dominated by those *datus* with the largest number of slaves; that is, by the sultan and certain *datus* on the coast who were most directly involved in Sulu's external trade. Second, the more dependent Sulu's economy was on slaves, the larger loomed the question of its supply of slaves. The only way for the Taosug to obtain the raw materials that formed the basis of their commerce was to secure more slaves, by means of long-distance raiding.

In this period, the rate of growth of the sultanate's population had not kept pace with its expanding commercial economy. Since it was the labour of slaves that made possible external trade, slavery rose markedly from this time and became the dominant mode of production. This explains why Jolo quickly became the principal centre in the zone for the importation of slaves and the outfitting of marauders.[96] Slave raiding in the Sulu Sultanate was highly organised. There were several types of expeditions: those which were equipped by the sultan and his kindred; those which were independently recruited with the encouragement of the sultan; and those conducted without the sanction of the sultan. While the right to organise raiding expeditions resided at all levels of the political system, the sultan and certain *datus* on the coast were in the best position to do so by virtue of their control over external trade and their more expansive network of alliances.

The military and economic activities of Samal-raiding populations were regulated closely by their Taosug patrons. They encouraged the Balangingi—an 'emergent' community who themselves or their forebears had been captives—to become fishers of human beings.[97] To meet the West's insatiable demand for produce acceptable in Chinese gourmet markets and, hence, the increased demands for slave labour in the zone, *datus* not only equipped Samal vessels, but also provided credit to the Iranun with advances in boats, powder and ball, cannon, rice, opium and additional crew.[98] Everything was to be repaid in captured slaves.[99] *Banyaga* familiar with distant coasts and local conditions often accompanied the Balangingi on long slave raids southwards to Celebes and north to Luzon—raids that gave cause for considerable anxiety to colonial governments as late as the 1870s. Thus, the capture of slaves whose surplus labour could be converted into a source of wealth was the principal aim of Taosug-sponsored Iranun/Balangingi attacks on Southeast Asian villages and *prahu* shipping.[100]

There are no statistics on the overall number of slaves imported into Jolo in the period under consideration, except for the divergent estimates of European observers. These range from 750 to as high as 4,000 captives per year from 1775 to 1848 for the Philippines alone. It is possible to reconstruct a clearer picture of the pattern of slave imports to the Sulu Sultanate on the basis of captives' statements and other sources. Slave imports to the Sulu Sultanate during the first 65 years (1780–1835) probably averaged between 2,000 and 3,000 per year. The steepest rise in the number of slaves brought annually to Sulu, between 3,000 and 4,000, occurred in the period from 1836 to 1848, when external trade was most intense at Jolo. The trade reached its apex in 1848 and slackened considerably in the next two decades with imports ranging between 1,200 and 2,000 slaves per year until it collapsed in the 1870s.[101] The figures appear to show that between 200,000 and 300,000 slaves were moved in Iranun and Samal vessels to the Sulu Sultanate in the period from 1770 to 1870.[102]

Conclusion

The second half of the nineteenth century proved to be a critical turning point in the history of the Sulu Sultanate, as it was in the rest of the non-Western world. Everywhere, challenges arose to confront the Sulu State's ability to create and reproduce the material and social conditions for survival. With increased cooperation among Western navies and more effective use of steam vessels, the Sulu world began to shrink. The first signs came with the destruction of Balangingi and Jolo by the Spanish between 1846 and 1852.[103] The *datu's* main source of wealth was his following. The destruction of Balangingi and Jolo placed serious constraints on the ability of the Taosug to retain control over the Balangingi Samal, their principal source of slaves. The grooved cannon and gunpowder of the West, which had first attracted Iranun and Samal to Jolo as clients and suppliers of captives, were now operating to drive them apart. There was a progressive fragmentation of Samal groups because of Spanish incursions and disruption of the Taosug economy. No longer could their harrying fleets expect to find coasts unprotected and towns defenceless. The era of long-range slave raiding was over.

The total collapse of the system only came with the concerted effort of Spain to end Sulu's autonomy. In the last three decades of the century, the trade was destroyed by the Spanish naval campaign, which systematically annihilated all *prahu* shipping in the Sulu Archipelago; by the development of a policy to compel the Taosug to settle down in villages as agriculturalists; and by the immigration of large numbers of Straits Chinese to Sulu in spite of, or perhaps because of, the naval campaign. Taosug control over the regulation of external trade collapsed, with drastic consequences. They were forced to curtail their commercial activities and become dependent on the merchant immigrants with contacts in Singapore. The traditional Taosug redistributive role was taken away, the zone disintegrated, and the pattern of life altered by the extinction of slavery. By the beginning of the twentieth century, the demise of the trading and raiding system had left the former Sulu State bereft of its importance as a major commercial entrepôt in the wider island economy and confronted with severe internal social and economic problems.

Two major conclusions can be drawn from this discussion of the place of the slave in Sulu society in the nineteenth century. The first is the decisive importance of the exploitation of slaves in the functioning of the social formation in Sulu. As Terray reminds us, 'A social formation cannot be understood except by beginning with an analysis of the relation of productions which are at its base'.[104] External trade spawned slavery in the Sulu Sultanate. The increase in external trade which affected state formation and economic integration made it necessary to import captives from the outside world to bolster the population. As goods from China, Europe and North America flowed to Jolo, the Taosug aristocrats thrived, and there emerged the Balangingi—a strong, skilled people who were the scourge of Southeast Asia, raiding in 18-metre-long *prahu*. The sea was the life-force of the sultanate, where tens of thousands of *banyaga* laboured annually to provide the specialties for external trade. The arrival of captive slaves on a hitherto unprecedented scale for intensive or skilled work, and their gradual absorption into the lower levels of Taosug and Samal society were central to the development and expansion of the Sulu redistributive system.

Second, the rise of Sulu as the dominant state in the trading zone at the end of the eighteenth century conforms to the more general process of state formation and economic integration that begins with the introduction of external trade. The Sulu Sultanate's history thus parallels the evolution of independent states and stateless societies beyond Southeast Asia where slaves played economic and social roles similar to those in the Abron Kingdom of Gyaman.

Chapter 6

The Balangingi Samal: The Global Economy, Maritime Raiding and Diasporic Identities in Nineteenth-century Philippines[1]

Introduction: Framing and sources

The aim of this chapter is to trace the formation of the Samal Balangingi as an ethnic group comprised of 'pirates' and their captives, and their continued sense of belonging to the island stronghold of Balangingi, even after its inhabitants were forcefully resettled in the decade between 1848 and 1858 (see Map 6.1). It is important to begin by tracing the evolution of Balangingi maritime raiding from its late eighteenth-century origins that supported the English supplies of tea from China, into the nineteenth century's systematic, regional-based slaving and marauding activity. It is also equally important to draw out the implications of that evolution for Spanish colonial systems of domination, development and discourse in the context of the advent of the China trade, empire building and corresponding ferocious rivalry with the Samal Balangingi. The seas of Asia, east by south, from Canton to Makassar, and from Singapore to the Bird's Head coast of New Guinea, crisscrossed by Balangingi raiding ships, Southeast Asian merchant vessels and colonial warships, have been the sites of extraordinary conflicts and changes often associated with the formation of ethnic groups and boundaries, political struggles and national histories (see Map 6.2).

The individual and collective fate(s) of the Samal Balangingi are detailed, after the Spanish conquest of their stronghold at Balangingi, focusing not only on leading slave raiders and warriors but also their wives and mothers. Stress is placed here on just how critical the resettlement policy directed against the deported Samal Balangingi was for the Balangingi's future cultural and social life. The experience of defeat and dispossession of a place of belonging was deeply engrained in their memory. However, the bombardment and destruction of Balangingi in 1848, far from progressing the Spanish campaign to 'eradicate' piracy and slave raiding, would actually trigger furious resistance from surviving Samal slave raiders. The remnant Balangingi, especially leaders like Panglima Taupan, came to see themselves as moulded by specific times with a deep sense of loss of a way of life and attachment to a particular place, their island stronghold. For these feared slave raiders, there was one historical event

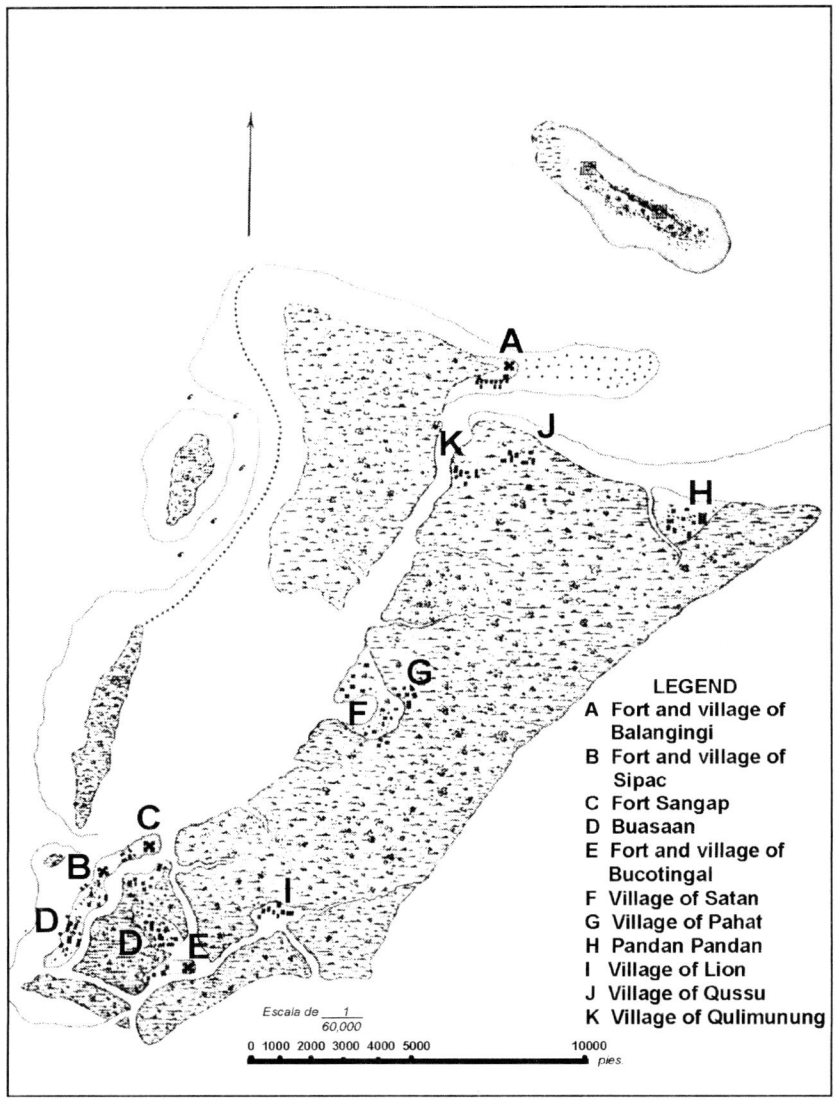

Map 6.1 A mid-nineteenth-century Spanish map of Balangingi, home of the feared Samal slave raiders. The islets in the Samal group were fringed with mangrove swamps awash at high tide, but exposed at low tide. Bits of land became separated from one another as the sand barrier inside the encircling reefs changed shape and elevation. Channels into the lagoon opened and closed during the year with tidal movements and shifting currents.

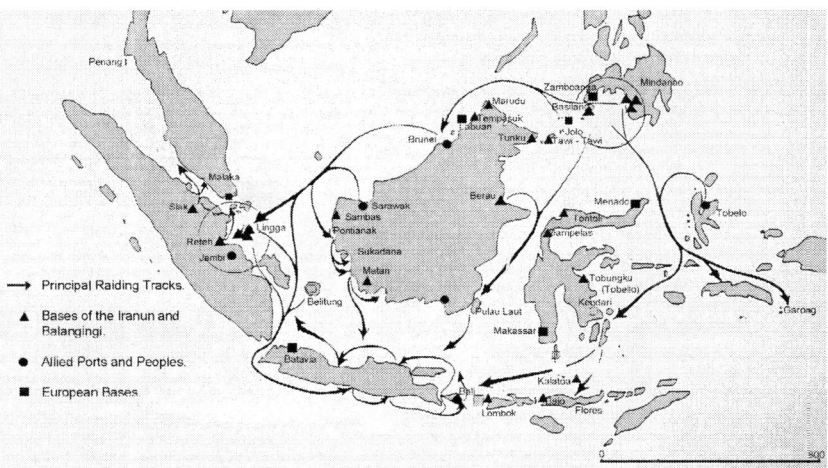

Map 6.2   Balangingi slave raiding in Southeast Asia

that acted as the background to all discussions about how people came to see themselves and look at the issue of identity and belonging in the Philippines in the latter half of the nineteenth century. That was the event of the Balangingi's dispossession of an island fortress that was once undeniably theirs and their subsequent forced relocation and settlement outside their homeland. They were spirited eight hundred miles away by the Spaniards in a conscious effort to deny them their very identity. This is an extraordinary story of an emergent Muslim maritime ethnic group attempting to overcome all odds.

For several centuries, the Sulu–Mindanao region has been known for 'piracy' (see Map 6.3). In the early nineteenth century, an entire ethnic group—the Samal Balangingi—specialised in state-sanctioned maritime raiding, attacking Southeast Asian coastal settlements and trading vessels sailing for the fabled Spice Islands, or for Singapore, Manila and Batavia. When people think of slavery in Southeast Asia, they rightly imagine tens of thousands of peoples stolen from their villages across the region and sent directly to work in the large fisheries and wilderness reserves of the Sulu Sultanate. The insatiable demands of the sultanate for labour to harvest and procure exotic natural commodities, such as sea cucumber and bird's nest, reached a peak in the first half of the nineteenth century as the China trade flourished. The large-scale forced migrations of the unfortunate mass of captives and slaves caught in the cogs of the Sulu economy, shaped the demographic origins of the Balangingi and the overall population trends and settlement patterns of much of the Philippines and Eastern Indonesia well into the end of the nineteenth century.

In this new globalised world, Sulu, Balangingi, Canton and London were all intimately interconnected. A major feature of this emerging global economy was that over two hundred years ago, Europe and the then emerging markets of East and Southeast Asia were tangled in a commercial and political web that was in many ways just as global as today's world economy. The Taosug of Sulu expanded their trade with China and the West, and increased their strike force, labour power and population of seafaring peoples. The Balangingi helped to

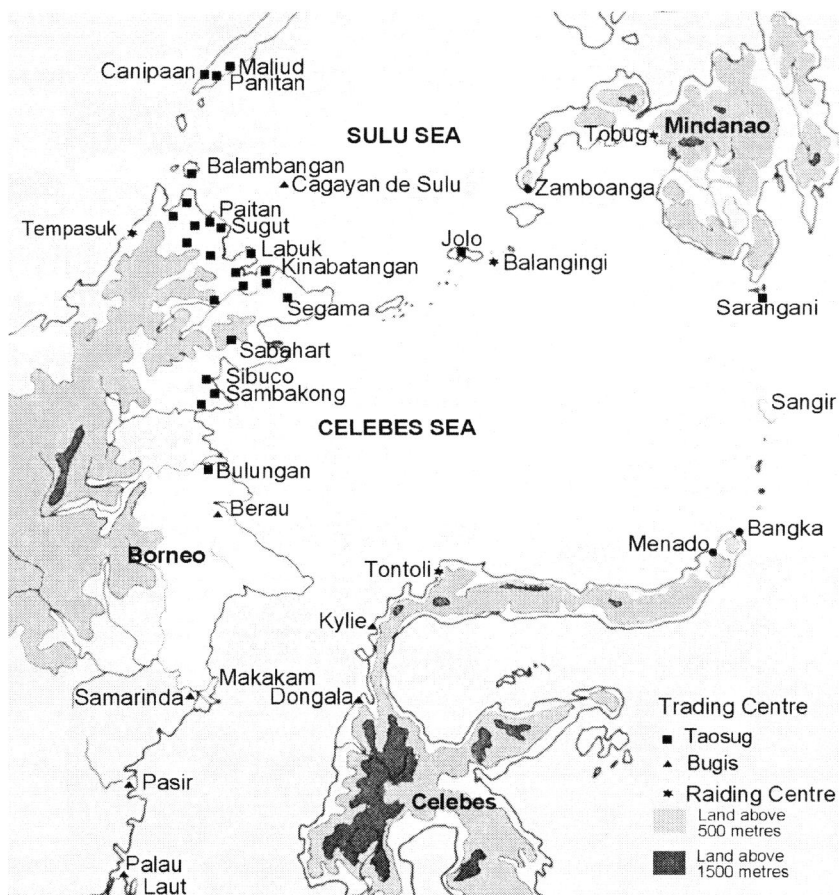

Map 6.3   The Sulu Zone constituted a Southeast Asian economic region with a multi-ethnic, pre-colonial, Malayo-Muslim state and an ethnically heterogeneous set of societies of diverse political backgrounds and alignments. These diverse ethnic groups could be set within a strategic hierarchy of kinship-orientated stateless societies: maritime, nomadic fishers and forest dwellers. In terms of world commerce and economic growth, the Sulu Zone was not an important economic region until the eighteenth century.

establish a system of slaving and redistributive trade that had very important consequences for the growth of Sulu's power and which, from one year to the next, yielded extraordinary profits to the Taosug.[2] The Balangingi profited from the expanding China trade, which they supplied with captives and slaves taken on the high seas and along the shores of Southeast Asia, in return for weapons, staples and luxury goods.

The history of Sulu and Mindanao has always been shaped by its landscape and especially by its relationship to the sea. The numerous islands of the Sulu Archipelago and coastal stretches of Southeast Asia were home to generations of Balangingi 'pirates' two centuries ago; their exploits were recorded by Spanish, English and Dutch naval officers, colonial officials, friars and merchant traders, and were often woven, myth-like, into the fabric of local folktales and colonial national histories. These memories and histories commemorated attempts to 'eradicate' the great Muslim threats of 'piracy' and slavery, and invariably failed to place Balangingi maritime raiding activity in a proper context. Past and present historians of the colonial period, in considering the Balangingi slave raids, have uncritically adopted the interpretation perpetuated by interests 'on the right side of the gunboat'.[3] They have relied heavily on sources inherently antagonistic to the nature of the society and values of the Balangingi raiders, such as the hostile accounts of the Spanish friars, the printed reports of Dutch and English punitive expeditions, and Sir Stamford Raffles and James Brooke's influential reports on 'Malay piracy'. In these Eurocentric histories, which dwell on the activities of the Balangingi at length, the term 'piracy' is conspicuously present in the titles.[4]

The main impetus for fashioning a new understanding of the Balangingi past has been the radical change in perspective that some historians have adopted to study the region's recent history and its continuing integration within the world capitalist economy. Here, I pay particular attention to the path-breaking book Eric Wolf wrote in the early 1980s, *Europe and the People Without History*.[5] Wolf argues that no community or nation is or has been an island, and the world, a totality of interconnected processes or systems, is not and never has been a sum of self-contained human groups and cultures. The modern world system, as it developed, never confined colonial capitalism to the political limitations of single states or empires. The point is that history consists of the interaction of variously structured and geographically distributed social entities that mutually reshape each other. The transformation of the West and China and the rise of the Balangingi in modern Southeast Asian history cannot be separated: each is the other's history. This viewpoint is a fundamental frame of reference. No ethnic group, not even one as apparently misunderstood as the Balangingi, can be studied in isolation from the maritime world(s) around and beyond them.[6]

In an effort to lay out the wide-ranging activities of these sea raiders—activities which extended from the Bay of Bengal to the Timor and Arafura seas—and to outline the structural basis of the system of social and political organisation that united them, it is necessary to piece together a description of their way of life from a variety of sources. These include explorers' accounts, like that of Alfred Wallace, the captivity narratives of Ebenezer Edwards and Luis de Ibañez y Garcia, and oral recollections, as well as the vitally important declarations or *testimonio* of fugitive captives and the statements of Balangingi prisoners.[7] The captivity narratives of Edwards and Ibañez y Garcia with the Balangingi, while highlighting motif images of the 'Moros' as barbaric and uncivilised, also contain important personal introductions to the subject of captivity itself, and to the raiders' warlike activities. Significantly, Ibañez y Garcia, who travelled with the celebrated Balangingi leader Panglima Taupan nine years after the destruction of his people's stronghold at Balangingi in 1848, offers a bird's-eye view of how Taupan's small band roamed the Visayan Sea in search of slaves, plunder and revenge. The historical record rarely provides sufficient insight into the career and fate of individual Balangingi leaders like Taupan, who achieved lasting fame through his daring exploits, travels and stubborn resistance to Spanish warships.[8] However, the orally transmitted local history of the exploits of such men and women in the Mindanao–Sulu region and in the Cagayan Valley of Northern Luzon also provides the historian with additional rare information about the activities, followers and fate of these people; detailed knowledge about aspects of global–local trade, slave raiding and the historical space between heredity and cultural heritage; and the exploration of the temporal and physical sites of dislocation and relocation. While the oral traditions of the descendants of the exiled Samal Balangingi are not conclusive in themselves, the documenting of these rememberings by anthropologists and historians demonstrates the sea of un-fished knowledge that is still extant within personal narratives today, despite the way state power both informs and re-forms cultural and historical identity.

The historian can also comprehend the forces that shaped the way of life of the Balangingi in the early nineteenth century, and explore the uprooted lives and fate of those captured and enslaved by studying the statements of fugitive captives and captured slave raiders. The statements of the fugitive captives (*cautivos fugados*) carry a self-affixed stamp of authenticity. Most statements and captivity narratives have a first person observer-narrator—an authentic voice of experience—attempting to present a narrative that usually shows similarities with other accounts dealing with the same subject(s), such as the dominant ways of organising maritime life, slave raiding, and the forms and allocation of labour—and whether it fits into a widely accepted social and cultural pattern. Set primarily in the years 1836 to 1862, at a time when the Balangingi were gradually losing the naval war in the seas of Southeast Asia, the testimony in the captive statements enables the historian to follow the Balangingi *garay* on their extended voyages (see Figure 4.2).[9] The crews endure boredom, chase small fleets of *tripang* fishers, attack coasting ships, get attacked in return by steam warships—all happening with a level of crushing realism as blood washes across the decks, among the splintered oars and carnage of dying slave rowers and raiders.

In the context of the global economy and the advent of the China trade, it should be understood that the slave raiding activities of the Balangingi, so readily condemned in blanket terms as 'piracy' by European colonial powers and later historians, were a means of consolidating the economic base and political power of the sultan and coastal chiefs of Sulu, and which functioned as an integral, albeit critical, part of the emerging statecraft and socio-political structure(s) of the zone. Thus, viewed from within the Sulu world of the late eighteenth and early nineteenth centuries, the term 'piracy' is difficult to sustain. However, in its practical devastating effects, particularly when Balangingi attacks were systematically directed against colonial coastal settlements and shipping, the Spanish, Dutch and English authorities could hardly be blamed for reacting to it in these terms, despite, from the late eighteenth century onwards, the word 'piracy' itself being bound up with larger colonial strategic policy implications and mythic resonances.

Balangingi: Place and the formation and maintenance of 'ethnicity'

Cruising expeditions against the Balangingi raiders promised no lasting results because the points to which they could retire were innumerable and often off the colonial charts. The Spanish officer, Don Jose Maria Halcon, providing naval intelligence about Balangingi maritime raiding to an English captain at Manila in 1838, compared their haunts to extensive 'nests or banks of rats' where they could fly from one refuge to another, with impunity.[10] Europeans, he believed, could never succeed in annihilating them. Hence, geography as destiny was a sinister friend, albeit an ally, of the Balangingi. The Balangingi needed a primary place from which to operate, somewhere to hide, and a means of converting their 'spoils', namely slaves, into 'modern' trade commodities—especially firearms and textiles.

Lying between Mindanao and Borneo, the Sulu Archipelago was the gateway to the Philippines for trade coming from the East Indies, and the gateway to the Moluccas for trade from China. Away from Jolo to the west and south, clusters of low-lying small coral and sand islands, islets, rocks, reefs and shoals, like Balangingi with its lagoons, mangrove swamp cover and particular pattern of tidal movements, stretched in an arc across the waters of the Sulu Sea (see Map 6.1). By the second quarter of the nineteenth century the Spanish, English and Dutch considered Balangingi to be the most dangerous of all the maritime raiding bases in Southeast Asia. The Balangingi, who, as late as 1838 were often confused with the Iranun of south-west Mindanao, were a highly organised, extremely expert slave raiding group, regional in scope, with significant resources in ships, munitions, capital, especially slaves and contacts. The Balangingi lived, along with other Samal-speaking groups and the Iranun, in a dozen or more villages and fortified settlements scattered along the southern shore of Basilan and on the islands of the Samalese cluster of which Balangingi was dominant.[11] As Sulu's trade with China and the West expanded at the end of the eighteenth century, Taosug *datus* increasingly retained neighbouring groups of seafarers as slave raiders. From Balangingi and related settlements on other islands, these Samal-speakers voyaged great distances; they swept the coasts from Luzon to Brunei and from Singapore to Menado, capturing slaves. But, who were the Balangingi? Although Francisco Combes and Thomas Forrest described the warlike activities and trade of the Samal in earlier periods, before the nineteenth century there are no historical references to the Balangingi as a separate ethnic group. In Western sources, Muslim maritime raiders, because of their slaving exploits, are first mentioned as Balangingi in the area of Singapore in the late 1830s. In 1838, several 'Illanun' *prahus* were destroyed by the steamboat *Diana* off the east coast of Malaya, and some of the badly shaken survivors, when interrogated, called themselves 'Balangingi' after the island that was their major base and home.[12] From that period the ethnic label, 'Balangingi', became, in the European literature, synonymous with 'pirate'. The Balangingi Samal seem to have acquired ethnic distinction as 'notorious pirates' only because they specialised in maritime slave raiding and because they incorporated an incredible number of non-Samal peoples into their society.[13]

The Samalese group comprised Balangingi Island (16 square kilometres) and Tunkil, a cluster of four islets (25 square kilometres) situated in the centre of the Sulu Archipelago, midway between Borneo and Mindanao. The islets were subject to change of size and shape, with tidal variations and modulations in the wind and weather patterns, separating into small parcels of coral and rock when inundated at high tide. They were fringed with mangrove swamps, and separated from neighbouring islands by an extensive series of connected reefs and winding channels through which swirled strong currents and counter-currents. At that critical moment in 'regional time', as Sulu's slave-based commodity-driven economy rapidly developed, Balangingi's low-lying impenetrable seascape constituted a tremendous strategic advantage for these emergent maritime raiders on the brink of forging a new Samal identity.

On these little islands, the Balangingi constructed wells and four forts (Balangingi, Sipac, Bucotingal and Sangap) to guard their villages and raiding *prahus*. The forts (*kota*), situated on raised ground and protected by coral reefs on three sides, were enormous stockades of two, three and four tiers of stout tree trunks, packed with rammed earth and coral to a height of more than 6 metres and defended with heavy cannon.[14] Remarkably, Hailan Kaligeran de Perez, aged ninety, still remembered from her childhood details of what her exiled father recounted to her about his youth on Balangingi. Most importantly, he explained to her that a remarkable natural asset located at the tip of the island—a hidden channel—protected the forts, godowns and a rough collection of houses. Diego Kaligeran told his young daughter one evening in the *sitio* of Tigbao, Zamboanga, that the only way of entering Balangingi was through this blind channel (*butas*).[15] From a purely defensive point of view, Balangingi was the best island natural fortification and large-scale maritime raiding base in the Malayo–Muslim world, during the age of sail.

However, Balangingi itself was not an ideal place from the standpoint of subsistence and everyday life. The island had to import virtually all the food its inhabitants required—especially rice and sago—from Jolo and Marudu Bay in North Borneo. With no surface water and little flora except the ubiquitous coconut palm, the Balangingi were incapable of maintaining the subsistence base required to support a dense population.[16] The islands and seas upon which the Samalan-speaking people of the Balangingi cluster lived placed them in an ecological bind that shaped their demographic origin and relationship to the Sulu Sultanate. The sole orientation of the Samal was, of necessity, towards the sea—from which, as specialists in maritime raiding, boat building and marine procurement, they derived their strength, security, and ultimately, wealth. Balangingi's proximity to Jolo as an outlet for retailing captives; its ecological dependence on larger, neighbouring volcanic islands like Jolo and Basilan as a source of rice, fruit and vegetables and trade goods; and the natural barriers surrounding it, help to explain why Balangingi became the home of one of the most feared maritime raiding groups of island Southeast Asia.[17]

To understand the important role played by the Balangingi in the slave trade in Southeast Asia, it is necessary to trace their history as an ethnic group.

The only historical work that deals with the Balangingi, *Piracy and Politics in the Malay World*, by Nicholas Tarling, does not consider their ethnic origins.[18] Avoidance of this question presents a deceptively static picture of an 'outlaw society' with an ethnically homogeneous population. Samal groups in the Sulu Archipelago were emergent populations; the success of the Balangingi as slave raiders was due in large measure to their ethnic heterogeneity and systems of kinship and social organisation that were exceptionally inclusive. Captives' statements present a picture of Samal populations undergoing constant cultural readjustments until 1848, as they established themselves as a different kind of people. At the beginning of the nineteenth century, there was an infusion of ethnically diverse captive people among the Balangingi—mostly through demands for labour on slave raiding *prahus* and in the *tripang* and pearl fisheries—that complicated the identity of Samal populations.

Many of the captives or slaves who were brought to Balangingi became Samal by borrowing language, religion and customs. Insufficient data prevents a precise reconstruction of the overall size and origin of Samal populations at the end of the eighteenth century.[19] What information there is for the nineteenth century has survived in the statements of fugitive captives. These testimonies show that the incorporation of other ethnic groups took place on a large scale, especially in the second and third generation. In 1836, it was estimated that only one-tenth of the male population were actually 'true' Balangingi Samal; the remainder were *renegados* (renegades), more particularly Tagalog and Visayan, and various Malay-speaking captives.[20] In essence, it is a historical fallacy to regard the Balangingi prior to 1848 as a monolithic ethnic, cultural and linguistic group. This homogeneous notion of the Balangingi obscures the extraordinary rate of incorporation and cultural accommodation taking place and the extent of internal ethnic differentiation.

The global economy of Sulu was expanding rapidly enough at that time for Samal populations to absorb ever-larger numbers of captives. A conscious recruitment policy of the Taosug *datus*, dictated by fluctuations in the trade economy and the hazards of the 'sea-war', changed the demographic structure and ethnic composition of Samal groups in less than two generations (1820–1845). Given that Barth considers a 10 per cent rate of incorporation in a generation drastic,[21] it can be argued that the social and cultural flexibility of the Sulu system was truly remarkable. Village populations in 1836 appear to have ranged from just over 300 people with ten to twelve raiding *prahus* (*garay*) at Tunkil to more than 1,000 people, with thirty to forty *prahus*, at Balangingi.[22] Six years later the size of the fleets at Balangingi were carefully monitored by the Spanish who estimated that up to 150 *garay* sailed on long-range raids each year.[23] In less than a decade, Balangingi's population roughly quadrupled; in 1845, the village had an estimated 4,000 people and 120–150 large vessels. The overall Samal population devoted to maritime raiding at Balangingi reached an upper limit, in 1848, with 10,000 people and 200 raiding *prahus*.[24] The consequence of this extraordinary population growth was the birth of an 'emergent' maritime raiding group within the Sulu Sultanate—the Samal Balangingi.

It must be remembered that slaving and slave ownership were among the principal means of enlarging and consolidating the political influence and wealth of upwardly mobile Taosug and Balangingi Samal chiefs. Slave ownership provided labour-power, prestige and, more importantly, differential access to force and authority in the socio-political hierarchy of Taosug and Balangingi society. The labour and skills of slaves, captured and transported by the Balangingi, made possible the complex elaboration of economic, political and social patterns in the Sulu Sultanate, which characterised the way of life and statecraft of the *datu* class and ensured their monopoly of trade goods and natural commodities, that became a crucial part of the global system of economic growth and interdependence with China and the West.

The raids and their impact

The Balangingi fortune was to be found on the sea. The pattern of Balangingi marauding activity was strongly influenced by the monsoon trade-wind system, the major ocean current structure and the distribution of settlement locations of these seafaring peoples. The Balangingi visited the Philippines twice annually, once in March and again in October.[25] It was the small settlements far from the *cabeceras* with little or no outside communication or defence, and those situated on offshore islands which could not be protected from the mainland, that were exposed to the greatest danger. On Luzon, these settlements were found principally on the Pacific coast. In favourable weather, the Balangingi came up from the south or circumnavigated the island in a clockwise direction to attack the weaker settlements. On their way north to the Pacific, the Balangingi made rapid attacks on west coast villages, and they appeared on the Zambales coast every year from 1836 to 1841. In the central and southern Visayas, the Balangingi continued to attack coastal villages on Panay, Negros, Cebu, Samar and Mindanao.[26]

In another direction, Brunei was within easy range of the Balangingi and from the middle of March to the end of November a squadron hovered about southern Palawan to seize Brunei inhabitants and cut off trade to North

Borneo.[27] In the same manner, the Maluso Samal of Basilan harried the settlers of Zamboanga. The raids made it impossible for townspeople to fish and, ironically, Zamboanga became dependent on its assailants for fresh supplies. In the south, the Balangingi disputed Bugis rights to subject peoples and to control marine produce off the coasts of northern Celebes (Sulawesi) and east Borneo.

In their heyday the Balangingi could muster at least 150 *garay*, often double banked and capable of carrying up to sixty warriors, that sailed in fleets of eight, ten, twelve, twenty or thirty *prahus*.[28] The Spaniards considered it useless to offer letters of marque against these maritime raiders as they navigated in vessels so 'ill-provided that they were frequently without any water to drink', and it was reported that the Balangingi were accustomed in case of emergency to drink their urine or seawater.[29] According to the oral accounts of elderly Balangingi, as a last resort they were also prepared to drink blood collected from the severed arms and opened veins of captives, in order to muster the strength to survive without food and water for weeks on end, until they managed to reach their island stronghold, and home.

The most notorious feature of their wind-driven operations was the systematic taking of captives who were either ransomed, sold as slaves in colonial cities hungering for labour or exchanged at Jolo and Sarangani Island off the coast of southern Mindanao. Balangingi raiding at the end of the eighteenth century, as has already been noted, was primarily a consequence of the onset of the China trade and was never a strictly Islamic enterprise. It was heavily commanded by Philippine and 'Malay' renegades in search of good fortune and a new way of life. It also used European merchants, including Spaniards, as intermediaries who frequently traded war stores for the spoils and deployed the labour of ransomed captives for their private commerce.

Less than two centuries ago, few homes in Southeast Asia's vast patchwork of coastal settlements had been left unscathed by the Balangingi. F. Mallari notes that when the south-westerly or 'pirate wind' blew from April until the end of October, those Filipinos who lived close to the San Bernardino Strait or along coastal stretches of the Samar or Sibuyan seas constantly scanned the horizons for the first sign of massed sails.[30] Many people lost their kin and were forever haunted by their loss. Victims snatched from coastal settlements—especially women and children—were generally welcomed as new members of this emergent maritime Muslim community to which they were forcibly taken, often hundreds of miles away. Most captives and slaves accepted their fate and adopted new roles, large numbers replacing Balangingi seafarers lost to the hazards of nature, battles and disease.

Certainly no ethnohistory of the Balangingi since the late eighteenth century, no description of the meaning and constitution of their 'culture', and no anthropologically informed historical analysis of the transformation of their society can be undertaken without reference to the advent of the China trade and the rise of the Sulu Sultanate; and the integral role in both those processes of Balangingi slave raiding—a role that was so forcefully felt by most ethnic groups right across island Southeast Asia.

Defeat, dispossession and diaspora

Spanish recovery in the sea war against the Balangingi would not seriously get under way until almost the middle of the nineteenth century, but then it came rapidly. The theory expressed by Spanish naval experts was to control Balangingi 'piracy' at the source, or at least check maritime raiding by establishing forward bases for naval operations and as places of refuge for victims of Balangingi slaving. However, the most effective blow against Balangingi slave raiding and 'piracy' would be struck from another quarter initially—by the able and liberal-minded Narciso Clavería, the Governor-General of the Philippines. In 1848, he secured pre-fabricated steam gunboats for the defence of the islands from Europe. The arrival of the steamers marked a turning point in the fifty-eight year 'sea-war' (1790–1848) against Balangingi slave raiding and marauding. Clavería's decision to launch steam warships against Balangingi vessels, fortifications and settlements across the archipelago and south of Mindanao was as much a telling message to the Sulu Sultanate as to Spain's colonial competitors that Madrid was watching—and that it would not tolerate any interventionism that might have threatened to disrupt the sovereignty that Spain claimed over the region. His campaign to punish them with *kapal api* (fire ships) marked the start of a new era of conflict with the Balangingi; an era that would signal the end of their way of life in less than twenty-five years. This was the defining moment when the slave hunters became the hunted.

Clavería understood the strategic importance of the control of Balangingi, which became the focal point of a new Spanish strategy. A daring naval attack aimed at the throat of Sulu, namely Balangingi, was the key to cutting the sultanate in two and stopping slave raiding in the Philippines. In 1845, he initially authorised an expedition against Balangingi and Tunkil and established a small fort and naval base on Basilan in the heartland of the Balangingi.[31] Although the expedition had been ill-prepared—lacking sufficient troops, artillery and scaling ladders—and ultimately failed, the Spanish managed for the first time to fully reconnoitre the Samalese group at close range, and thus form a detailed picture of the topography, defences and population of Balangingi.[32] Armed with this information, Clavería devoted the next several years to systematically organising a formidable taskforce comprised of the best trained and equipped colonial troops—an expedition that his personal honour and patriotism demanded he command himself. The fate of the Balangingi had already been sealed with the arrival of the new Governor and the first war steamers. He would dedicate his naval invasion to his Queen, projecting disparaging images of the Balangingi as 'savages' and 'barbarians' and Jolo, their principal entrepôt, as a place where Spanish subjects were enslaved and in danger of apostasy.[33]

The expedition, headed by Clavería himself, consisted of three war steamers, schooners, three transport brigs, brigantines, a detachment of the *marina sutil* (light navy) and several regiments of crack troops. The Governor ordered that no quarter be given as the steamers and taskforce approached Balangingi Island in the early hours of 16 February 1848. The three black ships belching smoke as they came over the horizon just before dawn, announced the arrival of Clavería's invasion force, and must have posed a terrifying sight to the stunned Samal sentinels in an age when the Balangingi still deemed their island base impregnable and virtually 'closed' off to the outside world.

The 1848 defeat of the Balangingi by Clavería and his sizeable taskforce is one of the most important military feats in the nineteenth-century history of colonial warfare in Southeast Asia. In the minds of local observers, in the campaign correspondence of Clavería and his officers, as well as in the oral traditions of the Balangingi, the desperate heroic battles of extermination between the slave raiders, especially at Sipac Fort, and the combined forces of the Spanish army and navy, represented to both sides their own great epic—their crusade or their Masada—but this epic proved no more true (or false) than any other (see Figure 6.1). In the end, the largest diaspora of Samal people in recent history, effected through invasion and total war, and forced removal and relocation, was accomplished.

Governor Clavería was a brave, ambitious and intelligent officer. With the three steam warships, he attacked Sipac, the largest fortress the Balangingi had ever built in Southeast Asia, from several sides simultaneously, while he mustered nearly 1,000 troops for the landing. He and his combined assault force wiped out the Balangingi at Sipac in an unbelievable murderous battle. From a distance, the advancing Spanish troops could see a large red flag with a raven that was unfurled by the Sipac defenders—red symbolising courage, the black raven signifying death.[34] For the Spanish forces the message was all too clear: the Balangingi were prepared to fight to the death. The Samal warriors fought ferociously and at Sipac, which was situated in the ravine of an isthmus,

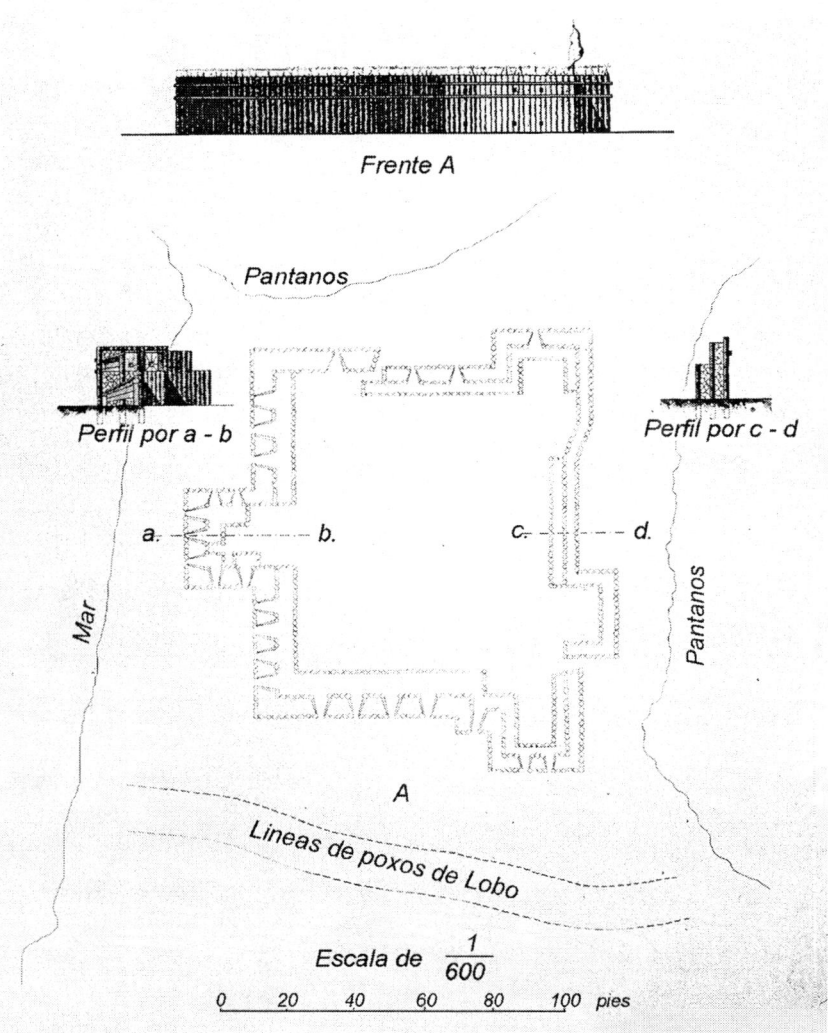

Figure 6.1 Spanish plans of the heavily fortified Samal stronghold (*kota*) of Sipac. The *kota* was situated on raised ground, protected by reefs, rocks, mangrove and a defensive moat, and defended by cannon

they drove the attackers from the walls of the fort three times, before the Spanish were able to penetrate the outer defences under the cover of artillery fire from the steamers. Once inside the stockade, the Spanish troops found the anguished Balangingi warriors who expected no quarter—killing their women and children out of sheer desperation, and then impaling themselves on the phalanx of Spanish bayonets.

The wanton slaying stopped, amid the cursing and weeping, only after the Spanish commander promised clemency to the warriors. The Samal men then submitted, put down their blood-soaked weapons and surrendered. They, along with over 150 terrified Samal women and children who had survived the carnage, were immediately marched as prisoners of war out of the devastated burning fortress to the waiting Spanish ships.[35]

The Balangingi warriors who died in the crazed battle totalled more than 450, along with 200 women and children, while another 350 men, women and children were taken prisoner. The Spanish liberated nearly 300 captives from the Philippine provinces and the Dutch islands.[36] In the five days following the assault on Sipac Fort, the Spanish engineers and soldiers burned the already decomposing bodies of their foes in pits and trenches, razed to the ground the four forts, destroyed seven villages and 150 vessels, as well as 7,000 to 8,000 coconut trees. Their scorched earth policy left Balangingi unfit for habitation. In the aftermath of the destruction of Sipac, Clavería spoke to the expedition forces about the mopping up operations with his usual sense of candour and patriotism suffused with a mixture of violence and action. The speech also contained positive imperatives for the eyes of the region, acknowledging a sense of great accomplishment with no remorse for the sorrow of war:

> The nations in the area should acknowledge and thank you for this very important service, and the many people who were rescued owe you their freedom. Very soon we shall occupy the rest of the island. We shall destroy their resources, their fortifications, the ships and boats they use for piracy. Then we shall rest, feeling proud of the fact that we accomplished a great service on behalf of mankind, especially in the Philippines. We shall leave these islands in a state of proof that no one can ever insult us without fear of being punished in the same manner.[37]

The Carthage-style conquest of Balangingi was complete and the expedition returned to triumphant welcomes in Zamboanga and Manila. Parades and festivities were held in honour of the victory and news of it was officially broadcast across the provinces on broadsheets in a variety of dialects. A

Te Deum was held in the capital's cathedral and Clavería was decorated and promoted to viscount by the Spanish queen, while many of the officers and men received citations for valour and were variously rewarded.[38]

Although many Balangingi were killed, others transported and their vessels burnt, the Spanish victory was not decisive as, when the attack occurred, more than half the warrior population had been either absent raiding or collecting provisions while hundreds of others had managed to elude their assailants and escape to Sulu.[39] In December 1848, some Samal attempted to re-establish themselves on Balangingi and Tunkil under Panglima Julano Taupan, who had been away purchasing rice to provision the strongholds when the Spanish attacked. He had taken refuge on Sulu, but had failed to convince the sultan and the *ruma bichara* (council of ministers) to assist him in getting back the Samal prisoners of war, especially the women and children being held hostage at Zamboanga. Owing to the successive Spanish campaigns, the Samals, more than ever before, were thrown on to their own economic, social and political resources. They still had a considerable number of *prahus* in 1850, but the action of the Spanish cruisers tended to scatter the Balangingi throughout the Sulu archipelago, and on to the coasts of southern Palawan, north Borneo and beyond.[40]

These Balangingi who had come face to face with mass death inside the Sipac Fort and survived, having come so close to being one of the statistics of Clavería's campaign of eradication, were unique, both psychologically and morally. It followed that a new social integration for these survivors was more difficult than anything that they had experienced before. And this was especially so for their leaders, particularly warriors like Panglima Taupan, Palawan Dando and Tumugsuc, who had been absent during the onslaught. The Balangingi Samal survivors of 1848, and in particular Julano Taupan, no longer regarded themselves as indestructible, but proved to be capable of integrating into their personality and character as a single ethnic group, one of the most trying experiences to which a Southeast Asian could be subjected—namely the horrors of confronting a common cast of colonial mind and set of attitudes and policies, a genocidal mentality and a dazzling array of weapons of mass destruction. In this context it is imperative to concentrate on the changing emotions of these warriors and the intense bond that developed between survivors under terrible stress. The Samal slave raiders had suffered heavy losses with the introduction of war steamers to the Philippines and had been driven from their strongholds on Balangingi. They would never be able to regain their former strength in the face of the major defeat and entrapment that had already taken place. But the Balangingi were not yet prepared to succumb to the threat the steamship posed to their future, and the colonial frame of mind that created and maintained that threat, portraying them as 'savages' and 'wildmen', who stood in the way of Christianity, progress and free trade.

In response, those Taosug who controlled the flow of the sultanate's global trade resorted to extreme violence, calling upon the assistance of the Spanish navy to eradicate the Balangingi. Taupan's ascendancy, leadership and raiding campaigns came to symbolise the process through which the Balangingi Samal had taken total control of maritime raiding in the aftermath of their defeat in 1848. Their hard-won separation was in many ways a response to the sultanate's campaign to collaborate with Spain against this development. After being driven out of their original island stronghold by the Spanish, many of the Balangingi survivors settled on islands in the Tawi-Tawi cluster, which became a major Balangingi base for attacks on Dutch and English shipping. As the Spanish and other colonial authorities cracked down on the old South China Sea and Moluccan slaving routes, the dispersed Balangingi responded by exploiting somewhat different routes and they used new as well as old tactics. Repeated long journeys, like those undertaken in the early 1800s, were far less common as the Balangingi tried a variety of routes through the Philippines and the Moluccas, using fewer ships in large numbers of smaller squadrons. After 1852, Taupan's actions triggered a general sea war that lasted until 1858. The second Balangingi campaign dragged on for six years, costing the Spanish colonial government hundreds of thousands of dollars, and countless more Balangingi and Filipino lives. Lieutenant Colonel Ibañez y Garcia's captivity narrative, *Mi Cautiverio: Carta que con motivo del que Sufrio entre los Piratas Joloanos y Samales en 1857*, proved that between 1848 and 1852, despite the Samal defeat and forced diaspora, Panglima Taupan was able to exert considerable leadership and authority over the dispersed Balangingi, temporarily reuniting them as a 'people'. Ibañez y Garcia's narrative contained many anecdotes about the heart-rending conditions he witnessed on the coasts of Leyte and Samar as Taupan stepped up intelligence and the tempo of Balangingi raiding efforts. The audacious *panglima* seized passenger and trading boats, put coconut and banana plantations to the torch and landed on the coast of Samar at Lauan to kill men, women and children, obviously haunted by the memory of the horror of Sipac Fort and the tragic circumstance of his imprisoned family in the cells of Fort Pilar at Zamboanga.[41]

Panglima Taupan, considered by the Spaniards to be the last of the great Muslim raiding chiefs, was also, in the eyes of his own people, one of the greatest. He was feared by his enemies and revered by his own society and followers. Taupan was fearless and a superb seafarer, but, after the destruction of Balangingi, the *panglima* had to chart a new course for his own life and for that of his followers. He and his survivors now lived in a complex fast-moving world of steam warships, new colonial naval strategies and regional security pacts. In the fateful years between 1848 and 1851, Panglima Taupan was forced to pause and reassess where he was in the world and what was truly important to him. It was because of a catastrophic event—the wholesale destruction and dispossession of his homeland and the death of many warriors and friends—that he reflected on what was important in the lives of the Balangingi as an ethnic group. Taupan had returned home from a provisioning voyage to a seemingly annihilated place and was overwhelmed and haunted by the alienation of the site of the horrific battle at Sipac, where so many members of his community died or were deported. It is understandable that Taupan's first visit was likely to have occasioned a painful meditation on past and present. What was at issue was the balance between the two for his people's future. It required real commitment to take stock and take some positive steps from the Sipac experience—horrible as it had been—to first assess then do something about their autonomy and future as an ethnic group: steps that would test their very will to survive. It is against this background of the scars of war that Panglima Taupan's maritime raiding exploits were to become the subject of so much conversation, consternation and controversy from the drawing rooms of Manila to the *conventos* of every province in the Visayas.

He was a man who was tied deep within himself to a concrete set of activities through which the Balangingi came to see themselves and a tragic historical situation—a globalising market-driven situation that bred slave raiding, violence, new ethnic identities and communal ways for Taupan's dispersed seafaring people. Yet, he was kept going, driving himself and his followers beyond endurance by the desire to see at least the Balangingi Samal hostages and his wife and children released back into that interconnected world that was so complex and alluring, but now dangerous for the Balangingi at every turn. In the end, when Taupan realised there was no other solution except shame and submission, and stunned by bewildering frustration over the initial hostage crisis, both the leader and his followers were compelled to extreme acts of violence and slave raiding. The Spanish terms were unconditional surrender.

The dispossessed Balangingi of the 1850s were under constant pressure from the Spanish to surrender and relocate, and they were to be another victim of the Spanish administration's mid-century removal policy, but with a difference—Taupan had initiated a sea war against Spain in the Philippines. He proceeded to wage a hit and run style war from the islands around the Visayas, with an inferior force and little popular support, and he was facing a technologically superior enemy. But the final result of Taupan's efforts was his treacherous seizure. Under a flag of truce, he was taken by the Spanish after he had agreed to meet with them to discuss an end to the six-year struggle and an exchange of hostages at Simisa, which included some members of his family.[42] Panglima Taupan had provided much of the 'life drive' for his people and their future. Everybody and everything in the fragmented world of the dispersed Balangingi, of necessity, depended in large measure on his great courage and inner security. But, in 1858, when the circumstances of his life were extremely harrowing and destructive, in the face of constant desolation, pain and living death, the battle-weary Taupan was ready to strike a truce. The previous year, in 1857, the Spanish 'light fleet' based at Basilan had launched a surprise attack on Simisa, a major Balangingi settlement, where they rescued seventy-six captives, and took 116 prisoners, including many current members of the families of Balangingi leaders. Later, on 7 July 1858, Panglima Taupan, Palawan Dando and Tumugsuc, against whom the lightning-like assault at Simisa had been specifically directed, voluntarily presented themselves to the Governor of Zamboanga to seek peace and exchange Samal prisoners—especially women and children—for sixty Christian captives, one priest and one European woman.[43] But the Spaniards betrayed these men. Their families were not returned to them and the celebrated Balangingi leaders were unceremoniously seized as prisoners of war.

The Spanish realised that the best stratagem to end this extraordinary man's career, short of life imprisonment or execution, was to banish him to the Cagayan valley, north central Luzon, along with Palawan Dando and Tumugsuc, who were to be sent to Nueva Viscaya and Isabella respectively. The official proponents of deportation argued that Spain's progress in the Philippines and their 'manifest destiny' were dependent upon the removal of the 'savage' Balangingi from the pathway of Spanish civilisation. The Governor-General, in his letters to Spain, justified his actions in removing the Balangingi by portraying himself as a humanitarian in an army uniform. Forced to face the reality of abandoning the sea, the symbol of their traditional life and current misfortune, Taupan and his commanders steadfastly refused to admit to the Spanish naval interrogators their purported crimes. The Balangingi warriors of Simisa, particularly the twenty-six who belonged to the elite group composed of *panglimas* and other principal leaders (over half of whom were born at the height of the China trade) were brought in chains by express steamship to Manila, where they were first confined at the Cavite Arsenal. They were later transferred to Fort Santiago and placed under heavy guard. Their fate had already been sealed. A large number of Samal still confined in the prison of Fort Pilar in the south, slated for deportation at local expense to other places outside the archipelago, including the Marianas, were instead to be settled at Zamboanga.[44]

While the principal Balangingi leaders remained closed in the dungeon of the fort, their families were in the same locality occupying space in the public prison, the *corregimiento* of Tondo. The personal fate and courage of these Balangingi women, who undoubtedly felt so uncomfortable in Manila, bearing the harrowing scars of the sea war, almost defies translation. Their only resources were tenacity, determination and each other. From the cell of the public prison of Tondo, Sabi, a wife of Palawan Dando from the island of Simisa, petitioned the government to be allowed to join her elderly mother Painon and her daughter Ymbag, who were both sent to the Hospicio de San Jose. Painon was to live at the Asilo de Beneficencia until the end of her life; Ymbag received Christian religious instruction which the foundation gave to orphaned children who stayed there. Because of her mother's extreme age, Sabi was torn between her role and duty as a wife and that of daughter and mother. With her child, she chose to join Painon, her mother, despite the fact that her husband, who had lost his right arm in the battle of Simisa, sorely needed her.[45] It was Tainun, Palawan Dando's mother who, despite her infirmity, had accompanied her badly wounded son from Zamboanga to Manila, and who ministered to him in his hour of greatest need. In a brief communiqué, dated 25 February 1860, the administrative Head of the Hospicio de San Jose announced that the *mora* Sabi, wife of the Balangingi leader Palawan Dando, who was incarcerated in Fort Santiago, had died on 27 December 1859. Sabi's badly injured husband, Palawan Dando, also died grief-stricken in solitary confinement the following April.[46] The petitions of women like Sabi, Nuyla and others help us to hear the unheard voices of the Sulu world in conflict—in this case, the voices of Balangingi women—who were imprisoned and exiled for their powerful political and religious beliefs and family ties. There is a strong sense here of the silence being broken with respect to the underside of the Samal–Spanish conflict. These are petitions, fragmentary narratives, in which Balangingi women emerge as central protagonists in the culmination of over a century of political and cultural conflict: fragments challenging the dominant political rhetoric of Spanish success and the stereotypes and policies of cultural submission that they so effectively perpetuated.

Panglima Taupan and his immediate followers had implored the clemency of the Spanish authorities in Manila, claiming that by virtue of the royal pardon granted to them by the Spanish Crown they should not be deported to Cagayan. The Balangingi Samal, as prisoners of war, were declared to be direct vassals of the Crown—like the Spanish colonists and Filipino subjects themselves. The

Balangingi prisoners' appeal to the Crown for clemency was accepted by Spain on the grounds that the influence of Islam, and not global-capitalism, had left its pernicious mark. In the Spanish mind, it was the inextricable link between Islam and 'piracy' that was so essential to the Balangingi's development and evolution as maritime slave raiders. This strongly held belief partly explains both the basis of the pardon and Spanish attempts to forcibly resettle the Balangingi in northern upland villages, thus freeing the Samal from enslavement to Islam and from the influence of their celebrated chieftains, particularly Panglima Taupan. The pardon was granted to guard against the future use of combinations of Samal Balangingi power that could rival the authority of the Spanish, and on the condition that they were banished from the sea and their homeland, forever. The key phrase in the royal order of 19 April 1859 rationalising the deportation of the Balangingi and the condemnation of Islam stated, 'piracy was an occupation that found a religious basis and was viewed not as a criminal act arising from moral degradation but rather, lack of civilization.'[47]

The trauma of the conquest was immense, but it was not adequately understood by the Balangingi until 1858. The primary message of the deportation sought to invalidate the totality of Balangingi life and replace it with Spanish-Christian values—largely by forced means. The dispossessed Balangingi were to practise the agriculture and arts of civilised 'man' and learn the worship of the true God. Islam, which sanctioned slavery, was to be replaced by Catholicism. At the same time, slave traffic, the basis of the wealth of Sulu's market, was to be replaced by the lucrative profits derived from the surplus value of the *deportados*' forced labour for the tobacco monopoly in the Philippines. The distant tobacco plantation in Cagayan would serve not only as an economic outpost of empire, it was also meant to be an agent of change among the banished seafarers. Farming was to be encouraged and Christianity taught in order to acculturate and assimilate the Balangingi. The Spanish were determined to break down the social structure, culture and religious beliefs of the Samal slave raiders, thus transforming them into 'Filipino' farmers and colonial subjects indistinguishable from their Yoggad neighbours, the original inhabitants of Isabella.[48] These events surrounding the betrayal, surrender and removal of the Balangingi provide real insight into Spanish attitudes and policy, and clearly display their ethnocentric approach to the Balangingi and strong antagonism towards Islam.

The Balangingi men deported to the Cagayan valley petitioned for their families, who were deliberately being held behind in Manila and Zamboanga, to also be relocated with them in the mountain fastness of Isabella so that they could live there permanently. It took some time due to lack of proper transport, but, on 19 March 1860, the incarcerated Samal women and children began the final leg of their bewildering epic journey northward into an unforgiving landscape—a journey that was directed towards getting rid of them as an independent seafaring people and depriving them by violent means of their island homeland.[49] The general removal of the Balangingi from the Mindanao–Sulu region under the provisions of Julano Taupan's surrender was, without a doubt, the most consequential event in recent Samal history. While the Spanish tribunal in Manila had decided to deport all Balangingi leaders to their respective destinations in north central Luzon, the government reserved final judgement on Panglima Taupan who remained in chains at Fort Santiago. He was placed under the jurisdiction of the Commander of the Navy and found guilty of piracy for the capture of the Spanish schooner *Soterana*. Instead of sending him to Bontoc in the Cagayan Valley, he was transferred to the Cavite Arsenal where he died in a cholera epidemic that swept the area in 1861.[50] Three years later, in October 1864, still deeply disturbed by the circumstances surrounding the remarkable *panglima's* death, 39-year-old Maria Manobo, a Balangingi, testified in Zamboanga, that while in Manila, she had heard that Panglima Taupan had died as a prisoner, shackled and alone in the Cavite Arsenal. She used words that she had undoubtedly spoken before to other Samal who possessed no such memories, and the Spanish were deeply concerned, realising that even in death their removal policy had failed to erase the memory of Panglima Taupan.[51]

Margarita Cojuangco, in *Kris of Valor*, has sympathetically recounted the odyssey of the Balangingi who were resettled in the Cagayan Valley to work on the Tabacalera plantations. She has reconstructed the history of the Samal Balangingi diaspora spanning four generations of exiles, offering new materials, insights and an ethnohistorical perspective based on several periods of fieldwork in Cagayan as well as in the Mindanao–Sulu region.[52] What meaning could the deported Balangingi find in their forced removal and their social response to it? Each generation of exiles had to cope with its own history. The most difficult part of this was coming to terms with the traumatic events surrounding the destruction of Balangingi in 1848, the assault on Simisa a decade later, and the removal process itself. For the first generation, these events were all part of the protracted Samal–Spanish sea war and the alien universe of the tobacco plantations. Clearly, some second- and third-generation exiles found that the easiest way to try and cope with the world taking shape around them was to adopt the attitude in part that one must live one's own life and not be bothered by what both revolutionised and traumatised the lives of their former seafaring parents. Within a generation, some of these Balangingi, who had been baptised into Catholicism, had intermarried with neighbouring Yoggad, Ilocano and

Tagalog migrants in Camarag and elsewhere.[53] However, Haji Datu Nuno, alias Antonio de la Cruz, the Jesuit-educated youngest son of Panglima Taupan, established the importance of the places in which the Balangingi had lived, and how much they grieved when they lost them. In 1881, he petitioned the government to return to Mindanao to utilise his services as a culture broker in a manner deemed most useful by the Zamboanga authorities. The local officials sought his assistance to facilitate the settlement of nearby Taluksangay, which was being populated by Samals.

Many Balangingi who had lost a place of profound importance found it unforgettable. Feelings about lost or destroyed places, namely Balangingi and Simisa, roused their deepest emotions. As Panglima Taupan tragically learned from the Spanish strategy of removal and the meaning of lost places, losing a home or a village or being forced to leave a homeland was also meant to be like losing a loved one. Taupan and his orphaned exiled son, each in his own way, had to confront and examine what it meant to lose a place of belonging forever, and why some of the first- and second-generation exiles kept on returning to those places so large in their memories. Both men, the father, a warrior, and the son, a man of letters, undoubtedly considered the meaning of the lost homes, villages and their seafaring way of life. Haji Datu Nuno's return to Zamboanga in 1881 tells a human story of grieving and loss that is also inspiring. He perceptively saw the beginning and the end of things for the banished Balangingi in the sea. The most apparent demonstration of this simple but profound realisation was provided when some Balangingi exiles who had lived in the Cagayan valley for more than forty years, who had not changed their attitudes and beliefs so radically, chose to return to their 'real life' and home in the south. For those Balangingi their choice suggested a (re)viewing of Balangingi and what it meant to be Balangingi or 'Moro' people from a far away 'outside' (Cagayan) on the edge of remembering, forgetting and imagining. In the end, the forced removal of the Balangingi from their homeland did not lead to a condition of permanent exile for everybody. At the beginning of the twentieth century, Haji Datu Nuno arranged with the American colonial authorities to repatriate some exiled Samal to Mindanao and Sulu. In 1905, 100 men, women and children returned to Zamboanga on the SS *Mauban*, and Haji Datu Nuno settled them at Taluksangay, Tigboa and Tupalic.[54]

In the early 1970s, C. A. Majul noted that the Christian descendants of the exiles in the Cagayan Valley were still recognisable, and the older ones could remember the Kalimah as recited by their grandparents. This tended to corroborate information given to me in 1974 that small isolated pockets of these people, Muslim Yoggads, who were located at some distance from

Echague, still read the Qur'an and traced their original settlement in the area to the forced removal of the Balangingi in 1848.[55] Some of those third- and fourth-generation Balangingi who did not return to Zamboanga maintained some semblance of cultural roots that resisted the process of political incorporation and cultural assimilation promoted by Spanish policies, and the subsequent increasing integration of local, regional and global economies. Cojuangco has highlighted the persistence of a Muslim identity in Yoggad society, which takes common Balangingi ancestry as the basis for membership, and promotes a collective trans-local/trans-regional identity, in a modern multi-ethnic state—the Philippines.[56] The rise and fall of the Balangingi in the nineteenth century demonstrates that there was no fixed 'Balangingi identity' before this century, but that it was always in flux, undergoing constant readjustment. Conversely, as a consequence of the emergence of the Samal Balangingi raiders as a distinctive ethnic group, any 'Filipino identity', actual or imaginary, was also in flux and equally precarious. Hence, in order to understand how Balangingi ethnicity evolved and was maintained and reconstructed over time, one has to take into account the political, economic and socio-cultural aspects of these identities as they were directly affected by colonialism, world commerce and slavery.

The problem of ethnic identity and the formation and maintenance of 'cultures' are elusive, complex and contested processes, practises and attributes that defy simple explanations and definitions. I have stressed the inextricable relationship between maritime raiding, slavery, forced migration, 'homeland' and cultural identity as being critical factors that led to the emergence of new ethnicities and diasporas. This expedient reconstructing of ethnicity and identities, resulting from the complex influences generated by the China trade, compels us to think about related notions of society and 'culture' in more processual ways.[57] Historians of the region need to locate the emergence, maintenance and abrogation of populations, and the 'cultures' and ethnic self-definitions they encompass, within the framework of a series of historically changing, imperfectly bounded, multiple and branching integrated sets of local, regional and global social and economic alignments.

In the Philippines today, it seems history is still being used and abused to shape the future. How does possible contestation over the nature and relevance of explaining the birth of Balangingi ethnicity itself give meaning to identities and broadly held societal views in the Philippine present? Today's Balangingi are principally descended from Christian captives arriving from the Philippines between 1800 and 1848. Fresh insights and undeniable evidence back up the view that wave after wave of captives transported from Luzon, Cebu, Negros, Leyte, Panay and Samar came to dominate the local Samal populations in Balangingi. The existing culture transmitted religion, language and certain maritime technologies and nautical skills, and the arriving peoples greatly affected the existing population and their history. Ethnohistorians like the Comaroffs, Leach, Keesing, Wolf and I have stressed that the genesis, persistence and transformation of ethnicities must be understood within a set of fluid self-defining systems, embedded in economic and political relations, and contingent upon specific historical forces and events.[58] We are now acutely aware of the 'origins' of Balangingi ethnicity to its present configuration, and of the dynamic and ecological aspects of 'culture' and place, as well as how ethnic identities have been constructed and reconstructed in local-regional history on a large scale.

Conclusion

Balangingi provides an exceptional case study of how collective identities were established, made real, and took on a particular ethnic and cultural content.[59] The case of the Samal Balangingi both prior to and after losing their homeland also shows that maintaining and managing ethnic self-identification and the writing of its history in the Philippines, have been both a dynamic process and a contested domain, and that cultural difference as signified and articulated by ethnicity is problematic and precarious. This manner of historically tracing the 'ethnicity' and 'culture' of the now quite distinct Samal maritime community leads us to a new way of framing and re-presenting a sense of what constitutes kinship identification, group solidarity, common culture and conflict, and particularly political struggles in Southeast Asia. By stressing the problems of self-definition and the reconstruction of identities, and the meaning of homeland and lost places, as a revealing social and psychological process in its own right, the case of the Balangingi challenges lineal notions of history and bounded static conceptions of 'culture' and ethnic groups that were imposed, imagined and maintained by Europeans both before and after colonisation. I have documented, through their own and other accounts of their lives and activities, the formation of Balangingi ethnicity, their participation in a regional search for slaves, their key role for statecraft in the capitalist world-dominated economy of Sulu, and their struggle for freedom against Spanish power, and the tragic fate of their home base, maritime raiding organisation, communities and networks.

Set against this background of dispossession and displacement, I now wish to ask a question that was of considerable contemporary importance in the Philippines—both then and now. How did the Balangingi experience and express their sense of belonging to a place they knew was taken by great force and cultural arrogance from its prior owners? Spanish authorities tried to erase their memory of the displacement and dislocation by forcibly assimilating them as 'normal' colonial subjects, teaching them agriculture and attempting to convert them to Christianity. But the parallel stories and memories of the realities of that past history of the place(s)—Balangingi, the Cagayan Valley and Taluksangay—where their great grandparents and grandparents fought and died and grew up were continuously maintained by the Samal Balangingi. Today, these people claim their ethnic identity based on these earlier interdependent acts of violence and 'remembering', and on the related universal issues of place and belonging.

Chapter 7

Savagism and Civilisation: The Iranun, Globalisation and the Literature of Joseph Conrad[1]

The Iranun Age

Lanun. The name struck fear into the hearts and minds of riverine and coastal populations across Southeast Asia nearly two centuries ago. Recently, ethnohistorical research has shown that where Lanun or Iranun maritime raiding is concerned, old traditions die hard. The terror of the sudden harsh presence of these well-armed alien raiders lives on in the oral recollections, reminiscences, popular folk epics and drama of the victims' descendants in the Philippines, Indonesia and Malaysia to this day.[2] Only in one part of the globe, in the latter part of the eighteenth century, did Europeans find 'piracy' flourishing extensively; pursued as a calling, not by individuals, as was the case with most of those who had followed the profession of buccaneering in the West, but by entire communities and states with whom it came to be regarded as the most honourable course of life—a profession.

The Iranun were frequently the enemies of every community and nation stretching from the Bird's Head Coast of New Guinea and the Moluccas (among the most productive spice islands of the Netherlands East Indies) to mainland Southeast Asia (see Map 7.1). Over two centuries ago, a Bugis writer chronicled that 'Lanun' in double-decked *prahus* from 27 to 30 metres long, rowed by more than 100 slaves and armed with an intricately wrought swivel cannon cast in bronze, were plundering villages and robbing Malay fishers in the Straits of Malacca and the Riau Islands (see Figure 7.1). Among other victims of their marauding were the coastal inhabitants of Thailand and Vietnam.[3] They would also raid in the Philippines, where the central and northern sections of the archipelago were under the control of Spain.[4] Iranun squadrons regularly plundered coastal villages and captured slaves. Their exploits and conquests had the immediate effect of either disrupting or destroying traditional trade routes. Chinese junks and traders were driven off from states such as Brunei and Cotabato, the erstwhile masters of the Iranun, robbing parts of the archipelago of the traditional trade and exchange of spices, bird's nests, camphor, rattans and other valuable items.[5] The Iranun earned a fearsome reputation in an era of extensive global commerce and economic growth between the West and China.

By the 1780s maritime raiding or 'piracy' in Southeast Asian waters—although common in the past—began to occur far more frequently, and with far greater ferocity of purpose than colonial authorities cared to admit. The regularity of the Iranun sweeps led the authorities in Singapore and other Straits Settlements to refer to the months of August, September and October as the *musim lanun*.[6] No one at the time seemed to know for certain whether the intrusion of Western traders in the affairs of China in the late eighteenth century helped create the 'Lanun' phenomenon. An ethnohistorically enigmatic case, the rise of Iranun maritime raiding requires contextualising within a cross-regional hemispheric framework. The period at the end of the eighteenth century was commonly recognised as the 'Age of Iranun'. For seventy years or more, these fiercely independent raiders sallied forth from their bases in the Sulu and Celebes Seas, and other parts of the archipelago, to prey upon the burgeoning intercontinental traffic sailing between Europe, India and China, and the regional traffic from Penang and the ports of Batavia and Makassar to the east. The coasts of Borneo, Sumatra and Sulawesi soon harboured Iranun communities that specialised in the trade. But, many Iranun raiders continued to think of Mindanao and Sulu as their homeland and main base.

From the end of the eighteenth century to the middle of the nineteenth, Southeast Asia felt the full force of the Iranun slave raiders of the Sulu Sultanate, as one coastal population after another was hunted down. Captive people from right across Southeast Asia in their tens of thousands, seized by these sea raiders were put to work in the sultanate's fisheries, in the bird's nest caves, or in the cultivation of rice and transport of commodities to local markets in the regional redistributive network. Thus, the Sulu state created and reproduced the material and social conditions for the recruitment and exploitation of slaves in the zone.[7] More than anything else, it was this source and use of labour power that was to give Sulu its distinctive predatory character, as a 'pirate and slave state', in the minds of Europeans in the nineteenth century. China's tea trade with England and the global economy changed the pattern of maritime warfare and economic and social relationships among particular Iranun populations in the Sulu–Mindanao region, increasing its intensity and scope across the region. It led to widespread decimation and displacement of entire populations throughout the lowland Christian Philippines and much of the rest of Southeast Asia.

Sulu was an ascendant trading state, standing at the centre of a widely spread redistributive network and economy. But, it was under Taosug sponsorship and in the service of that interdependent globalising economy that the Iranun raided throughout the Southeast Asian world. Taosug *datus* partially re-patterned the

Figure 7.1 An Iranun sea raider, attired in a cotton-quilted red vest and armed with a spear, *kris* and *kampilan* decorated with human hair. The portrait of this formidable warrior was done in the early 1840s on the northwest coast of Borneo.

social organisation and ethnic identity of particular Iranun groups to meet the soaring European and Chinese demand, and to gain direct access to Western technology and Chinese trade goods. In this way the exchange of Chinese tea and European firearms as entangled commodities, embedded within the framework of expanding economic growth and improved military organisation set the stage for the explosive emergence of particular Iranun maritime marauding populations in the space of just several decades. Moreover, these highly mobile raiding populations took it upon themselves to 'modernise' and acquire foreign technology, including firearms, to rapidly strengthen their strike force and social organisation, and to enhance their shipbuilding techniques and nautical skills. Indeed, the post-1780 era saw maritime raiding and slaving more widespread and intense than at any earlier time, as the Iranun borrowed both knowledge and technology from European and Chinese traders; Chinese compasses, European charts, compasses and brass telescopes were all widely used as 'weapons of war' by these intrepid raiders. The Iranun, armed with the latest navigation aids and modern weapons, struck fear into the hearts of coastal and riverine people throughout Southeast Asia. The local populace was soon afraid to live along unprotected stretches of the sea coast or come down to the ocean front from the interior of many islands. Until quite recently, villages in many parts of eastern Indonesia, particularly on Buton, were either situated well inland, or, if on the coast, on steep cliffs with extremely difficult access—the historical legacy of defence and flight against the threat of Iranun marauders and slave raiders.[8]

The large-scale forced migrations of the unfortunate mass of captives and slaves caught in the cogs of the Sulu economy, shaped the demographic origins of the Iranun and the overall population trends and settlement patterns of much of the Philippines and Eastern Indonesia well into the end of the nineteenth century. When people think of slavery in Southeast Asia, they rightly imagine tens of thousands of peoples stolen from their villages across the region and sent directly to work the large fisheries and wilderness reserves of the Sulu Sultanate. The insatiable demands of the sultanate for labour to harvest and procure exotic natural commodities, such as sea cucumber and bird's nest, reached a peak in the first half of the nineteenth century as the China trade flourished. Now in this new globalised world, Sulu, Mindanao, Canton and London were all intimately interconnected. A prime feature of this cross-cultural trade was that more than two centuries ago Europe and the markets of China and Southeast Asia were entangled in a commercial and political web of economic interactions and cultural flows that was, in many ways, just as borderless and complex as today's global economy. Yet, another characteristic of late eighteenth- and nineteenth-century globalisation was that it went hand in hand with degeneration and fragmentation. Even as economies of traditional trading states such as that of the Sulu integrated, others, for example the sultanates of Brunei and Cotabato, were disintegrating, while in the process regional populations across Southeast Asia were fragmented, scattered and re-located. In the context of the world capitalist economy and the advent of the China trade, it should be understood that the slaving and raiding activities of the Iranun, so readily condemned in blanket terms as 'piracy' by European colonial powers, later historians and literary figures, was a means of consolidating the economic base and political power of the sultan and Taosug coastal chiefs of Sulu, and which functioned as an integral, albeit critical, part of the emerging statecraft and socio-political structure(s) of the Sulu Zone.

The Iranun originally inhabited coastal stretches around the mouth of the Pulangi, Polloc Harbour and further round the eastern shore of Illana Bay. By the start of the seventeenth century, thousands had also migrated inland to the lake and plateau region at the south-west corner of the Tiruray Highlands. The maritime raiders, who, in the nineteenth century were labelled the *Illanun* (Illanoon), were, according to the Spanish, a distinct people, who inhabited the stretch of coast within the great bight of the Bay of Illana, from which they took their name, distinguishing themselves from other ethnic groups. This coast and bay, whose shorefront constituted a continuous line of impenetrable mangrove and swamps, was readily linked to the great lake behind it, which the Iranun considered their stronghold and home, and hence they were termed by the Spaniards in Zamboanga and Manila a 'distinct race', *los Ilanos de laguna*, or 'the Illanoons of the lake'.[9] The Iranun burst quite suddenly into Southeast Asian history in the second half of the eighteenth century with a series of terrifying raids and attacks on the coasts and shipping of the Philippines, the Straits of Malacca and the islands beyond Sulawesi. Their primary targets were unprotected coastal settlements and sailing boats that travelled throughout Southeast Asia bringing valuable commodities from China and the West back to the most remote parts of the archipelago. Many of these marauders were sponsored under the authority of their rulers from the trading states of Sulu, Cotabato, Siak and Sambas. They were soon described as 'Lanun' or 'Illanoon'—'pirates'—by those who suffered their depredations or either travelled with or hunted them, and wrote about their widespread impact on the Southeast Asian world.

Iranun long-distance maritime raiding operations ultimately depended on the land for supply of arms, food and shelter. Hence, island, riverine and interior shore bases were absolutely necessary for the success of the Iranun marauding

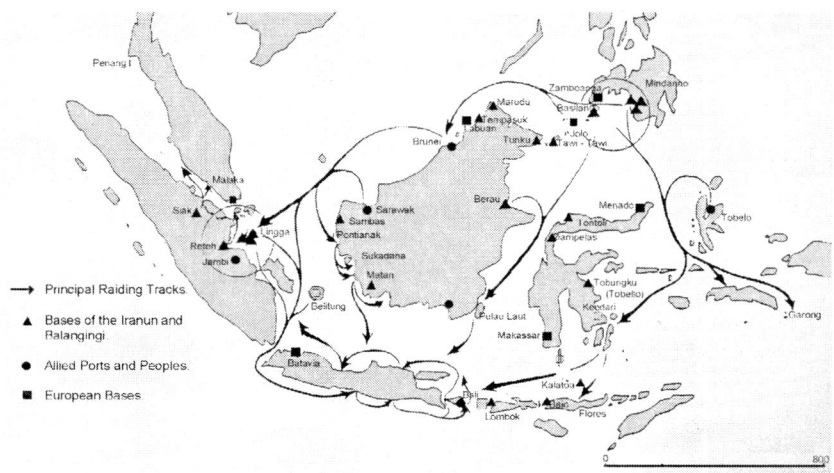

Map 7.1   Iranun–Balangingi maritime raiding and the Malay Archipelago in the first half of the nineteenth century

enterprise. The Iranun did not situate their raiding and slaving settlements on the peripheries of the various competing colonial empires at the end of the eighteenth century. On the contrary, dominating the seas of Southeast Asia, they established many of their bases close to the busiest shipping lanes and colonial port cities, namely those centred on Manila, Makassar, Batavia, Penang and Singapore. At the same time they allocated specific hunting territories to particular fleets, which operated from this chain of settlements and bases that stretched from Sulawesi in the east to Sumatra in the west. As the last quarter of the eighteenth century advanced, the distance and duration of Iranun voyages made the establishment of these satellite settlements, extending across the length and breadth of the major seaways, absolutely critical for the pursuit of their raiding and slaving activities. The raiding distances between Mindanao and Sulu and the edges of the Malay world, as they intersected with the Canton market, were very great. It would have been impossible for the Iranun to have carried on their widespread raiding operations year after year, from their 'haunts' in Illana Bay and the Sulu Archipelago, without strategic bases, set up within the target areas or at key crossroads and 'choke-points' along the major maritime routes. The migratory maritime raiders spread to the rest of Southeast Asia, establishing major bases in the Philippines, Sumatra, Lombok, Flores, Kalimantan and Sulawesi. These Iranun satellite bases that engaged in slave raiding and marauding were established by invasion, founded because of social unrest or natural catastrophe in their homeland, or through support rendered by a local ruler. Although the historical origins of these Iranun settlements differ to a certain extent, they also share much in common with respect to their basic purpose, settlement patterns and ultimate fate. In their heyday (1765–1845) the forward bases maintained a separate Iranun identity, but were sometimes aligned with neighbouring realms and, at other times, essentially non-aligned. Maritime raiding was the centre of their livelihood, but the majority of their inhabitants—women, children and slaves—were either engaged in subsistence agriculture, fishing or major local enterprises such as tin or gold mining. Located near the vital straits and rivers that they dominated, these Iranun settlements were comparatively large and prosperous.

At the end of the eighteenth century, as Western traders started to appear in Canton and began exporting tea, along with other goods, the expansion-bent Iranun set up forward bases across Southeast Asia, ignoring Dutch, Spanish and British authority with impunity. The trading operations of European corporate enterprises, particularly the British East India Company and the Dutch Vereenigde Oostindische Compagnie (VOC), as well as those of private Western traders, led, within the short span of three decades (1770–1800), to an unprecedented growth of Iranun society and population based on long-distance maritime raiding and its integration into the capitalist world economy. The Iranun sea warriors, like the Vikings, were worldly raiders who travelled in search of slaves, work and good fortune, sometimes for years on end, around the great ports of Manila, Makassar, Batavia, Penang and Singapore. They often spoke a variety of languages and were familiar with the traditions and religions of all quarters of Southeast Asia. Some were literate, able to negotiate a ransom or unravel the intricacies of the colonial legal system and they were all knowledgeable in the martial arts, weapons manufacture and seamanship. Some Iranun marines on their two- and three-masted *joanga* doubled, along with renegades, as translators and gunners. The sea and the opening of China were the key ingredients in all of this. When the region's economy boomed as part of the process of engagement with global commerce, both these factors became catalysts for the Iranun to make new lives for themselves as marines and conscripts aboard their sea raiders.

Blood upon the sand and sails

Between 1780 and 1815, from the shores of the Straits of Malacca to the coasts of the Moluccas, Iranun slave raiding and 'privateering', a tacit substitute for war, dominated the history of relations between the colonial powers. While maritime raiding and slavery were a feature of many societies around the archipelago at the time, colonial officials and historians have encouraged us to see only the 'Lanun', '*Moros*' and 'Sulu *zeeroovers*', the pirates of Islam but especially the Iranun, while conveniently forgetting Europe's involvement in the compounding of the Iranun ascendancy.[10] At the end of the seventeenth century, the Dutch, a new global maritime power, emerged along the cold grey coasts of the North Sea to challenge the mercantile supremacy of both the Spanish and the British throughout the ensuing centuries.[11] The larger international rivalries of these colonial powers—especially the British and Dutch—culminated in a protracted struggle for commercial dominance in the seas of Southeast Asia as both nations were inevitably drawn into the global macro-contact wars of the eighteenth century. In this context, international economic and political considerations played their part in aiding and abetting 'Lanun piracy', considerations that were often hidden from view within the larger confidential diplomatic manoeuvrings of the great European powers and their respective trading cartels.

What, for instance, can be made of the activities of the late eighteenth century English country traders and the Iranun? The powerful British East India

Company of the period was instrumental in introducing among the Iranun a tacit system dominated by both the indiscriminate sale of arms and opium and intelligence gathering, to assist the Bengal-based business organisation against its Dutch and Asian competitors.[12] The picture that emerges of Southeast Asia towards the end of the eighteenth century is one of a vast emporium for the China trade and for foreign influence over almost every aspect of life including politics, economics, statecraft, religion and the social fabric. A large proportion of the population—including the Iranun in Sulu, Cotabato, Sambas, Siak and elsewhere across the archipelago—were drawn into the propelling force of the global Chinese market economy. Important trade decisions were based on analysis of economic and political intelligence culled from Europe as well as the ships' logs and journals of private English country traders who were circulating war stores and sowing seeds of discontent in the farthest outposts of the Dutch trading empire. As the small states of the fabled spice islands struggled to stand up to the Dutch (with their own political and economic bloc), the British East India Company took advantage of political instability, production shortages and sustained losses in one area—Sulawesi and the Moluccas—to eliminate the Dutch as competitors, while profiting in another—the Straits of Malacca.

However, had Iranun mercenaries always operated according to the dictates of the English, the tacit 'privateering' system might well have functioned in the interest of the British and local Malay rulers. In practice, Iranun raiders proved too difficult to control, and once away from either the semi-official scrutiny of East India Company traders or official representatives of various Malayo-Muslim states, their maritime raiding and plundering were frequently indiscriminate. They tended to prey on the ports, towns and vessels of so-called friendly nations, not just those of the 'enemy', as Francis Light, the founder of the British East India Company factory and settlement at Penang, learned, much to his dismay in the early 1790s, as did his counterparts in the Moluccas a decade later.[13]

At the end of the eighteenth century, the Iranun maritime raids had a profound, albeit decisive impact on Southeast Asia. The Iranun have been rightly blamed for demographic collapse, loss of agricultural productivity and economic decline, as well as the break-up of the Dutch stranglehold on the Straits of Malacca and Eastern Indonesia. But the driving force for this process was still global and economic: the Iranun profited from Spanish, Dutch and English internal colonial problems and expansion, but were not the cause of the problems. In their remorseless search for captives and slaves the Iranun brought the 'border arcs', or moving frontiers of the margins of the Malayo-Muslim world and of the various colonial peripheries, home to the centres, striking back at the empire's heartland around Batavia and Singapore, in the Straits of Malacca and Manila Bay, and beyond, reaching right across the top of northern Australia. These fearsome alien marauders originated from areas beyond the pale—unknown sites still well outside the reach of colonial dominion. An analysis of Iranun maritime raiding highlights the fact that most attacks took place in the waters of local principalities and developing colonies—ports, towns and villages—close to the coast. Slave-taking and theft were the main motives. Their mobility, kinship and diplomatic connections and their capability to either protect or disrupt trade, enabled the Iranun to forge region-wide links, albeit a powerful fluid political confederation of sorts, that could make or break local mini-states and destroy colonial trade networks and population centres. James Brooke, the self-styled white Raja of Sarawak, an arch political rival and sworn enemy of the Iranun, interviewed the commanders of an 'Illanun' fleet in 1841, 'remonstrating with them on the crime of piracy', and describing their wide-ranging raiding exploits as a 'devastating system'.[14]

To the Spanish, the Iranun, irrespective of whether there was war or peace around the globe, were simply the archenemy—*Moros, piratas* and *contrabandistas*.[15] Rampaging from one end of the archipelago to another they carried out a 'pattern of tragedy so recurrent as to become almost tedious,'[16] as particular communities were repeatedly battered with a vengeance. They pillaged and burnt churches and towns, preyed on cargo-laden sailing vessels and merchant ships, and disrupted inter-island and regional trade, turning Philippine waters into a vast Muslim lake. At the end of the eighteenth century, no one in the coastal stretches of the Philippines was safe because of the global geo-political drama that had begun to unfold in a series of acts involving Britain's entry into the China market, the sudden rise of the Sulu Sultanate as an entrepôt for the Canton trade, and the widespread advent of the Iranun slavers.[17] A Spanish writer described the wholesale misery inflicted by the Iranun on the inhabitants of the archipelago as a chapter in the history of Spain and the Philippines 'written in blood and tears and nourished in pain and suffering.'[18] Iranun maritime raids affected virtually the entire coastline of Southeast Asia, and even stretches of New Guinea and the Bay of Bengal were not secure from slave raids. In the east, the Iranun sailed down the Makassar Strait to cross the Java Sea and South China Sea to attack the north coast ports on Java and the large tin-mining island of Banka. Iranun raided extensively in the Sangir Islands, Halmahera and to a lesser extent in the Moluccas. They also pushed beyond the defended limits of the Southeast Asian world, crossing the South China Sea to attack undefended stretches on the coastline of Thailand and Cochin China. At the opposite extremity they also raided, but failed to dominate, the dangerous coasts of New Guinea. In the 1790s, Iranun slave-hunters in search of captives extended the limits of their known world even further, sailing well into the waters of the Bay of Bengal, touching at the Andaman Islands and perhaps scouring the southern coast of Burma. Less than two centuries ago, few homes in Southeast Asia's vast patchwork of coastal settlements had been left unscathed by the 'Illanun'. Thousands of people lost their kin and were forever haunted by their loss. Sudden capture and swift retreat often marked the coastal raids by the Iranun in the nineteenth century. Victims—especially women and children—were generally welcomed as new members of these maritime Muslim communities to which they were forcibly taken, often hundreds if not thousands of miles away. Most captives and slaves accepted their fate and new roles, large numbers replacing Iranun mariners lost to the hazards of nature, sea battles and disease.

The greatest threat to late eighteenth-century seaborne trade came from the Iranun who operated from the mangrove-lined inlets, bays and reef-strewn islets in the waters around the southern Philippines and Borneo, especially the Sulu and Celebes seas. They preyed on the increasingly rich shipping trade of the Spanish, Dutch and English, and Bugis and Chinese, and seized their cargoes of tin, spices, rice, opium, munitions and slaves as the merchants headed to and from the trading centres of Manila, Makassar, Batavia and Penang. The Iranun had a stranglehold on this trade across Southeast Asia because it was so exposed along its entire course through numerous hazardous straits and channels among countless islands—islands frequented by a fearless sea-going people of predatory tendencies possessed of swift sailing *prahus*—which offered every opportunity for surprise attack. When small merchant *prahus* and Chinese junks made their halting voyages on the sea's calm waters, the Iranun were never far away, striking at all sized craft. The simply had to wait, sheltered behind a convenient island, headland or bay overlooking strategic sea routes, and sooner or later 'coastwise' targets, never straying out of sight of land, would cross their path. From England, the United States and Europe, other larger sailing ships, laden with arms, opium and textiles for the China market repeatedly ran the gauntlet of these narrow straits which were the hunting ground of the Iranun. At certain times of the year, in these bottlenecks and chokepoints, trading vessels generally had to slow down in the crowded or becalmed sea-lanes. The Iranun usually approached and boarded when the sea was calm and the air was still. With most crewmembers exhausted after a long chase, panic would set in. The British and Dutch realised that if they just ignored the Iranun they would become bigger, more dangerous and equipped with ever more sophisticated raiding technology. And that is exactly what happened in the first half of the nineteenth century with Indonesian waters having the highest risk of maritime attacks, and the number of cases increasing every year. Iranun maritime raiding increased in Southeast Asia at the start of the nineteenth century, as did the cost to the world economy in Asia and economic growth, which then topped hundreds of millions of pounds. Estimates of losses from maritime raiding reached as high as several million pounds a year. Most cargo insurers like Lloyds were helpless in the face of the onslaught. If challenged on the open sea, the Iranun did not hesitate to kill their victims, take over their ship and sell both the ship and its cargo in Sulu or on the black market region-wide.

Certainly no ethnohistory of the Iranun since the late eighteenth century, no description of the meaning or constitution of their 'culture', and no anthropologically informed historical analysis of the transformation of their societies can be undertaken without reference to the advent of the China trade and the rise of the Sulu Sultanate; and the integral role in both these processes of Iranun maritime raiding and slaving—a role that was so forcefully felt by most indigenous groups in island Southeast Asia. Yet, despite their major historical importance, the Iranun, the infamous 'Illanoon' and '*Moros*' still remain one of the least known and most misunderstood ethnic groups in the modern history of Southeast Asia.

The merciless savage and empire building

Spanish colonisation of Mindanao and Sulu began with the concerted naval campaigns against the Iranun after 1848 and culminated in the late 1880s with the occupation and conquest of the old ruling families that confronted the Spanish forward movement in mainland Mindanao. During that time, a period which witnessed the eventual economic and political collapse of the Sulu trading sphere and the consolidation of high colonialism, both the Spanish and English systematically created, in official documents and pronouncements, novels, short stories and theoretical productions, a composite image of the Iranun 'character', as an ideological prelude and intellectual justification for the mid- to late nineteenth-century conquest and colonisation. The allayed battle between savagism and civilisation, with glory for the Spanish, British and Dutch, and, ultimately, defeat and tragedy for the Iranun as its inevitable outcome, formed a major theme and metaphor of much of the official record and the literature—published and unpublished—depicting Iranun and 'Malay piracy' in the period under consideration here. One of the most enduring characteristics of three centuries of Muslim/Christian relations and conflict in the Philippines was the susceptibility of non-Muslims to think about the Iranun in stereotypes evoked by the Spanish of *Divide et Impera*, giving the Muslim and Christian Filipinos disparate identities. Over the previous three centuries, most Spanish and Filipinos cast all Muslims, particularly the Iranun, in stereotypical images that changed somewhat from time to time to suit new colonial needs and conditions, but which were invariably denigrating. They were collectively labelled *Moros*—an appellation carrying the burden of foreign connotations from the time when Islam challenged the Holy Roman Empire for the domination of Europe. By the 1850s, the Iranun, infamously labelled as *Moros*, were regarded simultaneously as depraved, uncivilised, subhuman savage warriors and shiftless, untrustworthy foreigners, who were unable to handle their own dispersed affairs and liable to annexation and conquest. Hence, in the aftermath of the Spanish conquest of late nineteenth-century Mindanao and Sulu, the Iranun were still branded *Moro*, which remained synonymous in Christian Filipino minds with pirate, savage and bandit. Such preconceived ideas and notions about the stereotypical meaning of *Moro* and a contested sense of time and space, had already been amplified in the metaphysics of Muslim-hating and empire building in the Philippines when the earlier tide of Iranun maritime raiding and the heresy and 'menace of Islam' swept over the archipelago in the later half of the eighteenth century.

The Iranun were considered in the minds of ordinary Filipinos and Malays to be well organised, numerous, fierce and ruthless. Their massive fleets and in-shore scouring operations were hallmarks of the Iranun. Flotillas of *lanong* attacked large trading ships and regional centres, while Iranun slave raiders, hundreds strong, harried small settlements along the coasts of the Philippines and Sulawesi, and left such a feeling of dread among the local populace that anything threatening or evil became synonymous in the minds of mothers and children with the 'Lanun' and *Moros*—the notorious 'pirate tribes of Mindanao and Sulu'. The lesson to be learned everywhere across Southeast Asia was deep and powerful, especially for ordinary Christian converts whose belief system was essentially Animist, but whose world under colonial rule was rapidly becoming 'modern'. On Luzon or Sulawesi, a Tagalog or Menadonese might see clearly what they might become if they did not live according to their highest evangelised nature. The Iranun warrior and seafarer became important for the European colonial mind, not for who they were and of themselves, but rather for what they showed 'civilised' colonised men and women they were not and must not be. Stemming from profound differences between the cultures of Spain and England, and the culture of the Iranun, as well as from Spanish and English colonial self-interest, convictions of superiority, and a chronic disinclination to view Iranun motives and actions from any perspective but their own, these myopic imperial images and beliefs signified by the signs *Moro* and 'Illanun' defamed and dehumanised the Muslim inhabitants of Sulu and Mindanao, reducing them in the European mind and imagination to something sinister and faceless, akin to the barbarians who resisted Roman rule and Christianity—barbarians who had to be cleared from the seas of Southeast Asia rather than the lands of Caesar's empire. Not only did the pejorative images associated with the labels *Moro* and 'Illanun', as ethnic pseudonyms, contribute to further misinformation, misunderstanding and hostility, but they justified and made more acceptable—as their lasting legacy does to this day—the final aggression and injustice.

The memory of the Iranun raiders lingered well into the first half of the twentieth century, long after they had ceased to pose an imminent menace. For example, Cullinane and Xenos stress, in their reconstruction of the regional demographic history of Cebu, that the memory and fear of '*Moro* depredations' is embedded in the legends and folk histories of many municipalities and parishes of Cebu to this day.[19] *Moro* came to symbolise all that was dangerous, dark and cruel about the tragic confrontation, and the Iranun's adherence to Islam. For the Spanish, the colonial enterprise in the Philippines was in many ways a religious enterprise. For the British, sea tenure and empire were also finally to be demonstrated from a different sort of theology—capitalism and industrial technology. But the fundamental characteristic and central focus of the centuries-long mutual conflict and uneasiness had always been the fact that almost everything that mattered to the Iranun had come to be defined and measured by the sea—the seas that in so many ways were invented, 'discovered' and eventually ruled by the Spanish and English. The central fact of domination and empire was the fundamental attitude and belief that the Iranun possessed their seas only as a natural right, since that possession, in the minds of the Spanish and English, existed prior to and outside of a properly civilised state. What followed then, was that the sea was technically *vacuum domicilium*, and that the Spanish and English, who would control the sea and make it productive for Christ and world commerce, who would give it order and regulate inter-regional trade, were obliged to take over and exterminate the *Moros* and Illanun of the 'eastern seas' in order that *laissez faire* trade and colonial Christian enterprise could be carried out successfully. This extreme posture and situation had always been incomprehensible to the Iranun of Sulu and Mindanao, and it was also clear that the central focus of these cultures in conflict had always been in the sea—the sea that, in more ways that one, was discovered by Spain and Britain, and functioned as a political instrument, a commodity, an empire lifeline, a national prerogative and aspiration. The Iranun were defined by it, measured by their domination and use of it, and were to be dispossessed of it. But, in the latter half of the nineteenth century, even as the last Iranun villages and raiding vessels were burned or broken up, the denigrating image of the *Moro* and Illanun as slave raider and savage pirate, now began to hold new moral meaning for both the European and Christian Filipino imagination. The myth of the 'savage' now both evoked and guaranteed the final success of the larger sacred–secular drama of colonisation, conquest and annexation, and the vision of the Filipino people's own place in it, just before the dawn of the twentieth century.

Joseph Conrad and the Iranun

In nineteenth-century Spanish literature on the *guerras piraticas de Filipinas* and English accounts about the Illanoon and Malay piracy, there is an association of the male Muslim physical and psychical self with the raw environment and nature that uses the sea as a canvas against which *Moro* and Illanun identity might be interrogated and problematised as a precursor to the cant of conquest. These images that were carved out of language(s) systematically by the Spanish and British were also imposed on the seas and islands of the Iranun, as a geographical sign of their dangerous, uncivilised, albeit contaminated character, and labelled as ominous, 'vile' sites, unclean sites beyond the pale. These sites of non-colonial space were important, as were the Iranun who lived in them, precisely because they were areas out of reach of colonial state control. The networks of atolls, rocks, shoals and submerged reefs were described as natural 'nests' and 'webs', signifying a breeding ground for rats, other vermin and spiders—frightening, dirty, destructive pests in people's minds that always caused harm. Hence, the best means of eliminating the danger of such sites of contamination and pollution, cunningly perceived to be 'infested' with rodents and arachnids and carefully masked by linguistic images of filth and disease, was to 'eradicate' them, meaning the wholesale extermination of the Iranun. This reading of the sea and the maritime world of the Iranun in mid-nineteenth-century European texts was not uncommon. The use of such pejorative powerful language to describe the presence of formidable seafarers from land-based representations associated with filth, pollution and danger does not, however, undermine a potent 'other' political-historical reality. Rather, it demonstrates the suspect nature of certain European histories and literary traditions, as their authors attempt to reinforce Western-centred myths, identities and traditions. Reconstructing and reinterpreting the ethnohistory of the Iranun in this way underpins the nineteenth-century reading positions made available by the hundred-year-long crisis in Spanish–Philippine history and the construction of Muslim–Christian relations and identity politics. The dialogue of difference, when reinforced, invokes violence and attempts to break down the cultural resistance and armed struggle declared within specific historical landscapes. Eradication actually meant the systematic attempt by the Spanish and English governments to wipe out the ethnic culture and maritime way of life of the Iranun.

Sir Stamford Raffles and James Brooke handed down the theory that 'piracy', the stealthy nemesis of free trade and British dominion, was a sign of decay and decline in the Malayo-Muslim world, and that various sultans and chiefs had turned to maritime raiding and slaving because their traditional local–regional trading activities and networks had been disrupted by the growing corporate commercial strength and interference of Europeans, particularly the Dutch. Aspiring nineteenth-century empire builders, such as Raffles and Brooke, had every reason to characterise the neighbouring territories and seas they hoped to rule or dominate in trade as areas or domains of decadence, turmoil and decline, and whether or not they were sympathetic to colonial rule, later historians and writers, such as Joseph Conrad, generally tended to adopt their view uncritically. Stamford Raffles and James Brooke had also repeatedly maintained in their writings and public pronouncements, especially Brooke, that the Illanun were 'fierce, numerous and warlike; without question the worst pirates in the archipelago.'[20] Brooke's essentialist, racist portrait of the Iranun based on deep-seated animosity and mistrust would be echoed half a century later in Joseph Conrad's influential fiction.

It was over thirty years since the Iranun defiantly gave up their last stronghold at Tungku on the east coast of Borneo in 1878. Though some of the racist and imperial writings of individuals like James Brooke had lost none of their sting in the intervening years, Conrad was more inclined to portray what it was about the Iranun background and their life that led them to act as they did in their relationships with Europeans. Conrad began writing his 'Eastern tales' in an age when the rhetorical aspect of the New Imperialism played an important role in a linguistic, albeit cultural re-appropriation of the Malayo-Muslim world of Southeast Asia. Besides the visible alteration of that world by colonial conquest and annexation, imperial writers, wielding their pens as instruments of empire, were fictionalising the environment, creating powerful literary structures that would frame and reinforce the patterns of dominance over particular geographical areas and conquered subject peoples.[21] The Iranun, as indomitable other, differentiated both racially and by creed, challenged this hegemonic imperial process and rhetoric and the narrative strategies of Conrad as he explored the encounter between Europeans and 'Illanuns' in his novels with an Indonesian setting. Conrad's fictional 'histories' of contact and colonialism focus uneasily on the cultural encounters between Europeans—merchant-adventurers, vagabonds and colonial officials—and non-European people, particularly the 'Illanun', reconstructing the experience of both sides between various extremes and collision, leading to the eventual destruction of previously autonomous maritime groups like the Iranun and weaker Europeans.

Relying primarily on Raffles, Brooke and Royal Navy captains like E. Belcher and Keppel as his principal ethnographic and historical sources on the 'Illanun', Conrad has shown in his fiction how many European men, all non-English, suffered from a deep malaise in the presence of the dreaded 'Illanun'. Many Dutch, German and Eurasian traders lived in fear that these Muslim maritime raiders would sweep them and their fledgling enterprises and daredevil schemes into oblivion; and several relied on opium to comfort themselves and assuage their anxiety in the face of the 'terror'.[22] In Conrad's fiction, 'Illanun', both noble and savage, had their destined place in the unfolding order of Anglo-Saxon imperial history according to the dictates of time. Both kinds of 'Illanun' would be eliminated through superior British moral values, technology and legal juridical processes, and the passage of time to make way for the presumed sovereign British way of life.

The noble 'Illanun' deserved Conrad's pity for his late nineteenth-century condition and his passing, but his roving maritime way of life, no less than that of the ignoble 'savage' raiders, demanded strict censure according to Darwin's evolutionary scale of progress and the passage of Anglo-Saxon history. Conrad's texts exemplify the position that these fiercely independent seafarers—'Illanun'—of Malayo-Muslim states such as Sulu were inscribed with shared values and shared norms through the structure of that state; a state framed and re-presented as a 'pirate' state and slave state. In the end, his fiction demonstrates there is legitimation of the dominant Anglo-Saxon group's interests (economic, class, racial and religious). This kind of legitimation is evident in his writings with his protagonist William Lingard's desire to 'clean up the pirates' because their values differ from and do not conform to the Anglo-Saxon ideas that are embodied in the dominant social order and with the legitimation of imperial and colonial practice. Conrad preached in his novels with an east Indonesian setting, about the inevitability of Anglo-Saxon civilisation and imperialism—Britannia—dominating the seas and superseding Malayo-Muslim savagism, regardless of courage or nobility. The children of his English and continental readers learned also from textbooks that were replete with similar images of maritime Asia, about travel, adventure, colour prejudice and the forging of empire.[23] An important legacy of the politically conscious literary output of Joseph Conrad in the years of high colonialism was his (un)masking of the ideological biases or wills to power that lay behind the pretensions to universality and impartiality of particular moral views. In other words, early twentieth-century readers were reminded of the way in which conceptions of 'reason' or of 'goodness' were the historical and contingent constructions of particular societies and cultures, and the links between such constructions and power.

Conrad's novels helped shape the vocabulary and the imagery that turn-of-the-century colonial administrators and settlers used to describe their actual experiences in maritime Southeast Asia, and the lifestyles they observed among its seafaring peoples, like the 'Illanun', Bugis and Samal–Bajau. In turn, the accounts of explorers, naval officers, missionaries and other travellers and adventurers provided the 'factual' basis, and therefore a validation, for the ethnographic image and imagining about 'other' people and places rendered by Conrad. This dark, refracted, albeit somewhat tempered version of the 'Illanun', as a symbol of the naturally free savage, persisted into the twentieth century, sometimes grudgingly advanced by a seemingly impartial Conrad. In the mid-1880s, he had briefly sailed in the Celebes Sea, as first mate in a Singapore-based, Arab-owned steamer, the SS *Vidar*, and, as a fellow seafarer, had found something to admire in the Iranun maritime way of life. Conrad spent only nineteen weeks serving in the *Vidar*. The future author's knowledge of the Iranun was not based on his own personal interaction with them, but rather on folk memory and hearsay collected on board ship and in port, particularly in the expatriate community clubs and tearooms of Singapore, and from the non-fiction accounts of other travellers and adventurers. But having had no actual first-hand contact with them, Conrad generally represented them as bloodthirsty raiders, intent on murder, pillage and slave-taking.

G. J. Resink, a professor of Indonesian legal history, used the writings of Joseph Conrad to show that there were still numerous independent Malayo-Muslim realms beyond Dutch Java at the end of the last century. According to Resink, a mixture of Iranun, itinerant European-merchant adventurers, Bugis and Arab traders were the most important *dramatis persona* visible on the horizon of the eastern archipelago under Joseph Conrad's Western eyes.[24] But, Conrad actually believed that in the judicial and administrative control of other peoples like the 'Illanun', the British had no ethical equals in the West. The English trait of 'simplicity of motive and honesty of gain' was not found in the business methods of most of the protagonists of Conrad's Indonesian fiction.²⁵ The reader does not have to be told their nationality; one only has to look at their names—Willems, Schomberg, Almayer and Hudig.²⁶ Conrad's novels and short stories set in the eastern archipelago explore the ambiguous self and that 'in between' space, for their moral thinking and their moral lives, arguing that the Anglo-Saxon imagination and technological superiority both resists and shows up the inadequacies of that larger dichotomy between the West and non-West as well as a host of other ones, including such philosophical distinctions among the English and continental Europeans between reason and emotion, fact and value, thought and experience. It is against this background of the reader being constantly reminded of Conrad's belief in the superior quality of Anglo-Saxon patterns of governance, judicial administration and trade that the historian must determine how the celebrated author has framed and represented the '*Illanun* character' in his novels.

The almost mythical Captain William Lingard—the model for Tom Lingard in Conrad's novels with an Indonesian setting—known as the *Raja Laut*, or Lord of the Seas, all over Southeast Asia from Singapore to Torres Strait, and from Timor to Mindanao, had made his fortune in the 1860s and 1870s by discovering a secret passage to sail up the Berau River in East Borneo. Tom Lingard, the celebrated *Raja Laut* in *The Rescue*, is also depicted as a man of 'high mind and pure heart' in accord with Conrad's conception of Anglo-Saxon superiority in administering the lives of Asian peoples. The author is able to forcibly demonstrate the English merchant-adventurer's innate Anglo-Saxon virtues of courage, objective justice, assumption of responsibility and trust, while attempting to effect control over the 'Illanun', a Muslim seafaring people with a philosophy totally alien to that of Lingard.

In *The Rescue* the 'Illanun' and their lord, Daman, a man of prowess, with his fleet of between thirty and forty raiding *prahus*, play a central role in the novel. They had come to help Hassim, the Wajo prince, reclaim his territory from which he had been expelled by civil war and Dutch intrigues. They were simultaneously on the lookout for gunpowder, arms and plunder during the course of their special mission. As Daman proudly tells his followers, 'The Illanuns seek booty on the sea…Their fathers and the fathers of their fathers have done the same, being fearless like those who embrace death closely.'²⁷ Conrad subtly portrays the 'Illanun' carrying out the dictates of their destiny and the not-so-subtle oppression and betrayal that such an autonomous destiny demands. Daman hates Europeans because of the treatment of his ancestors at their hands but Conrad adds tragic stature to Daman's view of life to keep the novel from becoming simply another romantic tale of Malay pirates and far-flung empire.

His father and grandfather (…having been hanged for an example twelve years before) had been friends of Sultans, advisers of Rulers, wealthy financiers of the great raiding expeditions of the past. It was hatred that had turned Daman into a self-made outcast.[28]

When the 'Illanun' lord and his chief captured two European men and held them for ransom, Daman's aim was to obtain sorely needed arms and gunpowder from both Lingard and a stranded European yacht, which was under the *Raja Laut*'s protection. Forced by circumstance and the drive of his own instinct, Daman entered into negotiations with Lingard:

> After all, it was perhaps a great folly to trust any white man, no matter how much he seemed estranged from his own people…Lingard's brig appeared to him a formidable engine of war. He did not know what to think and the motive for getting hold of the two white men was really the wish to secure hostages.[29]

Lingard himself was extremely wary of the Iranun lord, despite his own charismatic reputation as a great warrior, a *Raja Laut*—the King of the Sea, which had secured his safety at the parley up until then. But his life nearly gets turned upside-down when the sinister figure of Daman appeared. His purpose, his reason for seeking Lingard is unclear, but his motive was that the Iranun lord was intent on destroying him and seizing his brig and the stranded yacht. Lingard knew that 'not one of them but has a heavy score to settle with the whites.'[30] Wasub, a loyal friend, had also warned Lingard to exercise extreme caution in approaching Daman at the meeting:

> Daman is crafty and the Illanuns are very blood-thirsty. Night is nothing to them. They are certainly valorous…Tuan should take a follower with him… one…who has a steady heart…and with quick eyes like mine—perhaps with a weapon—I know how to strike.[31]

Lingard eventually secured the release of the hostages—he and Daman being sworn to keep their word as warriors.

The character Babalatchi, the skilful one-eyed 'prime minister' and *shahbandar* (harbour master), who features in *Almayer's Folly* and *An Outcast of the Islands* was also an 'Illanun' and had been a 'pirate'. Joseph Conrad did meet a Dongala trader called Babalatchi when he was on the *Vidar*, but it is not certain that aspects of the life of the historical and fictional characters match (see Figure 7.2).

Figure 7.2 Copy of a bill of lading from the SS *Vidar*, which Conrad sailed aboard, with the name of Babalatchi as the trader sending the goods (Courtesy of the Stirling Memorial Library, Joseph Conrad Collection, Yale University)

Conrad's character could also have been partially based on a seaman called Jadee. Jadee's lifecycle and background fit with Babalatchi's remarkably well—having been sold as a slave to Sulu pirates when he was very young. Both had similar careers as maritime raiders and *serangs*.[32] In *An Outcast of the Islands* the reader is given an insight into Babalatchi's 'Illanun' past:

> Babalatchi had blundered upon the river while in search of a safe refuge for his disreputable head. He was a vagabond of the seas, a true Orang-Laut, living by rapine and plunder of coasts and ships in his prosperous days; earning his living by honest and irksome toil when the days of adversity were upon him. So, although at times leading the Sulu rovers, he had also served as Serang of country ships…He gathered experience and wisdom in many lands, and after attaching himself to Omar el Badavi, he affected great piety…He was brave and bloodthirsty without any affection, and he hated the white men who interfered with the manly pursuits of throat-cutting, kidnapping, slave-dealing, and fire-raising, that were the only possible occupation for a true man of the sea. He found favour in the eyes of his chief, the fearless Omar el Badavi, the leader of Brunei rovers, whom he followed with unquestioning loyalty through the long years of successful depredation. And when that long career of murder, robbery and violence received its first serious check at the hands of white men, he stood faithfully by his chief.[33]

In Conrad's panoramic examination of history, the 'Illanun' were neither devoted to nor inspired by the Anglo-Saxon idea of 'simplicity of motive and honesty of aim'.³⁴ In the English writer's representation, where the 'Illanun' raided they intended to be masters and suffered no rivals. While Conrad admired the sea for being the home of the Iranun more so than the land, he still considered them, like the Arab traders, both unscrupulous and resolute.³⁵ Conrad, when writing about 'Illanun' character traits and reasons for 'Sulu piracy', drew upon the West's deep-seated distrust of the Islamic world. Despite the passage of more than a century, the echoes of religious wars fought by Muslims against Christian 'infidels' on Java and Sumatra reverberate through his fiction. Conrad, in *The Rescue*, depicts Daman and the 'Illanun' as Muslim pirates descended from nomad, camel-raiding ancestors, notwithstanding their inspired bold leader. The Europeans, whose yacht was perilously stranded, repeatedly use as synonyms 'moors', 'savages' and 'barbarians' when mentioning the menacing presence of the Iranun. Conrad, through this not-so-subtle process of negation, which unduly stresses Muslim religious zeal and fanaticism, makes the 'Illanun' seem even more dangerous—as the spectre of militant Islam served to prolong and nurture mutual hostility in the face of Western progress:

> [Daman]…advanced alone. The plain hilt of a sword protruded from the open edges of his cloak. The parted edges disclosed also the butts of two flintlock pistols. The Koran in a velvet case hung on his breast by a red cord of silk. He was pious, magnificent, and warlike.³⁶

In *An Outcast of the Islands*, Conrad also dwells on Islam, war and men of prowess, introducing the blind, dispossessed leader of Brunei rovers, Omar el Badavi, Babalatchi's ex-'pirate' chief, in a similar vein.

> I knew him well when he had many slaves, and many wives, and much merchandise, and trading praus and praus for fighting. Hai-ya! He was a great fighter in the days before the breath of the Merciful put out the light in his eyes. He was a pilgrim, and had many virtues: he was brave, his hand was open, and he was a great robber. For many years he led the men that drank blood on the sea: first in prayer and first in fight! Have I not stood behind him when his face was turned to the West? Have I not watched by his side ships with high masts burning in a straight flame on the calm water? Have I not followed him on dark nights amongst sleeping men that woke up only to die? His sword was swifter than the fire from Heaven, and struck before it flashed. Hai!…Those were the days and that was a leader, and I myself was younger;

and in those days there were not so many fireships with guns that deal fiery death from afar.[37]

Conrad thus perpetuated in the English-speaking world the *reconquista* '*Moro*' image of the Iranun—bloodthirsty thieving Muslims—as a legacy of the Spanish friars and other European colonisers. However, when considering maritime raiding and slaving activity in Southeast Asia, it must be remembered that the Iranun were invariably defending their religion as well as their political system(s) and right to trade, along with the hypocrisy that allied the English and the Iranun against the Dutch in the sea war of the late eighteenth century. Old Jorgenson, the former captain of *Wild Rose* and Lingard's fellow adventurer in *The Rescue* could remember the Padri War, and the name of the Sentot, who fought by the side of Prince Diponegoro and who, as a *Ratu Adil*, earned the title 'King of the South Seas of Java'. It is Sentot's grandson who is one of Daman's lieutenants. Conrad therefore links an Islamic revivalist movement of central Sumatra and *jihad* at the start of the century and the eventual elimination of 'Illanun piracy' at the end of the century to the final formation of a colonial state, the Netherlands East Indies, embracing the Indonesian archipelago.

Despite the celebrated author's literary efforts to dissect the social and psychological impact of European colonialism along the margins of a Malayo-Muslim maritime frontier, his attempts to embroider certain aspects of 'Illanun' character and traits fail. Conrad's portrayal in literature of the 'Illanun', Bugis and Arabs as 'Muslim souls', individuals with inner lives capable of depth or superficiality, whose capacities for moral understanding and growth were intrinsically bound up with their traditions and transitions, their imaginations, their preparedness to be surprised by and to wonder at each other and their Islamic world in conflict with the West, intentionally fostered a legacy of animosity and mistrust. In Conrad's case, moral understanding was inseparable from emotional response, and that to recognise a fact about the 'Illanun' was to be able to judge or value it, and that the capacity for serious and authentic thought about the 'big' facts of human existence in the maritime world of the Islamic Iranun was conditioned by his experience as a 'Polish nobleman, cased in British tar', and his reader's response to it. Conrad helped Western societies to remember the close of a traumatic period in Southeast Asia's history after nearly a century of upheaval and warfare from state-sanctioned maritime raiding by the Iranun that had directly affected hundreds of thousands of people and fostered a culture of fear and violence. His literature helped both citizens and institutions to forge individual and collective perspectives and memories of the 'Illanun', consideration of whose actions were still especially painful on personal grounds to many, and establish, (re)create and (re)interpret the mythological boundaries between the 'Illanun' and 'the reader'.

The real strength of this orphaned Slavic seafarer, who even later as a famous author among the British, but always British with a difference, was that he addressed some of the deepest moral and philosophical implications of the West's rise to world domination, in a manner which took seriously literature's distinctive way of thinking about language, self and the creation of a new Anglo-Saxon world under global capitalism and colonialism and the destruction of old societies and cultures within Asia, Africa and Latin America. Conrad's moral imagination and literary ethics were consciously Anglo-Saxon, deliberately privileging a particular sort of English conception of autonomous rationality and class-biased conceptions of social order that both framed and constructed negative images of maritime Islamic peoples and 'far eastern' landscapes. Images of the Iranun as 'Illanun' were fixed in Euro-American imaginations by the linguistic reappropriation and rhetorical processes of negation in Conrad's dramatic novels and short stories of the clash of savagism and civilisation between East and West.

Colonialism's pirates

The Iranun burst quite suddenly into Southeast Asian history in the second half of the eighteenth century with a series of terrifying raids and attacks on the coasts and shipping of the Philippines, the Straits of Malacca and the islands beyond Sulawesi. Their primary targets were unprotected coastal settlements and trading boats that travelled throughout Southeast Asia, bringing valuable commodities from China and the West back to the most remote parts of the archipelago. It is estimated that during the last quarter of this century (1774–1798) of maritime raiding and slaving against the Dutch and Spanish, between 150 and 200 raiding ships set out from the Mindanao–Sulu area each year. The sheer size of the vessels—the largest *lanong* measuring upward of 40 metres in length—and the scale of the expeditions dwarfed most previous efforts, marking a significant turning point in the naval strategy of Malay maritime raiding as it had been traditionally understood.[38] Rescued captives interrogated by colonial officials had often been traumatised by the violence they had witnessed during the sea attacks and settlement raids along the coastline. The oral traditions of their descendants still speak of 'the terror'. They tell of the terrifying landing on the beach and the way that the slave raiders ended years, perhaps even several decades of anonymity and a quiet life, that hid their ancestors from the war at sea and the machinations of the global economy. R. Barnes, in his classic study of Lamalera, a remote community on the south coast of the island of Lembata, near the eastern end of Flores, notes the village is really a 'twin settlement', with the lower one (Lamalera Bawah) on the beach and an upper one (Lamalera Atas) on a nearby cliff for protection from earlier Iranun maritime slave raids. Such villages in eyrie-like settings were usually palisaded, but in this case (as at Tira, the site of Southon's fieldwork in Buton) the main defence was inaccessibility. Heersink also notes that on Salayer most of the nineteenth-century settlements were situated in the interior. Here the northern and southern extremities of the island were the least safe, and suffered most from Iranun 'piracy', while the alluvial west coast became the prominent zone of security and trade.[39] New evidence has also emerged supporting the widespread fear and dread of the Iranun in the Java Sea. K. Stenross, researching the traditional sailing boats of Madura, recently accidentally came across people with terrifying memories of the Iranun still intact on the north coast, in a small isolated village. In Tamberu he found—while discussing photographs of Bajau grave-markers shaped like miniature boats—evidence of centuries-old oral traditions about the 'Lanun' that signify tales of cultural confrontations and conflicts. These confrontations originated in the violent intimacies of the encounter between expansive Iranun and struggling, oppressed coastal people. Obviously, the fear of the Iranun went a long way since their maritime raiding tracks crossed regional and ethnic boundaries like no other before, not bypassing even a tiny village like Tamberu, reaching extremes of pain and alienation among the Madurese coastal inhabitants there.[40]

But whether the Iranun were really any more wantonly cold-blooded than their colonial adversaries and neighbouring rivals was immaterial because by the end of the eighteenth century the traditional image of the Iranun warrior, as savagely cruel and destructive, had gained widespread acceptance. The complexities of relations in the struggle over power and autonomy on the seas, between the maritime Islamic world of the Iranun and the conflicting interests and machinations of the Western powers bent on controlling the oceans and sea-lanes, demonstrate how a pathology of physical and cultural violence associated with global macro-contact wars and empire building, particularly with political struggles between the English and Dutch in various parts of Southeast Asia, led to widespread conflicts and regional tragedies. The enormous increase in global trade that affected state formation, statecraft and economic integration made it absolutely imperative to import captives from outside the Sulu Zone to meet labour-power requirements. As commodities from China, Europe and North America flowed to Sulu, the Taosug aristocrats thrived, and there emerged the Iranun—strong, skilled maritime people who were the scourge of Southeast

Asia, as they raided in thirty-metre-long sailing ships. The sea and tropical forests were the life-force of the sultanate, where tens of thousands of captives and slaves laboured annually to collect and process exotic commodities for the China trade. The rising demand for captives and slaves from across Southeast Asia reshaped the character of the political economies of Sulu and China, and, as part of the same process, gave birth to the advent of highly specialised mobile communities of maritime raiders.

Thus, the history of slaving and the slave trade and the rise of the Iranun must be framed as part of a unitary historical process, which explains the major factors contributing to the formation and maintenance of their ethnic identity; namely, the intrusive roles played in their sudden development and expansion by the global economy and singular entangled commodities, particularly tea, sea cucumber, bird's nest and firearms. Maritime raiding, or what the Spanish, British and Dutch labelled 'piracy', was not a manifestation of savagism and dependence, but rather it was the result of phenomenal economic growth and strength. The state-sanctioned system of maritime raiding and slaving in Sulu was part of a vital effort to partake in and control a rapidly increasing volume of global commerce triggered by the advent of Europeans in the China trade in the late eighteenth century. Accusations of cultural decadence and barbarism that were repeatedly directed against the Sulu Sultanate and the Iranun by leading European participants in that trade are both ironic and incorrect when approached from the perspective of a unitary historical process.

Conclusion

Over the course of the nineteenth century, '*Moro*' and 'Illanun' emerged as terms of 'character' in colonial policy and practice and public discourse, wrongly implying a single group of people with a common language, territory and set of beliefs that carried the burden of savagism. Frake has stressed that the label '*Moro*', in the context of the Spanish *reconquista*, Inquisition and colonisation by Spain of the Philippines, became not only a religious label but an ethnic one as well; a label for a social identity and character to which defamatory behaviours and traits were ascribed.[41] By the repeated use of the appellation and the accusation, Spanish administrators and friars and English empire builders and literary figures such as Joseph Conrad, framed the Islamised inhabitants of Sulu and Mindanao, as dangerous fanatical 'rovers'—Muslim pirates—who transgressed local–regional borders and boundaries, boundaries only recently forcibly imposed and maintained by the colonial powers.

The Spanish and British used the labels '*Moro*' and 'Illanun' to obscure the nature and extent of internal ethnic differentiation that existed in the Sulu–Mindanao region. There was no fixed 'Iranun' identity prior to the imposition of colonial rule at the end of the nineteenth century. The formation and maintenance of their ethnicity was continually in flux because of competing forms of social organisation and discontinuities in space and time, caused by their integration into the global economy and fearful rise to regional prominence. Until quite recently, the appellations '*Moro*' and 'Illanun' were synonymous with a specific social disposition, 'cultural' attitude and behaviour; and associated with ignorance, depravity and treachery. These labels, by turning history into myth and stereotype, signified an Islamic people in Mindanao and the Sulu Archipelago who were still labelled and mythologised as 'savages', 'pirates' and 'slavers'. This view of the history of the Iranun was once orthodoxy; it is now under challenge as factually inaccurate, unjust and actually destructive.

Chapter 8

Rickshaw Coolie: An Exploration of the Underside of a Chinese City outside China, Singapore, 1880–1940[1]

Towards an approach

This chapter is concerned with the pursuit of some historical problems related to my research in progress on the urban social history of Singapore and the Chinese labouring class. The initial project focuses on one particular occupation, rickshaw coolie, in order to unveil the devastating poverty of the Chinese sojourner in the colonial city, and the disjunction between colonial order and the reality of life on the streets. *Rickshaw Coolie* brings to life the texture of experience of the labourers of urban Singapore, examining the origins and development of the rickshaw trade in Singapore; its control and regulation from the standpoint of the Chinese and British; the method of earning a livelihood by rickshaw pulling; and the ironies and often the despair of the rickshaw coolies' lives in urban Singapore. The other related project, titled *Ah Ku and Karayuki San: Prostitution in Singapore 1870–1940*, is concerned with a group of workers whose labour also helped build Singapore in the twentieth century. These women—marginalised in memory—travelled from China and Japan to work in Singapore as prostitutes. This project will sketch in the trade in women and children in Asia, and—making innovative use of Coroner's Inquests and other records—home in on the details of the prostitutes' lives in the colonial city: the daily brothel routine, personal crises and violence, social relations, leisure, mobility, disease and death.

I have been researching this subject for seven years with little company from historians of modern Southeast Asia. Recently, however, I sense among colleagues in Australia and Southeast Asia an increasing recognition of the need to focus their researches on the urban workplace, labour and the problems posed by everyday experience for the labouring class under colonial rule in Southeast Asia. Such efforts, if they are to be meaningful, must be translated, theoretically and empirically, against a background of real life. This approach poses grave historiographical problems as a tradition of theoretically informed urban historical inquiry is virtually nonexistent in Southeast Asian modern history. Historians, like anthropologists, have tended 'to graze in the field',[2] focusing their primary attention on rural societies of Southeast Asia.

Considerable work has been done on the potentialities and causes of peasant-based movements and opposition to colonial rule, but hardly any historical research has been conducted on the urban labouring class, of which the rickshaw coolies of Singapore formed a part. In the course of this decade new directions in the related fields of social history and colonial urbanism will help to redress the rather belated development of urban social history in the Southeast Asian region.

The tidewater colonial capitals of the nineteenth and twentieth centuries created new modes of human experience for immigrant Asians, but especially for *singkeh* (newcomers from China). The rapid development of Singapore at the end of the nineteenth century as a commercial centre and entrepôt port, dominated by import and export firms and banks, for Britain's imperial expansion and trade-oriented economy in Southeast Asia had a profound impact upon every aspect of economic and social relationships. It was most marked in the labour nexus, the spatial segregation, the extreme overcrowding of the lower-class Chinese who, as rickshaw pullers, coal coolies, stevedores and hawkers—the sinews of empire—helped to shape the expansion of Singapore (see Map 11.1).

To establish this background of 'experience', the notion of workplace and work must be carefully developed and refined within a 'total context and cultural setting'.[3] On this basis, Singapore, as a Chinese city outside China, is a resource, a field of action, a cockpit or social arena for understanding the economic and cultural aspects of labouring-class Chinese society, as specifically expressed and epitomised in the work entailed in pulling a rickshaw. It is in this context that an account of the material setting of Singapore is vital. Its physical mass concerns us here. Inadequate housing in the form of decrepit, Dickensian buildings; the interdependence of water supply and sewage disposal problems; and too few hospitals and cemeteries affected all areas of life of the flood of lower-class Chinese. This material environment included the setting of labour, as rickshawmen were actively employed throughout the city. We can gain valuable insight into how Singapore expressed itself in one way to the able bodied, but quite differently to the elderly, the sick and dependants of rickshaw pullers at various stages in the family cycle.

This more rounded approach to the private and public environment of the city enables the social historian to examine the workplace as a 'total concept and cultural setting',[4] and to explore with thoroughness one particular occupation, rickshaw pulling. A detailed exploration of this process of labour, of the rickshaw coolie, also enables the historian to describe and analyse how the structure and ideology of two world orders, namely Ching China and Great

Britain, combined to confine rickshaw coolies to an occupation characterised by low wages, hazardous working conditions, poor labour unions and uncommon death. By developing an approach set within the environmental context of a coolie town, where rickshawmen tried to live according to their own values, priorities and resources as the British colonial city of Singapore expanded, hitherto unanswered questions about insights into their home and workplace will surface from the 'underside'. A compelling picture can be fashioned of the conditions of employment, daily life, leisure, disease and death. Ordinary Chinese men tumble from the pages of historical record: they set out the forms of social organisation among the rickshawmen in the civic and entertainment districts of the city, and the contest between discipline and resistance against the British administration and the tumultuous urban life that swirled around them in the city. In short, the aim of this context-sensitive approach is to reconstruct the history of these rickshawmen and their interaction with the British colonial city that they made their home and workplace.

Inextricably bound up with this context-sensitive approach is the present state of our knowledge of the vast movement of coolies between China and the *Nanyang* (Chinese for the south seas), and their efforts to survive in colonial Singapore. What impact did this mass movement of immigrant labourers have on the colonial city and its municipal authorities as superficial contact and prolonged relationships developed? Cultural conflicts occurred and disputes arose over work practices, housing, sanitation and even sacred spaces such as burial grounds. There was an increasing disparity of experience between the ever-burgeoning Chinese immigrant population and the adequacy of the British administration and the city itself to cope with the scope and rate of change. An exploration of the cultural and social geography of an expanding colonial Singapore will reveal clashes of culture over two perceptions of work and the workplace in the cityscape of colonial Singapore. The city's administration consistently chose minimised planning costs, precipitating social conditions that inevitably forced rickshawmen over the poverty line. Despite these contradictions in the historic role of the city, expanding Singapore, especially at the peak of its growth, often seemed a place of hope and betterment compared to the countryside of China and the treaty ports. In the 1890s, the emigrants facing poverty and deprivation in China could not keep their growing families fed. Among the rickshawmen many decided to migrate temporarily from counties near Foochow.[5] By the mid-1920s they had begun to lay down their roots for future generations. Singapore, as revealed in the colonial records, offered the same hardships, but with a difference, at least for some *singkeh*—the promise of a future. Without such hope life is not worth living at all.

By focusing on the rickshaw coolies of Singapore, thanks to the lens of analysis provided by the Coroner's Records, one can also glimpse with some intimacy the society proper from which the migrants have come. The individual and collective lives of the rickshawmen as revealed primarily in this source open a 'window on China'[6] through which we can command a view of the circumstances of those who stayed behind. We can actually 'see' the relationship between clan organisations in Singapore and their links with villages and regions in China from where they originated. The clans emphasised the maintenance of cultural and philosophical traditions with the homeland and the pursuit of special interests within the political and economic order. It is within this context that the links between locality, kinship, migration and the immutability of occupation begin to fall into place. Family circumstances and relationships between family members of those who emigrated and those who stayed behind can also be identified: the birth of children, illness, destitution and death with its concomitant social and economic repercussions, the unrelenting pressure to remit money, and to return, as well as the spiral of failure. In a sense the study of the rickshawmen is a way of seeing China from without and, at the same time, looking from China downward at the world of the *Nanyang*, but especially the underside of Singapore.

An understanding of the impact of colonial policy and practice on the lives of the rickshaw coolies is also important to describe and analyse the key social relationships within the Chinese community, between puller and owner and puller and customer, and between the rickshawmen and Europeans—administrators, magistrates and Coroners on the one hand; and regular fares, tourists and reckless motorists on the other. The study of British attitudes and policies with respect to rickshaw coolies will enable us to penetrate the myth of the foulness of the rickshaw quarters, of the pullers' propensity to vice, and of criminality to clarify what took place in the structure of the society of the rickshawmen as a whole, and to understand how and why this myth was perpetuated.

In the context of the colonial history of the peninsula itself, it is of course a fact that changes in Singapore's material circumstance and increased prosperity have been connected with the period of increased Chinese immigration, and paramount economic and political dominance of the British in Malaya. The role and economic contribution of the Chinese immigrant was critical in formulating British developmental activities in urban settings. The importance of the subject is undeniable. While acknowledged in the historical and developmental literature, it has not yet received the careful attention it warrants. At the turn of the century, the rickshaw, as a cheap ordinary means of transport, revolutionised the life of Singapore, and although initially encouraged, by the 1920s the rickshaw and rickshawmen were felt by the British to present a physical challenge to development policy and the showcase image of Singapore as a 'modern city'. The demand for rickshaw transport throughout the inter-war years remained, as did the harsh social differences sustaining it. The British refused to encourage the trade, at times ignoring it, and then opposing it with a vengeance at the height of the Depression.

Finally, in this account of the urban workplace, labour and 'experience', there is the need to give due consideration to the inequality of life before death[7] as a major part of the social history of the rickshawmen in the period under consideration. An inherent economic and social inequality was linked with high morbidity and mortality in the Singapore of the rickshawmen, precisely because it was a 'coolie town'. Underlying the depressing economics and health hazards of rickshaw pulling there was a demographic pressure energetically crushing the Singapore Chinese that was a direct consequence of the symbiosis of colonial capitalism and migration from south-eastern China. Within the restricted urban setting of Singapore's Chinatown this pressure, in combination with a colonial policy of neglect, made an inequality of economic and social condition that was hardly bearable in the best of times, but which worsened in the 1920s, opening up an ever-widening gulf of prolonged poverty with each passing year that was difficult, if not impossible, for the rickshawmen to cross. The alternative to 'dust to be blown around', to excessive opium smoking, whoring and gambling, to excessive pain and illness, to excessive loss of strength and ageing, to excessive loneliness, without kin, was suicide.

In the first part of this chapter I have suggested how a historian should handle the rickshaw and the coolies who pulled them; Manuel Castells argued that 'cities are made *by people*'.[8] Of all the Chinese labourers who symbolised colonial Singapore, the rickshawmen were perhaps in the best position to know the city. What is needed is a revision of current urban social theory based upon research into a background of real life in the colonial urban context among groups such as the rickshaw coolies of Singapore.

A note on sources

I now want to consider briefly the nature, quality and coverage of the sources for this history. In order to understand what it meant to pull a rickshaw, historians must saturate themselves in the whole range of sources available on colonial Singapore in the late nineteenth and twentieth centuries. There is a wealth of tangential information about Chinese labouring classes in the colonial records waiting to be interpreted. These records can go a long way towards assisting us in our understanding of the course of Chinese life in a Chinese city outside China. The pattern of urban life for the Chinese labouring class can be reconstructed in detail with precision and painstaking care from these sources. Among the most important and interesting are the Coroner's Records for colonial Singapore, 1883–1940. I discovered them after considerable difficulty in the basement of the Subordinate Court in 1979. As I began to read the certificates, and inquests and inquiries, the rickshawmen, their kinsmen, clansmen and women of a forgotten past became my companions. They walked beside me. As a source of special interest to historians of the urban poor, these records bring the rickshaw coolie into the historical forefront; empirical evidence is provided on age, sex, marital status, address, place of birth, occupation, length of time in Singapore, diet, dress, sickness, death and suicide. The causes of death often depict the deprivation experienced in pulling a rickshaw. Much also can be learned about housing, health and poverty, and the almost hopeless struggle to survive, from literary sources, the detailed accounts of European and Asian observers of Singapore, and photographs that show the Singapore that the rickshaw pullers knew. Finally, another important and valuable technique for a breakthrough to the experience of Chinese working-class people involved participant observation, conducted while I lived in an 'unredeveloped' part of Singapore's Chinatown.

History and theory: A people's history

There is a need for new directions in historical writing about the overseas Chinese in Southeast Asia under colonial rule. There is scope for a whole range of historical studies of Chinese working-class men and women situated in the city that would not only suggest answers to questions about the relationship of immigrants, workplace and work in a colonial setting, but would also have direct implications for history writing and theory. A historical account of what the experience of rickshaw coolies has been would not in itself explain why their experiences have taken that form. History can only illuminate the past if it is given explanatory power through the development of theory. The task of developing the relationship between history and theory to understand the dynamics of historical change, and to see social structure within a larger temporal framework so as to deal more effectively and creatively with questions of immigration, labour and colonial capitalism, need not be left to the demographers, geographers and anthropologists.

The nature of the approach I wish to pursue combines close attention to a specific period with a desire for a theory of historical transformation to place the rickshaw coolie in circumstance. In time, I have confined myself to that of nineteenth- and twentieth-century colonial capitalism. Within this limited framework, I want to situate my enquiry 'in as local a setting as possible'[9]—in order to reach the underside of Singapore, to map its dimensions, to explore the big sectors and little crannies, to understand how the society of which the rickshawmen were a part worked, to describe on a minute scale what has not yet been described, in the manner of the ethnographer. Raymond Firth used the term micro-sociology in 1938 to describe such an approach: 'much of the anthropologists' work [and I would add historians of urban-social history in this case] has lain hitherto in what may be called micro-sociology—the study of small groups or small units in larger groups; of how relationships operate on a small scale, in personal terms.'[10] Microdynamism not only marks a fundamental change in the way we ordinarily describe and understand Singapore's past. It also makes it possible to grasp in a coherent pattern the economic, social and psychological manifestations of urban life on the rickshawmen of Singapore. The historiographical implications of this kind of ethnohistory dealing with the individual experience of an overseas Chinese 'community' at a particular moment in time, as if under a microscope, is 'to enlarge upon the ways in which one's forebears have *made a difference* in history [emphasis added]'.[11] To create such a history is to understand a totality of social relations, and the historian must range widely to match old questions to new knowledge.

Conclusion

I stressed earlier that documents and oral evidence are decisive in determining the answers to the questions the historian starts with. The 'experience' of rickshawmen and kin, both at work and home, can be rediscovered in sources like the Coroner's Records, through oral interviews and contemporary official reports and statistical analyses. It is the gaps in the everyday life of pullers and their perceptions of that experience that must be filled in and redefined against a backdrop of the larger world and events—the rhythm of boom and slump, a world depression, and the impact of war and peace. The historiographical thrust is on the recovery of subjective experience in a Chinese immigrant community; consequently, an equally fundamental change occurs in the way Singapore's past is described in the shift in emphasis from 'places' to 'faces', of being able to see the society of the rickshawmen from within, and a related concern with the quality of life. This historical writing is meant to present historical issues as they appeared to the actors, who have so often been hidden from history, and in such a way that reality can no longer be kept at bay. It must be categorically stated here that the main thrust of such history writing is not to concentrate on the rickshawmen. I have already stressed the methodological desirability of working outward and upward, from the categories of the rickshawmen and events in their lives, to illustrate underlying social processes. Our need then is to build facts about the overseas Chinese past in Singapore into a new historical analysis of what ought to be studied in a 'coolie town'—the life cycle of labourers, the material deprivation under which they worked and the transactions of everyday life.

Rickshaw Coolie is not meant to be a curative history. It is being written through a concern to expose the structures of experience of the Chinese labouring class under colonial rule in Singapore. At the same time, I hope that the study of the rickshaw trade and rickshawmen, based on the historiographical principles of a People's History, will contribute to a revision of Southeast Asian modern history, and equally important, in the context of present-day Singapore, to the notion of what is 'historical'.

Chapter 9

The Singapore Rickshaw Pullers: The Social Organisation of a Coolie Occupation, 1880–1940[1]

Following in the footsteps of the elders

This chapter integrates the history of the experience of rickshaw coolies into the larger history of Singapore in the period from 1880 to 1940. These were decisive years. They witnessed the extraordinary economic development of the vast potential for tin, rubber, oil palm and tobacco in the Malay peninsula, and on the east coast of Sumatra under colonial rule, and the evolution of Singapore as a 'coolie town', with a colonial administrative heart and an entrepôt port, with the birth of the rickshaw and a stream of immigrants from China who poured in faster and faster to pull it. This floodtide of *singkeh* came to Singapore with the hope of forming a foundation for a new and prosperous life. Expanding Singapore, especially at this stage of its growth from the third quarter of the nineteenth century, was often considered by the migrants as a place of hope and betterment. From the second half of the nineteenth century, when dire poverty and overpopulation plagued south-eastern China, there were in Singapore tens of thousands of Cantonese, Hengwah, Hockchia and Foochow sojourners who hoped to find a pipeline to prosperity.

But by no means everyone who emigrated did so because of local conditions. Colonial enterprise in Southeast Asia also went far towards determining the number of *singkeh* who emigrated in any year. Peasants were lured away from south-eastern China by knowledge of the development and expansion of colonial capitalism in rural agricultural enterprises—and in the public works, trade and finance sectors of the port cities—and adjusted to and were utilised in the colonial process. Sure of better paid employment, *singkeh* joined other Chinese migrants to mine tin in Perak, to open up the tobacco plantations of neighbouring North Sumatra, to pioneer rubber-smallholding in Sarawak, and also to pull rickshaws in Singapore, where life was said to be better.[2]

Potential *singkeh*, poor and leaving their villages to women's care, came in thousands on foot, by cart or by river *sampan* to a seaport where a passage to the *Nanyang* was sought. Huge profits were to be made in the traffic of importing coolies, commonly referred to as the 'pig business'. In the control and regulation of this immigration the secret societies were heavily involved.[3] Few Chinese peasants could afford to pay their own passage. Recruitment agents of each major society in Singapore or independent labour brokers competed to offer the peasant or labourer the starting sum while they waited to sail. The total cost of a credit-ticket was about 33–38 dollars; the recruited indebted immigrant usually took three years to repay the price of the assisted passage after it was transferred from the broker to a Singapore employer such as a rickshaw owner.[4] At the same time, other poor men were more fortunate as they came from families or sending villages where men of enterprise and wealth were willing to back their crossing.

Between 1881 and 1913, when colonial government reform was sought for labour contracts, 37,000 to nearly 103,000 men a year, mostly under indenture, sailed from Hong Kong to Singapore.[5] No other ports, including Swatow and Amoy, ever exceeded 70,000 a year. Hong Kong was the starting point of the scheduled sailings of the passenger steamers and sailing vessels of firms like Syme Muir and Co. and Jardine and Matheson and Co., and the principal port of call for competing German, Danish and Dutch sailing lines. But there were also junks going to the *Nanyang*, from harbours small and large all along the China coast.[6]

Singkeh were not always well cared for on the voyage down. Photographs show how small some of these ships were that made regular passages in the South China Sea with emigrants. Passengers were herded like cattle across a sea without the solace of kinship, in crowded, squalid and unsanitary living spaces onboard ship. Besides the usually appalling shipboard conditions there was the added terror of the unfamiliar—frequently being storm-battered on voyages of several weeks' duration.[7]

On arrival in Singapore, the new labourer was usually disposed of by secret society recruiters to an employer who spoke his own language. Language was one of the most important factors in establishing employment and a sense of place. Communication was the necessary first step towards the kind of community the newcomer had known in China; Hokkien mixed with Hokkien, Teochiu hired Teochiu. Cantonese *singkehs* followed Cantonese *towkays* and so forth. Recruitment conducted along speech–dialect lines meant that the stream of newly arrived immigrants had little to say about choice of occupation.[8] If a Hengwah *towkay* happened to be a rickshaw owner then *ipso facto* the Hengwah *singkeh* became a rickshaw puller.

The absence of the family, a pivotal force in traditional Chinese society, was the other important factor in the experience of newcomers[9] as they institutionalised their lives in Singapore. The major secret societies—the Ghee Hin, Ghee Hok and Hai San—which were often based on residential and occupational principles, not only found a place for newly arrived labour in the economic system; they also bridged the gulf between the traditional territorial and kinship systems that these men left behind in China, and the preponderantly male society they were forced to fashion in its place.

The voluntary associations were organised on the principle of a common surname, a fictive kinship, dialect group, or area of origin, from places near and far, neighbouring village to distant county or prefecture. Linguistic differences and alignments and recruitment on the basis of surname by clan associations fostered mock kinship, claimed loyalties, and established a framework of social and cultural life—a place of residence, a job, reliance on men of wealth and power—for *singkeh* from Fukien and Kwangtung.[10] It was the dialect and surname association's resources—traditional and new—which brought some semblance of strength and mutual aid to the society. In a non-kin environment, without family or lineage support, the immigrant associations were a linchpin.[11]

The associations created ritual and secular solidarity among members by providing 'kinsmen', 'descendants' and 'mourners' for festivities, ancestor worship and funerals.[12] Traditional anniversaries were ritually celebrated with dinners and visits, financial assistance ensured to those in need, disputes arbitrated, and bereavement and death looked after.[13] Clan associations were also used to tackle a broad range of other problems. The newly arrived member from China who faced problems of housing and work injustices quite correctly sought the help of the clan association. The voluntary associations, however, against the background of several generations of immigration by China-born men deprived of family and marriage, were not a sovereign remedy.[14] Yet, the bonds of artificial kinship did provide a measure of stability in an urban overseas world mainly without kin, however, lacking perduring generational bonds, could never provide an adequate substitute for the needs of the great mass of immigrants.

The city was changing in the 1880s, as Chinatown was fast on its way to having a population of several hundred thousand bachelor workers and destined to be called 'bullock cart water' in dialect—a filthy booming coolie town. The character of its transport and the pattern of traffic also began to change. Motor cars and buses did not exist yet, and carriages drawn by high-stepping Java ponies and horses filled the streets. Most people walked. In 1880, a large consignment of Japanese-manufactured rickshaws—'man-powered carriages'—made an impact on the then dominant mode of transport, horse carriage, and quickly became the popular means of transportation. Within the short space of five years, thousands of rickshaws were already engaged day and night negotiating the narrow back lanes of Chinatown with passengers, or carrying goods over short distances around the wholesale markets.

The Hengwah and Hockchia rickshaw pullers knew what they wanted. To begin with, facing poverty and deprivation in their own country, these *singkeh* had left their families behind in villages, counties and prefectures in Fukien and Kwangtung provinces. Significantly, they had their own 'ambition', and some were given the strength of a bull and possibly a long life to use it. Their sole goal in coming to all corners of the earth, especially to the promised city of Singapore, was to make money, then to return home to buy land and build a house. A beautiful dream, but one with a difference—Singapore offered the same hardships as rural China but with the promise of a future. The sojourners knew that without such hope their life was not worth living at all. They seized the opportunity to migrate, and to do the hard work of rickshaw pulling as the contraptions proved instantly popular, becoming at once an integral part of Singapore's history and of its society, economy and life. The sojourning dream gave them physical strength and a sense of purpose. It encouraged them; they felt pulling rickshaws was a relatively quick way of realising their ambition. But in reality it was not as simple as that; their expectations were rarely if ever realised. On the contrary, rickshawmen often were proven to be wrong, very wrong. Rickshaw pulling was a menial, hazardous occupation, and a coolie's personal and economic wellbeing inevitably rested on a combination of factors, including the attitude of the rickshaw owner as employer; the state of the puller's health and standard of living; interference of the relevant authorities, for example the Malay peons' extortion of the rickshawman; and administrative and transport policy for the city.

A distinctive feature of this emigration of rickshawmen was the absence of women. There were no formal families and lineages, and thus, no customary coherence, no customary stability. Emigration saw the widespread emergence of non-kin institutions rooted in the social structure of late nineteenth-century Chinese society in Singapore, in which secret societies and voluntary associations were shot through by small, 'private', shapeless kinship units, fragments of families and lineages, but possessing the closest of blood ties—brother–brother, father–son and uncle–nephew. These networks of weak family ties and affinity, crisscrossing South China and stretching as far down as Singapore, were a reservoir of energy, sympathy and misery among those who followed the same route to be pullers; on the other hand, thankfulness, exploitation and greed characterised employers and officials alike looking for periodic replacement of cheap labour to pull the rickshaws to keep pace with Singapore's growth and prosperity.

The credit ticket system, based on cash advances and a period of indenture, in combination with native place and language, tended to determine choice of occupation. But not all poor immigrants relied on the conventional means of labour organisation and recruitment, of brokers, secret societies and clan associations organised on the basis of sub-ethnic divisions, to secure initial employment. Some found job security by relying on kindred on the spot, who provided them with a fund of information on rickshaw pulling and found them employment. The significance of this fact of kin-folk suggesting an occupation, part of the role of elder brothers, fathers and uncles in economic life, is that the activity of rickshaw pulling was inextricably bound up with personalised economic, social and political values, and affiliations in the Chinese communities in Singapore that began with kinship and emigration, defined work, and the limits of success.

The pullers

At the beginning of the twentieth century one could readily recognise the place of origin of the very numerous men represented in the rickshaw trade by their speech, residence, place of worship and where they plied for hire. It is clear that most of the pullers were Hokkien and Cantonese before the abolition of the secret societies in 1890.[15] But within the short space of eight years the Hockchew and Hengwah were increasing rapidly and by their cheap labour driving the Hokkien and Cantonese and others out of the trade.[16] Described as being 'dreadfully ignorant' by officials, they came without families from eight different districts in and around Foochow, and from the prefecture of Hengwah. By 1902, the numbers of coolies engaged in rickshaw pulling suggested that the Foochow communities among the Chinese population exercised jurisdiction over much of the economy and organisation of the rickshaw trade in Singapore. Out of an estimated 22,000 rickshawmen, nearly 15,000 were Hengwah, Hockchia and Hwee An; who spoke different dialects of Foochow and Hokkien.[17] The Hengwahs and Hockchias formed the largest proportion. Most of them came direct from China from the Hokkien province through Amoy and then to Singapore.[18] Low Ngiong Ing vividly remembers these men from the days of his youth in early modern Singapore.

> The neighbourhood [Lower Victoria Street] was dirty and noisy, but full of life. Most of the rickshaw pullers were Hockchias and Hingwas, hailing from two adjoining counties south of Foochow. The Foochow dialect was understood by most of them, though they had their own patois which, like my own, sounded uncouth in finicky Foochow ears.[19]

Estimates of the number of rickshaw pullers plying for hire on the streets between 1880 and 1940 vary. Pullers themselves supplied hardly any information on their numbers in discussions with officials on the rare occasions when they were directly questioned by special commissions or boards of inquiry. The figures derived from the owners with a vested interest in the industry were not always based on the same calculus as that of officials, and discrepancies exist in the estimated number of men who earned their living by pulling rickshaws. The figures given, which were official statistics of the Rickshaw Department, were calculated on the assumption that there were two coolies to every rickshaw, and very often three by 1918.[20] These figures were a rough estimate because only the owners and not the pullers were registered (see Table 9.1).

It was commonplace for words like 'about', 'approximately', 'over' and 'exceeds' to be used in official reports to estimate the size of this transient workforce. Even the estimates of those best informed varied by as much as several thousand men. Alex Gentle, the Coroner and former president of the Municipal Commission, thought there were at least 15,000 rickshaw coolies in Singapore in 1908, but Mr Hooper, head of the Jinrickisha Department, roughly estimated there were over 20,000. Any reduction in the number of men who earned their living by pulling rickshaws was often attributed to fewer coolies arriving from China. In 1918 there were still over 20,000, but the numbers were coming down.[21] The

Table 9.1 Estimated number of Jinrickisha Coolies, 1888–1917

Year	Number
1888	5,046
1889	5,000 (approximately)
1890	5,877
1891	7,331
1893	11–12,000
1894	12,000 (over)
1897	15,000 (over)
1900	20,000
1902	22,000
1904	20,000 (estimated to be over)
1908	10,000 (about)
1917	10,000 (exceeds)

The estimates have been compiled from the annual reports of the Jinrikisha Department. See Singapore Municipal Annual Report, Jinrikisha Department, 1888, 1889, 1890, 1891, 1893, 1894, 1897, 1900, 1902, 1904, 1908, 1917.

coolies were not coming from China in the same numbers as they had ten years earlier, owing to expensive passage, low exchange value of Singapore currency and the high cost of living. In 1919 the demand for rickshawmen exceeded the supply and increased prices for the labour of rickshaw pullers were expected. However, by 1921, the number of rickshaws on the streets had increased from 8,022 to 9,244.[22] The rise in the number of pullers resulted from the falling off in employment available on estates in Johore and elsewhere. All the pullers were still China-born with practically no Singapore-born men coming into this kind of work.[23] Even during the 1930s the vast majority of them still started fresh from China.

The age distribution of the rickshawmen, which was a principal demographic feature of this emigration, was to have a marked effect on the character of the Chinese community, and upon the city itself. As to age, the only accurate statistics we have come from the Coroner's Records. Here we have to begin by saying that even our best estimates with regard to age structure and employment are somewhat skewed by death. Because we cannot estimate development in this distribution with any certainty, we are unable to pinpoint the age at which they came and began to pull rickshaws and the length of time they pursued this occupation; also, we are unable to say when they returned to China, but conclusive evidence does exist on age levels and death in employment. One thing is for certain, rickshaw pulling was an occupation for neither the fainthearted nor the elderly. The hard work called for physically strong men and preferably young when they were still in the prime of their life. Table 9.2 shows the age structure of a group of 102 rickshawmen.

Table 9.2 Age distribution of 102 rickshawmen who appeared in the Coroner's Records between 1902 and 1939

Age	Number
11–20	3
21–30	30
31–40	31
41–50	28
51–60	9
61–over	1

This table was compiled from data on Rickshaw pullers in the *Singapore Coroner's Inquest and Inquiries, 1902–1939*. An even more age-specific breakdown into groups is as follows: 11–15, 0; 16–20, 3; 21–25, 12; 26–30, 18; 31–35, 11; 36–40, 20; 41–45, 14; 46–50, 14; 51–55, 7; 56–60, 2; 61–65, 1; above 66, 0.

Their age at the time of their death ranged from 19 to 61 years old, but the work experience overwhelmingly represented was that of manhood, the period between 20 and 50 years of age. Sixty-eight per cent were between 21 and 40, a time for hard work. There were also 27 per cent between 41 and 50. Significantly only 3 per cent were under the age of 20, and 9 per cent above the age of 51, with one man, Lim Phua Sim, an elderly Hengwah puller, over 61 years of age.[24] The largest groups were in the age spread between 21 and 30 (30) and 31 to 40 (31); there were few youths between 16 and 20 years of age. The sudden sharp decrease in the numbers above the age of 50 is dramatic. Age was a sign to stop and step outside the shafts before it was too late. When men entered their fifties, rickshaw pulling began to take its toll on the body in a remorseless way, even upon the toughest street-wise pullers. The choice was simple. They had to slow down or die.

Single, transient, most rickshawmen lived in crowded two- and three-storey tenement houses. It has already been mentioned that the occupation of rickshaw pulling rested on the principles of kinship, speech and/or locality/origin. Residence was no exception. There are plenty of indications of the phenomenon of residential segregation. Rickshaw pullers of particular sub-ethnic groups congregated along certain streets next to one another, lodging house by lodging house. These areas where the men seem to have been living, from a few weeks to a number of years, were dominated by a distinctive identity and character that was Foochow or Hokkien and not, for example, Cantonese. And there were numerous signs on a street to symbolise this and to evoke the residents' way of life, from temples to dialect associations or the name of the street itself and its derivation, and a cacophony of daily sights and sounds all orchestrated in the dialect of its occupants.[25]

The number of men living in these houses, who dossed down in shifts, varied in 1918 from as few as 15 at No. 96 Queen Street to the very severe overcrowding of No. 124 Victoria Street with 175 occupants in the house—with the average number ranging between 35 and 60 along Johore Road, Bencoolen Street and New Market Road. The number of men in the two houses listed in 1918 as occupied by rickshaw coolies on Mosque Street, Nos 36 and 41, were high: 80 and 85 respectively. At No. 96 Bencoolen Street, a big compound house, crowding began to approach the unbearable with 110 coolies, at 70 dollars a month rent. As high as these figures are, they do not represent a considerable increase in prewar densities for some areas such as Kreta Ayer. It seemed reasonable, as early as 1904, to situate the new 'commodious and substantially built' rickshaw station at Kreta Ayer (which was renovated in 1985) in that 'crowded part of town, where so many *jinricksha* owners and pullers live'.[26] But by 1918 there was no more housing in the area; the pullers did not want to go far out of the city. Mr Hooper, appearing before the Housing Commission Inquiry that year, testified that Duxton Road and Craig Road near Kreta Ayer were 'very crowded, and the vicinity of Peoples Park'.[27] Manassah Lane, off Park Road, was described by him as a 'dreadful place'. Certainly more houses were required. All around Muar Road and Angullia Road the crowding was extremely bad. The head of the Rickshaw Department finished his testimony on a sombre note by saying that 'the houses in the [rickshaw] coolie districts are filled and overcrowded'.[28]

Many of these lodging houses were either owned or rented by rickshaw proprietors. Nearly forty-five years later, Ng Kar Eng could still remember where he went to hire his rickshaw as a young hopeful:

> Yes, the rickshaw belonged to the owner of the house where I stayed. There were only three or four rickshaws left then [1937]…they were used by some old men to make a living, while some younger men used trishaws.[29]

The pullers were nearly always under an obligation to go into the lodging house of their employer. There they lived in cramped dormitories, with friends and strangers, in minuscule cubicles, each occupied by several men, so as to gain a little additional income and defray the cost of rent. The length of time rickshawmen lived in a particular lodging house varied, and there was continual turnover, but if the atmosphere, despite overcrowding, was supportive, and that often depended on the presence or absence of kin, and current relations with the owner/landlord, a man would stay for years. Differences in rent payments tended to be manifested by the location and extent of overcrowding in a lodging house. The rents were apt to be higher in the downtown area or on its fringe in the less overcrowded rickshaw housing than anywhere else. There are also some indications that rent payments sometimes included the cost of the provision of a certain amount of *chandu* daily to regular pullers who smoked opium, but in moderation.

Rickshawmen who were married constituted a very small percentage of the total, and lived in coolie lodging houses with far from homogeneous populations. A report on the sanitary conditions of Singapore compiled in 1907 catalogues the household composition of the 64 residents living in a three-storey tenement house at 20–23 Sago Lane—a street in an overcrowded area of Chinatown.[30] The rents in the lodging house ranged from $1.50 to $4.50 per month. The report tells of a rickshaw puller and his wife and child occupying cubicle No. 6 on the first floor with an area of 8 square metres, and windowless.

The married man paid $2.80 a month to Lim Ah Keng, the sub-tenant, who slept in the passage. The occupations of the other tenants on the first floor included a seamstress, a tailor and a revenue officer who paid $4.50 per month rent, while a prostitute and her child lived directly above the married rickshawman's family on the second floor.[31] Under such circumstances, payment of rent was more difficult, as families could not crowd into cramped dormitory quarters in the big compound houses, nor sleep in shifts, to reduce rent.

In 1893, the average daily earnings of a rickshawman was about 40 cents. That was his gross earnings before he paid 8 to 10 cents for the hire of his rickshaw.[32] By 1908, an experienced man grossed between $1.70 and $2.00 per day, while at the same time the wages of the ordinary coolie was 45 to 50 cents a day; a day labourer in the tin mines earned 70 cents, and one dollar a day was the most a coal coolie ever earned.[33] The rickshaw puller's net earnings stabilised at about one dollar a day by 1924, but the inexperienced ones and opium addicts were fortunate if they could make 40 cents nett, to buy food and *chandu*.[34] By then, government legislation freezing the wage of rickshaw pullers and soaring inflation, taken together, had affected the rickshaw coolies, particularly those with families, to an appreciable extent. Accommodation, rice and staples such as salted vegetables and cooking oil were almost beyond their means. The pattern of a puller's monthly income in the inter-war years was complex because it rested not simply on what people were paid, but on personal circumstances: good health and the number of trips averaged a day, whether the wife was working, the owner and job security, and number of children. A wage which was a luxury for a nineteen-year-old Hengwah, Ong Teck Cheng, living with clansmen in a rickshaw coolie lodging house, or for a married couple who were both working with no children at home, was penury for a young married man like Lim Ong,[35] whose wife had to stay at home to look after two young children.

Rickshaw fares were cheap. For a journey up to one mile the charge was six cents in 1897. The set fares were gazetted by the Rickshaw Department, but in actual fact any distance was negotiable in money terms; bargaining went on between the passenger and the puller, and fares ranged from a few cents up to 60 cents according to the distance, time of day and weather. The small unexpected windfall usually came from generous foreigners—tourists, soldiers and sailors—visiting briefly, attracted by the 'city lights'. But for the regular inhabitants of Singapore the fares changed with the onset of wet weather. Rickshaw fares climbed sharply with sudden torrential downpours. However, it was not unusual at the end of the journey for inexperienced pullers or those lacking in cunning to be either caught in a wrangle over the sum agreed to or to be bilked.

It was not easy for the Singapore rickshaw coolie, despite his reputation for hard work and thrift, to become a *bona fide* owner of the rickshaw he pulled.[36] Few of their number were ever able to obtain sufficient funds for the purchase of a rickshaw, and to still eke out a satisfactory living withstanding the heavy liabilities with which they were saddled to meet the requisite expenditure. Perhaps two pullers in a hundred owned their rickshaws. The rest of the rickshawmen—there were 20,000 coolies registered in 1902[37]—rented their vehicles on a shift basis from rickshaw owners. The owners, because the rickshaw trade was labour intensive with a low capital overhead per vehicle, made a much better living out of rickshaws in Singapore than their pullers. The rickshawman's net income could only improve by getting rid of the rental he had to give to the owner; that is, if he owned his own rickshaw or shared the purchase of one with a group of pullers on an instalment basis. The rickshaw was central to the work and life of Hengwah, Hockchia and Hockchew immigrants, and ownership of one was their ray of hope. But the material investment involved to become an owner remained beyond the means of most of the men, struggling against rent capital, the high cost of living, and fluctuating exchange rates.

The owners

The owners of rickshaws usually came from the same area or dialect group in China as their pullers. Owners were primarily Hengwah, Hockchia and Hokkien in this century. Earlier, most had been Cantonese.[38] But other dialect groups normally accounted for the purchase and maintenance of some of the thousands of rickshaws in operation then in Singapore. The vast majority of owners were men. Women's names occasionally stood in the register of the Rickshaw Department as 'owner' of a numbered rickshaw—usually as wives of owners or widows.

On the face of the evidence few appear to have come up through the ranks of the rickshaw trade the hard way as pullers. But there were exceptions, particularly among those men who had enough capital to start in Singapore with their own rickshaw. A number of these went on to own fifteen or twenty and retire from pulling.[39] Owners were sometimes *towkays*, small-time rent capitalists, such as shopkeepers and lodging-house proprietors, who kept and maintained several rickshaws as a side investment. They usually operated in restricted areas of the city with a particularistically defined rental policy towards various sub-ethnic communities. Another category of rickshaw business was half ownership and half operator; in other words, the puller owned the rickshaw and rented it out, usually to kin, when he was not pulling it himself. These rickshawmen were rarely encountered on the streets, though, as they were the exception, as the cost of ownership ($160 for a new one in 1917) was prohibitive and most could not hope to save the capital sum necessary to become a rickshaw owner. Most often after a lifetime of trying to save money to buy their own vehicle, coolies still had insufficient capital to be able to settle their daily living expenses and debts, let alone purchase even a second-hand one. By far the most important category was the rickshaw entrepreneurs. They accounted for the vast majority of the rickshaws that thronged the streets of Singapore. These individuals, who frequently owned from thirty to fifty rickshaws, derived their income primarily from a monopoly of ownership and rentals. All their rickshaws were rented out to pullers. In some instances they did not restrict renting only to pullers of the same ethnic group; as long as members of other Chinese communities who wanted to ply for hire were considered trustworthy, the rickshaws were hired out.

Almost all fleet owners in Singapore rented their rickshaws for half a day. Rickshaws were usually hired out on two shifts. The day puller went out with his rickshaw at 6 a.m. and returned between 2 and 3 p.m. Night pullers worked a series of shifts, the most common times being 2 p.m. to midnight and 5 p.m. to 3 a.m., providing service throughout the city, but especially in the brothel districts and the vicinity of the harbour, till sun-up. Many coolies religiously came at certain hours to hire their vehicles for half a day or night. The rickshawman's routine preference for a particular hiring time also sometimes extended to going back for months, in some cases, even years, to an owner, who more often than not was from the same speech group or locality in China, and as a matter of course choosing a customary rickshaw. When the rickshaw owners were sufficiently well acquainted with the men, especially regulars and 'old hands' who lived in their boarding houses or close by and pulled their rickshaws, to comment not only on the idiosyncrasies of their hiring habits but on their character and personality too, and hence by inference on their relationship with them, it is not surprising to see them stress those qualities they deemed as both necessary and desirable in the making of a good puller, qualities that cost them next to nothing but immeasurably enhanced their authority, and profits from renting rickshaws, namely, cooperation and reliability, good health and physical strength, and common sense and being economical with money.

The prices the rickshaws were let out for by the owners to a rickshawman varied in different districts and according to quality. The usual rates between 1904 and 1916 can be seen in Table 9.3. The owners, because the rickshaw trade was labour intensive with a low capital overhead per vehicle, made a much better living out of rickshaws in Singapore than their pullers. The sweat and suffering of these hard-worked coolies made fortunes for the rickshaw capitalist from whom they had to rent rickshaws. For these men, inspired by the profit motive, the rickshaw was a lucrative investment, the return on capital being as much as 100 per cent per annum. The rental system made owners rich, the pullers hard-driven, exploited and poor. As long as the ownership of rickshaws was concentrated in the hands of rent capitalists there was no means for the puller to increase earnings, to save, to purchase a rickshaw, except to run harder, longer. Pulling like that could kill. Two elements, the high rental fee and restricted ownership, were a sign of the inequality of their life and death, and of the undue influence and power of rent capital in regulating the social relations of Chinese coolies in a colonial society.

Table 9.3 Prices for hiring rickshaws

Year	1st Class	2nd Class
1904	—	18–36 cents per day
1905	50–60 cents per day	18–38 cents per day
1906	50–60 cents per day	15–32 cents per day
1907	50–60 cents per day	22–28 cents per day
1908	45–60 cents per day	20–28 cents per day
1916	50–60 cents per day	15–32 cents per day

The social environment and morbidity

Most rickshawmen saw no future in marriage. They realised the impossibility of having a family and chose to live alone as bachelors. This is what it meant to pull a rickshaw in Singapore—to be solitary. Thousands upon thousands of men pulled rickshaws to a moronic rhythm of work, little or no leisure, and work for years on end. Apart from drawing a rickshaw, the single puller's life was strongly 'empty', lacking the joys of family life, parenthood, and for some, even friendship. There was no limit to the amount of work such a puller could do. His time and energy were his own. But it was precisely this concentration of energy that produced the abnormal willpower and strength to pull a rickshaw year after year, alone.

Work was compulsive for most rickshawmen. A more leisurely social life was constrained by absence of family and lack of money. But occasionally there was free entertainment in the neighbourhood. *Wayang-going* was a common way to break down the wall between work and life. Men could actually get away from it all to unleash the frustrations of pulling a rickshaw and living alone. The streets in the rickshaw quarter were a stage when a Chinese *wayang*, or street opera, played to the delight of the pullers. Temple and native-place associations often arranged such open-air entertainment in order to celebrate a religious holiday. The operas ran for many days with itinerant *wayang* troupes performing on makeshift stages from dusk to dawn; the surrounding streets became a hub of activity, alive with spectators socialising, filled with the sound of Chinese music, of clashing cymbals and drums, and hawkers providing delicious fare along the five footways for the marathon performances.

Besides *wayangs*, festivals and religious holidays, the art of living was maintained among rickshawmen by fulfilling their social obligations to a deceased puller. Death, from the point of view of the native-place association, called for a certain set of social activities and obligations that stressed ancestral worship, strengthened social ties among mourners and promoted clan solidarity. The personal and social relationships between two rickshawmen were expressed in the reciprocal rights and duties associated with the mourning ritual as fictive kin.[40] The rickshawmen played a part in the preparations for a simple burial and formed the funeral procession to a clan cemetery or the municipally run pauper's cemetery with its fixed grave plots.

Despite spartan living conditions and a colonial government whose control reached into the most intimate aspects of the rickshawman's work-a-day life, most of them—even those most left alone—managed to pursue their private passions. They found some solace in the four evils. The four evils were well known among the rickshaw pullers of Singapore, and the four went together in the city. They were opium smoking, prostitution, drinking and gambling. The four evils individually and in combination prevented many young hardworking pullers from fulfilling the 'inexorable duty of every son'[41]—the regular remittance of money to support destitute kin in their home villages in China. In their early years in Singapore especially, they sent their income at regular intervals. Being in a new land was no excuse for forgetting their past; the survival of the family depended on them pulling their rickshaws undyingly. But as time passed and men began to smoke opium or visit the brothels out of loneliness, remittances were apt to be sent less frequently. The bond of loyalty linking single rickshawmen to family and village in China began to fray, and then come apart as the years went by in Singapore. Men began to fritter the money away on opium, daughters of joy and flower girls, alcohol and cigarettes, and on gambling—money that their whole families relied on for income. When rickshawmen failed to remit money or answer the stinging letters reprimanding them for their laxity, kin, mostly wives, wearied of waiting. In the eyes of their people these men had been unsuccessful. Some of them finally left China to look for their brothers or husbands in Singapore, only to discover on arrival, once having found them, that they left a past at home perhaps a lot better and happier than the present. The cause of the paradox was that their brothers and husbands had become different men after long years of working alone with rickshaws in Singapore—they had become addicted to opium, alcohol, gambling and were infected with venereal disease.

The four evils were the sole recreation afforded to rickshawmen in Singapore. The paradox surrounding them was that they helped to make what in most respects was an intolerable life for the puller more tolerable, even exciting, joyous on occasion, if only for a moment, a few hours, or a day or two at most. But ultimately their health, ambition, sense of responsibility and dreams were consumed by the opium, sexually transmitted diseases, alcohol and gambling 'fever'. The four evils also destroyed the bonds of reciprocity between generations that linked filial sons to elderly parents in China. Their parents, the ancestors and the past were forgotten for the passion of the moment in a city that had slowly worn them down. The colonial government, on its part, was neither prepared to raise the pullers' wages nor create a more beneficial environment with appropriate housing, suitable recreational facilities and open spaces as a substitute for the sole means they had at their disposal to enjoy themselves.

An inherent economic and social inequality was linked with high morbidity and mortality in the Singapore of the rickshawmen, precisely because it was a 'coolie town'.[42] Underlying the depressing economics and health hazards of rickshaw pulling there was a demographic pressure crushing the Singapore Chinese that was a direct consequence of the symbiosis of colonial capitalism and migration from south-eastern China. Singapore, in the words of a senior army medical officer, was 'a nursery for disease' in 1872.[43] Rickshawmen were to live with disease-infectious death for more than half a century after he said that. Despite an unprecedented rise in the death rate from endemic killing diseases like typhoid, cholera, malaria and tuberculosis, both the colonial government and municipal authorities time and again refused to be put under pressure and to take effective steps for social care and the eradication of disease in Chinatown. The authorities consistently chose alternatives that minimised costs and therefore supplied a rational but less than humane approach to Singapore's housing, water supply and waste disposal problems. Slum property retained its inflated value right through the Depression—inflated precisely because it was overcrowded, and this was especially so in the rickshaw quarters. As long as the government was not prepared to pay the market price for this class of property, death from these diseases caused by poverty and overcrowding, particularly from tuberculosis and pneumonia, continued to take its toll of lives among rickshaw pullers. The city's decision to cope with its environment in this way from the 1880s till the 1930s meant that a puller came home each day to a neighbourhood that lived in the shadow of death. He knew what his friends were going through in this cramped, filthy, disease-ridden place called a city—the sleepless nights with malarial fever, the fear of not being spared by the cholera, the nights he lay awake because of the sound of the hacking cough of his tubercular clansmen coming through the dark from the floor below, but some nights he wondered amid all this death whether the disease would spare him. Yet, the truth of the matter was that it didn't really matter to him any more; he didn't seem to care as he knew that worse was coming. The environment of the city was gradually destroying him, too:

> Men have separated themselves from the animals but now drive their own kind back among the beasts. [He] remained in this...city but he was being transformed into an animal. Not a bit of it was his own fault. He had stopped thinking and, therefore, the human being in him was destroyed. He bore no responsibility for that at all. He'd never hope again. He'd just sink blindly, stupidly, lower and lower, into a bottomless pit. He ate, he drank, he whored, he gambled, he cheated, and all because he had no heart left in him. Others had taken it from him. All that remained was his big frame and now he waited for it to burst open like an abscess. He was getting ready for the potter's field.[44]

Most of them experienced the loss of human dignity because of this social and physical environment, and the reluctance of the colonial government to change all this. Examination of the major sequential decisions made by colonial Singapore in regard to the interdependence of housing, water supply, waste disposal and sewerage from the 1880s through the 1930s, shows that the city's rulers consistently chose alternatives that minimised costs at the expense of the coolie population. The tragedy was that rickshawmen and their families, because of these policies, were very vulnerable to disease, so pullers with very ill kin could only stand by helplessly and hopelessly. They were aware that the medical problem was not just a disease; it was the social and physical environment of the city and its policies that interfered with their state of wellbeing, and they felt the need to change it. But their failure to do so led some of them, after they had quarrelled over rent, contracted tuberculosis or syphilis, or gambled away their savings, to behave in a way that gave their kinsmen and clansmen anxiety as to their safety; they cried out in anger and shame as the vision that was planted in China swept them up and spat them out. In such circumstances—mounting health problems, income difficulties, and high levels of dependency among men who very often were unable to support their dependent members—in the course of time, drove them to the point of suicide.

The abolition campaign

In that furious time that stood between the two world wars, rickshaws and the men who pulled them were pencilled into the margins of Singapore's future. By the 1920s, the British felt that the rickshaw was a challenge to their development policy and the showcase image of Singapore as a 'modern city'. The demand for rickshaw transport throughout the inter-war years, however, continued, as did the harsh social differences sustaining it. The British refused to encourage the trade, at times ignoring it, and then opposing it with a vengeance at the height of the Depression. Officials believed that rickshaws were an uneconomical, slow and hazardous mode of conveyance, and that they would ultimately have to go to improve the flow of public transport. From this time on, the city's roads were restricted to motorised transport. The traffic-official argument was that rickshaws were slow-moving and snarled the flow of other vehicles. Thus, to free Singapore's public transport from traffic congestion, restrictions on rickshaws had to be introduced.

The rationale was wrong. The plain fact was that the rickshaws were far more manoeuvrable in dense traffic than any motor vehicle. They rarely broke down like the trams and buses, and handled most of the short distance trips on the small, congested streets and alleyways off the main roads where motorised public transport could not penetrate. There were no similar restrictions in these years on private cars and taxis, despite an appalling increase in motor vehicle traffic accidents. The planners were not to be deterred. The systematic removal of rickshaws, as 'slow-moving vehicles', began in 1928, but it did not improve the traffic situation on the main roads. From this time onward, the future of the rickshaw coolie was bleak. The Rickshaw Department began to withdraw licenses, while at the same time not issuing any more new licenses and cancelling expired ones. This sudden removal of thousands of rickshaws and the services they provided caused disruption among those living at the lowest income levels, who had to count every cent, for there was no alternative system of transport except to walk.

With admirable clarity, the 1930s demonstrated the ways in which the growing deprivation of the rickshawmen was being further aggravated by the policies of a government bent on gradually abolishing rickshaws in the interests of the motor car. The unequal distribution of wealth and power, and the advent of a large-scale motorised transport system combined against the puller's livelihood with a vengeance. The history of the inter-war years was to show that the experience of the rickshaw pullers was to be one of confrontation with the government and rickshaw owners, then one of 'temporary peace' through mediation and settlement, and then one of resistance and strikes. This cycle was to repeat itself several times over the course of these years, culminating in the coolie's display of solidarity in the strike of 1938 when the authorities and owners sought to end their way of life. The rickshaw pullers' future had been threatened before by owners, government officials and planners, but now they were fighting for survival. As more rickshaws were pulled off the streets in an effort to restrict their numbers, the owners raised the rental fee. In 1938, a life-and-death struggle with the owners erupted over the rental fee and manipulation of the pullers' contribution to the China Relief Fund to assist their countrymen who were then in 'deep water and scorching fire'. When the wage demands of the rickshaw pullers were not met they closed ranks, demonstrating against the owners and smashing their rickshaws.

The pullers had stopped work because of owner exploitation, hard times and the issue of the manipulation of the monthly donation to the China Relief Fund. They expected the Chinese public to rally to their cause. But the mass of Chinese in Singapore remained apathetic, even hostile at times, refusing to support them openly. The government condemned the stoppage. The owners refused to sit down and negotiate a prompt settlement. They relied on time, once all hope of a quick resolution had faded, hoping to starve the pullers into submission; and they were backed by the force of colonial law, as police constantly assisted them by patrolling affected areas, protecting their rickshaws, and arresting strikers. But by doing so the owners did not diminish the pullers' strength or resolution; the strike only magnified them.

Yet, despite a massive display of support and sacrifice from fellow pullers, some of whom earned as little as thirty cents a day, the rickshawmen had little reason for optimism. Throughout the strike, arbitration by various individuals and groups failed. The pullers also had to forgo tens of thousands of dollars, and a large section of them suffered from hunger and destitution, forcing some to take advantage of the government offer of repatriation. And, as a result of the policies of rickshaw abolitionists, the vast majority of vehicles remained firmly in the hands of a small number of *towkays*. Finally, and perhaps most importantly, the rickshaw strike had not reached beyond the confines of puller politics and community to touch the concerns of other Chinese coolies in order to confront the power and prejudice of a colonial system that was overwhelming them. Singapore was saved the humiliation and fear of having to face a general strike in the widest sense in the coolies' struggle against oppression and injustice. The pullers had obtained a considerable reduction in the rates of hire for their rickshaws, but the 1938 strike did not change anything else—the owners endured.

Conclusion

This chapter has described the social organisation of a coolie occupation; the role that rickshaws and rickshaw pullers played in Singapore's history; and the marginalised lives the coolies led. They can no longer be relegated to the back and side of the stage of Singapore history. Nor can they be seen as only the foundation of the stage. Now the experience, words and their voices come back to us—seventy or more years later—as their descendants in our time write a different epitaph on their past and their lives.

Chapter 10

Social History and the Photograph: Glimpses of Chinese and Japanese Labour in Singapore in the Early Twentieth Century[1]

The social history of Singapore Chinese society and the city's development, as a commercial centre and entrepôt port from 1870 to 1940, has been the setting of virtually all my work for the past two decades. *Rickshaw Coolie* and *Ah Ku and Karayuki-san* deal with turn-of-century Singapore, wedged between British Malaya and the Netherlands Indies, with its own startling tough 'history from below' and idiosyncrasies as a Chinese city outside China. These books examine the social conditions that spawned the rickshaw and prostitution industries and the way Chinese coolies and Japanese prostitutes lived their lives in conjunction with the big changes taking place in the development of colonial Singapore and Asia. Among the many groups of workers whose labour built Singapore in the first part of this century, there may be none as marginalised in memory as the men and women who travelled from China and Japan to work in Singapore as rickshaw coolies and prostitutes. Between 1880 and 1930 colonial Singapore attracted tens of thousands of Chinese immigrant labourers, brought to serve its rapidly growing economy. I have chronicled the vast movement of coolies between China and the *Nanyang*, and their efforts to survive in colonial Singapore. Focusing on one particular occupation, of rickshaw coolie, my research unveils the devastating poverty of the Chinese sojourner in the colonial city, the disjuncture between colonial order and the reality of life on the streets. I have also outlined the trade in women and children in Asia and homed in on the details of the Japanese prostitutes' lives in the colonial city: the daily brothel routine, crises and violence, social relations, leisure, morbidity, disease and death.

In 1981, Roland Barthes stated 'It is the advent of the photograph...which divides the history of the world.' Cognitively speaking, histories and pictorial framing are important ways of human world-making. Barthes' exemplary work stresses the fact that it is as true for photographs as it is for painting: 'Thanks to its code of connotation the reading of the photograph is thus always historical: it depends on the reader's "knowledge", just as though it were a matter of real language, intelligible only if one has learned the signs.'[2] Marx Wartofsky, a philosopher, in a provocative series of essays about the fields of proxemics and pictorial analyses, further clarifies Barthes' observation about the visual posture common in early twentieth-century Western photographs of colonial sites like Singapore: that of the detached spectator—the viewer who is relatively distanced or detached from what is being framed or watched based on a metaphor of the eye as a camera.[3] Wartofsky emphasises that pictorial or photographic representation of, for example, rickshaw pullers or Japanese prostitutes, was a cultural creative act with a historical basis that was 'not given but achieved; made, not discovered.'[4] Hence, in colonial port cities like Singapore, Europeans took pictures of the 'Chinese rickshaw puller' and the '*karayuki-san*' in order to appropriate and disarm the unfamiliar 'other' but, who, according to S. Matthews' study of Chinese photography, were 'unable to return the stares they received'.[5] These photographs imaging and imagining a form of visual captivity were 'read as proof of the justice of the imperial division of the world.'[6] While the contents of these photographs are either about Chinese or Japanese labourers in Singapore, the forms of the photographs remained explicitly Western, signifying an affirmation of the rationality of economic and scientific progress under colonial rule.

Photography and history: Rickshaw coolies

In order to grasp what the experience meant to pull a rickshaw in mid-1900, historians must immerse themselves in the whole range of sources available on Singapore in the late nineteenth and early twentieth centuries. There is a wealth of tangential information about the Chinese labouring classes in the colonial records waiting to be interpreted. An imaginative use of these official records can go a long way towards assisting us in our understanding the course of Chinese life, and lower class at that, in a Chinese city outside China, for whom they were not meant to extol. They bring the rickshaw coolies, their clansmen, kinsmen and women of a forgotten past into the historical forefront; empirical evidence is provided on age, sex, marital status, address, place of birth, occupation, length of time in Singapore, diet, dress, sickness and death. The causes of death often depict the deprivation experienced in pulling a rickshaw. Much also can be learned about housing, health and poverty, and the almost hopeless struggle to survive, from literary sources, the detailed accounts of European and Asian observers of Singapore, and by observing the yet 'unreconstructed' part of Singapore's Chinatown.

It must be stressed, however, that, as critical as these sources are for reconstructing a picture of the life and times of rickshawmen, generalisations regarding their experience cannot be based wholly on these records. If this detailed evidence is to be used to advantage in a representative account it must be supplemented by exceptional information in photographs and pictures that show the Singapore the rickshaw pullers recognised and understood.

There exists an important photographic record of rickshaws in Singapore. Intrepid photographers with unwieldy equipment and glass plate negatives were already taking interesting photographs of excellent quality at the time the rickshaw was invented and first introduced to Singapore in the early 1880s. It is their images of bygone Chinese society that remain to haunt Singapore in the present and bear witness to the past of the rickshaw puller. The most important photographs are found in the photograph and postcard collections of the National Archives and Record Centre; the photo files of newspapers; and in books, periodicals and magazines such as *British Malaya*.[7]

First, before discussing their significance as a source, it is necessary to draw attention to several problems involved in the use and interpretation of relevant photos of rickshawmen. In some respects, no medium was less appropriate for recording how rickshawmen ordinarily acted than the early camera. The stillness required of the puller, quite unnatural to him, was singularly unsuited to capturing accurately the motion of a rickshaw, and the strength and strain involved in pulling it. Later on, photographers—professional and novice—roamed the streets of Singapore with the Box Brownie cameras in hand seeking the exotic East, an ethnographic oddity, or simply to promote the tourist trade. These photographers, by their presence and activities, frequently turned rickshaw pullers, along with the street hawkers and beggars, into caricatured specimens for 'artistic effect', or for the fashionable genre of magazine pictures and picture postcards of the time.

Misunderstanding was created in the eye of the camera by insensitive Europeans who approached the rickshaw puller as simply one more curio Singapore offered to the traveller. Rickshawmen were asked to pose as still-life subjects (actually objects) against backgrounds that excelled in scenic beauty, such as the primeval setting of the Botanical Gardens or facing the sea on the Esplanade. By the use of these disguised settings, photographers distanced themselves from the image of the straining, sweating rickshaw coolie. The resultant photograph prevented persons from facing the depth of their emotions—anxiety, guilt, pity—over having been pulled in a rickshaw by a coolie. Instead, the exhausting life and the rickshaw became a pleasing sight to remember. Such photos inevitably robbed pullers of their humanity and, as objects of curiosity about a journey to the East, misrepresented what life they had. We know of at least one rickshaw puller though, who drew the line when his unthinking European passenger attempted to take a 'picturesque' photo of him; he took it as a sign of bad luck—an invasion of his soul: 'I came up here against a curious superstition, for my rickshaw puller refused to have his photograph taken, lest I might enclose his soul in the body of my camera.'[8]

On the other hand, especially in the Singapore of the 1930s, when pullers were living in appalling conditions, the sensitive photograph simply could not get it all in—the damp nocturnal world of the cubicle, limbs deadened by pain, and the worn weather-beaten faces of the men. While the results of the efforts of photographs like Julius Friend were not responsible for distorting reality at that time, they often could not capture its essence. The poverty and despair defied translation.

However, a 'reading' of the photographic record of Singapore is necessary to tell the story of the rickshawmen. A thoughtful analysis of still photographs can provide compelling information on a decisive moment in time and reveal in the process something about the behaviour of the rickshaw pullers, the physical details of rickshaws themselves such as the uncommon use of pneumatic tyres, and the characteristic environment of the men who pulled them. In this context, the images of these still photos, this moment rather than that, are a means of seeming to outwit time.

With these photographs, gathered from archives, newspaper files and magazines, I can delve into all corners of Singapore to develop an understanding of the city the rickshaw pullers knew—filthy, bustling, chaotic, swarming with the rickshaws at major street corners, idly parked outside the Raffles Hotel, and in motion along the Esplanade and Collier Quay from dawn to dusk. Just as significant is the immediate impression created by the snapshots of the kinds of work represented in the ordinary everyday life of the urban landscape, which ranged from the street vendors, a *singkeh* eating at a stall, a Chinese scribe engrossed in his work, to *Poh Sam* women plying their needles industriously. The rickshaw puller is there too, frozen in motion amid the confused pattern of traffic; so are the images of doomed older men captured in a rare moment of well-earned rest, sleeping in their rickshaw at twilight.

Bearing witness

Singkeh were not always well cared for on the voyage down. Photographs show how small some of these ships were that made regular passages in the South China Sea with emigrants. However, it is the posed photo depicted on the odd postcard and in travel accounts that speaks of the general character of an extraordinary exodus of young men going abroad to pull rickshaws in Singapore. Most of them came from the Kwangtung and Fukien provinces

Social History and the Photograph

in search of a new life. But they had no intention of staying. It was the ideal pattern of circular migration: 'men go abroad, earn, remit money, and return.'⁹ A singular photograph of a juvenile puller, kneeling between the shafts of his immaculately set out private rickshaw, wearing his best work shorts, his hair combed for the occasion, with his straw hat inconspicuously tucked away between the floorboard and the wheel, and looking straight into the eye of the camera; is a rare picture of a sojourning youth that would probably be sent to someone dear in China.

It was a common sight all over Singapore at dawn to see owners and pullers getting their rickshaws ready for the day. We can actually see and experience close-up this ritualistic daybreak activity by carefully 'reading' a period picture postcard entitled 'Jinrickisha Station'. The scene is Sago Lane in the Kreta Ayer section of Chinatown circa 1910. It has rained, the street is relatively deserted, the rain hoods have been put up on the rickshaws flanking both sides of the street; as one puller draws away on the puddle-soaked street with shaft held high, others stand or squat nearby chatting. In the left, foreground, an owner or puller leans down to clean, possibly repair, the mudguard on the rickshaw. The vehicle's rain-soaked hood, which has been taken off, is on the ground in

Figure 10.1   Young rickshaw puller.

Figure 10.2 Jinrickisha Station c. 1910.

a heap beside the shafts. Almost out of the picture in the left corner, another man, partially naked, stands between the shafts busily at work. Further down the street a puller bends over to check a wheel. While just across the way, on the upper right-hand side of the street, a rickshaw coolie wearing a conical-shaped straw fibre hat inspects the rainhood.

The amount of traffic in Singapore grew in direct proportion to the size of the town, its population, wealth and business in the latter part of the nineteenth century. Rickshaws were a significant part of that growth. In 1917, a twelve-hour survey at six main bridges in Singapore recorded 72,772 crossings of rickshaws. At the turn of the century there were no traffic regulations or road signs, nor does there appear to have been a hierarchy among road users. In old photographs and illustrations, such as 'The Padang, Singapore, circa 1905–10', Singapore traffic was seen to be difficult with private carriages, hack gharries, bullock carts, rickshaws, tramcars and hawkers carrying heavy loads in baskets, handcarts and pushcarts, with pedestrians on foot, and motor car drivers, all jostling for the right of way. On these streets, jammed with traffic, the motor vehicles sounded their horns at the pullers, the pullers shouted at the pedestrians, and the pedestrians tended to ignore both.

Figure 10.3 A typical Singapore traffic scene in New Market Road during the mid-1930s. Note how automobiles and lorries tend to dominate the space close to the drainage culvert on the left side of the street, forcing the rickshaw puller to veer out into the path of oncoming traffic.

Figure 10.4 Rickshaws lined up neatly outside Tank Road Railway Station, Singapore.

A hard and garrulous lot, rickshaw pullers knew almost every alley and side lane in their part of Chinatown like the backs of their hands. Old photos show that one could always expect to find scores of rickshaws around the luxury hotels (see Figure 10.10), the major market places, the railway station, the harbour and business districts catering to tourists, would-be shoppers and businessmen; they all turned to the rickshawmen, who sat in their bleached blue cottons and coarse straw hats— waiting, chatting, smoking or dozing between shafts.

Rickshaws were also hired by travellers. They would arrive by rail from the Federated Malay States at all hours. A postcard of the station at Tank Road shows nearly twenty rickshaws neatly

Figure 10.5 A rickshaw coolie sitting naked from the waist up, smoking an opium pipe. The photograph was taken prior to 1910.

lined up next to one another with foldable rain-proof hoods raised and lowered; the station clock showed the time to be nearly 5 p.m. The Tank Road railway station was so far from the business centre of the city and the Raffles Hotel that passengers who had come by train had to take a rickshaw from the station to their destination.

The structure of life

The following ensemble of photos bears witness to the rickshaw pullers of Singapore, chronicling their interaction with the city, and the causes and effects of immigration and colonial policy on their working and personal lives.

A rickshaw coolie's clothing, for example, at the beginning of the twentieth century normally comprised a pair of running shorts and a straw fibre hat. In 1900 pullers were prone to run on the streets naked from the waist up. Clothing became an essential item of expenditure when laws were passed requiring rickshaw coolies to wear certain clothes so as to look decent and not to offend unduly the sensibilities of the travelling public. A careful study of old photos shows that pullers were forced to become more clothes conscious and were dressed somewhat differently by 1914; they retained their traditional garb—

tight-fitting 'coolie blue' shorts or black baggy pants and straw hats, adding the ubiquitous loose-fitting coat-shirt to cover up the strain, sweat and nakedness.

In the overcrowded rickshaw districts, the lives of the rickshawmen and their families were bounded by the cubicles they lived in. The interior of the cubicles became their whole world: one of gloom in which the dust settled heavily, the air became stale, and the light was dim, even in the middle of the day. We know from turn-of-the-century photographs of the interiors of lodging houses, taken with a magnesium flash, that cubicles were pitch black and simply furnished. There were no windows and no means of lighting in many of them. Ventilation was poor and virtually non-existent in the windowless ones. Despite positive recommendations of the Emergency Housing Commission Report of 1918 calling for cubicles to be dealt with systematically, the dark cramped room portrayed in Dr Simpson's celebrated report of 1907 on housing in Singapore did not disappear from Chinatown, not even before the last rickshaw went off the streets in the 1950s.

The photographic record shows in detail the work-a-day world of the rickshaw coolie. These photographs of everyday life in old Singapore both document and challenge our assumptions about a place, a people and a time.

Figure 10.6 The central passage in the upper floor of a tenement house with cubicles on each side. By the first decade of the twentieth century, most of the rickshaw tenement houses were dreadful, decrepit, dangerous and old. This photo was taken with a magnesium flash in 1907.

Figure 10.7 There were no windows and no means of light in many of the cubicles. The lodging houses were densely packed, the heat and humidity almost unbearable at times, and visibility was rarely beyond the next few steps along the narrow passage.

Figure 10.8 A view of South Bridge Road at the turn of the century. By the mid-1900s rickshaws were the most popular form of public transport. The stinging competition of the rickshaws pressed hard on the hackney carriages.

Figure 10.9 A rickshaw puller in full stride with three passengers, on the stretch of New Bridge Road that runs parallel to Wayang Street, showing the Chinese Theatre Hall near the old Thong Chai Medical Institute.

Social History and the Photograph

Figure 10.10 Rickshaw stands scattered about the fronts of the best hotels in Singapore were considered to be lucrative spots to work by the pullers. This photograph, taken in 1921 by a West Australian hotelier, captures the daily activity of the rickshaw pullers around the Raffles Hotel.

Figure 10.11 Small peer groups on a sub-ethnic basis divided up different parts of the city and handfuls of rickshawmen could regularly be found occupying a particular place, huddling together. The photo depicts one such group of rickshaw coolies in front of the Clyde Terrace Market on Beach Road in the 1930s.

Figure 10.12 Food hawkers roamed the streets and set up wherever rickshaw pullers were found. There was no extravagance, but all of a sudden the facilities were there to enjoy a good cheap meal. On the docks, in Raffles Square, near the Railway Station, one could always see the itinerant Chinese hawkers with their cooking pots, lowering their poles to cater to the appetites of hungry rickshawpullers. One such scene took place near the Read Bridge in the early 1900s.

Figure 10.13 A new Rickshaw Station was opened in 1903 by the Jinrikisha Department for the licensing and inspection of rickshaws. This impressive building, which is situated at the southern end of South Bridge Road at the junction of Neil and Tanjong Pagar Roads, has been renovated by the Singapore government, and formerly housed a maternity and childcare centre. It is now the site of a seafood restaurant.

Photography and history: The *karayuki-san*

The camera arrived just in time to chronicle the astonishing wave of economic development that swept Singapore and left thousands of immigrants on its shores at the end of the nineteenth century. Innumerable black-and-white photographs depict the first years of the new century in Singapore. Familiar details of the prostitute's world that have since vanished were photographed: street scenes, buildings, transport, occupations and festivals are all portrayed.[10] Some of these photographs seem to capture almost the whole range of the women's existence, presenting it not as an unending catalogue of misery, but simply an experience. The photographs capture the *karayuki-san* away from Japan: thinking of family and friends; at work, posing at the behest of the brothel-keeper; at play, having a group picture taken with 'sisters'; and buying and selling, allowing a Chinese photographer to take a snapshot to be used as an 'exotic' postcard.[11] If one puts oneself in the place of the *karayuki-san* in the photographs, there is a thread of imagination, personal reminiscence and anecdote that are linked together.

The growth of brothel prostitution was to be expected at the end of the nineteenth century because of Singapore's rapid economic expansion. Trade and commerce were also to prove the main force in giving rise to the flourishing of photography in Singapore. In the last two decades of the nineteenth century, photographic studio sales grew annually as photographers resident in the colony, such as G. R. Lambert, T. Isshi, F. Ogata, and I. Fujisaki, saw potential for recording the human face, property and circumstances in the city.[12] Penny picture postcards introducing the equatorial colonies, their progress and the 'exotic' to people in the mother country also had a considerable impact. Thousands of photographic images of Singapore were recorded, but this pictorial record did not seem like an overkill in the eyes of the early photographers. Ordinary Londoners, local Singaporeans and villagers in northern Kyushu did not seem to reach saturation point in their desire to absorb the photographic subject. The *karayuki-san* reacted positively to the camera's assault on time, space and the imagination. It appears by the early years of the twentieth century that they simply could not have enough of photography's capacity to record their generation in Singapore for the future.

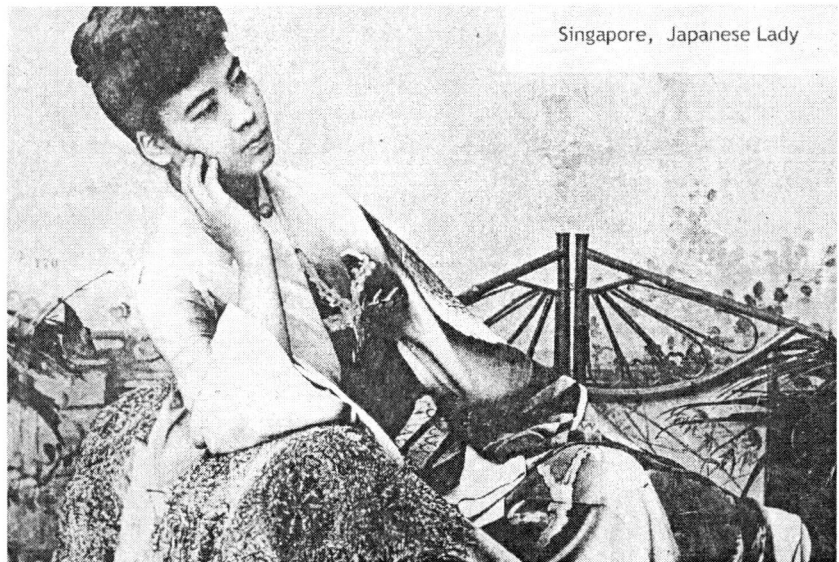

Figure 10.14 Some *karayuki-san* accepted offers to appear on picture postcards because the publicity and money were good. The image of Singapore as a centre of romanticism, exoticism and easy sex constituted a significant motive for travel to the city, as the advertising postcards of the Japanese 'ladies of the night' hoped to exploit. (Collection of Lim Kheng Chye, Courtesy National Archives, Singapore)

Through the eye of the camera

There were several kinds of photographs documenting the life of the *karayuki-san*. First, the type to be sent to family or friends in Japan, when every so often one of the women declared, 'Today let's go to the photographer's.' A full-length portrait in a gilt frame cost between six and seven dollars.[13] These photographs taken in a studio like G. R. Lambert's in Orchard Road could be done quickly—between 10 and 20 minutes, according to one of Singapore's master photographers.[14] The women invariably haggled over the price but still paid Isshi or Ogata, Lambert's employees, the cost of the group portrait. They never had photographs taken of places in Singapore—of the shops in the *suteretsu* or tropical landscape—only of themselves, and mostly in pairs or groups so it would not be so expensive. So their parents or kin had a singular image to show people in the village, they stared into the lens of the camera with a spartan simplicity; occasionally noble, frequently withdrawn, and the historian can sometimes glimpse in the sad expression and eyes a forlorn hope. Second, there were the registration portraits. The young Japanese women portrayed in some surviving photographs also saw themselves as members of a brothel family, one by one or all together. Looking back at themselves when they were younger, these photographs reminded some that the gulf between their youth, their past, and their country and their present situation was bigger, as they aged. The *karayuki-san* were not merely a handful of disgraced prostitutes overseas—certainly the picture presented in the Japanese media by 1918—but rather a class of females who had been forcibly dispersed throughout Southeast Asia, that was trying to survive in places like Singapore. Some were already old, grey-haired, alone, with only a photographic image and the memory of their passage through the 'family' and brothel, when the abolition edict was issued in 1921. Just occasionally, though, a *karayuki-san* like Oichi went to a photographic studio when she realised the bitter end was near. Oichi owed it to her sister to have a photograph taken before she gave up, abandoning Ofuku, her 'mother', and the burden. But she never went to the photographer, suicide claimed her first. Instead, on a table in her room was found a letter to the *okasan*,

Figure 10.15 A hard-edged arrival and registration portrait of a Japanese prostitute. The young woman stares into the lens of the camera with a spartan simplicity, and the historian can glimpse in the sad expression and eyes a forlorn hope. (Courtesy of the National Museum, Singapore)

Figure 10.16 The black-and-white arrival and registration of a portrait of a *karayuki-san*, c. 1900. (Collection of Gretchen Liu; courtesy of the National Archives, Singapore)

which requested her to send a photograph perhaps her arrival portrait, without comment, to her sister in Japan to bear witness to the reality of her passage from northern Kyushu to Singapore.[15]

Ah Ku and Karayuki-san contains some facets of the studio photographers' trade from the hard-edged arrival and registration portraits to the poignant and personal. Innumerable turn-of-the-century photographs of the women have not been saved; the glass plate negatives, especially by Japanese photographers, sadly, are also lost or destroyed. One of the best shots captured by Lambert's photographers is the 1890s portrait of four *karayuki-san*. Like many of the portraits that undoubtedly followed, the photograph was a gift or memento for the purpose of uniting the *karayuki-san* with loved ones or friends in Japan, a kind of talisman against the prostitute's fear that people at home would not remember her. Such photographs not only become tangible threads between prostitutes and the people who were important to them—which in turn could inspire, sadden, intrigue, and amuse them—they also invariably became physical extensions of the women's joy, sorrow and pain.

The turn of the century in Singapore saw photography practised with energy and a sense of fine art. The work of the Lambert photographic establishment was widely known, and its photographers had the time and desire to apply their cameras with artistic ambition. Capable of what is now regarded as sensitive

Figure 10.17 Kimono-clad 'hostesses' from Middle Road pose against a studio backdrop, c. 1900.

documentary photography, this studio nevertheless pursued the free expression of the medium. In Lambert's portraiture, especially in one of his better known images of four *karayuki-san*, the photographer renders great detail in accurate perspective while creating an aura of romanticism and elegance. The mind's eye is drawn to the idyllic soft focus canvas screen in the background, and the leopard skin in the foreground that three of the women are kneeling on. It lingers on the dark kimonos and their bits of jewellery—a cameo locket worn around the neck, and several gold rings. In the photograph their hair is worn traditionally, the bun just so, neatly held in place by ornamental pins and ribbons. To the uninitiated eye their kimonos do not look all that different from traditional ones. But *karayuki-san* introduced innovations in kimono wearing. To begin with, the *obi* or broad sash which binds the kimono together above the waist was usually narrower and more comfortable. Traditionally, unmarried young ladies from good families showed a proper upbringing by wrapping their *obis* tightly over their breasts, and to emphasise their puberty, such women were expected to wear white trim around their collars. The *karayuki-san* tended to ignore these gendered symbols that made them uncomfortable in a kimono. In fact, the bright orange and blue collars of orthodox design and low *obis* were the trademark of prostitutes in Singapore as late as the 1920s.

The camera's eye could be selective and untrustworthy. But Lambert let what he saw in the faces of these Japanese girls speak for themselves. This was their world in Singapore in the 1890s; like any photographer, he saw certain things in his own way, but he did not insist on a pose, that the woman on the extreme left lock arms with her 'sister', nor ask the *karayuki-san* in the light kimono, with a downcast look, to face the camera, before time momentarily stood still. This studio portrait of four Japanese women and others like it were remarkable for the degree of artistic conviction held by the photographers then working in the city. But the *karayuki-san*, above all, transcended this pursuit of photography as art with their obsessive concern with the photograph as a record of their activities. The portrait suggests that, beneath the photographer's work, a metaphor for their daily life and existence always remained. In this context, the image in this still photograph, this moment rather than that, was a means of seeming to outwit time while in Singapore.

The Singapore government found it impossible to suppress traffic in women and children and the abuses connected with it. Nor was it considered feasible to declare brothels illegal.[16] Because they could not be abolished, legislation was introduced under the Contagious Disease Ordinance (CDO) of 1870, imposing regulations on licensed brothels, but there was no formal policy with respect to control, still less prevention. To protect *karayuki-san* from enforced detention and

Figure 10.18 An extraordinary studio portrait of a young *karayuki-san*, her waist-length hair let down, capturing her other profile in the table mirror. (Collection of Gretchen Liu; courtesy of the National Archives, Singapore)

ill-treatment a system of registration and inspection of brothels and prostitutes was introduced. This was initially under the auspices of the Registrar-General's department.[17] This institutional system, which countenanced brothel prostitution, was in part designed to take British law into the brothels, and make illegal inmates free.[18] Documentary evidence shows that officials who approved of the system of registration and inspection believed it was the only method of safeguarding the liberty and welfare of the Japanese prostitutes in the tolerated houses.[19]

Figure 10.19 The *karayuki-san* Miyasaki Kechi in Singapore, 1892. Muraoka Iheiji noted on the back of her photograph that he had a considerable disagreement with this woman. (Courtesy of Muraoka Iheiji, *Muraoka Iheiji Jiden*)

The existing laws on the books, especially regarding traffic, without this system of registration and regulation were practically useless, as they could not prevent the importation, buying and selling of women and girls for brothel prostitution. On the other hand, registering officers had the power to limit the number of women residing in a brothel in accordance with its size, and could compel keepers to have their establishments always clean and well-ventilated.[20] The registration system also gave the Registrar, and later on the Chinese Protectorate, discretionary powers to investigate, break into and enter any house under suspicion of being a brothel, without a search warrant.[21] This system was simple in the extreme, but worked tolerably well. Every woman and girl in the public brothels was located and photographed. One photograph was retained by the Protectorate and the other by the *okasan* who pasted it in a record book kept in the brothel.[22] The photograph of the *karayuki-san* and the attached registration number, name and address printed in English made it more difficult for a brothel-keeper to get rid of a woman or abuse her, particularly because of periodic visits of the officers of the Protectorate. The *okasan* feared the brothel would be permanently closed if she was convicted of serious wrongdoing. The Protectorate's powers of suspension and/or cancellation of a licence enabled the government to make it in the interest of the *okasan* to treat their *karayuki-san* well, and for officials to carry out the regulations concerning women and the proper maintenance of the brothels, and to punish promptly any offences committed against prostitutes by keepers.

Yet the camera did not record a great deal. One is struck by the paucity of photographs of the women themselves. These prostitutes, especially the *ah ku*, and facets of their daily lives were rarely reproduced. Chinese keepers generally did not allow their women to be photographed as they might attempt to abscond on their way to and from the studio. Some women also felt that their souls could be captured by the magic of the camera and its 'shadow catcher'. Most of the photographs that exist enhance understanding of the material environment of prostitution, enabling the historian to glimpse details of the neighbourhoods in which the *ah ku* and *karayuki-san* lived. European photographers captured the monotonous exteriors of the brothels but they could not penetrate the dark humid cubicles of Malay Street, to re-create in stunning images the interior world of Singapore's most well-known brothel district.

What was the everyday life of the *ah ku* and *karayuki-san* like in the Smith and Malay Street brothels at the beginning of the twentieth century? The question can best be answered through observing the social relationships and activities of the 'family' in the neighbourhood up to late afternoon, before the carnival of the night began. For the historian of society this means

Figure 10.20 A rare photograph (c. 1914) showing a *karayuki-san* sitting in a wicker chair under the verandah of 26 Hylam Street where the louvred doors of the brothel swung open night and day for clients. It was in the brothel next door that Lance-Corporal Albert Chacksfield unsuccessfully attacked the prostitute Otoyo with a razor in 1912. (Collection of Paul Yap; courtesy of the National Archive, Singapore)

glimpsing their social life during the daytime—an angle rarely perceived. Old photographs and postcards show that silence characterised the brothel districts before midday. Thoroughfares like Malay Street, Smith Street, Tan Quee Lan Street and Trengganu Street were strikingly empty except for the odd sound of a coolie sweeping up the dirt and refuse from the previous night, when such spots were thronged and full of life.

The *ah ku* and *karayuki-san* were 'midnight people' and rarely got up before ten or eleven o'clock in the morning.[23] They infrequently appeared outside the district in the daytime; and the courtyard, foyer and reception halls of brothels were singularly empty.

What is lacking is a collection of brothel photographs taken inside the red-light districts of Singapore. There is not one of the interior of a brothel; none of an upstairs room with partitioned walls and a gilt iron-frame bed, barely lit up by a kerosene lamp; nor is there a single image of those incredible women sitting silently in the hall playing patience—pictures that would fill us with wonder about human character, contrasting different kinds of power, innocence and experience.

The few unforgettable photographs of *karayuki-san* that have survived, though, widen one's sense of what the Japanese women were like. Their pictures, which were printed on postcards and published in magazines, helped shape European stereotypes about them in Singapore. Romantic and occasionally surreal or elegiac in tone, these photographs broaden our perspective about changing times—the irrevocable rise of modern Japan and its push into the *Nanyo*, the drift of the women into overseas prostitution, and ultimately Japan's *volte-face* in 1921 against conveyor-belt sex overseas. Nearly all photographs of the *karayuki-san* in Singapore end in freeze-frames that were not casually taken by an insensitive amateur with a box camera. The women went singly or in pairs or small groups to a studio where a professional photographer snapped his image of them on a glass plate for posterity. Because there is not a great deal of personal material touching on what the *karayuki-san* of early twentieth-century Singapore were really like, an interpretive 'reading' of such photographs can be revelatory. Through the eye of the camera the historian can distinguish features in their coiffure, clothes and accoutrements. For example, subtle differences in the wearing of the kimono can be discerned, especially the manner in which the *obi*, or sash, was tied, to help clarify the origins of the women and professional distinctions between them.[24]

However, there was another kind of photograph taken of the *karayuki-san*. Chinese and European photographers, who created postcards and photographs of working people, liveried servants, and street scenes of city life, asked the *karayuki-san* living in Malay Street if they would pose in *juban* or kimono. Some accepted offers to appear on picture postcards because the publicity and money were good. It is difficult, however, to discern whether it was the harshness of their life in Singapore or the length of time required for the exposure that contributed more to the grim expression on some of their faces. Nevertheless, these reasonably polished, carefully calculated images provided a direct link for travellers and people around the world to the surface of the face of Singapore and the women of the *demimonde*. Not all strangers were interested in images of tropical palms, the burgeoning panorama of the city, lines of coolies trailing like ants from disgorging ships, or the commercial momentum and speed of material change affecting Singapore. Tourist advertisements for Singapore openly publicised sex and generally implied a certain feminine eroticism of the Japanese women. The image of Singapore as a centre of romanticism, exoticism and easy sex constituted a significant motive for travel to the city, this being the purpose of the advertising postcards of the *karayuki-san*. Many hotels and travel bureaus in the city indeed played to some degree on this 'exotic' image of the beauty of Japanese girls in traditional hairstyle, erotically clad in undergarments arranged against a pictorial screen. The flood of such cheap postcards, which were snapped up by travellers and invaded the privacy of Western homes, then made the unspeakable, the untouchable, and the inexpressibly beautiful and exotic real, but at a distance.[25] The *karayuki-san* were vividly 'visible', and they reacted favourably to this method of saturation advertising to boost their popularity. Postcards with their images were found everywhere, even in the poorest districts in Singapore. Matchboxes with drawings of their figures were also found in the Philippines.

In contrast to the *karayuki-san*, assimilation into Singapore Chinese society was a primary concern of the *ah ku*. Their everyday movements were constrained. Indeed, few photographs of these women, the majority of whom helped transform Singapore through their profession, appear to exist. Because of the nature of their work the *ah ku* remained out of sight, hidden away from the eye of the camera. In 1987, Yip Cheong Fung commented on the invisibility of the *ah ku*: 'I can't say why the Japanese women wanted to have their photographs taken. Chinese prostitutes definitely could not have their photographs taken like that as the *mamasan* would not allow it. She was afraid the woman would use the opportunity to escape.'[26]

The *karayuki-san* were migrants from another society. By the very act of working and being photographed for the public and posterity, they were asserting their discovery of new truths, while self-consciously differentiating themselves from the dominant local Chinese community. How these women

Figures 10.21 and 10.22 The *karayuki-san* never had photographs taken of places in Singapore—of the shops in the *suteretsu* or tropical landscapes—only of themselves, mostly in pairs or groups. Such photographs of the *karayuki-san* are both functional and symbolic objects that can make us gasp, grimace or smile; the black-and-white images are priceless snatches of Singapore life itself, each telling its own story. (Courtesy of the National University of Singapore Library, Rare Photograph Collection and National Museum, Singapore)

Figures 10.23 and 10.24 The image of Singapore as an 'exotic' destination constituted a significant motive for travel to the city that these 1903 postcards of the *geisha*, written by a French and a Dutch traveller, hoped to exploit. The image of the *geisha*—as lively, salacious silk-clad dolls—was supposed to be that of ladies of the evening, not ladies of the night like the *karayuki-san*. (Collections of Andrew Tan and K. C. Koh; courtesy of the National Archives, Singapore)

stayed Japanese had much to do with the enclaved nature of the *suteretsu*: the daily use of their Amakusa dialect among themselves ensured by a continuous stream of women as the sex trade grew, the desire to form bonds of quasi-kinship, and their insatiable engagement with the camera. But unlike the *ah ku*, the *karayuki-san* managed to forge a somewhat different way of life by day that drew on aspects of Japanese culture they brought with them and those they found in Singapore.

Conclusion

The current of history has been remorseless, unswervingly deaf to persuasion when it has come to finding a place for rickshaw coolies and prostitutes in Singapore's past. Their predominant presence in that past is all the more ironic as rickshaw pullers and the *karayuki-san* appeared in the background or foreground of nearly every photograph or pictorial postcard in their time, yet in a very real sense remained hidden, invisible to the naked eye but not to the camera.

These photos cannot give Singapore back what has been. But they do describe visually the role that prostitutes and rickshaw pullers played in Singapore's history, and the marginalised lives these labourers led. Old Singapore, unchanged in many respects for over eighty years, is almost gone now and can be found only in these types of photographs with their fugitive images of rickshaw coolies and Japanese prostitutes—only their images remain as an element of the past in Singapore's present.

Chapter 11

Living on the Razor's Edge: The Rickshawmen of Singapore between Two Wars, 1919–39[1]

This chapter reconstructs the world of the rickshaw pullers of Singapore in the period from 1918 to 1939,[2] examines the nature of their interaction and experience with the city, and the causes and effects of colonial policy and practice on their working and personal lives. There has been increasing recognition of the need to focus research on the urban workplace, labour and the everyday problems of the coolie class under colonial rule in Southeast Asia. Such efforts, if they are to be meaningful, must be posed, theoretically and empirically, against a background of real life. This approach raises grave historiographical problems because historians, like anthropologists, have tended 'to graze in the fields',[3] focusing their primary attention on rural societies of Southeast Asia. Considerable work has been done on peasant-based movements and opposition to colonial rule, but hardly any historical research has been conducted on the urban labouring class, of which the rickshaw coolies of Singapore formed a part.

The tidewater colonial capitals of the nineteenth and twentieth centuries created new modes of human experience for immigrant Asians, but especially for *singkeh*, the Chinese newcomers to Singapore.[4] At the end of the nineteenth century, Singapore rapidly developed as a commercial centre and an entrepôt port dominated by import and export firms and banks, and serviced Britain's imperial expansion and trade-oriented economy in Southeast Asia. This development had a profound impact upon every aspect of economic and social relationships, but it was most marked in the labour nexus, in the segregation and extreme overcrowding of the lower-class Chinese who, as rickshaw pullers, coal coolies and stevedores provided the sinews of empire and helped to shape the expansion of Singapore.

Linked to the structural changes in Singapore's economy was the social impact of mass migration on colonial Singapore, especially on work, behaviour, values and feelings of the Chinese labourers. There was an increasing disparity between the ever-burgeoning Chinese population and the city's ability to deal with growth and change. Singapore's administrators consistently chose alternatives that minimised planning costs, but created social conditions that inevitably forced rickshawmen over the poverty line. Despite these problems, Singapore, especially at the peak of its growth around 1900, often seemed a place of hope and betterment compared to the countryside of China and the treaty ports.

In order to understand the impact of colonial policy and practice in the lives of the rickshaw coolies, it is important to describe and analyse the key social relationships within the Chinese community between puller and owner, and between the rickshawmen and the Europeans who were administrators, magistrates and coroners. The study of British policies and attitudes with respect to rickshaw coolies will enable us not only to penetrate the myth of the foulness of the rickshaw quarters, of the pullers' supposed propensity to vice and criminality, but also to understand how and why this myth was perpetuated.

The sources for this slice of Singapore history—the life and struggle of the rickshawmen in the inter-war years and the circumstances surrounding their origins and demise—are mainly official reports and documents, contemporary social description, contemporary statistical analyses, photographs and oral history—'tales heard by the eyes'. In these sources an astonishing range of facts exist on all the factors at work in Chinese coolie society, encompassing not only the relative size of the population and the birth, marriage and death rates, but also statistics on accidental and violent deaths and suicide; figures for morbidity and mortality from circulatory, respiratory and sexually transmitted diseases; surveys by colonial social investigators on the nature of urban housing, on migration and the colonial economy; and several studies of changes in the economy, amount and consumption of opium.

On leaving China

The rapid increase in the 1880s and 1890s in the number of immigrating Chinese workers was the single most important demographic and social development in Singapore's history. Between 1880 and 1940, during the colonial period, millions left the two adjacent provinces of Fukien and Kwangtung in south-eastern China by sea, bound for the *Nanyang*. These men, mostly under indenture, sailed from Swatow, Amoy and Hong Kong to Singapore. Hong Kong was the starting point of the scheduled sailings of the passenger steamers and sailing vessels of firms like Syme Muir and Co. and Jardine and Matheson and Co., and the principal port of call for competing German, Danish and Dutch sailing lines. There were also junks going to the *Nanyang*, from harbours small and large all along the China coast.[5]

Many of these peasants were driven out by periodic poor harvests, flood-caused famines in all parts of South China and by the rising price of rice.[6] They were also forced out by local conditions of overpopulation and the policies of landlords. For many, survival meant escape from the impoverished domestic economy. Understandably, a multitude of *singkeh* left Fukien and Kwangtung in search of better prospects. They were indigent, barely knowing the written characters of their own language, but they carried with them the compass of culture, a will and a burning ambition. Their dream was one of hard work, a decent livelihood, and a return in some comfort to home and hearth in China.

The immigration of *singkeh* stamped an indelible image on Singapore. It was a coolie town, with a heterogeneous Chinese workforce, a disproportionate ratio of male to female, and an abnormal age structure. At the turn of the century Chinese males constituted over 72 per cent of the total population. Most of these men were either single or had left their wives and children behind. Alone, indebted, jobless on arrival, they accounted for almost all the able-bodied men of the working population. They were aged between fifteen and fifty-nine. There were few women (except for prostitutes), children, or old men among the Singapore Chinese in this period. A far more noticeable feature of this population in the early part of the century was the rate of return to China. *Singkeh* had come to do manual labour, to build, but not to stay. In the late 1890s only about 10 per cent of the Singapore Chinese were locally born. The average length of time spent in the city by those who immigrated was about seven years. Later, conditions were more favourable when compared to those in China, especially in the 1920s, and an increasing number of this immigrant transient community would settle in Singapore.

After arrival in Singapore, the newcomers joined forces within regionally based ethnic and sub-ethnic groups to carve out an economic niche for themselves. Initially, secret societies and later on speech groups sought to protect the occupational monopolies of particular sub-ethnic groups in various trades and occupations, such as the Hengwah, Hockchia and Foochow in rickshaw pulling. The role that the secret societies and voluntary associations played in economic and social relations among Singapore's rickshawmen was absolutely crucial. Their primary function was to provide financial assistance, social welfare and security for their members. As far as Singapore was concerned, solidarity among rickshaw pullers was forged on the anvil of the society they knew in China. Native place particularism and a network of voluntary associations helped to attract overseas sojourners into Singapore where, through their associations, they maintained special ties with the homeland as kinsmen and clansmen, and pursued special occupational interests like rickshaw pulling.[7]

The rickshaw was invented in Japan in 1869.[8] Originally called *jinrickshaw* from the characters meaning man-powered carriage, the '*jin*' was dropped from the term at the turn of the century and 'rickshaw' came into general use. The rickshaw became a modern form of transport throughout Asia in the late nineteenth and early twentieth centuries. The rickshaw combined new technology—superior Western-styled wheels—with cheap, seemingly indefatigable Asian labour. The two-wheeled wooden carriage was unquestionably an improvement over the Chinese-invented wheelbarrow, the sedan chair and animal-drawn vehicles. It is, after all, easier to pull a passenger along at a rapid pace than to carry or push them over a distance. Rickshaws, which required only one man, largely superseded sedan chairs, which required the labour of at least two, except in China's mountain resorts and in hilly Hong Kong.

The rickshaw spread across Asia and became the most popular way of getting around for most Asians. It soon became a familiar sight in the streets of larger cities like Yokohama, Beijing, Shanghai, Rangoon and Calcutta. The rickshaw first made its appearance in Beijing in 1886 and twelve years later appeared on the streets for public hire.[9] It was introduced into Calcutta by members of its Chinese community for carriage of goods around 1900. They later came into use for passenger service in 1914, and 'Chinese *rickshawalas* awaiting custom at the roadside were a familiar part of the Chowringhee scene.'[10] Rickshaws also found their way to South Africa where they became part of the urban landscape in Durban for many years.

The rickshaw was tried out for public transport in Singapore in 1880. The first consignment came from Shanghai, but they were imported from Japan the following year. They proved to be an immediate success. The apparently unheralded arrival of the rickshaw marked the beginning of a noticeable change in the traffic on Singapore's streets. Within a year of its advent, over 1,000 of these two-wheeled carriages were to be found plying for hire in the streets and alleyways of the city. Rickshaws were the pride of the road at the turn of the century. By 1924 the actual number of rickshaws active was estimated at 28,800. An inexpensive and convenient mode of transport around town, it was patronised by people from all walks of life, including schoolchildren, shoppers, hawkers, prostitutes, colonial officials and the indigent.

Most rickshawmen had been peasants in Fukien and Kwangtung. The pattern of their lives in village China was shaped by mud, rice and an old system of proprietary land owning. The life of the tenant farmer was locked in an endless struggle with nature—in planting and harvesting rice, digging canals and dikes, embanking rivers—and with landlords and enemies. Hengwah and Hockchia peasants had little hope of ever owning land, not even an acre of it. The selection of rickshaw pulling was not necessarily a personal choice. The economic and political conditions in Fukien and Kwangtung provinces compelled these men to go far afield in preference to slow starvation in their homeland. Hengwah and

Hockchia kin followed one another forming a chain, pushed from behind by wretched conditions in China, and drawn ahead by the remarkable economic activity of colonial Singapore, eventually linked to jobs as rickshaw pullers.

The crisis in pay, food and lodging

Because rickshaw rides were cheap, monthly income was fairly low as well, according to the Hockchia rickshaw owner, Lee Choon.[11] The rickshaw hire was twenty cents during the day and twenty-five to thirty cents during the night, which did not leave the puller very much.[12] A rickshaw coolie could make about one dollar a day (or $24 a month) in 1924.[13] He had to buy food out of that, for which a puller spent about thirty cents a day. That left him forty to fifty cents to buy clothes, send money to China, pay the prostitute and buy opium, if he smoked. Very few pullers made more than $20 a month, however. Since the cost of living was from $12 to $14 a month, the puller could count on $6 to $8 clear to either remit or fritter away on opium, daughters of joy and gambling.

Food cost less at home, even compared to the simple inexpensive meals eaten outside. While the average per capita monthly food expenditure was somewhat higher when the rickshawmen ate out, there were many who were loth to take the time to bargain in the market and cook at home, as the time and money saved in being the cook had to be balanced against time lost in real wages from pulling the rickshaw. Approximately 25–40 per cent of the puller's daily income was spent on food. Because the rickshawmen often earned irregular incomes they tended to live on a day-to-day basis. Thus they were forced to buy foodstuffs daily in small quantities from fresh food hawkers who lived close by. Their low incomes forced pullers to purchase primarily rice and vegetables. Naturally, for many, except the really poor among them, it made sense to pay a little extra to eat a meal with a bit of meat or fish at a stall on a regular basis where hawkers could also extend credit to their regular customers. It was difficult enough to work so hard, but to go hungry on top of that was a reality of life for rickshawmen in Singapore by the 1920s. A few cents really counted at the turn of the century. At that time a puller could eat well and still pay his rickshaw hire.

> A cup of coffee with milk was three cents in a coffee shop and two cents from a hawker...On the five footway, satay twice the size of that sold today and better in quality sold at two cents a stick; Kui-teow cost three cents for a large plateful. A big cupful of Hokkien mee, sufficient to satisfy one for a day, cost ten cents.[14]

However, by 1918, the wages of rickshawmen had fallen at least 20 per cent behind the increased cost of living. This was particularly noticeable with regard to the pattern of purchasing and consumption of food. The increase in the cost of the food, mostly condiments (soy sauce, sesame oil, vinegar) or preserved food from China was enormous. Salted cabbage, for instance, which was one of the main vegetables, increased from fifty cents to nearly three dollars per kilo. As a consequence of falling wages, rising prices for basic necessities and acceptance of lower nutritional levels, many of the pullers classified as offenders for being 'physically weak', 'decrepit', or 'ragged and dirty' were, in fact, suffering from malnutrition—a malnutrition that was virtually nonexistent among pullers two decades earlier. It was for these really poor men who found it difficult to muster the strength day after day to earn enough to get a reasonable meal that some wealthy '*Babas*' used to place pots of weak tea at the edge of the five footway in front of their houses.

> Two bowls, one filled with water and the other containing empty Chinese teacups, gave the weary rickshaw pullers…the opportunity of refreshing themselves with a drink whenever they walked past the homes of those Babas. The bowl of water was for them to wash the cups after they had their drink. This gesture of offering relief to hardship suffered by the less fortunate stemmed from the advice given to the *Babas* by priests, in whom they had great faith.[15]

Food became more expensive and difficult to obtain by the 1920s, as did housing. Singapore, with its free port status, was presented as a model of administrative and economic success for other colonial powers and the rest of the region; yet the vast majority of its Chinese inhabitants, including the rickshaw pullers, lived in dire poverty. The large common lodging houses used by the pullers ought to have been called 'Dickensian'. Upward of 30,000 rickshawmen lived in lodgings during the 1920s, most of which had neither running water nor toilets nor bathrooms. According to official municipal figures, each Chinese-Singapore resident had only a tiny amount of living space. The area of some cage-like cubicles or rooms was as little as 5.5 square metres per man. Some rickshawmen slept on the five footway or in the alleyway at the back, preferring that to soaring rents and the grimness of what was intended to be the basic accommodation for their kind. Sometimes when space was at a premium, men slept three ways in a room—on the wooden tiers, on the floor and on cots—or even, for the poorest, on the same bed with another puller. In Beijing in the 1920s, rickshaw firms accommodated on average 10.5 men for each room, although one case was found where sixteen men were living together.[16] By 1921, living space in Singapore was at such a premium that sixteen men living in one room was common.

A principal cause of the shortage of housing by 1918 was the proliferation of cubicles in most public lodging houses in Chinatown, and elsewhere. Property owners found it more profitable to subdivide their tenements rather than construct new housing. Large houses were subdivided into a honeycomb of temporary single rooms, or cubicles without separate kitchens and a common living area. This resulted in the worst sort of overcrowding imaginable. Because of the demand, a poor rickshawman could not afford to pay more than a share of the rent of a lodging house cubicle. Some rickshawmen did not even have a share of a cubicle; they occupied 'bunk space' in the narrow corridors of the lodging houses. Some ended up occupying these 'spaces' for years.

The difference in the amount of rent rickshawmen paid before World War I and after was dramatic. The effect of changes between 1919 and 1921 in the use of buildings from residential to shophouse and godown (warehouse) was to concentrate more and more men in less space. Thus for the years 1908, 1918 and 1921, a house in China Street had twenty, forty-two and sixty-five tenants; and another in Macao Street had twenty, twenty-seven and forty-nine respectively. Between 1908 and 1918 the rent increased by 40 per cent, while in 1923 it was 135 per cent higher than 1908.[17] It was a plain fact throughout the 1920s and 1930s that there was not enough lodging to house the number of rickshaw pullers. The supply of housing did not nearly approach the demand in the inter-war years, and thus there was no way to reduce the landlord's ability to force the men to pay exorbitant rents. Neither the private sector nor the colonial government was prepared to shoulder the expense of increased residential construction to ease the situation for the rickshaw pullers. The immensity of the problem and the cost were all too apparent to the colonial government: it simply said no. In the 1930s the government studiously ignored the housing problem and the vexed question of inordinate rents. This urban overcrowding of Singapore was largely a British failure.

By 1908, rickshaw coolies were already paying twice as much to rent a first-class rickshaw as a second-class one. Thereafter the first-class half-day rent was to remain higher than the second-class whole-day rent. By 1919 the daily takings of the pullers were estimated to be not less than 20,000 Straits dollars.[18] The rental system made owners rich and pullers hard-driven, exploited and poor. As long as the ownership of rickshaws was concentrated in the hands of small capitalists there was no means for the puller to increase earnings, to save, or to purchase a rickshaw, except to run harder and longer. Pulling like that could kill.

The prosperity of Singapore resulted from high trade levels in the marketing and distributing of primary products like sugar, copra, rubber and tin. It was a cruel irony for the puller that prosperity gave rise to the bad years with problems of acute overcrowding in the inner city, soaring rents, rice shortages and falling fares. In 1919, Singapore was entering a period of sustained prosperity based on soaring trade levels in primary products. Singapore was fast becoming a major centre for trade in primary products, but it was strapped for warehouse space. Something had to give. The boarding houses for pullers were rapidly stripped and turned into godowns for bulk storage of rice, copra and sugar. Not only were owners demanding more for hiring out rickshaws, but housing rents were also rising, even while pullers were being evicted from their lodgings near the waterfront.

Putting down the shafts

The Hengwah men of Tanjong Pagar were the first to put down the shafts. They were considered by the British to be the most truculent group among the pullers. They lived in one of the most dangerous districts, an area where their tenement houses were being confiscated in the interests of the commercial growth of Singapore.[19] The Hengwah men confronted City Hall demanding that the municipal commissioners double the rickshaw fares. But before the sanction of the commissioners for increased fares could be obtained, notices were posted on the walls of various rickshaw depots in Rochore Road, Muar Road, Victoria Street and Bain Street calling for a strike and a fare of fifteen cents per mile.

> Notice to inform our relatives and others that as things are getting dearer day by day and we the rikisha pullers find it very difficult to cope with the present high cost of living. The pullers of Kampong Glam and town sections have held a meeting and are now able to state that the fares from the 14 February 1920 would be raised to fifteen cents per mile. On the 13th instant pullers of both Kampong Glam and town are not to ply for hire. In conclusion we appeal for unity.[20]

The rickshawmen wanted immediate action on the matter of raising the fare, but the municipal commissioners, caught somewhat off guard by the radical nature of the demand, were not prepared to sit in conclave on such short notice to consider doubling the rates. They wanted at least a day to deliberate, and to have the last say on the matter. The psychology of the moment demanded time, for the sake of prestige. Their procrastination was a mistake. The lightning strike began on 13 February, with notices ordering the pullers not to ply for hire. For three days the majority of the public was inconvenienced by heavy downpours which held people up for work and dispelled the argument of some municipal officials that 'walking was always conducive to health'.[21]

Striking pullers stopped other pullers from plying for hire, especially on main thoroughfares and in the rickshaw districts themselves. Quite a number of cases of assault were reported in the Rochore section alone, which the strikers had sealed off. There were not more than 100 hire rickshaws operating in the Rochore, Kampong Kapor and Tanjong Pagar neighbourhoods, pulled only by desperate needier men, mostly opium smokers.[22] Another notice was posted the following day in the various depots, calling for rickshawmen to stand firm, to unite and to continue the strike:

> This is to notify one and all that the reason we did not go out for hire yesterday (Friday) was due to the Municipality not raising the rikisha fares. Those pullers who are not ashamed of themselves and go out to hire today (Saturday) will be assaulted and their rikishas damaged. We would not care, what nationality their passengers are. We ask our people not to create any disturbance, but to wait and not go out for hire till the fares are raised and lastly we plead for unity.[23]

Once again streets like Rochore Road, Victoria Street and Bencoolen Street came under police guard in case of threat, intimidation and violence to the public by the striking pullers. With the exception of privately owned rickshaws and pullers who received a monthly wage, the rickshawmen had been enjoined to keep off the roads and they did. Singapore's streets looked strangely empty without them.

> The roads were noticeable yesterday for the dearth of rikishas upon which so many depend for bringing them to work and which enable others to carry out their daily round of duties in town. Although there was the usual number of motor cars about, yet the streets did not wear their wanted busy aspect, as when the two-wheeled, man-drawn conveyance plied about for hire or carried passengers, the men between the shafts racing with one another and shouting to people to get out of the way. One also missed the long queues in Raffles Place, outside Johnston's Pier, and round the fountain in Raffles Square,

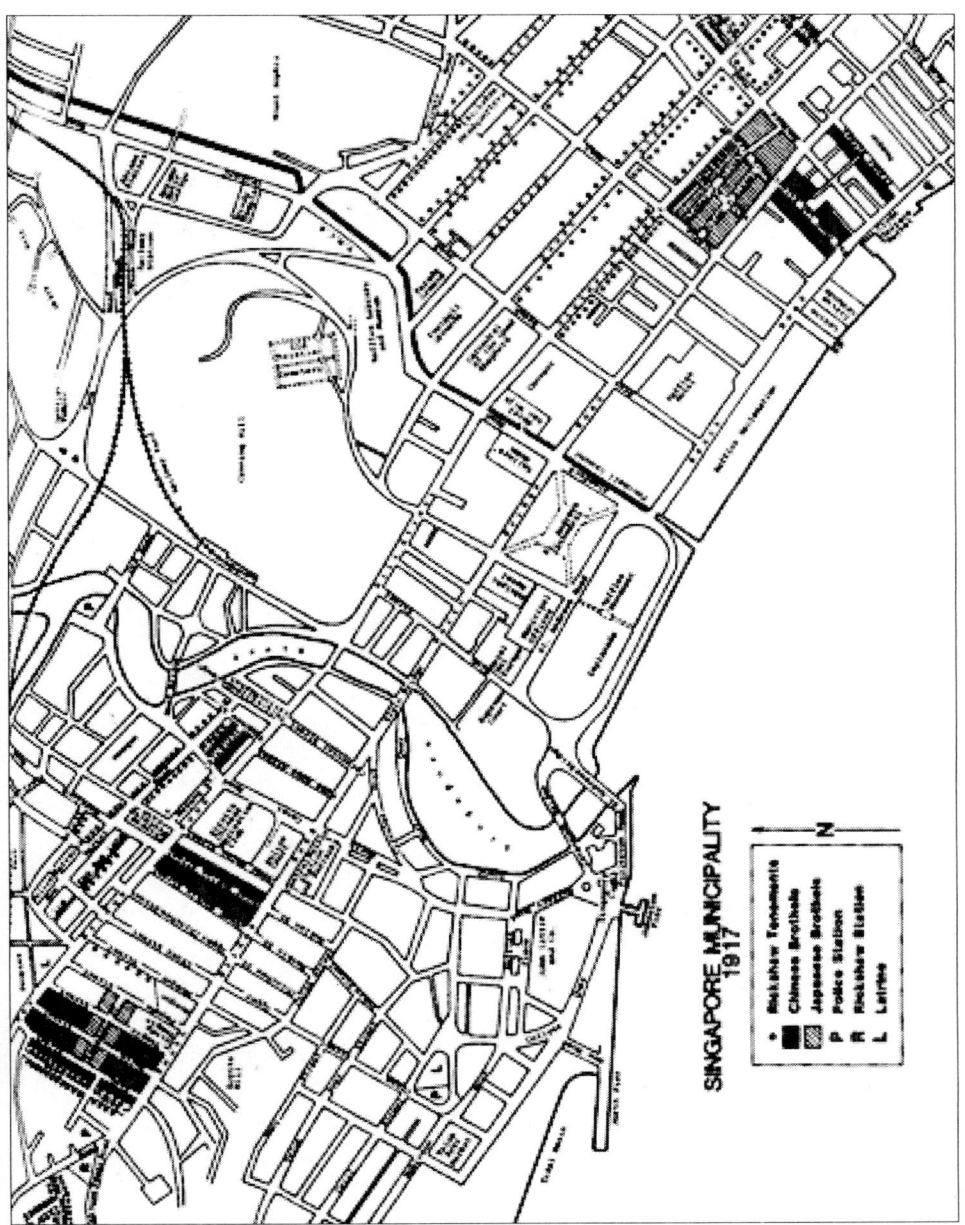

Map 11.1   Singapore municipality

and was led to think that it was either a Sunday, or some holiday but that the offices were open. The news of the men coming out [striking] was in the air the previous evening but not so widespread as to warn people to get away early the next morning in order to foot it and be in at business time.[24]

Public feeling was particularly hostile towards the pullers for striking on the very same day that their demand had been put to the commissioners.[25] There had been no period of grace—no time to arbitrate properly, all sense of decorum was lost, and the commissioners could not possibly avoid looking foolish. The pullers lightning-like action alienated what little public support there had been in favour of raising the rate before the strike. An angry commercial community recognised, much to its chagrin, that Singapore did not run an efficient tram service through all the principal parts of the town so people could go about their business. Instead, Singapore was dependent on the rickshawmen.

The question of increasing the fares was brought up at the commissioners' meeting on the afternoon of 13 February, and it was decided to allow an increase from five to seven cents for every half mile, but the commissioners insisted on the pullers' unconditional return to work, after which the terms would be announced.[26] By recommending an increase in the fare for the mile from ten to fourteen cents the pullers' demand had been practically met, and the status-conscious commissioners, who could not afford to be laughed at, refused to inform the public of the exact nature of their decision straightaway. The strike continued, much to the dismay of the public. The commissioners refused to convey the impression that they had yielded to the terms as a result of the strike, fearing pullers would take advantage of the precedent in the future whenever they felt the need for more pay.

Outside the chambers of the municipal building, Mr Hooper, the Registrar of Rickshaws, was at pains to counter a general view of the rickshaw puller as poverty stricken and an object of humanitarian pity. He gave some hypothetical figures on the earnings of men who had regular work at night pulling rickshaws in the brothel quarters to 'open the eyes of those who talk ignorantly'.[27] But there was ample evidence in current reports and boards of inquiry that a puller's monthly earnings were significantly lower and progressively declining in real terms, despite gross takings at the rate of $1.50 to $2.00 per day. The strike bore testimony to that harsh fact—a dwindling income and standard of living. It was left up to Mr Hooper (who had more experience than anybody else with pullers' protests and demonstrations) and several prominent owners to deliver the terms and obtain a return to work. Then, and only then, could the lines of the commissioners' recommendations be announced. The 'government's' position was explained to the strikers by him and the numbers of rickshaws gradually increased on the roads over the course of the next couple of days as the pullers began to sense the reality of the situation. Within a week the last few pullers who held out—not surprisingly, coming from the dock area where the strike had first begun—had again taken to the shafts. The deadlock had been completely broken. The rickshaw strike was over.[28] The pullers had won, but the clear-cut settlement had to be presented without humiliation. The tacit recommendation of the commissioners for increased fares was approved by the Governor in Council on 3 March.[29]

The strike of 1920 had revealed to the authorities that the pullers, who had been well organised, knew the value of the strike weapon and were prepared to use it on a moment's notice. Pullers united into a powerful force had wielded it successfully on this occasion against the city fathers. Coming together from all parts of the city, speaking different dialects and originating from different parts of Kwangtung and Fukien provinces, but all sharing a common purpose, the pullers acted to change their overcrowded, unhygienic, destitute condition under colonial rule. To be unafraid of striking against British authority and the *towkays* was an explicit political act. It was a powerful message. And it was to be adopted on a far-wider scale by rickshawmen in the Depression-ridden 1930s in Singapore to combat colonial authority and rent capital in an effort to save themselves.

Marriage and the elemental family

In the 1890s, peasants facing poverty and deprivation in China could not keep their growing families fed. Among the rickshawmen in Singapore, many had decided to migrate temporarily from counties near Foochow.[30] By the mid-1920s they had begun to put down roots for future generations. The tendency to establish elemental families[31] and settle permanently in Singapore came about because large numbers of single Chinese women started to flood into the city from war-torn China and because the British began to adopt a more relaxed attitude towards female immigration. A gradual but perceptible change in the nature of the rickshawmen's society began to take place with the coming of more women. Fate in the form of wives represented a break with the sojourning past, with China, and what remained of 'village China' in Victoria Street, Queen Street and other like neighbourhoods. For some men of this generation there was no longer any reason to go back to their village, despite improved means of transportation. But there was also a more immediate, deeper and even more profound break with village ties and clansmen in the local rickshaw houses:

a married couple could not live in the *pangkeng* of a rickshaw house; force of circumstance and privacy required them to find a cubicle elsewhere. A different pattern of living arrangement went along with being married that increased physical and social isolation. Cubicle living forced couples to be more highly individualised and privatised in their dealings with other tenants along a corridor.

In these low-status families, interpersonal relationships were of a different sort than in the traditional extended family. The structure of these new families with their elemental ties was characterised by a striking lack of convention and by 'poverty and powerlessness'.[32] A rickshawman, as a father, was not a strong patriarch because he had few if any resources at his disposal. He could not hope to have more than one son grow to manhood, yet there was no way he could make his grown son stay with him as in China. Brothers who married had to stand by their families and could not readily lend support to one another in the face of crushing poverty and hard work. The demography and economy of rickshaw families insured that they remained elemental in structure and organisation, small scale in size, of low status, therefore weak.

The attitude of married rickshawmen and their spouses towards birth control and family size was of crucial importance to their way of life. Rickshaw pullers and their wives faced economic crisis in the Depression, were themselves victims isolated in private cubicles, and did not generally desire large families. After marriage some form of contraception was deemed socially acceptable and necessary among rickshaw couples. Tragically, a rickshaw household rich in children was a household ruined, for the father could not possibly hope to feed all of them and bring them up. The small number of children in the families of rickshaw pullers was also the result of the high rate of mortality among infants and pre-school age children. Living in the cubicles of the tenement houses of Chinatown had a terrible effect on newly born Chinese children. Tragedy's alien face was a weary young rickshaw mother. Many of them were malnourished and cubicle-bound from morning to night, especially if they already had one young child at the breast. Early marriage and early death of children were very much part of Sim Kwee Geok's life. She married in Singapore when she was twenty and lived with her husband up to her death, at which time she was six months pregnant. She had been pregnant the year before too, but her newborn child only lived a few days.[33] Children like Sim Kwee Geok's suffered sometimes for weeks in the dark, cramped, oven-like cubicles, and the horror of malnutrition and infection were a brutal reality for most of them. Chinese infant mortality was well above a level that was considered normal for Singapore in the inter-war years. The cause of death of newborn Chinese children was usually linked to some form of gastrointestinal disease or beri-beri.[34]

In the elemental family the wife was apt to possess more strength of character as an individual than she might in the joint-extended family, because relations were limited to husbands and wives and on occasion wives and mothers. She was the matriarch and had sole responsibility for the activities and concerns of the family—that is, coordinating the domestic economy, housekeeping and child-rearing. But these women, who were married to pullers during the 1920s, were cut off economically and legally from their own families. Once married a woman's interests were bound up entirely with her husband and his people. The working out of social ties within the elemental family often meant that a wife's sole source of security and hope for a future was her husband. Brides from China rarely lived out their lives among kin, except when their brothers or fathers were rickshaw pullers. It was a lonely way to spend a lifetime, isolated from most other members of the husband's household also living in China, and trapped in a cubicle with a young family to rear.

Since rickshaw pullers were among the lowest paid workers in Singapore, frequently women worked until they had children. From the Coroner's Records it is obvious too that their desire to work grew as their marriages were placed under increasing pressure during the Depression. Wives of rickshaw pullers faced a basic contradiction in Singapore at that time: their position was central to the social and economic survival of the family unit, but they could not fulfil the social role of wife and mother and the economic role of worker at one and the same time within the framework of the elemental family. Rickshaw family units began to crumble under the strain because the woman's role as wife and mother had to be fulfilled at the expense of working to help meet the consumption needs of the family. Children meant an increase in the necessary labour within the home and an increase in household expenditure. The cost of living continued to climb while the families' existing income was at the mercy of currency fluctuations, and future capacity to earn waned.

Rickshawmen who were married constituted a small percentage of the total and lived in coolie lodging houses with far from homogeneous populations. Under such circumstances, payment of rent was more difficult, as families could not crowd into cramped dormitory quarters in the big compound houses, nor sleep in shifts, to reduce rent. The lives of the rickshawmen and their families were bounded by the cubicles they lived in. In one spartan cubicle:

> dark, confined, unsanitary, and without comfort may live a family of seven or more persons. Many of them sleep on the floor, often under the bed. Their

> possessions are in boxes, placed on shelves to leave the floor free for sleeping. Their food, including the remains of their last meal, is kept in tiny cupboards, which hang from the rafters. Their clothes hang on walls, or from racks.[35]

There were no windows and no means of light in many of the cubicles. The lodging houses were densely packed, the heat and humidity almost unbearable at times, and visibility was rarely more than a few steps along the narrow passage. Within this cell-like atmosphere, rickshawmen and their families struggled to bring some sense of quality to their lives and make their cubicle surroundings more tolerable. There was a simple poignancy about the potted flowers and herbs with which they decorated the window ledges and doors of those miserable lodging houses.

The rickshawmen's elemental family tended to break down in the face of the nightmare attempt to scrape a living in the Singapore streets. Witness the death of Sim Kwee Geok, the thirty-five-year-old wife of rickshawman Lim Jin San. After quarrelling with her husband over financial matters, and depressed by the recent death of her infant child, she drank a quantity of liquid caustic soda while six months pregnant.[36]

Lack of cash to meet the total monthly expenses of families (even with the earnings of a wife), short of borrowing from friends or pawnshops, led to breakdown of marriage and family life—ultimately to despair and death. In the cases revealed in the Coroner's Records the collapse of the elemental family reached unquestionable intensity. In them husbands and wives share their grief, dreams and nightmares, and allow the historian of society to weave a tapestry of the agony of the underside of Singapore in the 1920s and early 1930s. These are the voices of the dead, recounting the details of problems that were tearing their families apart. Rickshaw pullers were very poor indeed, between 1918 and 1921. Men were working for next to nothing, everything they needed—food, lodging, rickshaws— was too expensive and in short supply, everything, that is, except eligible illiterate women from China to marry. It was not an era in which a rickshawman could realistically expect to provide a woman with a proper home and family; yet, at the very same time, events in China had initiated a period of unprecedented female immigration to the *Nanyang* and Singapore that was not to end until World War II. One puller knew that marriage could finish rickshawmen, and he painted a dismal picture of the condition of married pullers at the end of 1920.

> But how could he take care of a family when he depended on pulling a rickshaw for his living? He knew about his long-suffering brothers in the mixed courtyards. The men pulled rickshaws, the women sewed, the children

scavenged...They gnawed on watermelon rinds dug out of garbage heaps... and they all went to get handouts of rice gruel.[37]

Poverty unleashed the violent demons of domestic discord. Marriages stretched thin and died in disputes over family expenses and actual expenditures. Lee Ah Toh, a Hengwah rickshaw puller, heard his sister arguing with her husband about some money. He lived in the same building in an upstairs cubicle, occupying a small cubicle at the rear of the first floor with his sister, brother-in-law and eleven-year-old son. Lee Ah Toh remonstrated with her and the matter was settled. He did not realise that his taking his brother-in-law's part against his sister would have fatal consequences. Her husband, Tan Moon Heng, then went out with his brother-in-law to a tea shop opposite the lodging house. By the time they came back three hours later Ler Cho Wing had hanged herself over twenty cents, having become very depressed and concerned about the consequences of her husband's spendthrift behaviour. Obviously, the death is attributable to their poverty. Tan Moon Heng described the sequence of events leading to his wife's suicide.

> On the 10th July 1935 at 5 pm I returned home after pulling my rickshaw for two hours. I went to our room. My wife was there. I found she had been paid one dollar, being repayment of a loan to someone. I took twenty cents of this one dollar and bought a durian...My wife scolded me for taking the money and threatened to throw the rest away. I went out again to a nearby teashop with my brother-in-law. I returned home again after 8 pm...that evening she accused me of spending money too freely.[38]

In a similar case, Gian Yeow Sun's husband refused to allow her to work as a hawker and she became upset about it. Her husband was concerned that she would be arrested for hawking without a licence. She stopped selling cakes about a week before her death.

> We did not quarrel about it. I am in regular employment myself. I do not know of any other reason [apart from wanting to be hawker] why my wife should commit suicide. I gave her all my earnings. She enjoyed good health and behaved normally. She did not threaten to take her own life. She was quite happy and joked with me on the night before her death.[39]

Of the thirty-one cases of suicide among rickshaw coolies known to us from the Coroner's inquests, twenty-six occurred between 1921 and 1939. All six recorded cases of suicide of wives of rickshaw pullers took place in the desperate years between 1929 and 1935.[40] They reveal the broken and heretofore forgotten lives of pullers and their families in close fearful touch with a world depression. The same problems that were responsible for increased poverty and the collapse of low-status families by strangling the puller's traditional sources of income also led to suicide. The difficulties of poor wives were acute in a society where women were considered generally to be little better than 'pieces of meat put on the table for men to slice'. Inequality in the family combined with the wretched existence of living in a tenement cubicle with several small children and where all were likely to suffer serious illnesses drove women to commit suicide. Their acts must be interpreted as an outcry against the cruelties of Singapore life in the late 1920s and 1930s.

Suicide was an indication of the grave social effect of the economic blight of the 1920s and 1930s on rickshawmen and their families, but the immediate cause of suicide among rickshawmen in the recession-depression times was loss of work. Rickshawmen, especially middle-aged ones in the thirty-five to forty age-bracket, had a strong identification with their vocation and way of life. If they lost their job through illness, or through violent injury or accident, they frequently suffered a loss of personal esteem, felt they were failures in the minds of their kindred, and had nothing to live for. About half the suicides in the Coroner's inquests were men aged between thirty-five and forty-five years of age, and they were overwhelmingly single. The decision to kill themselves seems to have been preceded by just that loss of personal self-esteem and of self-identity. The rise in suicide among men over forty was exceptionally sharp, and definitely higher than in most other coolie occupations. As rickshawmen became older the chances of killing themselves increased. They realised that there was now no possibility of ever owning a rickshaw, and thus they were sliding downhill in a narrowing circle of poverty and debt, waiting for the end. They kept on hiring rickshaws because it brought them more money than hawking or pig-rearing, but inside they knew the dream of their youth was dying, as so would they shortly.

Although the rickshaw was central to the work and life of Hengwah, Hockchia and Hockchew immigrants, and ownership of one was their ray of hope, the investment required to become an owner remained beyond the means of most of the men. The market value of the Japanese-made rickshaw rose from $38 at the end of the nineteenth century to $90 in 1917. In that same year the cost of new vehicles jumped from $90 to $160 for first class and from $45 to $75 for second class.[41] The dramatic price rise was principally due to the war and high freight rates prevailing, but the price never came down again to prewar levels. By 1921 the cost of new Japanese rickshaws had risen to $180 and in consequence rickshaws were being made locally but, as was the case in the past, these proved inferior to those imported.[42] Often after a lifetime of trying to save money to buy their own vehicle, pullers still did not have enough capital to settle their daily living expenses and debts, let alone purchase even a second-hand rickshaw.

In order not to mortgage their dreams and land in debt, bachelors accepted a low standard of living and depended upon kin and clansmen. They shared rental rooms in filthy, overcrowded tenements or 'rickshaw houses' from landlords who, in many instances, were primarily rickshaw owners besides being proprietors of coolie lodges. By the late 1920s the hard facts on wages and living conditions were grim—food and rent for the rickshaw accounted for almost three-quarters of all that the poorest pullers spent daily, and food meant mostly rice and vegetables. As income continued to decline during the 1930s, so pullers ate less, and they ate worse, living on credit. Health worsened and debts mounted.

The abolition campaign

By the 1920s, the British felt that the rickshaw was a challenge to their development policy and to the showcase image of Singapore as a 'modern city'. The demand for rickshaw transport throughout the inter-war years continued, nevertheless, as did the harsh social conditions for the pullers. The British refused to encourage the trade, at times ignoring it, and then opposing it with a vengeance at the height of the Depression. In the decade the rickshaw first appeared, traffic was made up of bullock carts, gharries and steam trams, but by the early 1930s street traffic was thoroughly mechanical, faster, more congested and obviously more dangerous. There were no gharries left and a bullock cart was a rare sight. Omnibuses and trolley buses replaced electric trams in the main part of the city, and swiftly moving motor vehicles, automobiles and lorries had spread rapidly. There were still plenty of rickshaws but the downward trend had begun. Rickshaws were now considered to be a public 'nuisance' and a 'traffic hazard', and were gradually being excluded from the streets. By the mid-1920s officials believed that rickshaws were an uneconomical, slow and hazardous mode of conveyance, and that they would ultimately have to go to improve the flow of public transport. From this time on the city's roads were restricted to motorised transport. The official argument was that rickshaws were slow moving and snarled the flow of other vehicles.

For the rickshaw pullers the reductions over the next five years meant unemployment, reduced incomes, or being forced to return to the rural poverty and unrest of south-eastern China. On several occasions government officials had publicly stated that they would prefer to remove rickshaws from Singapore streets completely. Singapore's urban expansion continued in face of the world depression. Urban planners believed that the march of progress was inexorable, that the antiquated rickshaw had to make way for modern motorised transport. The government restricted their numbers to a licence quota of 4,000 and banned their movements in certain parts of the city. Social reformers joined in urging a ban on rickshaws for humanitarian reasons, but this would remove 90 per cent of the transport used by poorer Singaporeans. The rickshaw pullers and the users—schoolchildren, invalids, the elderly and commuters for whom rickshaws were an essential service—were hurt badly.

By the late 1920s officials confidently predicted that the rickshaw was on the way out. Singapore was a trading and financial powerhouse with powerful old firms, financial institutions, thousands of little businesses and full of fast-moving vehicles. Rickshaws, symbolically, were an unpleasant reminder of constant poverty, and the straining and sweating Chinese labour behind it all. People were in a hurry, and the rickshaw no longer held a special place.

With admirable clarity the 1930s demonstrated the ways in which the growing deprivation of the rickshawmen and their families was further aggravated by the policies of a government bent on gradually abolishing rickshaws in the interests of the motorcar. The question of control and eventual abolition of rickshaws first came up in 1927 when the commissioners decided that unfit pullers and *singkeh* should be removed from the roads to prevent traffic congestion and in the interests of safety. It was hardly incidental that these men were also considered by Europeans to be eyesores on the streets. In 1928 the reduction of rickshaws by a stipulated percentage every year had begun, but not all pullers had time to seek another occupation before the full force of the slump hit Singapore.[43] By 1931 there were no opportunities except hawking for out-of-work pullers. By 1935 this weeding-out process based on automatic annual reductions had already resulted in a drop from 9,000 to 4,000 vehicles for public hire.[44] The experience of the rickshaw pullers in the inter-war years was one of confrontation with the government and rickshaw owners, one of 'temporary peace' through mediation and settlement, and then one of resistance and strikes. The cycle repeated itself several times before culminating in the coolies' display of solidarity in the strike of 1938 when the authorities and owners sought to end their way of life. The rickshaw puller's future had been threatened before by owners, government officials and planners, but now they were fighting for survival. As more rickshaws were pulled off the streets in an effort to restrict their numbers the owners raised the rental fee.

In 1938 a life-and-death struggle with the owners erupted over the rental fee and manipulation of the puller's contribution to the China Relief Fund to assist their countrymen who were then in 'deep water and scorching fire'.[45] When the wage demands of the rickshaw pullers were not met they closed ranks, demonstrating against the owners and smashing their rickshaws.

The 1938 rickshaw strike, which began on 4 October and lasted till 14 November, was the longest of its kind. Yet, despite its success, it seemed in the end only to hasten the cry for the abolition of rickshaws altogether. During the five weeks that both sides stubbornly held out, a large section of the travelling public suffered, particularly the elderly and children, who had to walk to school for a change. But Singapore was learning to do without rickshaws. The strike led to a large increase in the number of bicycles registered, which only pushed along the demise of the rickshaws.

Unlike past strikes the small community of Europeans did not appear to be very seriously affected by, or even care about, the absence of rickshaw transportation. But the question of the strike action of the rickshawmen was an altogether different matter. The Europeans on the whole did not have any sympathy or respect whatsoever for the pullers and their cause. They were just coolies, disobedient coolies, who had defied Crown law and, once again, disturbed the city's peace and prosperity. Although the pullers had organised themselves, albeit temporarily, into a Rickshawmen's Association to seek redress for owner exploitation, they were unable to draw such cases to the attention of the authorities, who refused to take the issue seriously, except in regard to the use of the strike.

The pullers had stopped work because of owner exploitation, hard times and the issue of the manipulation of the monthly donation to the China Relief Fund, and had expected the Chinese public to rally to their cause. But the mass of Chinese in Singapore remained apathetic, even hostile at times, refusing to support them openly. The government condemned the stoppage; the owners refused to sit down and negotiate a prompt settlement. The owners relied on time, once all hope of a quick resolution faded, intending to starve the pullers into submission. They were backed by the force of colonial law, for the police constantly assisted by patrolling affected areas, protecting their rickshaws, and arresting strikers. The government and owner opposition did not diminish the pullers' strength or resolution, but magnified it.

Despite a massive display of support and sacrifice from fellow pullers, the rickshawmen had little reason for optimism. Throughout the strike, arbitration by various individuals and groups had failed. The pullers lost tens of thousands of dollars, and many were reduced to hunger and destitution, and were forced to take advantage of the government offer of repatriation. Furthermore, as a result of the policies of rickshaw abolitionists, the vast majority of vehicles remained firmly in the hands of a small number of *towkays*. Finally, and perhaps most importantly, the rickshaw strike did not succeed in reaching beyond the confines of puller politics and community to touch the concerns of other Chinese coolies in a joint struggle to confront the power and prejudice of a colonial system that was overwhelming them. In the end, Singapore was saved the 'humiliation' of a general strike generated by the coolies' struggle against oppression and injustice.[46] The pullers did obtain a considerable reduction in the rates of hire for their rickshaws, but the 1938 strike did not change anything else—the owners endured.

Conclusion

The rickshaw coolies in Singapore during the inter-war years were victims of the changing structure of Singapore society. The economic growth of Singapore under colonial rule did not exist for them. For the rickshawmen in the 1920s especially, the setting was a city in decay. Singapore had one of the highest growth-death rates and some of the worst health conditions and housing of any city of comparable size in Asia. Rickshawmen and their families suffered accidents, the violence of congested areas and sudden attacks of illness while living in the slums of a coolie town in the Depression. The government measures and fines against the rickshawmen made the city richer, but the pullers' world of work pulsed with hunger, poverty, rush and death. Then, in that furious time that stood between the two wars, rickshaws and the men who pulled them were pencilled into the margins of Singapore's future. The puller's mad chase after a vision of life with hope that enabled him to endure almost anything in Singapore was halted by a deliberate policy of abolition.

Examination of the major decisions made by the colonial government of Singapore in regard to housing, water supply, waste disposal and sewerage from the 1880s through the 1930s, shows the city's rulers consistently chose alternatives that minimised costs at the expense of the coolie population. The tragedy was that these policies made the rickshawmen and their families vulnerable to disease and left the pullers with very ill kin with the only option of standing helplessly and hopelessly by. They were well aware that their medical problems were not just disease, but due to the social and physical environment of the city and the government policies that undermined their wellbeing. They felt the need to change things, but their failure to do so led some of them to lives which gave their kinsmen and clansmen anxiety. They quarrelled over rent, contracted tuberculosis or syphilis, or gambled away their savings. They cried out in anger and shame as the vision that was planted in China swept them up and spat them out, as circumstances drove them to the point of suicide.

Through the means of the rickshaw as their source of livelihood and the institution of marriage, men and women from China strove to create a better life in Singapore with families, but their future was foreclosed by colonial policy and practice and terminated in the Depression. The rickshawmen and their families in the inter-war years could hardly take satisfaction for their individual efforts and sufferings in the glory of Singapore's future. They were consumed by trying to earn a living pulling a rickshaw in Singapore during those two decades of the great economic growth and crisis.

Chapter 12

Placing Women in Southeast Asian History: The Case of Oichi and the Study of Prostitution in Singapore Society

Women's history and social history

The broadsheet for this colloquium stressing contributions focusing on the experiences of particular individuals or groups (for example, lepers, plantation workers, prostitutes, small farmers, merchants and artisans) unmistakably sets the tone of this chapter, and which, from the standpoint of social interpretation, presumes the history of society. In the first part of this chapter, I want to discuss some problems related to researching and writing working-class women's history in Southeast Asia with particular reference to overseas Japanese prostitutes—their life and society—in Singapore in the late nineteenth and twentieth centuries. The second part of the chapter examines briefly a range of issues pertaining to prostitution and Singapore society from lower-class women's work as overseas prostitutes and position in the labour force of a colonial economy to the *karayuki-san's* role as deserted people in Japan's rural culture of the 1930s.[1] My emphasis then is on working-class women's history in the *Nanshin* (Japanese for the southern ocean, referring to Southeast Asia) and not on those cast in the roles of wealthy upper-class matriarchs, or as blue-stocking workers. This is a much neglected area of Southeast Asian history, I feel, and, notwithstanding some pioneering work, a systematic study of it will be the product of years to come.

My interest in working-class women's history is related to the development and popularity of social history. When ordinary Southeast Asian people, rather than elites, are considered to be important subjects of historical study in their own right, then it is far more likely that women will be included. The pioneering work being done in the United States and Britain in this area has considerable relevance theoretically and methodologically for historians of Southeast Asia. However, the recent ascendancy of Southeast Asian social history in itself cannot ensure that lower-class women's experiences are integrated into history, for several reasons. First, the history of working-class women's past encompasses areas that are usually perceived as the domain of political, economic and even intellectual history, rather than social history, although the current concern of the social interpretation of history with the lives of ordinary people is influencing developments in these fields. Second, it is wrong to assume that being poor has the same implications for women as for men in terms of objective structures and subjective experience, when this is not necessarily the case. Unfortunately, in Southeast Asian social history at the moment, we know precious little about placing ordinary women, ideas, events and behaviour in the precise context of an overall community at any one time, let alone their transformation over time. Historians ought to be criticised for conspicuously assuming an interpretive 'unity of interest' in the lives of ordinary Southeast Asian people in the family, working-class life, and in patterns of social mobility, migration and urban history.[2] For instance, within the experience of overseas-Chinese working-class families of rickshaw pullers in Singapore, there is an evocation of a darker and more literal version of the sojourning era, which is basic to my new interpretation of the history of that city, that seriously undermines the supposed 'unity of interest' within the family; there is new evidence of a tendency in certain instances towards considerable disagreement between husbands and wives on such matters as migration, birth control and family size, and likewise, disturbing inferences about child-rearing, the place of women in the labour force and distinct standards of living within the family that led women to commit suicide.[3] Unless gender differences are taken into account, therefore, the findings of a social history may rest upon evidence and interpretation for which the author has little or no idea of the exact universe of lower-class working women. Hence, under these circumstances, even the most eminent social historians may well continue the practice of writing ordinary women out of history by acting as 'professional magicians',[4] making women disappear before our very eyes.

Most of the respected historians of Southeast Asia in various ways in their works either ignore lower-class working women, or confine their presence in history to a very narrow sphere.[5] In the course of writing *Rickshaw Coolie*, there was recognition that ordinary women have hitherto been swept under the rug of Southeast Asian social and economic history as effectively as out of the political past. I am studying in the larger context of a trilogy on overseas Chinese labour, Chinese and Japanese women, prostitutes, as wage earners and migrants, and I am also seeking to explain why women's sexuality in the servicing of labour power in the economy of colonial Singapore, and in the reproduction of labour power in the home in China and Japan, has remained invisible.

Women's history has received increasing notoriety in the last few years as a new field of historical study. It has institutionalised itself and can lay claim to organisations, methodologies and a system of publications. The emergence of women's history as a recognised field of inquiry in the context of Southeast Asian history reflects certain trends and developments in the discipline itself; it is clear that our generation of historians' re-creation of the past insists that women's history is not simply an appendage of social history, and that information on lower-class women cannot simply be thrust into the great lacunae left in the male account of ordinary everyday life of the Southeast Asian past.

In search of a methodology

Historians like Gerda Lerner have fought continuously against formal recognition of the impression that ordinary women the world over have not had a significant past,[6] a reality and subject not worth recording. Historians of Southeast Asia are starting to become aware of the problem and necessity to view the past through women's eyes too. To raise questions about the values and attitudes that historians have often brought to their interpretation of the Southeast Asian past unmistakably tells us about the methods by which that history has been studied, and consequently written. Gerda Lerner, Renate Bridenthal and Joan Kelly-Gadol have provided an illuminating set of insights about historians' conceptual tools invested with power to exclude women, being geared towards revealing more about male experience rather than human experience.[7] Lerner raised a key issue that will confront all Southeast Asian historians in the coming decade, 'What would history be like if it were seen through the eyes of women and ordered by the values they define?'

In their search for a new form of women's history these historians have emphasised methodology. Specifically, gender has been established as a category of analysis of the same order as class and race in the shaping and consideration of the past.[8] Ruthlessly exposing the thinking and technique behind the dominant conventional writing of the past, stressing the gender variable in history, these historians, in particular, are attempting to find new answers to the question 'What is history?' and new ways to do history so that the formative personal, intellectual and political experience of women's past, as well as men's past, is revealed.[9] Natalie Zemon Davis, the noted teacher and scholar of cultural and religious life in sixteenth-century France, concurs. She wrote in 1975:

> It seems to me that we should be interested in the history of both men and women, that we should not be working on only the subjected sex any more than an historian of class can focus exclusively on peasants. Our goal is to understand the significance of the sexes, of gender groups in the historical past.[10]

Almost by definition the category 'gender' challenges accepted interpretation—Lerner, Davis and other historians argue that only by objectively analysing the disparate experiences of men and women and their relationships can we make valid statements about the past, and not least, about human experience rather than male experience. For the Southeast Asian historian such a belief and application of a guideline is an attainable goal, but not without its revisionist consequences. This fundamental shift in emphasis and methodology has significant implications for Southeast Asian history as a discipline, for it necessarily entails a reassessment of accepted periodisation, subject matter and analysis. To find out what happened in Southeast Asian history to the *karayuki-san* in Singapore is not enough at the outset without trying from the very start to reverse the nature of the periodisation—to make sure of the 'why'. Obviously, we must leave the 'why' alone until after we have gathered and arranged the facts in a temporal sequence; the major turning points in time illuminating such a gender-based history could be those which affected the environment of family and home, sexuality and family structure, childbirth, the advent of notions of political patriotism, pollution and taboo, given their significance for the *karayuki-san's* lives.[11] However, this seemingly prefabricated kind of periodisation has made some of the feminist historians wince because it can lead potentially to the isolation of women's history, rather than to the need to find a basis for reform in historical study and historical writing.

Instead of a purely gender-based periodisation, Kelly-Gadol suggests 'relational periodisation'; that is, relating the history of women (i.e. *karayuki-san*/prostitutes) to that of men (rickshaw pullers/coolies). Traditional periodisation can provide a pattern and meaning for the most important structural changes taking place in the society, but what counts is the explicit analysis of the relationship between each change, each development, for its impact on women, as well as men. Rearranging the relation in this way between the *dramatis personae* and the past, means inverting our sense of what constitutes a 'history' and historical advance.[12] Lerner is even more definite on this point about writing the history of relationships between women and men. Periodisation ought to be more than a 'trick of the trade', a heuristic device, she notes, and adds cogently, that 'relational periodisation' is as much a function of class as gender.[13] Here, too, I agree with Lerner.

Second, in an effort to make historical methodology more relevant to the study of ordinary women, Southeast Asian historians must revise the categories of analysis that have evolved for studying the history of the region. In Southeast Asian historiography, knowing how things happened, why they happened and what an individual lived through has largely meant seeing man shaping his destiny. Now more than ever, when the historical categories relating to male forms of experience are so subject to question, women's historians are demanding a revision of concepts such as 'oppression'. As a category of analysis for opening up women's history, the idea of 'oppression' is severely limiting.[14] For example, the *karayuki-san* in Southeast Asia might be pitied if the concept of 'oppression' were to be used analytically, drawing our attention to the undeniable social, political and legal injustices these women experienced as 'victims' at various times and in various places. In such a history a woman like Oichi would be rendered completely passive by virtue of circumstance or chance, as if her life didn't matter at all. Oichi committed suicide at number 55 Malabar Street, Singapore, on 17 February 1906.[15] What appears to have been passive acceptance of an evil, dangerous or mad situation ending in suicide may have been a rational choice, a way to autonomy, or at least a defiant statement about survival in a distant land. The framework of oppression ignores the fact that women matter; it disregards the persisting power of women, despite the constraints imposed upon them.[16] Lerner stresses this point:

> Essentially, treating women as victims of oppression once again places them in a male-defined framework: oppressed, victimised by standards and values established by men. The true history of women is the history of their on-going functioning in this male-defined world, on their own terms.[17]

This view and method tries to see the *karayuki-san* as actors with power to affect their destiny, not simply be acted upon. It does not deny the significance of imposed constraints, but enables us, rather, to see women such as the *karayuki-san* making history, or at least struggling to cope with it, and this, to me, is the real stuff of Southeast Asian social history. Within this conceptual framework, since the public sphere was men's sphere traditionally, and public life the subject matter of history, historians of Southeast Asia must also demand a revision of such concepts as women's 'submission', 'dependence', 'work', 'power' and 'status'.[18]

The chief obstacle to the use of such categories to explore women's past is that they are potentially 'alien' to their life and experience, and can only serve to reinforce the belief that women have not mattered in history. What repeated usage of these categories really shows is that historians have not been able to break through the meshes of the wrong words and wrong questions, looking in the wrong places—a male-defined world. Women's history writing on Southeast Asia must come from inside the framework of experience of the women, showing what they have gone through (as overseas prostitutes in this case in the ports of Southeast Asia), exploring their consciousness and lifestyle, seeing how this would determine their attitude towards life, work and death— their destiny: in other words, to have a head start; to begin with a technical vocabulary that expresses itself historically with a female norm of behaviour.

Women historians' attempts to comprehend the experience and consciousness of an individual such as Oichi and a social group like the *karayuki-san* are particularly acute because prostitutes and coolies have left few written records, even as a twentieth-century phenomenon. Further, conceptual problems confront the historian who wishes to use informants or documentary sources to describe and analyse the social behaviour and the *mentalité* of ordinary women or groups. First-hand accounts of elderly informants are replete with difficulty from the standpoint of interpretation, since the historian in the serious study of their field (unlike the anthropologist) often is forced to carry on a dialogue with the dead, and cannot therefore verify an interpretation or hypothesis about the past and the reconstruction of a social world by simply talking to the living, whatever their insight or achievements.

Finding source material to piece together cultural landscapes in women's history in Southeast Asia is a difficult task, primarily because, like other socially subordinate groups, ordinary women have been, by virtue of their role and responsibility, largely inarticulate. The absence of a written record of ordinary women's lives is also partly a function of the traditional definition of history: just as the realm of interpretation supposedly rests upon a complete analysis of politics, economics and formal religion, so only documents relating to such areas have been considered as historical raw materials. This fact concerning sources and interpretation has affected ordinary women's lives and perceptions differently than men, and it has also affected the history of the working man too, the labouring classes; but, at least in a variety of cultures in Southeast Asia in the nineteenth and twentieth centuries, the effects have been more severe for women. Sources that will enable us to draw conclusions about the parts of lower-class women's society from its overall nature include the use of the occasional rare letters or personal papers articulating moments of change; photographs, travelogues and official accounts that tell us about the context and underlying story of those moments; culturally significant episodes that emerge from reports on migration, poverty and prostitution and in police and medical records; and legislation which indicates that different sex and class context is signified. Similarly, certain types of empirical data, especially demographic records in series, can yield first-rank data on marriage, childbirth, residential patterns and their reciprocal influences on the social and economic features of women's lives.

These source materials will provide us with invaluable information about ordinary Southeast Asian women. The subjective nature of these records is both their strength and weakness. That the material in the historical record may not be entirely representative of a given group like the Japanese-overseas prostitute, is a legitimate criticism, yet their potentially personal nature makes them intrinsically useful for writing women's history from below. However, the true test of their validity must lie in how the historian of society pieces them together (often from a variety of perspectives) to create a 'mosaic-like tableau', that indicates, most importantly, how a woman such as Oichi felt about her life and new circumstance in Southeast Asia. In an effort to reconstruct the universe of the *karayuki-san*, the historian must do original and meticulous work on such sources, building up a thorough picture of the lives of the women in the environment of family and home in Japan, and in the brothels of Southeast Asia. I myself have attempted to set out the detailed method of intensive presentation—'thick description'—in *Rickshaw Coolie*: the evocation of the experience of what it meant to become a rickshaw puller receives exhaustive consideration; the agony of deadened limbs and the beads of sweat pouring down one's face in 100 degree Fahrenheit temperature while pulling; the eyes rolling back, uplifted through the haze of opium smoke to the dream of a warm hearth and home in China; and the frantically protective arms of a younger puller gathering in the cold stiff body of an elderly infirm brother found hanged.

To create a portrait of small-time life and the struggles of inarticulate women and men to survive, the historian of society has to take care with the small details of faces and cultural artefacts of a person or 'event'. Oichi's sudden death, in an unforgettably frightening sequence, which strikes the little brothel at No. 55 Malabar Street in Singapore and disturbs its universe, I feel, is an example of just such an 'event'.[19] The most important insight gained from this method in my work as a historian and teacher of history—to see the past as alive—has been a newfound sensitivity for such women and men of a forgotten past. While I have always had this sense of empathy, it was not explicitly highlighted as necessarily relevant as part of my training to be creative as a historian. For example, I had not fully realised how terrifying and back-breaking an experience overseas prostitution was for many wretched young juveniles like Oichi, who were rounded up in poverty-stricken rural Japan, transported to the *Nanshin*, and shipped around from one brothel to another, at times, like cattle.[20]

The ultimate goal of this approach and method is not to shirk the realities of early twentieth-century Singapore life, but rather to explore its unpleasant portrait of Oichi's life 'from the bottom up'; indeed, to discover in the process the historical behaviour and consciousness of a *karayuki-san*, which is in many ways as compelling as her human story. The micro-dynamic approach ensures an outlook for the writing of Southeast Asian history that focuses on the use of the social relations of the sexes (a history of the common humanity of men and women) to make ordinary women visible.[21] In order to gain a better understanding of ordinary Japanese and Chinese women's place in Singapore society and social change, the writing of social history has to move beyond a split vision of two socio-sexual spheres (a private domain and a public domain) in which neat distinctions of sex and work, sex and class, family and society, production and reproduction are seen to be tenable, to a unified 'double' vision in which such relations are seen to be simultaneous.[22] Such a historical framework thereby gives value to ordinary women's conceptions of the world they lived in, and of their place in it.

The difficulties that attend an analysis of the full emotional complexity of the historical situation of the *karayuki-san* and the contradictions inherent in their lives—the exact combination of motives, pressures, values and feelings—perhaps, can be depicted only through a collective biographical form of presentation. This technique compels the social historian to pay close attention to the disparate experience, values and motives of a small group of individual women in diverse contexts and sequences of action, and to subsequently piece together and analyse in a convincing manner the pattern and meaning in their lives for the majority of the women.[23] A historical study of this kind not only involves an extension of the content and meaning of history; it also implies a revision of that content. If this process of reconsideration is taken to its logical disciplinary conclusions, then what emerges is Southeast Asia revised, with ordinary women and men as 'the measure of significance'.[24] One of the most promising aspects of this approach is that it offers a means of integrating women's history into social history. However, historians of Southeast Asian society will have to do more than merely pay attention to ordinary women's lives. I am finding that there are great difficulties in translating this personal vision of a people's history, embedded in structure and experience, into a method. I have not yet established all the necessary parameters by which to define and frame this kind of people's history. I am still in search of a historical approach and methodology that will enable most aspects of an ordinary woman's life, like that of Oichi, to be sketched in so that the re-creation of her women's society and human relationships are made a reality in the colonial pasts of Singapore and Japan. However, the task is clear. If social historians are to research and write about ordinary women in the Southeast Asian past—prostitutes, peasants and court dancers—they must first fashion a mode of presentation that integrates 'experience' (seeing the past of people as alive) with the techniques of microsociology and collective biography. Hence, the surprising result will surely be reconciliation of narration and analysis in our scrutiny of that past to understand the significance of the sexes.

Prostitution in Singapore society

The second part of this chapter briefly re-creates the world of Oichi's Singapore, and examines the nature of the *karayuki-san's* experience with the city, and the causes and effects of prostitution and colonial policy and practice on their working and personal lives. Between 1887, when the average number of brothels registered was 225, and the second decade of the twentieth century the Chinese labouring population of Singapore exploded from 86,000 to nearly 316,000. The rapid increase in the 1890s in the number of immigrating Chinese labourers was the single most important demographic and social development in Singapore's history. Many of these peasants were driven out by periodic poor harvests, flood-caused famines in all parts of South China and by the rising price of rice. They were also forced out by local conditions of overpopulation and the policies of landlords. For many, survival meant escape from the impoverished domestic economy. Understandably, a multitude of *singkeh* left Fukien and Kwangtung in search of better prospects. They were indigent, barely knowing the written characters of their own language, but they carried with them the compass of culture, a will and a burning ambition. Their dream was one of hard work, a decent livelihood, and a return in some comfort to home and hearth in China.[25]

The immigration of *singkeh* stamped an indelible image on Singapore. It was a coolie town, with a heterogeneous Chinese workforce, a disproportionate ratio of male to female, and an abnormal age structure. At the turn of the century Chinese males constituted over 72 per cent of the total population. Most of these men were either single or had left their wives and children behind. Alone, indebted and jobless on arrival, they accounted for almost all the able-bodied men of the working population. They were aged between fifteen and fifty-nine. There were few women (except for prostitutes), children or old men among the Singapore Chinese in this period. A far more noticeable feature of this population in the early part of the century was the rate of return to China.[26] *Singkeh* had come to do manual labour, to build, but not to stay. In the late 1890s only about 10 per cent of the Singapore Chinese were locally born. The average length of time spent in the city by those who immigrated was about seven years. Later, conditions were more favourable when compared to those in China, especially in the 1920s, and an increasing number of this immigrant transient community would settle in Singapore.²⁷

Despite spartan living conditions and a colonial government whose control reached into the most intimate aspects of the coolies' work-a-day lives, most of them—even those most left alone—managed to pursue their private passions. They found some solace in the four evils. The four evils were well known among the labouring classes of Singapore, and the four went together in the city. They were opium smoking, drinking, gambling and prostitution. In an overwhelming male society of poor immigrant Chinese labourers, prostitution was a basic phenomenon. Chinese and Japanese women like Oichi, in their thousands, occupied hundreds of brothels in streets nearby the working-class quarters to provide sexual gratification to a veritable army of immigrant labourers without wives and children. There was a definite relationship between the number of prostitutes and the size of the *singkeh* population, between the economic ascendancy of Singapore at the end of the nineteenth century and a notable increase in prostitution, and between the repeal of the Contagious Diseases Ordinances in 1887 in Singapore and the occupational distribution of venereal disease (VD). What is most significant here is that the incidence of sexually transmitted diseases increased dramatically among prostitutes and coolies from the 1890s onwards, and its tragic social significance is exhibited clearly in the Coroner's Records by the phenomenon of suicide.²⁸

In the period before the abolition of brothels in 1927, one of Singapore's foremost industries was prostitution, and camera-slung tourists, wealthy Chinese, drunken sailors and ordinary coolies were picked up by rickshaw pullers catering to the brothel trade and taken to the red light districts. Brothels were allowed in several sections of the city known as the 'district or quarter'. In 1898 the Chinese houses in Singapore were divided into public brothels, formerly registered under the Contagious Diseases Ordinance with the Chinese Protectorate, about 200 in number, with over 3,000 prostitutes, all Cantonese, and private or 'unregistered' brothels, about 150 in number, containing about 600 prostitutes, chiefly Teochiu.²⁹ For those visitors who wanted to get out of their hotels, offices or warships amid the smells and bustle of the city to visit the Japanese red-light district, there were 109 brothels and 633 *karayuki-san* to choose from in the vicinity of Hylam, Malabar, Malay and Bugis Streets in 1905—the year just prior to Oichi's death.³⁰

Each of these districts, with hundreds of brothels lining streets cheek by jowl, had their loyal clients. During the first part of this century Europeans—diplomats, officials and planters—favoured the discreet Japanese women of Malay and Malabar Streets. Foreign tourists, soldiers and especially Japanese sailors also sought their sexual favours, as well as visiting the unregistered haunts of Malay and Eurasian women scattered in the sidelines and alleys of the city. Rickshaw pullers made regular journeys to the brothels in Chin Hin Street, Fraser Street, Sago Street, Smith Street, Tan Quee Lan Street and Upper Hokkien Street. The pullers spent most of their time here carrying Cantonese prostitutes to rendezvous with wealthy *towkays*. They also ran errands for the women—for example, the purchase of additional packets of opium on behalf of a client—and pulled their ordinary customers, the teeming migrant coolie population, around the red light district established exclusively for the Chinese—no matter how drunk or disorderly they were.[31]

In 1927 the red light districts were closed down by the colonial government and public brothels abolished. Traffickers and brothel-keepers tried to carry on their business along other lines. Chinese and Japanese lodging houses and Chinese eating houses were, to a far greater extent than before, used for brothels. The number of unlicensed lodging houses was about three times the number necessary for *bona fide* business, and their main business was prostitution. The women connected with the lodging houses and 'sly prostitution' in the Depression years were Japanese, Chinese, Eurasian, Tamil, Javanese and Malay from the Peninsula.

The *karayuki-san*

It is against this background of economic growth under colonial rule and the changing structure of Singapore society that the social historian must pass over into the underside of modern Japan, in order to show how its 'economic miracle' too, widened the gulf, economically and socially, for ordinary Japanese, but especially for the poverty-stricken farmers and fishermen of Kyushu and the surrounding islands. If we are to see with fresh eyes the individual 'event' and meaning of the life and death of Oichi created by the tensions of changing social and economic circumstances, and the way of all *karayuki-san* in their social and productive relationships, we must first see what 'modern' Japan looked like from the bottom up; a conception of life of what it was like to be a typical young daughter of a poor farm family scourged by back-breaking labour and famine in Kumamoto Prefecture, where the hilly, arid Amakusa islands are located. I want to draw specific attention to the relationship between the impact of the economic growth of Meiji Japan on lower-class rural women and their tenant farming families in the Japanese countryside, and the economic geography of a particular place with high rents—the Amakusa Island. The primary reason for the immigration of poor women and girls from the Amakusa region, who travelled from Japan to Singapore to work as prostitutes or who were sold to brothels, was simple: crushing poverty.[32]

Early in the twentieth century, the daughters of poor rural families from Amakusa Island and Shimabara were sent into a life of juvenile prostitution in the ports of Southeast Asia.[33] The historical plight of young girls like Oichi who were forced to leave their Japanese homes in the 1890s, where parents were no longer able to support them, and settle in offshore cities and towns in Southeast Asia, where they often worked in brothels until they had enough money to return to their distant homeland, must be recounted by women's historians of Southeast Asia with the meticulous care an entomologist devotes to the collection and study of a rare insect, small, fragile, possibly endangered.

It is true that their story is immensely sad, for many were exploited as women, and as Japanese, and once back in their homeland after 1921, when a Japanese law abolished licensed prostitution in Singapore and elsewhere, they found that their own people and even their families now considered them an embarrassment, and rejected them. It is true that the lives of the *karayuki-san* are the story of one of Japan's deserted people. But *karayuki-san*, who often spent their lives in bondage in urban settings like Singapore or Sandakan in order to contribute to the traditional 'family economy', providing for destitute farm families at home, who were too ashamed to take them back, were not victims through any real fault of their own. They were victims of circumstances over which they had no control: changing times in Japan, a new world that was being born in Singapore, values that no longer functioned in survival in turn-of-the-century places where they took jobs as prostitutes in the *Nanshin*.

Recently, however, Japanese women's historians have begun to trace the lives of scores of these young women, many of whom were from outcast backgrounds, or simply so poor that their families sold them under duress into prostitution. As the lives of young, twentieth-century rural women studied by Morisaki Kazue and Yamazaki Tomoko gradually unfolded for these historians, by using memoirs, fiction, official testimony, eyewitness accounts and personal recollections, they could follow in some instances a pathetic young peasant girl's progress from kidnapping to Singapore and Sandakan in her youth, through prostitution, to a humble but proud old woman living an isolated life in rural Japan of the 1970s.[34] Other undefeated elderly women also survived outside Japan, preferring the life of expatriates, and still live in poverty in places where they were first stationed as *karayuki-san*.

The choice of prostitution and modern lower-class Japanese women in Singapore society as a subject, sets the *karayuki-sans'* actions against the socio-political currents of their times both in Japan and Southeast Asia; their

Figure 12.1 Kimono-clad 'hostesses' from Middle Road pose against a studio backdrop in the 1930s.

individual goals, loyalties and pursuits take on broader significance. The dynamic nature of their struggle to find either security and happiness, or the factors that conditioned their failure should be emphasised, in marked contrast to the usual interpretation of these women as 'victims'. The experience of the *karayuki-san* is not just the history of 'miserable women', the price Japan had to pay for its startling economic growth last century, and its thrust to colonise the south seas.[35] Temporally speaking, it is true that the factors which condition the experience of these women are part of a history that must link the agricultural poverty and the social costs of industrialisation in Japan with the rapid economic growth and urbanisation of Singapore—poor, picturesque, unsanitary and overcrowded. Yamazaki Tomoko, however, had inadvertently demonstrated in the experience of Osaki's life in *Sandakan Hachiban Shokan*, by contrasting the past with the present in a series of flashbacks, that it is the creativity of the oppressed that must be studied; in other words, their humanity—the *karayuki-san* behaving as active agents seeking to cope with an emergent reality. I have already suggested that the experience of these women shows that despite the extreme conditions of both rural poverty in Japan and a life of prostitution in the expanding towns of Southeast Asia, that the wretchedness in their life and circumstances could be mitigated by strategies that constituted an 'implicit philosophy', but perhaps in ways which some of us would find disturbing—witness the social cost of Oichi's death.

Conclusion

The state of the art of women's history, the search for an approach to write people's history in Southeast Asia, and the topic of prostitution in Singapore economy and society is an extremely complicated subject that requires moving on many fronts at once, perhaps too many. Let me try to write my way out, at least for now. In order to understand what the experience meant to be a juvenile prostitute from Japan, a *karayuki-san*, in Singapore at the beginning of the twentieth century, the historian of society must chronicle the rhythm of what was normal, describing the patterns and social networks of day-to-day life among the women in great detail. By the creative use of the technique of collective biography and a range of sources, telling us about what it was like to be an ordinary Japanese woman, the social historian will be able to capture and evoke a sector of the history of the Japanese population offshore whose outlook and experiences have not been adequately represented. Through the promise of these variegated sources available on Singapore and Japan in the late nineteenth and twentieth centuries, and this methodology, I hope to break down the historiographical barriers surrounding our understanding of prostitution and the experience of the *karayuki-san* in Singapore's past. It is the compellingly detailed examination of the structure of the lives of prostitutes at the micro-social level that will challenge our sense of the past and all that it implies in Singapore. The second volume of the proposed trilogy hopefully will put ordinary Japanese and Chinese women back into history without taking the economic, social and political forces out of it.

Chapter 13

Lives of the *Ah Ku* and *Karayuki-san* of Singapore: Their Lives, Sources, Method and a Historian's Representation[1]

Introduction: On space and time

Ah *ku* is a general term of address in Cantonese for a woman or lady irrespective of age. *Ah ku* was the polite way to address a Chinese prostitute in colonial Singapore. *Loi ku* or 'whore' was the opposite denigrating term in Cantonese. *Karayuki-san* was the word used traditionally by the Japanese of Amakusa Island and the Shimabara Peninsula, north-west Kyushu, to describe rural women who emigrated to Southeast Asia and the Pacific in search of a livelihood. The ideographs comprising *karayuki-san* literally mean 'going to China', as Kyushu, the place where most of the women were from, was the part of Japan closest to China. *Karayuki-san* in common parlance nowadays has become a popular term to describe women from the poorest sectors of society during the Meiji/Taisho periods who lived and worked abroad as prostitutes. This chapter attempts to explore sources, a method and an approach to analyse and explain the life circumstances of the *ah ku* and *karayuki-san*, and to portray their roles and the subject of brothel prostitution in Singapore, between 1870 and 1940, in a broader regional context. There have been few studies of prostitution in Southeast Asia that recognise that prostitutes, as a marginal group in society, have a history of their own.[2] Examinations of prostitution have primarily focused on the social, psychological and sexual services which women like the *ah ku* and *karayuki-san* traditionally provide for men. In this context, brothel prostitution in colonial Singapore has been viewed primarily in relation to another person, the male, often a coolie, and its effects on him or Singapore, rather than on the prostitute herself and her reaction to a particular situation and place in society.

The tidewater colonial capitals of the nineteenth and twentieth centuries created new modes of human experience for immigrant Asians, but especially for prostitutes and coolies. The rapid development of Singapore at the end of the nineteenth century as a commercial centre and entrepôt port, dominated by import and export firms and banks, for Britain's imperial expansion and trade-oriented economy in Southeast Asia had a profound impact upon every aspect of economic and social relationships. It was most marked in the labour nexus and spatial segregation of the *ah ku* and *karayuki-san*, and the lower class Chinese who, as rickshaw pullers, coal-heavers, stevedores and hawkers helped shape the expansion of Singapore.[3] The historian of society must concentrate on a particular place—the port-city of Singapore—though what is uncovered in this tidewater colonial capital resonates beyond its confined space and has relevance to many such ports of monsoon Asia and all sites of Chinese and Japanese brothel prostitution overseas.

This history would describe and analyse brothel prostitution in the urban areas of turn-of-the-century Singapore, situating the sexually repressive, exploitative institution in its proper social-historical context. The attempt here is to shape a conceptual and analytical framework for a social history of brothel prostitution based on links between large-scale processes and small-scale experience occurring in Singapore and in rural China and Japan in the years between 1879 and 1940. Broader issues of social change, and manners and morals in China and Japan, were mirrored in the actual circumstance of the women's lives as a strictly sexual commodity—beautiful merchandise. The environmental setting of Singapore as a port-city and 'coolie town', the geographical focus of such a social history, had a direct impact on the daily existence of the prostitutes and their clients.

The traumas attached to the life of this Chinese city—emotionally demanding and physically brutal—acutely affected the lives of the *ah ku* and *karayuki-san*. As the urban economy continued to expand in the 1890s and as immigration became increasingly critical, the number of male migrant clients seeking marginal employment swelled. The problems of prostitutes inevitably intensified. And only those Chinese and Japanese women who possessed balance and strength had any chance of surviving the paradoxes of the city's emerging economic and political developments. A central argument of this chapter is that brothel prostitution in Singapore, as a particular type of the city and social setting, represented the development of a process of labour regulation and segregation in which the structure and ideology of British, Chinese and Japanese societies combined to confine prostitutes to a profession typified by hazardous conditions, low wages and monotonous work. The insistent linkage of the individual fate of Chinese and Japanese prostitutes with Singapore's fate permits the social historian to avoid presenting the superficial past, by merely exploring the city's surface. The rhythms of this history and a particular vision tell the social historian what one understands as possible. The narrative ought to move between China, Japan and Singapore as it presents its evidence on the long-term forces, the structures that determined individual actions and everyday life and recounts the testimonies of the *ah ku* and *karayuki-san*.

A social history of the *ah ku* and *karayuki-san* would be organised chronologically and thematically, emphasising large-scale processes and small-scale experience. This research begins by insistently linking the big events in the Asian region to the lives of the *ah ku* and *karayuki-san*: tracing traditional patterns of work and family in rural societies torn apart by natural catastrophe, warlordism, a market economy or industrialisation; defining who they were, moving on to their experiences as prostitutes and migrant women in Singapore; and finally focusing on the other significant people in their lives—notably, members of the fictive brothel 'family', who looked after their routine existence, and clients. As a portrait of Singapore set at the beginning of the twentieth century, this history would explore how prostitutes viewed their profession, working conditions and changing social attitudes, during a critical period in the port-city's development.[4] Throughout this part of the study there would run a keen awareness that, in describing and analysing the life and circumstance of the prostitutes, the historian must place appropriate emphasis upon those issues and values that were important to them. A careful examination of what forces made women and girls choose prostitution as a way of life would also reflect the wider social, economic and political conditions of their particular time and place. There is a need here to capture the sense of time. As a social history, there would be telling insights into how grinding was the poverty and degradation of life in rural China and Japan just a hundred years ago. While Britain's imperialist administrators and merchants were establishing a nerve centre of trade and empire that made Singapore 'great', the ordinary women in areas such as Amakusa Island and the Pearl River delta, were crammed into poverty-stricken villages. Their wretched inhabitants, often malnourished and riddled with disease, attempted to scratch a living as best as they could. Local changes and subsequent events in the existence of these women would be placed repeatedly in the context of phenomena occurring in Singapore, Britain and north-east Asia, as well as other parts of the world.

A distinguishing feature of this social history should be the leaps in time and space when examining the causes and impact of poverty in the lives of the prostitutes, and the nature of their interaction with the growth of the city; and changes in colonial and local social policies with respect to prostitution. The social historian should compare something that happened in the life of a *karayuki-san* like Osaki or Oyoshi late in the nineteenth century in Japan, for instance, with a connected occurrence in their careers or that of another woman in the twentieth century in Singapore—so that one understands both more clearly.[5] At the Singapore end one should try to emphasise those factors that brought prostitutes and coolies into the developing life of the city, those which involved maintaining ties with family, village and homeland, as well as the pursuit of brothel prostitution within the framework of colonial capitalism. The task of developing the relationship between history and theory to understand the dynamics of change and to situate social structure within a larger temporal framework, in order to deal more effectively with questions of prostitution, labour and colonial capitalism, need not be left to the geographers, demographers and anthropologists.

On sources

Anthropology has provided significant insights into patterns of thought and behaviour as revealed in ritual, symbol and myth, but the social historian has to rely sometimes on far more oblique evidence of what went on in the minds of these Chinese and Japanese women to clarify the meaning of choice, motive and intent. Many factors remain unknown about the phenomenon of emigration and brothel prostitution in Singapore, as faceless and nameless as the women and girls were who were sent there from China and Japan. To resurrect the lives of the *ah ku* and *karayuki-san* from obscurity, the historian's findings must be based on a wide array of documents often used by political, economic and institutional historians, but seldom in a single study. The historian of society should draw upon a variety of primary source materials to reconstruct the careers of the Chinese and Japanese prostitutes who inhabited Singapore in this seventy-year period in order to give them a voice. Much of the evidence about the economic and social life of the *ah ku* and *karayuki-san* is fragmentary. But surviving sources, which only provide a point of entry into their lives, deal with issues that were very much a part of Singapore's sensibility in the early twentieth century, issues of gender and labour, and sexuality and physicality. The evidentiary skeleton of a history of the *ah ku* and *karayuki-san* should be quantitative, comprising names, dates, places of birth and employment, mined from obscure records of the Coroner's and Magistrate's courts, hospitals and asylums. These sources are fleshed out with other materials, including oral history accounts and photographs, to analyse both intentions and outcomes, and to grasp the sometimes subtle changes in aspiration and belief, as to how the daily experience of Chinese and Japanese prostitutes fitted into the life and work of Singapore.

The social historian finds within the Coroner's Records vivid, rich testimonies to the *ah ku* and *karayuki-sans'* lived experience, evoking a milieu and sentiment whose details were recognisably real and which were often clouded by an atmosphere of unease, irony and danger: of Loh Sai Soh's fatal objections to Lam Loh Su exiting from the brothel; of Otoyo and her penalised client of two years, Lance Corporal Albert Chacksfield, whom she called 'Checks'; of the beautiful Duya Hadachi, her experiences of a relationship strained beyond endurance, and of the deadly struggle between her paramours and of many, many, others.[6] Such ordinary people tumble from the pages of the record; they talk about choice of partners, love and betrayal, desperation and alienation, drawing us into their lives. In an effort to reconstruct the lives of the *ah ku* and *karayuki-san*, from small and not-so-small fragments of their collective biography and the history of their times, the unrecognised names of women like Oichi, Li Chin Ho and Ng Ah Weh also leap from the pages of the Coroner's Inquests and Inquiries.[7] Not necessarily accustomed to taking up courageous positions, sometimes unwilling to make rash sacrifices or large gestures, these young prostitutes—like so many before and after them—daily coped with a harsh 'fate' about which they felt perplexed and against which they bridled. In the course of the historian's search for their complexity of point of view, Oichi's inability to live up to her brothel-keeper's expectations, the impossibility of Li Chin Ho repaying her debt, and the determined practicality of Ng Ah Weh to leave a Trengganu Street brothel emerge. The depositions command respect at every stage for their frankly confessional nature, and make fascinating reading even for those historians whose predispositions tend to devalue the conclusions that can be gleaned from them, as an unusually rich and compelling source. Despite some apparent difficulties, it is clear that sources like the Coroner's Records can give us knowledge of both large matters of regional significance (a central concern of nomethically driven economists and political scientists preoccupied with the recent past), as well as make visible the micro-case experience of marginalised women like the *ah ku* and *karayuki-san*. The details of material life, workplace and working conditions, as well as 'family' activities recorded in them are incidental to the main purpose of the records, and hence are unlikely to be distorted. As so often when dealing with official colonial records, they are at their most useful when employed for purposes that their compilers would never have dreamt of.

In terms of sources, there is also a wealth of material to be collected on prostitution in the oral tradition and folklore of the Smith Street and Malay Street quarters of Singapore. Much of this tradition is held in the minds of an older generation with only a limited period before the grave buries their local knowledge with them. Yamazaki, Morisaki and Imamura have traced and interviewed elderly Japanese women who were sold into prostitution by their destitute farming families and worked in Japanese brothels in Singapore before World War II.[8] Their information, which brings a human element to this social history, comes from listening to the testimony of the veterans themselves, albeit decades after their careers ended, telling it how it really was—mostly pain, shame, passion, horror and luck. Because almost all *ah ku* and *karayuki-san* were illiterate, there are few written accounts of their personal experience and thoughts. And had they been literate, Yamazaki and others believe ingrained cultural constraints would have prevented them from committing themselves in writing for fear of disgracing their families. Yamazaki concluded that only through oral testimony from a surviving *karayuki-san* herself would the inner life of the overseas prostitute become known and understood. To help recover the life history of the *ah ku* and *karayuki-san* there are some remarkable elderly survivors of that era in Singapore who are formidable bearers of memories, but they are fast disappearing, In 1987, the author interviewed, with the assistance of Ms Tan Beng Luan, over a dozen Chinese women and men who had lived and worked in the brothel areas where Lam Loh Su and Otoyo and others spent their days and nights. They remembered the exact location of particular brothels, just how and when some prostitutes began work, and rich detail about observations on their personal life and people around them. Most of the informants were in the mid-seventies or eighties, several even in their late nineties, but some of them recalled, in a clear, wonderfully expressive language, a variety of experiences dealing with their earlier lives and work. These transcribed interviews run from several paragraphs to a few dozen pages. The authentic voices of elderly women and men have been captured vividly, remembering themselves as young people coming to terms with fear, a 'borrowed place', a way of life only dimly understood, friendship and death. But this evidence consists not just of remarkable recollections and fragments of the life histories of these women; it is also, in part, a slice of the social history of prewar Singapore. These reflections and floods of memories of elderly Chinese and Japanese informants should be used to re-create the social-cultural setting in Singapore's brothel districts. The social historian should attempt to faithfully record the 'sense of place', especially the particulars of what life was like for the *ah ku* and *karayuki-san*, who were definitely a part of, yet were never fully accepted into, Singapore society. There should be certain cautionary juxtapositions of Coronial evidence and interviews of women at eighty or more, from all these areas—China, Japan and Singapore—who vividly recall their childhood experiences as peasant daughters, with the later images of their working world—stationed in brothels in Singapore from 1915 to 1941. They were, after all, both as individuals and members of a particular social group, products of the same economic and social processes, sensibility and regional variation in standards and patterns.

The explication of evidence of prostitution in Singapore's past should also foreground questions about what non-verbal clues and three-dimensional documents of material culture, such as women's clothing, accessories and buildings, can tell historians about how to re-interpret and re-present the larger reality and hidden meanings of the history of Chinese and Japanese prostitutes in the city and brothel. Inferences gleaned from seemingly unimportant detail in building facades, kimonos, photographs and postcards capture otherwise unrecorded moments and aspects of culture. Photographs of the *karayuki-san* and the brothels which sprang up around Singapore during the years following peak migration were both functional and symbolic objects that can make us gasp, grimace or smile. The black and white images, from the hard-edged arrival and registration portraits to the poignant and personal ones, are priceless snatches of Singapore life itself, each telling its own story. Innumerable turn-of-the-century photographs of the women have not been saved, the glass-plate negatives, especially of Japanese photographers, sadly, also lost or destroyed.[9] However, among those rare portraits of the *karayuki-san* that have survived, there are photographs which were a gift or memento meant to join the *karayuki-san* and loved ones or friends in Japan, a kind of talisman against the prostitutes' fear that people at home would not remember. Such photographs not only became tangible threads between a prostitute and the people who were important to her, which in turn could inspire, sadden, intrigue and amuse them, they also invariably became physical extensions of the woman's joy, sorrow and pain. The methods employed by historians and social anthropologists of reading, inference, observation and listening in the interpretation of literary, visual and oral sources are the key points of departure in the analysis of historical evidence for such a social history.

On method: Lifespan and collective biography

Based on Coroner's Inquests and Inquiries, and other records and interviews, the historian of society should attempt to reconstruct the life cycle of Chinese and Japanese prostitutes and their day-to-day experience between 1870 and 1940. A lifespan approach takes into account matters of personality and chance, and how prostitutes at varying stages in their careers experienced historical change and the role of larger events differently. The historian is immediately drawn into the *ah ku* and *karayuki-san*'s world from early childhood to old age, based largely on changes in biology and kinship.[10] One should, in reconstructing the life cycle of a substantial minority of prostitutes, argue that brothel prostitution in Singapore was not a phase through which most Chinese and Japanese women passed. Relative life chances were affected directly by the hazards of a life of prostitution—alcoholism, drug abuse, indebtedness and disease—which formed almost insurmountable obstacles towards achieving a more conventional place in society. Starting with the village backgrounds, the hazards of the trade in women and an emigrant voyage, the historian should follow the *ah ku* and *karayuki-san* through their encounters with brothel life in general and with madams, pimps and clients in particular into the routines and crises of earning, spending, social relations, leisure, mobility, disease and death. This gender-conscious perspective does not just enrich the urban, social history of Singapore. It is also a historical account of human nature, of human relationships compelled by the pride and prejudice of the human spirit. In this social history, oppression, affectionate joy, utopia and desolation occurred together in real life for many of these women of negligible social origins. At the same time, a sense of filial responsibility, and the necessity of being emotionally strong and nourishing the opposite sex still mattered culturally to these women, despite their being forsaken by life. Furthermore, there was a real link with crime and criminality that must be recognised in forming a true picture of the exploitation and injustice of brothel prostitution. The narrative should also portray a darker side of the lives of the *ah ku* and *karayuki-san*, and the dangerous, disillusioned universe of extreme violence and drug addiction of an underworld of flesh traders and brothel owners.

This social history also employs prosopography, a collective-biographical approach, to develop a social-cultural understanding of the life cycle and careers of these women. The lives and circumstances of the *ah ku* and *karayuki-san* are too complicated to be kept within the bounds of the stereotyped image of the prostitute as simply poor, weak humanity thrust into the sordid conditions of a Singapore brothel. Complexity characterised their struggle to survive, personal associations with clients, friends and family, and how they fought, sometimes with indomitable courage, to empower their lives, despite the structural constraints imposed on their existence. So one is often forced back to a view of their activity as a complex striving towards ends that vary, conflict, and to a certain extent remain undefined. It is the task of the social historian to grasp this complexity. Combining a lifespan approach with prosopography should allow the historian to reconstruct a complex 'inner history' based on the lived experience of the *ah ku* and *karayuki-san*. It should enable the author not only to learn how these women were perceived by the society in which they worked, but also to know how they viewed themselves and their daily experience. The second half of this history would be essentially a collective-biographical portrait, a historical drama that engages us at the social, political, psychological and emotional human level. It is an ethnohistory in the fullest sense: accounts focused on particular tragedies of innocents forced into prostitution; individual stories of love, vengeance, sex and violence set against the backdrop of the social ills and squalor of colonial Singapore.

Clarity, balance and the sifting of history are required in piecing together scraps of information about events, reactions and influences in order to shed light on the past of such a group of women, usually inarticulate and rarely documented as individuals. The effort to recover their story from abstruse sources, the raw material for both history and anthropology, is based on the capacity of a creative imagination to evoke the daily patterns of a type of people like prostitutes, and the conviction that carefully accumulated detail or 'thick description', emphasising both experience and explanation, is the best way to take the true measure of their times.

This social history, as ethnography, would be peppered with jarring anecdotes and terse tales from the Coroner's and police records. These short vignettes turn out to have remarkable implications for the pace and texture of collective biography, and for stitching together a tapestry of poverty, sexual antagonisms, subordination and conflict in the social history of prostitutes' and coolies' experiences. The historian, in building up a prosopography from statistical evidence and individual illustrative cases, with its broad social sweep, stumbles on to dissonances and long-hidden aspects of the *ah ku* and *karayuki-san's* lives characterised by physical hardship, tormented images, addiction, debilitating and often fatal diseases and, frequently, extreme loneliness. Collective biography is critical in creating a much-needed non-institutional thematic framework for part of this social history, focusing on women at work, demonstrating interdependence and impermanence between China, Japan and Singapore; and encompassing dynamic elements in that history. Schematically, we can represent the social history of the *ah ku* and *karayuki-san* as in Table 13.1.

It is in light of this historical method that the notion of women's choice and control or lack thereof over life and circumstance is a critical issue, in reconstructing and interpreting both the shaping of achievement, and the discovery and growth of purpose in historical situations of brothel prostitution. This is a choice, not of private citizens, but of prostitutes, both individually and collectively—a choice as an enabling condition either to fully participate in or exit from the social and communal life of the brothel world. The framework of traditional historical analysis that regards these choices and distinct actions such as going abroad, shifting brothels, a willingness to experience the disturbance of passion, refusing to accept a client, and suicide, as less relevant or irrelevant ignores the fact that women matter. It disregards the persisting power of the *ah*

Table 13.1 Schematic representation of the social history of the *ah ku* and *karayuki-san*

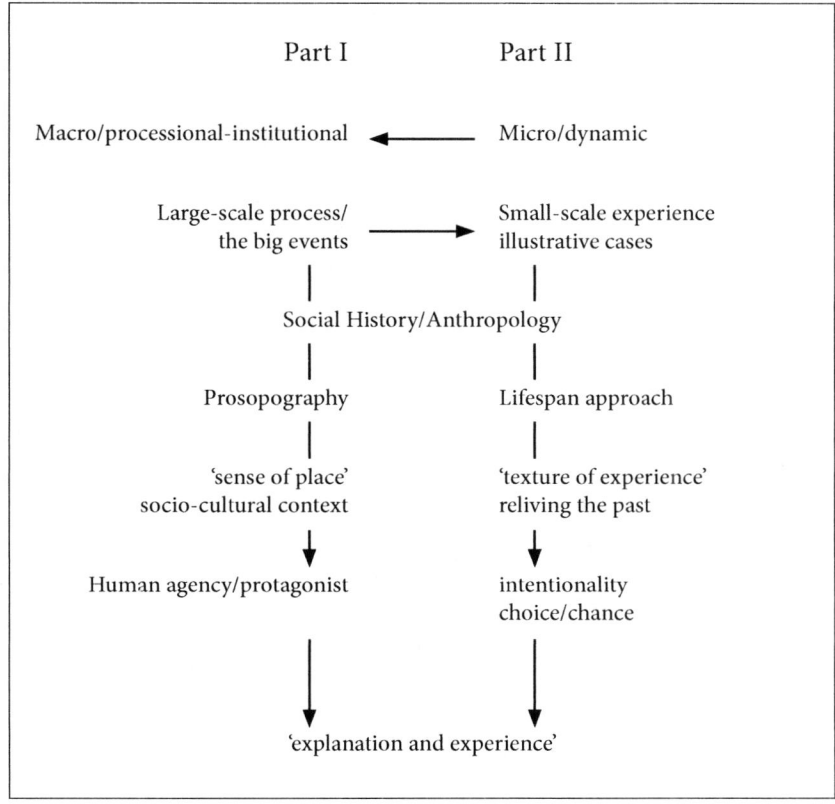

ku and *karayuki-san*, despite the constraints imposed upon them, as well as the role of chance in human choice.

The balance between a specific choice and act, and all their social and cultural significance, can be superbly revealed by a careful analysis of the pattern of actions in the cases listed in the Coroner's Records. Admittedly, in instances of suicide, judgements were made; however, the ironies of the scene and decision were often left to speak for themselves. In a sustained, detailed and extraordinary list in Table 13.2, 'Chinese and Japanese Prostitutes: Suicide', what appears to have been passive acceptance and painful resignation to a dangerous oppressive situation ending in suicide may have been a rational choice—a way to autonomy and peace, or perhaps a haunting, defiant, vengeful statement about a harsh struggle to survive in a distant land. The *ah ku* and *karayuki-san's* hard-earned wisdom, knowledge of life and knowing humour were not

Table 13.2 Japanese and Chinese prostitutes: suicide

Japanese prostitutes: suicide

Name	Age	Sub-communal group	Address of brothel	Period of residence	Name of brothel-keeper	State of deceased's health	Opium smoker	Date of suicide	Cause of suicide	Place of suicide	Suicide due to	Inquest number	Year
Otama	21		24 Malay Street	4 years	Osutsu	Headaches/nightmares		5/6/1900	Post-traumatic stress	Cubicle/brothel	Cutting her own throat	59	1900
Onatsu	32		11-1 Malay Street		Otomo	Pale, thin, depressed		17/12/02	Debt?	Cubicle, 32 Malabar St	Strangulation	184	1902
Oahki	22		26 Hylam Street	More than 3 years	Oasan	Depressed		27/5/03	Debt	Sea near vessel G.G. Meyer	Asphyxia drowning	58	1903
Ohichi	24		55 Malabar Street	2½ years	Ofuku			17/2/06	Debt/problem with mistress	Cubicle/brothel	Asphyxia hanging	82	1906 CCVS
Oyoshi	39		6-2 McPherson Road (private residence)			Depressed/ill health		17/11/16	Persistent ill health	Small house, 6-2 McPherson Rd	Burns—Set fire to herself	229	1916

Chinese prostitutes: suicide

Name	Age	Sub-communal group	Address of brothel	Period of residence	Name of brothel-keeper	State of deceased's health	Opium smoker	Date of suicide	Cause of suicide	Place of suicide	Suicide due to	Inquest number	Year
Lee Chong Fong	20	Cantonese	121 Hong Kong St	5 months	Leong Guan Eng		no	22/12/82		Cubicle/brothel	Overdose of opium	147	1883
Ng Ah Weh		Cantonese	36 Trengganu St	More than 8 months			no	2/10/87	Wanted to leave the brothel	Cubicle	Overdose of opium	104	1887
Chan Sye Kaw		Cantonese	60 Upper Hokkien St	3 months			Occasional	6/9/98		Cubicle/brothel	Overdose of opium	117	1898
Liong Chai Ho	25	Cantonese	40 Trengganu St	3 months	Chan Ah See			26/10/07		Cubicle/brothel	Overdose of opium	170	1907

Chinese prostitutes' suicide

Name	Age	Dialect	Address	Duration	STD	Complaints	Date	Place	Method	Reason		Year
Li Chin Ho	20	Cantonese	5 Tan Quee Lan St			Complaining of headaches	6/5/08	Cubicle/brothel	Overdose of opium	Debt	14	1908 CCVS
Sin Chow	21	Cantonese	4 Trengganu St	1 year			13/7/08	Cubicle/brothel	Overdose of opium	Gambling	23	1908 CCVS
Lee Ah Choi	22	Cantonese	61 Upper Hokkien St	1 year	Chan Ah Ng Gonorrhoea	Occasional	9/9/08	Cubicle/brothel	Overdose of opium	Gambling?	159	1908
Yip Mui Chai	17	Cantonese	9-6 Canal Rd (unlicensed)	4 months	Chan Ah Yee	No		Cubicle, 12 Sago St	Overdose of opium	Wanted to leave the brothel	218	1908
Chow Chat Hui	30	Cantonese	64 Upper Hokkien St		Wong Ah Yee	Complaining of headaches	21/7/09	Cubicle/brothel	Overdose of opium	Gambling	129	1909
Wong Mau Tan	24	Cantonese	15 Sago St	8 days	Chu Ah Thai	Severe cough, headaches	11/01/12	Cubicle/brothel	Overdose of opium	Persistent ill health	160	1912
Leong Tong Fook	20	Cantonese	67 Smith St (unlicensed)	2 years		Syphilis	5-6/5/21	Master Attendant's pier	Floating in the sea	Persistent ill health	168	1921
Tan Moh Tan	19	Cantonese	77 Pagoda St (unlicensed)	1 year			2/11/24	Sea off the Esplanade	Asphyxia drowning	Fear of losing lover	439	1924
Wong Ah Yeok	26	Cantonese				Pregnant	10/2/34	SunWah Lodging House Peck Seah St window	Jumped from 2nd floor	Six months pregnant was worried	61	1934
Ho Hong Min	20	Hokkien	27 Tanjong Pagar Road			Syphilis	13/2/37	No	Cubicle, 12 Aliwal Street	Overdose of opium	Debt – ill health	105	1937
Chan Ah Kuan	25	Cantonese	216-3 Syed Alwi Road	2 weeks		Gonorrhoea	4/2/38	Rm 216-3 Syed Alwi Road	Lysol poisoning	Debt – ill health	68	1938

Source: CCVS Certificate Coroner's View Singapore

essentially conservative. The true history of the prostitutes' choices, on their own terms, in the male-defined world of Singapore, was often all about survival and mobility. In managing social change some prostitutes responded positively to outside influences and adapted to these in dynamic ways that maintained both their communal and individual integrity. The historian must not lose sight of the fact that there were many *ah ku* and *karayuki-san* who were functioning well. Not all Chinese and Japanese prostitutes' lives inevitably led to misery and premature death.[11] For some of these women, especially among the *karayuki-san*, prostitution constituted a transitional stage in their lives, eventually leading to marriage or respectable employment. Turning to prostitution had been a calculated decision for some of them. They chose to work in offshore brothels with the hope of obtaining, after several years, some windfall capital. However, money to assist a family wasn't the only motive. Some were catching up with life. The *karayuki-san* were often better fed and clothed in a Singapore brothel than in their farm village or while working for a thread mill. If the choice was back-breaking agriculture, factory sweatshop or a brothel overseas, it is not difficult to envision why the latter alternative was felt to be more lucrative and less physically demanding by some. For a few prostitutes, who were upwardly mobile and had managed to achieve self-sufficiency, it was possible to finish up with an aura of respectability, running a hotel, café or bar. But the vast majority remained destitute.

What the historical record should show the historian, and he or she should find awesome, is the strength and resiliency of the human personality of particular prostitutes. Here is quite a different focus, a willingness, in view and method, to perceive the *ah ku* and *karayuki-san* as women with power to affect their destiny, not simply as the oppressed 'victims' of undeniable social, political and legal injustices. Such a view does not deny the significance of imposed constraints, but enables us rather to see the Chinese and Japanese women making history, or at least struggling to cope with the flow of life. This, to me, is the essence of Southeast Asian social history. The historiographical thrust is on the recovery of subjective experience in a female marginal community; consequently, an equally fundamental change occurs in the way Singapore's past is described, in the shift in emphasis from 'places' to 'faces', in being able to see the society of the prostitutes from within, and in a related concern with the quality of life. This historical writing would present historical issues as they appeared to the actors, who have so often been hidden from history, and in such a way that reality can no longer be kept at bay.

Retrieving prostitutes' lives

This detailed historical account of the 'texture of experience' of the prostitutes' lives should necessarily be comparative, requiring both analysis of Chinese and Japanese women separately, and a comparison between their two worlds; it should also involve an examination of the social relations between the women and clients, and what happened among the *ah ku* and *karayuki-san* when they were by themselves. In a sense, this ethnography created by the historian of society not only can, but must, analyse and argue from the clues in documents and other cultural artefacts to social realities. The historian, by pursuing this line of inquiry in depth into the records, can fashion an inner history of women that overcomes the public–private split, challenges the longstanding division of the history of Singapore into separate components—race, gender and class—and yet is not cut off from mainstream chronological and geographical connections. But in amassing the life-like detail to fit together the pieces of the ethnohistorical mosaic mirroring the careers of these silent and forgotten women, the social historian must comprehend the fact that for many areas, conceptually speaking, the historical record is silent. Singapore life in the *demimonde* was chaotic, fragmented, random and discontinuous: in a word, absurd, if not silent. Here the historian's concern reaches the limits of innovative investigative work, in that it touches on absences and the role chance plays in life. The historian finds that certain details and moments of the women's past, often coloured by irony and outrage, will remain unknowable and that the history that one can recover and write is based only on innumerable fragments of past lives. The conventional wisdom of social history and anthropology must recognise such lacunae or great silences, as well as areas where the historian holds no more than a 'thin shrivelled tissue in the hand'.[12]

It is important to reiterate that such a social history takes the prevalent structures and experiences of the prostitutes' lives seriously. This interdisciplinary approach—rich, contextual and close to the ground—attempts to establish a methodological and conceptual framework of historical analysis acceptable to Gayatri Spivak's challenge:

> …There has to be a simultaneous…focus; not merely who am I? But who is the other woman? How am I naming her?…Is this part of the problematic I discuss?[13]

As in Spivak's case, the historian will discover in this approach and evidence the 'power of the powerless' and the actual forces that animated their lives.

Socio-historical phenomena previously considered to be sufficiently described and understood in the city assume completely new meanings because of the altered scale of observation. A medley of characters, situations and reflections will pass before the historian about the real nature of turn-of-the-century Singapore in all its starkness and joy. By organising the illustrative case material around themes relating to workplace and working conditions, the social historian can convert a mass of detailed depositions into an 'inner history'—an ethnographic image of what actually happened in the lives of the prostitutes of Singapore. The freshness and immediacy of the testimony of the *ah ku* and *karayuki-san* echoes down the corridor of time to inform us what it was like to live and work in a brothel in Malay Street or Smith Street. This highly detailed and personal view, 'the texture of experience', firmly situates these women in the port-city circa 1900. The picture shocks, for it removes forever the idea of Singapore as a pleasant place, an economic showcase, 'the Clapham Junction of the Eastern Seas', and replaces it with an image of harshness, full of outrages and injustices, but also of stubborn persistence of courage and hope when these should have disappeared; it makes ordinary women—prostitutes—three dimensional, not simply cardboard cut-outs.

Conclusion

What the social historian should attempt to create is a personal history of the prostitutes' times closely based on intimate experience, while still paying careful attention to the larger historical influences—the institutions, processes and interactions—which determined their fates. The author has already stressed the methodological desirability of working outward and upward, from the categories of the *ah ku* and *karayuki-san* and events in their lives, to illustrate underlying social processes. Our need, then, is to build facts about the overseas Chinese and Japanese past in Singapore into a new historical analysis of what ought to be studied in a 'coolie town'—the life cycle of prostitutes, the material deprivation under which they worked and the transactions of everyday life—in order to understand the *ah ku* and *karayuki-san*, as far as the social historian is able, in light of their own experience and their own reactions to this experience.

Chapter 14

Karayuki-san of Singapore: 1877–1941[1]

Introduction

A new-found interest in social history, recent developments in historical thought and methodology, and a fresh awareness of the importance of gender-specific experience have led historians to question an 'ordinary woman's place' in Singapore's past.[2] In the historiography of Singapore, there is a need to foreground the critical importance of the *karayuki-san* in the sex, politics and society of the city, stressing not only alterations in their life and circumstance, but also variations in the role of the colonial government and changes in the ideology of sex and social policy.[3]

The history of Japanese prostitution in Singapore is a subject that not only raises the issues of women's work and status, but links these with the much less tractable questions of sex, race and colonialism, as well as male sexuality and women's exploitation of other women. Prostitution, in the period from 1880 to 1940, was determined by complex social and economic forces in Singapore, China and Japan. Therefore, the assumptions, meaning and experience in the lives of the *karayuki-san* comprise a historical unity that was formed and affected by these forces and historical transformation. Women's history must answer questions about the ways in which prostitution has been organised and regulated in a period of fundamental change; a historical era which witnessed the emergence of Singapore as the hub of an imperial system in Southeast Asia, and as a 'coolie town' where tens of thousands of Chinese immigrants were becoming part of a larger urban society—a Chinese city outside China.[4]

The study of prostitution in Singapore should concentrate on the *karayuki-san* over a relatively short span of time, sixty years, to describe and analyse the lives of the women themselves, and place the subject of brothel prostitution and traffic in women and children in a broader context. Emphasis must first be placed on the macro-social forces and cultural values that shaped the character of prostitution. The social historian must examine the patriarchal system of society and government responsible for the selling of women and young girls abroad. The record of prostitution in Singapore is part of the history of international traffic and procuring in Japan where women were oppressed by the dual yoke of sex and class.[5] Second, the social hierarchy within the profession, exploitation, the economic factors and its benefits, must also be part of a new interpretive framework that gives meaning to the lived experience of these women.

The second part of a study of prostitution in Singapore should give us a sense of the circumstance of the women themselves, of a pattern, a life cycle, that we often don't get about our own lives. The drive here is to investigate the unique experience of these women, emphasising the origin and identity of the prostitutes, their relationships with family, friends and other people who helped fashion their careers and destinies—the procurers, brothel-keepers, colonial officials and clients. The experiences of the *karayuki-san* can show that for some of them prostitution was a form of employment as a migrant, but often involving limited rights in self. Japanese women were not all 'total victims', as some found prostitution to be in their own interest, but, on the other hand, prostitution was not a well thought out career path for many; as 'outsiders' they had no choice. In terms of revisionism, their domination by a patriarchal system must be considered to be the starting point in examining the process of historical change and women's lives in Japan and Singapore.

Demography is vital in giving an answer to why prostitution is so important to the history of Singapore. The development and expansion of the city was the direct result of a vast immigration of Chinese labourers that continued steadily from the 1880s. The population quadrupled in forty years. This massive influx altered the character of Singapore. The labour market could absorb them, but such an unprecedented increase created serious problems; nearly all the immigrants were bachelors. These coolies crowded into working-class tenements in Chinatown and the density rates soared. As more and more *singkeh* (newcomers) moved in, the demand for prostitutes soared just as rapidly. Ordinary Japanese were swept up by Singapore's 'economic miracle' and pushed from behind by the uneven development of Japan and a patriarchal family structure. Japan in this paradoxical century of incredible economic growth and deprivation in rural areas tended to export labour. It is against this background of social upheaval, and economic expansion and the changing structure of Singapore society, that the historian must pass over into the underside of modern Japan. To show how its 'economic miracle' also widened the gulf for ordinary Japanese, but especially for the poverty-stricken farmers and fishermen of Kyushu and surrounding islands. The historical plight of girls like Oichi, who in the 1890s were forced to leave their homes and settle offshore in the colonial cities and towns in Southeast Asia, was directly linked to how Japan's startling economic growth and modernisation actually opened the gulf economically and socially between the rich and the poor, and between the city and the countryside. The economic geography of a particular place, Amakusa

Island, brought grinding poverty that forced stricken parents in typical farm families to sell their daughters into Japan's brothels.[6]

At the beginning of the twentieth century the coolie class was mostly single and poor. Colonialism was in its heyday. Singapore was booming as the region was opened up to economic development. Everybody was in work. In a very real sense a new class of migrant labourer was born. The *karayuki-san* lived on the edges of the coolie districts, as well as on the margins of the law. This demographic perspective provides a startling different view of the history of Singapore. For most Japanese from farms and port cities, migration was something that happened to them. Demography and sojourning had massive effects on the lives of people, born or unborn, on the lives of children, women like Oichi, bachelor labourers, elderly people—all who shared in the migration to Singapore. This 'turning point' in history represents the same situation for women as for men when the historian considers the role of the *karayuki-san* as migrant labourers rather than merely as socially unassimilated—'fallen women'. The emphasis on deviant behaviour and the 'sinful nature' of prostitution has obscured the prostitutes' contribution to the growth of Singapore society; simply because their way of life does not appear 'noble' or socially acceptable does not make it less important. The lives and experiences of these women—their feelings, sensitivity and the capacity for joy, hope, fear, sorrow and caring—are inextricably bound up with emergence of Singapore, and with the fate of modern Japan.[7]

This phase in Singapore's history, the Hua-Ch'iao period, is rarely described from the prostitutes' perspective in history books.[8] The extraordinary importation of ragged and poverty-stricken peasants from China to build roads, railroads, government buildings, load and unload cargo and supplies, and work in godowns and factories, was part of a dynamic urban scene in which the prostitutes were indispensable. The character of Singapore, both as a Chinese city outside China and as a coolie town under British rule, shaped the careers of the *karayuki-san*. The need for cheap labour, the demand for the women's services, a colonial policy of controlling brothel prostitution through registration and medical inspection, the stigma of Victorian racism and patriarchy, provide the historical context and social setting which determined the lives and choices of Singapore's Japanese prostitutes.

Poverty, patriarchy and prosperity

Prostitution in Singapore was linked to economic factors in rural China and Japan. Congenital poverty, weak family economies and rising economic expectations were all part of a set of prevailing conditions that created a vast source of supply of Japanese women and young girls for international traffic. These influences show up far more plainly when attention is focused on regional demography and the lack of occupational choices for rural daughters of poor fishing and farming villages of southern Japan who emigrated. Those who left these impoverished areas to become *karayuki-san* were to bear much of the burden and social cost of the early industrialisation and urbanisation of Japan.⁹ Extreme conditions of agrarian poverty, overcrowding and falling levels of productivity became almost impossible to bear. One of the few ways such rural conditions of wretchedness could be mitigated was to leave Japan to work abroad. In the late nineteenth century anyone who left western and northern Kyushu to work in another country as seasonal labourers were called *karayuki-san* 'one who goes to China', *kara* being the word used for China at that time.¹⁰ Men and women left Amakusa Island and Shimabara Peninsula to work on the railways in Siberia. Work and job prospects were advertised by emigration agents and shipping companies. These migrant-labourers, who saw themselves as '*karayuki-san*', also laboured on the pineapple plantations of Hawai'i and went to the frozen wastes of Western Canada's timber camps. Later on, only after World War II, did the meaning of the word *karayuki-san* change, to specifically describe those women and young girls, primarily from Kyushu, who went abroad as prostitutes.¹¹ Yamazaki explains how this altered meaning of *karayuki* is linked directly to a historical understanding of the relationship between the institutionalisation of capital and the growth of agrarian poverty on a regional basis throughout Japan.

> *Karayuki-san* is a word derived from two longer words which mean 'One who has travelled to China', but means itself an overseas prostitute who, from the middle of the nineteenth century to the end of the First World War, had left behind her homeland of Japan and gone abroad to sell herself to foreigners; such prostitutes went not only to China and Siberia in the North and to the countries of Southeast Asia in the South, but also to India and Africa. They came from Japan as a whole, but especially it is said, from Kyushu: from the island of Amakusa and the Shimabara peninsula. That most shared this origin was due, basically...to the poverty of those regions...Indeed, these prostitutes and the poor peasant women of Shimabara and Amakusa undoubtedly represent two branches of the same tree.¹²

The impoverishment of the rural farm families of southern Japan during the Tokugawa period was due to a large extent to the increasing rate of taxation that had to be paid in kind, usually rice or barley. The peasants of Amakusa and

Shimabara had to turn over up to 50 per cent of their harvest to the *daimyo* or *bakafu* as a land tax. This usually amounted to 15,000–18,000 *koku* annually.[13] A host of other taxes also were levied on the necessities of life, including the farmer's house, doors and windows, on cloth, sake, beans and hemp, and, significantly, on female children.[14] Debts rose, so did the rate of abortion and female infanticide.[15] Even after the Meiji Restoration of 1868, the burden of taxation and the new penetration of capital into the villages were to be salient causes for peasant-farmers being forced off their land.

> The Meiji government, 'new' though it was called, and irrespective of the fact that it had toppled the Tokugawa Shogunate, merely changed what had been a tax in kind to a tax in money and made no attempt whatever to lower the tax rate in any significant way.[16]

The Shimabara Peninsula, which is located in Nagasaki prefecture, and the arid mountainous Amakusa Island, which faces the peninsula from across the Kayosaki Strait, in Kumamoto Prefecture produced the largest number of *karayuki-san*. These fishing and farming areas of northern Kyushu were among the most impoverished in Japan. Shimabara Peninsula and Amakusa Island were well known for their destitution.[17] This lack of resources and economic want was the result of a number of natural and social phenomena, which in turn had affected all levels of Kyushu society during the Tokugawa era. M. Hane has shown, from a detailed analysis of village registers, population and taxation records, that between 1691 and 1856 the population of Amakusa rose dramatically, more than trebling in size, but rice production lagged behind, increasing by a factor of only 1.08.[18] The striking increase in population should have meant a commensurate growth in labour power, and agricultural productivity should have risen. However, because of the island's poor fertility, the increased population only led to an intensification of poverty. The barren ash-ridden soil couldn't yield enough to meet the needs of Amakusa's burgeoning community.[19] Population continued to increase in the three decades after 1868, and infanticide was now considered a capital crime. Agrarian poverty also increased, which was the dismal cause of this migration of rural women and young girls from Japan's southern provinces. Amakusa villagers realised that to make further gains, as neither their farms nor fisheries were masterpieces of efficiency with scarce arable land, heavy seas and overpopulation, they would have to turn increasingly on an individual basis to emigration. The geographical proximity of Amakusa Island and Shimabara Peninsula to the Chinese mainland and the countries of the *Nanshin*, and to the port of Nagasaki, greatly facilitated the exodus of Kyushu women who went in search of work abroad at extremely low wages to help set a full table.

The truth is that there are some things we can learn from the experience of these young women who were forced to migrate or were sold by their parents into prostitution. The most important was the value that a peasant family placed on a female child in a poorer overpopulated region when it was difficult to make ends meet. Japanese agriculture was back-breakingly labour intensive and in difficult times every bowl of rice meant a struggle. As a society, rural farmers and fishers saw survival as a primary social and individual goal. The exchange of a daughter, who was regarded as an object to be invested in or sold, was for peasant families devoid of natural resources and with a profound, historical sense of vulnerability, the only guarantee of a possible future. Patriarchy in traditional Japanese culture was responsible for the exploitation of women financially, physically, sexually and emotionally.

Implicit in the traditional status of women in the patriarchal family system is the notion that their position, due to cultural and religious beliefs, has been comparable to that of an 'outsider'. Male-centred Japanese households operated in such a fashion that a woman had no say in family matters, except towards the end of her life as a mother-in-law or widow. She could neither inherit property nor hold any except for a dowry. Domestic labour and childbearing were her principal duties—to produce sons for the family line. The historian of society must emphasise patriarchy as much as agrarian poverty as a basic cause for prostitution in Singapore, and the status and condition of Japanese women as migrants and prostitutes. The history of the *karayuki-san* in this context, which is deeply embedded in the moral and legal framework of traditional patriarchal families, in reality is also the history of Japanese men—of their attitudes, schemes and manipulations.

Female children were considered expendable by peasants living on the margin of despair, who could not afford another mouth to feed. A daughter represented a drain on the family economy with little hope of future compensation. This extreme devaluation of females within the patriarchal family system, short of infant abandonment and infanticide, led ultimately to prostitution. Many baby girls owed their lives to their parents considering them a possible source of future revenue through sale or pawning as domestic servants to wealthier families or other 'benefactors' who made money on them by re-selling them into prostitution in Singapore.

In many cases *karayuki-san* entered prostitution mainly to obtain much-needed financial assistance for parents or kin. The appeal to an ill-fed daughter's filial devotion, by starving or irresponsible parents during periods of pestilence or famine, resulted often in her going abroad to take up a life of prostitution in a brothel in Singapore, under the compromise of debt.[20] Ironically, in a case where either parents or relatives had received the amount of the pledge upon her entry into a Singapore brothel, the unselfish motive of filial loyalty towards them often compelled the young *karayuki-san* to respect the contractual obligation and honour the debt. Parents took full advantage of this ideology to raise money on the saleable value of their filial daughters as they would on any negotiable property. In one such case a villager on Amakusa applied at the local police station for a passport for his child to emigrate. A policeman was sent to dissuade the father from such a rash course of action. However, upon discovering their miserable lot, he had no choice but to assist the family in sending their daughter to Southeast Asia:

> Besides the fact that the parents were ill, there were eight children, including the eighteen year old daughter, freezing and starving in a dilapidated shack. The money which the young girl might have earned as a textile-mill worker would not have been nearly enough to feed nine mouths. If she had become a prostitute in Japan, she would have only earned enough to support them for half the year. So the daughter with the policeman's help went to Singapore. She became one of the most popular prostitutes in the brothel quarter, and was able to send home regularly seventy dollars a month over a six year period.[21]

The traditional conception of filial piety placed the female child at a severe disadvantage. If the situation arose that a Japanese family had to part with a child because of agrarian poverty or over-population, it was naturally to the girls that the parents first turned. Female children of eleven or under were often sold by hopeless parents to procurers to save the rest of the family. In such circumstances it was not unusual for these parents who could not take care of their daughter to consent to the unconditional transfer of the child to anyone who claimed to be in a position to feed and clothe her. Thus the Japanese patriarchal system constantly produced women and young girls for prostitution abroad, who were sold or pawned by their own fathers or sometimes their brothers to complete strangers who, in turn, after having paid the usual indemnity money to the parents or brother, had the right to transfer the child again against the same kind of indemnity to a brothel keeper in Singapore.

International traffic and brothel prostitution

This trade in women for prostitution occurred in a unique context in which a vigorous market for prostitutes existed in the colonial port towns of Southeast Asia. Brothel districts in major cities like Singapore were sanctioned by colonial governments to cater to the sexual needs of tens of thousands of migrant bachelor labourers. The manipulation of women in Japan by their families, when harvests failed and famine arrived, for economic, social and sexual purposes helped to legitimise this traffic in women for prostitution overseas. Prostitution was a flourishing business in Singapore at the end of the nineteenth century. It had become a multi-million dollar network linking remote villages in rural Japan with ports like Nagasaki and Kobe to the dockside in Hong Kong and brothels in Singapore. The flood of *singkeh*/coolies arriving to work in Singapore had created gender imbalance in the city, and the demand for prostitutes by migrant labourers was responsible for an extensive and organised traffic in young women and girls.[22]

In an investigation of the role of prostitution in modern Singapore history, an appraisal of the social relations between the *karayuki-san* and migrant labourer, as prostitute and coolie, must also take into account Japan's changing attitude and response to the existence of the *karayuki-san*. The Japanese had little trouble excusing the migration of women, prostitution and the spread of brothels throughout Southeast Asia in the name of capitalism and the state from 1895 to 1920. The overriding acceptance of the national need for prostitution and the 'flesh' trade overseas reflected the nature of Japanese society and an extreme nationalism. Some *zegen* who sent young women overseas as prostitutes managed to justify their activities under the banner of imperial glory, asserting that the sex trade was benefiting everyone. There was truth in the embarrassing position of these 'flesh traders'. It did not take long for small Japanese businesses to be established in the areas of Singapore where the *karayuki-san* resided. Kimono salesmen, pharmacists, photographers, florists, launderers, restaurateurs, cabinet-makers, doctors and dentists all set up businesses, or practices, in and around the brothel district, pinning their future success on the presence of the *karayuki-san*. In this way, the Japanese, who were still too weak to advance politically and militarily into Southeast Asia, progressed first economically by tacitly encouraging overseas migration and prostitution to develop their economic base. It was just after the Russo–Japanese war that the influence and wealth of the Japanese community began to visibly expand. There were nearly 700 *karayuki-san* in Singapore by then. These young women, in brightly coloured kimonos, would call out from under shining lanterns in Hylam, Malay and Malabar streets to passing coolies, sailors and soldiers. They called Singapore 'Shinkinzan', the new goldmine.[23]

Traffic in women and children from Japan and licensed brothel prostitution in Singapore were inextricably linked. Both flourished by the early twentieth century. The primary incentive for this trade that made Singapore a major destination for women and young girls was the organised houses of prostitution. They brought in big money catering to a vast, predominantly Chinese immigrant labour force. Notwithstanding the existence of brothel prostitution in Japan, this international traffic was promoted to a far greater extent by a network of brothels in Singapore and other seaports in Southeast Asia. Social conditions surrounding Singapore's rapid commercial development in the last decades of the nineteenth century made the brothels a necessity.[24] And consequently, the houses in the Malay Street and Smith Street areas became a major source of supply for procurers and traffickers—'flesh traders'. The trade in *karayuki-san* was extremely lucrative. The demand for Japanese women was so great in the region at the turn of the century that it could not be fully met, and large sums of money exchanged hands in the process of buying and selling. Japanese girls were sought after as *karayuki-san* throughout Asia including India, Burma, Thailand, the Netherlands Indies, in the French colonial city of Saigon, and in US-controlled Manila. Some girls were even sent by *zegen* to the far-flung pearling centre of Broome in north-western Australia, and to Sandakan on the east coast of Borneo.[25] Various groups of Japanese traffickers were extremely active, targeting lucrative places for their business in the last decades of the nineteenth century. The opportunities for prostitutes brought over by these traffickers were extraordinary around the tin-mining centre of Ipoh, and in Medan, where tobacco plantations were being opened up, while Johore, with its rubber estates and proximity to Singapore, was singled out. Singapore, which offered practically unrestricted possibilities to traffickers, was the hub for the movement of Japanese women intended for prostitution in Southeast Asia. The port-city was the distributing centre for traders who wished to place the girls not only in Johore and the Federated Malay States, but also in Siam, Borneo and the Netherlands Indies. The scenario was very similar to that in Hong Kong a decade earlier except Singapore was now the place of transit and the number of destined targets multiplied a hundredfold as the region lay at the doorstep of the city.

The *karayuki-san*, *zegen* and Japanese brothel-keepers were well acquainted with the various China ports and Hong Kong. Shanghai and Hong Kong were recognised centres of prostitution and used as depots for the supply of

Japanese prostitutes to other ports of China in the 1870s and 1880s. In other Asian ports, such as Saigon and Haiphong in French Indo-China, and Hainan Island and Macao, there were no large colonies of *karayuki-san* but only a Japanese brothel here and there. By 1895 the centre of Japanese traffic had shifted from one British port, Hong Kong, to another, Singapore. In both ports, sanction had been given by the British government for the establishment of Japanese brothels, side by side with respectable Japanese businesses, and it proved extremely difficult under such circumstances for the imperial government to carry out its intention of ending traffic in Japanese girls for brothel prostitution in both colonies.[26] As early as 1885 the Japanese Minister for Foreign Affairs had requested the colonial government in Hong Kong to restrict the number of licences granted to Japanese women for prostitution to no more than fifty at any one time. The Minister informed the Colonial Secretary that his government was attempting to take more stringent measures to prevent as much as possible the departure of these women from Japan for China and Korea.[27]

Japanese prostitutes were resident in most Chinese and Korean ports during the 1880s. There were an estimated 800 *karayuki-san* in Shanghai tugging on the sleeves of customers in 1882. The Japanese Consul there had between 500 and 600 sent back to Japan.[28] The remainder evaded the dragnet and were shifted farther south to Cochin China and Singapore, which was shortly to become the major centre for the distribution of *karayuki-san* throughout Southeast Asia. The Kobe *Yushin Nippo* published the life history of an eighteen-year-old girl who was returned to Kobe by the Japanese Consul to Singapore, and her account gave the authorities some idea of the widespread destinations and organisation of the *zegen*. She was taken from Osaka to Kobe, from Kobe to Hong Kong, and then she and another girl were transported first to Singapore, and then handed over to a Japanese brothel-keeper in Batavia, who also owned a house in Sumatra. The keeper paid 450 yen for her. When he opened a second establishment in another part of Sumatra the girl was transferred there. The *karayuki-san* became so ill working there that she had to be sent to a hospital. Through the good offices of the Japanese Consul in Singapore she was returned at the expense of the brothel-keeper to Kobe. On the same day she was originally sent to Singapore from Hong Kong, nine other girls being detained with her were shipped to Australia.[29] Here we can also make serious use of popular evidence, such as a contemporary sorrowful song sung to the *samisen* about the *karayuki-san*, literally telling social historians about the demand, range of geographical destinations, and ultimate fate of many girls from Kyushu, the part of Japan closest to China.

> Carried on the drifting current
> Her destination will be
> In the west, Siberia;
> or in the east, Java.
> Which country will be her grave?
> Lover's chatter
> Is like the dust
> Of any country.[30]

When famine and crop failure struck the farming villages of northern and southern Japan, peasants starved to death and girls were sold to *zegen* by their families. There were at least fifteen major famines in the Meiji-Taisho era with villagers on Hokkaido and north-eastern Honshu suffering most severely.[31] In famine years the number of young rural girls destined for brothels abroad skyrocketed; two of the worst famines occurred in 1905 and 1934. Twenty-nine years after Japan's major victory over Russia, and the last devastating catastrophe in the north, isolated starving peasants in Honshu still had to sell their daughters to traffickers as late as 1934, in order to save the rest of their household. In that one year alone nearly 16,000 girls were sent from the six northern prefectures to work in urban brothels, geisha houses, restaurants and cafés. An additional 36,540 also sought work in cities further south as maids or textile mill workers.[32]

It was *zegen* like Muraoka Iheiji and his henchmen who went to the stricken northern prefectures and to Kyushu and the surrounding islands in search of girls to purchase for the Singapore market. Traffickers like Muraoka were directly involved with brothel owners in Singapore in a highly organised network. Ginji Shibuya, Gajero Nihonda and Tambaya were the king pins in the organisation of traffic in women and children, and the control of brothels in turn-of-the century Singapore.[33] Supply followed demand in the years from 1895 to 1900. Thereafter, the number of *karayuki-san* in Singapore kept increasing, and with the steady rise came even more *zegen* who preyed upon them for a living. Mr Tomijiro Onda, an eighty-year-old prewar barber who had lived most of his life in Singapore, told Yamazaki Tomoko that the influential traffickers included Akijiro Kusada and his brother from Shimabara Peninsula, the Shimada family from Isahaya, the Naka family from Fukuoka and the Meyosaki family from Nagasaki.[34] But among these leading names in the Japanese overseas vice trade it was only Muraoka who ever wrote about his activities as a *zegen*. He left Japan for Hong Kong in 1885, serving as a deckhand on a British ship. In Tientsin he left the vessel and moved on to Shanghai and Amoy before establishing his own brothel and headquarters in Singapore between 1890 and 1894. In the short space of four years, he claimed, in somewhat exaggerated fashion, to have presided over the smuggling from Japan to Singapore of more than 3,200 women destined to become *karayuki-san*. Muraoka despatched them as far west as Mauritius and as far east as Australia for anywhere from 400 to 2,000 yen. After leaving Singapore in 1894, the year brothel registration was abolished, he helped to pioneer the trade in Borneo, the Netherlands Indies and the Philippines by the turn of the century.

There were also prostitute brokers actively involved in the traffic between villages in northern and southern Japan; and ports like Kobe, Osaka and Nagasaki. They helped to organise lots that were taken to the seaports on an advance payment of as little as two or three yen per girl; they were then transferred to the likes of Muraoka to be shipped overseas.[35] Most of these peasant girls had been deceived by brokers into believing they would obtain decent wage-paying jobs in Osaka or Tokyo, rather than in foreign countries, as domestic servants, waitresses or nursemaids. Perhaps as many as one-fifth, though, went voluntarily. They knew what they were letting themselves in for by going abroad to be a *karayuki-san*.[36] The increasing complexity of this traffic for brothel prostitution was reflected in the fact that Japanese girls were being labelled in sets according to destination and demand by 1912, as bound 'for Korea', 'for Siberia' or 'for America'. Many of them were thus sold and transported in batches as '*Chosen yuki*', 'Siberia yuki' or 'Ameyuki-san'.[37]

The majority of women were smuggled overseas on coal ships plying the route between Nagasaki and Shanghai. Sailors, whose steamers regularly berthed in Kobe or Nagasaki, were often bribed by *zegen* into taking girls on board as stowaways. From Shanghai, they generally went first to Hong Kong where they spent some time in the brothels, and were required to learn some English. After a short stay in the colony, often of several months' duration, the girls were again stowed aboard as secret passengers in the hold of a ship and taken southward to Singapore.[38] Increasing recognition of the extent of this organised traffic to Singapore was the frequency with which the phrase 'illegal female emigrants' began to appear in newspapers in the Fukuoka prefecture. The girls who had been purchased or kidnapped in Japan, and smuggled in the bilge or coalbunkers of steamships without proper passports or documents, were sold at the wharf to brothel-keepers, as soon as they landed in Singapore. The price of an attractive young woman could be as much as 2,000 yen once lodging and transportation costs were calculated.[39]

As no passports were required for Japanese citizens going to Chinese and Korean ports it was difficult for Japanese authorities to control this traffic. A series of regulations and instructions to Japanese consuls abroad led to some prevention against *zegen* taking women and girls overseas for brothel prostitution.[40] But there was no way the marine police and emigration authorities could watch all the boats, especially foreign vessels and railway stations, and question closely all possible persons suspected of being *zegen* or possible victims of traffic. As a consequence of these problems, the Japanese government promulgated an important law in 1896 to prevent women from openly leaving the country to engage in prostitution abroad. Henceforth, unless given permission by the proper administrative authorities, no immigrant woman could take passage to a foreign country.[41] But traffic in Japanese women to Southeast Asia was not reduced to any extent by these measures in the period 1890–1914, because of the twin factors that made the international trade in women and young girls possible; first, the highly profitable well-organised brothel system set up to meet colonial demand abroad, which was tightly controlled by key families, syndicates and *zegen*; and, second, the economic impact the *zegen* and *karayuki-san* had as they spread out from Singapore to the Malay Peninsula, and into the neighbouring islands of the Netherlands Indies, fostering the prosperity of local Japanese merchants, and sending back much-needed foreign exchange to Japan. The exact number of Japanese prostitutes imported to Singapore annually during the latter part of the nineteenth century is not known. But several sources are available to estimate the dramatic increase in the number of *karayuki-san* between the late 1870s and 1914. The social and demographic data in the Japanese consular records for Singapore and other parts of Southeast Asia indicate a high degree of under-registration.[42] In most tabulations of female occupations the categories 'others' and 'special' tacitly meant prostitution in the consul's brief, as a large proportion of the women who had not registered with the consulate had been smuggled out of Japan, and they would not have shown up in the census otherwise. As a consequence, the number of *karayuki-san* cited in Japanese consular records for various Southeast Asian countries were at best conservative estimates. For example, Muraoka stated that in 1906, the number of unregistered *karayuki-san* in Manila alone was near the 400 mark.[43] From census data on Singapore taken from Consular Records, one can see just how unreliable the estimates were on the increase in both the number and percentage of Japanese women arriving there between 1877 and 1914.

Singapore's connection with Japanese traffic and brothel prostitution was established by 1877. There were already two brothels present and fourteen Japanese women had arrived there—all of them *karayuki-san*. From this inauspicious beginning the *karayuki-san* went on to work in brothels throughout Southeast Asia by 1905, and their early arrival in Singapore was to

Table 14.1 This table shows how unreliable the estimates were of the increase in both the number and percentage of Japanese women arriving in Singapore between 1877 and 1901.

	1871	1881	1891	1901
Japanese males	1	8	58	188
Japanese females	0	14	229	578
Total	1	22	287	766

Source: Song Ong Siang, *One Hundred Years History of the Chinese in Singapore*

open the door for many more Japanese who also came to the *Nanshin* 'to earn a living'. In the aftermath of victory in the Sino–Japanese war in 1895 the number of women sent abroad increased, in part fanned by the flames of militarism, national pride and the patriotic virtue of '*chukun aikaku*'—Emperor worship and love of country.[44] At the turn of the century there were between 2,000 and 3,000 Japanese living in Singapore, Muraoka said. According to the *zegen*, 80 per cent of them were women and they were all involved in traffic and brothel prostitution. The census, of all documents, only declared that there were 578 Japanese females in Singapore in 1901.[45] However, by the early 1900s it was estimated that 500 to 600 girls from poor families were sent to Hong Kong and Singapore alone each year. In Hong Kong they fetched upward of $250 each, and in Singapore the market price was up to $350. It was believed that *zegen*, like Muraoka, made a profit of around $200 on each girl, and could readily earn in the vicinity of $100,000 a year.[46] The *Fukuoka Nichinichi*, in discussing the treatment of Japanese women as 'illegal immigrants' and prostitutes abroad, provided an estimate that is closer to Muraoka's figure, of the scale of the traffic; by 1900 Singapore's Japanese population was approximately 1,800 of which more than half were *karayuki-san*.[47]

After Japan's victory over Russia in 1905, the lesson of the economic necessity of the expansion of a strong mother country was further driven home, and many Japanese shops were opened in Singapore. Ambitious, practically minded Japanese moved into the *Nanshin* seeking their fortunes: not just men but women, too. *Karayuki-san* arrived continuously in Singapore from this time. The traffic was nearing the height of its prosperity. In the immediate aftermath of the Russo–Japanese war many *karayuki-san* were repatriated from Vladivostok and the interior of Siberia to Japan. Unable to adjust and settle down to village life once back home, they left Japan again to go to Singapore, Sumatra, Borneo and Australia. The traffic continued to grow and peaked during the Taisho era, when the largest number of *karayuki-san* operated in Singapore.[48] There were over 300,000 Japanese working overseas in 1906, and almost 10 per cent of them, more than 22,000, were *karayuki-san*.[49] Singapore had not only become the focal point for Japan's supply of prostitutes to the region by that time, it was also reputed to have the largest number of *karayuki-san* as can be seen by the following figures: Singapore, 2,086; Vladivostok, 1,087; Batavia, 970; Shanghai, 747; Hong Kong, 485; Manila, 392; and Saigon, 192.[50] Not just in British Singapore, but also in the Dutch East Indies, the US Philippines and French Indo-China there existed well-organised Japanese brothel districts, which were run by big-time operators like Tambaya of Nagasaki.[51] In the following year, 1907, Singapore's *karayuki* population steadily increased, assisted in part by the northern invasion of 'Siberia-*yuki*', although the registry book in the Office of the Chinese Protectorate showed only 620 Japanese prostitutes who were active.[52] There were in addition many unregistered prostitutes particularly among the newly arriving girls from Russia. One can imagine how busy the brothels were at this time as victorious Japanese sailors celebrated their shore leave in Singapore by visiting the brothels, and how prosperous the traffic was then for the *zegen*.

In 1915 it was asserted by an old ship captain, who had lived in the port for many years and was well informed on the subject of the 'flesh trade', that there were 1,500 Japanese prostitutes in Singapore alone. Others estimated as few as 402 in the public brothels in the same year. But besides the public brothels, many of the Japanese teahouses, bars, restaurants and hotels were also used as brothels and kept *karayuki-san* for hire. This would bring the number up to something like the shipmaster's estimate, perhaps, a little more than 1,100,[53] but I think it is still somewhat over the true figure. In March of 1917, there were only 328 Japanese females of all ages in the whole of Singapore island, according to a confidential letter sent to the Colonial Secretary by Sir Arthur Young, the Governor.[54] Whatever was a fair average in point of numbers for the *karayuki-san* at this time, it is certain that traffic to Singapore fell off sharply in the next few years. By 1921 the Japanese prostitute population had been dramatically reduced as a result of an imperial decree, which abolished brothel prostitution abroad, and recalled the women to Japan. This measure, and the concerted efforts of British officials to assist the Japanese Consul in its implementation, had a ruinous impact on the activities of the *zegen* in this leading city in Southeast Asia where there were so many Japanese brothels and prostitutes. The primary focus of their traffic now shifted back up north, as the *zegen* attempted to organise a legion of women to follow the Japanese army into China. Those *karayuki-san* deliberately remaining behind in Singapore were forced to live and work as 'sly prostitutes' in the Malay and Banda Street areas.

Brothels and prostitutes

Prostitution in Singapore was carried on by *karayuki-san* in public brothels registered under the Contagious Diseases Ordinance in two parts of the city that were recognised as brothel areas; in public brothels in the city outside these two areas; in private brothels, which were unregistered and not recognised by the Chinese Protectorate, and which were generally known as 'sly' brothels; by *karayuki-san* who did not live in brothels; and by Japanese women and young girls who were not professional prostitutes, but who occasionally prostituted themselves in lodging houses.[55]

In Singapore between the 1880s and 1920s the recognised red light districts served as a 'natural' form of boundary maintenance. Licensed brothels were confined to specific localities catering for Chinese and non-Chinese clients, including Europeans. The licensed brothels for Chinese were primarily clustered in the 'big town' south of the river where the largest number of coolie labourers were found. Brothels for non-Chinese were chiefly concentrated at the north end of the city. The primary colonial administrative aim of this 'natural' segregation of brothels into districts for Chinese and non-Chinese clients was to separate, control and regulate the behaviour of the prostitutes and curb the spread of VD.

While the carefully bounded brothel quarters were subject to regulatory control, geographically and socially, the character of the two 'safe zones' was also shaped by the fact that the Smith Street area was situated in the heart of Chinatown, and the Malay Street area was in an entertainment district and urban slum not far from the central business centre of Singapore. This spatial overlap between the recognised districts where prostitution flourished and Chinatown was a direct consequence of Singapore's expansion. As the economy and port grew, so did the migrant labouring populations of the city. However, the brothel-keepers, merchants, cabinet-makers, clothiers, florists, launderers, restaurant owners and doctors, whose prosperity depended on the patronage of the *karayuki-san*, accounted for only a small fraction of that population, compared with the vast army of labourers who lived and worked in these Chinese working-class districts. Strictly speaking, segregated prostitution did not exist in Singapore, according to colonial authorities, because there were public brothels both inside and outside the special districts. But by tolerating the existence of these red light areas in marginal working-class neighbourhoods, in the heart of the city, the colonial government was inadvertently highlighting the importance of prostitution. This policy of toleration and transgression with respect to the locality of the brothels sought to set social and economic boundaries, and regulate the sexuality and behaviour of Chinese and non-Chinese:

Simply by staying out of this section, one could avoid taking cognizance of the business or its practitioners. But by locating the district at its very Centre, the city emphasized its existence and heightened its visibility. In some cities, [like Singapore], citizens almost had to avoid the red light district consciously, thus intensifying their awareness of its existence.[56]

By 1905, Malay Street was ablaze with colourful Japanese lanterns by night which winked from the doorways of brothels that housed the *karayuki-san*. Some of the most progressive houses in the *suteretsu* stayed open into the small hours of the morning, and *karayuki-san* who made no secret of their desire to please, also worked into the wee hours in the *suteretsu*. This local term used by the *karayuki-san* to refer to the Malay Street area was neither Malay nor Chinese, but rather a corruption of the English word 'streets', which had been distorted by the hearing and pronunciation of the rural women from Amakusa and Shimabara.[57] A Japanese reporter described the *suteretsu* in 1910 for the people of Kyushu in a local newspaper, the *Fukuoka Nichinichi*:

> Around nine o'clock I went to see the infamous Malay Street. The buildings were constructed in a western style with their facades painted blue, under the verandah hung red-gas lanterns with numbers such as one, two or three, and wicker chairs were arranged beneath the lanterns. Hundreds and hundreds of young Japanese girls were sitting on the chairs calling out to passers-by, chatting and laughing...Most of them were wearing *Yukata* of striking colours...Their hair was arranged in the pompadour style with big ribbons attached. Most of them were young girls under twenty years of age. I learned from a maid at the hotel that the majority of these girls came from Shimabara and Amakusa in Kyushu.[58]

When Yamazaki visited Singapore in the mid-1970s she found, much to her disappointment, that telltale signs of the *suteretsu* had all but disappeared as it had been totally swallowed up by then in the urban renewal of the city. The only tangible evidence of the earlier existence of the once discreet Japanese brothel quarter appeared to be the street names themselves, emblazoned on the side of a corner building, especially 'Malay Street':

> I walked along these streets filled with deep emotion. But the old Japanese brothel quarters were nothing but slums. Row after row of three-storey buildings flanked both sides of the street...Most of the buildings facing onto the street were Chinese shops...I could see wash hanging from poles, as there

were no windows except those facing onto the street...many brightly coloured shirts and trousers were hanging from them. Most of the buildings were at least sixty or seventy years old, and the plaster was peeling off the facades revealing the bricks underneath. The walls were painted various colours in the rooms but it only tended to intensify the overall slum-like atmosphere.[59]

While the physical locality of the buildings revealed very little to Yamazaki, the memory of the presence of the *karayuki*-women in these 'streets' lingers in local minds. Interestingly, elderly Chinese residents still use the term *yap pun kai* to refer to specific streets in the two different brothel districts where the Japanese women once resided. I was told this in 1987, despite the fact that the *karayuki-san* have been absent from Malay Street, Hylam Street and Spring Street for more than sixty-six years, since the abolition of licensed Japanese prostitution in Singapore occurred in 1921.[60]

The southern area was located principally in North Canal Road, and in Hong Kong, Chin Chew and Chin Hin Streets in the first three decades of the second half of the nineteenth century. Cantonese women, who received only Chinese, resided in these houses which were generally ill-ventilated and dirty. Teochiu *ah ku* also resided in brothels in North Canal, New Bridge and North Bridge Roads, while the 'all nationality' women, primarily European and Malay prostitutes, frequented North Canal and Rochore Roads, and Chin Chew Street.[61] However, by the 1890s the centre of the red light district had shifted six blocks further south into the heart of Chinatown—the Kreta Ayer area—as it expanded in the last years of the nineteenth century, the southern area by then was taken to comprise Smith Street, Sago Street, Trengganu Street, Upper Hokkien Street and Chin Hin Street.[62] These five streets were occupied chiefly by Chinese and Japanese brothels. Sago Street had at least three establishments labelled 'Japanese house' in letters over 30 centimetres high, above the door.[63] It was a common sight in this street before World War I to see ten or twelve prostitutes on view in each brothel soliciting from the doorways. Often referred to as Little Temple Street by Cantonese, because of a local landmark, the Toh Peh Kong Temple built in 1895, Sago Street had at least twenty-eight brothels in 1902.[64] An old man who grew up there remembered the exact locality of some of these less classical examples of shophouse architecture. He began by producing a small list of street names and brothel locations that he had been thinking about since we last met. I then showed him a photograph of Sago Street in 1910. He responded, 'there were more brothels on the right hand side of the street if one was standing at the New Bridge Road end and fewer on the left hand side.'[65] Neighbouring Banda and Spring Streets were also known in Cantonese as *Phan*

Tsai Mei, 'lane of foreign prostitutes', because so many *karayuki-san* were found there.[66] Spring Street is still locally known in the Kreta Ayer area as *Yap Pun Kai*. The term 'Spring Street' would only be used with a non-dialect speaker, or non-Chinese.[67]

There are limitations on the data available for plotting distribution, numbers and changing patterns of location, and size of brothels in the period of the heyday of coolie migration and organised prostitution. Here, I have to rely on a combination of seemingly unrelated statistical materials in order to build up a picture of the distribution and size of brothels that is convincing in terms of fact. First, the report of the committee appointed to enquire into the working of the Contagious Diseases Ordinance in 1877 provides a valuable appendix listing licensed brothels and the number of prostitutes in each house for the month of February. Second, a copy of a letter from the Protector of Chinese to the Colonial Office, to which was attached a list of brothels in particular streets, requesting police assistance, with the number and name of the keeper, as well as a rare official return of licensed brothels and prostitutes from the records of the Chinese Protectorate for 1905.[68] Another source and form of official intervention, a 1902 list of brothels and coolie lodging houses to which water meters were attached, with a statement of receipts before and after the introduction of meters, also enables the social historian to 'discover' on which streets *karayuki-san* were most apt to congregate, in order to be near potential custom.[69] Finally, the Coroner's Inquests and Inquiries can provide systematic evidence, in this case about residential patterns, which will also yield information on the addresses of the brothels where the prostitutes were living in a particular year.

An immense increase in the number of brothels, invading parts of the city where they had never been seen before, occurred in the 1890s. Their rapid spread was as a result of the repeal of the Contagious Diseases Ordinance in 1887, the abolition of the registration of brothels in 1894, and a record increase in the migrant-labour force during those years. The statistics provided to the government by the Inspector-General in 1898 did not comprise all the brothels in the city. Possibly as many as one half of them may have escaped his lists, which were presumed to be more accurate with respect to the Japanese and European houses. Nevertheless, he located 308 Chinese brothels, whose inmates were returned by their keepers as 1,751. The Inspector-General also listed 121 other brothels containing 335 prostitutes, women of 'other nationalities'.[70] By 1917 the overall numbers had dropped off dramatically. In the six streets of the northern or Malay Street area, there were 337 multi-storey houses, of which 171 were brothels; their inmates were 910 *ah ku* in

120 brothels and 255 *karayuki-san* in 51 houses. In the southern or Smith Street area comprising five blocks there were 373 terraced houses, of which 63 were brothels. The inmates were 660 Chinese prostitutes, overwhelmingly Cantonese, in 61 houses and 12 Japanese in two houses.[71]

The number of women who could reside in a brothel depended entirely upon the size and accommodation of a house. While the overall number of brothels steadily increased in Chinatown between 1877 and 1905, the real dramatic growth occurred in the Smith Street area where the houses were mostly three and four storeys high, and the number of *ah ku* cramped in them rose accordingly—by 100 per cent. By 1905, a typical house in Sago and Trengganu Streets contained fourteen women, and the bigger brothels housed as many as seventeen or eighteen prostitutes. By way of comparison, the size of the Japanese brothels varied little from the end of the nineteenth century into the first part of the twentieth century, averaging between five and seven *karayuki-san* per enterprise, with more prostitutes and larger brothels being located on the southern fringe of Chinatown (see Table 14.2). Size-wise the two brothels situated in Sago Street were atypical establishments with twenty-three *karayuki* women in residence between them. The rapid growth of the Japanese brothels had been dramatic in both parts of the city. On the northern side they were concentrated in the few blocks of the Malay Street area. In 1878, two Japanese brothels had already opened their doors for business in Malay Street. Thereafter, the number of brothels continued to increase, and by 1887 there were more than 100 *karayuki-san* in Singapore. In 1902, there were 83 brothels and 611 women, and by 1905, thirty-seven years after the Meiji Restoration, and the year of the advent of the Russo–Japanese war, the number of Japanese brothels and prostitutes officially known to the Chinese Protectorate had reached 109 and 633 respectively (see Table 14.3).[72]

The long rows of shuttered Japanese brothels in the *suteretsu* were divided into higher and lower grade houses, but the Japanese, unlike the Chinese, rarely discriminated against clients on the basis of race. The *karayuki-san* were generally prepared to have sexual intercourse with any man who could pay the fee, providing they were not compelled to engage in abhorrent sexual behaviour. Mizuya Tsuboachi, in his early twentieth century travel account, described the visible signs of class distinction between the higher and lower grade brothels in the Malay Street area:

> Every brothel had a table and a few chairs in front of it, as well as benches along the wall. These were placed there for the *karayuki* girls to sit and wait for customers…and the girls…who all have chalk white faces like winter melons,

which look even more pale under the glow of the lamp…are calling out to any stranger, it doesn't matter whether he is a Chinese coolie or a black Tamil labourer.[73]

This was the usual way the *karayuki-san* went about their business, but there were also upper-class brothels where the women and girls were waiting for customers inside instead of actively displaying themselves in front of the brothel. There were no chairs and tables outside these higher class establishments, simply 'a carpet stretching from the entrance to the upper floor'.[74] Eating houses nearby served as annexes to the brothels in the *suteretsu*, creating a great blaze of electric light and colours: with customers coming and going, and *karayuki-san* everywhere. The three-storey restaurants were expensively furnished with electric fans, many pictures and mirrors, and served by efficient staff. However, despite all this nearby illumination the Japanese brothels were generally lit by

Table 14.2 The size of brothels in selected streets in the Southern Area in 1877 and 1905.

Locality	1877			1905		
	Number of Brothels	Number of Prostitutes	Average Number of Prostitutes	Number of Brothels	Number of Prostitutes	Average Number of Prostitutes
New Bridge Rd	33	205	6.2	0	0	0
North Canal Rd	20	95	4.8	4	14	3.5
Chin Hin St	12	65	5.4	17	133	7.8
Upper Hokkien St	36	360	10.0	36	310	8.6
Upper Cross St	4	5	1.2	10	32	3.2
Totals	105	730		67	489	
		Average number of prostitutes = 7.5			Average number of prostitutes = 7.3	
Smith Street				17	237	13.9
Trengganu Street				7	119	17.0
Sago Street				13	194	14.9
Spring Street				5	38	7.6
Banda Street				12	72	6
Totals				54	660	
					Average number of prostitutes = 12.2	

Source: This table has been compiled from List of Licensed Brothels for the month of February 1877, Appendix M, pp. LXI–LXIII, in Report of the Committee appointed to enquire into the working of Ordinance XXIII of 1870, commonly called the Contagious Diseases Ordinance, in *Straits Settlements Legislative Council Proceedings 1877*, Appendix 7, and Return of Brothels and Prostitutes Brothels known as the Protectorate, SSAR, 1905, p. 652.

Table 14.3 The size of Japanese brothels in selected streets in Singapore in 1905.

Locality	Number of brothels	Number of prostitutes	Average number of prostitutes
Hylam Street	26	153	5.8
Malabar Street	27	143	5.2
Malay Street	32	179	5.6
Bugis Street	6	30	5.0
Sago Street	2	23	11.5
Banda Street	11	67	6.0
Spring Street	5	38	7.6
Total	109	633	
		Average number of prostitutes = 5.8	

Source: Return of Brothels and Prostitutes Brothels known as the Protectorate, SSAR, 1905, p. 652.

only a single oil lamp in the entrance hall. A more sombre red gas lamp, meant to guide customers, with the street number on it, was hung out over the five footway in front of the house.[75]

Japanese brothels usually housed fewer women than the Chinese ones, and as a result the interiors of their houses were somewhat different, too. The entrance hall was much smaller than in a Chinese brothel and there was also a woven bead curtain hanging just behind the main door as one entered the house.[76] The Chinese brothels had a different sort of entrance, a vertical two-piece plank door that opened inward, set behind a slatted horizontal bar frame that slid in and out on a track across the entrance. This security system of double doors meant that the plank could be swung open, enabling people on the street to peer inside while the bar door remained shut, locked in place, preventing pedestrians or clients from entering or leaving the house without express permission.[77] The rooms upstairs in the Japanese houses in the *suteretsu* were somewhat more spacious; averaging about six *tatami* mats in width, which was a standard size for an average room then, and not nearly as dark or squalid as the cubicle-like rooms in many of the Chinese brothels.[78] However, none of the rooms used by the *karayuki-san* had toilets or cooking facilities; there was a common bathroom on each floor and a kitchen at the back of the house, which suggests that the Japanese brothels were certainly no exception to the rule concerning a general lack of amenities in working-class housing throughout Singapore.

Brothel prostitution was a lucrative form of business for Japanese and Chinese entrepreneurs in Singapore when it was undergoing rapid economic expansion and development. Running brothels in the city was considered one of the easiest ways to accumulate capital before the turn of the century.[79] Most of the pioneering Japanese enterprises in Singapore were involved with brothel prostitution in one way or another. The proprietors of these businesses, however, were obsessed with their respectability in a foreign land, and attempted to remain hidden behind other more legitimate economic investments, while continuing to extract considerable profit from the labour of the *karayuki-san*. One of the few genuine Japanese stores in the early days that was not a front for brothel prostitution was the Yamato Company.[80] On the other hand, well-to-do respectable Chinese did not think it at all demeaning to themselves and their interests to own brothels, and as law-abiding citizens to build houses on their property as brothels towards the end of the nineteenth century.[81]

To obtain an accurate picture of the earnings of a Japanese brothel in the turn-of-the-century period in the *suteretsu*, the social historian can conservatively calculate the brothel-keepers' earnings from available information. According to Yamazaki, Tarazo, a brothel-keeper, paid 300 yen for Osaki.[82] At that time an ordinary *karayuki-san* received from one to eight customers per day. There would have been on average five girls on the evening shift when Osaki started her first one with Tarazo. The Japanese houses operated twenty-four hours a day, seven days a week. Kikuyo Zendo, a contemporary of Osaki, told the celebrated filmmaker Shohei Imamuru that it was possible to earn up to 300 yen monthly after expenses in the Malay Street area. She grossed on average up to 420 yen a month.[83] That meant the tiny woman had to see at least 210 men monthly who paid two yen and the house took 40 per cent, but she got extra for doing extra. Every girl would average about 250 yen a month, so a Malay Street house would have roped in about 18,000 yen. The outstanding places would take nearly twice as much annually and there were at least 109 Japanese brothels in Singapore in 1905.

Brothel prostitution played an important economic role in providing the capital for the growth of Chinese and Japanese enterprise in Singapore at that time. Mori's fieldwork in Amakusa in the 1950s drew attention to the significant role of the *karayuki-san* and brothel prostitution in Japan's economic advance in Singapore and elsewhere in the *Nanshin*.[84] Kimono shops, restaurants, drugstores, confectionery shops, florists, boarding houses and many other ventures were soon bound up with the fate of the *karayuki-san*. If a *karayuki* girl was suddenly swept away like Oahki of 26–2 Hylam Street in 1903, the heads of many small establishments were bound to sustain a loss. From the medley of witnesses called to identify Oahki's body, we learn about the nature of some of the businesses that were directly dependent on brothel prostitution. These establishments included a coffee house at 26 Hylam Street managed by Otsuka who told the Coroner:

> The corpse that I have just seen…is that of Oahki, a prostitute living near me in Hylam Street…I last saw her alive about ten or eleven a.m. yesterday.[85]

O'Haru was a tailor. In his shop right across the street at 26–3 Hylam Street, he mended kimonos for girls like Oahki. European and Japanese physicians also made considerable money out of brothel prostitution, running private lock hospitals and providing weekly professional services on a full-fee-paying basis, as well as certificates of good health under the auspices of the Contagious Diseases Ordinance. So did the merchant banks handling remittances and other economic transactions on behalf of the prostitutes and neighbourhood business associates. The largest percentage of bank savings depositors and money order clients were predominantly people from the *suteretsu*.

Yamazaki and others have stressed how economically important were the retail shops and businesses that developed in Singapore because of the presence of the *karayuki-san*, and the foreign exchange sent back to Japan by women like Osaki and Oahki during this period. It was migrant women working primarily as *karayuki-san* that were at the cutting edge of Japan's economic expansion in the *Nanshin*. First came the brothels and the *karayuki-san*, then the merchants, shopkeepers and doctors, and finally the bankers. The establishment of the brothels and the growth of the *suteretsu* fostered the development of much-needed capital for economic diversification within both Singapore and Japan. The timing is important here. Japan could not yet compete successfully with the West as a modern industrial nation for markets and products, and was desperately in need of overseas currency to foster the will and capacity to do so in the foreseeable future. Mitsui in Singapore started by retailing Asahi beer in the *suteretsu*. Shortly afterwards, Yatabe Company became the sole agents for Henode beer, and a popular brand of cigarettes. Japanese textile shops such as Koyoma, Mizuno and Marato opened their doors wherever the *karayuki-san* were to be found. Singapore was no exception and the list of Japanese textile and dry good stores in the business directories and magazines by 1912 was long.[86]

The income flowing back to Japan from the *karayuki-san* was considerable. It is difficult to determine the level of official sanction of a policy by the Japanese government to deliberately foster the establishment of brothel prostitution and the sending of rural women abroad to earn much-needed foreign currency. Yamazaki and Hane's work is really saying that Japan's actions at the time implied such a policy was in place. A leading political theorist in Japan, Fukuzawa Yukichi, encouraged the emigration of women as prostitutes, especially to port cities and places undergoing rapid economic development—places like Singapore, Hong Kong and Vladivostok. Fukuzawa argued that since there was no future for these women in Japan, except as prostitutes, it would be far better for them and the nation for them to go abroad to accumulate foreign currency. He stated: 'Their going abroad should not be criticised; rather, since immigration is being encouraged, they should be given the freedom to do so.'[87]

It is difficult to assess the actual extent to which Fukuzawa's ideas influenced government thought and policy. It is clear though that while the Japanese government did not openly support the emigration of these women, little was done either to discourage it, or the growth of brothels overseas. This was due to the fact that the amount of money coming back to Japan from the establishment of the brothels abroad in places like Singapore was enormous. The Nagasaki post office alone was said to have dealt with over 200,000 yen a year, the basic amount annually sent back home in remittances from *karayuki-san* working in Southeast Asia.[88]

Total abolition

For Japanese women who came to Singapore in the early 1900s, lured by prospects of a better way of life, the mean living conditions of the city and sometimes dangerous work in brothels were considered insignificant compared to their chief hurdle at the end of World War I—the pride and honour of their nation back home. The background to the hotly contested issue of the future of overseas prostitution began in the late 1880s when a divided public vigorously debated the pros and cons of the *karayuki-sans*' role in helping to spearhead Japan's climb towards economic ascendancy in the region. The Japanese government established a consulate in Singapore in 1889, only one year after the repeal of the Contagious Diseases Ordinance, and six years before the outbreak of war with China.[89] The consuls, from the very beginning, viewed the presence of the *karayuki-san* in Singapore as a national disgrace, pointing to their increasing numbers as a tangible sign of Japan's continued weakness, and advised the Meiji government to adopt a more balanced economic policy. But the opinion of the likes of Nakagawa Tetsuro, the first consul, was sorely lacking in history and in sensitivity to Amakusa and Shimabara realities. Peasant women had performed the magnanimous task of working abroad as prostitutes, remitting desperately needed money to family and benefactors in the impoverished south, while their urban-industrialising neighbours in central Honshu were reluctant to share part of the modernisation burden. Some things did not change. Individuals such as Nakagawa Tetsuro had quickly analysed the economic, political and social costs of such personal sacrifice and reached the conclusion that they were unacceptable. The *karayuki-san* were a source of embarrassment to other Japanese who could afford to lead more dignified lives on their own terms in the city. The problem, as the consul put it in one of his first reports, was that:

> Not only the Chinese but also the Indians and Malays are quite cunning and arrogant. They despise and ridicule the Japanese in the extreme. It cannot be helped though because hitherto, the bulk of the Japanese population here are prostitutes, traffickers and pimps, most of whom are ex-sailors, who live off their earnings, except for a few small merchants and hawkers. Even gentlemen and wealthy merchants visit the brothels in transit to and from Japan. That is why they scorn us, they believe that all Japanese are involved in the prostitution racket.[90]

In a similarly frank letter to the consul in 1892, a high-ranking Japanese naval officer who passed through Singapore en route to France to take command of a new dreadnought, expressed his feelings of indignation against the lukewarm attitude of his Government in permitting wholesale Japanese prostitution in Singapore. 'It grieves me greatly,' he said,

> being aware of the pains and sacrifices which my government is making and has been making for so many years to advance in every respect towards the highest standard of civilization and morality, and thus merit the respect and esteem of outside nations, to see the fruits of those efforts partially marred by the lowest and vilest class of my country women. What must foreigners, who have never set foot in our country think of its social condition when the only class whom they encounter outside of it consists almost solely of our lowest class of society. Surely they must, on this account naturally be inclined to despise our nation, and, so far, they are not to be blamed for doing so. It is true that in our country, as well as in all others, there are numbers of prostitutes but then there are certain places which are set apart exclusively for their residence and which are always on the outskirts of the cities and towns, so that respectable persons are not shocked by coming in contact with them while they are parading their vice before the eyes of the public, as is the case in

this place, where they reside in the centre of the city and within a stone's throw of the public place of worship.[91]

There was nothing beneficial at all about the women in the young officer's mind and his attitude hardened even more at the end of his letter, leaving no grounds for his countrymen to go soft on the presence of the *karayuki-san*:

> I most emphatically assert that there is no reason whatsoever why there should be in Singapore or any other foreign place Japanese prostitutes, and such likewise, I am sure, is your opinion, my brother officers, and that of every respectable Japanese. However, such a state of things might in my estimation be easily remedied if our consuls were more stringent in their dealing towards this class of persons, and even if our government were to be more cautious in according them passports by which they are enabled to leave Japan, though I have been told that many of them, if not the greater majority, have succeeded in arriving in foreign ports through the aid and abetting of a low class of foreigners who, so to say, have smuggled them over in the guise of housekeepers, servants and nurses. It may perhaps be utterly impossible to have the whole of them expelled from Singapore, but most assuredly the evil might be greatly minimized if our consul were to take the matter into his serious consideration…Even the few respectable country women of ours who reside here complain that they are occasionally, when passing along the streets, mistaken by foreigners as belonging to the low class mentioned, and are insulted.[92]

However, public thought in Japan was split over the future of the *karayuki-san*. Influential opinion-makers like Fukuzawa Yukichi stressed their reputation for helping to forge a modern free-enterprise economy. To those desperate for foreign capital, and committed to the transformation of Japan's urban-industrial sector along disciplined modern lines, the financial contribution of the *karayuki-san* was a national asset. The attitude of these modernisation theorists about the work of the *karayuki-san* was wholly pragmatic. On the other hand, the abolitionists called for more care in the future development and welfare of rural Kyushu society, which compelled women to become prostitutes and migrate abroad. However, the *karayuki-san* in the 1890s had no time to debate with diplomats, naval officers, politicians and businessmen about the merits or demerits of whether their presence abroad was a 'national humiliation' or a 'national asset'. These women, many already victims of Japan's uneven economic development, were attempting to put their lives and future on an equal footing.

Because prostitution was one way to live, their supporters and families in Japan benefited, as the capital they remitted boosted tiny local markets and poverty-stricken villages, both as a means of converting debt to equity and of financing economic growth through purchasing of land and other assets. But in 1894 the Meiji government announced guidelines for a new immigration policy to regulate migrant labour. The bill, which was passed in the same year that the registration of brothels was withdrawn in Singapore, contained a provision phasing out women working overseas as prostitutes and brothel-keepers. It also sharpened and defined future employment for migrant women, which was to be limited to the domestic sphere. But problems of implementation and local control remained unresolved. The government wanted rural officials and police to play a major role, but this development placed them in a quandary. They could not always resist the exhortations, bribes and fear of reprisal from traffickers and local families desperately seeking to fill the economic vacuum in remote rural areas, to cooperate in sending their daughters overseas as *karayuki-san*.

By 1909, some influential members of the Japanese community in Singapore and several missionaries had begun to call for an end to Japanese brothels. For abolitionists, it was a question of national honour and prestige, and of being viewed as a 'civilised' nation in the eyes of the West.[93] In the minds of critics and reformers, Japan had been foolish to try and emulate the West's economic example to be modern and potentially self-sufficient by trying to sacrifice the human resources of the nation, especially the women, in the interests of national policy. European powers like Britain and France with resource-rich colonies and a moral mission were bound to question the wisdom of an economic policy that made the impoverished outer islands of its archipelago, namely Hokkaido and Kyushu, so dependent on Honshu, the emergent urban-industrial centre, that their women had to work abroad as prostitutes, otherwise their regional economies would collapse, and their people starve. As Japan's global links strengthened, embarrassed Japanese residents in Singapore began to challenge the belief that the *karayuki-san* had to be tolerated. Legitimate businessmen and Christian-inspired Japanese missionaries with ties to the Salvation Army advocated eventual prohibition of *karayuki-san* and tighter control of brothels in the city during the five years preceding the Great War.

The parts began to fall into place for the abolitionists in 1913. For that year the movement received a real boost when Consul Fujii cooperated with colonial authorities to curb traffic in women. He expelled all known Japanese traffickers and pimps from Singapore. As a result of the consul's efforts, seventy-two Japanese men involved in the 'shameful' business were deported.[94] However, this measure did not prove decisive in putting an end to traffic because of the vital role brothels played in the economy of the Japanese community in Singapore, as well as in the different prefectures in Japan where the women came from. After the 1913 campaign the *zegen* disappeared from public view, but they continued to lurk behind the scenes, manipulating the *karayuki-san* and sexual economy in a city where colonial authorities continued to tolerate brothel prostitution.

In the course of the next several years there was factional strife among leading *zegen* in Singapore in the power reshuffle to fill gaps that occurred in the aftermath of the first wave of expulsions. Anonymous reports began to reach the Japanese consulate as *zegen* became increasingly active once again, and there was more than one public confrontation among themselves, as they became more suspicious of one another in an atmosphere of unleashed competition and bloodletting. The Japanese Consul took advantage of these troubles to capture four principal traffickers in April 1914; one managed to escape shortly afterwards, but the other three were arrested, imprisoned and subsequently deported. Despite having respectable white-collar fronts as a dentist, plantation owner and manager of a retail store, they made no effort to contest the issue of their deportation, lacking the will to resist the decision of the British authorities to expel them.[95] Once again, *zegen* and others with brothel connections packed up and fled in face of the crackdown, leaving behind only their official photographs as a telltale sign of the role they had played in brothel prostitution.[96] The British authorities had been for some time in communication with the consul and it was decided in June 1915, in the immediate aftermath of this second exodus, that no more Japanese women were to enter the colony for the purposes of prostitution. As a result of this decision, it was hoped their numbers would diminish until none were left. The consul considered that the national honour of Japan was at stake, and interested himself keenly in the matter.[97]

But, once again, just when Japan, on the basis of reports from its consulates in Southeast Asia was prepared to finally take effective measures against brothel prostitution abroad, the imperial proclamation banning it was postponed because of economic uncertainties. Japan developed the economic jitters in 1915. Chinese merchants in Southeast Asia staged an extraordinary regional boycott, protesting against the twenty-one demands Japan had presented to China, which forced many Japanese merchants to the wall as monetary strategies and credit policies fell apart.[98] Japan's policy of raising foreign currency and maintaining liquidity at levels necessary to sustain economic growth while preserving price and exchange rate stability verged on collapse. Consequently, in the years leading up to the end of World War I no policy shift occurred from

Japan's earlier economic strategy of expecting *karayuki-san* to remit capital, as its economy geared up for a recovery stimulated in part by foreign exchange the women sent back to prime the pump to induce consumption. The Japanese government did not give any reason for the silence, but the demand for capital and the necessity for economic advance during the First World War ended the debate over policies to ban prostitution abroad. The boycott by overseas Chinese merchants which had precipitated these jitters brought little relief to the disgruntled consul in Singapore as the favourable climate to move against brothel prostitution was lost in the economic turmoil and backlash of 1915.[99]

Despite the initial economic setback caused by the Chinese boycott, the development of Japanese business interests and population was steady during the remaining years of the war.[100] Japan was able to take advantage of a surge in trade and investment opportunities in Southeast Asia created by the withdrawal of German and British economic interests to feed the war effort. Within a short space of time, more Japanese shipping firms, import and export businesses and numerous small investors, so necessary to strengthen Japan's drive to become Asia's most powerful nation, were attracted to Singapore, than seemed possible a few years earlier. Out of the fifty leading houses in 1919, comprising banks, shipping corporations, import and export agencies and general stores, which altogether employed some 450 men, no less than thirty-five had been opened since 1916.[101] The Japanese Association of Singapore, the public organisation of the community in the city, increasingly undertook research and provided services pertaining to legal matters, fiscal regulations and future economic concerns. When the Singapore government passed an *Aliens Registration Act* in May 1917 the Japanese Association took charge of this matter, to ensure that none of its residents, including prostitutes, failed to register; almost half the community in the city in 1917, numbering 1,805 men, were engaged in mercantile pursuits, photography and hairdressing. The census listed 947 women, the majority of whom were *karayuki-san*.[102]

Japanese economic development in Southeast Asia had been influenced directly by the course of events during World War I. The Ministry of Foreign Affairs was especially concerned to promote an image of Japan, among the fraternity of victorious powers, as an economically progressive Asian nation. The *karayuki-san* were to pay dearly as Japan searched for a formula to impress the West that it had successfully modernised.[103] By 1920 Japan had established itself as a result of several years of unprecedented growth in trade from its exports, which brought in large amounts of income and recoverable credit, as Asia's major economic power in the region. However, the beneficiaries of this record-breaking trade in Southeast Asia were not the rural women of Amakusa and Shimabara who had been smuggled from their coastal villages and farms to brothels in Singapore. They were worst hit. The comparative slackening of deposit growth from *karayuki-san* meant that the currency coming from these hard-pressed women assumed less national significance in the new postwar economic climate. The women were to be badly victimised by their country's obsession to develop and compete economically and politically along capitalist–militarist lines with Western powers. The Japanese government recognised the danger of adverse propaganda that could be directed against it by Britain and other European nations, as to whether Japan really was a culturally sophisticated, enlightened society, if it continued to condone a system of brothel prostitution abroad. Capitalism and being 'modern' now took on a different meaning as Japan prepared to abolish the livelihood of the *karayuki-san*. When Japan opened her doors to the West in the second half of the nineteenth century it had little of value to trade with the outside world. The women of Kyushu and Honshu who were encouraged to go abroad in ensuing decades to work as prostitutes and remit much-needed foreign currency could no longer live on the edge of Japanese society's toleration by 1919. The continued presence of the *karayuki-san* was considered a national disgrace, and proof that Japan still lacked an innovative approach to developing its economy in a competitive world. Japan came under increasing pressure from foreign governments to close its brothels overseas if it wanted to share in the political and economic privileges enjoyed by a select group of Western nations.

Because the continued presence of *karayuki-san* in European colonies and foreign countries adversely reflected on the prestige of Japan and affected the sound development of Japanese interests abroad, the imperial government ordered its consular representatives to take steps to bring about repatriation of all Japanese prostitutes overseas. The women were in no case to be repatriated forcibly, but it was the duty of consuls to persuade them to leave.[104] They were to be assisted in their efforts by local Japanese, who banded together to bring pressure to bear on *karayuki-san* to return to Japan for the sake of its national development. Nowhere was the abolition policy carried out more swiftly and with remarkable energy than in Singapore, where, after a long series of instructions from the Ministry of Foreign Affairs, more than nine-tenths of the *karayuki-san* in the city were compelled to leave for Japan within the space of several years. The consul's concern over possible economic loss and the image of Japanese women, as other than 'grasping vixens' tugging on the sleeves of European gentlemen walking down the street of an international port-city, led to collaboration with British authorities to deport all *karayuki-san* in 1920.[105] Yamazaki Heikichi, the Deputy Consul, sensed the timing was right and moved decisively. He brought together leading representatives from the Japanese community for a two-day conference to make a decision on the abolition of prostitution. There may have been some who would have disagreed under other circumstances, but at the conference table they also swam with the tide in an atmosphere that claimed objectivity and fairness. In a letter to the Singapore government he explained the importance of colonial cooperation in closing the brothels:

> I have the honour to state that, at a meeting of the representatives of the Japanese societies and other bodies in the colony...which was held on the 5th and 6th instant [January] at Singapore, a resolution was passed that they will do their endeavours to see all Japanese brothels now existing in the colony... closed by the end of this year, if possible...All Japanese brothels in Penang were closed in December last by the efforts of the Protector of Chinese there, and those in Singapore are now busy in making preparations to disengage their ill-fame business by the end of June next, in accordance with my advice and request which I gave them in December last in consultation with the Protector of Chinese at Singapore...I should, however, ask for the kind assistance of the Government...which is necessary...to achieve this task. Under the circumstances, I am to request that you would be so good as to arrange that no fresh case of a Japanese brothel...may henceforth be permitted...and also that the competent authorities...may render good offices in bringing forth the abolition of the existing Japanese brothels.[106]

The abolition edict sent shock waves through the Malay Street community, and small businesses that were kept going by the brothels either experienced hard times, or folded under pressure from the consulate. The strict enforcement of the law by the consul created turmoil and panic among women and brothel operators because they considered the deadline for deportation to be unrealistic.[107] The evacuation was too soon and its planned implementation caused real hardship for *karayuki-san* in Singapore, and in other parts of Southeast Asia.[108] Differing from the popular image of *karayuki-san* in Japan, these women, although poor and lacking security, nonetheless were not lacking in self-esteem. They protested both individually and collectively in cities like Manila, where fourteen cases were filed at the Court of First Instance, against the humiliating edict and the power of the police to enforce it.[109] The official record also shows the *karayuki-san* of Singapore reacting against prevalent social attitudes and legislation. They were still in a position to make some decisions about the future of their own lives, and found ways to protest their treatment and public humiliation. Some women simply disappeared. They operated as private prostitutes rather than being out of a job. Others refused to leave and managed to find work as waitresses in restaurants or cafés, or became mistresses of former clients.[110] Yet some were unable to get to Japan. They had borrowed money or purchased goods on credit, and a large percentage of them had VD.

In dealing with the West, the Japanese government was now able to declare that it had abolished prostitution overseas and curtailed traffic in women. But many *karayuki-san* affected by the ruling, who had returned to Japan, were at a loss as to what to do with their lives. They had earned millions of yen for Japan since the Russo–Japanese War and helped in no small measure to usher in their nation's modern century. Yet they experienced discrimination in Japan against themselves. They had also experienced discrimination in Singapore under British rule, but realised now that the same thing existed in Japan. The muted response to their repatriation pointed out one of the flaws of the emerging doctrine of a Greater East Asia co-prosperity sphere. To the end most of these women would be proud of being Japanese, but not always proud of Japan, especially in the charged atmosphere of reaction and backlash displayed towards them in the 1920s. What comes through in the accounts of elderly women about their work and these times was the difficulty of adjusting to civilian life, and the feeling of being ostracised by villagers and younger urban-dwellers with more modern views, who forgot the sacrifices *karayuki-san* had made on their behalf, and were ashamed of them.[111] These hapless women who had sex overseas with Europeans, Chinese, Malays, Indians, merchant mariners and military personnel, became the butt of some of the worst sort of village gossip and discrimination at home. *Karayuki-san* like Osaki-san in *Sandakan Hachiban Shokan* (Sandakan No. 8 brothel), came home to a nation that did not care what they had been through in Singapore, Manila or Sandakan, or what they had endured since then—the broken ties, lost years and nightmares. Yamazaki has argued Japan only prohibited prostitution after it was economically secure. Japanese officials repatriated *karayuki-san* in a distinctly shabby fashion. They were dumped at the nearest port of arrival with no financial assistance and without any real regard as to the underlying reasons for their plight. The Japanese generally did not have any sympathy or respect for Osaki's generation, who went abroad to Singapore and other port cities and prostituted themselves, to keep their relatives alive and make Japan economically self-sufficient. A whole generation of women had nowhere to go and didn't feel anything but lonely. Forced to fend for themselves, it is not surprising that some of them turned their backs on their families and villages out of a sense of shame and anger, and followed the Japanese army into China.[112] Other more elderly women who could not rebuild their lives, along lines other than sex and alcohol, suicided.

Now in Singapore, gonorrhoea was more likely to be contracted by copulation with a Japanese prostitute. After 1920 Japanese prostitution was no longer under strict control as brothels became sly, and the infection rate among remaining *karayuki-san* was much higher.[113] 'Sly' brothels sprang up all over the city and Japanese women were continually moving from one quarter to another to escape police surveillance. Private medical examination was less frequent, and many inmates were infectious. *Karayuki-san* found their better-class customers, who used to frequent the tolerated houses, falling off. They began to receive more lower-class patrons with the result that many sly brothels eventually became the haunts of Malay and Tamil coolies. Banda Street was one spot where fashionably dressed Japanese women were to be seen more frequently now. An elderly Chinese businessman said that the Cantonese used to call Banda Street and neighbouring Spring Street, *Phan Tsai Mei*, which meant 'Lane of Foreign Prostitutes', giving an idea of the social life there in the early 1920s, when many Japanese prostitutes moved into the neighbourhood.[114] Some of the women became servants in nearby coffee shops, but clandestinely carried on their old occupation. But many of them continued to operate from premises within the Japanese residential area around Middle Road, Hylam Street and Malay Street. *Zegen* and brothel-keepers solved the problem of the imperial ban by setting up the remaining *karayuki-san* in restaurants, boarding houses and cafés, as well as using blocks of private lodging houses, scattered about outside the Japanese residential area, beyond the supervision of the municipal authority and government. In the years following World War I, moves also began which were to culminate in the establishment of Lavender Street as the heart of the Japanese red light district by the mid-1930s.[115] The government's efforts to regulate the hundred or so Japanese sly brothels scattered over the inner areas of the city were rarely successful.

Conclusion

The incentives for the daughters of rural farmers in Kyushu to migrate were partially dire poverty and the ideology of the patriarchal family system, and partly the employment opportunities created by the demand for prostitutes in a burgeoning Singapore with its huge pool of single coolies, as well as a lack of alternative employment opportunities closer to home. The attraction of escaping the unending drudgery experienced in farm life for young peasant women is also not hard to imagine. Some had no regrets about leaving their villages. The 'pull' of Singapore where money was to be made, and the hard times experienced living on farms, lured them away.

The coolie traffic, a market for prostitution and Singapore's economic development were interrelated factors that were crucial in shaping the meaning and experience of the *karayuki-san*, and the history of the city. The presence of these women was indispensable in maintaining the *singkeh*/coolie labour force so necessary for Singapore's growth and expansion. Equally important, large profits were to be extracted from the prostitutes as cheap migrant-labourers, which would enable Japanese entrepreneurs to accumulate capital and diversify their economic interests in colonial Singapore. Agrarian poverty, patriarchy and rising urban prosperity all had a direct impact on creating a situation of drastic gender imbalance in Singapore at the end of the nineteenth century, on the choice of a rural Japanese woman to become a prostitute, or to fall victim to the traffic destined for that market, as well as on the lives of the masses of men who visited the Japanese brothels.

Chapter 15

Prostitution and the Politics of Venereal Disease: Singapore, 1870–98[1]

Introduction: Migration and prostitution

Prostitution in Singapore was linked to economic factors in rural China and Japan. Congenital poverty, weak family economies and rising economic expectations were all part of a set of prevailing conditions that created a vast source of supply of Chinese and Japanese women and young girls for international traffic.[2] Life in both countries was exceptionally difficult in the second half of the nineteenth century. Although China had considerable wealth, most lived a hand-to-mouth existence in the over populated rural areas. Poverty in the villages and outlying districts of south-eastern China, where many agrarian families lived on the edge of starvation, not only drove women and girls out of the countryside into the ports, but acted as a lever on parents already bowed under financial strain. Privation was a handicap that struck hardest at the daughters of peasants and rural labourers. Unable to feed the many mouths they were responsible for, and suffering from chronic economic insecurity, parents sold their daughters to would-be benefactors, totally unaware of the future fate in store for so many of them who were taken to Singapore. Poverty and desperate hungry Chinese families were root causes of brothel prostitution in Singapore at the end of the nineteenth century.

This trade in women for prostitution occurred in a unique context in which a vigorous market for prostitutes existed in the colonial port towns of Southeast Asia. Brothel districts in major cities like Singapore were sanctioned by colonial governments to cater to the sexual needs of tens of thousands of migrant bachelor labourers. The manipulation of women in China and Japan by their families, when harvests failed and famine arrived, for economic, social and sexual purposes helped to legitimise this traffic in women for prostitution overseas. In traditional China and Japan the young would-be *ah ku* and *karayuki-san* seemed to subscribe to the rightness of their own subordination. The values of filial piety and the patriarchal family system were so ingrained that it was almost taken for granted that they might have to enter a profession abroad specifically to entertain men sexually. Its rightness was seldom questioned. The young women would submit and endure.

Prostitution was a flourishing business in Singapore at the end of the nineteenth century. It had become a multi-million dollar network linking remote villages in rural China and Japan with ports like Nagasaki and Canton to the dockside in Hong Kong and brothels in Singapore. The flood of *singkeh* arriving to work in Singapore had created gender imbalance in the city, and the ever-increasing demand for prostitutes by migrant labourers was responsible for an extensive organised traffic in young women and girls.[3] Brothels became a boom industry by the mid-1890s in Singapore, whose streets were continuously thronged with thousands of single Chinese labourers and sailors from the navies and merchant marines of most nations, especially England, Germany and Japan.

The intensity of the demand for women who were sexually willing was great enough to justify the existence of the *ah ku* and *karayuki-san* in the eyes of the colonial government. British officials could not resolve the paradox of the indispensable link between prostitution, immigration and urban-economic development, to give migrant labourers a more 'normal' life. Prostitution had existed from the start of Singapore's history, primarily because of the sizeable number of bachelor coolies in the colony. But the economic development of Singapore and the Malay Peninsula in the 1880s and 1890s gave prostitution a real boost throughout the city. More and more Chinese and Japanese brothels appeared on the streets around the labouring quarters. By the mid-1890s they were so well established that both sides of the city had their respective red light districts. During this period of rapid economic growth and development, prostitution was viewed by the colonial authorities as a necessary evil; since there were so few eligible Chinese women to go around, migrant-labourers who did not have wives would have to visit prostitutes. The social life of these sojourning Chinese was in no sense a natural one, lacking the ordinary comforts of a wife and family. The coolies had to make a stark choice between celibacy, homosexuality or patronising prostitutes. The vast majority chose to visit the brothels. The presence of the *ah ku* and *karayuki-san* was especially important for these men because of the unequal gender ratios for Chinese immigrants in the late nineteenth century.

The Contagious Diseases Ordinance (CDO): Regulation and registration

The Singapore government found it impossible to suppress traffic in women and children and the abuses connected with it. Nor was it considered feasible to declare brothels illegal.[4] Because they could not be abolished, legislation was introduced, under the Contagious Diseases Ordinance of 1870, imposing regulations as to the conduct of licensed brothels, but there was to be no formal policy with respect to control, still less prevention. To protect *ah ku* and *karayuki-san* from enforced detention and ill-treatment, a system of registration and inspection of brothels and prostitutes was introduced in Singapore, which initially was under the auspices of the Registrar-General's department.[5] This institutional system, which countenanced brothel prostitution, was in part designed to take British law into the brothels and make illegal inmates free.[6] Documentary evidence shows that officials who approved of the system believed it was the only method of safeguarding the liberty and welfare of Chinese and Japanese prostitutes in the tolerated houses.[7] They were to repeatedly stress throughout the 1880s and 1890s that the system of segregation and regulation of brothels had nothing to do with the compulsory medical examination of prostitutes, rather that government registration and inspection was a way of protecting *ah ku* and *karayuki-san*, who could not help themselves to escape from virtual bondage and dependency.[8]

The system of registration of brothels in Singapore was part of a larger regulatory code for the compulsory examination of prostitutes, the Contagious Diseases Ordinance. The CDO, which was a consequence of a strong mid-Victorian interest in sanitary reform, owed its origins to a series of Acts passed between 1864 and 1869 under a legislative title usually applied to measures concerned with foot and mouth disease.[9] The coy sub-title of the *Contagious Diseases Act* actually meant 'venereal disease, including gonorrhoea'. The first of three Acts was carefully passed through Parliament in 1864 to curb the effects of sexually transmitted diseases, especially syphilis, in the armed forces stationed in Britain's garrison and seaport towns.

The Singapore government was also prompted by this Victorian fear of high rates of infection of soldiers and sailors in garrison and dock towns, to legalise a system of segregation and isolation, to control prostitution and the spread of venereal disease (VD) in the port-city. From the perspective of senior colonial officials the introduction of the CDO was essential to protect British soldiers and sailors, who were mostly lower class, and could not afford to support wives and families in Singapore.[10] Lacking the 'high moral standard required' for sexual continence, it was their general opinion that the 'other ranks' had neither the education nor self-restraint that would keep them away from the brothels. Parliament did not condone the regimental brothels of the French and German armies for British soldiers overseas except in India.[11] Hence, the official rationale for compulsory registration and medical treatment of Singapore's prostitutes was to protect British servicemen from the ravages of uncontrolled sexually transmitted diseases. One thing was explicitly clear: the introduction of the CDO was not meant primarily for the protection of the Chinese coolie populace, who would have to turn to homosexuality or masturbation if they did not visit brothels in the two zones where prostitutes underwent periodic medical examination.[12] The CDO of 1870 was passed with a view to preventing the spread of venereal diseases, but almost entirely for the protection of Her Majesty's sea and land forces. However, once it was put into force, its regulations embraced the entire population of the city, of which the labouring Chinese formed the vast majority. The CDO came into operation on 2 September 1872 on the south side of the Singapore River, and in November of the same year on the north side, but examination of prostitutes did not begin until March 1873.[13] Initially, there was very strong opposition to the Ordinance, and for some months little or nothing could be done by way of medical examination. The most serious difficulty experienced in working the Ordinance was the resistance of Chinese women to submit themselves to examination.[14] Officers were foiled by inmates absconding, and brothel-keepers closing their houses, professing to retire from their occupation.[15] Opposition, however, gradually weakened as *kwai po* perceived that the government was determined to carry the Ordinance out, so that by the end of the year the Registrar was able to accomplish something resembling regular medical inspection. But A. F. Anderson, the Colonial Surgeon, still met difficulties in getting women to submit to examination. He had to regularly go among the brothel-keepers and/or brothel owners and persuade them, as the Ordinance gave him no power to force them to comply.[16]

Several hundred 'all nationality' class women were examined every week, including Japanese, Europeans and Indians. The examination of the 'strictly Chinese' class used to take at least a week in each month. After examination, the doctor signed an order for admission of those who were sick into the Lock Hospital, under provisions of the Ordinance. The 'all nationality' women found well were provided with a card on which was noted the state of their health.[17] Significantly, both officials and doctors refused to extend the practice of issuing certificates of good health to Chinese women. They felt it could not be done without difficulty and would yield no beneficial result. This negative attitude with respect to Chinese women was singular in colonial medical circles in Singapore at the end of the nineteenth century, and it was to do incalculable damage by helping to foster a dangerous situation where Chinese males, especially coolies, were not made aware of the risks involved in sexual contact with *ah ku*.

The average number of women registered yearly up to the end of 1875 was 1,400. However, there was every reason to believe that this figure fell far short of reality, even in the known brothels. The situation with respect to examining Chinese women quickly became futile, there was too much substitution going on, and, in the opinion of the Colonial Surgeon, the only means to prevent it was by having the women photographed.[18] The sole way to ascertain whether all *ah ku* of a brothel attended or that the women present were licensed, was by the *kwai po* producing the list of inmates of the house. However, the Registrar, deputy inspectors and doctors under the CDO had no means whatsoever of ascertaining if other women were put forward to impersonate sick inmates of a brothel, except in very few cases.[19] The substitution was often carried out by a brothel servant, *tai pang po*, coming forward for examination in the place of an *ah ku* who had contracted a sexually transmitted disease, and wished to avoid the Lock Hospital.[20] There was a great deal of substitution going on with the sanction of brothel-keepers between 1872 and 1881, but doctors were only able to establish the fact in rare instances by certain marks on the women.[21] The records that were kept in the hospital were not of much use either in establishing proper identification because women were frequently changing their names and locality. To make matters worse, the Ordinance did not provide adequate punishment for a *kwai po* who substituted a healthy woman for a diseased one at an examination, other than prosecuting her for not bringing up the proper woman she was summoned to produce. The magistrate's fines in such cases usually only ranged from 25 to 100 dollars.[22]

Steps were taken by the Registrar's Department and the newly formed Chinese Protectorate to rectify the problem of substitution. In 1881 the Protectorate took charge of the CDO. The difficulties experienced in making *kwai po* and heads of secret societies accept the examination system led to the innovation of registration, whereby each woman was photographed and furnished with a ticket on which was printed, in Chinese, a notice to the effect that she was at all times, at liberty to apply to the Registrar or Colonial Surgeon in case of grievance or ill-treatment, or if she wished to leave the brothel.[23] The ticket also contained, in English, the number of the brothel and that of the *ah ku* as she was entered in the Registrar's books. The *kwai po* protested, plainly saying they were afraid of losing large sums invested in their girls. After threatening the law, possible riots, boycotts, the closing of shops, and making extraordinary scenes throwing down their licence boards, dancing on the floor with wooden clogs, and shouting furiously, they ultimately gave in to the measure.[24]

The sexually transmitted disease mostly encountered in the 1870s and early to mid-1880s was gonorrhoea; secondary syphilis was hardly met with then.[25] It was clear to all concerned, right from the start, that the monthly examination of Chinese prostitutes was not frequent enough to prevent further spread of venereal infection. It was possible for a woman or man to acquire and convey gonorrhoea in less than a month. It was the failure to systematically examine men as well as women that made the possible success of the CDO doubtful from the very beginning. Medical officials felt Chinese women could not be examined once a week, like the 'all nationality' prostitutes, let alone their menfolk, simply because of the workload—it would have taken one medical officer all his time to do it. This callous attitude meant that British doctors, like J. H. Robertson, did not expect the Chinese in the city to ultimately escape the wave of venereal infection of the 1880s.[26] It was a slow developing wave, but potentially a much greater wave of infection, in which prostitutes and coolies were increasingly at risk as immigration increased, but there was an official consensus that nothing more needed to be done formally with the Chinese to contain the spread.

Once the CDO came into force, apothecaries like L. Schrieder sold drugs used for venereal complaints more widely than ever before. He not only prescribed for Chinese prostitutes upon their own statement of their disease; where he considered it necessary, he examined them.[27] On the other hand, a druggist like R. A. Miles worked in partnership with a doctor to whom he would send prostitutes who came to him asking for treatment or wanting to purchase drugs for themselves. He stated before an inquiry that many Chinese doctors purchased medicine from him, primarily mercury, in ointment or pill form, which was used by *ah ku* living in brothels who had contracted a sexually transmitted disease.[28] *Sinseh*, educated in Canton, or who were trained in hospitals of the city, dispensed mercury in the form of calomel and cinnibar, but indiscriminate use of mercury, however, often led to loss of teeth, baldness and kidney ailments.[29]

The CDO: Moral reform and repeal

To prevent the spread of sexually transmitted diseases, illegal traffic in women and children, and the infiltration of secret societies, a strict system of registration and stringent health measures developed under a single government authority—the Chinese Protectorate—from 1881 onward.[30] There had been strong backing for the introduction of the CDO because any move to rigidly control the tolerated brothels and regulate prostitution would also contribute to the government's ability to extend its authority over the labouring Chinese, by the means of such a measure.

On the surface the Singapore government's plan to regulate and control the city's brothels under the CDO seemed a realistic solution to a vexing problem.

However, this Ordinance to stem the rising incidence of sexually transmitted diseases and access of England's soldiers and sailors to the city's prostitutes did not seem to the Colonial Office and the British public a straightforward solution.[31] There was a protracted conflict between the Chinese Protectorate and the Colonial Office throughout the 1880s over the CDO and brothel prostitution; a basic fact of life in Singapore Chinese society due to gender imbalance. It was a classic power struggle with W. A. Pickering attempting to extend the force and provisions of the CDO, and his own personal authority as Protector, at the expense of the colonial magistrates. He was determined to curb illegal traffic and isolate and punish its agents as severely as possible.[32] On the other hand, Whitehall thought it dangerous to invest officials on the spot in cities like Singapore with discretionary legal power pertaining to the regulation of prostitution—especially a man like Pickering, who always had been prone to act on his own initiative, and who had also been trained in Chinese language and customs, which few other colonial officials had mastered. He was to struggle in vain though to get the CDO amended to give the Protectorate greater powers for prevention of traffic. If such authority could not be granted, he argued in August 1882, then he and his officers would have to continue 'protecting women and children by our wits'.[33] In his tug-of-war with the Colonial Office, Pickering emphasised little could be learned from the Hong Kong experience and the pattern of its legislation with respect to the CDO. In his long reports on Chinese affairs, especially those on traffic in women and brothel prostitution, he repeatedly argued for changes to the CDO based solely on the experience of Singapore.[34] There was no doubt, as Pickering claimed, that the introduction of the Ordinance had been effective in combating sexually transmitted diseases, and, to a certain extent, had benefited the women themselves, but in the end colonial policy was still directed from London. There, on the other side of the world in the seat of Empire, the CDO arrangements in Singapore came to offend not only Whitehall, but also became a grave cause of concern to the Victorian evangelical conscience by 1887, with dire consequences for Singapore Chinese society.

Mid-Victorian paternalistic authoritarian morality and attitudes made a mockery of the issue of sexuality and gender in the Acts. In the wider context of public and private definitions of deviant sex, all oppression was directed at women and, *a priori*, any woman infected with a VD was treated as a criminal. The failure of the Victorian sexual system to apply the same standard and law to upper-class gentlemen, soldiers and sailors, in order to protect the privacy of male individuals as carriers, defeated the Act's purpose, exposing the double standard of the age, and sexual prejudice among 'respectable' classes towards prostitution and the poor.

Moral reformers, feminists, missionaries and civil libertarians charged that the provisions for the protection of human rights were inadequate. Many felt that the measures were also immoral and ineffective. From the early 1870s until repeal was won in 1886, a combination of pressure groups waged an active campaign in and out of Parliament to defeat the law's purpose of making 'sinning safe'. The repeal campaign to influence the law regarding state regulation of prostitution, through public opinion in the early years and the successful attempt to prevail upon the Liberal Party by the 1880s, was fashioned out of a complex network of radical and nonconformist movements for moral and social reform.[35] Josephine Butler's charismatic role and ideas, and the Ladies National Association for the Repeal of the Contagious Diseases Acts (LNA), were central to the success of the abolition movement. The LNA, the most militant of the repeal organisations, seized the issue of the double standard of sexual morality embodied in the Acts as a rallying point for their abolition. It mounted campaigns in the subjected districts, calling for registered women to boycott the Acts, and conducted rescue work among prostitutes.[36] This feminist commitment to individual liberty and militant activism became closely tied to the concerns of evangelical and other moral reform groups by the early 1880s. Butler pressed home the public debate about the impact of the Acts on private and working-class life, writing statements for the press, addressing church congregations and working men's associations, appealing to philanthropic societies, and organising mass prayer meetings all over the country with the assistance of the Society of Friends and the Salvation Army.[37] In the end though, in the social and political circumstances of the 1880s, it was not the independent action on parliament and prayers of the 'new abolitionists' that was to get the Acts off the statute book, but rather a strategy of having repeal adopted as part of the Liberal Party platform through the efforts of James Stansfield, as Parliamentary Chief.[38] The long campaign of Josephine Butler and other leaders of Victorian political culture to repeal the *Contagious Diseases Acts*, which was brought to a successful end in 1886, had widespread repercussions throughout the Empire, particularly in Singapore. The provisions of the CDO were felt to be too obsessed with confinement and punishment in the regulation of prostitution, in order to curb the spread of sexually transmitted diseases among troops in local garrisons.

Standards enforcing social discipline and the limits of sexual behaviour were set by the Colonial Office for Chinese society in Singapore, as a consequence of the repeal of the *Contagious Diseases Acts*, despite an imprecise understanding of the nature of recent demographic development and social needs in the city. Nowhere in Southeast Asia was a VD epidemic to have a more drastic impact than in Singapore, a city in 1888 that included at least 2,500 prostitutes in a population of over 86,000 Chinese males.[39] And nowhere was the acute effect of Josephine Butler's moral crusade more strongly felt than in the Kreta Ayer area in the 1890s, where *ah ku* and their customers were to sicken, move away, or die at an alarming rate after contracting a sexually transmitted disease. The venereal epidemic about to break was to be a community-wide problem. The large-scale immigration of Chinese migrant labour, the extreme excess of males, and Dickensian living conditions of the mass of migrant workers made prostitution in Singapore a complicated and difficult problem to handle, but not one that the Victorian conscience could grasp, let alone condone. Influential churchmen and reformers lobbied Parliament, clamouring for the suppression of prostitution in addition to the repeal of Singapore's CDO, a system of registration which they felt oppressed and corrupted Chinese and Japanese women, making their rehabilitation difficult if not impossible, and for the prohibition of lock hospitals.[40]

Pickering was hand-picked by the government to respond to a question from the Colonial Office as to whether the interests of Singapore absolutely required the CDO. He was undoubtedly the best suited person to answer this difficult political question because of his intimate knowledge of Chinese, and first-hand experience of his office. But Pickering's somewhat unorthodox views with respect to the governance of Chinese society, his inherent antipathy to the principal objectives of the CDO and his deeply held Christian beliefs found explicit expression in what he wrote, ultimately weakening the overall impact of the conclusions of the rapidly prepared lengthy report.[41]

There was no doubt under Pickering's administration of the Chinese Protectorate, that the CDO had been used by him in such a manner to secure some benefits for *ah ku* and *karayuki-san* in registered brothels, but the majority of the Executive Council felt his report was wide of the mark.[42] They knew the city was in fact engaged in a desperate struggle against the spread of sexually transmitted diseases caused by a direct overlap between the government's policy to encourage immigration of unmarried Chinese men, and the necessity to regulate institutionalised prostitution:

> If even an Ordinance should be introduced abrogating these laws, I would introduce a section prohibiting the immigration of men into the Colony unless accompanied by a due proportion of women. That, I think, would open people's eyes to the true bearings of the question. As long as a Government enforces (as in the case of soldiers at home), or encourages (as in the case of immigration here) modes of life that are out of accord with the laws of nature,

it is bound, I think, to look to the consequences. We know that our system of unrestricted male immigration leads, and will lead, and must lead, to certain lamentable consequences. We allow it to go on for a variety of reasons, which may be summed up in the general term of expediency.[43]

Under such circumstances the question of whether the Ordinance could be repealed or not was almost entirely a medical one. Maxwell's views on problems posed by increased immigration and the spectre of epidemic, reveal an administrative ideology bent on retaining the CDO to attract cheap Chinese labour to working-class districts of the city, without having to ferociously sacrifice them to a wave of VD:

> Arguments founded on peculiar views in religion or ethics have been needlessly, in my opinion, imported into this question at home and elsewhere. As a matter of practical administration, the question for us seems to be: Has the Contagious Diseases Ordinance caused any perceptible lessening of the diseases which it is its object to prevent? If so, its use in large seaports like Singapore and Penang, which are also garrison towns may be conceded…The registration of brothels and their inmates, their periodical inspection etc., seem to be essential.[44]

There was an overwhelmingly firm view in Singapore government and civilian circles to retain the legislation as long as the system of unrestricted male immigration continued. The Ordinance had to be kept on the books to contain the spread of sexually transmitted diseases—an inevitable consequence of the immigration policy—within tolerable limits. Nevertheless, the domestic–social interests of Singapore Chinese society were to be sacrificed to the pragmatic ones of Victorian political culture by a Secretary of State who was prepared to turn a deaf ear to all arguments put before him on the question of discontinuing the Contagious Diseases Ordinance. The Secretary of State felt it politically expedient to follow the course that had been resolved upon in England to repeal compulsory examination, while retaining in force the system of registration and supervision of brothels in Singapore, and all parts of the Ordinance which were directed against brothel slavery. The CDO had been originally introduced because of the prevalence of VD among British soldiers and the seamen on board Royal Navy vessels stationed in Singapore waters. But, the paradoxical argument in Pickering's report, not to enforce monthly medical examinations in the strictly Chinese brothels, while at the same time stating that it was absolutely critical to maintain registration of licensed brothels to ameliorate conditions of inmates, had carried the day in the Colonial Office. Any new Ordinance would have to show that its basic purpose was the general protection of women and girls, and not merely the prevention of sexually transmitted diseases. After giving due consideration to the reports, appendices and attached letters enclosed in the Governor's despatch by various medical officers and others who argued the case to retain the legislation from a purely medical point of view, pointing to a probable increase in VD otherwise, and acknowledging that the subject was one of 'great difficulty and complication', the instruction for the repeal was callously issued by the Secretary of State:

> These arguments were strongly urged in this country, but were over-ruled by Parliament, and I feel compelled *in the absence of any special local reasons* [emphasis added], to act in accordance with the decision of Parliament. I have, therefore, to instruct you to prepare an Ordinance for the repeal of all such parts of the law as enforce compulsory examination of women, but I hope that, with a free lock hospital, and with knowledge brought to these unfortunate women that they can freely avail themselves of it, the danger arising from the change may not be as great as is feared. At the same time, I am not prepared, for the present at all events, to do away with the registration of brothels and their general supervision by Government.[45]

A disbelieving angry Governor, Sir Frederick Weld, hesitated to issue the order. He doubted, on the one hand, whether his government could fully carry out instructions to maintain registration and supervision of brothels, strictly enforce penalties on brothel-keepers for infringement of rules, and provide a free lock hospital; and on the other, still hope to convince the Secretary of State that there were exceptional local reasons for maintaining compulsory examination in the Colony, sufficient in themselves not to adopt the decision of Parliament with regard to the English towns.[46]

Weld's trenchant efforts between July and September of 1887 to persuade the Colonial Office and the British government to take his objections seriously only led to dismissal. His reluctance to implement the new policy was considered by his superiors to be a substantive breach of discipline. The end of the year brought a new hardline Chinese-speaking Governor, Sir Cecil Clementi-Smith, who was prepared to do the Colonial Office's bidding, and with him the repeal of the CDO, which had been in force in the colony since 1870. Pickering's new Ordinance for the Protection of Women and Children and registration of brothels and inmates took its place, but all compulsory medical examinations and the collection of fees for the treatment of patients in lock hospitals from *kwai po* ceased at the beginning of 1888. The new law was politic rather than just.

Josephine Butler's successful campaign against state regulation of prostitution in England and the pragmatic politics of a conservative British government and Colonial Office, that ran roughshod over local opinion, ramming through the abolition of the medical examination in Singapore, were the two most decisive factors responsible for the making of a 'real calamity'—the spread of syphilis and gonorrhoea on a pandemic basis in the Singapore Chinese community by 1890.

The abolition of registration: The rise of VD

On 31 December 1887, the registration fee and compulsory medical examination ceased in Singapore, but provisions for protection of prostitutes in licensed brothels were still carried out.[47] The Chinese Protectorate spared no effort to induce *kwai po* and *ah ku* to take advantage of the free medical treatment and support. The regulation school of thought in official circles had maintained that it was not possible to suppress brothel prostitution. It was a necessary social evil. However, officers of the Protectorate and colonial surgeons now faced the unenviable task of making access to a comprehensive range of medical services work for prostitutes with a sexually transmitted disease on a voluntary basis. In a chilling letter the new Governor, Sir Cecil Clementi-Smith, having earlier downplayed the threat of epidemic as a consequence of the repeal of the CDO to satisfy the Colonial Office, now exposed a tragic web of deceit, stupidity and helplessness. It involved everyone from *kwai po* to officials of the Protectorate—not to mention the *ah ku* themselves, many of whom refused to stay in the free hospital, continuing to indulge in indiscriminate sexual activity when it was obvious they were placing themselves and the public in the path of a dangerous contagion.[48]

The repeal of the compulsory clauses of the CDO had practically rendered the lock hospitals useless by the end of 1888. Few women sought entry, and among those admitted, the majority left before they were cured, but they were still given free medicine in the battle to contain the spread of VD.[49] It is evident from his correspondence though that as early as September 1889, Clementi-Smith was already beginning to see Singapore's struggle against VD as hopeless. The emerging epidemic could be envisaged, from the standpoint of the Governor's urgent necessity for detailed statistical information, as a triangle: clustered in the tip of the triangle were the growing number of diagnosed cases of VD—primarily from military and institutional hospitals. In the middle layer of the triangle were the bulk of the unrecorded cases of VD; people, many of them Chinese coolies, with symptoms of infection (such as weight loss, rheumatic pain, recurrent headaches, skin rashes, chest pains and shortness of breath) had a gonorrhoea or syphilis diagnosis, but the vast majority did not consult public health authorities. At the base of the triangle were the 'silent' cases of prostitutes—many of whom were infected with gonorrhoea, but who showed no symptoms of the illness in the years immediately following the repeal.[50]

It was to be a devastating decade for Singapore. The Chinese community was forced to confront an emerging epidemic in a state of anger and frustration, constantly struggling against a set of cultural myths and unexamined assumptions of bureaucrats in the Colonial Office. The greatest increase in venereal cases, found at the tip of the triangle in 1889, was in returns from the pauper hospitals, but cases grew in number in reports coming in from all hospitals.[51] The colonial surgeons agreed that secondary syphilis was more common than before, and once it started replicating the opportunities for infection were bound to increase in a transient population of coolies and merchant seamen.[52] VD continued to spread both in terms of the number of cases treated and severity of type met with, as was shown by disturbing reports from various hospitals in Singapore, over the next two years.[53]

The Secretary of State did not challenge the mounting evidence on the rise of VD in Singapore. He simply did not believe the empirical data persuasive enough to consider making any major changes in the new system for the protection of women and girls and regulation of brothels. He turned his back on any suggestion to re-enact the CDO, responding to British public opinion and Conservative Party political culture and needs:

> As I informed you in my despatch of 30 November 1888 I am not at present prepared to discuss the question of this increase of disease following upon the prohibition of compulsory examination of prostitutes. As that prohibition was based upon other than medical grounds.[54]

The spotlight of moral reform societies in Britain fell on Singapore throughout the early 1890s with renewed revelations about registration of brothels and a system of licensed prostitution in an overseas colony garrisoned by British soldiers and sailors. Written appeals, speeches and questions raised in Parliament focused attention on this system of questionable practices, which countenanced brothel prostitution. It had been abolished at home, and the repealers were determined to shut down the registration system in Singapore as well as Hong Kong. They could not accept the fact that brothels were necessary in such colonies. Unacceptable as it was to many, there were sound arguments in favour of brothel prostitution that had repeatedly been put before the government. The same kind of public pressure that had been brought to bear on Joseph Chamberlain, Colonial Secretary in the Conservative British government of the early 1890s, was now exerted on a new Secretary of Colonies, Lord Ripon, to end the system of registration of brothels. Ironically, the major question in the mind of the Singapore community in the aftermath of the repeal of the CDO was whether registration and inspection were adequate any more. The abolition of the registration system in 1894 meant no proper control of brothels and inmates; medical examination, personal treatment, health standards and rules-of-the-house now depended on self-regulation which varied from one brothel to another. The Protectorate had practically no check on the *kwai po* after 1894, as its officers no longer had the power to periodically inspect brothels.[55] There was no consideration given to whether this measure would further hinder efforts to prevent the spread of sexually transmitted diseases by withdrawing all effective assistance from prostitutes. With the abolition of the registration system by Lord Ripon, the Protector of Chinese and his staff ceased, except when special information was provided, to visit brothels in the city. The end of registration rendered the Protectorate helpless to protect a class of migrant worker who needed security and welfare assistance more than any other—the Chinese prostitute. The Protector no longer knew where an *ah ku* went once she left his office, after examination or arrival from China, and knew absolutely nothing about the prostitute's movements to other parts of Southeast Asia from Singapore.

The end of the registration system in 1894 saw a steady growth in both the number of cases and the virulence of sexually transmitted diseases, and Singapore became infamous within the space of several years, as one of the unhealthiest spots in the Empire. VD became a major issue in Singapore in 1889, an even bigger one after 1894, but officially a real grave problem only in the late 1890s, when sexually transmitted diseases among troops and in the Chinese community reached pandemic level. Singapore's escalating concern about VD had not been fuelled by irrational fears that usually raced ahead of rumoured epidemics, causing panic, and often provoking discrimination against members of high-risk groups. Because of the success of the British moral reform lobby in forcing the Singapore government to effectively abandon the lock hospital system and registration of brothels, there had been a large increase in the number of private houses of resort. The location of these brothels offered special grounds for objection because they quickly spread to parts of the city where they had never been seen before. The collapse of the containment policy, and the sudden rise in facilities for sly prostitution, further increased the spread of VD.[56]

Coolies, soldiers and sailors could not be kept out of the brothels, and with no controls, labourers and armed forces had resorted to the lowest and most diseased in search of warmth, comfort and sex. There was a dramatic rise in VD among the British garrison and navy stationed in Singapore. VD also reached staggering heights in the Chinese community after 1895. The results of Whitehall's policies between 1888, the year of the repeal of the CDO, and 1894, the year of the abolition of inspection of brothels, which had been forced upon Singapore without due consideration of different conditions of life and circumstances were, as had been locally anticipated, disastrous. The appalling extent of the epidemic was revealed by the findings of an investigative committee of the Straits Settlement Association. The inquiry was confined exclusively to Singapore, and although it proved impossible to ascertain the full extent of VD in the community at large, the statistics available for certain classes and institutions, limited though they are in certain respects, were still revealing and representative in character.[57]

There was little evidence to suggest that visiting British soldiers and sailors brought VD into the city. On the contrary, medical authorities shared the view that the armed forces were more likely to take VD out with them than bring it in. Drunken soldiers and seamen were particularly at risk and liable to be infected through a casual contact in one of the unregistered private houses.

Table 15.1 compares conditions in the 1880s and 1890s of the Hong Kong Garrison with respect to sexually transmitted diseases with the state of the Singapore Garrison and Tanglin Barracks, and shows the greater extent and virulence of VD in Singapore by 1896.[58] The significance of the widespread prevalence of VD among soldiers in Singapore is even more striking, when compared with documentation on its frequency among the armies of Prussia, France and the United States in the second half of the nineteenth century, with rates of 70 to 120 per 1,000 men.[59]

Table 15.1 VD admissions into hospitals in Hong Kong and Singapore in 1884 and 1896 of sailors stationed in the Singapore Garrison and Tanglin Barracks.

Year	Ratio per thousand	
	Hong Kong	Singapore
1884	145	123
1886	360	567

Let us now turn to an examination of those records associated with VD and rates of infection, concerning the general state of health of the city population, about which it is more difficult to comment. The official data available primarily examine the high percentages of recognisably 'at risk' groups, highlighting when possible the rates of infection between sexes, influence of the age factor in infection, the problem of gender imbalance, promiscuity and brothel prostitution, and the role played by coolies and prostitutes. Colonial records such as hospital returns, jail reports and annual statements from the lunatic asylum not only provide background information on the context of the epidemic, but also its social significance and impact in the city, especially among the Chinese community.[60] While sexually transmitted diseases did not discriminate on the basis of ethnicity, class and gender, particular types of people acquired higher rates of infection in Singapore, because it was a coolie town and port, falling into readily distinguishable groups, as hard labourers, prisoners, the indigent and insane, and prostitutes.

After 1888, the admissions for VD to various city hospitals began to climb year by year. In 1892, 682 patients were admitted for secondary syphilis alone, and 37 of these died.[61] The proportion of the number of infected women was close to that of men, due to the disparity between the sexes, and a society where a system of medical inspection was no longer compulsory. In 1892, 95 women, primarily prostitutes, presented themselves voluntarily for examination. As in 1891 the majority were Japanese, and of these 83 were found to be diseased, a proportion of 87 per cent, as against 75 per cent in 1891, and 29 per cent in 1890.[62] These tests that concentrated largely on prostitutes had yielded significant facts, identifying in no uncertain terms both carriers of VD and the effect of the abolition of registration. In the annual medical reports between 1892 and 1896, Dr M. F. Simon, Principal Civil Medical Officer, began each account by making a grave statement about the continued rise in the number of cases of VD treated in various hospitals in the Colony. VD admissions constituted nearly one-tenth of all hospital admissions in 1893; during 1894 there was a slight downturn in the number of cases admitted, but still it was over 2,000, while the number of deaths credited to secondary and tertiary syphilis showed a marked increase—seventy-six patients having died in hospital from this disease in 1894, as against 111 in 1895, and 135 by 1896.[63] More numerous cases of diseases of syphilitic origin were also turning up with ominous regularity at the outdoor dispensaries. The sustained high death rate for secondary and tertiary syphilis showed the increased virulence of the disease in a society where gender imbalance already presented very serious difficulties.

The number of cases of sexually transmitted diseases admitted to Tan Tock Seng Pauper Hospital after 1888 was far in excess of the figure for the years prior to the repeal of the CDO, and it produced a set of undesirable problems and consequences, both for the institution and government. The increased prevalence of VD among the destitute and unemployed led the steering committee of the hospital, which was already badly overcrowded, to select patients to be admitted on the basis of their means rather than upon the kind of disease from which they were suffering.[64] Venereal patients who could afford to pay were referred to the General Hospital, while those who were destitute but could walk about and look after themselves were relegated to the class of outpatients.[65] The committee subsequently notified the government that the number of charitable admissions due to cases of VD continued to be so great, that it was causing a financial crisis and overcrowding in the already beleaguered hospital, and that they had been left with no choice but to refuse to admit any further cases, except in the most extreme circumstance as of April 1890.[66] It was among the underclass though, people living below the poverty line or involved in more dangerous lifestyles and sexual experimentation, that it was impossible to stop the spread of infection. The jail reports for the years 1890–96 showed that the epidemic was raging out of control at a startling rate among people in the civil community that fell into the recognisable group 'criminal' or 'prisoner'. Of the 3,497 prisoners admitted to the Criminal Prison during 1896, 1,732 showed signs of having been infected at some time or other, as against 1,692 in 1895 and 597 in 1894, while in 1890, the number of prisoners that had been admitted was 4,856 of whom only 202 had VD.[67] The figures in this disturbing trend speak for themselves. From 1890 to 1896, colonial doctors working in the criminal prison found that while the number of prisoners admitted declined, the percentage of prisoners with gonorrhoea or syphilis continued to rise. Table 15.2 shows that in the last three years sexually transmitted diseases trebled among individuals of the civil community furnishing the jail population, and it had multiplied itself between eight and nine times in six years.[68] The number of infected men far exceeded women. The proportion per thousand of population by 1896 was 495, which was near to the average among troops stationed at Tanglin during those years.

I noted earlier that the VD epidemic could be envisaged as a triangle with prostitutes at its base. While the contribution prostitution made towards the incidence of VD in Singapore varied in time, prostitutes continued to be the source of at least 80 per cent of infection throughout the 1890s. Bunched together at the apex and middle layer of the triangle were tens of thousands of diagnosed and undiagnosed cases of VD in the civil community—largely

Table 15.2 Prisoners with VD admitted to the criminal prison between 1890 and 1896.

Year	Prisoners admitted	Infected
1890	4,856	202
1891	4,404	—
1892	4,510	—
1893	3,446	609
1894	2,979	597
1895	3,028	1,692
1896	3,497	1,732

Source: Straits Settlement Association to the Colonial Office, 8 November 1897, Co 882/6

a consequence of the great disparity of the sexes in the city. The statistics on sexually transmitted diseases from military and civilian hospitals were an index of the condition of prostitutes, numbering nearly 3,000 by 1896, who now practised their profession without hindrance or medical supervision. Dr Mugliston, Colonial Surgeon, felt that in his opinion 'all of these women either have now, or have had, venereal disease.'[69] If he was only partially correct, more than 2,000 Chinese and Japanese women were carriers of VD, but this figure is not by any means a liberal estimate for the 1890s. When Dr Ellis, as Acting Health Officer, visited recognised brothels in 1893 to inspect their sanitary condition, he looked at 1,710 prostitutes, without special local examination, and found that in a large number of cases signs of VD in various forms were present. He pointed to the hopeless situation of twenty-two babies and children in these houses who had contracted congenital syphilis, and many other children who thus far showed no symptoms of the disease, but were suspected of carrying it.[70]

VD was extremely prevalent among *ah ku*. European doctors who treated prostitutes privately felt cases of VD among Chinese women were often the worst because they were so badly neglected.[71] Most of them were almost totally cut off from the outside world and forced by *kwai po* to continue to receive customers when sick.[72] After 1888 *ah ku* could no longer be compelled to go to hospital. The *kwai po* determined whether an infectious woman received medical treatment; she could have a doctor attend her or not, as she pleased. During Dr Ellis's inspection of brothels in 1893 he came across one Chinese girl in a state of high fever. She attracted his special notice, and when the *kwai po* casually left the room the *ah ku* burst into tears, stating that she was extremely ill with VD, and that she had been made to receive three men in succession the previous night. Ellis felt it was impossible to stop the spread of infection among Chinese labourers while the majority of *ah ku* were under coercion to remain at work, and when many knew themselves to be unfit, and felt so terribly sick, alone and alienated.[73]

But some Chinese women were not aware that they required treatment, and allowed gonorrhoea and syphilis, which could more readily be cured at an early stage, to develop until they were absolutely incurable. Primary syphilis, which *ah ku* thought relatively harmless, affected its victims with frequently recurring sores causing varying degrees of itch, rash and pain.[74] Many women initially suffered mild outbreaks of these lesions, which caused a tingling or itching sensation in the lower part of their body. Later more severe episodes of syphilis, sometimes years afterwards, caused intense bone-breaking pain, especially at night. But numerous Chinese prostitutes had such mild infections at first, they were not aware that they had the disease, and became part of a reservoir of symptomless carriers spreading VD among male migrant labourers. An *ah ku* rarely did anything for the outbreak of sores developing on her body, or she usually had the *kwai po* or Chinese doctor simply put on a little caustic.[75] Despite showing symptoms warranting VD diagnosis, she often denied that the disease existed, and sometimes refused to accept the fact that it could be sexually transmitted by continuing to work, allowing scores of clients to contract it. Chinese prostitutes often could give up sex only when their VD became cases for operation with large ulcerous sores and skin diseases, otherwise they rarely went to the doctor. *Ah ku* who finally sought admission to private hospitals were often brought in in a deplorable state of health, suffering from advanced stages of secondary and tertiary syphilis. 'I doubt whether the Chinese understand the importance of the sore [lesion],' Dr Mugliston said. 'I think that is the reason they do not come [to hospital]. They look upon it as they look upon a sore on the finger. They don't know that it will lead to constitutional trouble.'[76]

As the rate of infection for Chinese artisans, hawkers and coolies rose, some consulted private doctors, including Europeans, who were supposedly competent in the management of VD, especially syphilis.[77] Some men had had the disease for years and what treatment they received was generally inefficient and expensive. Few doctors at the time were able to provide much information about a genuine cure for syphilis. While it is true that not all VD victims suffered such physical pain, apart from those in the agonising later stages of syphilis, there was, nevertheless, a devastating psychological effect that every person— coolie and prostitute—contracting a sexually transmitted disease experienced. Syphilis rendered an individual leprous, as there was no cure, and the disease was socially stigmatised. Any sexual contact by a carrier with a prostitute put the woman at risk. Thus a syphilitic person bore a social stigma and was unable to enter a relationship in good conscience without the trauma of revealing their affliction.[78] Coolies and prostitutes suffered drastic lowering of self-confidence and self-esteem, and encountered constant difficulties and moral dilemmas in interpersonal relationships and in the workplace. This psychological and social damage to the fabric of the Chinese community was neither mentioned nor fully understood by most of the doctors who appeared before the Commissioner's Committee to give evidence on the rise of VD. The mounting personal anxiety over not being able to work only added to the devastating psychological trauma that VD victims suffered.

Despite their efforts to prevent the spread of sexually transmitted diseases and mounting anxiety over the virulence of the syphilis replicating itself in the Chinese community, the government found it difficult to acquire epidemiological data through contact tracing highly infectious women.[79] Patients, especially at outdoor dispensaries, invariably refused to give any information about promiscuous women who could possibly effect an outbreak, or their place of residence. The difficulties of tracing and the related problem of under-registration meant that VD figures quoted from the official record on its frequency were not by any means the whole story of the epidemic in Singapore. The statistics obtained from the hospitals did not take into account the mass of Chinese who sought care elsewhere, either from *sinseh*, or their workmates. The Principal Civil Medical Officer believed that, in addition to the cases treated in government hospitals, a large number of individuals were cared for by private practitioners and in private hospitals, which were not included in government returns. The Coroner's Records, which inadvertently dealt with some of these invisible VD cases, also show that the annual statistics of the Health Department did not indicate the total incidence of sexually transmitted diseases in the city. The extent of the problem was seriously underestimated in the Chinese community, especially in the case of syphilis, perhaps by as much as 40 per cent, if all 'silent' cases were included.[80]

The government felt it was not making any headway in containing the spread of the epidemic. The number of VD cases admitted to hospitals continued to increase. In 1897, the Governor again pressed his case that Singapore was a fear-ridden city and that it should be allowed to take effective measures to deal with sexually transmitted diseases, brothel prostitution and promiscuity.[81] Nearly all infectious female syphilis occurred among prostitutes during the 1890s. The disparity between female and male statistics on syphilis was also heightened because so few Chinese women migrated, or imported it to Singapore, other than prostitutes. The burgeoning migrant labour traffic in and out of the colony during the 1890s threatened to further exacerbate this tragic state of affairs as the number of prostitutes with early signs of syphilis continued to increase.[82] Unfortunately, it was difficult to determine exactly how common sexually transmitted diseases were in the Chinese labouring population because there were no statistics on its spread among them.[83] Sir Cecil Clementi-Smith had felt it his duty in view of Colonial Office instructions regarding the CDO to initially prevent Heads of the Medical Department and Chinese Protectorate from collecting and supplying information on the increase of VD in the Chinese population, or to attend before a Committee of Inquiry of the Commissioners to give evidence on that problem in 1889.[84] If this dangerous epidemic was to be controlled, even he realised though within the short space of two years, that accurate statistics were vital to help prevent it from spreading.[85] VD had already become a public health issue of grave concern in Clementi-Smith's mind by 1891, and no longer purely a political policy matter. By 1898, the number of cases of VD admitted to hospital had reached a record high with the incidence of syphilis among coolies being very large, judging from post-mortem examinations held at hospitals and the asylum, and reported on by the Coroner and pathologist.[86]

One of the main aims in this examination of the venereal disease epidemic of the 1890s is to clarify the changing mixture of motives and attitudes between policy functionaries in the Colonial Office and Singapore officials, and to link certain political assumptions and policy, bureaucratic behaviour and cultural myths with a specific historical 'event'—the repeal of the CDO and the appalling spread of VD. A conscious paternal mandate, control of the Chinese poor, and regulation of their sexual economy through implementation of the CDO were somewhat different motives that coexisted in the minds of colonial officials, especially among those serving in the Chinese Protectorate and Colonial Medical Service. In the absence of government-enforced medical examination, private schemes gained tacit approval in the 1890s for purposes of social control and development of the economy, so that gonorrhoea and syphilis could be rapidly detected and treated in a milieu of large-scale urban growth and migration.

The most important brothel medical club established for Chinese in the 1890s was run by the Colonial Surgeon, Dr Mugliston. His system operated throughout the two brothel zones where nearly all of the Cantonese houses were located. There were four clubs in the scheme with names like Ping On Tong and Po On Tong, to which most *kwai po* in their respective parts of the city belonged.[87] The subscription fees charged by Dr Mugliston were either paid solely by the *kwai po* when a woman was handing over all her earnings to the house, or divided equally between *kwai po* and *ah ku* in cases where the woman was either indebted to the brothel-keeper or was a free agent in the house. All medicine supplied to brothel-keepers on Dr Mugliston's stationery was purchased by arrangement over the counter at the Government Dispensary at discounted prices that could not be obtained elsewhere in the city.[88] The Colonial Surgeon saw no conflict of interest between his public role and private practice in prescribing these drugs at cut-rate prices to brothels and prostitutes. In fact, he knew the favourable outcome of his scheme rested upon recognition of his official experience; the success of the establishment of the Cantonese medical clubs was due primarily to the fact that Dr Mugliston knew all the brothel-keepers from long involvement with them in carrying out the CDO, and inspection of their houses while the Women and Girls Protection Ordinance was in force prior to 1894. For their part, *kwai po* preferred to engage a medical man of his status, influence and experience whom they could trust, rather than a complete stranger.[89]

There existed among many people in Victorian England a repression of sexuality—a prudish attitude—in the middle and upper classes that publicly led to table legs being covered for decorum and privately to a thriving subculture of pornography and prostitution. The English doctors running brothel medical clubs in Singapore had ambivalent feelings and attitudes based on sexual repression and racial hostility about their work. They regularly confronted Chinese women who were socially repugnant to them and possibly infectious. On the whole, as members of a mid-nineteenth-century English educated culture, they argued for recognition of prostitution in Singapore as an inevitable social necessity, the 'Great Social Evil', with government regulation as the only hope for establishing VD limits. However, the medical profession involved in brothel clubs showed little interest or concern in the *ah ku* as real people, often condemning them as 'prostitutes'—women who were morally degraded and unfit, and as such not worthy of their help or consideration under the circumstance. These partisans of regulation were culturally predisposed to dominate and dislike these women. In their reports, especially Mugliston's, there is no sense of compassion or pity, describing Chinese women who contracted VD occasionally as 'beasts', or 'mindless' and 'sub-human'. They found the condition of most of these women to be utterly appalling and dangerous because VD was so widespread in Singapore by 1894. Not surprisingly, under such circumstances, they tolerated those who exploited the women accepting without reservation regular payments from *kwai po*, and did their best to support brothel prostitution. They also tried to foil any attempt to suppress the club system, which was one of the most efficient and profitable ways a government physician could augment his salary.

Blame for the VD epidemic, however, could not be directed wholly at prostitutes, as its beginning was the direct result of moral and political measures taken in Whitehall and the House of Commons. Medically, the spread of sexually transmissible diseases in Singapore should have been managed like any other infectious disease, but politicians and moralists in Britain had continued to refuse to treat them in this fashion. It was also a consequence of promiscuity and poor standards of health and recreational care among labourers in a coolie town who engaged in sex with prostitutes. A prostitute was not initially infected by another prostitute, but by a client. Yet little was ever said in the official record about VD also being spread by men who patronised prostitutes. The problem of VD in Singapore was always specifically associated with brothel prostitution, but the government felt the houses could be regulated and the disease contained prior to 1888. The question of an incontinent male migrant labour force, and a low standard of living and personal care associated with the way of life of these men who engaged prostitutes, was something the government repeatedly refused to address, claiming their housing, social and recreational needs were insoluble. But the Straits Settlement Association pinpointed this extraordinary feature of the Singapore population—the stream of coolies moving back and forth from China without women—as being at the very heart of an explanation of the VD crisis that the city was going through. The Association argued that the future wellbeing of Singapore hung in the balance, precisely because of this exceptional circumstance. The VD question affected the whole community:

> The Association is not disposed to undervalue the effect of moral influences in opposing the progress of vicious habits, and frankly recognises the honourable motives of those who are opposed to all forms of compulsory legislation, but it would respectfully and earnestly urge that the enormous disproportion of the sexes, the migratory character of the population, and the general conditions of life…are so exceptional as to demand exceptional legislation.[90]

Conclusion

In the contest to persuade the Colonial Office to rescind its policy on the CDO, the importance of a lobby like the Straits Settlement Association could not be understated, bringing expert knowledge and enormous pressure to bear in Parliament and the corridors of the Colonial Office. Although the organisation's proposals on behalf of the Singapore government were not adopted, the unswerving position of the Association on unrestricted migration, brothel prostitution and the rise of sexually transmitted diseases was made clear to politicians and bureaucrats in London. In the end, the Acting Governor, Sir J. H. Swettenham, was forced to convene a special committee of inquiry on the VD problem in 1898. Evidence was taken at seven meetings from doctors, the Protector of Chinese, the Inspector-General of Police and other knowledgeable witnesses to deal more effectively with the spread of VD and brothel prostitution. The evidence gathered for the Secretary of State only further supported the need for a large degree of autonomy to regulate the city's brothel zones:

> The Executive Council has decided that the report of the Committee should be laid before you with the statement that the Council agreed with the conclusions of the Committee, but was willing to adopt any means which offered a fair prospect of checking venereal disease. For checking this disease an elaborate system was tried locally and repealed in deference to public sentiment in the United Kingdom. It is I believe an axiom in matters politic that he who objects to a remedy for an admitted evil, must be prepared with an alternative scheme and it is to be regretted that the abolitionists were not compelled to devise an efficacious one for this Colony before destroying the only barrier which warded off disease from the population. You have desired me to advise what course short of the old system of registration is likely to prove the most effective check on brothel slavery. I could devise a scheme, but despair of inventing one which would not be objected to by a large body of public opinion in the United Kingdom because, to write frankly, that public opinion appears unable to grasp or contemplate such a state of law or morals as obtains in this Colony.[91]

Chamberlain's refusal, however, to consider re-enactment of the CDO in Singapore was based on certain 'facts and conditions' that were partly political. While acknowledging the disastrous increase of sexually transmissible disease since the Ordinance was repealed, he frankly reiterated that any effort to place the CDO on the statute books again would undoubtedly face strong opposition in England.[92] British moral and political attitudes towards sexual behaviour were once again forcefully imposed on Singapore Chinese society. The Secretary of State could not sanction the re-introduction of any system involving either compulsory registration of women, or registration of brothels and prostitutes, fearing that at the first opportunity such measures would be repealed.[93] To have recommended otherwise meant incurring the moral and political wrath of Josephine Butler's followers and other abolitionists, as well as members of his own Conservative Party. He was not about to commit political suicide, but hoped 'other means' could now be adopted locally, which would halt the epidemic. Chamberlain had been forced to recognise that prostitution could never be completely suppressed in the city, and that there was a need for supervision of brothels to ensure that their activities were confined to areas where law and order could be maintained, and traffic and the further spread of VD contained. Ironically, he was saying to the government and people of Singapore that he was now prepared to restore some measure of authority to the Chinese Protectorate, which had been deliberately circumscribed by the Colonial Office a decade earlier, in order to make it more responsible for supervision of brothels. He consciously engineered a metamorphosis of the Protectorate's role, and legal measures pertaining to the Protection of Women and Girls Ordinance, which enabled the Singapore government to now use discretionary power at its disposal to close a brothel or tolerate it, as a basis for maintaining an extra-legal system of publicly recognised houses.[94] The Chinese Protectorate kept an in-house list of tolerated brothels, their keepers and inmates. Those houses catering to Europeans, especially Japanese brothels, received special attention. Newly arrived prostitutes were interviewed as in the past, and keepers on the unofficial list had their women regularly inspected by private doctors under threat of penalty of shutting their premises. The development of this quasi-system of regulation helped contain the spread of infection in brothels catering for Westerners, but the majority of Chinese were increasingly placed at risk in the new century. This came as no surprise to the government because in Singapore sexually transmitted diseases had been a heterosexual problem involving prostitutes and coolies from the outset. Venereal disease continued to spread in this way as immigrant Chinese labour kept on increasing up to World War I.

Chapter 16

A Tale of Two Centuries: The Globalisation of Maritime Raiding and Piracy in Southeast Asia at the End of the Eighteenth and Twentieth Centuries[1]

Introduction: Connections and problems of framing and definition

In this final chapter, I want to explore similarities and differences between maritime raiding and slaving in Southeast Asia at the end of the eighteenth century, with maritime raiding and piracy as they manifest in the late twentieth century, especially in relation to globalisation. Maritime raiding already existed when the Portuguese arrived in Asia in the sixteenth century.[2] But the incidence of piracy in Southeast Asia (the region encompassing all the countries within a boundary defined by India, China, Australia and New Guinea) only rises dramatically in direct response to colonialism and Western enterprise. There is a strong inter-connective relationship between the ascendancy of long-distance maritime raiding or 'piracy' on a regional scale, and the development of an economic boom in Southeast Asia linked to the China trade at the end of the eighteenth century. In this context, maritime raiding was also closely linked to slaving and slavery as a social and economic phenomenon that became a crucial part of an emergent global commercial system and economic growth in the region.

As I have argued in Chapter 7, during the Iranun Age from 1768 to 1878, Iranun and Samal Balangingi influence covered a huge expanse, reaching from the Bay of Bengal in the west and the Timor and Arafura Seas in the south, throughout the central and northern Philippines, across the South China Sea, and it touched the homelands of diverse distant indigenous groups in the south of Cochin China and in western parts of northern Australia.

In addition to being fierce warriors and slavers of popular stereotype, the Iranun were master craftsmen (smiths, shipwrights, weavers and carvers), shrewd traders and fearless intrepid explorers. Their raiding and trading activities stimulated political, demographic and ecological changes right across Southeast Asia, and in Europe, China and America. Their activities created new societies, identities and patterns of settlement in the present-day Philippines,

Indonesia and Malaysia, and led to major conflicts between the Western imperial powers, the Malayo-Muslim maritime world and Islam more than 200 years before Osama Bin Laden threw down the gauntlet to the United States and the Western world.

The comparative temporal perspectives in this chapter, which covers the latter part of both, the late eighteenth and the late twentieth centuries, lends considerable explanatory power to my treatment of the multi-faceted links and changes between Iranun maritime raiding, on the one hand, and on the other, modern-day crime on the high seas in Southeast Asia, with the China connection, growing commodity flows and the fluctuations of the global economy.[3] Just as maritime raiders and slavers became generally active due to global economic development and disruption(s) in Asia in the 1790s, the incidence of piracy, or crime and terrorism on the high seas in Southeast Asia has steadily increased in a time of desperation at the end of the twentieth century, the final decade of which was marked by widespread ethnic and political conflict and the near total collapse of global financial systems and associated regional trade.

One way to make sense of this extraordinary burst of maritime raiding at the end of the eighteenth century is by viewing it from the standpoint of the interests, perspectives and conceptual frameworks marking the initial opening of China to the West, and the emergence of new global ethnoscapes, such as the Sulu Zone. This framework can be compared and contrasted with China's recent momentous economic transition that has paralleled bouts of trans-national maritime crime and piracy in Southeast Asia at the end of the twentieth century. Iranun 'pirates' were among the first real predators of global commerce in the eyes of the West by the end of the eighteenth century, and, as a new high-seas breed, were well organised and financed and ruthless. Their latter-day counterparts would be on the rise after 1968 in the Straits of Malacca, the Gulf of Thailand, the South China Sea and in the waters surrounding the Sulu Archipelago.

Central to my notion of late-eighteenth-century globalisation is the realisation of the inter-connectivity of local day-to-day activities and events, either read or construed as maritime raiding or 'piracy' on one side of the globe, namely Southeast Asia, and the removal of the civilisational, societal, ethnic and regional boundaries on the other side of the regional out-there, and of the globe.[4] The discovery of the global phenomenon as a condition for the advent of Iranun maritime raiding in the 1790s, requires a specific shift in subjectivity and framing. It marks, on one level, recognition of the continuing struggle of the reified 'other', Iranun, or latter-day criminal and terrorist, against the history of modernity and the four centuries of Western efforts to gain hegemony over the oceans and seas of Asia. Eric Wolf, in his path-breaking book, *Europe and the People Without History*, traces the development and nature of the chains of causes and consequences of the complex relationship between Europe and the rest of the post-1400 world. By emphasising a common past, he persuasively argues that European expansion created a market of global magnitude by incorporating pre-existing networks of exchange and by creating new itineraries and historical trajectories between continents that linked European and non-European populations and societies. This pattern of historical processes and international commodity exchange would also foster regional specialisation and initiate worldwide movements of commodities. At the end of the eighteenth century, this history of connection between European and non-European societies also gave rise to long-range maritime raiding or 'piracy' in Southeast Asia on a hitherto unknown scale. Essentially, the growth of European trade and dominion—capitalism—would bring about a qualitative change not only in the regnant mode of production, but also in the commercial network connected with it.[5]

The Sulu Zone was an area of great economic vitality at the end of the eighteenth century. This vitality was based on global–local links to the China trade. Commodities—marine and jungle products found within the Zone— were highly desired on the Canton market, and as Sulu chiefs prospered through strict regulation of the redistributive economy, they required more and more labour to collect and process these commodities. It was the Iranun, clients of the Sultan of Sulu, who scoured the shores of the island world in their swift raiding boats, to find slaves to meet this burgeoning labour demand. In the context of the development of the law of international sea piracy, the global economy and the advent of the China trade, it should be understood that the maritime raiding and slaving activities of the Iranun, so readily condemned in blanket terms as acts of 'piracy' by European colonial powers and later historians, were a traditional means of consolidating the economic base and political power of the sultan and coastal chiefs of Sulu, and which functioned as an integral, albeit critical, part of the emerging statecraft and socio-political structure(s) of the Zone. Thus, viewed from inside the Sulu world of the late eighteenth century, the term 'piracy' is difficult to sustain.

The term 'piracy' was essentially a European one. Significantly, Carl Trocki notes that the term appears in the Malay literature as a developing concept and a new terminology only in the latter half of the eighteenth century.[6] The term subsequently criminalised political or commercial activities in Southeast Asia that indigenous maritime populations had hitherto considered part of their statecraft, cultural–ecological adaptation and social organisation. Trocki,

Esther Velthoen and I have demonstrated that it was the dynamic interplay between raiding—*merompak* (Malay) or *magooray* (Iranun)—and investment in the maritime luxury goods trade that was a major feature of the political economies of coastal Malay states. In effect, maritime raiding was an extension of local–regional trade and competition, and a principal mechanism of state formation, tax collection and the processes for the in-gathering—forced and voluntary—and dispersion of populations in the post–late-eighteenth-century Southeast Asian world. Wolf's influential theoretical work shows that European expansion not only transformed the trajectory of societies like Sulu, but also reconstituted the historical accounts of their societies after intervention, introducing powerful new concepts, myths and terminologies linked to patterns of dominance, as in the case of the invention of the term 'piracy' in the Malay world at the end of the eighteenth century.

Because the way to power in Southeast Asia lay in control over slaves and dependent labour, guns and trade goods, it is not surprising that slaving in the region was bound up with maritime raiding and warfare. Captives were a main source of booty and, not surprisingly, they were also one of the leading items of regional trade.[7] The trading kingdoms and states in Southeast Asia were continually faced with the problem of a lack of labour power, and they were all, without exception, states that organised and conducted wars and systematic raids both over land and sea to seize labour power.[8] The problem of a severe shortage of labour power was most acute in the coastal kingdoms that did not have an irrigated wet-rice core, and that depended on systems of trading, raiding and slaving for the development and evolution of statecraft and social structure.[9]

One major result of the rise of globalising, cross-cultural commerce and wars of rival empires of trade was a systematic shift to maritime raiding and slaving on a more general scale than before by Southeast Asian coastal states now determined to seize labour power from wherever possible and by whatever means. The accelerated growth of global trade, especially with the Dutch and English, led to the widespread practice of the acquisition of slaves, by way of raiding, warfare or purchase, as a labour force to collect exotic products of the forests and seas as commodities for export to China, and to build and maintain public works and port facilities in the major port cities of Southeast Asia from the seventeenth to the late eighteenth centuries. Because much of this activity took place at a time that coincided with the advent of large, standing maritime populations of seafaring, trading-raiding peoples throughout the Southeast Asian region, the Malay sovereigns, as Christian Pelras, Barbara and Leonard Andaya and Velthoen have shown, often had recourse to particular Bugis and

Bajau people whose skills and energies were cultivated for slave trafficking, the procurement of exotic marine products, particularly tripang, and who, under the sponsorship of various states and local lords, received encouragement to raid coastal shipping or neighbouring shores in the spice islands and the Straits of Malacca.[10]

'Piracy' suddenly appears at the end of the eighteenth century because of the economic boom developing across Asia with the greatly increased flow of commodities between Southeast Asia, China and the West. Here I want to resolve an apparent temporal paradox in Southeast Asian history about 'piracy' and politics in the Malay world and European imperial policy and expansion in the region. The paradox is that the rise of the Sulu Sultanate increased maritime raiding, and the opening and imminent decline of China at the hands of Europe took place at much the same time (the eighteenth and first half of the nineteenth centuries) as the introduction of tea, an important commercial plant from China, to Europe.[11] By the end of the eighteenth century, Britain's insatiable desire for this commodity was to change the face of Asian history and shape the future destinies of both Sulu and China. The capitalist world economy came to dominate Malay states like the Sulu Sultanate and its environs. Chinese demand for exotic commodities that were suddenly of great interest to Europeans, encouraged both the establishment and 'takeoff' of sub-regional trade networks and the production of commodity flows. New entrepôts emerged, especially in the area of the Sulu Sea and Borneo. The island of Jolo became a major centre for cross-cultural trade in the recent history of Asia, and the Sulu Sultanate flourished. The Taosug became locked into a vast web of trade and exchange involving the exploitation of the rich tropical resources of the area, with producers, distributors and controllers involved in a complex set of relationships and structural dependency. For the sultan, with his capital located on the seacoast, the entrepôt and neighbouring areas incorporated a set of cultural–institutional practices typical of centralised trading states based on redistribution for the production and acquisition of goods, on the one hand, and kinship, warfare, slavery and other forms of organisation and culture on the other. As the sultanate and the Malay states organised their economies around the collection and distribution of marine and jungle commodities, there was a greater need for large-scale recruitment of labour to do the intensive work of procurement. An estimated 68,000 men laboured each year alone in the Sulu Zone's tripang fisheries to provide the popular Chinese exotica, a standard banquet fare that appeared on so many menus, sometimes braised with geese's feet or abalone. The Taosug, with their retainers and slaves, collected about 10,000 piculs of tripang in any one season in the first half of the nineteenth century (one picul is equivalent to 133 pounds or 60 kilograms).¹² Bird's nest for the Qing cuisine had to be obtained in the wilderness of Borneo. The Iranun, the slave raiders of the Sulu Zone, met this need for a reliable source of workers. Within three decades (1768–1798) their raids encompassed all of insular Southeast Asia.

Certain lessons and examples from history about global economic–cultural interconnections and interdependencies tend to explain historical processes, patterns and events that have formerly been glossed over. For example, sugar 'demanded' slaves and the Atlantic slave trade. Similarly, tea, inextricably bound to sugar as product and fate, would also inadvertently 'demand' slaves in the Sulu–Mindanao region and elsewhere, and thus lead to the advent of Iranun maritime slave raiding or what the British, Dutch and Spanish decried as 'piracy'. Since the British primarily wanted sea cucumber, sharks' fin and bird's nest for the trade in China tea, the issue of the nature of productive relations in Sulu—slavery—suddenly became primary at the end of the eighteenth century. The demand for certain local commodities in return for imports affected the allocation of labour power and the demand for fresh people throughout the Sulu Zone, as well as in other sectors of Southeast Asia. In this globalising context, tea was more than simply the crucial commodity in the development of trade between China and Britain, it was also a plant that was instrumental in the stunning, systematic development of commerce, power and population in the Sulu Zone; a commerce which changed the regional face and history of Southeast Asia, and inadvertently gave birth in the Malay world to the essentially European term 'piracy'. Past and present historians of the colonial period, in considering the Iranun maritime raids and slaving activity, have uncritically adopted the interpretation perpetrated by interests 'on the right side of the gunboat'.¹³ They have relied heavily on sources inherently antagonistic to the nature of the society and values of the Iranun raiders, such as the hostile accounts of the Spanish friars, the printed reports of Dutch and English punitive expeditions, and Sir Stamford Raffles and James Brooke's influential reports on 'Malay piracy'. In these Eurocentric histories, which dwell on the activity of the Iranun at length, the term 'piracy' is conspicuously present in the titles.¹⁴ While there are references to them in earlier histories, travel accounts and official reports, historians have had to burrow deeper and deeper into the fragmented sources in various archives in Europe and Southeast Asia, especially the Philippine National Archive, in order to reconstruct a detailed ethnohistorical account of these maritime people. As I have shown in *The Sulu Zone*, particular sources are of critical importance, but they are of little value unless the historian knows what to do with them.¹⁵ The main impetus for fashioning a new understanding of the Iranun past has been the radical change in perspective that some historians have adopted to study the region's recent history and its continuing integration within the world capitalist economy. These changes in perspective attempt to combine the historiographical approaches and ideas of the Annales historians with the conceptual framework of world system theorists and solid ethnography.[16] Here, I again pay particular attention to the well-written, stimulating book Wolf wrote in the early 1980s, *Europe and the People Without History*.[17] Wolf argues that no community or nation is or has been an island, and the world, a totality of interconnected processes or systems, is not and never has been a sum of self-contained human groups and cultures. The modern world-system, as it developed, never confined capitalism to the political limitations of single states or empires. Wolf's postulations, if accepted, imply that an analysis of capitalism not limited to the study of single states or empires will be more complete and, in certain ways, less static. The point is that history consists of the interaction of variously structured and geographically distributed social entities that mutually reshape each other. The transformation of the West and China and the rise of the Iranun in modern Southeast Asian history cannot be separated: each is the other's history. In this chapter, this ethnohistorical viewpoint is a fundamental frame of reference. No ethnic group, even those as apparently misunderstood as the Iranun, can be studied in isolation from the maritime world(s) around and beyond them.[18]

The Iranun: A deadly force

Thomas Forrest noted that some of the Iranun–Maranao migrants and warriors, who had formerly held a lowly rank within the traditional hierarchy of the Magindanao and Taosug involved in the China trade, became men of power and prowess, both master and lord, when they became 'Illanun'. A key factor in the late-eighteenth-century Sulu expansion was global trade, which certainly provides the most convincing explanation of the origins of Iranun maritime raiding and slaving to the north and south. Slave raiding was used to increase Sulu's population. The late-eighteenth century was a time of growing political instability and macro-conflict among rival European powers in Asia. The resulting region-wide economic competition led to an increase in trade with the Sulu Sultanate, which was an important source of exotic natural commodities for China, such as sea cucumber, bird's nest and pearls, as well as more mundane commodities such as wax and rice. The spread of large-scale Iranun maritime raiding by the mid-1770s implies the presence of something worth plundering, so the increased global trade with the English and Spanish also encouraged Taosug-sponsored Iranun marauding. By the latter half of the eighteenth century, the Iranun had already begun to establish themselves in settlements like Tempasuk and Pandassan, west of the Sulu Sea. These villages were specifically established as forward bases for maritime raiding and the collection of slaves that the Taosug could use to procure and process natural commodities to supply European traders for the China market.

Blood upon the sails and sand

It is estimated that during the last quarter of this century (1774–1798) of maritime raiding and slaving against the Dutch and Spanish, between 150 and 200 raiding ships set out from the Mindanao–Sulu area each year. The sheer size of the vessels—the largest *lanong* measuring upward of 39 metres in length—and the scale of the expeditions dwarfed most previous efforts, marking a significant turning point in the naval strategy of Malay maritime raiding as it had been traditionally understood. Armed with the latest firearms, the Iranun slave raiders struck fear into the hearts of coastal and riverine people throughout Southeast Asia. Large settlements were targets of fleets of forty to fifty *prahus*. The boats carried 2,500 to 3,000 men, as well as heavy artillery. The regularity of these raiding sweeps for slaves was as predictable as the winds which carried the Iranun boats to their target areas. Customary warnings were issued each year by the Dutch, Spanish and English to coastal towns and small craft on the approach of the 'pirate wind' in August, September and October that brought these fishers of men. Physical evidence of the Iranun raids can still be found in the Philippines today. Scattered along the coastlines of the Philippine archipelago are remnants of the century-long terrifying presence of these raiders. An old stone watchtower, a crumbling church-cum-garrison, or the remains of a Spanish fort and cemetery can be found along the coasts of Catanduanes, Albay, Leyte and Samar, bearing witness to the advent of sudden affluence in the zone and deep despair throughout the Philippines.[19] So notorious were the Iranun slave raiders that they are recalled in the exploits of local heroes who drove them off, in the folktales of Virac, Catanduanes and the Riau Archipelago and Madura in Indonesia. The number of people plucked by the Iranun from the shores of Southeast Asia in a span of 100 years was staggering. Several hundred thousand slaves were moved in Iranun vessels to the Sulu Sultanate in the years between 1768 and 1848.[20]

The greatest threat to late-eighteenth-century seaborne trade came from the Iranun who operated from the mangrove-lined inlets, bays and reef-strewn islets in the waters round the southern Philippines and Borneo, especially the Sulu and Celebes seas. They preyed on an increasingly rich shipping trade of the Spanish, Dutch and English, and Bugis and Chinese, and seized their cargoes of tin, opium, spices, munitions and slaves as the merchants headed to and from the trading centres of Manila, Makassar, Batavia and Penang.[21] The Iranun had a stranglehold on this trade across Southeast Asia because it was so exposed along its entire course through numerous hazardous straits and channels among countless islands—islands frequented by a fearless sea-going people of predatory tendencies possessed of swift sailing *prahus*—which offered every opportunity for stealth and surprise attack. When small merchant prahus and Chinese junks made their halting voyages on the sea's calm waters, the Iranun were never far away, striking at all sized craft. They simply had to wait, sheltered behind a convenient island, headland or bay overlooking strategic sea routes, and sooner or later 'coastwise' targets, never straying out of sight of land, would cross their path. From England, the United States and Europe, other larger sailing ships, laden with arms, opium and textiles for the China market repeatedly ran the gauntlet of these narrow straits that were the hunting ground of the Iranun. By the end of the eighteenth century, the British East India Company had moved to establish trading bases in the Straits of Malacca. While the authorities in Bengal began to exert some influence over the commercial affairs of the Straits Settlements, the Royal Navy did not dominate the seas of the area. Iranun maritime raiding and slaving in this region were complex phenomena confronting several global powers, namely Britain, the Netherlands and Spain, and a number of local sultanates, Kedah, Riau–Lingga, Jambi, Siak and Palembang, all located in the area of highest risk, within a long narrow rectangle drawn to link Banka Island and Billiton to the Riau Archipelago, Singapore and the Malay Peninsula. According to Dutch and British reports and figures, between 1800 and 1830 Iranun slave raids and marauding accounted for almost half of all the incidents reported in this region. The West's developing involvement in the China trade and the subsequent founding of Singapore contributed to the Malacca Strait and its environs experiencing one of the highest rates of maritime raiding in Southeast Asia at that time. The annual value of Singapore's entrepôt trade in 1833 was estimated at about two million Spanish dollars, but it was in fact worth far more as the settlement acted as the central redistributive point for the circulation of goods throughout Southeast Asia, in every direction. Wong Lin Ken suggests that Iranun marauding in the Straits of Malacca seriously damaged English commerce as losses of cargoes and *prahus* to these sea raiders pushed up local prices and led to an overall decline in Singapore's country trade.[22]

At the end of the eighteenth century the Iranun maritime raids had a profound, albeit decisive impact on Southeast Asia. The Iranun have been rightly blamed for demographic collapse, loss of agricultural productivity and economic decline, as well as the break-up of the Dutch stranglehold on the Straits of Malacca and Eastern Indonesia. But the driving force for this process was still global and economic: the Iranun profited from Spanish, Dutch and English internal colonial problems and expansion, but were not the cause of the problems. In the 1790s, a top-heavy administratively moribund Dutch East India Company (Vereenigde Oostindische Compagnie) could barely keep the vast archipelago—already fraying at the edges—together. Few parts of eastern Indonesia seemed more prone to Iranun raiding and violence than Buton and neighbouring islands. For the first two decades of the nineteenth century, it was wracked by Iranun–Tobello violence that left thousands of people dead and tens of thousands of others homeless as they abandoned the coastline and fled to the interior.

Rescued captives interrogated by colonial officials had often been traumatised by the violence they had witnessed during the sea attacks and settlement raids along the coastline. As I discussed in Chapter 7, the oral traditions of their descendants still speak of 'the terror'.

While the terror of the distant past continues to be revealed in memories, changes in the distant past itself were challenging the very survival of slavery in different parts of Southeast Asia, as elsewhere in the world. The main slave raiding zones in the South China Sea and the waters of Eastern Indonesia attracted the intense naval pressure of Britain, Spain and the Netherlands for more than a quarter of a century; by the 1880s, the numbers of slaves moving across the region had been reduced to a trickle. Consequently, forced sales into slavery and debt bondage to ensure the survival of the economies of states like Sulu rose in the second half of the nineteenth century as the autonomy of traditional Malay states, and maritime raiding and slaving, all declined under the combined pressure of modern colonial navies.[23]

Borders, state power and crime on the high seas, 1968–2000

In the latter half of the twentieth century, the Asia–Pacific basin is a major contributor to the world economy, and particularly to those Southeast Asian nations that its seas and oceans touch directly. It provides low-cost sea transportation between Asia—especially China, Japan and South Korea, and the West—as well as extensive fishing grounds and offshore oil and gas fields.[24] Southeast Asia, since the 1970s, has become one of the global 'hot spots' of attacks on vessels—to service illegal migrancy and the global traffic in women and children, and to steal the cargo. At the end of the twentieth century, more than half of all reported attacks on vessels worldwide occurred in this region.[25] The entire area of Southeast Asia, including the South China Sea, once again has come to be considered a danger zone, as was the case at the end of the eighteenth century. The waters off Indonesia, Malaysia, Singapore and the Philippines are the predominant areas of incident occurrences as commercial and wealthy yachting interests are attacked with increasing frequency.

The earlier terrifying days of the lateen square-rigged Iranun raiders flying the raven flag are gone, but some of the world's most murderous and bloodthirsty 'pirates' have roamed the waters of Southeast Asia since the 1970s. The spots pinpointed by the IMB (International Maritime Bureau) as the most vulnerable to attack and hijacking currently include the South China Sea area between the northern Philippines, China, Taiwan, and Hong Kong and Macao, the Gulf of Thailand, the sea north of Java in Indonesia; and the narrow Strait of Malacca off Singapore, where 60 per cent of the world's merchant tonnage passes.[26] For example, statistics compiled over the seven-month period from May to December 1993 showed that forty-two incidents were reported in the East and South China Sea out of sixty-seven worldwide. Most of the attacks took place in international waters and, in many cases, firearms were used.[27] The geographical challenges defy solutions to curb piracy. It was the case at the end of the eighteenth century, and it remains the case at the end of the twentieth, that geography remains a sinister ally of modern Southeast Asian pirates. In 1996, Mr Martin, IMB regional manager for Southeast Asia, stated:

> You look at the Philippines, it has such a long coastline…you will need at least ten thousand patrol boats. Indonesia is the same, there are thousands of islands for pirates and hijackers to hide.[28]

The geography of insular Southeast Asia also offers fresh insights into the complex and various ways in which international frontiers have encouraged maritime raiding, slaving and modern-day crime on the high seas. Just as maritime borders became barriers against the hot pursuit of raiders and pirates in relation to earlier competing colonial powers, nowadays the borders of hostile nations in the region provide similar barriers. Many Southeast Asian states in the worst affected areas—South China Sea, Straits of Malacca, Gulf of Thailand and the Sulu Sea—are not capable of policing a jurisdiction that extends 200 nautical miles (370 km) from their coasts. In congested areas, these jurisdictions overlap and are often the subject of bitter international legal disputes and boundary squabbles. When a foreign vessel is attacked in these worst affected areas, the navies of other nation-states cannot help either because the vessel is within a particular jurisdiction. These other Southeast Asian states cannot always also help because they either have insufficient resources or they are aiding and abetting the piracy and crime on the high seas. In the last three decades of the twentieth century, 'piracy' has no longer been linked to the slave trade in a conventional historical sense. It is directly linked to global traffic in illegal migrants and women and children destined for prostitution, right across Asia. Thus, piracy, or the exercise of extreme violence and theft on the high seas of Southeast Asia, has become a major criminal activity linked up with emergent globalised culture and regional states. The late-twentieth-century pirates of Southeast Asia—be they Thai fishers, Vietnamese pirates, Indonesian shipjackers or Sulu 'terrorists'—are all products of new postcolonial relationships where globalisation, wars and ethnic-political struggles have enhanced material crime relationships on the sea. A comparison with the sudden emergence of the Iranun at the end of the eighteenth century highlights in both cases crucial processes of engagement and disengagement from world commerce and economic growth, and the development of a colonial-state system. Such a comparison also shows which regional states formed, stagnated or fragmented under the impact of these global processes, as new groups of 'brokers in violence' emerged and ruled the seas of Southeast Asia.[29] The Iranun were among the first predators of global commerce in Asia to seriously attract the attention of the West, which was bent on expanding economically into China at the beginning of the nineteenth century. But South Seas 'piracy' is on the rise again and the new breed is well organised and financed and no less ruthless than the Iranun.

On the one hand, the economic boom of the 1970s and 1980s enabled former Indonesian President B. J. Habibie to turn Batam, the island twenty kilometres south of Singapore, into the headquarters of a dark alliance between triad-linked figures, space-age pirate gangs armed with the latest technology, and Indonesian marine officials. On the other hand, economic hardship, fuelled by the Asian currency crisis of the late 1990s, a new generation of technology and a lack of law enforcement among governments, especially in the South China Sea and the Sulu Zone, have helped push the extreme violence of a new wave of pirates to unprecedented heights. Piracy and violence in the modern manner—with machine guns, grenade-launchers, fast boats, rape and death—pose a very serious challenge to Asian states and navies. In this context, crime on the high seas must be understood in the same terms as any other major market force, with pirates in the region ranging from opportunistic Thai, Vietnamese and Taosug fishers, common criminals and rogue elements in various regional naval forces, to members of sophisticated Asian crime syndicates, namely composed of Chinese overseas. Consequently, the current economic and political conditions in both Indonesia and the Philippines throughout the 1990s have left many Indonesians, Filipinos and foreign observers with the impression that both nations have become, in the language of Thomas Friedman, 'messy states'—states in very severe difficulties and where corruption is overwhelming.[30] Similarly, in the Netherlands Indies at the end of the eighteenth century, global trade and Iranun maritime raiding and slaving were largely shaped and reinforced by one another. Two centuries ago, in the period just before the Dutch East India Company fell (1795), the Company was also in a 'messy state', governed by a ring of officials united by self-interest and unable to control the maritime raiding and slaving that it had inadvertently helped to create.

The globalising forces emanating from changing scales of production and consumption in Southeast Asia today, and this relationship to crime on the high seas, including human traffic or the new slavery, cannot be denied or wished away. Further, by reviewing certain acts of 'piracy' occurring after the 1970s, and by contrasting these acts with the Iranun type of incidents occurring two centuries before, it becomes obvious that the conventional articles on piracy now do not apply to many of the acts of crime found in current reports of the IMB and newspaper accounts of the incidents. This was also the case in the 1790s with Iranun maritime raiding in contrast to the western buccaneers and swashbucklers of the seventeenth-century Caribbean basin and Spanish Main.

On modern-day definitions of 'piracy' in Southeast Asia

The term 'piracy' has a narrow definition in the eyes of many modern governing bodies in Asia. The United Nations Law of the Sea defines piracy as: 'illegal acts of violence or detention, or any act of depredation, committed for private ends by the crew or passengers of a private ship and directed on the high seas or in a place outside the jurisdiction of the state.'[31] For statistical purposes the IMB defines 'piracy' as: 'An act of boarding or attempting to board any ship with the intent to commit theft or any other crime and with the attempt or capability to use force in the furtherance of that act.'[32] This definition, thus, also covers actual or attempted attacks whether the ship is berthed, at anchor or at sea. However, a review of illegal acts of 'piracy' occurring across Southeast Asia between the years 1970 and 2000 highlights the fact that the conventional definitions of piracy and the scholarly interpretation of legal issues do not apply to many types of incidents nowadays. I do not wish to dwell here on the semantics of what may actually define an act of piracy. Rather, this chapter is concerned with comparing the operational aspects of maritime raiding and slaving with piracy and/or the even narrower definition of maritime terrorism at the tail end of two centuries; namely, slaving, sea robbery, vessel hijacking, human traffic and other related maritime crimes.

It is important to distinguish between three forms of piracy in Southeast Asia in the recent period (1970–2000) under consideration. The first type is more mundane, takes place in inshore waters, and is perpetrated by bands of impoverished fishers, ill-organised gangs or idle roustabouts.[33] They opportunistically approach and board larger vessels where the concentrations of shipping are greatest, or where the law enforcement is weakest. Thousands of ships pass each month through the Malacca Straits between Indonesia and Malaysia, or call at Singapore at the southern end of the straits. There is also an extraordinary concentration of ships in the South China Sea plying well-established shipping lanes to Hong Kong, Taiwan, South Korea and Japan. These ships, particularly at anchor, are easy prey for the pirates, who board from small speedboats, armed with guns or machetes, threaten the crew, and make off with cash and valuables such as mooring ropes and paint.[34]

Indonesian coastal communities, over the past three decades, have suffered from the emphasis on commercial exploitation for short-term profit-making. Indonesia's fishing communities are among the poorest of the poor because of large-scale illegal fishing operations, fish bombing and the destruction of coral reefs. In some cases, even a few thousand dollars of stolen goods constitutes a fortune for individuals and coastal communities that rely on traditional fishing methods to subsist. The continual lack of response from the authorities against the practices that have destroyed the resources of these communities (particularly trawling, fish bombing and cyanide poisoning) has ended in unilateral action—raids by local people on illegal fishing boats and merchant vessels.[35] For all its size and mass, a deep draught vessel, like a small tanker or cargo ship, is a vulnerable target because of its own tonnage. When confined to narrow and restrictive channels, and operating at night or times of limited visibility, these vessels are extremely susceptible to hostile boarding. Typically, many of these attacks occur at night with the ship at anchor. In the late 1970s and 1980s, fishing vessels, particularly around the southern Philippines, also received the attention of pirates and armed robbers. The bandits operated swiftly and accurately from faster boats, taking the fish catch, boat engines, fuel, personal effects, or worse, the boat itself.[36] The single linking factor was that many were driven to piracy by poverty and the coastal resource crisis facing Indonesia, the Philippines and Thailand, particularly in times of thin fishing or poor harvests.[37]

During the 1970s and 1980s, attacks on merchant ships began to increase in a general climate of growing commodity flows and patterns of Japanese investment and shipping. It was at this time that shipowners and their crews became increasingly alarmed about a relatively new and far more sophisticated, well-organised type of crime: the high seas hijacking of ships and cargoes by international crime syndicates based across the Asian region. Over the past three decades, the actions of these syndicates, which are comparable to the Iranun in operational terms, argues Arthur Bowring, director of the Hong Kong Shipowners' Association, are nothing less than 'high seas terrorism'.[38] This far more serious type of piracy in Southeast Asia usually targeted small tankers or larger vessels, and stole the entire cargo. In such incidents, it was not unusual, after hijacking a ship, for a second pirate-directed vessel to move alongside the hijacked vessel to siphon off the oil, to collect the bulk cargo, or both. This type of operation required a far higher degree of organisation than the piracy conducted by bands of impoverished fishers, and was/is orchestrated by gangs who follow shipping schedules on the Internet.[39] International Maritime Organisation reports say that most of the attacks occurred at night, with armed gangs boarding the ships usually while they were anchored or berthed. Regardless of where these strikes happen in the region, nearly all attackers of high-tonnage vessels have intimate knowledge of vessel design and layout, being able to make their way through a ship quickly. After the late 1970s, the lack of effective watch, on targeted vessels standing at anchor or pier side, often further increased vulnerability in many incidents. In addition to the hijacking of ships and the theft of cargo, the main targets of Southeast Asian attackers appear to be cash in the ship's safe, crew possessions and any other portable ship's stores, including coils of rope.[40]

Dangerous areas within the region

In this period between 1970 and 2000, the most pitiful victims of Southeast Asia's pirates were the defenceless boat people in the Gulf of Thailand. For those who headed across the gulf to Thailand the journey could be a nightmare if they found Thai fishing boats in their path. The attacking fishers were often part-timers, pirates of opportunity, who could make up for a bad catch by stealing the passengers' valuables. The attacking fishers were also capable of extreme brutality, murdering scores of people heading for southern Thailand. Women were systematically taken off refugee boats and raped by the crew of a fishing boat, and then passed to another fishing boat and then on to another. After 1987, Thailand, with some success, began to crack down on the pirates who robbed and terrorised refugees fleeing Vietnam.[41]

Refugees fleeing from Indochina, the boat people, were the pirates' easiest targets. But pirates were preying with growing frequency on ships in the sea-lanes of Southeast Asia, especially in the Sulu Zone, with authorities in the region largely unable to cope with them. In the late 1970s, the most pirate-infested waters were those around the southern Philippines and Borneo, the Sulu and Celebes seas. Armed with heavy weapons left over from the Indochina war, the pirates were halting fishing boats, yachts, coastal steamers and even small ocean-going freighters on the high seas, and taking their cargo and other possessions. Often there were violent clashes as the Taosug and Samal pirates fired heavy machine guns, grenade-launchers, recoilless rifles and mortars at their victims, and casualties increased. The vessels were frequently taken as prizes by the pirates, and the hapless crews and passengers were left to swim for shore. Sometimes, in scenes reminiscent of the Iranun, the victims were held for ransom. The Malaysian authorities accused these pirates of also sabotaging navigation buoys and lights so that ships would go aground on the numerous reefs of the Sulu Sea—making them sitting ducks for plunder. The pirates' stratagem of shooting up navigation beacons in the Sulu Sea in apparent attempts to force ships aground was partially successful. In December 1978, Philippine Air Force aircraft were forced into action to rescue a grounded Panamanian freighter from armed raiders. More than 100 pirates attacked and seized the ship, holding it until the Philippine Air Force drove them away.[42] Japanese shipping lines now considered southern Philippine waters so dangerous that the majority of their vessels bound for Indonesian ports began to detour westward into the South China Sea.

The 1980s was to see a major increase in piracy around Southeast Asia. But the Gulf of Thailand and the Sulu Zone were still considered two areas where it was most prevalent. However, by the late 1980s attacks on merchant ships began to increase sharply in the Straits of Malacca, the Strait of Singapore and the Phillip Channel—major shipping lanes that connect the South China Sea with the Indian Ocean. In 1986, armed pirates used grappling hooks to board large freighters off Indonesia and Singapore, and strip them of their cargoes. In addition, Taosug pirates cum Muslim insurgents, who could not find a ship to plunder, took over the east coast town of Semporna (where I lived from 1967 to 1969), locked the inhabitants in the community hall and looted its banks and all the shops. The daylight raid was the second on the remote town in six weeks. The incidents had shaken the state of Sabah, and the town's residents in particular. The raids highlighted the inadequacy of the Malaysian Navy and police who lacked the staff to effectively patrol Sabah's long east coast. The deadly trail of these ominous incidents, at opposite ends of the region, would set the tone for the late 1980s: a decade that would be wracked by violence and crime on the high seas of Southeast Asia on a scale hitherto unprecedented, except for the scope and magnitude of the freewheeling Iranun operations in the 1780s when they burst from the Bay of Illana to prey upon the China trade and coastal villages across the region.

Pirate attacks against large ships have tripled during the 1990s, to 300 a year. Nearly three-quarters of all the world's pirate attacks now take place in Southeast Asia. The waters and ports around Indonesia alone accounted for one-third of all attacks.[43] The International Chamber of Commerce has designated Indonesia as 'the most piracy prone country in the world'.[44] This is not surprising as, under the New Order, problems were solved by using violence and corruption in a state where those who held the economic reins of power were loth to surrender them. In fact, by 2000, pirate attacks in Indonesia's sea-lanes alone outnumbered all attacks in the Middle East, Africa and Latin America combined[45]. More than 300 incidents of pirate attacks on shipping in south and Southeast Asia took place in 2000, making it the worst year on record. The most dangerous waters were around Indonesia where well-armed gangs were responsible for 43 per cent of the total number of attacks.[46] Regardless of the statistics, it is also not unrealistic to project that less than half of all incidents in Indonesian waters are actually being reported. Hence, these already damning figures can only serve as nominally reliable regional indicators of piratical activity, particularly in Indonesia, where most ports experience robbery and hostile boardings of vessels at berth and anchor. Ships calling at the Indonesian ports of Belawan, Jakarta, Merak Panjang, Samarinda and Tanjang Priok have reported numerous attacks while at anchor and berth.[47] Local government and law enforcement agencies within Indonesia have had little or no ability to respond in an appropriate manner to such attacks against shipping or yachts and other pleasure craft.[48] Nor are there any signs that the number of attacks will drop unless Indonesia takes serious steps.

Singapore, located between Malaysia and Indonesia, is a global centre for transnational capital and regional trade, with strong service and manufacturing sectors, and international trading links that allowed the port-city to weather the effects of the Asian financial crisis better than its neighbours. Singapore in the 1990s, according to regional security analysts, also became the prime transit point for all sorts of contraband going to the United States, Western

Europe and the Third World.⁴⁹ Ship attack and piracy activity has become a regular occurrence in the Singapore Strait in a decade of growing commodity flows of drugs, arms, fauna and human beings. In the waters around Singapore, teams of pirates with high-powered rifles, operating from speedboats, began to attack slow-moving cargo ships in a series of hit-and-run robberies in the early and mid-1990s. Piracy against ships in these waters rose sharply over the following five years. One of the main reasons for this, apart from Singapore's obvious economic success and globalised culture, was the disastrous economic and political situation in Indonesia after 1997.

The Malacca Strait, at 800 kilometres long, is the world's longest strait, and it is the main seaway connecting the Indian Ocean to the China Sea. It varies in width from 17 to 300 kilometres, and the entire strait is peppered with wrecks and shifting shoal banks.⁵⁰ The strait, in some stretches, is shallow and narrow, and requires precise navigation. Prior to 1989, the Malacca Strait was considered to be relatively safe, with seven cases of piracy and armed robbery being reported annually from the area. But, in 1989 the figure rose to twenty-eight and by 1991, it had gone up to fifty a year.⁵¹ The Malacca Strait is one of the world's busiest shipping lanes now used by over 600 vessels a day. It has become the most pirate-infested channel in the world, which was also the case during the Iranun age at the height of the China trade. In the Malacca Strait, in terms of the political economy of crime and globalisation, piracy is one of the thriving trades, alongside industrial development, slick resorts and prostitution.

In the Straits region as a whole, most of the attacks have occurred in the Phillip Channel in the Malacca Strait or the Singapore Strait. In these areas, ships generally have to slow down to avoid collisions in the crowded sea-lanes. At the beginning of 2000, the Malacca Strait recorded the second-highest number of attacks, after the waters around Indonesia, with fifty, followed by the area around Chittagong port in Bangladesh at forty-six.⁵² The IMB, which monitors piracy attacks globally, said that ongoing political and economic turmoil in Indonesia has made the Malacca Strait and surrounding waters more risky than ever for ships.⁵³

Another factor that often did not receive the recognition it deserved was the effect these attacks had on the seafarers involved. The annual reports of the IMB Piracy Reporting Centre in Kuala Lumpur highlight that modern piracy, particularly in the three decades under consideration, has become more violent, bloody and ruthless. For shipowners, and the staff and fishers who crew their ships and trawlers, maritime crime is a serious and dangerous business. According to Captain Jayant Abhyanker, the IMB Deputy Director, it is made all the more fearsome because its victims know they are usually alone and defenceless. He said, 'It is impossible for those of us here to fully appreciate the trauma pirate attacks cause, both physically and mentally.'[54] Hapless seafarers in the Gulf of Thailand, the Straits of Malacca and the Sulu Sea were often threatened with guns, knives, machetes or other weapons; and were tied up, beaten and stripped of all their possessions. In some cases, crewmembers were murdered. In others, whole crews were cast adrift in lifeboats. Many victims have never fully recovered from the trauma they experienced and have not gone to sea again. The greatest violence in maritime crime attacks is related to the seizing of refugee boats and 'phantom ships'. In the recent hijacking of a Panamanian cargo vessel, the MV *Cheung San*, the pirates confessed to the Chinese authorities that they gathered the twenty-three crewmembers on deck and shot them. In a similar bloody incident, a hijacked Japanese-owned cargo vessel, MV *Tenyu*, was found in China with a new crew. The fate of the original fourteen crewmembers is still unknown, although they too are feared to have been murdered.

The impact of widespread environmental disaster and pollution is another potential by-product of maritime crime that is often overlooked—and waiting to happen—in Southeast Asia, particularly in the Malacca Strait, where the cost implications of environmental pollution are huge. Tankers, bulk carriers and cargo ships have often been left uncrewed during attacks. In the 1990s, pirates have, on several occasions, endangered navigation by leaving vessels, including fully laden tankers, under way and without command, dramatically increasing the risk of collision or grounding in the narrow congested shipping lanes. The resulting ecological and navigation implications of such reckless behaviour are enormous. Such a nightmare had almost come to pass in 1992; an ecological disaster was only narrowly averted, after pirates boarded a Panamanian registered ship, taking control of the 305 metre ship. They tied up its twenty-four crew and left. Fortunately, one of the crew members managed to break free fifteen minutes after the raiders had gone and took control of the 305 metre ship, which had been steaming unguided at night through one of the most crowded channels in the world—Phillip Channel off Singapore. The risk of a collision or grounding was very real and it was a matter of pure luck that the hulking supertanker did not run aground, creating a worse oil spill than that of the *Exxon Valdez* disaster off Alaska. The near-fatal incident became a closely kept secret by the Straits authorities and the shipowner, but it galvanised the local maritime world into action against Indonesia where the pirates had sought a safe haven.

Four Asian syndicates with Mafia-style dons in Indonesia, the Philippines, Hong Kong and mainland China seem to have had the right amount of transnational sophistication to make money from crime on the high seas during the 1980s and 1990s. The leaders of these syndicates, whose working vessels are equipped with satellite dishes, computers and automatic weapons, can control dangerous region-wide operations from a great distance—for example, from an office building in Hong Kong, Singapore or Manila, or from a flashy brothel or resort golf course on the Indonesian island of Batam. Other branches are based in Johore Bahru in Malaysia and Taipei in Taiwan. The syndicates robbed the crews and stole their ships. In this way they direct the criminal operations that hijack ships heading for Singapore, which is the world's busiest harbour. At the end of the twentieth century, this act of hijacking in Southeast Asia crossed all boundaries and involved all nationalities. The modern-day masterminds of crime on the high seas are well-suited businessmen, sitting in plush offices hidden behind ghost companies, stealing ships and goods, sometimes via the Internet. The same Hong Kong- and Singapore-based syndicates were also already heavily involved in illegal immigration based on using stolen ships. The syndicate in Indonesia, which is believed to be linked to former President Suharto's closest business associates, was almost certainly behind the surge in Indonesian and, especially, Chinese stowaways transported on 'phantom ships' that over the past seven or eight years have turned up in Canada, the United States and Australia.[55]

In a sense, these pirates and criminals are obviously being used as pawns in the struggle for power in Jakarta and elsewhere across the region. This is not new, given the close links between the New Order regime (particularly the generals), capital and the globalisation of crime that has occurred over the past two decades. Military personnel like Suharto's son-in-law, Prabowo Subianto, allegedly have found it in their interest to cultivate crime on the high seas in all its manifest forms—shipjacking, traffic in illegal aliens, the arms trade— to serve their political interests in the context of both national and global transition. This new wave of pirates, who rule the waters of the South China Sea, have turned Batam, a small Indonesian island across the strait from Singapore, developed by B. J. Habibie, into the headquarters of pirate gangs with links to the Indonesian navy. The island of about half a million people is only an hour by ferry from Singapore. In the late 1970s, Dr Habibie, as the young protégé of President Suharto, was appointed head of the Batam autonomous area and he boldly drafted liberal legislation inviting foreign investors, mostly from Singapore, Taiwan and Japan, to build golf course resorts, electronics and other middle-size factories in Batam. What Habibie had not planned for was the growing sex industry. Rapid industrial development and the influx of foreign tourists, particularly Singaporean Chinese and Japanese looking for young girls, have made Batam a strategic location for doing business. One of the thriving businesses on the island, home to manufacturing, ship repair and prostitution, has become piracy in the Malacca Strait. The region's authorities have learnt from interviews with seamen, shipping agents, coast guard officers and prostitutes that this modern piracy or crime on the high seas is controlled from Batam by a murky alliance between pirates, the Indonesian coastal patrol and other marine officials.[56]

Like the case of the Iranun at the end of the eighteenth century, due in part to the technology transfer, maritime security forces increasingly proved to be no match for well-organised pirates in the Malacca Strait, the Gulf of Thailand, the South China Sea and Sulu Sea. In the last three decades of the twentieth century, these space-age raiders have used computers and the Internet to select vessels and itineraries; they have relied on radar to locate targeted vessels; they have gathered intelligence from radio transmissions and informers, and have carried out night attacks using swift, small motorised boats and automatic weapons. These raiders have easily escaped in boats that are simply too fast or that blend in with hundreds of other small ships in Southeast Asian waters.[57] On board some of these vessels, ASEAN naval forces have found sets of handcuffs, face masks, fake immigration stamps, paint of various colours, welding equipment and ship stamps with which the pirates could turn hijacked vessels into phantom ships. Theoretically, a ship stolen in the region could simply turn up in another part of Asia, with a different name and flag, as far away as southern China or Chittagong.[58] While they have not been ignored, between the late 1970s and 2000, and as a major feature of an emergent globalised culture, the pirates and criminals on the high seas of Southeast Asia have become more numerous, more dangerous and equipped with more sophisticated crime technology.

Containing modern piracy

At the end of the twentieth century, forms of consumerism and significant market forces in China and the West, and the rhythm of Chinese history, have continued to affect development and modernity in Southeast Asia. In the 1990s, China was repeatedly accused of being soft on piracy and has been identified as the country in which the majority of pirates and criminals in Southeast Asia sell hijacked cargoes and vessels. Most of the missing ships were registered in Honduras and Panama, and conveyed bulk cargoes such as timber, fuel and minerals that were easy to dispose of in China's booming economy. However, as the Chinese authorities have reluctantly started to crack down on the pirates, criminal syndicates in Southeast Asia have recently begun to go further afield to dispose of hijacked cargoes, with India and Iran being favoured destinations.[59]

Conclusion

Maritime raiding, slaving and modern crime on the high seas, when framed from this angle of vision and context, are part of a larger globalising process of a sub-region engulfed by an economic boom (1768–1800) and a financial crisis (1990–2000). It is widely recognised as encompassing the first and second openings of China with global, albeit predominantly Western, financial systems and transnational trade. Recognition of this fact, that Southeast Asia in its pre-colonial, colonial and post-colonial pasts has experienced unhindered flows of commodities, capital and coerced labour, especially in productive zones like Sulu, enables us to understand the economic–political relationships between maritime raiding, slavery and state formation at the end of the eighteenth century. On the other hand, it highlights the link between modern piracy and crime, as agents of social change, in the context of the stark reality of economic crisis and global transition with its social and political consequences for restructuring the new order in Southeast Asia.

However, in global comparative terms, the problem of the resurgence of piracy on the high seas of Southeast Asia can also be represented as one of the historical imagination—of the ability to imagine alternative interpretations and futures. This creative shift in perspective shows that between 1768 and 1800, and 1968 and 2000, Iranun maritime raiding and slaving and space-age piracy and criminally related matters on the high seas of Southeast Asia, were as much forces of engagement with world commerce and economic growth then as globalisation is a force for maritime crime in Southeast Asia now. The shaping of economic and political violence associated with maritime raiding, slaving and the criminalisation of piracy in Southeast Asia in both the past and present contexts belonged to a new moment(s) (1768–1800 and 1968–2000) in history. There is a strong continuity in certain respects between late-eighteenth-century Malay trade-based states like the Sulu Sultanate and the post-1970s new order state of Indonesia, the Philippines and Thailand, using 'pirates' and criminals on the high seas to galvanise their economies and get things done in a region beset by political and economic instability. International pressure has not been able to force Indonesia to act against piracy. Indonesia continues to suffer severe political and economic turmoil, and the Indonesian navy, tainted by allegations of corruption and crime on the high seas, is understaffed and short of resources.[60] Operations such as human traffic in illegal migrants, illegal fishing by trans-national trawlers and attacks on vessels and shipjacking in the Malacca Strait, have relied on the collusion of local naval authorities and regional crime syndicates. By the late 1990s, the most obvious obstacles preventing effective anti-piracy activities in Indonesian waters have been the adverse impact of regional autonomy, especially in the Riau–Bantam region, the devastating effects of the economic crisis, and increased communal tension and political violence across the archipelago.

Regional cooperation in Southeast Asia under these circumstances remains untenable, as Indonesia continues to be wracked by political and economic turmoil, and real law enforcement in China remains an abstract concept, when it comes to prosecuting piracy and crime in Asian waters. Globalisation and emergent globalised culture continue to enhance material crime relationships linked to piracy in Southeast Asia. As was the case at the end of the eighteenth century, with respect to Iranun maritime raiding and slaving, space-age piracy and crime on the high seas are on the increase in Southeast Asia at the dawn of the twenty-first century. And so too is the cost to industry, trade, local fishers, coastal inhabitants and regional consumers, which now tops billions of dollars. Estimates of losses from piracy and related criminal activity in Southeast Asia reach as high as twenty-five billion dollars annually. Most cargo insurers and shipping companies are helpless in the face of this criminal trend in the context of regional change and global transition. In the 1780s and 1790s, there appeared to be little prospect of a solution within the foreseeable future to what had become a major problem in Southeast Asia's sea-lanes when the Iranun launched their large-scale operations, carried out by well-organised fleets of large raiding *prahus*, that ushered in a major transformation of regional history. Nowadays, as the world contracts through ever-increasing connected ventures, a somewhat different mirror image has appeared on the horizon once again, as new-wave pirates and ship thieves rule the seas of Asia.

Notes

Introduction: Passing Over

1. J. Dunne, *The Way of All the Earth*, Sheldon Press, London, 1972, pp. 135–56.
2. H. Dick, 'Indonesian economic history inside out', in *Review of Indonesian and Malaysian Affairs*, vol. 27, (1993): 1–12, p. 6; J. F. Warren, *The Sulu Zone 1768–1898: The Dynamics of External Trade, Slavery and Ethnicity in the Transformation of a Southeast Asian Maritime State*, Oxford University Press, Singapore, 1981.
3. Dick, 'Indonesian economic history inside out', p. 1.
4. J. Comaroff and J. Comaroff, *Ethnology and the Historical Imagination*, Westview Press, Boulder, 1992, p. 22.
5. E. R. Leach, *Political Systems of Highland Burma, A Study of Kachin Social Structure*, London School of Economics and Political Science, London, 1954, pp. 4, 212.
6. Warren, *The Sulu Zone*, pp. xi–xvi, 252–5.
7. R. M. Keesing, 'Asian cultures?' in *Asian Studies Review*, vol. 15, no. 2 (1991): 43–50, p. 46.
8. ibid.
9. E. R. Wolf, *Europe and the People Without History*, University of California Press, Berkeley, 1982, p. 387.
10. P. Burke, *History and Social Theory*, Polity Press, Oxford, 1992, pp. 38–9.
11. C. Ginsburg, *Clues, Myths and the Historical Method*, Johns Hopkins University Press, Baltimore, 1989, p. 156.
12. Warren, *The Sulu Zone*, pp. 299–315.
13. G. Marcus, 'Problems of ethnography in the modern world system', in *Writing Culture. The Poetics and Politics of Ethnography*, ed. J. Clifford and G. Marcus, University of California Press, Berkeley, 1986, pp. 165–93, p. 190.
14. R. Darton, *The Great Cat Massacre and Other Episodes in French Cultural History*, Vintage Books, New York, 1985, p. 3.
15. Wolf, *Europe and the People Without History*, p. 390.
16. Comaroff and Comaroff, *Ethnology and the Historical Imagination*, p. 44.
17. Warren, 'The Port of Jolo and the Sulu Zone Slave Trade: An 1845 Report' (unpublished paper), 2005.
18. K. Prewitt, 'Presidential items', in *Items—Social Science Research Council*, vol. 50, no. 1 (1996): 15–18, p. 16.
19. V. Lieberman, 'An age of commerce in Southeast Asia? Problems of regional coherence—a review article', in *The Journal of Asian Studies*, vol. 54, no. 3 (1995): 796–807.
20. S. Schama, *Dead Certainties: Unwarranted Speculations*, Granta Books, London, 1992, p. 31.
21. Certificate Coroner's View Singapore (CCVS), Oichi, N.82, 17/2/06.
22. Schama, *Dead Certainties*, 1992, p. 322.
23. Schama, 'In search of history's muse', in *Dialogue*, vol. 9, no. 3 (1992): 62–6, p. 62.

24 Warren, *Rickshaw Coolie: A People's History of Singapore (1880–1940)*, Oxford University Press, Singapore, 1986, p. 177; *Ah Ku and Karayuki-san: Prostitution in Singapore 1870–1940*, Oxford University Press, Singapore, 1993, p. 304.

25 Ong Keng Sen, in program booklet, *Broken Birds: An Epic Longing*, TheatreWorks Production, Fort Canning Green, March 1995.

26 R. H. Crawford, M. Clark and G. Blainey, *Making History*, Penguin Books, Fitzroy, 1985, pp. 64, 66–7.

27 Joseph Campbell cited in D. K. Osborn (ed.), *A Joseph Campbell Companion*, Harper Collins, New York, 1991, p. 26.

Chapter 1: The Sulu Zone

1 This chapter first appeared in *Archipel*, vol. 18 (1979): 223–30.

2 See J. C. Van Leur, *Indonesian Trade and Society*, Van Hoeve, The Hague, 1967.

3 Notable exceptions are the significant studies that have been published in the past decade on the Sultanate of Aceh (1607–1636) and Johor (1641–1728), which use a vast array of sources to portray the cosmopolitan urbanism of ruler and merchant in the maritime Malay world of the seventeenth century. See Denys Lombard, *Le Sultanat d'Atjeh au temps d'Iskandar Muda*, 1607–1636, Maisonneuve, Paris, 1967; and Leonard Andaya, *The Kingdom of Johor, 1641–1728, Economic and Political Developments*, Oxford University Press, Kuala Lumpur, 1975.

4 Van Leur, *Indonesian Trade and Society*, p. 163.

5 See Nicholas Tarling, *Piracy and Politics in the Malay World*, F. W. Cheshire, Melbourne, 1963; Lennox A. Mills, *British Malaya, 1824–1867*, Oxford University Press, Kuala Lumpur, 1966, pp. 323–4, 328–9; L. R. Wright, *The Origins of British Borneo*, Hong Kong: Hong Kong University Press, Hong Kong, 1970, pp. 5, 39; and C. A. Majul, *Muslims in the Philippines*, University of the Philippines Press, Quezon City, 1973, chapters VII, VIII, pp. 249–316.

6 See James F. Warren, *The Sulu Zone 1768–1898: The Dynamics of External Trade, Slavery, and Ethnicity in the Transformation of a Southeast Asian Maritime State*, Singapore University Press, Singapore, 1981; reprinted, Quezon City, Philippines: New Day Publishers, 1985.

7 Extensive ethnological research has been conducted among the Taosug by Thomas Kiefer; among the Balangingi Samal by William Geoghegan; among the Samal Bajau Laut by Harry Nimmo, Clifford Sather and Carol Warren; among the Yakan by Carol Maloney; among the Maranao by David Barradas; and among the Subanun by Charles Frake.

8 The *estados* are the early ship registers for the port of Manila. The *almojarifazgo* are the records of the ad-valorem tax on departure of a vessel. See Appendix F, 'The Manila-Jolo trade, 1786–1830', in Warren, *The Sulu Zone*, pp. 265–78.

9 See Appendix R, 'The statements of the fugitive captives of the Sulu Sultanate, 1836–1864', in Warren, *The Sulu Zone*, pp. 299–315. Two years (1968–1969) of living in a Samal Bajau Laut community on the north-east coast of Borneo, an area once part of the periphery of the Sulu Sultanate, has provided me with a perspective from its edge and an attachment to this maritime world that was the initial impetus for the study.

10 The idea of a distant assemblage of islands constituting the hinterland of a port town was developed by Spoehr in the context of contemporary culture change in the Pacific. See Alexander Spoehr, 'Port town and hinterlands in the Pacific Islands', in *American Anthropologist*, vol. LXII (1960): 568–92.
11 Tarling, *Piracy and Politics in the Malay World*, pp. 20, 146–85.
12 Majul, *Muslims in the Philippines*, pp. 107–316.
13 I have estimated that the number of slaves imported over the period from 1770 to 1870 varied from a low estimate of 201,350 to a high estimate of 302,575. See Warren, *The Sulu Zone*, pp. 208–11.
14 Vestiges of the traditional patterns of trading and raiding persist to this day. These patterns, now labelled 'smuggling', continue to operate across national boundaries now dividing this once integrated zone.

Chapter 2: Joseph Conrad's Fiction as Southeast Asian History

1 A version of this chapter first appeared in *The Brunei Museum Journal* (1977): 21–34.
2 G. J. Resink, 'De archipel voor Joseph Conrad', in *Bijdragen tot de Taal-Land-en Volkenkunde van Nederlandsch-Indie*, vol. CXV (1959), II, pp. 192–208; Resink, 'The eastern archipelago under Joseph Conrad's western eyes', in *Indonesia's History between the Myths*, ed. G. J. Resink, Van Hoeve, Hague, 1968, pp. 307–23; N. Sherry, *Conrad's Eastern World*, Cambridge University Press, Cambridge, 1966, pp. 89–139; J. Allen, *The Sea Years of Joseph Conrad*, Methuen and Co., London, 1967, pp. 187–241.
3 The Sulu Zone in the late eighteenth and nineteenth centuries comprised the Sulu Archipelago, the north-east coast of Borneo, the foreland of southern Mindanao and the western coast of Celebes. See James F. Warren, *The Sulu Zone 1768–1898: The Dynamics of External Trade, Slavery, and Ethnicity in the Transformation of a Southeast Asian Maritime State*, Singapore University Press, Singapore, 1981; reprinted, Quezon City, Philippines: New Day Publishers, 1985, pp. xx–xxii.
4 R. Broersma, *Handel en Bedrijf in Zuid-en Oost-Borneo*, G. Noeff, Gravenhage, 1927, p. 170.
5 ibid., p. 228.
6 ibid., p. 174.
7 Joseph Conrad described the animated atmosphere of Makassar at the time as follows:
> At that time Macassar was teeming with life and commerce. It was the point in the islands where tended all those bold spirits…in search of money and adventure. Bold, reckless, keen in business, not disinclined for a brush with the pirates that were to be found on many a coast as yet, making money fast, they used to have a general 'rendezvous' in the bay for purposes of trade…the Dutch merchants called them English pedlars…most were seamen; the acknowledged king of them all was Tom Lingard…whom the Malays…recognised as 'Rajah Laut'—the King of the Seas.
>
> See Conrad, *Almayer's Folly: A Story of an Eastern River*, London; J. M. Dent and Sons, Ltd., London, 1947, pp. 6–7.

8   Secretan was a wealthy merchant of Lombok and Bali. It is possible that he inherited King's trading interests when the latter shifted his activities from Lombok to Borneo. He owned the ships *Nina* and *Swan* in which Lingard sailed to Java, Celebes and Borneo. Secretan died in May 1864 and in his will appointed Lingard guardian of his two children by a Balinese woman, Sumanty. Within a week of his death, Lingard, who had already taken the liberty to cancel a 13,000 florin debt owed to Secretan by the Sultan of Gunung Tabor, had bought a part ownership in the *Coeran* with Thomas Morgan Craig, another of Secretan's ship masters. See no. 31 De Gouveneur van Celebes en Onderoorigheden (hereafter GVC), aan Gouveneur General van Nederlandsch Indie, 27 June, 1863, Geheim, no. 2107, Kabinet 270, AR-Schaarsbergen, Kolonien Archief 1398; Sherry, *Conrad's Eastern Sea*, pp. 92–3.

9   Conrad recalled that the crew of the *Vidar* picked 'up the [Lingard] beacon at the mouth of the river just before dark and the tide serving. Captain C— was enabled to cross the bar and there was nothing to prevent him going up the river at night.' See Conrad, *A Personal Record*, J. M. Dent and Sons, Ltd., London, 1950, p. 77.

10 No. 31, GVC aan zyne Excellentie den Gouveneur General van Nederlandsche Indie de Batavia, 27 June, 1863, AR-Schaarsbergen, Kolonien Archief 1398.

11 ibid.

12 ibid.; Sherry, *Conrad's Eastern World*, p. 92.

13 Der Luitenant ter zee ter Kommandant ter Maritieme middelen bij te Expeditie in de Zuiden Ooster Afdeeling van Borneo aan den Resident ter Zuider ooster Afdeeling van Borneo te Banjdarmassin, 4 March 1863, AR-Schaarsbergen, Kolonien Archief 1398.

14 ibid.; A. Van Marle, 'De Rol van de Buitenlandse Avonturier', *Bijdragen en Mededelingen Betreffende de Geschiedenis Der Nederlanden*, vol. LXXXVI, no. 1 (1971): 32–9, p. 34.

15 No. 31, GCG, aan zyne Excellentie den Gouveneur General van Nederlandsche Indie te Batavia, 27 June, 1863, AR-Schaarsbergen, Kolonien Archief 1398.

16 Sherry, *Conrad's Eastern World*, p. 97.

17 Charles Olmeijer was born in Surabaya in 1848; his father was a government clerk in the city and his mother was the 'native woman Amina'. In 1874, four years after he went to Berau, Olmeijer married a Eurasian girl of seventeen, Johanna Maria Cornelia van Lieshout; her father was a non-commissioned Dutch officer and her mother a Menadonese. They had a large family—five sons and six daughters—although she died in 1892 at thirty-five. As a morose, frustrated, lonely man, Olmeijer spent his closing years with his son, Willy, a local trader in Samarinda. He died in the Surabaya hospital in September 1900 after an operation for cancer. For years Olmeijer's son had kept his father's diary in an office safe in Samarinda, only to have it lost (and undoubtedly destroyed) when the Japanese invaded Borneo in 1942. See J. S. Holmes and A. van Marle, 'Joseph Conrad in Indonesia', unpublished lecture, University of Munster, 1961, pp. 15–22; statement of Kang Si Gok, Chinese resident of Tanjong Redeb, age 82, in Mr R. Haverschmidt to Dr J. G. Reed, 24 August 1952, Haverschmidt Papers. Records compiled in 1951–1952 in Berau by Mr R. Haverschmidt, late manager, N. V. Steenkolen Maatschappij Parapattan, Teluk Bajur, Berau.

18 Statement of Adji Bagian, age 53, in Mr R. Haverschmidt to Dr J. G. Reed, 24 August 1952, Haverschmidt Papers; Olmeijer, who was to watch their trade at Berau grow and thrive in the 1870s, and gradually diminish and stagnate in the 1880s, hoped to secure his fortune not only in trade but mining; by panning for gold in the alluvial stream beds of interior Borneo he hoped to strike it rich. As late as 1890 he was to request official permission from the Dutch authorities to enter into a contract with the Sultan of Sambaliong to prospect for gold. 'Almayer's thoughts were often busy with gold, gold he had failed to secure, gold the others had secured…or gold he meant to secure yet.' See Conrad, *Almayer's Folly*, p. 3.

    He [Almayer] must patiently try and keep some little trade together. It would be alright. But the great thing—and here Lingard spoke lower—the great thing would be the gold hunt up the river. He—Lingard—would devote himself to it. He had been in the interior before. There were immense deposits of alluvial gold there. Fabulous. He felt sure. Had seen places. Dangerous work? Of course! But what a reward!

    See Joseph Conrad, *An Outcast of the Islands*, J. M. Dent and Sons, London, 1947, p. 149.

19 Statement of Hadji Bagian, age 53, in Mr R. Haverschmidt to Dr J. G. Reed, 24 August, 1952, Haverschmidt Papers.

20 ibid.

21 Conrad, *A Personal Record*, London: J. M. Dent and Sons, 1924, pp. 74–5.

22 Interview with Mrs C. C. Oehlers, the daughter of Jim Lingard, by Dr J. G. Reed, 13 April 1951, Reed Papers. Papers of the late Dr J. G. Reed of Perak, Malaysia, relating to his research into the life of Joseph Conrad in the John Neilson Conrad Collection, Oamaru, New Zealand.

23 Statement of Anang Dachlan, age 77, in Mr R. Haverschmidt to Dr J. G. Reed, 24 January 1952; Mr Haverschmidt to Dr J. G. Reed, 30 July 1951, Haverschmidt Papers. When Jim Lingard came to Berau he married a Eurasian named Site who was a relative of the prominent Chinese merchant Po Eng Sing. The young man travelled widely in the interior, spoke the local dialect fluently, and, according to his daughter, 'was much loved and respected by the natives'. Jim became a successful trader, but to support his family of six children (one daughter, five sons) as they grew up, he began to lend money through Po Eng Sing at exorbitant rates. In later life, Jim stopped trading altogether and lived in Po Eng Sing's house off the interest of the money lent by the Chinese merchant. According to his daughter, he died in Sumatra after a prolonged illness at Berau in about 1916 at the age of fifty-four. Statement of Kang Si Gok, Anang Dachlan and the Ratu of Gunung Tabor, widow of Sultan Achmud, in Mr Haverschmidt to Dr J. G. Reed, 24 January 1951, Haverschmidt Papers; interview with Mrs C. C. Oehlers by Dr J. G. Reed, 13 April 1951, Reed Papers.

24 Broersma, *Handel en Bedrijf in Zuid-en Oost-Borneo*, p. 228.

25 Until the end of 1873 Lingard owned the following ships: the schooners, *Coeran* and *Fanny*, the small schooner-rigged steamer, *Johanna Carolina*, and the large three-masted barque, *West Indian*. The *Coeran* was sold in February 1874 in Singapore. See Sherry, *Conrad's Eastern World*, p. 98.

26 The total picture of the pattern of Lingard's trading activities only emerges from an analysis of the shipping and harbour statistics in both Straits newspapers and the *Makassarsch Handelsblad*. See Tables 2.1 and 2.2.

27 Letter to the editor dated 30 November 1875, *Makassarsch Handelsblad*, 4 January 1876, no. 1.
28 See Table 2.2; Conrad, *Almayer's Folly*, p. 8.
29 Crocker to Sir Rutherford Alcock, 19 September 1887, CO 874/244.
30 Birch to Martin, 18 October 1901, CO, 874/268.
31 Crocker to Sir Rutherford Alcock, 10 September 1887, CO 874/243.
32 For example, in the course of two trips between January and June of 1878, the N.I. Steamship, *Tromp*, alone exported 1,776 piculs of gutta-percha from Berau to Makassar. However, by 1892 it was estimated that the export of gutta-percha from Berau and Bulungan together totalled only 3,000 piculs per year. The supply of raw rubber that the Kuran/Berau region yielded had dwindled because of the rapacity with which the trade was conducted after 1878. Inside two decades, vast tracts of virgin forests had been systematically felled by gutta collectors (they did not tap the trees but simply cut them down) and rattan cutters with a total disregard for its future preservation. Jim Lingard estimated that the forests of Berau and Bulungan would be exhausted of gutta percha by 1894. See Table 2.2; 'Report on Berouw', 1892, K.P.M. survey of Berau Borneo: conditions and trade possibilities, 24–26 July 1892, Haverschmidt Papers.
33 El consul de Espana en Singapore a Senor Ministro de Estado, 20 April 1876, Archive de Ministerio de Asuntos Exteriores, Correspondencia Consulados Singapore, p. 2067.
34 Statements of Kang Si Gok and Anang Dachlan, in Mr Haverschmidt to Dr J. G. Reed, 24 January 1951, Haverschmidt Papers; Syed Mohsin came to Singapore as a young man in an Arab vessel. He made a number of voyages in a trading ship and saved enough money to open a modest shop on Singapore's Arab Street. In time he prospered and came to own several large trading vessels and steamers. He had been a rich man, but towards the end of his life he was practically ruined by his sons-in-law. See Charles Buckley, *An Anecdotal History of Old Time Singapore*, University of Malaya Press, Kuala Lumpur, 1965, p. 656, first published in 1902. Conrad who saw Syed Mohsin by chance, on a wharf in Singapore, six or seven years before his death in 1894 at about the age of 80, recorded his observations:
> I myself saw him but once…quite accidentally…an old, dark little man blind in one eye, in a snowy robe and yellow slippers. He was having his hand severely kissed by a crowd of Malay pilgrims to whom he had done some favours, in the way of food and money. His alms giving, I have heard, was most extensive, covering almost the whole archipelago.

See Conrad, *The Shadow Line: A Confession (and) Within the Tides: Tales*, J. M. Dent, London, 1950, pp. 4–5.
35 Statements of Kang Si Gok and Anang Dachlan, in Mr Haverschmidt to Dr J. G. Reed, 24 January 1951, Haverschmidt Papers.
36 'That must have happened many years before…I knew that Almayer founded the chronology of all his misfortunes on the date of that fateful event…' (the founding of a permanent Arab trading station at Berau): Conrad, *An Outcast of the Islands*, p. x.
37 Diary of William Pryer, 27 June 1880, CO 874/69; Pryer to Read, 31 July, 1880, CO 874/192.

38 Crocker to Alcock, 10 September 1887, CO 874/243.

39 Treacher to Sir Rutherford Alcock, 31 December 1882, CO 874/232; Treacher to Sir Rutherford Alcock, 30 July 1885, CO 874/239; Pryer to Brown, 15 January 1886, CO 874/240; Treacher to Sir Rutherford Alcock, 19 February 1886, CO 874/240.

Chapter 3: Who Were the Balangingi Samal?

1 A version of this chapter first appeared in *The Journal of Asian Studies*, vol. 37, no. 3 (1978): 477–90.

2 See E. R. Leach, *The Political Systems of Highland Burma*, London School of Economics, London, 1954, and 'The frontiers of Burma', in *Comparative Studies in Society and History*, vol. III, no. 1 (1960): 49–68; F. K. Lehman, *The Structure of Chin Society*, Studies of Anthropology, no. 3, University of Illinois Press, Urbana, 1963, and 'Ethnic categories in Burma and the theory of social systems', in *Southeast Asian Tribes, Minorities and Nations*, ed. P. Kunstadter, vol. I, Princeton University Press, Princeton (1967): 93–124; M. Moerman, 'Who are the Lue?', in *American Anthropologist*, vol. LXVII (1965): 1215–230 and 'Accomplishing ethnicity', in *Ethnomethodology*, ed. R. Turner, Penguin Books, London, 1974, pp. 54–68. For general articles relating to the genesis and persistence of ethnic boundaries, the incorporation of ethnic groups, and the organisation of interethnic relations in polyethnic social systems, see F. Barth (ed.), *Ethnic Groups and Boundaries: The Social Organization of Culture Difference*, Allen & Unwin, London, 1969; and L. A. Despres (ed.), *Ethnicity and Resource Competition in Plural Societies*, Mouton, The Hague, 1975.

3 See Thomas Kiefer, *The Tausug: Violence and Law in a Philippine Moslem Society*, Holt, Rinehart & Winston, New York, 1972; and 'The Tausug polity and the Sultanate of Sulu: A segmentary state in the southern Philippines', in *Sulu Studies*, no. 1 (1972): 19–64. Kiefer has published numerous articles and monographs on the extensive ethnological research he conducted, principally in the years 1966 to 1968, on the Taosug (Tausug; Tawsug; Suluk; Su'ug).

4 For a cogent discussion of the advent of Islam in Sulu and Mindanao, and its relationship to Southeast Asian Islam until the coming of the Spaniards in the sixteenth century, see chapter 2 of C. Majul, *Muslims in the Philippines*, University of the Philippines Press, Quezon City, 1973, pp. 35–78.

5 William Geoghegan, 'Balangingi Samal', in *Ethnic Groups of Insular Southeast Asia*, ed. F. M. Lebar, Human Relations Area Files Press, New Haven, vol. 2, 1975: 6–9, pp. 6–8. Ethnographic studies of the Samal Bajau Laut, spanning nearly a decade, have been conducted in the environs of Tawi-Tawi in the Sulu Archipelago. See Harry Arlo Nimmo, 'The structure of Bajau society', PhD dissertation, Department, of Anthropology, University of Hawai'i, 1969.

6 See Warren, *The Sulu Zone 1768–1898: The Dynamics of External Trade, Slavery, and Ethnicity in the Transformation of a Southeast Asian Maritime State*, Singapore University Press, Singapore, 1981; reprinted, Quezon City, Philippines: New Day Publishers, 1985, pp. xx–xxii.

7 ibid., pp. 5–143 provides a detailed discussion of the various trading patterns.

8 In these Euro-centred histories, which dwell on the activity of the Iranun and Balangingi at length, the term 'piracy' is conspicuously present in the titles:

V. Barrantes, *Guerras Piraticas de Filipinas contra Mindanaos y Joloanos*, Imprenta de Manuel H. Hernandez, Madrid, 1878; Emilio Bernaldez, *Resana Historico de la Guerra a Sur de Filipinas, sostenida por las armas Espanoles contra los piratas de aquel archipielago, desde la conquista hasta nuestraos dias*, Imprenta del Memorial de Ingenieros, Madrid, 1857; Jose Montero y Vidal, *Historia de la Pirateria Malayo Mahometans en Mindanao, Jolo y Borneo*, Imprenta de M. Tello Madrid, 1888; Nicholas Tarling, *Piracy and Politics in the Malay World*, F. W. Cheshire, Melbourne, 1963.

9   Ann L. Reber, 'The Sulu world in the eighteenth and early nineteenth centuries: A historiographical problem in British writings on Malay piracy', MA thesis, Cornell, 1966. In fact, as Reber points out, Raffles could have reached very different conclusions regarding the subject of piracy and the Sulu Sultanate. He seems to have been unaware of the accurate published accounts and the manuscript material on the Sulu world written by Alexander Dalrymple, Thomas Forrest and James Rennel at the end of the eighteenth century; and available in the archives of the East India Company.

10 See Lennox A. Mills, *British Malaya, 1824–1867*, originally published 1925, Oxford in Asia, Historical Reprints, Kuala Lumpur, 1967, pp. 323–4, 328–9; Tarling, *Piracy and Politics in the Malay World*, pp. 20, 146; K. G. Tregonning, *A History of Modern Sabah 1881–1963*, University of Malaya Press, Singapore, 1966, p. 186; L. R. Wright, *The Origins of British Borneo*, Hong Kong University Press, Hong Kong, 1970, pp. 5, 39; Majul, *Muslims in the Philippines*, chapters 7, 8, pp. 249–316.

11 See Blake to Maitland, 13 August 1838, Public Records Office, London (PRO), Admiralty 125/133; Declaraciones de todos los cautivos fugados de Jolo y acogidos a los Buques de la expresada division, con objeto de averiguar los puntos de donde salen los pancos piratas, la clase de gente que los tripulan, la forma en que se hacen los armamentos y otros particulares que arrogan las misnias declaraciones, Jolo, 4 October 1836, Philippine National Archive, Manila (hereafter PNA), Mindanao/Sulu (hereafter M/S) 1803–1890, pp. 1–72; Relacion de los 45 cautivos venidos de Jolo sobre el Bergantin Espanol *Cometa*, 19 Marso 1847, PNA, Piratas 3; Verklaringen van ontvlugten personen uit der handen der Zeeroovers van 1845–1849, Arsip Nasional Republik Indonesia, Jakarta, Menado 37.

Freed captives and captive marauders expressed their own attitudes towards raiding in numerous statements and interrogations, recorded over several decades. These were occasionally published in Dutch scholarly journals. See A. J. F. Jansen, 'Aantekeningen omtrent Sollok en de Solloksche Zeeroovers', in *Tijdschrift voor Indische Taal-, Land -en Volkenkunde, uitgegeven door het (Koninklijk) Bataviaasch Genootschap van Kunsten en Wetenschappen* (hereafter *TBG*), vol. 7 (1868): 212–43; 'Berigten omtrent den Zeeroof in den Nederlandsch-Indischen Archipel, 1857', in *TBG*, XV (1968–1972): 436–57; 'Berigten omtrent den Zeeroof in den Nederlandsch-Indischen Archipel, 1858', in *TBG*, vol. XX (1873): 302–26; W. R. Van Hoevell, 'De Zeerooverijen der Soloerezen', *Tijdschrift voor Nederlandsche Indies*, Vol. II (1860): 99–105.

12 See N. Tarling, 'Some notes on the historiography of British Borneo', in *Southeast Asian History and Historiography*, ed. C. D. Cowan and O. W. Wolters, Cornell University Press, Ithaca, 1976, pp. 285–95, p. 293.

13 Edward Kuder, 'The Moros in the Philippines', in *Far Eastern Quarterly*, vol. 4, no. 2 (1946): 119–26, p. 123; Najeeb Saleeby, 'The Moros', 1906, no. 161 in Beyer and Holleman, Papers on Philippine Customary Law, II, p. 10; also, introductory chapters

of Melvin Mednick, 'Encampment of the lake: The social organization of a Moslem Philippine people', PhD dissertation, Department of Anthropology, University of Chicago, 1965.

14 N. 839, De Resident van Menado, Jansen, aan den Gouveneur der Moluksche Eilanden te Amboina, 8 June 1856, Algemeen Rijksarchief-Schaarsbergen, Kolonien, 6873.

15 Saleeby, 'The Moros', p. 11.

16 Admiralty to Under Secretary of State, 14 July 1862, PRO, Foreign Office, London (hereafter FO), 12/30.

17 F. Combes, *Historia de las Islas de Mindanao y Jolo*, Madrid, 1667, W. E. Retana & P. Pastells, 1897, cols. 23–32; T. Forrest, *A Voyage to New Guinea and the Moluccas from Balambangan: Including an Account of Magindano, Sootoo and Other Islands*, G. Scott, London, 1779, pp. 372–4; Geoghegan, 'Balangingi Samal', p. 4.

18 Several 'Iranun' *prahu* were destroyed by the steamboat *Diana* on the east coast of Malaya in 1836, and some of the survivors when interrogated called themselves Balangingi after the island that was their home. See Warren, *The Sulu Zone 1768–1898*, pp. 297–8.

19 In regard to the treacherous character of these currents, Bernaldez wrote: 'They usually swirl about at six or seven miles an hour...we have seen a steam warship dragging both anchors, after letting out more than 60 fathoms of chain on each anchor in Balangingi waters', Bernaldez, *Resana Historico de la Guerra a Sur de Filipinas*, p. 15, see also p. 153.

20 El Gobierno Politico y Militar del Zamboanga a El Gobernador Capitan General (hereafter GCG), 30 May 1842, PNA, M/S 1838–1885.

21 Bernaldez, *Resana Historico de la Guerra a Sur de Filipinas*, p. 153.

22 El Gobierno Politico y Militar de Zamboanga a GCG, 30 May 1842, PNA, M/S 1838–1885; statements of Francisco Gregorio, Diomicio Francisco and Mariano Sevilla in Expediente 12, Declaraciones de todos los cautivos fugados de Jolo, 4 October 1836, PNA, M/S 1803–1890 (Exp. 12, unless otherwise specified, will hereafter refer to this set of Declaraciones); J. Farren to Viscount Palmerston, 29 February 1848, PRO, FO, 72/749.

23 Kiefer, 'Tausug polity', in *The Tausug*, p. 51; C. Majul, 'Political and historical notes on the old Sulu Sultanate', in *Journal of the Malaysian Branch Royal Asiatic Society*, vol. XXVIII, pt. 1 (1965): 23–43, pp. 39–40.

24 Statements of Juan de la Cruz and Jose Ruedas in Exp. 12; Van Hoevell, 'De Zeerooverijen der Soloerezen', p. 102.

25 Tarling, *Piracy and Politics in the Malay World*, pp. 146–85.

26 Exp. 12, statements of Angel Custodio, Juan Salvador, Domingo Candelario and Juan Santiago; Diary of William Pryer, 9 March 1879, Colonial Office, London, 874/68; Warren, *The Sulu Zone 1768–1898*, Appendix XVIII: 'The statements of the fugitive captives of the Sulu Sultanate', 1836–1864, pp. 299–315.

27 Barth, 'Introduction', in *Ethnic Groups and Boundaries*, ed. Barth, p. 22.

28 Exp. 12, Jose Ruedas, Gabriel Francisco and Matias de la Cruz.

29 El Gobierno Politico y Militar de Zamboanga a GCG, 30 May 1842; 15 February 1845 letter of Jayme Simo in Expediente 12, sobre haber salido la expedicion contra Balangingi, 17 February 1845, PNA, M/S 1836–1897.

30 Information obtained by Charles Grey at Singapore from Wyndham relating to Sulo, 24 February 1847, PRO, A 125/133; Van Hoevell, 'De Zeerooverijen der Soloerezen', p. 102.
31 Tarling, *Piracy and Politics in the Malay World*, pp. 146–85; Majul, *Muslims in the Philippines*, pp. 271–77.
32 J. Hunt, 'Some particulars relating to Sulo in the archipelago of Felicia', in *Notices of the Indian Archipelago and Adjacent Countries*, ed. J. H. Moor, Frank Cass and Co. Ltd., London, 1968 (first edition 1837), pp. 31–60, p. 40.
33 Blake to Maitland, 8 August 1838, PRO, A 126/133; Jansen, 'Aantekeningen omtrent Sollok en de Solloksche Zeeroovers', pp. 217, 229.
34 Hunt, 'Some particulars relating to Sulo', pp. 35–7, 50–61.
35 Statement of Silammkoom, 31 May 1838, in Bonham to Maitland, 28 June 1838, PRO, A 125/133.
36 Exp. 12: Matias Domingo and Juan de la Cruz; extract from *Singapore Free Press*, 6 April 1847, in PRO A 125/133. Majul, *Muslims in the Philippines*, fails to recognise the important redistributive role of the Taosug raiding, and its relationship to the economy of the Sulu Sultanate. He wrote, 'All the evidence points to the fact that the Sulu Sultan and chief *datus* never encouraged or approved of piracy by Samal or Iranun *datus*, for they were themselves traders having an interest that all shipping lanes be kept safe especially for traders going or coming from Jolo' (p. 285).
37 Jansen, 'Aantekeningen omtrent Sollok en de Solloksche Zeeroovers', pp. 216, 227.
38 Charles Wilkes, 'Jolo and the Sulu', in *The Philippine Islands 1493–1898*, ed. E. Blair and J. Robertson, Arthur H. Clark, Cleveland, 1906, vol. 43, pp. 128–92, p. 180.
39 Dumont d'Urville, *Voyages au pole sud et dans l'Oceanie sur les corvettes l'Astrolobe et la Zelee*, Gide et J. Baudry, Paris, 1844, vol. VII, pp. 179, 303–8; Edward Belcher, *Narrative of the Voyage of H.M.S. Samarang, during the Years 1843–1846*, Reeve, Benham & Reeve, London, 1848, p. 270; Exp. 12: Juan Santiago, Juan Sabala, Francisco Zacarias, Pedro Antonio and Vicente Remigio.
40 Exp. 12: Juan de la Cruz; Bonham to Maitland, 28 June 1838, PRO A 125/133.
41 Jansen, 'Aantekeningen omtrent Sollok en de Solloksche Zeeroovers', p. 228.
42 Bonham to Maitland, 28 June 1838, PRO, A 125/133.
43 Exp. 12: Juan Florentino, Manuel Feliz, Diomicio Francisco and Mariano Sevilla; extracts from *Singapore Free Press*, 6 April 1847, PRO A 125/133; Numero 137, Carlos Cuarterón, prefecto apostolico, a GCG, 12 August 1878, PNA, Isla de Borneo (2); Tomas de Comyn, *State of the Philippines in 1810 being an historical statistical and descriptive account of the interesting portion on the Indian Archipelago*, Filipiniana Book Guild, Manila, 1969, p. 124; Barrantes, *Guerras Piraticas de Filipinas contra Mindanaos y Joloanos*, pp. 108, 161, 265–6.
44 Statements of Abdul and Sendie in Verklaringen van ontvlugten personen uit der handen der Zeeroovers van 1845–1849, Arsip Nasional Republik Indonesia, Jakarta, Menado 37; Jansen, 'Aantekeningen omtrent Sollok en de Solloksche Zeeroovers', p. 225.
45 Jansen, 'Aantekeningen omtrent Sollok en de Solloksche Zeeroovers', pp. 215, 222–4.

46 ibid., p. 222; Bonham to Maitland, 28 June 1838, PRO, A 125/133.
47 Exp. 12: Angel Custodio, Alex Quijano, Mariano Sevilla.
48 Exp. 12: Mariano Sevilla and Juan Santiago.
49 Exp. 12: Francisco Basilo and Mariano Sevilla.

Chapter 4: The *Prahus* of the Sulu Zone

1 A version of this chapter first appeared in *The Brunei Museum Journal*, (1985): 42–53.

2 For a detailed discussion of the multi-ethnic zone of which Sulu was the centre, see J. F. Warren, *The Sulu Zone 1768–1898: The Dynamics of External Trade, Slavery, and Ethnicity in the Transformation of a Southeast Asian Maritime State*, Singapore University Press, Singapore: 1981; on Iranun and Samal *prahu* construction, see Arturo Sociatas y Garin, 'Memoria sobre el Archipielago de Jolo', in *Boletin de la Sociedad Geografica de Madrid*, vol. 10 (1881): 110–33, 161–97, p. 196; for articles on the type, size and construction of *prahus* in the Philippines and eastern Indonesia, see G. Adrian Horridge, *The Design of the Planked Boats of the Moluccas; the Lambu or Prahu Bot, the Konjo Boatbuilders and the Bugis Prahus of South Sulawesi*, Maritime Monograph and Reports Nos. 39 and 40, National Maritime Museum, Greenwich, 1978–1979; *The Lashed-lug Boat of the Eastern Archipelagoes, the Alcina Ms and the Lomblen Whaling Boats*, Maritime Monograph and Reports no. 54, National Maritime Museum, Greenwich, 1982; William Henry Scott, 'Boat building and seamanship in classic Philippine society', in *Philippine Studies*, vol. 30, no. 3 (1982): 335–76; C. C. Macknight and Mukhlis, 'A Bugis manuscript about prahus', in *Archipel*, vol. 18 (1979): 271–82.

3 Thomas Forrest, *A Voyage to New Guinea and the Moluccas from Balambangan: Including an Account of Magindano, Sooloo and Other Islands*, G. Scott, London, 1779, p. 184.

4 ibid., p. 196.

5 Statement of Mariano Sevilla in Expediente 12, 4 October 1836, PNA, M/S 1803–1890; Apuntes sobre la Isia de Basilan 1892, Society of Jesus Archives of the Philippine Province, XIV–9, p. 32; Livingston, 'Constabulary monograph of the province of Sulu', Beyer-Holleman collection of original sources in Philippine Customary Law, vol. 1, paper 160, no. 1, p. 5.

6 Statement of Marcelo Teafilo in Expediente 12, 4 October 1836, PNA, M/S 1803–1890; W. R. Van Hoevell, 'De Zeerooverijen der Soeloerezen', in *Tijdschrift voor Nederlandsche Indie*, 2 (1860): 99–105, p. 102; E. B. Christie, 'The Moros of Sulu and Mindanao', Paper 162, vol. vi, no. 23, Beyer-Holleman collection of original sources in Philippine Customary Law, (BH-PCL), p. 38.

7 Diary of Leonard Wood, 6 January 1906, Leonard Wood Papers, The Library of Congress, Washington, D.C., container 3; Livingston, 'Constabulary Monograph of the Province of Sulu', Walker, 'Report of the 53rd Census District' (Tawi-Tawi), vol. 2, paper 161, no. 11, p. 38, Beyer-Holleman collection of original sources in Philippine Customary Law; A. J. F. Jansen, 'Aantekeningen omtrent Sollok en de Solloksche Zeeroovers', in *Tijdschrift voor Indische Taal-, Land-en Volkenkunde*,

uitgegeven door het (Koninklejk) Bataviaasch Genootschap van Kunsten en Wetenschappen, vol. 7 (1858): pp. 212–39, p. 220; Sociatas y Garin, 'Memoria sobre el Archipielago de Jolo,' p. 196.

Chapter 5: Slavery and the Impact of the External Trade

1. A version titled 'Slavery and the Impact of External Trade: The Sulu Sultanate in the Nineteenth Century', first appeared in *Philippine Social History, Global Trade and Local Transformation*, ed. E. de Jesus and A. McCoy, Ateneo de Manila University Press, Quezon City, 1982, pp. 414–44.
2. The zone comprising the Sulu Archipelago, the north-east coast of Borneo, the foreland of southern Mindanao and the western coast of Celebes set the geographical framework of the study.
3. My study, 'Trade, raid, slave: The socio-economic patterns of the Sulu Zone, 1770–1898', PhD dissertation, Australian National University, 1976, on which this chapter is primarily based, stresses the impact of a rapidly expanding foreign trade on the economy and society of the Sulu Zone, and provides a background to a discussion of slavery as an established feature of the Sulu Sultanate in this period.
4. Extensive ethnological research on the Taosug (Tausug, Tawsug, Suluk, Su'ug) conducted by Thomas Kiefer principally in the years 1966–1968 has been published in numerous articles and several monographs. See, T. Kiefer, *The Tausug: Violence and Law in a Philippine Moslem Society*, Holt, Rinehart and Winston, New York 1972; 'The Tausug polity and the Sultanate of Sulu: A segmentary state in the southern Philippines', in *Sulu Studies*, no. 1 (1972): 19–64.
5. For a cogent discussion of the advent of Islam in Sulu and Mindanao, and its relationship to Southeast Asian Islam until the coming of the Spaniards in the sixteenth century, see C. Majul, *Muslims in the Philippines*, University of the Philippines Press, Quezon City, 1973, chapter 2, pp. 35–78.
6. W. H. Geoghegan, 'Balangingi Samal', in *Ethnic Groups of Insular Southeast Asia*, ed. F. M. Lebar, Human Relations Area Files Press, New Haven, 1975, vol. 2, pp. 6–9. Ethnographic studies of the Samal Bajau Laut, spanning nearly a decade, have been conducted in the environs of Tawi-Tawi in the Sulu Archipelago. See H. A. Nimmo, 'The structure of Bajau society', PhD dissertation, Department of Anthropology, University of Hawai'i, 1969; and *The Sea People of Sulu*, Chandler Publishing Company, San Francisco, 1972.
7. For a detailed discussion of the traditional patterns of trade of the Sulu Sultanate, see Warren, *The Sulu Zone, 1768–1898 The Dynamics of External Trade, Slavery, and Ethnicity in the Transformation of a Southeast Asian Maritime State*, Singapore University Press, Singapore: 1981, pp. 6–16; see also my article, 'Sino–Sulu trade in the late eighteenth and nineteenth centuries', in *Philippine Studies*, vol. 25 (1977): 73–93.
8. Warren, *The Sulu Zone*, pp. 5–148.
9. ibid., pp. 147–211
10. ibid., pp. 216–51.
11. I rely heavily on the anthropological studies of Thomas Kiefer and also acknowledge the pioneering work of John Gullick and Melvin Mednick concerned with the

historical reconstruction of traditional Muslim political systems in Southeast Asia. See Kiefer, *The Tausug*, pp. 104–12; 'The Tausug polity and the Sultanate of Sulu', pp. 19–64; 'The Sultanate of Sulu: Problems in the analysis of a segmentary state'; 'Traditional states of Borneo and the Southern Philippines', in *Borneo Research Bulletin*, ed. Clifford Sather, vol. 3 (1971): 46–50; J. Gullick, *Indigenous Political Systems of Western Malaya*, The Athlone Press, London, 1958; M. Mednick, 'Some problems of Moro history and political organization', in *Philippine Sociological Review*, vol. 5 (1957): 39–52. See also D. Brown, *Brunei: The Structure and History of a Bornean Malay Sultanate*, Brunei Museum, Brunei, 1970.

12 See Appendix P, 'The Manila-Jolo trade, 1786–1830', in Warren, *The Sulu Zone*, pp. 265–78.

13 In these Euro-centred histories the term 'piracy' is conspicuously present in the titles. V. Barrantes, *Guerras Piraticas de Filipinas contra Mindanaos y Joloanos*, Imprenta de Manuel G. Hernandez, Madrid, 1878; J. Montero y Vidal, *Historia de la Pirateria Malayo Mahometans en Mindanao, Jolo y Borneo*, M. Tello, Madrid, 1888.

14 See Blake to Maitland, 13 August 1838, Public Records Office (PRO) London, Admiralty 125/133; Declaraciones de todos los cautivos fugados de Jolo y acogidos a los Buques de la expresada division, con objeto de averiguar los puntos de donde salen los pancos piratas, la clase de gente que los tripulan, la forma den que se hacen los annamentos y otros particulares que arrogan los mismas declaraciones, Jolo, 4 October 1836, Philippine National Archive (PNA), M/S 1803–1890, 1–72; Relacion de los cuarenta y cinco cautivos venidos de Jolo sobre el bergantin Espanol *Cometa*, 19 March 1847, PNA, Piratas 3; Verklaringen van ontvlugten personen uit der handen der Zeeroovers van 1845–1849, Arsip Nasional Republik Indonesia, Jakarta (hereafter ANRI), Menado 37. Numerous statements and interrogations of freed slaves and captive marauders, recorded over several centuries and expressing their own attitudes towards the place of slaves and raiding in the Sulu world, were also published occasionally in Dutch scholarly journals. See A. J. F. Jansen, 'Aantekeningen omtrent Sollok en de Solloksche Zeeroovers', TGB VII (1858), TBG XX (1873), pp. 302–06; W. R. Van Hoevell, 'De Zeerooverijen der Soloerezen', in *Tijdschrift voor Nederlandsch Indies* (hereafter TNI) vol. 2 (1850): 99–105.

15 See Appendix R, 'The statements of the fugitive captives of the Sulu Sultanate, 1836–1864', in Warren, *The Sulu Zone*, pp. 299–315.

16 C. Coquery-Vidrovitch, 'An African mode of production', in *Critique of Anthropology*, vols 4 and 5 (1975) 37–71; Coquery-Vidrovitch, 'Recherches sur un mode de production Africain', in *La Pensee*, vol. 144 (1969): 61–78; S. Amin, 'Sous-developpement et dependence en Afrique noire', in *Partisans*, vol. 64 (1972): 3–34; Y. Person, 'Enquete d'une chronologie Ivoirienne', in *The Historian in Tropical Africa*, ed. J. Vansina, R. Mauny and L. U. Thomas, Oxford University Press, London 1964, p. 332. See also C. Meillassoux (ed.), *The Development of Indigenous Trade and Markets in West Africa*, Oxford University Press, London 1971.

17 E. Terray, 'Long-distance exchange and the formation of the state: The case of the Abron Kingdom of Gyaman', in *Economy and Society*, vol. 3 (1974): 316–45.

18 J. Hunt, 'Some particulars relating to Sulo in the archipelago of Felicia', in *Notices of the Indian Archipelago and Adjacent Countries*, ed. J. H. Moor, Frank Cass and Co. Ltd., London, 1968, p. 37 (first edition 1837).

19 For an important article on the problems of defining slavery, see E. R. Leach, 'Caste, class and slavery—the taxonomic problem', in *Caste and Race: Comparative Approaches*, ed. A. de Reuck and J. Knight, Churchill, London, 1967, pp. 83–94. See also R. A. Padgug, 'Problems in the theory of slavery and slave society', in *Science and Society*, vol. 40 (1976): 3–27.

20 Diary of William Pryer, 25 November 1878; 26 June 1879, Colonial Office, London (hereafter CO), 874/68.

21 M. Mednick, 'Encampment of the lake: The social organization of a Moslem Philippine (Moro) people', PhD dissertation, Department of Anthropology, University of Chicago, 1965, pp. 60–1; Kiefer, 'The Tausug polity and the Sultanate of Sulu', p. 30.

22 A. Gunther, 'Correspondence and reports relating to the Sulu Moros', (Jolo and Manila 1901–1903), Beyer-Holleman collection of original sources in Philippine Customary Law, (hereafter BH-PCL), paper 162, vol. VI, no. 16, pp. 10–12; E. B. Christie, 'The non-Christian tribes of the northern half of the Zamboanga peninsula', Paper 162, vol. VI, no. 25, BH-PCL, p. 87; L. W. V. Kennon, D. P. Barrows, J. Pershing and C. Smith, 'Census report relating to the district of Lanao Mindanao', BH-PCL, paper 162, vol. VI, no. 28, p. 4; N. Saleeby, *Studies in Moro History, Law and Religion*, Bureau of Printing, Manila, 1906, pp. 92–3.

23 Scott to Governor, 30 June 1904, H. L. Scott Papers, Library of Congress, Washington, D.C., Container 55; Saleeby, *Studies in Moro History*, p. 94.

24 Saleeby, *Studies in Moro History*, pp. 66, 81, 89.

25 ibid., pp. 71, 83, 93.

26 ibid., p. 93.

27 Diary of William Pryer, 14 March 1878, CO 874/68.

28 W. Pryer, 'Notes on north eastern Borneo and the Sulu Islands', in *Royal Geographical Society*, vol. 5 (1883): 90–6, pp. 92–3.

29 J. K. Reynolds, 'Towards an account of Sulu and its Bornean dependencies 1700–1878', MA thesis, University of Wisconsin, 1970, p. 81.

30 Pryer, 'Notes on north eastern Borneo and the Sulu Islands', p. 92.

31 T. Forrest, *A Voyage to New Guinea and the Moluccas from Balambangan: Including an account of Magindano, Sooloo and other islands*, G. Scott, London, 1779, p. 330.

32 Diary of William Pryer, 14 March 1878, CO 874/68.

33 W. Briskoe, Journal, vol. 2, Department of the Navy, US National Archives and Records Service, entry for 5 February 1842. See also statement of Vicente Santiago in Expediente 12, 4 October 1836, PNA, M/S 1803–1890, 70.

34 Warren, *The Sulu Zone*, pp. 228–9; Mednick, 'Some problems of Moro history and political organization', p. 48.

35 See the statement of Francisco Enriquez in P. de la Escosura, *Memoria sobre Filipinas y Jolo redactada en 1863 y 1864*, Imprenta de Manuel G. Hernandez, Madrid, 1882, p. 373.

36 O. J. W. Scott and I. C. Brown, 'Ethnography of the Magandanaos of Parang', (1908), BH-PCL, Paper 163, vol. VI, no. 34, p. 16; A. Sociats y Garin, 'Memoria sobre el Archipielago de Jolo', in *Boletin de la Sociedad Geografica de Madrid*, vol. 10 (1881): 110–33, 161–97, p. 171.

37 See the statements in Relacion jurada de los individuos cautivos venidos en la Fragata de guerra. Inglesa Samarang, 15 March 1845, PNA, Piratas 3; Hunt, 'Some particulars relating to Sulu', p. 50.

38 S. Elkins, 'Slavery and its aftermath in the Western World', in *Ciba Foundation Symposium on Caste and Race: Comparative Approaches*, ed. A. V. S. de Reuck and J. Knight, J. & A. Churchill, London, 1967, p. 200.

39 Hunt, 'Some particulars relating to Sulu', p. 50.

40 El Gobernador Capitan General a Senor Presidente del Consejo de Ministro de Guerra y Ultramar, 9 December 1858, Archive Historico Nacional, Madrid, Ultramar 5184; Hunt, 'Some particulars relating to Sulo', p. 50.

41 Numero 133, Carlos Cuarterón, prefecto apostolico, a Senor Gobernador Politico y Militar de Jolo, 3 December 1878, PNA, Isla de Borneo.

42 Decreto numero 9, El Consejo de las Indias, 18 December 1776, Archivo General de Indias, Seville (hereafter AGI), Filipinas 359; P. Vicomte de Pages, 'Travels round the World in the years 1767, 1768, 1769, 1770, 1771', in *Travel Accounts of the Islands 1513–1787*, The Filipiniana Book Guild, Manila, 1971, pp. 127–84, p. 156; F. de Sainte-Croix Renouard, *Voyage Commercial et Politique aux Indes Orientales, aux Iies Philippines, a la Chine, avec des nations sur la Cochin Chine et le Touquin, pendant les annees 1803, 1804, 1805, 1806 et 1807*, Clement, Paris, 1810, vol. 2, p. 276; Forrest, *A Voyage to New Guinea*, p. 330; Barrantes, *Guerras Piraticas*, pp. 160–1; Montero y Vidal, *Historia de Filipinas*, vol. 2, p. 369.

43 C. Wilkes, 'Jolo and the Sulus', in *The Philippine Islands, 1493–1898*, ed. E. H. Blair and J. A. Robertson, Arthur H. Clark, Cleveland, 1903–1909, vol. 43, pp. 128–42.

44 See statements of Mariano de la Cruz and Francisco Gregorio, in Expediente 12, 4 October 1836, PNA, M/S 1803–1890; El Gobierno Politico y Militar del Zamboango a Gobernador Capitan General, 9 June 1847, PNA, M/S 1838–1885.

45 Extracts from *Singapore Free Press*, 6 April 1847, Public Record Office (PRO), Admiralty 125/133; F. P. Williamson, 'The Moros between Buluan and Punta Flecha', (1903), BH-PCL, VI, Paper 162, vol. VI, no. 26, p. 103; Mednick, 'Encampment of the lake', p. 62.

46 The Chinese manufactured mother-of-pearl articles in the form of beads, fish counters, fans and combs. See W. Milburn, *Oriental Commerce; containing a geographical description of the principal places in the East Indies, China, and Japan, with their produce, manufactures and trade, including the coasting or country trade from port to port; also the rise and progress of the trade of the various European nations with the Eastern world, particularly that of the English East India Company from the Discovery of the passage round the Cape of Good Hope to the present period; with an account of the company's Establishments, Revenues, Debts, Assets, at home and abroad*, Black, Parry and Company, London, 1813, vol. 2, p. 513.

47 See 'List of products of Sulu and its immediate dependencies', 26 February 1761, PRO, Egremont Papers, 30/47/20/1; 'List of goods to be had at Sooloo', MS, included with the log of the ship *Albree*, 656/1833A, Salem Peabody Museum, Salem, Massachusetts; Hunt, 'Some particulars relating to Sulo', p. 48.

48 In 1859 the Singapore price of a picul of mother-of-pearl shell varied according to the quality between 300 and 600 dollars. It was not unusual to pay up to 850 dollars to re-export it to Ceylon. See Numero 83, El Consul de Espana en Singapore a el

primer Secretario de estado, 3 July 1860, Archive de Ministro de Asuntos Exteriores, Madrid (hereafter AMAE), Correspondencia Consulados Singapore 2067.

49 This estimate has been arrived at by using the few examples in the literature, archival documents and private manuscripts to provide ratios between the number of people involved in marine procurement and their annual output at small collecting centres in the zone. I have used these figures in conjunction with the statistic for the estimated volume of *tripang* (10,000 piculs) and mother-of-pearl (12,000 piculs) exported from Jolo in the 1830s to establish the relative size of the labour force. For example, Hunt wrote that at Towson Duyon in Sandakan Bay (north-east Borneo), 'A Hundred bajow or fishermen [are] employed in catching and curing tripang; they obtain about fifty piculs annually', and at Loo-Loo, 'There are...thirty to forty Bajow fishermen employed in catching tripang; twenty or thirty piculs are cured here annually'. On Tawi-Tawi there were 'eight hundred Islams, chiefly the slaves [clients?] of Datu Mulut Mondarosa and Datu Adanan. They produce annually for the Sulo market three hundred piculs of Kulit tepoy [mother-of-pearl], forty piculs of beche de mer...and some very valuable pearls'. At Basilan 'fifteen hundred Islams produced twenty piculs of black birds nests, three hundred piculs of Kulit tepoy, a few pearls, some tortoise shell, and twenty or thirty prows of paddi for annual export'. See Hunt, 'Some particulars relating to Sulo', pp. 54–55, 59. These figures tend to support the conclusion that the collecting and curing of a picul of *tripang* or a picul of mother-of-pearl shell required the average annual labour of two men for *tripang* and four men for mother-of-pearl. This means that in the first half of the nineteenth century an estimated 68,000 men laboured in Sulu's fisheries. In 1880 a Spanish naval officer alluded to the size of the groups employed in Jolo's mother-of-pearl fisheries: '...in order to collect mother-of-pearl shell, they [the Taosug] assembled innumerable expeditions which are often led by a *datu*. I guarded one [expedition] of 2,200 fishermen and three *datus*.' Comision Reservada a Borneo y Jolo 1881–1882, bound MS, Biblioteca de Palacio, Madrid, p. 38.

50 Warren, *The Sulu Zone*, pp. 67–103.

51 Crocker to Sir Rutherford Alcock, 10 September 1887, CO 874/243.

52 Hunt, 'Some particulars relating to Sulo', p. 37.

53 Statements of Alex Quijano, Francisco Sacarias and Domingo Francisco in Expediente 12, 4 October 1836, PNA, M/S 1803–1890. See also statement of Juan Florentine, in Relacion jurada de los dos individuos venidos en la corbetta de guerra *Francesa Salina* procedente de Sumalasan en el Archipielago de Jolo, PNA, Piratas 3; Treacher to Sir Rutherford Alcock, 3 July 1884, CO 874/237.

54 Pryer to Treacher, 5 October 1881, CO 74/229, N.8; Pryer, 'Notes on north eastern Borneo and the Sulu Islands', p. 92.

55 Pryer, 'Notes on north eastern Borneo and the Sulu Islands', p. 93.

56 S. St. John, *Life in the Forests of the Far East*, Smith Elder and Company, London, 1862, vol. 2, p. 250.

57 T. J. Jacobs, *Scenes, Incidents and Adventures in the Pacific Ocean, or the Islands of the Australasian Seas, During the Cruise of the Clipper*, Margaret Oakley, Harper and Brothers, New York, 1844, p. 335.

58 M. Yvan, *Six Months among the Malays and a Year in China*, James Blackwood, London, 1855, pp. 258–9.

59 Wilkes, 'Jolo and the Sulus', p. 181.
60 Statement of Alex Quijano, in Expediente 12, 4 October 1836, PNA, M/S 1803–1890.
61 Jansen, 'Aantekeningen omtrent Sollok en de Solloksche Zeeroovers', p. 222; Bonham to Maitland, 28 June 1838, PRO, Admiralty 125/133.
62 Statements of Alex Quijano, Domingo Candelario and Mariano Sevilla, in Expediente 12, 4 October 1836, PNA, M/S 1803–1890; statement of Mah Roon, 2 June 1838, in Bonham to Maitland, 28 June 1838, PRO, Admiralty 125/133.
63 Statements of Juan Florentine, Manuel Feliz, Domingo Francisco and Mariano Sevilla, in Expediente 12, 4 October 1836, PNA, M/S 1803–1890; extracts from *Singapore Free Press*, 6 April 1847, PRO, Admiralty 125/133; Numero 137, Carlos Cuarteron, prefecto apostolico a Gobernador Capitan General, 12 August 1878, PNA, Isla de Borneo (2); T. de Comyn, *State of the Philippines in 1810 being an historical statistical and descriptive account of the interesting portion on the Indian Archipelago*, Filipiniana Book Guild, Manila, 1969, p. 124.
64 Statements of Abdul and Sendi, in Verklaringen van ontvlugten personen uit de handen der Zeeroovers van 1845–1849, ANRI, Menado 37; Jansen, *Aantekeningen omtrent Sollok en de Solloksche Zeeroovers*, p. 225.
65 S. Osborn, *My Journal in Malayan Waters*, Routledge, Warne and Routledge, London, 1861, p. 41. In some instances slaves redeemed themselves by acts of bravery which indebted their masters to them. Slaves involved in raiding were most apt to receive their freedom under such circumstances. See Witti to Treacher, November 1881, CO 874/229; C. Majul, 'Political and historical notes on the old Sulu Sultanate,' in *Journal of the Malaysian Branch of the Royal Asiatic Society*, vol. XXVIII (1965): 23–43, pp. 35–6; Kiefer, *The Tausug*, p. 41. The following example illustrates the circumstances under which a master might have exercised the right of redemption by a sacred promise to God:

Dato meldrum of Johor states that he saw Pengeran Mahomet of Brunei wearing a baju ranti [chain mail] at Pandassan, in the early fifties. The Pengeran had married an Illanun wife who was settled there and who claimed rule over the river. Pengeran Mahomet said he had been pirating on the coast of China, more than once along with the Illanuns, on one occasion he fell into the sea with his baju ranti on but was saved by a slave who dived and fished him up.

British North Borneo Herald and Official Gazette (hereafter NBH), 16 September 1895, p. 236.
66 Kiefer, *The Tausug*, p. 10.
67 Farren to Palmerston, 17 January 1851, CO 144/8; Corbett to the Secretary of the Admiralty, 6 October 1862, Foreign Office (FO), 71/1.
68 Statements of Pedro Antonio, Vincente Remigio and Francisco Augustino, in Expediente 12, 4 October 1836, PNA, M/S 1803–1890; Witti to Treacher, November 1881, CO 874/229.
69 Statements of Vincente Remigio and Francisco Augustino, in Expediente 12, 4 October 1836, PNA, M/S 1803–1890; Witti to Treacher, November 1881, CO 874/229.
70 Statements of Juan Sabala and Vincente Remigio, in Expediente 12, 4 October 1836, PNA, M/S 1803–1890.

71 Statements of Matias de la Cruz and Francisco Sacarias, in Expediente 12, 4 October 1836, PNA, M/S 1803–1890; Verklaring van Chrishaan Soerma, 10 August 1846, ANRI, Menado 50; W. Pryer, 'Diary of a trip up the Kinabatangan', in *Sabah Society Journal*, vol. 5 (1970): 117–26, p. 119.

72 Verklaring van Chrishaan Soerma, 10 October 1846, ANRI, Menado 60.

73 Pryer, 'Diary of a trip up the Kinabatangan', p. 119.

74 Diary of William Pryer, 14 March 1878, CO 874/67.

75 ibid.

76 Briskoe, *Journal*, vol. 2, 5 February 1842; Diario de mi Comision a Jolo en el vapor Magallanes, Jose Maria Peneranda, 19 March 1848, PNA, M/S unclassified bundle; Jansen, 'Aantekeningen omtrent Sollok en de Solloksche Zeeroovers', p. 214.

77 De la Escosura, *Memoria sobre Filipinas y Jolo redactada en 1863 y 1864*, p. 371; Diary of William Pryer, 8 March 1879, CO 874/68.

78 Wilkes, 'Jolo and the Sulus', p. 166; J. S. C. Dumont D'Urville, *Voyages au pole sud et dans l'Oceanie sur Les Corvettes l'Astrolabe et la Zelee...pendant les annees 1837–1838–1839–1840*, Gide et J. Baudry, Paris, 1841–1846, vol. 7, p. 170.

79 Wilkes, 'Jolo and the Sulus', p. 161.

80 Statement of Jose Ruedas, in Expediente 12, 4 October 1836, PNA, M/S 1803–1890, 32.

81 Statement of Gabriel Francisco, in Expediente 12, 4 October 1836, PNA, M/S 1803–1890, 71.

82 Forrest, *Voyage to New Guinea*, p. 330; Hunt, 'Some particulars relating to Sulo', p. 40; D'Urville, *Voyage au pole sud et dans l'Oceanic sur Les Corvettes l'Astrolabe et la Zelee*, vol. 7, pp. 308, 313; Wilkes, 'Jolo and the Sulus', p. 165.

83 Forrest, *A Voyage to New Guinea*, p, 330; Hunt, 'Some particulars relating to Sulo', p. 40.

84 Jansen, 'Aantekeningen omtrent Sollok en de Solloksche Zeeroovers', pp. 216, 227.

85 Prefettura Apostolica de Labuan Su Dipendenze Ecc. Nella Malesia Orientale, Carlos Cuarterón, 10 November 1878, PNA, Isla de Borneo (1). See also statement of Simona Plasa, in Expediente 34, Gobernador Militar y Politico de la Provincia de Zamboanga a Gobernador Capitan General, 1 February 1852, PNA, M/S 1838–1885; Verklaring van Chrishaan Soerma, 10 August 1846, ANRI, Menado 50.

86 Wilkes, 'Jolo and the Sulus', p. 168.

87 Witti to Treacher, November 1881, CO 874/229.

88 Statement of Manuel de los Santos, in Expediente 12, 4 October 1836, PNA, M/S 1803–1890.

89 Statement of Jose Ruedas, in Expediente 12, 4 October 1836, PNA, M/S 1803–1890.

90 Wilkes, 'Jolo and the Sulus', p. 166.

91 Montero y Vidal, *Historia de la Pirateria Malayo Mahometans en Mindanao Jolo y Borneo*, p. 69. In 1903 General Leonard Wood described Panglima Hassan as: 'Originally a slave born on Pata island, and little by little has worked up until he is now the most important Chieftain in the island of Jolo, next to the Sultan and Datu Jokanian.' See Leonard Wood Papers, Library of Congress, Washington, D.C., container 3, Diary of Leonard Wood, 18 August 1903.

92 Terray, 'Long-distance exchange and the formation of the state', pp. 316–445.
93 Warren, *The Sulu Zone*, pp. 42–3, 48–60, 60–2.
94 Warren, *The Sulu Zone*, pp. 19–26, 43–8. See also Warren, 'Balambangan and the rise of the Sulu Sultanate, 1772–1776', pp. 74–83.
95 Terray, 'Long-distance exchange and the formation of the state', pp. 335–6.
96 Warren, 'Slave markets and exchange in the Malay World: The Sulu Sultanate, 1770–1878', in *Journal of Southeast Asian Studies*, vol. 8 (1977): 162–75, p. 162; *The Sulu Zone*, pp. 198–9.
97 Warren, *The Sulu Zone*, pp. 182–5.
98 Statements of Matias Domingo and Juan de la Cruz, in Expediente 12, 4 October 1836, PNA, M/S 1803–1890; extract from *Singapore Free Press*, April 1847, PRO, Admiralty 126/133. Majul fails to recognise the important redistributive role of the Taosug in raiding and its relationship to the reproduction of the social formation: 'All the evidence points to the fact that the Sulu Sultan and chief datus never encouraged or approved of piracy by Samal or Iranun datus, for they were themselves traders having an interest that all shipping lanes be kept safe especially for traders going or coming from Jolo,' see Majul, *Muslims in the Philippines*, p. 286.
99 Statement of Juan de la Cruz, in Expediente 12, 4 October 1836, PNA, M/S 1803–1890; El Gobierno Politico y Militar de Zamboanga a Gobernador Capitan General, 30 May 1842, PNA, M/S 1838–1886.
100 Blake to Maitland, 8 August 1838, PRO, Admiralty 126/133; Jansen, 'Aantekenigen omtrent Sollok en de Solloksche Zeeroovers', pp. 217, 229.
101 Warren, 'Slave markets and exchange in the Malay world: The Sulu Sultanate, 1770–1878', p. 174; *The Sulu Zone*, p. 208.
102 Farren to Palmerston, 16 March 1861, CO, 144/8; Warren, 'Slave markets and exchange in the Malay world: The Sulu Sultanate, 1770–1878', p. 174–76; *The Sulu Zone*, pp. 342–44. For a precise calculation on slave imports to Sulu 1770–1870, I have used the figure of 20.5 slaves per boat based on the statements of slaves seized 1826–1847 minus 4,800 to 8,000 (1,200 to 2,000 per year) for the period 1848–1862. From the calculations it therefore follows that the number of slaves imported over the period 1770–1870 varied from a low estimate of 201,360 to a high estimate of 302,676. See Table 4 in 'Slave markets and exchange in the Malay world: The Sulu Sultanate, 1770–1878', p. 174.
103 Warren, *The Sulu Zone*, pp. 190–7.
104 Terray, 'Long-distance exchange and the formation of the state', p. 340.

Chapter 6: The Balangingi Samal

1 A version of this paper was published in *Asian Ethnicity*, vol. 4, no. 1, February (2003): 7–29.
2 J. F. Warren, *The Sulu Zone 1768–1898: The Dynamics of External Trade, Slavery and Ethnicity in the Transformation of a Southeast Asian Maritime State*, Oxford University Press, Singapore, 1981, pp. 150–3.
3 ibid., p. 147.

4   V. Barrantes, Guerras Piraticas de Filipinas contra Mindanaos y Joloanos, Imprenta de Manuel H. Hernandez, Madrid, 1878; E. Bernaldez, *Resana historico de la guerra a Sur de Filipinas, sostenida por las armas Espanoles contra los piratas de aquel archipielago, desde la conquista hasta nuestros dias*, Imprenta del Memorial de Ingenieros, Madrid, 1857; J. Montero y Vidal, *Historia de la Pirateria Malayo Mahometans en Mindanao, Jolo y Borneo*, 2 vols, Imprenta de M. Tello, Madrid, 1888; N. Tarling, *Piracy and Politics in the Malay World: A Study of British Imperialism in Nineteenth-century Southeast Asia*, Donald Moore, Singapore, 1963.

5   E. R. Wolf, *Europe and the People Without History*, University of California Press, Berkeley, 1982.

6   J. F. Warren, 'Who were the Balangingi Samal? Slave Raiding and Ethnogenesis in Nineteenth Century Sulu', in *Journal of Asian Studies*, vol. 37, no. 3 (1978): 477–90.

7   Parliamentary Papers, House of Commons, 1851, vol. LVI, pt. 1 [1351], Papers respecting the Operations against the Pirates on the Northwest coast of Borneo; O. Rutter, *The Pirate Wind Tales of the Sea-robbers of Malaya*, Oxford University Press, Singapore, 1986, pp. 45–8; L. de Ibañez y Garcia, *Mi Cautiverio; carto que con motive del que sufrio entre los moros piratas Joloanos y Samales en 1857*, G. Allhambra, Madrid, 1859; Warren, *The Sulu Zone 1768–1898*, pp. 299–315; A. R. Wallace, *The Malay Archipelago: The Land of the Orang-Utan, and the Bird of Paradise: A Narrative of Travel with Studies of Man and Nature*, 2 vols, Macmillan, London, 1869.

8   M. De Los Reyes Cojuangco, *Kris of Valor: The Samal Balangingi's Defiance and Diaspora*, Manisan, Manila, 1993.

9   Warren, *The Sulu Zone 1768–1898*, pp. 237–51, 298–315.

10 Blake to Maitland, 13 August 1838, Public Records Office (PRO), Admiralty, Sulu Piracy, 125/133.

11 Warren, *The Sulu Zone 1768–1898*, pp. 182–3.

12 Bonham to Maitland, 28 June 1838, PRO, Admiralty, Sulu Piracy, 125/133.

13 Warren, *The Sulu Zone 1768–1898*, p. 184.

14 Bernaldez, *Resana historico de la guerra a Sur de Filipinas*, p. 153.

15 ibid., p. 382.

16 Warren, *The Sulu Zone 1768–1898*, p. 183.

17 ibid.

18 Tarling, *Piracy and Politics in the Malay World*.

19 T. Forrest, *A Voyage to New Guinea and the Moluccas from Balambangan: Including an Account of Magindano, Sooloo and Other Islands*, G. Scott, London, 1779.

20 Exp. 12, 4 October 1836, Philippine National Archive (PNA), Mindanao–Sulu 1803–1890.

21 F. Barth (ed.), *Ethnic Groups and Boundaries: The Social Organization of Culture Difference*, Allen & Unwin, London, 1969, p. 22.

22 Exp. 12, 4 October 1836, PNA, Mindanao–Sulu, 1803–1890.

23 Exp. 12, 17 February 1845, PNA, Mindanao–Sulu, 1803–1890.

24 Wyndham to Gray, 24 February 1847, PRO, Admiralty, Sulu Piracy, 125/133.

25 A. J. F. Jansen, 'Aantekeningen omtrent Sollok en de Solloksche Zeeroovers', *Tijdschrift voor Indische Taal-, Land -en Volkenkunde, uitgegeven door het*

(Koninklijk) Bataviaasch Genootschap van Kunsten en Wetenschappen, vol. 7 (1858), pp. 212–39.
26 Farren to Clarendon, 9 March 1854, PRO, Foreign Office 72/663.
27 Loney to Farren, 10 July 1861, PRO, Foreign Office 72/1017.
28 *Singapore Free Press*, 6 April 1847, PRO, Admiralty, Sulu Piracy, 125/133.
29 Notes on the Island of Mindanao, PRO, Admiralty, Sulu Piracy, 125/133.
30 F. Mallari, SJ, 'Peneranda and the Bicol Defense System', in *Kinaadman*, vol. 14, no. 2, (1992): 105–22.
31 Farren to Palmerston, 27 December 1849, PRO, Foreign Office 72/761; Bernaldez, *Resana historico de la guerra a Sur de Filipinas*, pp. 151–3.
32 Exp. 12, 17 February 1845, PNA, Mindanao-Sulu 1836–97.
33 Clavería to the Minister of War, 12 April 1845, PNA, Cartas, 1945.
34 E. Baja, *The Philippine National Flag and Anthem*, Philippine Education Company, Manila, 1936, p. 34.
35 ibid.
36 GCG to Secretary of State, 28 February 1848, PNA, Cartas 1847–1848; Bernaldez, *Resana historico de la guerra a Sur de Filipinas*, p. 163.
37 GCG to Secretary of State, 28 February 1848, PNA, Cartas 1847–1848; Bernaldez, *Resana historico de la guerra a Sur de Filipinas*, p. 164.
38 Bernaldez, *Resana historico de la guerra a Sur de Filipinas*, p. 167; Cojuangco, *Kris of Valor: The Samal Balangingi's Defiance and Diaspora*, pp. 81–96.
39 Farren to Palmerston, 29 February 1848, PRO, Foreign Office 72/749.
40 Jansen, 'Aantekeningen omtrent Sollok en de Solloksche Zeeroovers', p. 231.
41 Ibañez y Garcia, *Mi Cautiverio*, pp. 12–18.
42 Julio Tolosa, Secretary of State, 10 July 1858, PNA, Mindanao-Sulu.
43 ibid.
44 ibid.
45 Julio Tolosa, Secretary of State, 12 October 1859, PNA, Mindanao-Sulu 1859–1861.
46 Leonardo Castello y Castro, Secretary of State, 28 April 1860, PNA, Mindanao-Sulu 1860.
47 Julio Tolosa, 18 April 1859, PNA, Mindanao-Sulu.
48 Cojuangco, *Kris of Valor: The Samal Balangingi's Defiance and Diaspora*, p. 137.
49 ibid.
50 Julio Tolosa, 8 September 1859, PNA, Mindanao-Sulu 1859–1861.
51 Maria Manobo, PNA, Mindanao-Sulu 1863–1894.
52 Cojuangco, *Kris of Valor: The Samal Balangingi's Defiance and Diaspora*, pp. 129–65.
53 ibid., p. 346
54 R. F. Wendover, 'The Balangingi Pirates', *Philippine Magazine*, vol. 38, no. 8 (1941): 337–8.

55 C. A. Majul, *Muslims in the Philippines*, University of the Philippines Press, Quezon City, 1973, p. 15.
56 Cojuangco, *Kris of Valor: The Samal Balangingi's Defiance and Diaspora*, pp. 27–38, 137–54.
57 Wolf, *Europe and the People Without History*, p. 387.
58 J. Comaroff and J. Comaroff, *Ethnography and the Historical Imagination*, Westview Press, Boulder, 1992, p. 44.
59 ibid.

Chapter 7: Savagism and civilisation

1 A version of this chapter first appeared in *Journal of the Malaysian Branch of the Royal Asiatic Society (MBRAS)*, vol. LXXIV, part 1, (2001): 43–69.
2 C. O. Frake, 'Abu Sayyaf displays of violence and the proliferation of contested identities among Philippine Muslims', in *American Anthropologist*, vol. 100, no. 1 (1998): 41–54; B. Sandin, *The Sea Dayaks of Borneo before White Rajah Rule*, Macmillan, London, 1967, pp. 63–5; J. F. Warren, *The Sulu Zone, the World Capitalist Economy and the Historical Imagination*, VU University Press/CASA, Amsterdam, 1998.
3 Raja Ali Haji ibn Ahmad, *The Precious Gift of Tuhfat Al-Nafis*, Oxford University Press, Kuala Lumpur, 1982.
4 Warren, *The Sulu Zone 1768–1898: The Dynamics of External Trade, Slavery and Ethnicity in the Transformation of a Southeast Asian Maritime State*, Singapore University Press, Singapore, 1981, pp. 147–56, 165–81.
5 ibid., pp. 152–3.
6 ibid., p. 154; O. Rutter, *The Pirate Wind Tales of the Sea-Robbers of Malaya*, Oxford University Press, Singapore, 1986.
7 Warren, *The Sulu Zone, the World Capitalist Economy and the Historical Imagination*, pp. 9–16.
8 M. Southon, *The Navel of the Perahu: Meaning and Values in the Maritime Trading Economy of a Butonese Village*, Research School of Pacific and Asian Studies, Canberra, 1995, p. 22; R. Barnes, *Sea Hunters of Indonesia: Fishers and Weavers of Lamalera*, Oxford University Press, New York, 1996, p. 44.
9 Blake to Maitland, 13 August 1838, Public Records Office (PRO), Admiralty 125/133 Sulu Piracy.
10 V. Barrantes, *Guerras Piraticas de Filipinas contra Mindanaos y Joloanos*, Imprenta de Manuel H. Hernandez, Madrid, 1878; E. Bernaldez, *Resana historico de la guerra a Sur de Filipinas, sostenida por las armas Espanoles contra los piratas de aquel archipielago, desde la conquista hasta nuestros dias*, Imprenta del Memorial de Ingenieros, Madrid, 1857; J. Montero y Vidal, *Historia de la Pirateria Malayo Mahometans en Mindanao, Jolo y Borneo*, 2 vols, Imprenta de M. Tello, Madrid, 1888; N. Tarling, *Piracy and Politics in the Malay World: A Study of British Imperialism in Nineteenth-century Southeast Asia*, Donald Moore, Singapore, 1963.

11. C. Boxer, *The Dutch Seaborne Empire 1600–1800*, Penguin Books, London, 1973; K. Glamman, *Dutch Asiatic Trade, 1620–1740*, Nijhoff, The Hague, 1958; L. Blusse, *Strange Company: Chinese Settlers, Mestizo Women and the Dutch in VOC Batavia*, KITLV, Dordrecht, 1986.

12. H. Furber, *John Company at Work: A Study of European Expansion in India in the Late Eighteenth Century*, Harvard University Press, Cambridge, 1951; M. Greenberg, *British Trade and the Opening of China, 1800–1842*, Cambridge University Press, London, 1951; S. B. Singh, *European Agency Houses in Bengal, 1783–1833*, K. L. Mukhopadhyay, Calcutta, 1966, pp. 1–3.

13. Light to G. G., 22 December 1791 Straits Settlements Factory Records (SSFR); H. P. Clodd, *Malaya's First British Pioneer: The Life of Francis Light*, Luzac and Co., London, 1948, p. 75; R. Bonney, *Kedah 1771–1821 The Search for Security and Independence*, Oxford University Press, Kuala Lumpur, 1971, pp. 90–2.

14. Brooke to Stanley, 4 October 1842, Parliamentary Papers House of Commons (PPHC), 1852, vol. XXXI, Borneo Piracy.

15. Warren, *The Sulu Zone, the World Capitalist Economy and the Historical Imagination*, p. 9; C. O. Frake, 'The genesis of kinds of people in the Sulu Archipelago', in *Language and Cultural Description*, Stanford University Press, Stanford, 1980, pp. 314–18; F. Mallari, 'Muslim raids in Bicol 1580–1792', in *Philippine Studies*, vol. 34, (1986): 257–86, p. 257.

16. N. G. Owen, *Prosperity without Progress: Manila Hemp and Material Life in the Colonial Philippines*, University of California Press, Berkeley, 1984, p. 27.

17. Warren, *The Sulu Zone, the World Capitalist Economy and the Historical Imagination*, pp. 9–19; Warren, *The Sulu Zone 1768–1898*, pp. 252–5.

18. P. Fernandez, *History of the Church in the Philippines, 1521–1898*, National Book Store, Manila, 1979, p. 203.

19. M. Cullinane and P. Xenos, 'The growth of population in Cebu during the Spanish era: Constructing regional demography from local sources', in *Population and History: The Demographic Origins of the Modern Philippines*, ed. D. Doeppers and Xenos, University of Wisconsin, Center for Southeast Asian Studies, Madison, 1998, pp. 71–138, p. 89.

20. R. Mundy, *Narrative of Events in Borneo and Celebes down to the Occupation of Labuan, from the Journals of James Brooke, esq., Together with a Narrative of the Operations of H.M.S. Iris by Capt. Rodney Mundy, R.N.*, John Murray, London, 1848, vol. 2, pp. 13–14.

21. E. Said, *Orientalism*, London: Routledge and Kegan Paul, 1978; J. Raskin, *The Mythology of Imperialism*, Random House, New York, 1971; J. Allen, *The Sea Years of Joseph Conrad*, Methuen, London, 1967; N. Sherry, *Conrad's Eastern Sea*, Cambridge University Press, Cambridge, 1966.

22. G. J. Resink, 'The eastern archipelago under Joseph Conrad's western eyes', in *Indonesia's History between the Myths*, ed. G. J. Resink, Van Hoeve, The Hague, 1968, pp. 307–23; J. Warren, 'Joseph Conrad's fiction as Southeast Asian history: Trade and politics in East Borneo in the late nineteenth century', in *The Brunei Museum Journal*, (1977): 21–34.

23. C. Parrish, *The Image of Asia in Children's Literature: 1814–1964*, Centre for Southeast Asian Studies, Monash University, Melbourne, 1977.

24   Resink, 'The eastern archipelago under Joseph Conrad's western eyes', pp. 305–23.
25   J. Conrad, *An Outcast of the Islands*, Penguin, London, 1975, pp. 20–1.
26   Conrad, *An Outcast of the Islands*; *The Rescue*, J. M. Dent and Sons, London, 1924; *Almayer's Folly*, Penguin, London, 1976.
27   Conrad, *The Rescue*, chapter 3, p. 223.
28   Conrad, *The Rescue*, chapter 2, p. 296.
29   Conrad, *The Rescue*, chapter 2.
30   Conrad, *The Rescue*, chapter 7.
31   Conrad, *The Rescue*, chapter 10.
32   Sherry, *Conrad's Eastern World*, p. 150.
33   Conrad, *An Outcast of the Islands*, part 1/5, p. 50.
34   Conrad, *An Outcast of the Islands*, part 1, no. 2, pp. 20–1.
35   Conrad, *An Outcast of the Islands*, p. 26; *The Rescue*, p. 295.
36   Conrad, *The Rescue*, chapter 2.
37   Conrad, *An Outcast of the Islands*, part 1/5, p. 33.
38   Warren, *The Sulu Zone 1768–1898*, pp. 147–8, 256–8.
39   R. Barnes, *Sea Hunters of Indonesia: Fishers and Weavers of Lamalera*, Oxford University Press, New York, 1996, p. 44; C. Heersink, 'Environmental adaptations in southern Sulawesi', in *Environmental Challenges in South-East Asia*, ed. V. T. King, Curzon, London, 1988, 95–120, pp. 103–4.
40   Stenross to Warren, personal correspondence, 8 March 2000.
41   Frake, 'The genesis of kinds of people in the Sulu Archipelago', p. 314.

Chapter 8: Rickshaw Coolie

1   A version of this chapter first appeared in *Itinerario*, vol. 1, no. 2 (1984): 38–51.
2   The language of the late Maurice Freedman. M. Freedman, *The Study of Chinese Society: Essays by Maurice Freedman*, Stanford University Press, Stanford, 1979, p. 401; see J. F. Warren, *Rickshaw Coolie: A People's History of Singapore (1880–1940)*, Oxford University Press, Singapore, 1986.
3   R. Samuel, 'Local history and oral history', in *History Workshop*, vol. 1 (Spring 1976): 192–208, p. 202.
4   ibid.
5   See, for example, Singapore Municipal Annual Report 1898, p. 102; for 1900, p. 30; Low Ngiong Ing, *Chinese Jetsam on a Tropic Shore*, Eastern Universities Press, Singapore, 1974, p. 73.
6   Freedman, *The Study of Chinese Society*, p. xiii.
7   For a fine discussion of this approach see L. Chevalier, *Labouring Classes and Dangerous Classes in Paris during the First Half of the Nineteenth Century*, Routledge and Kegan Paul, London, 1973, pp. 320–60.
8   M. Castells, *The Urban Question: A Marxist Approach*, Edward Arnold, London, 1979, p. x.

9   R. Samuel (ed.). *People's History and Socialist Theory*, Routledge and Kegan Paul, London, 1981, p. 414.
10 Freedman, *The Study of Chinese Society*, p. 388; Samuel, *People's History*, p. 413.
11 D. K. Emmerson, 'Issues in Southeast Asian history: Room for interpretation—a review article', in *Journal of Asian Studies*, vol. XI, no. 1 (November 1980): 43–86, p. 67.

Chapter 9: The Singapore Rickshaw Pullers

1   A version of this chapter first appeared as 'The Singapore rickshaw pullers: The social organization of a coolie occupation, 1880–1940', in *Journal of Southeast Asian Studies*, vol. 15, no. 1 (1986): 1–16.
2   'Commission of Enquiry into the State of Labour in the Straits Settlements and Protected Malay States', Singapore, 1890; W. L. Blythe, 'Historical sketch of Chinese labour', in *Journal of the Malayan Branch of the Royal Asiatic Society*, vol. xxx, no. 1 (1947): 64–114.
3   'Commission of Enquiry', pp. 8–14. Mak Lau Fong, *The Sociology of Secret Societies: A Study of Chinese Secret Societies in Singapore and Peninsular Malaysia*, Oxford University Press, Kuala Lumpur, 1981, p. 22; M. Freedman, *The Study of Chinese Society: Essays by Maurice Freedman*, Stanford University Press, Stanford, 1979, pp. 73, 82.
4   'Commission of Enquiry', p. 10; Mak Lau Fong, *The Sociology of Secret Societies*, p. 46; J. Ee, 'Chinese migration to Singapore, 1896–1941', in *Journal of Southeast Asian History*, vol. ii (1961): 33–51, pp. 41–2.
5   I have rounded the figures off. The exact number of Chinese immigrants leaving Hong Kong for Singapore were 37,341 in 1881 and 102,997 in 1913. See *Straits Settlement Government Gazette* (SSGG), 1881, Table B, p. 323, and *Straits Settlement Annual Report* (SSAR), Chinese Protectorate, 1913, Table A, p. 52.
6   Many emigrants still relied on the traditional mode of emigration from South China to the *Nanyang* during the transition period from sailing junks to steam navigation at the end of the nineteenth century. The bows of the Amoy junks were painted green, while those from Swatow were varnished red. Hence, the emigrant ships were popularly called the Green junks and the Red junks. Ta Chen, *Emigrant Communities in South China. A Study of Overseas Migration and Its Influence on Standards of Living and Social Change*, Secretariat, Institute of Pacific Relations, New York, 1940, p. 261.
7   ibid., p. 262. Ee, 'Chinese migration to Singapore', p. 33; SSAR, 1884, p. C147, 'Passenger Ship Amendment Bill'.
8   Mak Lau Fong, *The Sociology of Secret Societies*, p. 45; Freedman, *The Study of Chinese Society*, p. 174.
9   Freedman, *The Study of Chinese Society*, p. 72.
10 H. D. R. Baker, *Chinese Family and Kinship*, Macmillan Press, London, 1979, pp. 164–5.
11 Freedman, *The Study of Chinese Society*, p. 74.
12 ibid., pp. 74–83; Yen Ching-hwang, 'Early Chinese clan organisations in Singapore and Malaya, 1819–1911', in *Journal of Southeast Asian Studies*, vol. 12, no. 1 (1981): 62–92, pp. 66–7, 75–6.

13. Baker, *Chinese Family and Kinship*, p. 170; Freedman, *The Study of Chinese Society*, pp. 76, 135–6.
14. Yen, 'Early Chinese clan organisations', pp. 75–6; Freedman, *The Study of Chinese Society*, pp. 136, 183; Baker, *Chinese Family and Kinship*, p. 171
15. Straits Settlement Opium Commission, 1908, evidence of Mr Hooper, p. 26.
16. *Singapore Municipal Annual Report*, Jinrikisha Department, 1898, p. 102.
17. ibid., p. 30.
18. *Straits Settlement Opium Commission*, evidence of Mr Foodland, 1908, pp. 30–1.
19. Low Ngiong Ing, *Chinese Jetsam on a Tropic Shore*, Eastern Universities Press, Singapore, 1974, p. 73.
20. *Proceedings and Report of the Commission Appointed to Inquire into the Cause of the Present Housing Difficulties in Singapore, and the Steps Which Should Be Taken to Remedy Such Difficulties* (henceforth *Housing Commission Report*), Singapore: Government Printing Office, 1918, evidence of Mr Hooper, p. B-91.
21. ibid.
22. *Singapore Municipal Annual Report*, Jinrikisha Department, 1919, p. 2–E.
23. *British Malayan Opium Commission*, 2/12/1924, p. B-28.
24. *Singapore Coroner Inquest and Inquiry* of Lim Phua Sim in no. 597, 2/12/33.
25. Mak, *The Sociology of Secret Societies*, pp. 29, 60; Freedman, *The Study of Chinese Society*, p. 174.
26. *Singapore Municipal Annual Report*, Jinrikisha Department, 1904, p. 3.
27. *Housing Commission Report*, evidence of Mr Hooper, p. B-90.
28. ibid.
29. Interview with Ng Kar Eng, Archive and Oral History Department, Singapore, Reel 3.
30. Simpson, *Report on the Sanitary Conditions of Singapore*, 1908, pp. 17–24
31. ibid.
32. *British Malayan Opium Commission*, evidence of Lee Choon, 1924, p. C-47.
33. *Straits Settlement Opium Commission*, 1924, pp. 32, 279.
34. *British Malayan Opium Commission*, 1924, pp. B-29, C-47
35. *Singapore Coroner Inquest and Inquiry* of Ong Teck Cheng in no. 174, 4/4/29.
36. *Singapore Municipal Annual Report*, Jinrikisha Department, 1890.
37. *Singapore Municipal Annual Report*, Jinrikisha Department, 1902, p. 30.
38. *Singapore Municipal Annual Report*, Jinrikisha Department, 1898, p. 102.
39. *Straits Settlements and Federated Malay States Opium Commission*, 1908, the evidence of Mr Hooper, p. 28.
40. Freedman, *The Study of Chinese Society*, p. 242; Yen, 'Early Chinese clan organisations', pp. 63, 80–1.
41. Yap Pheng Geek, *Scholar, Banker, Gentleman Soldier, The Reminiscences of Dr. Yap Pheng Geek*, Times Books International, Singapore, 1982, p. 10.

42 For a fine discussion of this approach see L. Chevalier, *Labouring Classes and Dangerous Classes in Paris during the First Half of the Nineteenth Century*, Routledge and Kegan Paul, London, 1973, pp. 320–50.

43 C. M. Turnbull, *A History of Singapore 1819–1975*, Oxford University Press, Kuala Lumpur, 1977, p. 116.

44 Lao She, *Rickshaw* (the novel *Lo-T'o Hsiang Tsu*), trans. Jean M. James, University Press of Hawaii, Honolulu, 1979, p. 233.

Chapter 10: Social History and the Photograph

1 This chapter was read at the Representation of Labor in Singapore Symposium, National Museum of Singapore, May 2003.

2 R. Barthes, 'The photographic message', in *The Camera Viewed: Writings on Twentieth Century Photography*, ed. P. R. Petruck, vol. 2, Dutton, New York, 1979, p. 198.

3 M. Wartofsky, 'Picturing and representation', in *Perception and Representation*, ed. C. F. Nodine and D. F. Fisher, Praeger, New York, 1979, pp. 272–83; 'Visual scenarios: The role of representation in visual perception', in *The Perception of Pictures*, ed. M. A. Hagan, vol. 2, Academic Press, New York, 1980, pp. 131–52; 'Art, history and perception', in *Perceiving Artworks*, ed. J. Fisher, Temple University Press, Philadelphia, 1980, pp. 23–41; and 'Cameras can't see: Representation, photography, and human vision', in *Afterimage*, vol. 7, no. 9 (April 1980): 8–9.

4 Wartofsky, 'Picturing and representation', p. 273.

5 S. Matthews, 'Chinese photography: Notes towards a cross-cultural analysis of a western medium', in *Afterimage*, vol. 9, issue 6 (January 1982), p. 45.

6 J. Berger and J. Mohr, *Another Way of Telling*, Writers and Readers Pub. Coop., London, 1982, p. 97. See also: R. Barthes, *Erté*, Franco Maria Ricei (Romain de Publications Tirtoff), Parma, 1972.

7 Valuable photographs can turn up in the oddest places; a photo of rickshaw pullers standing in front of the Raffles Hotel was found among the personal papers of Reg Harrison, a prominent Perth hotelier, who briefly visited Singapore and the island of Java as part of a trade delegation in 1921, by a Murdoch University honours student in the course of her women's work in the hotel, catering and restaurant industries in Western Australia. The photograph is in bundle no. 3 of PR. 549411–4 in the Battye Library, Western Australia.

8 R. H. J. Sydney, *Malay Land*, C. Palmer, London, 1926, p. 19.

9 *Housing Commission Report*, Singapore, 1918, p.a.–37.

10 On the importance of photographs to the social historian, see H. Becker, 'Photography and sociology', in *Studies in the Anthropology of Visual Communication*, vol. 6 (1974): 3–26; J. Falconer, *A Vision of the Past: A History of Early Photography in Singapore and Malaysia, The Photographs of G. R. Lambert and Co., 1880–1910*, Times Editions, Singapore, 1987; J. F. Warren, 'Social history and the photograph: Glimpses of the Singapore rickshaw coolie in the early 20th century', in *Journal of the Malaysian Branch of the Royal Asiatic Society*, vol. 58, no. 1 (1985): 29–43.

11 *Singapore Retrospect through Postcards: 1900–1930*, Sin Chew Jit Poh and Archives and Oral History Department, Singapore, 1982.

12 Falconer, *A Vision of the Past*, pp. 190–1.
13 Yip Cheong Fung, interview held with assistance of Ms Tan Beng Luan, Singapore, 1 October 1987.
14 ibid.
15 Certificate Coroner's View Singapore of Oichi, no. 82, 17 February 1906.
16 No. 274, Minute of Mr Meade in Sir F. Weld to the Earl of Derby, 27 August 1883, CO 273/121.
17 Appendix O, Testimony of A. V. Cousins, Registrar-General, 21 November 1876, CO 273/91.
18 No. 25, Memorandum by the Secretary for Chinese Affairs, G. T. Hare, 12 June 1898, in Acting Governor Sir J. H. Swettenham to Mr Chamberlain, 8 September 1898, CO 882/6.
19 No. 132, Testimony of C. Phillips, Inspector under the Contagious Diseases Ordinance, in Lt-Colonel Anson to the Earl of Carnarvon, 21 April 1877, CO 273/91.
20 Appendix O, Testimony of A. V. Cousins, Registrar-General, 21 November 1876, CO 273/91.
21 ibid.
22 No. 60716, Sir Arthur Young to Walter Lord, 13 July 1917, CO 273/457.
23 Fong Chiok Kai, interview held with the assistance of Ms Tan Beng Luan, Singapore, 1 October 1987.
24 On the language of kimono wearing, see L. C. Dalby, *Geisha*, University of California Press, Berkeley, 1983, p. 282.
25 P. Stallybrass and A. White, *The Politics and Poetics of Transgression*, Cornell University Press, Ithaca, NY, 1986, p. 139.
26 Yip Cheong Fung, interview held with assistance of Ms Tan Beng Luan, Singapore, 1 October 1987.

Chapter 11: Living on the Razor's Edge

1 This chapter first appeared in *The Bulletin of Concerned Asian Scholars*, vol. 16, no. 4 (1984): 38–51.
2 This chapter represents work in progress that is based on a trilogy I am currently researching and writing on the Chinese labouring classes in Singapore. The initial volume, *Rickshaw Coolie, A People's History of Singapore*, was published in 1986. The other two volumes are provisionally titled 'Prostitution and Singapore Society: A Social History' and 'Chinese Suicide in Singapore, 1883–1939'. I want to thank the former Registrar-General, Mr Khoo Oon Soo, and the staff of the Subordinate Courts Library for their kind cooperation and assistance in facilitating my researches with the Coroner's Records.

   In 1978, I was given access to a collection of several hundred unclassified bound and unbound volumes stacked on the floor, more than a metre high, against the wall of a storeroom in the Subordinate Courts Building. The records had been moved several times from one repository to another under British rule, and again, as late as 1975. This had resulted in damage and loss on each occasion. Not sure where to start without a checklist or guide, I began to rummage among the stacks closest to me. I randomly located and read the first inquest statements of rickshaw pullers and their kin, finding expressions of personal grief, of pain and frustration, of the misery that colonial rule and the Depression had inflicted on them, of an extreme structural poverty reflected in the incidence of suicide, and of life's small pleasures like a special meal of chicken, rice wine and noodles shared with friends. I realised that the contents of this repository would yield up with skill and patience the living testimony of Chinese people who did not know how to express themselves in print and who did not have access to people with power.

3 The language of the late M. Freedman, *The Study of Chinese Society: Essays by Maurice Freedman*, Stanford University Press, Stanford, 1979, p. 401.

4 An immigrant, on landing in Singapore, was called a *Singkeh*, or a new man, or newcomer by the Teochiu, and *Sin-hak* by the Cantonese.

5 Many emigrants still relied on the traditional mode of emigration from South China to the *Nanyang* during the transition period from sailing junks to steam navigation at the end of the nineteenth century. The bows of the Amoy junks were painted green, while those from Swatow were varnished red. Hence, the emigrant ships were popularly called the Green junks and the Red junks. Ta Chen, *Emigrant Communities in South China. A Study of Overseas Migration and Its Influence on Standards of Living and Social Change*, Secretariat, Institute of Pacific Relations, New York, 1940, p. 261.

6 *Straits Settlement Annual Report* (SSAR), Chinese Protectorate, 1910, p. 173; 1911, p. 173; J. Ee, 'Chinese migration to Singapore, 1896–1941', in *Journal of Southeast Asian History*, vol. 2, (1961): 33–51, p. 34.

7 Freedman, *The Study of Chinese Society*, p. 243.

8 J. K. Fairbank, E. O. Reischauer and A. M. Craig, *East Asia, Tradition and Transformation*, George Allen & Unwin, London, 1973, pp. 524–5; 'Economic study of the Peking ricshaw puller', in *China Economic Monthly*, vol. 3, no. 6 (June 1926): 253–65, p. 253.

9 'Economic study of the Peking ricshaw puller', p. 253.

10 *Rickshaws in Calcutta*, UNNAYAN in association with T. H. Thomas, UNNAYAN, Calcutta, 1981, p. 1.

11 *British Malayan Opium Commission*, evidence of Lee Choon, p. C–47.

12 ibid.

13 In 1908 the wages of an ordinary coolie were 45–50 cents a day, a day labourer in the tin mines earned seventy cents, and one dollar a day was the most a coal coolie ever earned. A rickshaw puller's earnings stabilised about one dollar a day by 1924, but the inexperienced and opium addicts were fortunate if they could net forty cents to buy food and *chandu* (prepared opium). *Straits Settlements and Federated Malay States Opium Commission*, 1908, pp. 32, 279; *Proceedings of the Committee Appointed by His Excellency the Governor and High Commissioner to Inquire into Matters Relating to the Use of Opium in British Malaya*, Government Printing Office, Singapore, 1924, pp. B–29, C–47.

14 J. Cuylenburg, *Singapore through Sunshine and Shadow*, Heinemann, Singapore, 1981, p. 48.

15 F. Chia, *The Babas*, Times Book International, Singapore, 1980, p. 48.
16 'Economic Study of the Peking Ricshaw Puller', pp. 253–65.
17 No. 57, *Report of a Committee appointed to consider the alleged shortage of houses*, 3 September 1923, in CO 275/109.
18 *Singapore Municipal Annual Report*, Jinrikisha Department, 1919, p. 1–E.
19 Singapore faced four major rickshaw strikes in the twentieth century: 1903, 1919–1920, 1935 and 1938. The anatomy of each of these strikes is somewhat different, but rent capital, public authority and the world economy were all distinctive factors, in differing combinations. In all of these strikes the Hengwah rickshaw coolies of the waterfront area were to play a decisive role.
20 *Singapore Free Press*, 16 February 1920.
21 ibid., 17 February 1920.
22 ibid., 16 February 1920.
23 ibid.
24 ibid., 14 February 1920.
25 ibid., 16 February 1920.
26 ibid.
27 ibid., 18 February 1920.
28 ibid., 19 February 1920.
29 *Singapore Municipal Annual Report*, Jinrikisha Department, 1921, p. 5.
30 See, for example, *Singapore Municipal Annual Report* 1898, p. 102; for 1900, p. 30; Low Ngiong Ing, *Chinese Jetsam on a Tropic Shore*, Eastern Universities Press, Singapore, 1974, p. 73.
31 Despite the more pervasive pattern of a bachelor society with village links to China, between 10 and 15 per cent of rickshaw pullers had families with them in Singapore by the 1920s. These simple or elemental families were developed on rather short notice—a decade or two at most—from the 1920s onwards, and faced serious demographic and social problems right from the start. They were in form and size the exact opposite of the large, joint family in China. The simple or elemental family in Singapore among rickshaw coolies was never likely to be larger than six or seven souls, and could be reduced in the case of childless couples to two or even dissolution, when a husband or wife was left in the aftermath of an accident or suicide. Some households could from time to time include a grandmother, and the occasional guest, a nephew or person with the same surname and coming from the same village, newly arrived in Singapore.
32 Freedman, *The Study of Chinese Society*, pp. 235–6.
33 Singapore, *Coroner's Inquest and Inquiry* of Sim Kwee Geok in no. 619, 11/12/29.
34 *Singapore Municipal Annual Report*, 1938, p. 10; 1939, p. D-56.
35 B. Kaye, *Upper Nankin Street Singapore. A Sociological Study of Chinese Households Living in a Densely Populated Area*, University of Malaya Press, Singapore, 1961, p. 2.
36 Singapore, *Coroner's Inquest and Inquiry* of Sim Kwee Geok in no. 619, 11/12/29.
37 Lao She, *Rickshaw* (the novel *Lo-T'o Hsiang Tsu*), trans. Jean M. James, University Press of Hawaii, Honolulu, 1979, p. 61.

38 *Singapore Coroner's Inquest and Inquiry* of Ler Cho Wing in no. 303, 10/7/35.
39 *Singapore Coroner's Inquest and Inquiry* of Gian Yeow Sun in no. 319, 17/7/36.
40 At first glance, the number of notifiable cases of suicide among rickshaw pullers would appear to be demographically insignificant, only affecting several hundred people at most, as compared to the massive statistics available on all deaths in the colonial records. To make that assumption, however, would be to commit a serious fallacy. The very few cases of suicide of rickshaw pullers can tell us much about the complexities of life and its patterns, and about the social problem of thousands of pullers and tens of thousands of other poor Chinese who survived. Their deaths epitomised the plight of other Chinese who were the victims of colonial and municipal policies of unemployment, suffered high death rates from such infectious diseases as cholera and tuberculosis, and were hurt by the withdrawal of most funds and support from social welfare. The statements of those who came to the inquests of deaths labelled as suicide rise with unforgettable force above much of the illusion of the writing in Singapore's colonial/nationalist historical genre.
41 *Singapore Municipal Annual Report*, Jinrikisha Department, p. 8.
42 *Singapore Municipal Annual Report*, Jinrikisha Department, 1921.
43 *Singapore Free Press*, 23 February 1935.
44 ibid.
45 'The Heng Wah People and Their Development in Various Transport Trades', unpublished manuscript, Singapore, Nanyang University, c. 1950, p. 38.
46 One of the underlying reasons for the failure of other Singapore coolies, including some Hokkien groups of pullers, to rally behind the rickshaw coolies in 1938 was the heterogeneity of Singapore Chinese society with its numerous speech groups and surname 'clanship' ties, each with a distinctive version of culture deriving from south-east China. Cultural differences among these communities reflected a lack of solidarity that surfaced behind closed doors and affected their strategy with respect to the strike. Ho Swee Bee, an elderly clan leader from Duxton Road, pointed to clan resistance to the strike as a root cause for the failure of Singapore's coolie class to unite.

> From what I saw of the rickshaw pullers south of the river around Duxton Road, those who supported the strike were few, very few. The reason for this being that most of the *hokkien* pullers were clan oriented. That is why so few responded to the efforts of the labour organisers north of the Singapore River. On the other side of the river, the rickshawmen were united; the rickshaw owners were even afraid to venture out on the street for fear of being attacked. But south of the river, in the Duxton Road area, on this side, it was completely different. As I have just said, the reason why those of us in Duxton Road did not aggressively support the strike was because of our clan relationships. That is why the response from this side of the river [was not ideal]. Rickshaw pullers from north of the river wanted desperately to recruit people from Duxton Road for the strike but there was no way for them to do this because of the clan relationships. The growing militancy and organisations of the rickshawmen north of the river was perceived as a sort of threat to the clans and as such made them unacceptable to enter our territory to recruit for the strike.
>
> Interview with Ho Swee Bee, Archive and Oral History Department, Singapore, February 1982, reels 12 and 13.

Chapter 12: Placing Women in Southeast Asian History

1. *Karayuki-san* was the word used traditionally by the Japanese of Amakusa and Shimabara, Kyushu Island, to describe rural women who emigrated to Southeast Asia and the Pacific in search of a livelihood. The ideographs comprising *karayuki-san* literally mean 'going to China', as Kyushu, the place where most of the women were from, was the part of Japan closest to China. *Karayuki-san* in common parlance nowadays has become a popular term for describing women from the poorest sectors of society during the Meiji period, who lived abroad specifically as prostitutes. See Yano Tooru, *Nippon-no Nanyo Shikan*, Chunkou Shinsho, Tokyo, 1979, pp. 131–3.

2. R. Rapp, E. Ross and R. Bridenthal, 'Examining family history', in *Feminist Studies*, vol. 15, no. 1 (Spring 1979): 183–89.

3. J. F. Warren, 'Living on the razor's edge: The rickshawmen of Singapore between two wars, 1919–1939', in *Bulletin of Concerned Asian Scholars*, vol. 16, no. 4 (October–December 1984): 38–51.

4. D. B. Schmidt and E. R. Schmidt, 'The invisible woman: The historian as professional magician', in *Liberating Women's History*, ed. B. A. Carroll, University of Illinois Press, Chicago, 1976, pp. 42–54, p. 42.

5. For example, the David Joel Steinberg-edited book, *In Search of Southeast Asia: a Modern History*, a landmark in the interpretation of Southeast Asian history, pays scant attention to women's role in history, or the impact of historical events on women's lives, especially peasant and labouring women. While 'women's history' has been neglected, some pioneering attempts have been made to place women in Southeast Asian history. See S. Abeyasekere, 'Women as cultural intermediaries in nineteenth century Batavia', in *Women's Work and Women's Roles: Economics and Everyday Life in Indonesia, Malaysia and Singapore*, ed. L. Manderson, The Australian National University, Development Studies Centre Monograph no. 32, Canberra, 1983, pp. 15–29; C. Dobbin, 'The search for women in Indonesian history', in *Kartini Centenary: Indonesian Women Then and Now*, ed. A. T. Zainer'ddin et al., Monash University, Melbourne, 1980, pp. 42–51; L. Manderson, *Women, Politics and Change. The Kaum Ibu UMNO, Malaysia 1945–1972*, Oxford University Press, Kuala Lumpur, 1980; Ngo Vinh Long. *Vietnamese Women in Society and Revolution: 1. The French Colonial Period*, Vietnam Resource Center, Cambridge, Mass., 1974; N. G. Owen, 'Textile displacement and the status of women in Southeast Asia', in *The Past in Southeast Asia's Present*, ed. G. P. Means, Secretariat, Canadian Society for Asian Studies, Canadian Council for Southeast Asian Studies, Ottawa, 1978, pp. 157–70; and J. G. Taylor, *The Social World of Batavia European and Eurasian in Dutch Asia*, The University of Wisconsin Press, Madison, 1983.

6. G. Lerner, 'Placing women in history; a 1975 perspective', in *Liberating Women's History*, ed. B. A. Carroll, University of Illinois Press, Chicago, 1976, pp. 357–67.

7. See R. Bridenthal and C. Koonz (eds), *Becoming Visible. Women in European History*, Houghton Mifflin Co., Boston, 1977.

8. G. Lerner, 'The majority finds its past', in *Current History*, vol. 70, no. 416 (1976), p. 195.

9. See J. Kelly-Gadol, 'The social relations of the sexes: Methodological implications of women's history', in *Signs: Journal of Women in Culture and Society*, vol. 2, no. 4 (1976): 809–24.

10   N. Z. Davis, ' "Women's history" in transition; the European case', in *Feminist Studies*, vol. 3, nos. 3–4 (1975): 83–103, p. 90.

11   On periodisation being revised, see Kelly-Gadol, 'The social relations of the sexes,' p. 812; Davis, ' "Women's history" in transition', pp. 92–3.

12   Kelly-Gadol, 'The social relations of the sexes', pp. 810–12.

13   Lerner, 'Placing women in history: A 1975 perspective', p. 364.

14   A. Davin, 'Women and history', in *The Body Politic: Writings from the Women's Liberation Movement*, ed. M. Wandor, Xerox, London, 1969–1972, pp. 217–23.

15   Certificate Coroner's View Singapore (CCVS), Oichi, No. 82, 17 February 1906. Osuji, another prostitute in the brothel at Number 55 Malabar Street, was sent as usual at 2 a.m. on 17 February 1906 to collect the money from the other women. When she came to Oichi's cubicle, Osuji found the door fastened on the inside and could get no answer to her call. She looked under the partition and saw Oichi hanging from her bedpost. On Oichi's table was found a suicide letter to Ofuku, the mistress of the house, which as translated by the authorities, thanked her for her kindness, told her not to worry about her death, and asked her to send a photo of herself to her sister in Japan.

16   See C. C. Lougee, 'Modern European history', in *Signs: Journal of Women in Culture and Society*, vol. 2, no. 3 (1977): 628–50, p. 648.

17   G. Lerner, 'Placing women in history: definitions and challenges', in *Feminist Studies*, vol. 3 (Fall 1975): 5–14, p. 6.

18   Davin, 'Women and history', pp. 217–23.

19   CCVS, Oichi, No. 82, 17/ February 1906.

20   See M. Kazue, *Karayukisan*, Asahi Shinbunsha, Tokyo, 1976; and Yamazaki Tomoko, *Sandakan Hachiban Shokan-Teihen Joseishi Josho*, Chikuma Shoboo, Tokyo, 1972; *Sandakan no Haka*, Bungeishunjuu, Tokyo, 1977.

21   On the significance of microdynamism as an approach for this kind of history dealing with the individual experience of an overseas Japanese 'community' at a particular moment in time, as if under a microscope, see J. F. Warren, 'The coroner and the rickshaw coolie of Singapore: Materials, problems and opportunities for writing the history of overseas Chinese laborers', paper prepared for the Asian Studies Association of Australia, Fifth National Conference, 1984, pp. 6–7.

22   Kelly-Gadol, 'The doubled vision of feminist theory: A postscript to the "Women and Power" Conference', in *Feminist Studies*, vol. 6, no. 1 (Spring 1979): 224–7; R. Bridenthal, 'The dialectics of production and reproduction in history', in *Radical America*, vol. 10 (March–April 1976): 3–11.

23   On the significance of prosopography as a technique for writing Southeast Asian social history, see Warren, 'The coroner and the rickshaw coolies of Singapore', pp. 7–8; and *The Sulu Zone 1768–1898: The Dynamics of External Trade, Slavery and Ethnicity in the Transformation of a Southeast Asian Maritime State*, Singapore University Press, Singapore, 1981, pp. 237–51.

24   Lerner, 'The majority finds its past', p. 196.

25   Warren, 'Living on the razor's edge', p. 39.

26   ibid.

27   ibid., p. 40.

28. See Warren, 'The spiral of failure: Suicide among Singapore rickshaw coolies', *Southeast Asian Journal of Social Science*, vol. 13, no. 2 (October 1985): 47–66.
29. Enclosure in no. 227 Acting Governor Sir J. H. Swettenham to Mr Chamberlain, 5 August 1898, CO 882/6.
30. 'Return of Brothels and Prostitutes Brothels Known As the Protectorate', *Straits Settlement Annual Report*, 1905, p. 652.
31. ibid.
32. Yamazaki Tomoko, 'Sandakan No. 8 Brothel', in *Bulletin of Concerned Asian Scholars*, vol. 5 (1975): 52–60, pp. 56–8.
33. See the pioneering work of Morisaki Kazue, *Karayuki-san*; Yamazaki Tomoko, *Sandakan Hachiban Shokan-Teihen Joseishi Josho*; *Sandakan No Haka*; and Yano Tooru, *Nippon-no Nanyo Shikan*.
34. Yamazaki Tomoko, 'Sandakan No. 8 Brothel', pp. 54–5.
35. Yano Tooru, *Nippon-no Nanyo Shikan*, pp. 131–3.

Chapter 13: Lives of the *Ah Ku* and *Karayuki-san*

1. This chapter originally appeared in the *Southeast Journal of Social Science*, vol. 20, no. 1 (1992): 80–92.
2. R. Foster and O. Ranum, *Deviants and the Abandoned in French Society*, Johns Hopkins University Press, Baltimore, 1978, p. vii; J. F. Warren 'Retrieving prostitutes lives. Source materials and an approach for writing the history of the *ah ku* and *karayuki san* of Singapore', in *Itinerario: European Journal of Overseas History*, vol. 8, no. 1 (1990): 96–122.
3. J. F. Warren, 'Rickshaw coolie: An exploration of the underside of a Chinese city outside China: Singapore', in *Itinerario: European Journal of Overseas History*, vol. 1, no. 2 (1984): 80–91.
4. G. Hershatter, 'The hierarchy of Shanghai prostitution, 1870–1949', in *Modern China*, vol. 15, no. 4 (1989): 463–98, p. 464; S. Gronewold, *Beautiful Merchandise: Prostitution in China 1860–1936*, The Haworth Press, New York, 1982, p. 74.
5. Yamazaki Tomoko, 'Sandakan No. 8 Brothel', in *Bulletin of Concerned Asian Scholars*, vol. 7, no. 4 (1975): 52–60; *Sandakan Hachiban Shokan-Teihen Joseishi Josho*, Chikuma Shoboo, Tokyo, 1972; SCII (Singapore Coroners Inquest and Inquiry) Oyoshi, No. 229, 17/11/16.
6. SCII (Singapore Coroners Inquest and Inquiry), Chacksfield, Albert, No. 178, 7/11/12; Duya Hadachi, No. 452, 8/11/24; Loh Sai Soh, No. 10, 17/1/03.
7. Certificate Coroners View Singapore (CCVS), Li Chin Ho, N.14, 6/5/08; Oichi, N.82, 17/2/06; SCII.
8. Yamazaki Tomoko, 'Sandakan No. 8 Brothel'; *Sandakan Hachiban Shokan-Teihen Joseishi Josho*; and *Sandakan no Haka*, Bungeishunjuu, Tokyo, 1977; Morisaki Kazue, *Karayuki-san*, Asaki Shinbunsha, Tokyo, 1976.
9. J. Falconer, *A Vision of the Past: A History of Early Photography in Singapore and Malaya. The Photographs of G. R. Lambert and Co. 1880–1910*, Times Editions, Singapore, 1987.

10 S. Gronewold, *Beautiful Merchandise: Prostitution in China 1860–1936*, p. 2.

11 J. Best, 'Careers in brothel prostitution: St Paul, 1865–1883', in *The Journal of Interdisciplinary History*, vol. 12, no. 4 (1982): 597–617, p. 598.

12 R. Samuel, 'What is social history?' in *What Is History Today?*, ed. J. Gardiner, Atlantic Highlands, N.J.: Humanities Press, 1988: 42–48, p. 47.

13 G. C. Spivak, 'French feminism in an international frame', in *Feminist Readings: French Texts, American Contexts, Yale French Studies*, ed. C. Gaudin et al., Yale University Press, New Haven, Conn., vol. 62 (1981): 154–84, p. 179.

Chapter 14: *Karayuki-san* of Singapore

1 A version of this chapter appeared in the *Journal of the Malaysian Branch of the Royal Asiatic Society*, Volume LXII, part II, 1989, pp. 45–80.

2 See O. Zunz, *Reliving the Past: The Worlds of Social History*, University of North Carolina Press, Chapel Hill, 1985; J. F. Warren, *Rickshaw Coolie: A People's History of Singapore (1880–1940)*, Oxford University Press, Singapore, 1986, p. 218.

3 J. F. Warren, 'Placing women in Southeast Asian history: The case of Oichi and the study of prostitution in Singapore society', in *At the Edge of Southeast Asian History*, New Day Press, Quezon City, 1987, pp. 148–64.

4 J. F. Warren, 'Rickshaw coolie: An exploration of the underside of a Chinese city outside China, Singapore, 1880–1940', in *At the Edge of Southeast Asian History*, New Day Press, Quezon City, 1987, pp. 73–81.

5 On locating the *karayuki-san* within a wider framework of analysis see Morisaki Kazue, *Karayuki-san*, Asaki Shinbunsha, Tokyo, 1976; Yamazaki Tomoko, *Sandakan Hachiban Shokan-Teihen Joseishi Josho*, Chikuma Shoboo, Tokyo, 1972; *Sandakan no Haka*, Bungei-shunjuu, Tokyo, 1977; 'Sandakan No. 8 Brothel', in *Bulletin of Concerned Asian Scholars*, vol. 5 (1975): 52–60; Mikiso Hane, *Peasants, Rebels and Outcastes: The Underside of Modern Japan*, Pantheon Books, New York, 1982, pp. 207–25.

6 Warren, 'Placing women in Southeast Asian history: The case of Oichi and the study of prostitution in Singapore society', pp. 156, 164.

7 See Lucie Cheng Hirata, 'Free, indentured, enslaved: Chinese prostitutes in nineteenth century America', in *Signs: Journal of Women in Culture and Society*, vol. 5, no. 1 (1979): 3–29.

8 For the significance of the term Hua-Ch'iao in Southeast Asian modern history see Wang Gung-wu, 'Southeast Asian Hua-Ch'iao in Chinese History Writing', in *Journal of Southeast Asian Studies*, vol. 12, no. 1 (1981): 1–14.

9 Morisaki, *Karayuki-san*, pp. 17–18; Yamazaki, 'Sandakan No. 8 Brothel', p. 60; Hane, *Peasants, Rebels and Outcastes*, p. 218; Motoe Terami-Wada, '*Karayuki-san* of Manila; 1890–1920', in *Philippine Studies*, vol. 34 (1986): 287–316, p. 303.

10 Morisaki, *Karayuki-san*, pp. 17–18; Yamazaki, 'Sandakan No. 8 Brothel', p. 52.

11 Yano Tooru, *Nippon-no Nanyo Shikan*, Chunkou Shinsho, Tokyo, 1979, pp. 131–3.

12 Yamazaki, 'Sandakan No. 8 Brothel', p. 52.

13 ibid, pp. 56–7; Hane, *Peasants, Rebels and Outcastes,* pp. 6, 103–4, 218.
14 ibid.
15 Hane, *Peasants, Rebels and Outcastes,* p. 209.
16 Yamazaki, 'Sandakan No. 8 Brothel', pp. 56–7.
17 Hane, *Peasants, Rebels and Outcastes,* p. 218; Yamazaki, 'Sandakan No. 8 Brothel', pp. 56–7; Terami-Wada, '*Karayuki-san* of Manila; 1880–1920', p. 303.
18 Hane, *Peasants, Rebels and Outcastes,* p. 218.
19 Yamazaki, 'Sandakan No. 8 Brothel', pp. 56–7.
20 League of Nations, *Report of the Commission of Enquiry into the Traffic in Women and Children in the East,* (CETWCE) Geneva, 1933, pp. 44, 73.
21 *Nanyo no Gojunen Shingaporu o Chusin ni Doho Katsuyaku,* Tokyo: Nanyo oyobi Nippon Jinsha, 1937, p. 156.
22 Warren, *Rickshaw Coolie,* pp. 14–19, 161–5, 249; J. Ee, 'Chinese Migration to Singapore, 1896–1941', in *Journal of Southeast Asian History,* vol. 2 (1961): 33–51, p. 37; Hirata, 'Free, Indentured, Enslaved: Chinese Prostitutes in Nineteenth Century America', pp. 5–7.
23 No. 59232, General Officer Commanding the Troops, Straits Settlements to the Secretary, War Office, 25 February 1919, FO 371–4243, p. 372.
24 League of Nations, *Report of the Commission of Enquiry into the Traffic in Women and Children in the East,* pp. 21–2, 51, 96; *Nanyo no Gojunen,* p. 160.
25 See Yamazaki, 'Sandakan No. 8 Brothel', *Sandakan no Haka;* D. C. Sissons, '*Karayuki-san*: Japanese Prostitutes in Australia, 1887–1916–1', in *Historical Studies,* vol. 17, no. 68 (1977): 323–41.
26 Consul for Japan at Hong Kong to Acting Colonial Secretary, 20 October 1895, Japanese Ministry of Foreign Affairs (JMFA), 4/2/2/34; Acting Colonial Secretary to Consul for Japan at Hong Kong, 5 November 1885, JMFA, 4/2/2/34.
27 Consul for Japan at Hong Kong to Acting Colonial Secretary, 20 October 1885, JMFA, 4/2/2/34.
28 Morisaki, *Karayuki-san,* p. 96; Consul for Japan at Hong Kong to Acting Colonial Secretary, 20 October 1885, JMFA, 4/2/2/34.
29 *Singapore Free Press,* 11 September 1897.
30 Sissons, '*Karayuki-san*: Japanese Prostitutes in Australia, 1887–1916–1', p. 323.
31 P. R. Greenough, 'Famine', in *Encyclopedia of Asian History,* vol. 1, ed. Ainslie T. Embree, Charles Scribner's Sons, New York, 1988, p. 459; Hane, *Peasants, Rebels and Outcastes,* pp. 7, 207, 210; Terami-Wada, '*Karayuki-san* of Manila: 1890–1920', pp. 302–3.
32 Hane, Peasants, *Rebels and Outcastes,* pp. 114–15.
33 *Nanyo no Gojunen,* pp. 152–3; Yamazaki, *Sandakan no Haka,* p. 48.
34 Yamazaki, *Sandakan no Haka,* p. 48.
35 Hane, *Peasants, Rebels and Outcastes,* p. 129; Morisaki, *Karayuki-san,* p. 29.
36 Terami-Wada, '*Karayuki-san* of Manila: 1890–1920', pp. 293, 303.
37 Morisaki, *Karayuki-san,* p. 18.
38 'Japanese women abroad', in *Japan Weekly Mail,* 30 May 1896, p. 609.

39 Yamazaki, *Sandakan no Haka*, p. 49.
40 League of Nations, *Report of the Commission of Enquiry into the Traffic in Women and Children in the East*, p. 114.
41 ibid., p. 112.
42 Terami-Wada, '*Karayuki-san* of Manila: 1890–1920', pp. 290–1.
43 ibid., p. 299.
44 Hane, *Peasants, Rebels and Outcastes*, p. 20.
45 Song Ong Siang, *One Hundred Years History of the Chinese in Singapore*, Methuen, London 1923; reprinted University of Malaya Press, Kuala Lumpur, 1967, and Oxford University Press, Singapore, 1987.
46 *Nanyo no Gojunen*, p. 155.
47 Morisaki, *Karayuki-san*, pp. 179–80.
48 Hane, *Peasants, Rebels and Outcastes*, p. 218.
49 Yamamuro Gunpei, *A Theory of Social Purification*, Chuo Koron, Kakuskin-ron, Tokyo, 1977, pp. 252–5.
50 ibid.
51 *Nanyo no Gojunen*, p. 155.
52 ibid., p. 144.
53 No. 60716, Sir Arthur Young to Walter Lord, 13 July 1917, CO 273/457.
54 ibid.
55 No. 60716, Sir Arthur Young to Walter Lord, 13 July 1917, CO 273/457.
56 N. L. Schumsky, 'Tacit acceptance: Respectable Americans and segregated prostitutes 1870–1910', in *Journal of Social History*, vol. 19, no. 4 (1986): 665–79, p. 667.
57 Yamazaki, *Sandakan no Haka*, p. 46–7.
58 *Fukuoka Nichinichi*, 25 May 1910, cited in Morisaki, *Karayuki-san*, pp. 179–80.
59 Yamazaki, *Sandakan no Haka*, p. 72.
60 Yip Cheong Fung, interview held with the assistance of Ms Tan Beng Luan in Mr Yip's shop situated at the lower end of Kreta Ayer Road, Singapore, 1 October, 1987; Yamazaki, *Sandakan no Haka*, p. 38.
61 Report of the Committee appointed to enquire into the working of Ordinances XXIII of 1870, commonly called the Contagious Diseases Ordinance, in *Straits Settlement Legislative Council Proceedings*, 1877, Appendix 7, p. XLIII.
62 John Cowen to the Association for Moral and Social Hygiene, 18 December 1916, CO 273–452.
63 ibid.
64 *Chinatown: An Album of a Singapore Community*, Times Books International, Archives and Oral History Department, Singapore, 1983, p. 100.
65 Yip Cheong Fung's recollection of the location of the brothels was correct. See houses used as brothels in 1901 in Sago Street in *Chinatown: An Album of a Singapore Community*, p. 100; Yip Cheong Fung, interview held with the assistance of Ms Tan Beng Luan.
66 *Chinatown: An Album of a Singapore Community*, p. 110.

67 Fong Chiok Kai, interview held with the assistance of Ms Tan Beng Luan in the Committee Room of the Kreta Ayer Community Centre, Singapore, 1 October 1987.
68 List of Licensed Brothels for the month of February 1877, Appendix M, pp. LXI–LXIII, in Report of the Committee appointed to enquire into the working of Ordinance XXIII of 1870, commonly called the Contagious Disease Ordinance, in *Straits Settlements Legislative Council Proceedings* 1877, Appendix 7; No. 69, Sir C. Mitchell to the Marquess of Ripon, 2 March 1895, CO 273/202; and Return of Brothels and Prostitutes Brothels Known As the Protectorate, *Straits Settlements Annual Report*, 1905, p. 652.
69 SMAR, 1901, Appendix A, 'List of Brothels, Coolie Lodging Houses and Private Houses to Which Meters Have Been Attached', pp. 1–19.
70 No. 227, Acting Governor Sir J. H. Swettenham to Mr Chamberlain, 5 August 1898, CO 882/6, p. 52.
71 No. 60716, Sir Arthur Young to Walter Lord, 13 July 1917, CO 273/457.
72 Return of Brothels and Prostitutes Brothels Known As the Protectorate, SSAR, 1905, p. 652; Yamazaki, *Sandakan no Haka*, pp. 45–6.
73 Yamazaki, *Sandakan no Haka*, p. 47.
74 ibid.
75 No. 60716, Sir Arthur Young to Walter Lord, 13 July 1917, C0273/457.
76 Yip Cheong Fung, interview held with the assistance of Ms Tan Beng Luan, Singapore, 3 October 1987.
77 ibid.
78 Yamazaki, *Sandakan no Haka*, pp. 43–4.
79 No. 132, Testimony of Ah Jeok in Lt Colonel Anson to the Earl of Carnarvon, 21 April 1877, CO 273/9.
80 *Nanyo no Gojunen*, pp. 138, 163.
81 No. 227, Acting Governor Sir J. H. Swettenham to Mr Chamberlain, 5 August 1898, CO 882/6, p. 71.
82 Yamazaki, 'Sandakan No. 8 Brothel', p. 54.
83 Kikuyo Zendo, interview held with Shohei Imamura in producing the film *Karayuki-san*.
84 Katsumi Mori, *Jin shin BaiBai*, Shibundo, Tokyo, 1959, p. 20.
85 Singapore Coroners Inquest and Inquiry (SC) of Oahki, no. 58, 29/5/1903.
86 *Nanyo no Gojunen*, pp. 144–5.
87 Motoe Terami-Wada, '*Karayuki-san* of Manila: 1890–1920', p. 307.
88 *Nanyo no Gojunen*, pp. 155–6.
89 ibid., p. 137.
90 *Nanyo no Gojunen,* Diary from the Consulate-General in Singapore, Shimada Shizuo, p. 523.
91 Japanese Consul Singapore to the Minister of Foreign Affairs, 23 February 1892, JMFA, vol. 1.
92 ibid.

93 Hane, *Peasants, Rebels and Outcastes*, pp. 224–5; Yamazaki, *Sandakan no Haka*, pp. 71–2.
94 *Nanyo no Gojunen*, pp. 147–9; Morisaki, *Karayuki-san*, p. 180; Yamazaki, *Sandakan no Haka*, p. 72.
95 No. 60716, Sir Arthur Young to Walter Lord, 13 July 1917, CO 273/457; Japanese Consul Singapore, Fuji, to Ministry of Foreign Affairs, 30 May 1914, JMFA, 2/2/2/7, vol. 6; *Nanyo no Gojunen*, pp. 147–8.
96 *Nanyo no Gojunen*, pp. 148–9.
97 No. 60716, Sir Arthur Young to Walter Lord, 13 July 1917, CO 273/457.
98 Yamazaki, 'Sandakan No. 8 Brothel', p. 59.
99 ibid.
100 No. 59232, General Officer Commanding the Troops, Straits Settlements to the Secretary of the War Office, 25 February 1919, FO 371-4243.
101 ibid.
102 No. 57751, General Officer Commanding the Troops, Straits Settlements to the Secretary of the War Office, 20 January 1918, FO 371-3235; General Officer Commanding the Troops, Straits Settlements to the Secretary of the War Office, 28 February 1919, FO 371-4243.
103 *Nanyo no Gojunen*, p. 153; Yamazaki, 'Sandakan No. 8 Brothel', p. 59.
104 ibid.
105 Hane, *Peasants, Rebels and Outcastes*, pp. 224–5; *Nanyo no Gojunen*, pp. 149–50; League of Nations, *Report of the Commission of Enquiry into the Traffic in Women and Children in the East*, pp. 149–50.
106 Yamazaki Heikichi to the Secretary, High Commissioner, Straits Settlements, 30 January 1920, JMFA, 4.2.2.27., vol. 5.
107 Morisaki, *Karayuki-san*, p. 232.
108 *Nanyo no Gojunen*, pp. 149–50, 157; Motoe Terami-Wada, '*Karayuki-san* of Manila: 1890–1920', pp. 311–12.
109 ibid.
110 Kikuyo Zendo, interview held with Shohei Imamura in producing the film *Karayuki-san*.
111 No. 1975, Count Michimasa to Mr Henderson, 24 March, FO 371-15521; Hane, *Peasants, Rebels and Outcastes*, p. 37.
112 League of Nations, *Report of the Commission of Enquiry into the Traffic in Women and Children in the East*, pp. 68–9, Morisaki, *Karayuki-san*, p. 233.
113 'Report of Venereal Diseases Committee', Council Paper No. 86, Proceedings of the Straits Settlements Legislative Council (1923), CO 275/109, pp. C290–1.
114 Yip Cheong Fung, interview with the assistance of Ms Tan Beng Luan, Singapore, 3 October 1987.
115 J. Perkins, *Kampong Glam, Spirit of a Community*, Sendirian Berhad, Times Publishing, Singapore, 1982, p. 23.

Chapter 15: Prostitution and the Politics of Venereal Disease

1. A version of this chapter appeared in the *Journal of Southeast Asian Studies*, vol. 21, no. 2 (1990): 360–88.

2. League of Nations, *Report of the Commission of Enquiry into the Traffic in Women and Children in the East*, Geneva, 1933, p. 132; S. E. Niccol-Jones, 'Report on the problem of prostitution in Singapore', CETWCE, Geneva, 1941, p. 23; Yen Ching-Hwang, *A Social History of the Chinese in Singapore and Malaya, 1800–1911*, Oxford University Press, Singapore, 1986, p. 250; M. Hane, *Peasants, Rebels and Outcastes: The Underside of Modern Japan*, Pantheon Books, New York, 1982, p. 6; Yamazaki Tomoko, 'Sandakan No. 8 Brothel', in *Bulletin of Concerned Asian Scholars*, vol. 5 (1975): 52–60, pp. 56–7.

3. *Ah ku* is a general term of address in Cantonese for woman or lady irrespective of age. *Ah ku* was the polite way to address a prostitute. *Loh Kui* or 'whore' was the opposite denigrating term in Cantonese. *Karayuki-san* was the word used traditionally by the Japanese of Amakusa and Shimabara, Kyushu Island, to describe rural women who emigrated to Southeast Asia and the Pacific in search of a livelihood. The ideographs comprising *karayuki-san* literally mean 'going to China', as Kyushu, the place where most of the women were from, was the part of Japan closest to China. *Karayuki-san* in common parlance nowadays has become a popular term for describing women from the poorest sectors of society during the Meiji period who lived abroad specifically as prostitutes. See J. F. Warren, 'Placing women in Southeast Asian history: The case of Oichi and the study of prostitution in Singapore society', in *At the Edge of Southeast Asian History*, New Day Publishers, Quezon City, 1987, pp. 148–64; on Chinese migration see J. F. Warren, *Rickshaw Coolie: A People's History of Singapore (1880–1940)*, Oxford University Press, Singapore, 1986, pp. 14–19, 161–65, 249; J. Ee, 'Chinese migration to Singapore, 1896–1941', in *Journal of Southeast Asian History*, vol. 2 (1961): 33–51, p. 37; L. Cheng Hirata, 'Free, indentured, enslaved: Chinese prostitutes in nineteenth century America', in *Signs: Journal of Women in Culture and Society*, vol. 5, no. 1 (1979): 3–29, pp. 5–7.

4. No. 274, Minute of Mr Meade, in Sir F. Weld to the Earl of Derby, 27 June 1883, CO 273/121.

5. Appendix O, Testimony of Registrar-General A. V. Cousins, 21 November 1876, CO 273/91.

6. No. 25, Memorandum by Secretary for Chinese Affairs, G. T. Hare, 12 June 1898, in Sir J. A. Swettenham to Mr Chamberlain, 8 September 1898, CO 882/6.

7. No. 321, Testimony of Mr C. Phillips, Inspector under the CDO, in Lt Colonel Anson to the Earl of Carnavon, 21 April 1877, CO 273/91.

8. No. 25, Memorandum by Secretary for Chinese Affairs, G. T. Hare, 12 June 1898, in Sir J. A. Swettenham to Mr Chamberlain, 8 September 1898, CO 882/6.

9. For a classic social history of the state regulation of prostitution and the successful campaign for the repeal of the Acts, see J. R. Walkowitz, *Prostitution and Victorian Society: Women, Class and the State*, Cambridge University Press, London, 1980; and P. McHugh, *Prostitution and Victorian Social Reform*, St Martin's Press, New York, 1980.

10. House of Commons, vol. LVII, 1887, Contagious Diseases Ordinances (Colonies), enclosure 3, Principal Civil Medical Officer to the Colonial Secretary, 28 February

1887, in Sir F. Weld to Sir H. T. Holland, 20 April 1887; Sir H. Ord to the Duke of Buckingham and Chandos, 1 July 1868, CO 273/20.

11 The exception to the rule was India, where, in order to preserve the health and vigour of the British soldier, cantonments, or permanent military camps were established with Lal Bazars and lock hospitals. See K. Ballhatchet, *Race, Sex and Class under the Raj: Imperial Attitudes and Policies and Their Critics, 1793–1905*, Weidenfeld and Nicolson, London, 1980.

12 House of Commons, vol. LVII, 1887, Contagious Diseases Ordinances (Colonies), enclosure 3, Principal Civil Medical Officer to the Colonial Secretary, 28 February 1887, in Sir P. Weld to Sir H. T. Holland, 20 April 1887.

13 No. 132, Lt Colonel Anson to the Earl of Carnavon, 21 April 1877, CO 273/91.

14 ibid.

15 No. 42, Sir H. Ord to the Earl of Kimberley, 13 February 1873, CO 273/65.

16 No. 132, Lt Colonel Anson to the Earl of Carnavon, 21 April 1877, CO 273/91.

17 ibid.

18 No. 132, Testimony of A. F. Anderson, Colonial Surgeon, in Lt Colonel Anson to the Earl of Carnavon, 21 April 1877, CO 273/91.

19 No. 132, Testimony of C. Phillips, A. V. Cousins, R. F. Anderson in Lt Colonel Anson to the Earl of Carnavon, 21 April 1877, CO 273/91.

20 No. 132, Testimony of J. W. Wheatley in Lt Colonel Anson to the Earl of Carnavon, 21 April 1877, CO 273/91.

21 No. 132, Lt Colonel Anson to the Earl of Carnavon, 21 April 1877, CO 273/91.

22 No. 132, Testimony of Mr J. E. Cooper in Sir J. A. Swettenham to Mr Chamberlain, 5 August 1898, CO 882/6.

23 No. 274, Sir F. Weld to the Earl of Derby, 27 August 1883, CO 273/121.

24 ibid.

25 No. 227, Memorandum of Dr M. F. Simon in Sir J. A. Swettenham to Mr Chamberlain, 5 August 1898, CO 882/6.

26 No. 132, Testimony of J. H. Robertson, M.D. in Lt Colonel Anson to the Earl of Carnavon, 21 April 1877, CO 273/91.

27 No. 132, Testimony of L. Schrieder in Lt Colonel Anson to the Earl of Carnavon, 21 April 1877, CO 273/91.

28 No. 132, Testimony of R. A. Miles in Lt Colonel Anson to the Earl of Carnavon, 21 April 1877, CO 273/91.

29 No. 25, Memorandum of Dr Welch in Sir J. A. Swettenham to Mr Chamberlain, 8 September 1898, CO 882/6; No. 227, Testimony of Mr Wispauer in Sir J. A. Swettenham to Mr Chamberlain, 5 August 1898. CO 882/6.

30 No. 4, Sir F. Weld to Edward Stanhope, 10 January 1887, CO 273/143.

31 No. 274, Sir F. Weld to the Earl of Derby, 27 August 1882, CO 273/121.

32 No. 274, Sir F. Weld to the Earl of Derby, 27 June 1883, CO 273/121; No. 285, Sir F. Weld to the Earl of Derby, 4 July 1883, CO 273/121.

33 No. 274, Sir F. Weld to the Earl of Derby, 27 August 1882, CO 273/121.

34 No. 285, Sir F. Weld to the Earl of Derby, 4 July 1883, CO 273/121.

35 Walkowitz, *Prostitution and Victorian Society*, pp. 113–36.
36 ibid.
37 G. Petrie, *A Singular Iniquity: The Campaigns of Josephine Butler*, Macmillan, London, 1971, p. 205; R. S. Morton, *Venereal Diseases*, Penguin Books, London, 1966, p. 32.
38 Walkowitz, *Prostitution and Victorian Society*, pp. 233–45; Petrie, *A Singular Iniquity*, pp. 144–5.
39 Statistics of the Registration Office, Contagious Diseases Ordinance, 1888, CO 275/33.
40 House of Commons, vol. LVII, 1887, Contagious Diseases Ordinances (Colonies), enclosure 2, in Sir F. Weld to Sir H. T. Holland, 20 April 1887.
41 ibid, Enclosure 1.
42 ibid.
43 ibid., Testimony of Mr C. J. Irving in enclosure 2.
44 No. 128, Sir H. T. Holland to Sir F. Weld, 2 July 1887, CO 275/14.
45 ibid.
46 No. 373, Sir F. Weld to Sir H. T. Holland, 10 September 1887, CO 275/34.
47 No. 128, Sir H. T. Holland to Sir F. Weld, 2 July 1887, CO 275/14; No. 215, Sir C. Smith to Lord Knutsford, 17 May 1888, CO 273/152.
48 No. 552, Sir C. Smith to the Colonial Secretary, 10 December 1887, CO 275/34.
49 Annual Medical Report of the Principal Civil Medical Officer, Straits Settlement Annual Report, 1888, p. 2.
50 No. 451, Sir C. Smith to Lord Knutsford, 21 September 1889, CO 273/161.
51 No. 210, Sir C. Smith to Lord Knutsford, 3 May 1889, CO 273/160; Annual Medical Report of the Principal Civil Medical Officer, Straits Settlement Annual Report, 1890, p. 2.
52 No. 210, Sir C. Smith to Lord Knutsford, 3 May 1889, CO 273/160.
53 Annual Medical Report of the Principal Civil Medical Officer, *Straits Settlement Annual Report*, 1890, pp. 2, 8; No. 274, Sir C. Smith to Lord Knutsford, 15 June 1892, CO 273/181.
54 No. 368, Lord Knutsford to Sir C. Smith, 5 November 1889, CO 273/161.
55 No. 311, Sir C. B. H. Mitchell to the Marquess of Ripon, 25 September 1894, CO 882/6.
56 No. 227, Sir J. H. Swettenham to Mr Chamberlain, 5 August 1898, CO 882/6; Straits Settlement Association to the Colonial Office, 8 November 1897, CO 882/6.
57 Straits Settlement Association to the Colonial Office, 8 November 1897, CO 273/232.
58 ibid.
59 D. Llewellyn-Jones, *Sex and V.D.*, Faber & Faber, London, 1974, p. 83.
60 Straits Settlement Association to the Colonial Office, 8 November 1897, CO 273/232.
61 Annual Medical Report of the Principal Civil Medical Officer, Straits Settlement Annual Report, 1892, p. 3.
62 ibid.; No. 274, Sir C. Smith to Lord Knutsford, 15 June 1892, CO 273/181.

63 Annual Medical Report of the Principal Civil Medical Officer, *Straits Settlement Annual Report*, 1893-97; Straits Settlement Association to the Colonial Office, 8 November 1897, CO 882/6.
64 No. 569, Sir C. Smith to the Earl of Knutsford, 20 December 1889, CO 273/162.
65 ibid.
66 ibid.
67 Straits Settlement Association to the Colonial Office, 8 November 1897, CO 273/232.
68 ibid.
69 Testimony of Dr Mugliston in Straits Settlement Association to the Colonial Office, 8 November 1897, CO 882/6.
70 Straits Settlement Association to the Colonial Office, 8 November 1897, CO 273/232.
71 No. 227, Testimony of Dr Mugliston in Sir J. H. Swettenham to Mr Chamberlain, 5 August 1898, CO 882/6.
72 Straits Settlement Association to the Colonial Office, 8 November 1897, CO 273/232.
73 ibid.
74 Morton, *Venereal Diseases*, pp. 54-5, 58; Llewellyn-Jones, *Sex and V.D.*, pp. 14-15; No. 227, Testimony of Dr Mugliston in Sir J. H. Swettenham to Mr Chamberlain, 5 August 1898, CO 882/6.
75 No. 227, Testimony of Dr Mugliston in Sir J. H. Swettenham to Mr Chamberlain, 5 August 1898, CO 882/6.
76 ibid.
77 No. 227, Testimony of Mr Wispauer in Sir J. H. Swettenham to Mr Chamberlain, 5 August 1898, CO 882/6.
78 Morton, *Venereal Diseases*, p. 112; Llewellyn-Jones, *Sex and V.D.*, p. 12.
79 No. 187, Sir C. Smith to Lord Knutsford, 7 May 1888.
80 ibid.; House of Commons, vol. LVII, 1887, Contagious Diseases Ordinances (Colonies), enclosure 3, Principal Civil Medical Officer to the Colonial Secretary, 28 February 1887, in Sir F. Weld to Sir H. T. Holland, 20 April 1887.
81 No. 295, Sir C. B. N. Mitchell to Mr Chamberlain, 1 September 1897, CO 882/6.
82 Straits Settlement Association to the Colonial Office, 8 November 1897, CO 882/6.
83 No. 227, Sir J. H. Swettenham to Mr Chamberlain, 5 August 1898, CO 882/6.
84 No. 552, Sir C. Smith to the Earl of Knutsford, 9 December 1889, CO 273/162.
85 ibid.
86 No. 227, Testimony of Dr Mugliston and Mr Wispauer in Sir J. H. Swettenham to Mr Chamberlain, 5 August 1898, CO 882/6.
87 No. 113, Sir C. B. H. Mitchell to the Marquess of Ripon, 8 April 1895, CO 882/6; No. 227, Testimony of Dr Mugliston in Sir J. H. Swettenham to Mr Chamberlain, 5 August 1878, CO 882/6.
88 ibid.

89 No. 113, Sir C. B. H. Mitchell to the Marquess of Ripon, 8 April 1895, CO 882/6.
90 Straits Settlement Association to the Colonial Office, 8 November 1897, CO 273/232.
91 No. 227, Straits Settlement Association to the Colonial Office, 1 September 1898, CO 273/237; No. 227, Sir J. H. Swettenham, to Mr Chamberlain, 5 August 1898, CO 882/6.
92 No. 35, Mr Chamberlain to Sir C. B. H. Mitchell, 18 February 1898, CO 882/6.
93 ibid.
94 No. 121, Mr Chamberlain to Sir C. B. H. Mitchell, 28 April 1899, CO 882/6; No. 110, Mr Chamberlain to Sir C. B. H. Mitchell, 11 May 1899, CO 882/6.

Chapter 16: A Tale of Two Centuries

1 A slightly longer version of this chapter was published in the *Asia Research Institute Working Paper Series*, National University of Singapore, no. 2, June 2003.
2 Tomé Pires, c. 1468–c. 1540, *The Suma Oriental of Tome Pires: An account of the East…and, The book of Francisco Rodrigues: Rutter of a voyage in the Red Sea / tr. from the Portuguese MS in the Bibliotheque de la Chambre des Deputes, Paris*, and ed. by Armando Cortesao, Kraus Reprint, Nendeln, Liechtenstein, 1967, reprint of Hakluyt Society, 1944, vol. 1, p. 147; vol. 2, p. 233.
3 James F. Warren, *The Sulu Zone 1768–1898: The Dynamics of External Trade, Slavery and Ethnicity in the Transformation of a Southeast Asian Maritime State*, Singapore University Press, Singapore, 1981; *The Sulu Zone, the World Capitalist Economy and the Historical Imagination*, VU University Press/CASA, Amsterdam, 1998; *Iranun and Balangingi: Globalization, Maritime Raiding and the Birth of Ethnicity*, Singapore, Singapore University Press, 2002.
4 A. Giddens, 'Affluence, poverty and the idea of a post-scarcity society', in *Development and Change*, vol. 27 (1996): 365–77.
5 E. Wolf, *Europe and the People Without History*, University of California Press, Berkeley, 1982, pp. 386–9.
6 C. A. Trocki, 'Piracy in the Malay World', in *Encyclopedia of Asian History*, vol. 3, ed. Ainslie T. Embree, Charles Scribners, New York, 1988, p. 262.
7 Warren, 'Slavery in Southeast Asia', in *A Historical Guide to World Slavery*, ed. Seymour Drescher and Stanley L. Engermen, Oxford University Press, New York, 1998, pp. 80–87; A. Reid, *Slavery, Bondage and Dependency in Southeast Asia*, University of Queensland Press, St Lucia, 1983.
8 Warren, 'Slavery in Southeast Asia', pp. 80–7; *The Sulu Zone, the World Capitalist Economy and the Historical Imagination*; J. Scott, 'The state and the people who move around', in *IIAS Newsletter 20*, pp. 3, 45.
9 Warren, 'Slavery in Southeast Asia', pp. 80–7; *The Sulu Zone, the World Capitalist Economy and the Historical Imagination*; J. Scott 'The State and the people who move around', pp. 3, 45; L. Sears, 'The contingency of autonomous history', in *Autonomous Histories, Particular Truths: Essays in Honor of John Small*, ed. L. Sears, University of Wisconsin, CSEAS, Madison, 1993, pp. 3–35, pp. 6–9.

10 Christian Pelras, *The Bugis*, Blackwell, Oxford, 1996; L. Andaya, *The Kingdom of Johor 1641–1728; Economic and Political Developments*, Oxford University Press, Kuala Lumpur, 1975; B. Andaya, *To Live As Brothers: Southeast Sumatra in the Seventeenth and Eighteenth Centuries*, University of Hawai'i Press, Honolulu, 1993; E. Velthoen and G. Acciaioli, 'Fluctuating states and mobile populations: Shifting relations of Bajo to local rulers and Bugis traders in Colonial Eastern Sulawesi', unpublished paper presented at the International Seminar on Bajau Communities, LIPI, Jakarta, 22–25 November, 1993; Velthoen, 'A historical perspective on Bajo in Eastern Sulawesi', unpublished paper, Perth: Murdoch University, 1994.

11 Warren, *The Sulu Zone, the World Capitalist Economy and the Historical Imagination*, p. 15.

12 Warren, *The Sulu Zone 1768–1898*, pp. 61–2, 69–75.

13 Warren, *The Sulu Zone 1768–1898*, p. 147.

14 V. Barrantes, *Guerras Piraticas de Filipinas contra Mindanaos y Joloanos*, Imprenta de Manuel H. Hernandez, Madrid, 1878; E. Bernaldez, *Resana historico de la guerra a Sur de Filipinas, sostenida por las armas Espanoles contra los piratas de aquel archipielago, desde la conquista hasta nuestros dias*, Imprenta del Memorial de Ingenieros, Madrid, 1857; J. Montero y Vidal, *Historia de la Pirateria Malayo Mahometans en Mindanao, Jolo y Borneo*, 2 vols, Imprenta de M. Tello, Madrid, 1888; N. Tarling, *Piracy and Politics in the Malay World: A Study of British Imperialism in Nineteenth-Century Southeast Asia*, Donald Moore, Singapore, and F. W. Cheshire, Melbourne, 1963.

15 Warren, *The Sulu Zone, the World Capitalist Economy and the Historical Imagination*, pp. 51–8.

16 P. Burke, *The French Historical Revolution: The Annales School 1929–89*, Stanford University Press, Stanford, 1990; P. Baran, *The Political Economy of Growth*, Monthly Review Press, London, New York, 1957; A. G. Frank, *World Accumulation, 1492–1789*, Macmillan Press, London, 1978; I. Wallerstein, *The Modern World System: Capitalist Agriculture and the Origins of the European World Economy in the Sixteenth Century*, Academic Press, New York, 1974.

17 Wolf, *Europe and the People Without History*, pp. 384–91.

18 Warren, 'Who were the Balangingi Samal? Slave raiding and ethnogenesis in nineteenth century Sulu', in *Journal of Asian Studies*, vol. 37, no. 3 (1978): 477–90.

19 René B. Javellana, S. J., *Fortress of Empire: Spanish Colonial Fortifications of the Philippines, 1565–1898*, photographs by Jose Ma, Lorenzo P. Tan, Bookmark, Makati City, 1997.

20 ibid., pp. 208–11.

21 For an important study of how Southeast Asia became a crucial part of a global commercial system between the fifteenth and mid-seventeenth centuries, see A. Reid, *Southeast Asia in the Age of Commerce, 1450–1680: Expansion and Crisis*, 2 vols, Yale University Press, New Haven, 1993.

22 Wong Lin Ken, 'The trade of Singapore, 1819–1869', in *Journal of Malaysian Branch of the Royal Asiatic Society*, vol. 33, pt 4 (1960): 1–315, pp. 82–3.

23 Warren, *The Sulu Zone 1768–1898*, pp. 200–16.

24 'Intelligence File: Pacific Ocean', in *MaritimeSecurity.com*, online <http://www.maritimesecurity.com/research/pacific_ocean.htm>, accessed 15 July 2000.

25 'Worldwide maritime piracy', in *MaritimeSecurity.com*, '1999 Piracy Report', at <http://www.maritimesecurity.com/archive.htm>, June 1999, p. 8, accessed 15 July 2000.

26 A. Tan, 'The Asian waters, sea pirates eschew eye patches, steal ships via internet', in *Christian Science Monitor*, 13 June 1996, p. 7.

27 'Piracy and armed robbery at sea', in *Focus on IMO*, January 2000, p. 4.

28 Tan, 'The Asian waters, sea pirates eschew eye patches, steal ships via internet', p. 7.

29 Henk Schulte Nordholt, 'A state of violence', *IIAS Newsletter*, 23 October 2000, p. 3.

30 J. McCarthy, 'Why Indonesia is now easier to like', in the *Age*, Melbourne, 21 November 2000.

31 'Worldwide maritime piracy', p. 4.

32 International Chamber of Commerce (ICC), 'Weekly piracy report', online: <http://www.iccwbo.org/home/news_archives/1999/weekly_piracy_report.asp>, 4–10 July 2000, accessed 24 October 2006.

33 'South sea piracy: Dead men tell no tales', in *The Economist* online: <http://www.economist.com/displayStory.cfm?Story_ID=327568>, 16 December 1999, accessed 24 October 2006.

34 'The perils of rising piracy in Asia', in *Jane's Defence Weekly*, 15 November 2000.

35 'Indonesia's coastal resources in crisis', in *Down to Earth—International Campaign for Ecological Justice in Indonesia, Newsletter*, 47, November 2000.

36 'Piracy and armed robbery at sea', p. 4.

37 A. Eames, 'Modern piracy not so yo ho ho', in *Times*, 9 May 1998.

38 'South sea piracy: Dead men tell no tales.'

39 'The perils of rising piracy in Asia.'

40 'Guidance to ship owners and ship operators, ship masters and crews for preventing and suppressing acts of piracy and armed robbery against ships', IMO, MSC/Circ. 623, 16 June 1999, p. 1.

41 M. Hanlon, 'Thailand cracks down on pirates who terrorize fleeing boat people', in *Toronto Star*, 4 January 1987.

42 'Piracy resurgence on the high seas', in the *Australian*, 8 November 1978.

43 'South sea piracy: Dead men tell no tales.'

44 'The perils of rising piracy in Asia.'

45 J. J. Brandon, 'High-seas piracy is booming—it's time to fight harder', in *The Christian Science Monitor*, 27 December 2000.

46 'Indonesia's dangerous waters: Pirate attacks at record high', in *Deutsche Presse-Agentur*, 4 January 2001.

47 ICC, 'Weekly piracy report'.

48 'Intelligence File: Indonesia', in *MaritimeSecurity.com*, online: <http://www.maritimesecurity.com/research/intel_file_indonesia.htm>, 2001, accessed 20 May 2001.

49 'Intelligence File: Singapore', in *MaritimeSecurity.com*, online: <http://www.maritimesecurity.com/research/intel_file_singapore.htm>, accessed 15 July 2000.

50 'Worldwide maritime piracy.'
51 'Piracy and armed robbery at sea', p. 3.
52 'Indonesia's dangerous waters: Pirate attacks at record high.'
53 'Pirates attack ships near southern Malaysian port', *Associated Press*, 4 January 2001.
54 Ellen, 'Bringing piracy to account', in *Jane's Navy International*, vol. 102–3 (April 1 1997), p. 29.
55 'South sea piracy: Dead men tell no tales.'
56 Andreas Harsono, 'New wave pirates rule dark seas', in the *West Australian*, 17 April 1999.
57 J. J. Brandon, 'High-seas piracy is booming—it's time to fight harder', in *The Christian Science Monitor*, 27 December 2000.
58 ibid.
59 ICC, 'Weekly piracy report', 4–10 July 2000.
60 'The perils of rising piracy in Asia.'

Glossary

a'ata	slaves
ah ku	general term of address in Cantonese for a woman or lady irrespective of age. *Ah ku* was the polite way to address a Chinese prostitute in colonial Singapore
almojarifazgo	import-export duty
ambas	slaves
anja kansanan	Malay rank title
Babas	a small, highly Malayanised and Anglicised Chinese group in the Straits Settlements
bakafu	feudal lords
banyaga	chattel-slave who was either the victim or the offspring of victims of slave raids
barang karajaan	symbols of royal office
baroto	a canoe-like vessel with or without outriggers employed as an auxiliary craft for inshore raiding
Bisayan	variant of Visayan. Refers to the people who inhabit the central section of the Philippine Archipelago commonly known as the Visayas.
bugis paduwakan	from south Sulawesi: traditional two-masted all wooden sailing boats whose basic design has not altered for several hundred years
buitengewesten	Dutch term for the 'outer islands'; area beyond the Law
butas	channel
cabeceras	a town or capital of a parish; provincial capital
chandu	prepared opium
chukun aikaku	worship of the Japanese Emperor and love of country
contrabandista	smuggler
convento	rectory, residence of a priest, commonly attached to a Catholic church
corregimiento	public prison
daghregisters	daily accounts of proceedings of the Dutch East India Company
daimyo	feudal lords
dammar	resin obtained from a tree especially of genus *agathis* or *thorea*
datu	chief or aristocrat
deportados	those people forcibly moved from Balangingi to work in the tobacco plantations of the Cagayan Valley
divide et impera	Latin, divide and rule
estados	report or account
five footway	a verandah, and open arcade or light-roofed gallery extending along the front of shop houses and tenement dwellings as a continuous walkway

Glossary

gantang	dry measure equivalent to 3.1 kilograms
garay	Balangingi maritime raiding vessel of the nineteenth century
guerras piratacas de Filipinas	pirate wars of the Philippines
gutta-percha	a natural polymer, chemically the same as natural rubber; got from the latex of various Bornean trees
hakim	judge
hatib or *imam*	leader of the mosque or *surua* organisation; person who read the Qur'an, led prayer recitation, and acted as legal arbiter and judge when disputes arose between the commanders and their crews on board the Balangingi slave raiding vessels
indio	term used by the Spaniards to refer to the inhabitants of the Philippines
joanga	large raiding vessel the Iranun used for long cruises; the *joanga* measured on average 24–27 metres in length, and 6 metres in the beam
juban	kimono
julmuri or *juru mudi*	experienced officers who acted as steersmen and were responsible for the crew and the maintenance of the slave raiding vessel
juru batu	pilot on the slave raiding vessels whose job it was to tend the anchor and keep watch for reefs, shoals, rocks, trading ships and the enemy
jurumudi	see *julmuri*.
kain	cloth
kakap	a canoe-like vessel with or without outriggers employed as an auxiliary craft for inshore raiding
kampong	village
kapal api	lit. fire ships; steam warships
karayuki-san	'those who travel to China'; the word refers specifically to Japanese prostitutes who went abroad, not only to China, but Southeast Asia, India and North America between 1880 and 1920
kayus	pieces of coarse cotton cloth 20 fathoms in length
kebun rotan	rattan reserve
kerajaan	colonial Malayo-Muslim state
kiapangdilihan	bond slaves
Kolonial-Verslag	Dutch term for annual government report
koku	Japanese term for volume. 1 *koku* = 5 imperial bushels; 5.1 US bushels; 47.6 US gallons.
kota	fort
kris	a distinctive Malay or Javanese asymmetrical dagger, that is used for both ceremonial occasions and as a weapon.
kwai po	female brothel-keeper
lanong	see *joanga*

Illanun	The term 'I-Lanaw-en', popularised by the coastal inhabitants of Southeast Asia, and their European rulers as 'Illanun' (Illanoon, Illanaon, Lanun or Illano) to describe the Maranao and non-Maranao maritime peoples of southern Mindanao and the Sulu Archipelago in the late eighteenth and nineteenth centuries
loi ku	'whore', a denigrating term in Cantonese
magooray	Samal–*Iranun* term for maritime raiding
mamasan	brothel madam
mandau	ceremonial sword
marina sutil	light navy or antipiracy force
merompak	Malay term for raiding
moro/mora	term used by the Spanish to refer to the Muslims
Musim lanun	the months of August, September and October when Muslim raids were most likely to occur
nakodah	master of a sailing craft
Nanihin	Japanese for the Southern Ocean; refers specifically to Southeast Asia
Nanshin	Southern Ocean
Nanyang	Chinese for the South Seas; refers specifically to Southeast Asia
Nanyo	Japanese term for the Southern Ocean; refers specifically to Southeast Asia
okasan	'mother'
orang kaya	a commoner and a man of means
Orang-Laut	Malay sea people
orang tua	elderly chief of the Balangingi Samal
panco	or *garay* or *penjajap*; a raiding ship of lighter construction than a *lanong* or *joanga* used by the Balangingi as their principal craft
pangeran	lord
pangkeng	the common room for Chinese labourers in a dormitory or coolie house
panglima	commander
penjajap	see *panco*
perahu pinisi	from south Sulawesi: traditional two-masted all wooden sailing boats whose basic design has not altered for several hundred years
picul	133 pounds or 60 kilograms
pirata	pirate
poh sam	woman who mends clothes
prahu	Malay for sailing craft
pueblo	a municipal district
Raja Laut	Malay term for admiral
Ratu Adil	'Just Prince'; the Javanese Messiah prophesied by Djajabaja

Reconquista	refers to the period between 722 and 1492 CE during which the Christians liberated Spain and Portugal from Muslims. The form of Catholicism that travelled from the Iberian Peninsula to the New World and the Philippines was thus imbued with anti-Muslim sentiment.
renegade	renegade
rickshawala	also referred to as rickshaw coolie or puller
Ruma bichara	council of ministers serving the Sultan
sakay	crew in Balangingi slave raider
salisipan	also called *vinta, baroto,* or *kakap*; a canoe-like vessel with or without outriggers employed as an auxiliary craft for inshore raiding
samisen	a three-stringed Japanese musical instrument
shahbandar	harbour master
singkeh	newcomers from China
sin-hak	Cantonese term referring to an immigrant landing in Singapore
sinseh	doctor of traditional Chinese medicine or teacher
suteretsu	colloquial term in Amakusa dialect, referring to the Malay Street brothel area of Singapore, which was a corruption of the word 'street'
tai pang po	brothel servant
tali lanun	cheap rope of excellent quality
tatami	reed-covered straw matting in traditional Japanese rooms
towkay	businessman, shopowner, leader of dialect association; headman or 'boss'
tripang	sea cucumber
vacuum domicilium	Latin, empty, vacant or unoccupied; similar to *terra nullius*.
vinta	see *salisipan*
wayang-going	Chinese street opera in Singapore
yap pun kai	refers to specific streets in the two different brothel districts in Singapore where the Japanese women once resided
yukata	Japanese summer garment; or casual form of *kimono*
zeeroover	Dutch for pirate
zegen	professional procurers of prostitutes or 'pimps'

Bibliography

Unpublished official records

Britain
Public Records Office

Colonial Office Records (CO)
CO 144 Labuan, original correspondence, 1844–1906, vols 1–81
CO 273 Straits Settlements, original correspondence, 1867–1941
CO 275 Straits Settlements, sessional papers, 1870–1940
CO 874 British North Borneo papers 1878–1915
CO 882 Confidential print, Colonial Office

Foreign Office Records (FO)
FO 12, Borneo, 1842–1875
FO 71, Sulu, 1848–1888, vols 1–19
FO 72, Spain, 72/663, 72/749, 72/761, 72/1017
FO 371, General, Annual Reports from various British Territories for transmission to League of nations/White Slave Traffic, file 4243

Admiralty Records
Admiralty, 125/133, Sulu Piracy.

Egremont Papers
'List of products of Sulu and its immediate dependencies,' PRO, 30/47/20/1
Records of the East India Company, India Office Library, London

Bengal Public Consultations
P 13/13

Factory Records Straits Settlements, Vols 1–3

Parliamentary Papers, House of Commons
1851, LVI, pt. 1 [1351], Papers respecting the Operations against the Pirates on the Northwest coast of Borneo
1851, vol. LVI, pt I [1390], 'Historical Notices upon the Piracies committed in the East Indies and upon measures taken for surpassing them, by the government of the Netherlands within the last thirty years,' abstracted from articles by Cornets de Groot in the *Moniteur des Indies*
1852, vol. XXXI, (1538) 473. Borneo Piracy
1887, vol. LVII, Contagious Diseases Ordinances (Colonies)

Indonesia
Arsip Nasional Republik Indonesia, Jakarta (ANRI)
Menado 37

Japan

Japanese Ministry of Foreign Affairs (JMFA), Diplomatic Record Office, Tokyo
JMFA 4/2/2/34 Miscellaneous matters pertaining to laws and regulations on Japanese Traffickers, vol. 2, 1882–1926
JMFA, 4/2/2/27 Miscellaneous matters concerning Japanese Traffickers, vol. 7, 1877–1938

Netherlands

Records of the Auxiliary Repository, Schaarsbergen
Ministrie van Kolonien No. 1398, 5873

Philippines

The Records of the Philippine National Archives (PNA), Manila

Mindanao y Sulu
Bundles 1803–1890, 1836–1897, 1838–1885, 1838–1886, 1859–1861, 1860, 1863–1894, 15 unclassified bundles.

Cartas
Bundles 1845, 1847–1848

Isla de Borneo
Bundles I–II

Piratas
Bundles I–III

Singapore

National Archives and Records Centre
Straits Settlements Annual Reports (SSAR), 1861–1941
Straits Settlements Legislative Council Proceedings 1867–1941
Straits Settlement Factory Records 1791
Singapore Municipal Administration Reports 1888–1939
Straits Settlement Government Gazette (SSGG), 1881

Subordinate Court
Certificate of Coroner's Views Singapore 1906–1940
Singapore Coroner's Inquests and Inquiries 1882–1939

Spain

Archivo General de Indias (AGI), Seville

Seccion Audiencia de Filipinas
359–368 Consultos, Decretos, Ordenes Originales, 1770–1850
Archivo Historico Nacional, Madrid

Ultramar
Legajo 5184
Archivo de Ministerio de Asuntos Exteriores, Madrid

Correspondencia Consulados Singapore, 1848–1920
Legajo 2067–1848–1880

Biblioteca de Palacio, Madrid
Comision Reservada a Borneo y Jolo 1881–1882, bound MS

The United States

National Archives and Records Administration, Washington, D.C.
Department of the Navy
Records of the United States Exploring Expedition under the Command of Lieutenant Charles Wilkes 1838–1842
Roll 13—The Journal of William Briskoe, Armorer, aboard the *Relief* and the *Vincennes* (18 August 1838–23 March 1842)

Library of Congress Washington D.C.
The Leonard Wood Papers
Container 3, Diary, May 1902–31 January 1906
H. L. Scott Papers, Library of Congress, Washington, D.C.
Container 55–56, Official letters January 1900–1905

Salem Peabody Museum, Salem, Massachusetts
'List of goods to be had at Sooloo', MS, included with the log of the ship *Albree*, 656/1833A

Collections

Beyer-Holleman collection of original sources in Philippine Customary Law (hereafter BH-PCL). Typescript, Library of Congress, Washington D.C. and the 5873 Philippine Studies Program, University of Chicago.

Paper 160, vol. 1, no. 1, Major Charles Livingston, 'Constabulary monograph of the province of Sulu', 1915.

Paper 161, vol. 2, no. 8, Najeeb Saleeby, 'The Moros', 1906.

Paper 161, vol. 2, no. 11, K. Walker, 'Report of the 53rd Census District' (Tawi-Tawi), 1903.

Paper 162, vol. 6, no. 16, A. Gunther, 'Correspondence and reports relating to the Sulu Moros', Jolo and Manila, 1901–1903.

Paper 162, vol. 6, no. 23, E. B. Christie, 'The Moros of Sulu and Mindanao'.

Paper 162, vol. 6, no. 25, E. B. Christie, 'The non-Christian tribes of the northern half of the Zamboanga Peninsula', 1903.

Paper 162, vol. 6, no. 26, F. P. Williamson, 'The Moros between Buluan and Punta Flecha', 1903.

Paper 162, vol. 6, no. 28, L. W. V. Kennon, D. P. Barrows, J. Pershing and C. Smith, 'Census report relating to the district of Lanao Mindanao', 1903.

Paper 163, vol. 6, no. 34, O. J. W. Scott and I. C. Brown, 'Ethnography of the Magandanaos of Parang', 1908.

Harrison Collection, Battye Library, Western Australia

Harrison Papers
Reg Harrison, Personal Papers, bundle no. 3 of PR. 549411-4.

Haverschmidt Collection, Heerlen, Netherlands

Haverschmidt Papers
Records compiled in 1951-1952 in Berau by Mr R. Haverschmidt, late manager, N. V. Steenkolen Maatschappij Parapattan, Teluk Bajur, Berau.

John Neilson, Joseph Conrad Collection, Oamaru, New Zealand: Reed Papers
Papers of the late Dr J. G. Reed of Perak, Malaysia, relating to his research into the life of Joseph Conrad in the John Neilson Conrad Collection, Oamaru, New Zealand.

Published official records

Straits Settlement Government Gazette, 1881.
Commission of Enquiry into the State of Labour in the Straits Settlements and Protected Malay States, Singapore: Government Printing Office, 1890.
Straits Settlements and Federated Malay States Opium Commission, 1908.
Proceedings and Report of the Commission Appointed to Inquire into the Cause of the Present Housing Difficulties in Singapore, and the Steps Which Should Be Taken to Remedy Such Difficulties, Singapore: Government Printing Office, 1918.
Proceedings of the Committee Appointed by His Excellency the Governor and High Commissioner to Inquire into Matters Relating to the Use of Opium in British Malaya, Singapore: Government Printing Office, 1924.
League of Nations, *Report of the Commission of Enquiry into the Traffic in Women and Children in the East*, (CETWCE) Geneva, 1933.

Newspapers

British North Borneo Herald and Official Gazette, 16 September 1895.
Singapore Free Press, 1847-1935.
Japan Weekly Mail, 1896.
Makassarsch Handelsblad, 1876.
Malay Mail, 1965.

Interviews

Fong Chiok Kai, interview held with the assistance of Ms Tan Beng Luan, in the Committee Room of the Kreta Ayer Community Centre, Singapore, 1 October 1987.
Interview with Ho Swee Bee, Archive and Oral History Department, Singapore, February 1982, reels 12 and 13.
Interview with Ng Kar Eng, Archive and Oral History Department, Singapore, Reel 3.
Kikuyo Zendo, interview held with Shohei Imamura in producing the film *Karayuki-san*.
Yip Cheong Fung, interview held with the assistance of Ms Tan Beng Luan in Mr Yip's shop situated at the lower end of Kreta Ayer Road, Singapore, 1 October 1987.

Unpublished material

Holmes J. S. and A. van Marle, 'Joseph Conrad in Indonesia', unpublished lecture, University of Munster, 1961, pp. 15-22.

'The Heng Wah People and Their Development in Various Transport Trades', unpublished manuscript, Singapore, Nanyang University, c. 1950.

Velthoen, E., 'A historical perspective on Bajo in Eastern Sulawesi', unpublished paper, Perth: Murdoch University, 1994.

Velthoen, E. and G. Acciaioli, 'Fluctuating states and mobile populations: Shifting relations of Bajo to local rulers and Bugis traders in Colonial Eastern Sulawesi', unpublished paper presented at the International Seminar on Bajau Communities, LIPI, Jakarta, 22-25 November 1993.

Warren, J. F., 'The coroner and the rickshaw coolie of Singapore: Materials, problems and opportunities for writing the history of overseas Chinese laborers', unpublished paper prepared for the Asian Studies Association of Australia, Fifth National Conference, 1984, pp. 1-15.

Warren, J. F., 'The Port of Jolo and the Suln Zone Slave Trade: An 1845 Report', unpublished paper, 2005.

Warren, J. F., 'Social history and the photograph: Glimpses of Chinese and Japanese labour in Singapore in the early twentieth century', unpublished paper presented at the 'Labor and Migration in Asia Symposium', National Museum of Singapore, Singapore, May 2003.

Dissertations

Mednick, M., 'Encampment of the lake: The social organization of a Moslem Philippine (Moro) people', PhD dissertation, Department of Anthropology, University of Chicago, 1965.

Nimmo, H. A., 'The structure of Bajau society', PhD dissertation, Department of Anthropology, University of Hawai'i, 1969.

Reber, Ann L., 'The Sulu world in the eighteenth and early nineteenth centuries: A historiographical problem in British writings on Malay piracy', MA thesis, Cornell, 1966.

Reynolds, J. K., 'Towards an account of Sulu and its Bornean dependencies, 1700-1878', MA thesis, University of Wisconsin, 1970.

Velthoen, E., 'Contested coastlines: diasporas, trade and colonial expansion in Eastern Sulawesi 1680-1905', PhD dissertation, Murdoch University, 2002.

Warren, J. F., 'Trade, raid, slave: The socio-economic patterns of the Sulu Zone, 1770-1898', PhD dissertation, Australian National University, 1976.

Books

Ahmad, Raja Ali Haji ibn, *The Precious Gift of Tuhfat Al-Nafis*, Kuala Lumpur: Oxford University Press, 1982.

Allen, J., *The Sea Years of Joseph Conrad*, London: Methuen and Co., 1967.

Andaya, B. W., *To Live as Brothers: Southeast Sumatra in the Seventeenth and Eighteenth Centuries*, Honolulu: University of Hawai'i Press, 1993.

Andaya, L., *The Kingdom of Johor, 1641-1728*, Economic and Political Developments, Kuala Lumpur: Oxford University Press, 1975.

Baja, E., *The Philippine National Flag and Anthem*, Manila: Philippine Education Company, 1936.

Baker, H. D. R., *Chinese Family and Kinship*, London: Macmillan Press, 1979.

Ballhatchet, K., *Race, Sex and Class under the Raj: Imperial Attitudes and Policies and Their Critics, 1793-1905*, London: Weidenfeld and Nicolson, 1980.

Baran, P., *The Political Economy of Growth*, London, New York: Monthly Review Press, 1957.

Barnes, R. *Sea Hunters of Indonesia: Fishers and Weavers of Lamalera*, New York: Oxford University Press, 1996.

Barrantes, V., *Guerras Piraticas de Filipinas contra Mindanaos y Joloanos*, Madrid: Imprenta de Manuel H. Hernandez, 1878.

Barth, F. (ed.), *Ethnic Groups and Boundaries*, The Social Organization of Culture Difference, Allen & Unwin, London, 1969.

Barthes, R., *Erté (Romain de Tirtoff)*, Parma: Franco Maria Ricei Publications, 1972.

Belcher, E., *Narrative of the Voyage of H.M.S. Samarang, during the Years 1843-1846*, London: Reeve, Benham & Reeve, 1848.

Berger J. and J. Mohr, *Another Way of Telling*, London: Writers and Readers Pub. Coop, 1982.

Bernaldez, E., *Resana Historico de la Guerra a Sur de Filipinas, sostenida por las armas Espanoles contra los piratas de aquel archipielago, desde la conquista hasta nuestros dias*, Madrid: Imprenta del Memorial de Ingenieros, 1857.

Blusse, L., *Strange Company: Chinese Settlers, Mestizo Women and the Dutch in VOC Batavia*, Dordrecht: KITLV, 1986.

Bonney, R., *Kedah 1771-1821 The Search for Security and Independence*, Kuala Lumpur: Oxford University Press, 1971.

Boxer, C., *The Dutch Seaborne Empire 1600-1800*, London: Penguin Books, 1973.

Braudel, F., *The Mediterranean and the Mediterranean World in the Age of Philip II*, 2 vols, New York: Harper Row, 1972.

—— *Civilisation matérielle, économie et capitalisme: XVe-XVIIIe siècle* (Capitalism and Material Life, 1400-1800), Paris: Librairie Armand Colin, 1979.

—— *On History*, London: Weidenfeld and Nicolson, 1980.

Bridenthal R. and C. Koonz (eds), *Becoming Visible. Women in European History*, Boston: Houghton Mifflin Co., 1977.

Broersma, R., *Handel en Bedriff in Zuid-en Oost-Borneo*, Gravenhage: G. Noeff, 1927.

Brown, D., *Brunei: The Structure and History of a Bornean Malay Sultanate*, Brunei: Brunei Museum, 1970.

Buckley, C. *An Anecdotal History of Old Time Singapore*, Kuala Lumpur: University of Malaya Press, 1965.

Burke, P., *The French Historical Revolution: The Annales School 1929-1989*, Stanford: Stanford University Press, 1990.

—— *History and Social Theory*, Oxford: Polity Press, 1992.

Castells, M., *The Urban Question: A Marxist Approach*, London: Edward Arnold, 1979.

Chevalier, L., *Labouring Classes and Dangerous Classes in Paris during the First Half of the Nineteenth Century*, London: Routledge and Kegan Paul, 1973.

Chia, F., *The Babas*, Singapore: Times Book International, 1980.

Chinatown: An Album of a Singapore Community, Times Books International, Singapore: Archives and Oral History Department, 1983.

Clodd, H. P., *Malaya's First British Pioneer: The Life of Francis Light*, London: Luzac and Co., 1948.

Cojuangco, M. De Los Reyes, *Kris of Valor: The Samal Balangingi's Defiance and Diaspora*, Manila: Manisan, 1993.

Comaroff, J. and J. Comaroff, *Ethnology and the Historical Imagination*, Boulder: Westview Press, 1992.

Combes, F., *Historia de las Islas de Mindanao y Jolo*, 1667, Madrid: W. E. Retana & P. Pastells, 1897.

Conrad, J., *The Rescue*, London: J. M. Dent and Sons, 1924.

——*Almayer's Folly: A Story of an Eastern River*, London: Penguin, 1976.

——*An Outcast of the Islands*, London: Penguin, 1975.

——*A Personal Record*, London: J. M. Dent and Sons, 1950.

——*Lord Jim*, London: Blackwood, 1900.

——*The Shadow Line: A Confession (and) Within the Tides: Tales*, London: J. M. Dent, 1950.

Crawford, R. H., M. Clark and G. Blainey, *Making History*, Fitzroy: Penguin Books, 1985.

Cuylenburg, J., *Singapore through Sunshine and Shadow*, Singapore: Heinemann, 1981.

Dalby, L. C., *Geisha*, Berkeley: University of California Press, 1983.

Darton, R., *The Great Cat Massacre and Other Episodes in French Cultural History*, New York: Vintage Books, 1985.

de Comyn, T., *State of the Philippines in 1810 being an historical statistical and descriptive account of the interesting portion on the Indian Archipelago*, Manila: Filipiniana Book Guild, 1969.

de Ibañez y Garcia, L., *Mi Cautiverio; carto que con motive del que sufrio entre los moros piratas Joloanos y Samales en 1857*, Madrid: G. Allhambra, 1859.

de la Escosura, P., *Memoria sobre Filipinas y Jolo redactada en 1863 y 1864*, Madrid: Imprenta de Manuel G. Hernandez, 1882.

de Sainte-Croix Renouard, F., *Voyage Commercial et Politique aux Indes Orientales, aux lies Philippines, a la Chine, avec des nations sur la Cochin Chine et le Touquin, pendant les annees 1803, 1804, 1805, 1806 et 1807*, Paris: Clement, 1810.

Despres L. A. (ed.), *Ethnicity and Resource Competition in Plural Societies*, The Hague: Mouton, 1975.

Doeppers, D. and P. Xenos, *Population and History: The Demographic Origins of the Modern Philippines*, Madison: University of Wisconsin Press, CSEAS, 1998.

Dumont d'Urville, J. S. C., *Voyages au pole sud et dans l'Oceanie sur Les Corvettes l'Astrolabe et la Zelee…pendant les annees 1837–1838–1839–1840*, Paris: Gide et J. Baudry, 1841–1846.

Dunne, J., *The Way of All the Earth*, London: Sheldon Press, 1972.

Fairbank, J. K., E. O. Reischauer and A. M. Craig, *East Asia, Tradition and Transformation*, London: George Allen & Unwin, 1973.

Falconer, J., *A Vision of the Past: A History of Early Photography in Singapore and Malaysia, The Photographs of G. R. Lambert and Co., 1880–1910*, Singapore: Times Editions, 1987.

Fernandez, P., *History of the Church in the Philippines, 1521–1898*, Manila: National Book Store, 1979.

Forrest, T., *A Voyage to New Guinea and the Moluccas from Balambangan: Including an Account of Magindano, Sooloo and Other Islands*, London: G. Scott, 1779.

Foster, R. and O. Ranum, *Deviants and the Abandoned in French Society*, Baltimore: Johns Hopkins University Press, 1978.

Frank, A. G., *World Accumulation, 1492–1789*, London: Macmillan Press, 1978.

Freedman, M., *The Study of Chinese Society: Essays by Maurice Freedman*, Stanford: Stanford University Press, 1979.

Furber, H., *John Company at Work: A Study of European Expansion in India in the Late Eighteenth Century*, Cambridge: Harvard University Press, 1951.

Ginsburg, C., *Clues, Myths and the Historical Method*, Baltimore: Johns Hopkins University Press, 1989.

Glamman, K., *Dutch Asiatic Trade, 1620–1740*, The Hague: Nijhoff, 1958.

Greenberg, M., *British Trade and the Opening of China, 1800–1842*, London: Cambridge University Press, 1951.

Gronewold, S., *Beautiful Merchandise: Prostitution in China 1860–1936*, New York: The Haworth Press, 1982.

Gullick, J., *Indigenous Political Systems of Western Malaya*, London: The Athlone Press, 1958.

Hane, M., *Peasants, Rebels and Outcastes: The Underside of Modern Japan*, New York: Pantheon Books, 1982.

Hodgson, M. G. S., *The Venture of Islam 3*, Chicago: The University of Chicago Press, 1974.

—— *Rethinking World History, Essays on Europe, Islam and World History*, Cambridge: Cambridge University Press, 1995.

Horridge, G. A., *The Design of the Planked Boats of the Moluccas; the Lambu or Prahu Bot, the Konjo Boatbuilders and the Bugis Prahus of South Sulawesi*, Maritime Monograph and Reports Nos. 39 and 40, Greenwich: National Maritime Museum, 1978–1979.

—— *The Lashed-lug Boat of the Eastern Archipelagoes the Alcina MS and the Lomblem Whaling Boats*, Maritime Monograph and Reports No. 54, Greenwich: National Maritime Museum, 1982.

—— *The Prahu: Traditional Sailing Boat of Indonesia*, Singapore: Oxford University Press, 1985.

Jacobs, T. J., *Scenes, Incidents and Adventures in the Pacific Ocean, or the Islands of the Australasian Seas, during the Cruise of the Clipper, Margaret Oakley*, New York: Harper and Brothers, 1844.

Javellana, S. J., *Fortress of Empire: Spanish Colonial Fortifications of the Philippines, 1565–1898*, photographs by Jose Ma, Lorenzo P. Tan, Makati City: Bookmark, 1997.

Junker, L., *Raiding, Trading and Feasting: The Political Economy of Philippine Chiefdoms*, Quezon City: Ateneo de Manila University Press, 2000.

Katsumi Mori, *Jin Shin BaiBai*, Tokyo: Shibundo, 1959.

Kaye, B., *Upper Nankin Street Singapore. A Sociological Study of Chinese Households Living in a Densely Populated Area*, Singapore: University of Malaya Press, 1961.

Kiefer, T., *The Tausug: Violence and Law in a Philippine Moslem Society*, New York: Holt, Rinehart & Winston, 1972.

Lao She, *Rickshaw* (the novel *Lo-T'o Hsiang Tsu*), trans. Jean M. James, Honolulu: University Press of Hawaii, 1979.

Leach, E. R., *The Political Systems of Highland Burma, A Study of Kachin Social Structure*, London: London School of Economics and Political Science, 1954.

Lehman, F. K., *The Structure of Chin Society*, Studies of Anthropology, No. 3, Urbana: University of Illinois Press, 1963.

Llewellyn-Jones, D., *Sex and V.D.*, London: Faber & Faber, 1974.

Lombard, D., *Le Sultanat d'Atjeh au temps d'Iskandar Muda, 1607–1636*, Paris: Maisonneuve, 1967.

Low Ngiong Ing, *Chinese Jetsam on a Tropic Shore*, Singapore: Eastern Universities Press, 1974.

Majul, C. A., *Muslims in the Philippines*, Quezon City: University of the Philippines Press, 1973.

Mak Lau Fong, *The Sociology of Secret Societies: A Study of Chinese Secret Societies in Singapore and Peninsular Malaysia*, Kuala Lumpur: Oxford University Press, 1981.

Makepeace, W. E., R. St J. Braddell and G. E. Brooke (eds), *One Hundred Years of Singapore*, London: John Murray, 1921; reprinted Singapore: Oxford University Press, 1991.

Manderson, L., *Women, Politics and Change. The Kaum Ibu UMNO, Malaysia 1945–1972*, Kuala Lumpur: Oxford University Press, 1980

McHugh, P., *Prostitution and Victorian Social Reform*, New York: St Martin's Press, 1980.

Meillassoux, C. (ed.), *The Development of Indigenous Trade and Markets in West Africa*, London: Oxford University Press, 1971.

Milburn, W., *Oriental Commerce; containing a geographical description of the principal places in the East Indies, China, and Japan, with their produce, manufactures and trade, including the coasting or country trade from port to port; also the rise and progress of the trade of the various European nations with the Eastern world, particularly that of the English East India Company from the discovery of the passage round the Cape of Good Hope to the present period; with an account of the company's establishments, revenues, debts, assets, at home and abroad*, London: Black, Parry and Company, 1813.

Mills, L. A., *British Malaya, 1824–1867*, originally published 1925, Kuala Lumpur: Oxford in Asia, Historical Reprints, 1967.

Montero y Vidal, J., *Historia de la Pirateria Malayo Mahometans en Mindanao, Jolo y Borneo*, 2 vols, Madrid: Imprenta de M. Tello, 1888.

Morisaki Kazue, *Karayuki-san*, Tokyo: Asaki Shinbunsha, 1976.

Morton, R. S., *Venereal Diseases*, London: Penguin Books, 1966.

Mundy, R., *Narrative of Events in Borneo and Celebes down to the Occupation of Labuan, from the Journals of James Brooke, esq., Together with a Narrative of the*

> Operations of H.M.S. Iris by Capt. Rodney Mundy, R.N., London: John Murray, 1848.

Nanyo no Gojunen Shingaporu o Chusin ni Doho Katsuyaku, Tokyo: Nanyo oyobi Nippon Jinsha, 1937.

Ngo Vinh Long, *Vietnamese Women in Society and Revolution: 1. The French Colonial Period*, Cambridge, Mass: Vietnam Resource Center, 1974.

Nimmo, H. A., *The Sea People of Sulu*, London: Chandler Publishing Company, 1972.

Osborn, D. K. (ed.), *A Joseph Campbell Companion*, New York: Harper Collins, 1991.

Osborn, S., *My Journal in Malayan Waters*, London: Routledge, Warne and Routledge, 1861.

Owen, N. G., *Prosperity without Progress: Manila Hemp and Material Life in the Colonial Philippines*, Berkeley: University of California Press, 1984.

Parrish, C., *The Image of Asia in Children's Literature: 1814–1964*, Centre for Southeast Asian Studies, Melbourne: Monash University, 1977.

Pelras, C,. *The Bugis*, Oxford: Blackwell, 1996.

Perkins, J., *Kampong Glam, Spirit of a Community*, Singapore: Sendirian Berhad, Times Publishing, 1982.

Petrie, G., *A Singular Iniquity: The Campaigns of Josephine Butler*, London: Macmillan, 1971.

Pires, T., c. 1468–c. 1540, *The Suma Oriental of Tome Pires: An account of the East... and, The book of Francisco Rodrigues: Rutter of a voyage in the Red Sea / tr. from the Portuguese MS in the Bibliotheque de la Chambre des Deputes, Paris, and ed. by Armando Cortesao*, Nendeln, Liechtenstein: Kraus Reprint, 1967, reprint of Hakluyt Society, 1944.

Raskin, J., *The Mythology of Imperialism*, New York: Random House, 1971.

Reid, A., *Slavery, Bondage and Dependency in Southeast Asia*, St Lucia: University of Queensland Press, 1983.

Reid, A., *Southeast Asia in the Age of Commerce 1450–1680: Expansion and Crisis*, 2 vols, New Haven: Yale University Press, 1993.

Rickshaws in Calcutta, UNNAYAN in association with T. H. Thomas, Calcutta: UNNAYAN, 1981.

Rutter, O., *The Pirate Wind Tales of the Sea-Robbers of Malaya*, Singapore: Oxford University Press, 1986.

Said, E., *Orientalism*, London: Routledge and Kegan Paul, 1978.

Saleeby, N., *Studies in Moro History, Law and Religion*, Manila: Bureau of Printing, 1906.

Samuel, R. (ed.), *People's History and Socialist Theory*, London: Routledge and Kegan Paul, 1981.

Sandin, B., *The Sea Dayaks of Borneo before White Rajah Rule*, London: Macmillan, 1967.

Schama, S., *Dead Certainties: Unwarranted Speculations*, London: Granta Books, 1992.

Scott, W. H., *Slavery in the Philippines*, Manila: De La Salle University Press, 1991.

——*Barangay: Sixteenth Century Philippine Culture and Society*, Quezon City: Ateneo de Manila University Press, 1994.

Sears, L. (ed.), *Autonomous Histories, Particular Truths: Essays in Honor of John Smail*, Madison: University of Wisconsin, 1993.

Sherry, N., *Conrad's Eastern World*, Cambridge: Cambridge University Press, 1966.
Singapore Retrospect through Postcards: 1900-1930, Singapore: Sin Chew Jit Poh and Archives and Oral History Department, 1982.
Singh, S. B., *European Agency Houses in Bengal, 1783-1833*, Calcutta: K. L. Mukhopadhyay, 1966.
Song Ong Siang, *One Hundred Years History of the Chinese in Singapore*, London Methuen, 1923; reprinted Kuala Lumpur: University of Malaya Press, 1967, and Singapore: Oxford University Press, 1987.
Southon, M., *The Navel of the Perahu: Meaning and Values in the Maritime Trading Economy of a Butonese Village*, Canberra: Research School of Pacific and Asian Studies, 1995.
St John, S., *Life in the Forests of the Far East*, London: Smith Elder and Company, 1862.
Stallybrass P. and A. White, *The Politics and Poetics of Transgression*, Ithaca: Cornell University Press, 1986.
Steinberg D. J. (ed.), *In Search of Southeast Asia: A Modern History*, New York: Praeger, 1971.
Sydney, R. H. J., *Malay Land*, London: C. Palmer, 1926.
Ta Chen, *Emigrant Communities in South China. A Study of Overseas Migration and Its Influence on Standards of Living and Social Change*, New York: Secretariat, Institute of Pacific Relations, 1940.
Tarling, N., *Piracy and Politics in the Malay World: A Study of British Imperialism in Nineteenth-century Southeast Asia*, Singapore: Donald Moore, and Melbourne: F. W. Cheshire, 1963.
Taylor, J. G., *The Social World of Batavia European and Eurasian in Dutch Asia*, Madison: The University of Wisconsin Press, 1983.
The Century Dictionary, London: The Times, 1899.
Tregonning, K. G., *A History of Modern Sabah 1881-1963*, Singapore: University of Malaya Press, 1966.
Turnbull, C. M., *A History of Singapore 1819-1975*, Kuala Lumpur: Oxford University Press, 1977.
Van Leur, J. C., *Indonesian Trade and Society*, Hague: Van Hoeve, 1967.
Walkowitz, J. R., *Prostitution and Victorian Society: Women, Class and the State*, London: Cambridge University Press, 1980.
Wallace, A. R., *The Malay Archipelago: The Land of the Orang-Utan, and the Bird of Paradise: A Narrative of Travel with Studies of Man and Nature*, 2 vols, London: Macmillan, 1869.
Wallerstein, I., *The Capitalist World-Economy*, Cambridge: Cambridge University Press, 1979.
Warren, J. F., *The Sulu Zone 1768-1898: The Dynamics of External Trade, Slavery and Ethnicity in the Transformation of a Southeast Asian Maritime State*, Singapore: Singapore University Press, 1981; reprinted, Quezon City: New Day Publishers, Philippines, 1985.
——*Rickshaw Coolie: A People's History of Singapore (1880-1940)*, Singapore: Oxford University Press, 1986.
——*At the Edge of Southeast Asian History*, Quezon City: New Day Press, 1987.

—— *Ah Ku and Karayuki-san: Prostitution in Singapore 1870–1940*, Singapore: Oxford University Press, 1993.
—— *The Sulu Zone, the World Capitalist Economy and the Historical Imagination*, Amsterdam: VU University Press/CASA, 1998.
—— *Iranun and Balangingi, Globalization, Maritime Raiding and the Birth of Ethnicity*, Singapore: Singapore University Press, 2002.
Wolf, E. R., *Europe and the People Without History*, Berkeley: University of California Press, 1982.
Wright, L. R., *The Origins of British Borneo*, Hong Kong: Hong Kong University Press, 1970.
Yamamuro Gunpei, *A Theory of Social Purification*, Tokyo: Chuo Koron, Kakuskin-ron, 1977.
Yamazaki T., *Sandakan Hachiban Shokan-Teihen Joseishi Josho*, Tokyo: Chikuma Shoboo, 1972.
—— *Sandakan no Haka*, Tokyo: Bungei-shunjuu, 1977.
Yano Tooru, *Nippon-no Nanyo Shikan*, Tokyo: Chunkou Shinsho, 1979.
Yap Pheng Geek, *Scholar, Banker, Gentleman Soldier, The Reminiscences of Dr Yap Pheng Geek*, Singapore: Times Books International, 1982.
Yen Ching-Hwang, *A Social History of the Chinese in Singapore and Malaya, 1800–1911*, Singapore: Oxford University Press, 1986.
Yvan, M., *Six Months among the Malays and a Year in China*, London: James Blackwood, 1855.
Zunz, O. (ed.), *Reliving the Past: The Worlds of Social History*, Chapel Hill: University of North Carolina Press, 1985.

Articles

Abeyasekere, S., 'Women as cultural intermediaries in nineteenth century Batavia', in *Women's Work and Women's Roles: Economics and Everyday Life in Indonesia, Malaysia and Singapore*, ed. L. Manderson, The Australian National University, Development Studies Centre Monograph No. 32, Canberra, 1983, pp. 15–29.
Amin, S., 'Sous-developpement et dependence en Afrique noire', in *Partisans*, vol. 64 (1972): 3–34.
Barthes, R., 'The photographic message', in *The Camera Viewed: Writings on Twentieth Century Photography*, ed. P. R. Petruck, vol. 2, Dutton, New York, 1979.
Becker, H., 'Photography and sociology', in *Studies in the Anthropology of Visual Communication*, vol. 6 (1974): 3–26.
'Berigten omtrent den zeeroof in den Nederlandsch-Indischen Archipel, 1857', in *TBG*, vol. XV (1868–1872): 436–57.
'Berigten omtrent den zeeroof in den Nederlandsch-Indischen Archipel, 1858', in *TBG*, vol. XX (1873): 302–26.
Best, J., 'Careers in brothel prostitution: St Paul, 1865–1883', in *The Journal of Interdisciplinary History*, vol. 12, no. 4 (Spring 1982): 597–617.
Blythe, W. L., 'Historical sketch of Chinese labour in Malaya', in *Journal of the Malayan Branch Royal Asiatic Society*, vol. xxx, no. 1 (1947): 64–114.
Brandon, J. J., 'High-seas piracy is booming—it's time to fight harder', in *The Christian Science Monitor*, 27 December 2000.

Bridenthal, R., 'The dialectics of production and reproduction in history', in *Radical America*, vol. 10 (March–April 1976): 3–11.
'Coastal resources in crisis', in *Down to Earth—International Campaign for Ecological Justice in Indonesia, Newsletter*, vol. 45, May 2000.
Coquery-Vidrovitch, C., 'An African mode of production', in *Critique of Anthropology*, vols 4 and 5 (1975): 37–71.
Coquery-Vidrovitch, C., 'Recherches sur un mode de production Africain', in *La Pensee*, vol. 144 (1969): 61–78.
Cullinane M. and P. Xenos, 'The growth of population in Cebu during the Spanish era: Constructing regional demography from local sources', in *Population and History: The Demographic Origins of the Modern Philippines*, ed. D. Doeppers and Xenos, University of Wisconsin, Center for Southeast Asian Studies, Madison, 1998: 71–138.
Davin, A., 'Women and history', in *The Body Politic: Writings from the Women's Liberation Movement*, ed. M. Wandor, Xerox, London, 1969–1972: 217–23.
Davis, N. Z., '"Women's history" in transition; the European case', in *Feminist Studies*, vol. 3, nos. 3–4 (1975): 83–103.
Dick, H., 'Indonesian economic history inside out', in *Review of Indonesian and Malaysian Affairs*, vol. 27, (1993): 1–12.
Dobbin, C., 'The search for women in Indonesian history', in *Kartini Centenary: Indonesian Women Then and Now*, ed. A. T. Zainer'ddin, et al., Monash University, Melbourne, 1980, pp. 42–51.
Eames, A., 'Modern piracy not so yo ho ho', in the *Times*, 9 May 1998.
'Economic study of the Peking ricshaw puller', in *China Economic Monthly*, vol. 3, no. 6 (June 1926): 253–65.
Ee, J., 'Chinese migration to Singapore, 1896–1941', in *Journal of Southeast Asian History*, vol. 2 (1961): 33–51.
Elkins, S., 'Slavery and its aftermath in the Western World', in *Ciba Foundation Symposium on Caste and Race: Comparative Approaches*, ed. A. V. S. de Reuck and J. Knight, J. & A. Churchill, London, 1967.
Ellen, E., 'Bringing piracy to account', in *Jane's Navy International*, vol. 102–3 (April 1 1997): 29.
Emmerson, D. K., 'Issues in Southeast Asian history: Room for interpretation—a review article', in *Journal of Asian Studies*, vol. XL, no. 1 (November 1980): 43–86.
Fairbank, J. K., E. O. Reischauer and A. M. Craig, 'Economic study of the Peking ricshaw puller', in *China Economic Monthly*, vol. 3, no. 6 (June 1926).
Frake, C. O., 'The genesis of kinds of people in the Sulu Archipelago', in *Language and Cultural Description*, Stanford University Press, Stanford, 1980, pp. 314–18.
——'Abu Sayyaf displays of violence and the proliferation of contested identities among Philippine Muslims', in *American Anthropologist*, vol. 100, no. 1 (1998): 41–54.
Geoghegan, W. H., 'Balangingi Samal', in *Ethnic Groups of Insular Southeast Asia*, ed. F. M. Lebar, Human Relations Area Files Press, New Haven, 1975, vol. 2: 6–9.
Giddens, A., 'Affluence, poverty and the idea of a post-scarcity society', in *Development and Change*, vol. 27 (1996): 365–77.
Greenough, P. R., 'Famine', in *Encyclopedia of Asian History*, vol. 1, ed. Ainslie T. Embree, Charles Scribner's Sons, New York, 1988: 459.

'Guidance to ship owners and ship operators, ship masters and crews for preventing and suppressing acts of piracy and armed robbery against ships', IMO, MSC/Circ. 623, 16 June 1999.

Hanlon, M., 'Thailand cracks down on pirates who terrorize fleeing boat people', in *Toronto Star*, 4 January 1987.

Harsono, Andreas, 'New wave pirates rule dark seas', in the *West Australian*, 17 April 1999.

Heersink, C., 'Environmental adaptations in southern Sulawesi', in *Environmental Challenges in South-East Asia*, ed. V. T. King. Curzon, London, 1988, pp. 95–120.

Hershatter, G., 'The hierarchy of Shanghai prostitution, 1870–1949', in *Modern China*, vol. 15, no. 4 (1989): 463–98.

Hirata, L. Cheng, 'Free, indentured, enslaved: Chinese prostitutes in nineteenth century America', in *Signs: Journal of Women in Culture and Society*, vol. 5, no. 1 (1979): 3–29.

Hunt, J., 'Some particulars relating to Sulu in the archipelago of Felicia', in *Notices of the Indian Archipelago and Adjacent Countries*, ed. J. H. Moor, Frank Cass and Co. Ltd, London, 1968 (first edition 1837): 31–60.

'Indonesia's dangerous waters: Pirate attacks at record high', in *Deutsche Presse-Agentur*, 4 January 2001.

'Intelligence File: Indonesia', in *MaritimeSecurity.com*, <http://www.maritimesecurity.com/research/intel_file_indonesia.htm>, 2001, accessed 20 May 2001.

'Intelligence File: Pacific Ocean', in *MaritimeSecurity.com*, <http://www.maritimesecurity.com/research/pacific_ocean.htm>, accessed 15 July 2000.

'Intelligence File: Singapore,' *MaritimeSecurity.com*, <http://www.maritimesecurity.com/research/intel_file_singapore.htm>, accessed 15 July 2000.

International Chamber of Commerce (ICC), 'Weekly piracy report,' <http://www.iccwbo.org/home/news_archives/1999/weekly_piracy_report.asp>, 4–10 July 2000, accessed 24 October 2006.

'International Maritime Bureau warns for pirates in Singapore Strait', in *Alexander's Gas and Oil Connections*, vol. 4, no. 12, (30 June 1999), <http://www.gasandoil.com/GOC/reports/rex92790.htm>, accessed 12 March 2007.

Jansen, A. J. F., 'Aantekeningen omtrent Sollok en de Solloksche Zeeroovers', *Tijdschrift voor Indische Taal-, Land -en Volkenkunde, uitgegeven door het (Koninklijk) Bataviaasch Genootschap van Kunsten en Wetenschappen*, vol. 7 (1858): 212–39.

'Japanese women abroad', in *Japan Weekly Mail*, 30 May 1896.

Keesing, R. M., 'Asian cultures?' in *Asian Studies Review*, vol. 15, no. 2 (1991): 43–50.

Kelly-Gadol, J. 'The social relations of the sexes: Methodological implications of women's history', in *Signs: Journal of Women in Culture and Society*, vol. 2, no. 4 (1976): 809–24.

—— 'The doubled vision of feminist theory: A postscript to the "Women and Power" Conference', in *Feminist Studies*, vol. 6, no. 1 (Spring 1979): 24–227.

Kiefer, T., 'Traditional states of Borneo and the Southern Philippines', in *Borneo Research Bulletin*, ed. Clifford Sather, vol. 3 (1971): 46–50.

—— 'The Tausug polity and the Sultanate of Sulu: A segmentary state in the southern Philippines', in *Sulu Studies*, no. 1 (1972): 19–64.

Kuder, E., 'The Moros in the Philippines', in *Far Eastern Quarterly*, vol. 4, no. 2 (1946): 119–26.

Leach, E. R., 'The frontiers of Burma', in *Comparative Studies in Society and History*, vol. III, no. 1 (1960): 49–68.

—— 'Caste, class and slavery—the taxonomic problem', in *Caste and Race: Comparative Approaches*, ed. A. de Reuck and J. Knight, Churchill, London, 1967, pp. 83–94.

Lehman, F. K., 'Ethnic categories in Burma and the theory of social systems', in *Southeast Asian Tribes, Minorities and Nations*, ed. P. Kunstadter, vol. 1, Princeton University Press, Princeton (1967): 93–124.

Lerner, G., 'Placing women in history: definitions and challenges', in *Feminist Studies*, vol. 3 (Fall 1975): 5–14.

—— 'Placing women in history; a 1975 perspective', in *Liberating Women's History*, ed. B. A. Carroll, University of Illinois Press, Chicago, 1976: 357–67.

—— 'The majority finds its past', in *Current History*, vol. 70, no. 416 (1976).

Lieberman, V., 'An age of commerce in Southeast Asia? Problems of regional coherence—a review article', in *The Journal of Asian Studies*, vol. 54, no. 3 (1995): 796–807.

Lougee, C. C., 'Modern European history', in *Signs: Journal of Women in Culture and Society*, vol. 2, no. 3 (Spring 1977): 628–50.

Macknight C. C. and Mukhlis, 'A Bugis manuscript about *prahus*', in *Archipel*, vol. 18 (1979): 271–82.

McCarthy, J., 'Why Indonesia is now easier to like', in the *Age*, Melbourne, 21 November 2000.

Majul, C. A., 'Political and historical notes on the old Sulu Sultanate', in *Journal of the Malaysian Branch of the Royal Asiatic Society*, vol. XXVIII, pt. I (1965): 23–43.

'Malaysian marine police capture Indonesian pirates', in *ABC online*, 17 December 2000, World News Section.

Mallari, F., S. J., 'Muslim raids in Bicol 1580–1792', in *Philippine Studies*, vol. 34, (1986): 257–86.

—— S. J., 'Peneranda and the Bicol Defense System', in *Kinaadman*, vol. 14, no. 2, (1992): 105–22.

Marcus, G., 'Problems of ethnography in the modern world system', in *Writing Culture. The Poetics and Politics of Ethnography*, ed. J. Clifford and G. Marcus, University of California Press, Berkeley, 1986: 165–193.

Matthews, S., 'Chinese photography: Notes towards a cross-cultural analysis of a western medium', in *Afterimage*, vol. 9, issue 6 (January 1982).

Mednick, M., 'Some problems of Moro history and political organization', in *Philippine Sociological Review*, vol. 5 (1957): 39–52.

Moerman, M., 'Accomplishing ethnicity', in *Ethnomethodology*, ed. R. Turner, Penguin Books, London, 1974: 54–68.

—— 'Who are the Lue?', in *American Anthropologist*, vol. LXVII (1965): 1215–30.

Niccol-Jones, S. E., 'Report on the problem of prostitution in Singapore', CETWCE, Geneva, 1941.

Ong Keng Sen, in program booklet, *Broken Birds: An Epic Longing*, TheatreWorks Production, Fort Canning Green, March 1995.

Owen, N. G., 'Textile displacement and the status of women in Southeast Asia', in *The Past in Southeast Asia's Present*, ed. G. P. Means, Secretariat, Canadian Society for Asian Studies, Canadian Council for Southeast Asian Studies, Ottawa, 1978: 157–70.

Padgug, R. A., 'Problems in the theory of slavery and slave society', in *Science and Society*, vol. 40 (1976): 3–27.

'The perils of rising piracy in Asia', in *Jane's Defence Weekly*, 15 November 2000.

Person, Y., 'Enquete d'une chronologie Ivoirienne', in *The Historian in Tropical Africa*, ed. J. Vansina, R. Mauny and L. U. Thomas, Oxford University Press, London, 1964.

'Piracy and armed robbery at sea', in *Focus on IMO*, January 2000: 4.

'The piracy and slave trade of the Indian Archipelago', in *Journal of Indian Archipelago and Eastern Asia*, vol. 4 (1850): 45–52, 144, 162, 400–10, 617–28, 734–46.

'Piracy resurgence on the high seas', in the *Australian*, 8 November 1978.

'Pirates attack ships near southern Malaysian port', *Associated Press*, 4 January 2001.

Prewitt, K., 'Presidential items', in *Items—Social Science Research Council*, vol. 50, no. 1 (1996): 15–18.

Pryer, W., 'Notes on north eastern Borneo and the Sulu Islands', in *Royal Geographical Society*, vol. 5 (1883): 90–6.

——'Diary of a trip up the Kinabatangan', in *Sabah Society Journal*, vol. 5 (1970): 117–26.

Rapp, R., E. Ross and R. Bridenthal, 'Examining family history', in *Feminist Studies*, vol. 15, no. 1 (Spring 1979): 183–9.

Resink, G. J., 'De archipel voor Joseph Conrad', in *Bijdragen tot de Taal-Land-en Volkenkunde van Nederlandsch-Indie*, vol. CXV, no. II (1959): 192–208.

——'The eastern archipelago under Joseph Conrad's western eyes', in *Indonesia's History between the Myths*, ed. G. J. Resink, The Hague: Van Hoeve, 1968: 307–23.

Samuel, R., 'Local history and oral history', *History Workshop*, vol. 1 (Spring 1976): 192–208.

——'What is social history?', in *What Is History Today?* ed. J. Gardiner, Atlantic Highlands, N.J.: Humanities Press, 1988, pp. 42–48.

Schama, S., 'In search of history's muse', in *Dialogue*, vol. 9, no. 3 (1992): 62–66.

Schmidt D. B. and E. R. Schmidt, 'The invisible woman: The historian as professional magician', in *Liberating Women's History*, ed. B. A. Carroll, Chicago, University of Illinois Press, 1976, pp. 42–54.

Schumsky, N. L., 'Tacit acceptance: Respectable Americans and segregated prostitutes 1870–1910', in *Journal of Social History*, vol. 19, no. 4 (1986): 665–79.

Scott, J., 'The state and the people who move around', in *IIAS Newsletter 20*, 1999: 3, 45.

Scott, W. H., 'Boat building and seamanship in classic Philippine society', in *Philippine Studies*, vol. 30, no. 3 (1982): 335–76.

Sissons, D. C., '*Karayuki-san*: Japanese prostitutes in Australia, 1887–1916-1', in *Historical Studies*, vol. 17, no. 68 (1977): 323–41.

Sociats y Garin, A., 'Memoria sobre el Archipielago de Jolo', in *Boletin de la Sociedad Geografica de Madrid*, vol. 10 (1881): 110–33, 161–97.

'South sea piracy: dead men tell no tales', in *The Economist*, <http://www.economist.com/displayStory.cfm?Story_ID=327568>, 16 December 1999, accessed 24 October 2006.

Spivak, G. C., 'French feminism in an international frame', in *Feminist Readings: French Texts, American Contexts, Yale French Studies*, ed. C. Gaudin, New Haven, Yale University Press, vol. 62, (1981): 154-84.

Spoehr, A., 'Port town and hinterlands in the Pacific Islands', in *American Anthropologist*, vol. LXII (1960): 568-92.

Tan, A., 'The Asian waters, sea pirates eschew eye patches, steal ships via internet', in *Christian Science Monitor*, 13 June 1996, p. 7.

Tarling, N., 'Some notes on the historiography of British Borneo', in *Southeast Asian History and Historiography*, ed. C. D. Cowan and O. W. Wolters, Ithaca, Cornell University Press, 1976: 285-95.

Terami-Wada, M., '*Karayuki-san* of Manila; 1890-1920', in *Philippine Studies*, vol. 34 (1986): 287-316.

Terray, E., 'Long-distance exchange and the formation of the state: The case of the Abron Kingdom of Gyaman', in *Economy and Society*, vol. 3 (1974): 316-45.

Trocki, C. A., 'Piracy in the Malay world', in *Encyclopedia of Asian History*, vol. 3, ed. Ainslie T. Embree, New York: Charles Scribners, 1988.

Van Hoevell, W. R., 'De zeerooverijen der Soloerezen', in *Tijdschrift voor Nederlandsche Indies*, vol. II (1860): 99-105.

Van Marle, A., 'De rol van de buitenlandse avonturier', in *Bijdragen en Mededelingen Betreffende de Geschiedenis der Nederlanden*, vol. LXXXVI, no. 1 (1971): 32-9.

Velthoen, E., 'Wanderers, robbers and bad folk: The politics of violence, protection and trade in Eastern Sulawesi 1750-1850', in *The Last Stand of Autonomous States, 1750-1870: Responses to Modernity in the Diverse Worlds of Southeast Asia and Korea*, ed. Anthony Reid, London, Macmillan, 1997, pp. 367-88.

Vicomte de Pages, P., 'Travels round the world in the years 1767, 1768, 1769, 1770, 1771', in *Travel Accounts of the Islands 1513-1787*, The Filipiniana Book Guild, Manila, 1971: 127-84.

Wang Gung-wu, 'Southeast Asian Hua-Ch'iao in Chinese History Writing', in *Journal of Southeast Asian Studies*, vol. 12, no. 1 (1981): 1-14.

Warren, J. F., 'Joseph Conrad's fiction as Southeast Asian history: Trade and politics in East Borneo in the late nineteenth century', in *The Brunei Museum Journal*, (1977): 21-34.

—— 'Sino-Sulu trade in the late eighteenth and nineteenth centuries', in *Philippine Studies*, vol. 25 (1977): 73-93.

—— 'Slave markets and exchange in the Malay World: The Sulu Sultanate, 1770-1878', in *Journal of Southeast Asian Studies*, vol. 8 (1977): 162-75.

—— 'Who were the Balangingi Samal? Slave raiding and ethnogenesis in nineteenth century Sulu', in *Journal of Asian Studies*, vol. 37, no. 3 (1978): 477-90.

—— 'The Sulu Zone: Commerce and evolution of a multi-ethnic polity, 1768-1898', in *Archipel*, vol. 18 (1979): 223-30.

—— 'Slavery and the impact of external trade: The Sulu Sultanate in the nineteenth century', in *Philippine Social History, Global Trade and Local Transformation*, ed. E. de Jesus and A. McCoy, Quezon City: Ateneo de Manila University Press, 1982: 414-44.

——'Living on the razor's edge: The rickshawmen of Singapore between two wars, 1919-1939', in *Bulletin of Concerned Asian Scholars*, vol. 16, no. 4 (October-December 1984): 38-51.
——'Rickshaw coolie: An exploration of the underside of a Chinese city outside China: Singapore', in *Itinerario: European Journal of Overseas History*, vol. 1, no. 2 (1984): 80-91.
——'Social history and the photograph: Glimpses of the Singapore rickshaw coolie in the early 20th century', in *Journal of the Malaysian Branch of the Royal Asiatic Society*, vol. 58, no. 1 (1985): 29-43.
——'The spiral of failure: Suicide among Singapore rickshaw coolies', *Southeast Asian Journal of Social Science*, vol. 13, no. 2 (October 1985): 47-66.
——'The *prahus* of the Sulu zone', in *The Brunei Museum Journal* (1985): 42-53.
——'The Singapore rickshaw pullers: The social organization of a coolie occupation, 1880-1940', in *Journal of Southeast Asian Studies*, vol. 15, no. 1 (1986): 1-16.
——'Placing women in Southeast Asian history: The case of Oichi and the study of prostitution in Singapore society', in *At the Edge of Southeast Asian History*, New Day Press, Quezon City, 1987, pp. 148-64.
——'Rickshaw coolie: An exploration of the underside of a Chinese city outside China, Singapore, 1880-1940', in *At the Edge of Southeast Asian History*, New Day Press, Quezon City, 1987, pp. 73-81.
——'Retrieving prostitutes lives. Source materials and an approach for writing the history of the *ah ku* and *karayuki san* of Singapore', in *Itinerario: European Journal of Overseas History*, vol. 8, no. 1 (1990): 96-122.
——'Slavery in Southeast Asia', in *A Historical Guide to World Slavery*, ed. Seymour Drescher and Stanley L. Engermen, Oxford University Press, New York, 1998, pp. 80-87.
Wartofsky, M., 'Picturing and representation', in *Perception and Representation*, ed. C. F. Nodine and D. F. Fisher, Praeger, New York, 1979: 272-83.
——'Art, history and perception', in *Perceiving Artworks*, ed. J. Fisher, Temple University Press, Philadelphia, 1980, pp. 23-41.
——'Cameras can't see: Representation, photography, and human vision', in *Afterimage*, vol. 7, no. 9 (April 1980): 8-9.
——'Visual scenarios: The role of representation in visual perception', in *The Perception of Pictures*, ed. M. A. Hagan, vol. 2, Academic Press, New York, 1980, pp. 131-52.
Wendover, R. F., 'The Balangingi pirates', in *Philippine Magazine*, vol. 38, no. 8 (1941): 337-8.
Wilkes, C., 'Jolo and the Sulus', in *The Philippine Islands, 1493-1898*, ed. E. H. Blair and J. A. Robertson, Arthur H. Clark, Cleveland, 1903-1909: vol. 43, 128-92.
Wong Lin Ken, 'The trade of Singapore, 1819-1869', in *Journal of the Malaysian Branch of the Royal Asiatic Society*, vol. 33, pt. 4 (1960): 1-315.
'Worldwide Maritime Piracy', in *MaritimeSecurity.com*, '1999 Piracy Report', <http://www.maritimesecurity.com/archive.htm>, June 1999, p. 8, accessed 15 July 2000.
Yamazaki T., 'Sandakan No. 8 Brothel', in *Bulletin of Concerned Asian Scholars*, vol. 7 (1975): 52-60.
Yen Ching-hwang, 'Early Chinese clan organisations in Singapore and Malaya, 1819-1911', in *Journal of Southeast Asian Studies*, vol. 12, no. 1 (1981): 62-92.

Index

Illustrative material is indicated with **bold** page numbers.

A Personal Record (book), 33
Adultery, and slavery, 77, 78
Ah Ku and Karayuki-san (book), 15, 18, 20, 21, 146, 173, 188
Ah ku, xi, 194, 197, 372; and the Chinese Protectorate, 292, 295, 297, 301–3; and collective biography, 19, 238, 240–3; and filial piety, 284; and historiography, 19, 234–7, 239, 246, 248; and migration, 237, 285; and patriarchy, 284; and prostitution, 192–3, 234, 246, 248, 266, 267–8, 284, 285, 305; and social history, 236, 237, 238, 239, 247, 248, 284; and suicide, 243, 245; and sexually transmitted disease, 285–9, 292, 301–5
Akijiro Kusada, and trafficking, 259
Aliwal Street (Singapore) and prostitute suicide, 230
Almayer's Folly (book), 33, 37, 137, 138, 335, 337
Amakusa, dialect, 197, 265
Amakusa Island, 252; and *karayuki-san*, 234, 364, 372; and migration, 252; and prostitution, 265, 271, 273; and rural poverty, 230–1, 236, 250–1, 253, 255; and trafficking of women, 279
Amin, Samir, 74
Amoy, Port of, and migration, 155, 158, 199, 259, 357, 361
An Outcast of the Islands (book), 33, 138, 139, 140, 337, 338
Andaya, Barbara, 312
Andaya, Leonard, 312
Anderson, A.F. colonial surgeon, 287
Angullia Road (Singapore), 162
Arab Street (Singapore), 338

Australia, 146, **183**, 359; and maritime raiding, 127; and modern-day piracy, 309, 328; and prostitution, 257, 258, 260, 262
Australian National University, 3

Bachelors, as labourers, 156, 166, 250, 251, 256, 284, 285; and living standard, 215; and prostitution, 251, 256, 284, and society, 362
Bain Street (Singapore), 205
Bakafu, and land tax, 153
Bali and George Peacock King, 34; and Secretan, 336
Balangingi Samal, 23, 28, 70–1, **94, 95**, 309; captives, 8, 12; destruction of, 23, 32, 90, 93; ethnicity, 24, 32, 47–60; ethnohistory, 22; female prisoner, 8; fortifications, **107**; identity, 93–119; maritime raiding, 9–12, 22, 23, 31, 47–60, **63**, 75, 77–8, 89–90, 91, 93–119, **95, 124**; *prahus*, 61–9, **66-9**; and slavery, 5, 8, 12, 32, 61, 80–2, 87, 90; and trade, x, 87, 93–119; women, 23, 93, 98, 108, 113
Banda Street (Singapore), 263, 266, 269, 270, 282
Banka, and maritime raiding, 128; and modern-day piracy, 317
Banyaga, 77–91; as currency, 87; labour of, 81–7, 90, 91; legal position of 78; and literacy, 85–6; and manumission, 80–1; and marriage, 84; status of, 79–80, 82, 83–6, 88, 90; in the Sulu Sultanate, 77–8; and trade, 85. *See also* slavery and chattel-slave
Barnes, R. 142
Barth, F., 54, 102, 339
Barthes, Roland, 173–4
Batam Island and modern-day piracy, 320, 328–9

Batavia, and captives, 79; and maritime raiding, 125–6, 128, 129, 317; and Netherland East India Company (VOC), 34; and 'piracy' 95, 121; and prostitution, 258, 263

Beach Road (Singapore), **183**

Beijing, and the rickshaw, 201, 203

Belcher, Edward, 135

Bencoolen Street (Singapore), 161, 206

Bernaldez, Emilio, 341

Bird's nest, 13, 31, 43–5, 49, 61, 71, 82, 95, 120, 121, 123, 144, 314, 315, 348

Bond-slaves, 77. *See also kiapangdilihan*

Borneo, 54, 63, **66**, 70, 71, 72, 335, 344; and Conrad, 33–5, 37, 38, 41, 48, 50; 52, 53, 137; and the Iranun, **122**, 134; and modern-day piracy, 324; and Olmeijer, 336; and prostitution, 257, 260, 262; and Pryer, 78, 85; and slavery, 78; and Spanish campaigns, 109; and trade, 72, 82, 99–100, 101, 102–3, 104, 121, 129, 313–4, 316, 336, 337, 348; and Warren, 334

Bowring, Arthur, 323

Braudel, Fernand, ix, 4

Bridenthal, Renate, 222

British East India Company, and maritime raiding, 125, 127, 317; and trade, 61, 71

British Government and prostitution in Singapore, 190, 258, 277, 279, 285, 286, 294, 295, 297

British Malaya, 175

Broken Birds: An Epic Longing (stage production), 20, 21

Brooke, James, 35, 50, 51, 97, 128, 134–5, 314

Brothel family, 187, 192, 236

Brothel-keeper, 185, 191, 230, 238, 241, 244–5, 250, 255, 257, 258, 260, 264, 271, 276, 282, 287, 288, 294, 305. *See also Mamasan* and *Okasan*

Brothels, 18, 20, 146, 165, 167, 173, 185, 189, **192**, 193, 226, 229, 265–70, 272, 273, 278, 279; abolition of, 229, 230, 234, 235, 241, 242, 246, 260, 267–71, 273–4, 276, 279–80, 281, 295–6; and British Government, 190, 286, 296–7, 307; and Contagious Diseases Ordinance, 189–90, 229, 264, 267, 285–90, 292, 293–4, 297–9, 307; and crime, 241; and historiography, 235, 237, 238–42, 248–9; and Japanese Imperial Decree, 263, 277, 282; and migration, 231, 237, 256; and modern-day piracy, 328; Ordinance for the Protection of Women and Children, 294, 308; regulation of, 191, 228, 229, 251, 264, 267–70, 276, 286, 294; and rickshaw pullers, 208, 229, 230, 285, 287; and the Russo-Japanese war, 256, 268; and sexually transmitted diseases, 282, 285–90, 292, 293–4, 295–8, 301, 303, 304, 305–8; and suicide, 244–5, 365; and violence, 272; and the traffic in women and girls, 191, 238, 251, 255, 256–63, 276–7, 278–9, 283, 284–5, 290; and the Yamoto Company, 271

Buckley, Charles, 338

Burma, and historiography, 7; and *karayuki-san*, 257; and E. R. Leach, 4–5, 47; and maritime raiding, 129

Butler, Josephine, and the Contagious Diseases Act, 291, 292, 295, 307

Calcutta, and the rickshaw, 201

Camphor, 31, 49, 61, 71, 120

Cantonese, 266, 282, 361, 372; prostitution, 229, 234, 244–5, 266, 268, 304, 305; rickshaw pullers 154, 155, 158, 161, 230; *towkay*, 155, 164

Castells, Manuel, 150

Celebes, 2; and Conrad, 36; and Forrest, 63; and maritime raiding, 49, 52, 71, 72, 90, 104; and the Samal, 48, 52; and Secretan, 336

Celebes, Dutch warship, 35

Celebes seas, and Conrad, 136; and maritime raiding, 121, 129, 317; and modern-day piracy, 324; and the Sulu Zone, 3–4, 28, 30–1, 70, 344; and trade, 11

Chacksfield, Lance-Corporal Albert, **192**, 238

Chamberlain, Joseph, and Contagious Diseases Ordinance (CDO), 307; prostitution, 297, 308

Chandu, and rickshaw pullers, 162, 163, 361. *See also* opium

Chattel-slave, 77. *See also banyaga*

Children, 149; Balangingi, 23, 108; killed by Taupan, 110, and Lingard, 336, 337; and migration, 251; mortality of, 210–11; and Ordinance for the Protection of Women and Children, 294; as prisoners of war, 109, 111–13, 115; as readers of Conrad, 135; repatriated, 116; and rickshaw pullers, 163, 201, 210–11, 212–13, 216, 217; and sexually transmitted diseases, 301; in Singapore, 200, 228–9; of *singkeh*, 200, 228; and slave raiding, 125, 131; as slaves, 11, 78, 129; and tax in Japan, 253; traffic in, 146, 173, 189, 249, 254–5, 257, 259, 285, 289, 290, 318–19, 320

Chin Chew Street (Singapore), 266

Chin Hin Street (Singapore), 230, 266, 269

China, xi, 61, 201–2, 234, 235, 236, 237, 249, 257–8, 263, 273, 277, 282, 284, 309; culture in Singapore, 17, 18, 22, 167, **182**, **184**, 290, 307; and globalisation, 3, 4, 22, 61, 62, 71, 81, 91, 99, 103, 126, 128, 242, 310–11; and migration, 285; modern-day piracy, 310, 318–21, 327–31; and prostitution in, 258, 260; trade, x, 7, 8, 9, 10–13, 22, 28, 30–1, 36, 49, 50, 61, 71, 72, 81–3, 88, 89, 91, 93, 95–7, 99, 100, 104, 105, 112, 117, 120, 121, 122, 123–4, 127, 142, 143–4, 309, 311–7, 326

China Relief Fund, 171, 217

China Street (Singapore), 204

China tea trade, 10, 11, 12, 13, 22, 61, 71, 93, 121–2, 125, 313, 314; and slavery, 144, 314

Chinatown (Singapore), 150, 156–7, 162, 180, 181, 204, 250, 264, 266, 268; and disease, 168, 177

Chinese, 265–7, 269, 273, 277, 281, 282, 286, 290; and disease, 168, 287–9, 291–308; infant mortality, 210–11; and Iranun, 129–30, 317, 320, 325; migrants, x–xi, 15, 16, 20, 32, 63, 91, 146–53, 154–60, 164–8, 171, 173–7, 185, 192, 193, 194, 198–219, 221, 226, 228–9, 249–51, 292; and prostitution, 229, 230, 234, 235, 237, 239–41, 243–6, 251–3, 257, 264, 266, 267–8, 270–1, 277–8, 284, 285, 287, 288, 292, 298–306; remittance of money, 167, 202; and slavery, 85; women, 200, 209, 210–12, 227, 228, 229, 233, 235, 237, 239, 247, 253, 284, 285, 287, 289

Chinese Protectorate, 191, 229, 263, 264, 267, 268, 280, 288, 289–90, 292, 295, 297, 304, 307, 308

Clavería, Narciso, Governor-General of the Philippines, 105–6; destruction of Balangingi, 108–9

Clementi-Smith, Sir Cecil, and sexually transmitted diseases, 294, 295, 304

Cochin China, and *karayuki-san*, 258; and maritime raiding, 128, 309

Cojuangco, Margarita, *Kris of Valor* (book), 115, 117

Collective biography, 9, 10, 19, 24, 227, 228, 233, 238, 240–2
Collective identity, 6, 10, 12, 117, 118
Colonial government, and anti-piracy, 51; and prostitution, 230, 249, 256, 258, 264; and rickshaw pullers, 167–9, 204, 218, 229; and slave raiding, 90; and *singkeh*, 155
Comaroff, Jean and John Comaroff, 118
Combes, Francisco, 52, 100
Conrad, Joseph, 33–46, **36**; 120–45; *Almayer's Folly* (book), 33, 37, 137, 138, 335, 337; *An Outcast of the Islands* (book), 33, 138, 139, 140, 337, 338; *A Personal Record* (book), 336; and Borneo, 33–5, 37, 38, 41, 48, 50; 52, 53; *Lord Jim* (book) 33, 36; and pre-colonial trade, 33; and Malay world, 33; and Netherlands Indies, 33; and *SS Vidar*, 33; and Jim Lingard, 36; Tom Lingard, 33, 37, 137–8, 141; and Charles Olmeijer, 33, 35, 37, 38; and *The Shadow Line: A Confession (and) Within the Tides: Tales* (book), 338; *The Rescue* (book), 137, 140, 141
Contagious Diseases Act, 286; and Josephine Butler, 291
Contagious Diseases Ordinance (CDO), 189, 229, 264, 267, 269, 272, 273, 285–98, 300, 304–7
Coolie strike, 205–7, 208–9; and strike of 1938, 171–2, 216–8, 362, 363
Coolies, x, 14, 18, 19, 193, 194, 198–200, 229, 251; coal, 147, 163, 198; the Contagious Diseases Ordinance, 256; gender imbalance, 256, 285, 299, 306, 362; and historiography, 151–3, 174, 197, 198, 223, 225, 236–7, 242; and homosexuality, 285, 287; housing of, 161–2, 163, **181**, 198, 204, 211, 215, 218, 250, 267; and human trafficking, 154; as migrants, 148, 159–60, 173, 198, 236, 256, 267; and prostitution, 230, 234, 251, 256–7, 264, 267, 269, 282–3, 285, 299; rickshaw, 15, 18, 146–53, 154–72, 173–5, 178, **180**, 181, **183**, 197, 198, 199, 202, 218; town, 147, 150, 153, 154, 156, 168, 228, 235, 248, 249, 251, 299; and sexually transmitted diseases, 229, 287, 289, 296, 298, 299, 302, 303, 304, 306, 308; social conditions of, 154–72, 173, 175, suicide amongst, 213–14; wages of, 163, 361. *See also* rickshaw pullers
Copra, as trade item, 205
Coquery-Vidrovitch, Catherine, 74
Coroner's Records, and collective biography, 149, 211, 212, 237, 238, 240, 242, 267; and death, 18, 20, 160; and demographic features, 160; and historiography, 16, 17, 18, 19, 146, 149, 151, 152, 237, 360; and murder, 272; and sexually transmitted diseases, 303–4; and suicide, 16, 17, 213–14, 229, 243, 245, 365
Craig Road (Singapore), 162
Cullinane, M. and P. Xenos, 132
Culture, 8, 10, 13, 22, 47, 70, 97, 116, 220, 225, 240, 254, 291, 293, 296; meaning of, 6, 14, 105, 136; in history, 1, 3, 4, 5, 6, 7, 18, 117, 118, 130; reproduction of, 6, 24, 117, 132, 200, 228, 291, 193, 296, 305, 313, 363; transformation of, 1, 8, 12, 17, 114, 117, 118, 131, 134, 141–2, 148, 197, 315, 320, 326, 329, 331

D'Urville, Dumont, 86
Daimyo, and land tax, 253
Dando, Palawan, 109, 112, 113
Darnton, Robert, 10
Davis, Natalie Zemon, 222, 223
de Ibañez y Garcia, Luis, 98, 110

Diponegoro, Prince, and the Padri War, 141
Dunne, John, 1, 25
Dutch, 2, 24, 126; and conquest, 39; and Conrad, 33, 136–7, 141; East Indies, ix; history, 27, 28, 50, 85; and immigration, 155, 199; and *karayuki-san*, **196**; and Lingard, 34, 37; and maritime raiding, 52, 97, 99–100, 110, 125, 129–130, 134, 135, 142, 143, 144, 314, 316–18; and prostitution, 263; scholars, 33; and slavery, 86, 108, 312; and trade, 51, 127, 312; VOC, 125, 318, 321; warship *Celebes*, 35
Duxton Road (Singapore), 17, 162, 363
Duya Hadachi, 238

Edwards, Ebenezer, 98
Ellis, Dr, 301–2
Ethnic diversity, 3, 4, 6, 13, 27–32, 47, 52, 59, 65, 69, 70, 73, 77, 87, **96**, 117, 143, 145, 158
Ethnic identity, 47, 51, 53, 93, 95, 117, 118, 122, 130; maintenance of, 6, 22, 24, 124, 144
Ethnicity, and Balangingi, 99–105, 111, 109, 117–19; conceptions of, 6, 7, 100, 102, 130, 132, 144; and history, 10, 14, 22, 23, 24, 29, 47, 54, 72, 93, 97, 100, 117, 118–19, 315; maintenance of, 4, 109, 111, 145, 161, 164, 165, **183**, 200, 339; and modern-day crime, 310, 320; and prostitutes, 299; and rickshaw pullers, 161, 164, 165, **183**, 200, 299; and slavery, 78, 80, 87, 99, 99–105; transformations of, 5, 6, 7, 8, 12, 22, 27–32, 49, 59–60, 74, 111, 117–18, 134
Ethnohistory, and *Ah Ku and Karayuki San* (book), 15; and *Iranun and Balangingi* (book), 24; as method, 2–3, 5–7, 13–14, 19, 105, 120–1, 130, 133, 152, 242, 247, 315; and *Rickshaw Coolie* (book), 15; and *The Sulu Zone* (book), 3, 8, 13, 14, 22, 24, 314; *The Sulu Zone, The World Capitalist Economy and the Historical Imagination* (book), 24
Europe and the People Without History (book), 97, 311, 315

Female, behaviour, 225; children, 253, 255; 254; devaluation of, 254; disproportionate ratio of, 200, 228; historiography, 246; immigration, 200, 212, 260; infanticide, 253; prisoners, 8; prostitution, 187, 261, 262, 263; slaves, 78, 81, 86, syphilis, 303
Firearms, and maritime raiding, 316; and modern-day piracy, 319; trade in, 37, 88–89, 99, 122, 144. *See also* rifles, munitions and gunpowder
Flores, and maritime raiding, 125, 143
Foochow, 154, 158, 161, 200, 209
Forrest, Thomas, 52, 63, 65, 86, 100, 315, 340
Frake, Charles, 144, 334
Frank, Andre Gunder, 4
Fraser Street (Singapore), 230
Friedman, Thomas, and 'messy states', 321
Fujisaki, I., photographer, 185
Fukuoka Nichinichi, 262, 265
Fukuoka, 259, 260
Fukuzawa Yukichi, 273, 275

Gajero Nihonda, and trafficking in women and girls, 259
Gelanee, Tuan Imam, 85
Gender, and Contagious Diseases Ordinance (CDO), 290; and historiography, 221, 222–3, 249; and prostitution, 189, 237, 241, 247, 256, 283, 285, 299; and venereal disease (VD), 290, 299
Geoghegan, William, 334

Ginji Shibuya, and trafficking in women and girls, 239
Ginsburg, Carlo, 9
Girls, xi; and the Contagious Diseases Ordinance, 288, 294, 305, 308; and death, 20; Eurasian and Olmeijer, 336; and migration, 20, 230, 231, 237, 249, 250, 253; and prostitution, 20, 167, 189, 194, 230, 231, 236, 237, 249, 255, 257-60, 263, 264-5, 268-9, 271-2, 328; and sexually transmitted diseases, 296, 301; status of, 254-5; trafficking of, 191, 231, 249, 252, 255-6, 257-62, 263, 284-5
Globalisation, and Conrad, 120-45; 309-32; and economic opportunities, 11; in eighteenth century, 3, 123, 309, 310; and maritime raiding, 309, 320, 326, 328, 330, 331; in nineteenth century, 123; and slavery, 10; and social change, 12; in twentieth century, 309; in twenty-first century, 14
Gold, and Conrad, 337; and *karayuki-san*, 189; and Lingard, 35; mining, 125, 337
Gonorrhoea, 304; and Chinese prostitutes, 288-9, 296, 302; and Chinese community, 295, 296; and Contagious Diseases Act, 286; and Japanese prostitutes, 282; and prisoners, 300; and suicide, 245. *See also* sexually transmitted diseases.
Gullick, John, 344
Gunpowder, and maritime raiding, 32, 54, 72, 88-90, 137, 138; and trade, 37, 72. *See also* munitions, firearms and rifles
Gunung (Goenoeng) Tabor, 34, 35, 36, 37, 336, 337
Gutta-percha, 33, 35-8, 41-6, 338

Habibie, President B.J., 320, 328
Halmahera, and maritime raiding, 128
Hane, Mikiso, 253, 273
Heersink, C., 143
Hengwah, rickshaw pullers, 154, 155, 157, 158, 161, 163, 164, 200, 201, 205, 213, 214, 362
Historical imagination, 330
Historiography, and *Ah Ku and Karayuki-san* (book), 15; and *Broken Birds*, 21; and Manning Clark, 25; and Joseph Conrad, 33-46, 120-45; and culture, 6-7; and Robert Darnton, 10; and Natalie Zemon Davis, 222-3; and ethnicity, 6, 22, 47-60, 93-119; and Carlo Ginsburg, 9; and global-regional economic systems, 8, 10, 12, 13, 14, 120-45, 309-32; and Joan, Kelly-Gadol, 222-3; and historical sources, 8, 9, 16, 19, 28, 150-1, 237-40; and *Iranun and Balangingi* (book), 22, 24; and Gerda Lerner, 222-3; and maritime raiding, 11, 70-92, 93-119; and global maritime trade network, 4-5; and Marshall Hodgson, 4; and the Indonesian Archipelago, 27; and methodology, 4, 14, 16, 18, 19, 21-2, 30, 146, 315; of the people, 15, 17, 18, 20, 21, 25, 146-53, 154-172, 198-219, 249-83; and photography, 173-97; and prosopography, 10, 240-6; and representation, 234-248; and *Rickshaw Coolie* (book), 15, 221; and the Samal Bajau Laut, 2, 3, 15; and sexually transmitted diseases, 284-308; and slavery, 9; and John Smail, 4; and *The Sulu Zone* (book), 5-6, 7, 9, 13, 14, 15, 22, 24; and Warren's work, ix-xi; and Eric Wolf, 97, 311, 315; and women, 220-34, 249-82

Index

Ho Swee Bee, 363
Hockchia, rickshaw pullers, 154, 157, 158, 164, 200, 201–2, 214
Hodgson, Marshall, 4
Hokkien, 155, 202; owners or *towkay*, 164; prostitution, 269; rickshaw pullers, 158, 161, 363; Street, 230, 244–5, 266
Holmes, J.S., 336
Homosexuality, 285, 287
Hong Kong Street (brothel in), 244
Hong Kong, and the Contagious Diseases Ordinance, 290; and indentured labour, 155, 199; and licensed prostitution, 296; and modern-day piracy, 319, 322–3, 327–8; and Muraoka, 259; prostitution in, 266; and the rickshaw, 201; and sexually transmitted diseases, 298; and trade, 34; trafficking of prostitutes, 256, 257, 258, 260, 262–3, 273, 285
Hunt, J., 55, 74, 82, 86, 348
Hylam Street (Singapore), **192**, 229, 257, 266, 270, 271, 282; and murder of prostitutes in, 271–2; and prostitute suicide, 244;

Illunan, *see* Iranun
Imagined communities, ix, 7, 118
Imamura, Shohei, 238
India, and prostitution, 252, 257, 274, 281, 286, 287, 373; and maritime raiding, 121; and modern-day piracy, 309, 330; and trade, 71, 88
Indian Ocean, and modern-day piracy, 324, 326
Indo China and prostitution, 263
Indonesia, x, 4; and corruption, 321, 328; and Iranun, 23, 120, 123, 127, 318; and maritime raiding, 31, 60, 95, 310, 316; and modern-day piracy, 319, 322–8, 330, 331; and the Sulu Zone, 29

Indonesia, and the Dutch, 127, 141, 318; and historiography, x, 4, 7, 27, 28; and the Iranun, 23; and Islam, 27–8, 141; and Joseph Conrad, 135–7, 141; and maritime raiding, 31, 50, 60, 95, 120, 123, 130, 310, 316, 318; and modern-day piracy, 319–26, 327–31; and trade, 27
Infanticide, female, 253, and status of female babies, 254
Iranun (Illanun), x, 314; captives, 8; collapse of, 32, 90; and Conrad, 120–45; and culture, 6; ethnohistory of, 22, 23, 315; identity, 10, 24, **122**; and Islam, 52; maritime raiding, 5, 9, 12, 22–4, 31, 49, 51–2, 55, 58, 60, 71, 100, **124**, 309–10, 311, 314, 315–19, 320–1, 323–5, 329, 331; and modern-day pirates, 310, 316; *prahus* of, 61–9; **66–9**, slavery, 11, 12, 31, 50, 55, 56, 58, 61, 75, 85, 87, 90, 314, 316, 331; society and politics, 53, 311; and trade, 312, 315, 317; and VOC, 318
Iranun and Balangingi (book), 22, 24
Isahaya, 259
Islam, and Joseph Conrad, 133, 136–7, 140–1, 144; and ethnic identity, 95, 116–17; and the Samal, 49, 70; and slavery, 80, 97, 100, 104
Isshi, T., photographer, 185, 186

Jansen, A.J.F., 340
Japanese brothels, 273; abolition of, 280, 281; and business, 258
Japanese Government, and migration, 261, 273; and prostitution, 261, 273, 274–5, 279; and remittance from prostitutes, 272–3, 278
Java, and Conrad, 33, 136; and Harrison, 359; and Lingard, 336; and maritime raiding, 50, 52, 63, 128, 143; and modern-day piracy, 319; and Prince Diponegoro, 141;

ponies and horses, 156; and prostitution, 259; and Raffles, 74; and religious wars, 140; and trade, 34
Javanese tobacco, *see* tobacco
Javanese women and 'sly prostitution', 230
Jinrickshaw, 200
Johore Road (Singapore), 161

Kaligeran de Perez, Hailan, 101
Kalimantan, and maritime raiding, 125
Kayosaki Strait, 253
Keesing, Roger, 6, 118
Kelly-Gadol, Joan, 222, 223
Kiapangdilihan, 77
Kiefer, Thomas, 334, 339, 344
Kikuyo Zendo, 271
King, George Peacock, 34
Kobe, 258; Port of, 256, 260
Kongsi, 18
Korea, 2; and prostitution, 258, 260; and twentieth-century shipping, 318, 322
Kreta Ayer (Singapore), 161-2, 177, 266-7, 292
Kumamoto Prefecture, and *karayuki-san*, 253; and rural poverty in Japan, 230
Kwai po (female brothel-keeper), 287, 288, 295, 297, 301, 302, 304-5
Kyushu, xi, 185, 188, 230, 234, 250, 252, 253, 254, 258, 259, 265, 275, 276, 279, 282, 364, 372

Lambert, G.R., photographer, 185, 186, 188, 189
Lane of Foreign Prostitutes (Singapore), 267, 282
Lavender Street (Singapore), 282
Leach, E.R., 4-5, 118; and *Political Systems of Highland Burma* (book), 47
Lehman F.K., 47

Lerner, Gerda, 222-4
Light, Francis, 127
Lim Phua Sim, 161
Lingard, William, 33, 34-7, 38, 40-1; 45-6, 135, 137; *pangeran*, 34; and Raja Laut Kapitan de Berau, 34; Anja Kansanan, 34; and *Coeran*, 34-5, 40-1, 43-4, 336, 337
Little Temple Street (Singapore), 266
Lombard, Denys, 334
Lombok, and maritime raiding, 125; and rice trade, 34; and Secretan, 336
Lord Jim (book), 33, 36
Low Ngiong, Ing, 158

Macao Street (Singapore), 204
Majul, C.A., 116, 339
Makassar, and Conrad, 335; and Lingard, 34-5; and maritime raiding, 22, 50, 93, 121, 125-6, 128, 129, 317; and trade, 34, 36-7, 38, 40-1, 338
Malabar Street (Singapore), 257, 270; and prostitute suicide, 224, 226, 229, 244, 365
Malay, captives, 57, 72, 83-4, 86, 104, 330; economic development, 154; ethnicity, 7, 34, 102, 274; geographical location, 8, **124**; and the Iranun, 125, 127, 142; literature, 311; maritime raiding, 316-8; piracy, 50-2; 97, 130-1, 133, 137, 312-13, 314; prostitution, 281-2; and rickshawmen, 157; and rickshaws, 180; states and prostitution, 257, 261, 285; women, 230; world and Tarling, 102
Malay Street (Singapore), 17, 192-4, 229, 238, 244, 248, 257, 263, 264-6, 267, 268, 270, 271, 280, 282
Malaya, ix, 15, 52, 56, 149, 173; and Balangingi, 100
Malayo-Muslim State, 30, **96**, 101, 127, 134, 141, 310, 312; and Conrad, 33, 134-5; and Resink, 136

Malaysia, x, 2; and the Iranun, 23, 120; and modern-day piracy, 310, 319, 322, 324–5, 328, 330: and slave raiding, 29, 52

Males, Balangingi demographics of, 54, 102; disproportionate ratio of 156, 200, 228–9, 262, 292–3; historiography of, 222–4, 234; *indio*, 81; migration of, 235, 293; Muslim, representation of, 133, and privilege, 254; and prostitution, 246, 249, 306; and sexually transmitted diseases, 287, 290, 29, 302, 303; slavery, 78, 81, 86

Mallari, F., 104

Mamasan (brothel madam), 194

Manassa Lane (Singapore), 162

Manila, 334; archive repository, 28; and defeat of Balangingi, 108, 112–15; and maritime raiding, 99, 111, 125–6, 317; and modern-day piracy, 328; and prostitution, 257, 261, 263, 280, 281; and Spanish colonialism, 29, 99, 113, 115, 124; and trade, 28, 49, 61, 72, 95, 129, 317

Manila Bay and maritime raiding, 50, 128

Manumission, 80

Mathews, S., 174

McPherson Road (Singapore), and prostitute suicide, 244

Mednick, Melvin, 344

Meiji Government, 270 273, and prostitution, 276, 268, 364, 372; Restoration, 253 268

Meiji-Taisho, 234, 259; and *Broken Birds*, 20

Meyosaki family, and trafficking, 259

Middle Road (Singapore), **188**, **232**, 282

Miyasaki Kechi, **191**

Modern history, xiii, of Southeast Asia, 1–26

Moerman, M., 47

Moluccas, and the British East India Company, 127; and maritime trade, 28, 61, 100; and slave raiding, 72, 110, 120, 126, 128; and the Sulu Zone, 72

Morisaki, Kazue, 231, 238

Moro, 116, 130, 133; label, 51–2, 126, 131–3, 144–5; representation of, 98, 128, 131–3, 141, 144–5; wars, 30

Mosque Street (Singapore), 161

Mother-of-pearl, 44, 49, 61, 71, 81–2, 347, 348. *See also* pearl shell

Muar Road (Singapore), 162, 205

Mugliston, Dr, and sexually transmitted diseases, 301, 302, 304, 305

Munitions, and maritime raiding, 100, 129, 317; trade in, 41, 43, 129, 317. *See also* firearms, gunpowder and rifles

Muraoka Iheiji, photographer, 191; trafficker, 259–62

Musim lanun, 24, 121

Muslim raiding, 23, 24, 30, 97, 100, 104, 110, 128–9, 135, 324; representation of, 51, 52, 130–2, 133, 144; and Taupan, 104

Muslim social system, 3, 11

Muslim–Christian relations, 24, 28, 52, 97, 116–17, 130–2, 134, 140, 310

Nagasaki, 254, 259, 263, 273; Port of, 254, 256, 260, 285

Naka family, and trafficking, 259

Nakagawa Tetsuro, 273, 274

Nanshin, and prostitution, 226, 262, 271–2; and rural poverty, 254–5; and working-class women's history, 220, 226, 262

Nanyang, and migration of coolies, 148, 149, 154–5, 173, 199, 357, 361; and migration of prostitutes, 212

Netherlands East India Company (VOC), 34, 125

Netherlands, 24, 317, 318

Netherlands Indies, 15, 120, 141, 173, 257, 260, 261, 321; and Conrad, 33
New Bridge Road (Singapore), **182**, 266
New Market Road (Singapore), **179**
Ng Kar Eng, 162
Nimmo, Harry Arlo, 334
North Borneo Chartered Company, 2, 37
North Canal Road (Singapore), 266
Nuyla, 113

O'Haru, and Japanese kimonos, 272
Oahki, 244, 271, 272
Ogata, F., photographer, 185, 186
Ohichi, 244
Oichi, Japanese prostitute, 17, 187, 220, 224–32, 238, 250, 251, 365
Okasan (brothel mother), 187, 191
Olmeijer, Charles, 35, 37, 38, 336, 337; and Conrad, 33
Onatsu, 244
Ong Keng Sen, *Broken Birds: An Epic Longing* (stage production), 20–1
Opium, 244; and prostitution, 230; and rickshaw pullers, xi, 150, 162, 163, 167–8, **180**, 199, 202, 206, 226, 229, 361; and slave raiding, 56, 90; and slaves, 87, and suicide, 244–5; and trade, 37, 41–5, 72, 83, 88, 127, 129, 135, 317. *See also chandu*
Orchard Road (Singapore), 186
Osaka, 258; Port of, 260
Osaki, 236, 271, 272, 281
Otama, 244
Otoyo, **192**, 238–9
Oyoshi, 236, 244

Pagar Road (Singapore), and prostitute suicide, 245
Palawan Dando (Balangingi warrior), 109, 112, 113, death of, 113
Park Road (Singapore), 162
Passing over, as historical methodology, 1–3, 22, 24–5, 230, 250

Pearl shell, 54, 84, 86, 348. *See also* mother-of-pearl
Pearls, 13, 31, 54, 60, 62, 75, 102, 257, 315, 348
Pelras, Christian, 312
Penang, and the Contagious Diseases Ordinance, 293; and Francis Light, 127; and maritime raiding, 121, 125, 126, 129, 317; and prostitution, 280
Percival Road (Singapore), 20
Person, Yves, 74
Philippines, ix, x, 22, 47, 61, 70, 309; and captives, 8, 31, 60, 72, 90, 117, 118, 123; and Clavería, 105, 108; and *deportados*, 114; historiography, 4, 117; and Iranun, 23, 31, 128, 129, 142, 309, 316; and *karayuki-san*, 194, 260, 263; maritime raiding in, **64, 76**, 84, 93, 95, 103, 105, 109, 110, 120, 121, 123, 124, 125, 128, 129, 131, 142; maritime trade, 28, 100; and modern-day piracy, 319, 321, 322–4, 327, 330; and Muslims, 131–2, 144; state and ethnic politics, 23, 57, 117; and Taupan, 111–12
Pickering, William Alexander, and prostitution, 290, 292, 293, 294
Piracy and Politics in the Malay World (book), 104
Pirate, as label, 100, 124, 131, 133, 134, 145; states, 27, 75, 121, 135; wind, 104, 316
Pirates, 310, and the Balangingi, 53, 55, 93, 97; of Basilan, 86; and Conrad, 135, 137–8, 140; of Islam, 126, 140, 144; modern-day, 319–20, 322–30, 331; and the Sulu Sultanate, 51
Political Systems of Highland Burma (book), 47
Politics, 21, 238; and the Balangingi, 59, 93, 99, 102, 103, 109, 113, 117–18; and Britain, 127, 128,

132, 143, 149, 209, 291–3, 295–6, 306–8; and capitalism, 5; and Chinese migrants, 149, 158, 171, 201, 209, 218, 233, 235, 237, 241–2, 246; in east Borneo, 33–46; and the Dutch, 127, 143, 321; and ethnicity, 23, 52, 93, 118, 320; and gender, 220–233, 236, 273–4; and global systems, 4, 27–30, 50–1, 96, 97, 99, 123, 126–7, 128, 133, 279, 309, 311, 312, 315; and highland Burma, 4–5, 47; and identity, 134; and Indonesia, 321, 326, 330–1; and the Iranun, 128, 132, 141, 311; and James Brooke, 128; and Japanese migrants; 231, 233, 235, 237, 241–2, 246, 249, 256, 273–5, 279; and Joseph Conrad, 33–46, 136; and sexually transmitted diseases, 284–308; and slavery, 74, 77, 80, 85, 87, 128, 141, 144; and maritime raiding, 89, 98; and maritime Southeast Asia, 2–5, 7, 22, 24, 118, 123, 143, 309, 310–12, 321, 330; and the Philippines, 321; and modern-day piracy, 320, 326, 328, 330–1; and Spain, 109, 113, 130, 132, 134; and the Sulu Zone, 2–4, 6, 15, 27–32, 48, 61, 70, 88, **96**, 99, 103, 123, 130, 311, 312, 315; and the Taosug, 55, 57, 85, 103, 123

Post-colonial, 330, world, 15
Prewitt, Kenneth, on global/local, 13
Prosopography, as methodology, 9–10, 19, 241–2, **243**, 365
Protection of Women and Girls Ordinance, 294, 296, 308
Pryer, William, 78, 79, 82, 85

Queen Street (Singapore), 161, 209

Raffles Hotel, 136, 180, **183**, 359
Raffles Place, 206
Raffles Square, **184**, 206

Raffles, Sir Stamford, 50–1, 74, 97, 134, 135; 314, 340
Raja Laut, 34–6, 38, 39, 40, 137–8
Rangoon, and the rickshaw, 201
Rattan, 33, 35, 37–8, 42, 44–6, 67, 120; cutters, 338
Reber, Anne L., 51, 340
Resink, G.J., and Conrad, 33
Rice, x, 312; and maritime raiding, 53, 56, 90, 101, 109, 129; and poverty in China, 199, 201, 228; and poverty in Japan, 252–3, 254; and rickshaw pullers, 163, 202, 205, 213, 215; and slavery, 56, 81, 87, 121; trade in, 31, 34, 37, 41–5, 109, 315; wine, 17, 361;
Rickshaw, xi, 15, 17, 18, 19, 147, 154, 156, 159–61, 162, 163, 164, 170, 171, 174–5, 176, 177, 178, **179**, 180, **182**, **183**, **184**, 200–1, 214–15; abolition of, 170–1, 215–17; fares, 163; hire of, 204–5; and historiography, 150; station, 161; trade, 146, 149–50, 151, 153, 154, 157, 158, 164, 165–6, 174, 202
Rickshaw Coolie (book), x, 15, 18, 146, 153, 173, 221, 226, 360
Rickshaw owners, 155, 157, 162, 164–6, 171, 199, 204–5, 215, 217; women as, 164
Rickshaw pullers, x–xii, 15, 16, 146, 154–72, 157–60, 164–6, 170, 176, **177**, **179**, 180, **182**, **183**, **184**, 198–219; and age distribution, 160–1; and alcohol, 167, 168; and death, 167, 168; and endemic diseases, 168–9; and ethnic identity, 158, 161, 200, 201, 214, 363; and gambling, 167, 168; and historiography, 16–20, 147–8, 150, 151, 152–3, 174–5, 197, 221, 223, 226, 359, 361; and housing, 147, 149, 161–2, **181**, 203–4, 210, 215; and income, 163, 164, 202–3, 361;

and marriage, 162–3, 166, 209–13, 219; and migration, 148–9, 150, 176, 198; and opium, 167, 168; and poverty, 148, 150, 198, 203, 212, 213; and prostitution, xi, 19, 167, 168, 229, 230, 235; and remittance, 167; and secret societies, 155, 200; and sexually transmitted diseases, 168; and social organisation, 154–72; and social status, 149, 150, 200; and suicide, 17, 151, 213–14, 363; and *wayang-going*, 167–8, and women, 210–13, 219

Rickshaw pullers and strike of 1938, *see* Coolies and strike of 1938

Rickshawalas, 201

Rifles, and maritime raiding, 87; and modern-day piracy, 324, 326; trade in, 37. *See also* firearms, munitions and gunpowder

Rochore Road (Singapore), 205, 206, 266

Russo–Japanese War, 256, 259, 268

Sabi, 113, death of 113

Sago Lane (Singapore), 162, 177

Sago Street (Singapore), 230, 266, 268, 269, 270, 369; and prostitute suicide, 245

Saigon, and *karayuki-san*, 257, 258, 263

Salvation Army, and prohibition of prostitution, 276, and Contagious Diseases Act, 291

Samal Bajau Laut, 2, 14, 28, 334; and Tuan Imam Gelanee, 85

Samarinda, and George Peacock King, 34; and modern-day piracy, 325; and Charles Olmeijer, 336; and trade, 61, 72

Sandakan, and prostitution, 231–2, 257, 281; and Pryer, 85; and slavery, 79; and trade, 38, 44, 348; and tribute, 85

Sandakan, Hachiban Shokan (book title), 232, 281

Sangir Islands, and maritime raiding, 128

Schindler's List (film), 21

Sea cucumber, *see tripang*

Secretan, Francis James, 34, 336

Sex industry, ix, 193, 194, 197, 228, 230, 234, 235, 256, 264, 284, 285; and *ah ku*, 284, 285; and *karayuki-san*, **186**, 193, 194, 197, 268, 277, 281, 284, 285; and males, 249, 256, 284, 287, 298; and modern-day crime, 328; and suicide, 282

Sex, biological, 151, 174, 225, 227; demographic, 306, and social relations, 227, 228, and violence, 242

Sexual exploitation, 235, 242, 249, 254, 256, 284

Sexual inequality, 20

Sexual intercourse and slavery, 77–8

Sexual morality, repressive, 291, 305, 307

Sexuality, and filial piety, 241, and historiography, 249; women's, 221, 223, 235, 237

Sexually transmitted diseases, 168, 199, 229, 286–94, 295, 297–304, 306, 307, 308

Shanghai, 201, 257, 258, 259, 260, 263

Shimabara, 231, 253, 265, 273, 279, 364, 372; Peninsula, 234, 252, 253, 259

Shimada family, and trafficking, 259

Siberia, and *karayuki-san*, 259, 260, 262, 263; as migration destination, 252

Simisa, and Panglima Taupan, 112–13; and Spanish aggression, 115, 116

Simon, Dr. M.F., and venereal disease (VD), 299

Singkeh, 176, and migration, 147, 148, 154, 176, 198, 200, 228; and ethnic identity, 155, 156, 157; and abolition of rickshaws, 216; and prostitution, 229, 250, 256, 283, 285

Index

Slave labour, 11, 31, 55, 56, 58, 62, 72, 74–5, 81, 82–3, 84, 85–7, 88–90, 91, 95, 103, 312, 313

Slave raiding, 4, 6, 10, 145, 318; and the Balangingi, 5, 9, 10, 11, 22, 31–2, 47, 49, 50, 54–5, 58–9, 61, **63, 64, 69**, 71, 75, 77, 87, 90, 93, **94, 95**, 97, 98, 99–100, 102, 104–5, 109, 111, 114, 117, 118; and children, 125; and the China trade, 71, 95, 123, 144, 310; and Clavería, 105–6; and ethnogenesis, 47–60; and Joseph Conrad, 136, 139–42; and the Iranun, 5, 9, 10, 11, 22, 50, 61, **66**, 75, 87, 120–2, 125–6, 127–9, 130–1, 133, 142, 143, 309, 310, 311, 314, 315–17, 330–1; and *Iranun and Balangingi* (book), 24; and Jolo, 71–2; and 'messy states', 321; modern-day piracy, 309, 319, 321, 322, 330–1; in the Philippines, **76**, 105, 123, 128; in the Sulu Zone, 5, 9, 30–1, 50, 55, 59, 60, 61, **62**, 75, 77, 83, 84, 89–90–2, 93, 121, 129, 142, 144, 314; in *The Sulu Zone* (book), 6, 24; and the Taosug, 11, 52, 54–5, 57, 59, 75, 78, 81, 83, 88–9, 91, 95, 313; and women, 125

Slave trade, 1, 9, 11, 12–13, 104, 129, 318; and the Balangingi, 54, 55; at Jolo, 29, 32, 52, 71, 72, 81, 86, 88, 89, 90, 104, 313; and Joseph Conrad, 37; in *The Sulu Zone*, 12; the Sulu Zone, 31, 56, 74, 87, 88; and van Leur, 27

Slavery, 4, 95; brothel, 293, 307; and children, 11, 129; and culture, 6, 9, 81; and the economy, 8, 30, 87, 312; escape from, 80, 89; and ethnogenesis, 9, 47–60; and the Europeans, 11; and a gendered division of labour, 81, 83, 86; and globalisation, 5, 47, 312, 314, 321; and historiography, 8–9, 10, 14, 17, 30, 56, 72–4, 75, 84, 98–9, 101, 123, 144, 314, 320; and Islam, 9, 73, 97, 100, 114, 129, 133, 134, 135, 140; and manumission; 80; and the Spanish, 10, 29, 52, 91, 93, 105–6, 110–11, 114, 128, 142; and the Sulu Zone, 10, 27, 30–1, 70, 72, 75, 88, 101; and van Leur, 27; and violence, 79; and women, 11, 93, 129

Slaves, x, 5, 56, 63, 142, 312, 318; and the Balangingi, 9; Christian, 88; and ethnicity, 6, 10, 59, 117–8; and identity; 6, 12, 51, 54, 72, 77, 79, 117–18; ownership of, 55, 57, 70, 74–5, 78–80, 84, 87, 89, 103, 312; social position of, 53, 55, 77–80, 82, 83, 84–7, 88, 91; and sexual relations, 78; Spaniards as, 8; in the Sulu Zone, xii, 5, 6, 8, 72; and *The Sulu Zone*, 9, 10

Sly prostitution, and the depression years, 230; and sexually transmitted diseases, 297–8

Smail, John, 4

Smith Street and prostitution, 17, 192, 193, 230, 238, 245, 248, 257, 264, 266, 268, 269

Social history from below, 16, 18–19, 21–2, 70, 73, 126, 151–3, 173, 284–308; and women, 220–33, 234–48, 249–83, 284–308

Society of Friends and Contagious Diseases Act, 291

Soerma, Chrishaan, 85

Song Ong Siang, 262

South Bridge Road (Singapore), **182, 184**

Southeast Asian history, ix, x, xii, 1–3, 7, 9–10, 11, 13–15, 17, 22, 25, 27, 33, 47, 49, 51, 54, 55, 97, 106, 124, 130, 141–2, 146–7, 153, 220–33, 311, 313–15, 330–1; and the Balangingi, 12, 98–9, 115, 118–19; and Conrad, 135–6, 140–1; and the Iranun, 12, 126, 128, 130, 142, 144–5, 310;

and the Philippines, 22, 60, 98, 117, 119, 132–3; and Singapore, xii, 16–7, 18–19, 21, 22, 146–8, 149–50, 154, 157, 171–2, 173–97, 199; 220–33, 234–48, 249–83, 284–308; and the Sulu Sultanate, 4, 5, 7, 9–10, 12, 13, 90, 92, 97

Southon, M., 143

Spenser, St. John, and women traders, 82

Spice Islands, 23, 95, 120, 127, 313

Spices, 41, 43, 120, 129, 317

Spivak, Gayatri, 247

Spring Street (Singapore), 266–7, 269, 270, 282

Standpoint, 1, 101, 146, 220, 225, 295, 310

Stenross, Kurt, 143

Subaltern voice, ix

Sugar, 37; and slavery, 12, 314; and trade, 41, 43–4, 205;

Suharto, President, 328

Sulawesi, and the British East India Company, 127; and historiography, 2; and maritime raiding, 104, 121, 124–5, 131, 142; and the Sulu Sultanate, 61

Sulu pirates, label, 51, and the English, 52; and the slave trade, 84, 139

Sulu Sultanate, x, 2, 4, 8, 9, 11–13, 17, 27–32, 48, 53; and Balangingi, 110; and *prahus*, 61, and slavery, 47, 49, 50–1, 53, 55, 59–60, 62, 70–92, 95, 101, 103, 105, 121, 123, 144, 313, 316, 317; and trade, 70–92, 101, 110, 121, 128, 130, 313, 315, 330

Sulu Zone, ix; cultural and social forms, 6, 13, 123, 344; as geographic space, x, 22, 28, **29**, **48**, 61, **62**, **73**, **96**; ethnicity, 7, 8, 27; historiography, 3, 7, 8, 10, 13, 22, 30, 310; and Joseph Conrad, 33; and *prahus*, 61–9; 343; and modern-day piracy, 320, 324; and slavery, 11, 12, 13, 50, 56, 61, 63, 72, 75, 77, 143, 314; and trade, 9, 10, 39, 61, 71, 96, 311, 313, 344

Sumatra, and colonialism, 154; and Conrad, 141; and Lingard, 337; and maritime raiding, 23, 31, 52, 84, 121, 125; and prostitution, 258, 262; and religious wars, 140, 141; and *singkeh*, 154

Suteretsu, and photography, 186, **195**; and prostitution, 197, 265, 268, 269, 270, 271, 272

Swatow, Port of, and migration, 155, 199, 357, 361

Swettenham, Sir, J.J., and venereal disease (VD), 307

Syed Alwi Road (Singapore), and prostitute suicide, 245

Syphilis, 169, 219, 288, 299; and the Chinese community, 295–6, 302–4; and Chinese prostitutes, 301, 302, 303–4; and the Contagious Diseases Act, 286; and Japanese prostitutes, 301; and prisoners, 300; and suicide, 245

Tainun, 113

Tambaya, and trafficking in women and girls, 259, 263

Tan Quee Lan Street (Singapore), 193, 230; and prostitute suicide, 245

Tank Road (Singapore), **179**, 180

Taosug, x, 28, 52, 70, 84, 91; and agriculture, 32, 91; *datus*, 5, 11, 31, 52, 53–7, 59, 75, 82, 87, 89, 100, 102, 121; and Islam, 48; and maritime raiding, 49–9, 55, 89–90, 143–4, 316; and modern-day piracy, 320, 324; and slavery, 10, 11, 31, 32, 50, 54, 72, 75, 77–8, 80–1, 82, 83, 85, 86, 87, 88, 90, 103, 313; society, 6, 8, 10, 31, 48, 55, 59, 103, 123; and trade, 30–1, 49, 61, 72, 85, 88–9, 91, 96–7, 110, 121, 313, 315, 316; women, 83, 86

Tarazo, brothel keeper, 271

Tarling, Nicholas, *Piracy and Politics in the Malay World* (book), 102
Taupan, Panglima Julano, 98, 109
Teochiu, 361; rickshaw pullers, 155; and prostitution, 229, 266
Terray, Emmanuel, 74, 89, 91
Textiles, and maritime raiding, 99, 129, 317; trade in, 37, 41–5, 72
Thailand, and maritime raiding, 120, 128, 330; and modern-day piracy, 310, 319, 323–4, 327, 329, 330; and prostitution, 257
The Rescue (book), 137, 140, 141
The Shadow Line: A Confession (and) Within the Tides: Tales (book), 338
The Sulu Zone (book), 5, 6, 7, 9, 10, 11, 12, 13, 14, 15, 16, 22, 24, 314
The Sulu Zone, World Capitalist Economy and the Historical Imagination (book), 24
Tientsin, and Muraoka, 259
Tin, 129, 154, 205, 317; mining of, 125, 128, 154, 163, 257, 361
Tobacco, 154, 257; and forced labour in the Philippines, 114–15; from Java, 37, 44; Spanish, 88; trade in, 44–45, 83
Tokugawa Period and rural poverty, 252, 253; and taxation, 253
Tokyo, and the trafficking of women, 260
Tomijiro Onda, 259
Tortoise shell, 71, 348
Towkay, 155, 164, 171, 209, 218, 230
Traffickers, 230, 259, 274, 276; capture of, 277; expulsion of, 276
Trafficking, 258, 260, 290, 328; of children, 189, 249, 257, 259, 285, 289, 318–19, 320; of coolies, 154, 283; of girls, 191, 252, 256, 258, 259, 260, 261, 263, 284, 285; human, xii, 321, 322, 331; of prostitutes, 21, 303; and sexually transmitted diseases, 303, 308; slave, 11, 12, 31, 55, 80, 87, 114, 313;
of women, 189, 191, 241, 249, 252, 256, 257, 259, 260, 261, 262, 276, 281, 283, 284, 285, 289, 290, 318–19, 320
Trans-national, viii, 310, 331
Trans-regional, viii, 117
Trengganu Street and prostitution, 193, 238, 244–5, 266, 268, 269
Tripang (or sea cucumber), 13, 31, 42, 44, 49, 54, 60, 61, 62, 71, 75, 81, 82, 84, 95, 99, 102, 123, 144, 313, 314, 315, 348
Trocki, Carl, 311–12
Tumugsuc, 109, 112

Upper Hokkien Street (Singapore), 230, 266, 269; and prostitute suicide, 244–5

Van Leur, J.C., 2, 4, 27, 28
van Marle, A., 336
Veltoen, Esther, 312
Venereal disease (VD), and children, 301; in Chinese community, 298, 303; and colonial legislation, 306–8; and Contagious Diseases Act, 286, 291; and Contagious Diseases Ordinance (CDO), 229, 287, 289, 294, 295, 296, 298, 304; and Chinese labourers (coolies), 229, 293, 296, 302–3, 306, 308; and merchant seamen, 296; and poverty, 300; and prostitution, 229, 284–308; and rickshaw pullers, 168, 293; in Singapore, 297, 298, 299, 300, 303–5, 306; and military personnel, 286, 293, 298, 301; and prisoners, 300–1; Victorian attitudes to, 286, 289–92, 296, 297, 303, 305, 306–7
Vereenigde Oostindische Compagnie (VOC), 34, 125
Victoria Street (Singapore), 17, 158, 161, 205, 206, 209
Vidar Steamship and Conrad, 33

Vietnam, and maritime raiding, 120; and modern-day piracy, 320, 324
Vladivostok, and prostitution, 262, 263, 273

Wallace, Alfred, 98
Wallerstein, I., x
Warren, James Francis, *Ah Ku and Karayuki-san* (book), 15, 18, 20, 21, 146, 173, 188; *Iranun and Balangingi* (book), 22, 24; *Rickshaw Coolie* (book), x–xi, 15, 18, 146, 153, 173, 221, 226; *The Sulu Zone* (book), 5, 6, 7, 9, 10, 11, 12, 13, 14, 15, 16, 22, 24, 314; *The Sulu Zone, World Capitalist Economy and the Historical Imagination* (book), 24
Wartofsky, Marx, 173–4
Wax, 31, 35, 37, 41–5, 49, 61, 71, 82, 315
Wayang, Street, **182**
West Indian, 40, 45; and Lingard, 37
Wilkes, Charles, 56, 79, 83, 86–7, 88
Wolf, Eric, 118, *Europe and the People Without History* (book), 97, 311, 315
Woman, as subjected sex, 222
Women, xi, 16, 151, 154, 211, 236; abuse of, 323; Balangingi, 21, 58, 108–9, 110, 112–13, 115–16; and colonial mindset, 131; and the Contagious Diseases Ordinance, 267, 288–92, 294–5, 296, 305, 307–8; and filial piety, 241, 284; and gender imbalance, 157, 200, 135, 257, 283–5; marginalised, 238; and marriage, 211–12, 214, 219, 246; migrants, 146, 173, 193, 209, 231–2, 234, 236, 237, 241, 251, 252–4, 256–7, 261, 262, 272, 273, 276–7, 284, 364; and prostitution, xi, 19, 20, 146, 173, 185, 186–7, 188–9, 191, 192, 193, 194, 197, 220–33, 234, 236; 238, 239, 240–2, 246, 247, 248, 249, 250, 251, 256–7, 258, 261, 262, 263, 264–6, 268–70, 272–8, 284, 365, 371; repatriation to Japan, 263, 280–2; remittances, 272–3, 273–4, 278–9; as sexual commodity, 235; and sexually transmitted diseases, 282–3, 287–92, 294–5, 296, 299–303, 305–7; and slave raiding, 11, 104; and slavery, 82–3, 88, 104, 125, 129; and social history, 16, 18, 20, 21, 98, 146, 151, 174, 220–33, 239–42, 246, 247, 249, 250, 251, 364; in Southeast Asian history, 151, 220–33, 364; status of, 254–5; and suicide, 214, 221, 242; Taosug, 83; and trade, 82–3, 164, 176; traffic in, 249, 252, 256–7, 259–62, 263, 278–9, 281, 284–5, 290, 318, 320; as underclass, 14, 18; working, 211, as victims, 104, 129, 210, 224, 231, 232, 246, 250, 261, 275, 279, 283, 302
Wong Lin Ken, 317

Yamazaki Heikichi, 279–80
Yamazaki Tomoko, 231, 232, 238, 239, 252, 259, 265, 266, 271, 272, 273, 281
Yap pun kai, 266, 267
Yip Cheong Fung, 194
Yokohama, and the rickshaw, 201
Yvan, Melchior, 83

Zegen, and prostitution, 256, 257, 258, 258, 259, 260, 261, 262, 263, 277, 282